The Documentary Handbook

The Documentary Handbook takes a thematic approach to documentary, including chapters on the many myriad forms we watch today – from the cinematic releases of Michael Moore to low-budget internet efforts like *Video Nation*, from 'shock docs' to reality television.

The Documentary Handbook is a critical introduction to the documentary film, its theory and changing practices. The book charts the evolution of the documentary from screen art to core television genre, its metamorphosis into many different types of factual TV programmes and its current emergence in forms of new media. It analyses those pathways and the transformation of means of production through economic, technical and editorial changes.

The Documentary Handbook explains the documentary process, skills and job specifications for everyone from industry entrants to senior personnel, and shows how the industrial evolution of television has relocated the powers and principles of decision-making. Through the use of professional 'expert briefings' it gives practical pointers about programme-making, from researching, developing and pitching programme ideas to their production and delivery through a fast-evolving multi-platform universe.

Peter Lee-Wright is a documentary filmmaker with 30 years' experience working for the BBC and Channel 4. He is currently Senior Lecturer in Media and Communications at Goldsmiths, University of London. His most recent writing includes critical overviews of sports documentary and trade union documentary in *Encyclopedia of the Documentary Film* (2005) and analysis of the changes taking place in multimedia news, notably in *New Media, Old News* (edited by Natalie Fenton, 2009).

Media Practice

Edited by James Curran, Goldsmiths, University of London

The *Media Practice* handbooks are comprehensive resource books for students of media and journalism, and for anyone planning a career as a media professional. Each handbook combines a clear introduction to understanding how the media work with practical information about the structure, processes and skills involved in working in today's media industries, providing not only a guide on 'how to do it' but also a critical reflection on contemporary media practice.

The Documentary Handbook

Peter Lee-Wright

Routledge
Taylor & Francis Group

LONDON AND NEW YORK

First published 2010
by Routledge
2 Park Square, Milton Park, Abingdon, Oxon OX14 4RN

Simultaneously published in the USA and Canada
by Routledge
270 Madison Avenue, New York, NY 10016

Routledge is an imprint of the Taylor & Francis Group, an informa business

Typeset in Times New Roman and Helvetica Neue
by Florence Production Ltd, Stoodleigh, Devon
Printed and bound in Great Britain
by CPI Antony Rowe, Chippenham, Wiltshire

British Library Cataloguing in Publication Data
A catalogue record for this book is available from the British Library

Library of Congress Cataloging in Publication Data
Lee-Wright, Peter
   The documentary handbook/Peter Lee-Wright.
      p. cm. – (Media practice)
   Includes bibliographical references and index.
   1. Documentary films – History and criticism.   I. Title.
   PN1995.9.D6L384 2009
   070.18–dc22   2009022687

ISBN10: 0–415–43401–7 (hbk)
ISBN10: 0–415–43402–5 (pbk)
ISBN10: 0–203–86719–X (ebk)

ISBN13: 978–0–415–43401–0 (hbk)
ISBN13: 978–0–415–43402–7 (pbk)
ISBN13: 978–0–203–86719–8 (ebk)

To Linda – support beyond words

Contents

Part IV Entertainment for all

Illustrations

....

Acknowledgements

This book draws on such a rich weave of personal experience, critical conversation and convivial support that it will be impossible to name all who have contributed to it. But the spheres of influence in which I have worked I acknowledge with heartfelt gratitude, from the BBC and Channel 4 to the National Film and Television School, Southampton Solent University and Goldsmiths, University of London. I particularly thank my colleagues at Goldsmiths for their unstinting support and vital comments on the text: James Curran, Tony Dowmunt, Natalie Fenton and Noel Hines. I also had invaluable detailed feedback from broadcast journalist Mat Charles and documentary filmmaker Tracy Bass, both of whom also teach at Goldsmiths. The former Head of the Short Course Unit at the NFTS, Deanne Edwards, gave early and timely advice on the book's focus.

Conversations and interviews are acknowledged within the text, but I would particularly like to mention Kevin Sutcliffe, Deputy Head of News and Current Affairs at Channel 4, and Martin Turner, Head of Newsgathering Operations at the BBC, for their regular advice. Richard Klein – former documentary commissioner at the BBC, now Controller, BBC4, Angus Macqueen – former Head of Documentaries at Channel 4, Sue Davidson – former commissioner of science documentaries at Channel Five and Emma Read – commissioning editor for factual entertainment and specialist factual at Sky, lead a long list of key contributors from the commissioning carousel that ensures they will be in other posts by the time of publication. Producers and filmmakers who gave generously of their time include Vicki Barrass, Ed Braman, Mike Flood Page, David Dunkley Gyimah, Abigail Harvey, Sean Langan, Gavin MacFadyen and Helen Veale. The BBC Natural History Unit in Bristol were especially welcoming and I am most grateful to Miles Barton, Alastair Fothergill and Nigel Pope. Among those who contributed to the expert briefings, all of whom I should like to thank, I should mention Murray Dick, Shiva Kuma Naspuri and Hannah the Journalist.

I would also like to thank my editor Aileen Storry for her constant confidence through the lengthy gestation of this book, and my wife Linda for her undying support.

Peter Lee-Wright

Introduction

....

Film is more than the twentieth-century art. It's another part of the twentieth-century mind. It's the world seen from inside. We've come to a certain point in the history of film. If a thing can be filmed, the film is implied in the thing itself. This is where we are. The twentieth century is on film . . . You have to ask yourself if there's anything about us more important than the fact that we're constantly on film, constantly watching ourselves.

Don DeLillo, *The Names*, ch. 8, New York 1982

If you want to tell the untold stories, if you want to give voice to the voiceless, you've got to find a language. Which goes for film as well as prose, for documentary as well as autobiography. Use the wrong language, and you're dumb and blind.

Salman Rushdie 'Songs Don't Know the Score',
Guardian, London, 12 January 1987

When British-born terrorists bombed London on 7 July 2005, killing 52 and injuring many more, Londoners found resources and strengths within themselves more familiar from folk memory of the Blitz in 1940 and 1941. Many of the images Britons treasure from wartime were made under the auspices of the Crown Film Unit, a part of the Ministry of Information, tasked with keeping up public morale. The title alone of Humphrey Jennings's 1940 short *We Can Take It* (GPO Film Unit) conjures up an impression of the chippy little cockney standing up to the incoming bombs of the Third Reich. His more famous Crown Film Unit films, *Listen to Britain* (1942) and *Fires Were Started* (1943), enshrine the carefully constructed myth of an indomitable resilience in the face of peril. Historians have begun to revise that myth and reveal the government incompetence and public panic that began to take hold as people found insufficient refuge from the onslaught of German bombers. Painful truths will not diminish Jennings's iconic status in the documentary canon, tragically ensured by his premature death on location in 1950, but this casts a useful light on the plastic nature of documentary and the role it serves in the public consciousness.

The undisputed art of filmmakers such as Jennings, Watt and Rotha helped elevate the documentary form to a podium where purists like to encase it in a formalist shroud. Early television documentarists laboured under a uniform conception of their craft, in a tradition seamlessly transmitted from Grierson and Reith to Wheldon and Attenborough. This unitary model often obscures the truths that documentary sometimes unwittingly reveals, reflecting different meanings in a constantly changing society. Despite leftist sympathies, Jennings's generation saw no compromise in propagandist work for the war effort, nor conflict between his poetic sensibilities couched in a classically educated voice and his populist objectives. If alive today he would probably find it difficult to get work from commissioners desperate to attract young audiences through a popular argot. Equally, a contemporary society in which most people have access to some means of video recording, many can receive over 500 channels of television and – as Londoners reputedly are – can be caught on CCTV surveillance cameras up to 300 times a day creates a totally different visual context. Cultural change has always been reflected in the different forms of representation. If Jennings represents the 'documentary as high art' orthodoxy of a formal, conservative mid-twentieth-century Britain, the liberalisation of the 1960s onwards gave rise to the 'documentary as unmediated reality' myth, arguably an even more restrictive straitjacket that yet has a certain currency.

On that fearful 7 July, television news bulletins carried grainy video of the Underground nightmare grabbed on survivors' mobile phones, a novel use of available technology to help record and make sense of their trauma. David Blunkett MP, then a member of the Cabinet emergency committee, commented on how the media outpaced the government's own internal information system:

> In fact the news media were ahead of the material being presented to us. They had eyewitnesses sending through video footage, photographs and on-the-spot accounts. It was, in essence, the first time I think that reporting was as much about the men and women on the ground as it was about professional reporters themselves . . . We were entering a new era.[1]

This has been heralded as some kind of emergent citizen journalism, but that is to elevate the automatic pressing of a record button to the same level as the making of informed decisions, which none of these people were in any position to make, nor pretended to be. The context of those images' presentation and the interpretative commentary is what defines their meaning, and that remains in the reporters' and editors' control. Yet the thirst for instant reaction and first-hand experience has created a market for the ill-considered.

When another fatal incident took place on the London Underground just eight days later, no one had their phone on video record, but many confused first-hand accounts were broadcast to the world. Traumatised commuters had to make sense of armed police bursting into their carriage and shooting a fellow passenger dead with multiple shots to the head. It is a natural human reaction to try and retrospectively make narrative sense of the sounds and images that preceded this shooting. Thus the instant myth was born that Jean Charles de Menenez had vaulted the turnstiles in flight from the police, wearing a suspiciously bulky puffer jacket. In fact, it was the pursuing police that had done this, and their innocent target had strolled onto the train wearing his summer clothes and carrying a free newspaper. Even after admitting their mistake in shooting the Brazilian electrician dead, the police persisted in the post-rationalised view of events to justify their extreme actions – and it wasn't until Lana Vandenberghe, a secretary at the Police Complaints Commission, leaked the truth to ITN that it emerged publicly. At least a camera recording would have made that deliberate misinformation harder to sustain but – coincidentally and despite the heightened state of security – all the Stockwell station's many CCTV cameras were allegedly 'not working'.

So we must always strive to know for whom the cameras are working (or not), before we can know how to read the images they record, or exclude. As the founder of the English documentary school, and originator of the term 'documentary film' (to describe Robert Flaherty's 1926 film *Moana*), even John Grierson was aware of the many 'different qualities of observation, different intentions in observation, and, of course, very different powers and ambitions at the stage of organising material'.[2] That neat triptych can also serve to help define the ambition and scope of this handbook. It is my contention that those different qualities of documentary observation have evolved with the proliferation of views and voices that the progressive democratisation of the media has allowed. This has paralleled an equal explosion in different intentions, just as the monolithic monopoly of the BBC, charged by Reith to 'inform, educate and entertain' has been challenged by a vast and growing range of channels and other platforms peddling every conceivable kind of message. And the different powers and ambitions range from the global objective of Rupert Murdoch's News Corporation – to control as wide a range of global media as possible and influence governments so as to ensure a beneficial business environment – to ultra-low-budget video serving special interest groups, normally distributed through web connections. These three features together have been responsible for a multiplication of filmic forms that make up a significant proportion of our twenty-first-century visual culture, not just through the dominant means of television's many genres, but also reinvigorating cinema, giving much to the internet and invading the art gallery and the theatrical stage. Many of these emergent, maybe transient forms are not documentary in a form that Grierson and the founding fathers would recognise – and are also dismissed as trivial, formulaic and worse by some leading practitioners and theoreticians – but undeniably play a significant role in the ways in which factual information is framed, transmitted and viewed today.

It is this broader field of documentary and related factual programming that *The Documentary Handbook* addresses. While recognising and celebrating the antecedents and achievements of the classic documentary form, I feel it pointless to erect an ivory tower around it and its memory, denying all worth to the bastard forms it has spawned. Many of these programmes, in a fast-evolving multi-platform universe, are poor, though so were quite a few made during the so-called Golden Age of television in the 1960s and 1970s, when there was much less competition for resources and audiences. Furthermore, it is disproportionately in these new forms that many industry entrants will expect to work. Inexperience in production staff can be mitigated by better education and training, though poorly paid and resourced jobs are bound to continue with the marginal economics of niche channels. It is possible to elevate the ambition of this generation of programme-maker and enhance their critical skills, at least more readily than anyone can expect commercial stations to compromise their profitability in the service of art.

In today's fragmented marketplace, even the major terrestrial channels cannot take their audiences for granted and can no longer produce 'must-see' television for all the family, such as the legendary Christmas *Morecambe and Wise Show*, which used to attract over 20 million viewers in the 1970s. Not only do families infrequently sit together or share tastes, but the young audiences have separate TV sets, watch digital channels such as Bravo and MTV, and more often take their information and entertainment from the internet through the likes of YouTube and video download. Finding ways to access that audience is the key driver of change in TV programming, with technological evolution providing the instruments for those changes. Increasing consideration is given to audience wants and reactions, encouraging the endless repetition of successful formulae above formal innovation. Few focus groups produce innovative programme ideas.

Television reflects changes in society as much in the way it conceives, organises and prioritises its programmes as in its choice of subjects and their treatment. Television production was traditionally undertaken in departments specialising in particular subject genres – News, Current Affairs, Documentaries, Music and Arts, Drama Series and so on – but changes in the economics and corporate management of the industry have contrived significant collapse of these divisions. The BBC, for instance, appears to have spent the last 15 years in a constant, fevered state of internal reorganisation, culling whole departments and thousands of staff as it struggles to find more efficient models of production that best fit the fast-evolving new media landscape. Now what was the Production division has become 'Vision' and jobs are constructed with titles like 'Head of Multimedia Knowledge Commissioning'. The BBC has fared well in the development of new media, with its website a world-beater and its digital channels offering successfully clear propositions, but arguably at cost to the finances supplied by the licence fee payers to the core terrestrial services for which they thought they were paying.

Old verities and values have been swept away in this transformative tsunami. Current Affairs, once journalistically distinct and physically distant from News, has now been downsized and rolled into the News Division. Documentaries, long one of the key departments that anchored the schedules and gave the BBC its world renown, has been so diminished and demoralised that in a recent voluntary redundancy offer all its remaining executive producers applied. Not all of them have left and some great, classic documentaries are still made by the BBC, but not so many as in the past. This is due in part to the growth of the independent sector, where the majority of documentary filmmakers now ply their often lonely trade, but it is also due to the emergence of a whole host of other programme genres that better serve the television channels' attempts to retain audience loyalties in a crowded, fragmenting marketplace. Many of these employ what are essentially documentary techniques, and people skilled in those techniques, and it is the object of this book to chart this evolution and the multiple metamorphoses of the documentary form.

A vital part of that process is to understand the drivers of change and the conflicting ideas they represent. The classic authored television documentary that was once the gold standard proudly represented by the BBC is now seen by many as somewhat anachronistic, representative of a former imperial dominance of ideas and forms. The Latin American documentary has fulfilled an important role in giving voice to emergent groups in South America. The fast-emerging media markets of the world, notably India and China, mould the form to suit their different needs. But the empire of ideas is not dead, as Britain is second only to the USA in global television sales, and it is precisely in these documentary formats and other formulae that they are supreme. So this book, while trying to avoid charges of ethnocentricity through referring to other national forms, will take as its primary text English language documentary and its offspring. It will also explore the causes and impact of a revival in cinema documentary, which is integrally related to the rise and fall of other media.

The book is organised in five parts, grouping together particular types of documentary sub-genre that share a common thread. Thus Part 1 is called *Talk to the camera*, grouping together essentially informational programme forms in which people tend to address the camera directly. Chapter 1 deals with the various forms of *Reportage*, which remains the staple journalistic form in most parts of the television world, whether it is a seasoned reporter journeying in some far flung foreign part, or a specialist correspondent exploring a feature of the local economy. Chapter 2 concentrates on the *Exposé*, including undercover investigations where intrepid reporters risk personal harm to reveal wrongdoing in the otherwise unfilmable underbelly of society, and the work of the solo journalist. Chapter 3 describes the evolution of the lantern-slide *Lecture series* into grand, often globe-trotting documentary series in which experts reveal the features of their world, be it of history, art, music or philosophy. These are often known as 'landmarks'. Chapter 4 traces the emergence of the *Vox populi*, the voice of the people, from early socialist efforts allowing ordinary people to address the camera to latter-day individual forms like video diaries.

Part 2 is called *Observe the people*, and charts the evolution of the observational documentary, which is what most people understand by the term 'documentary'. Chapter 5 covers *Real life* and its central subject matter for the American proponents of Direct Cinema, the UK founders of Free Cinema and the French conceptualists of *cinéma vérité*. Chapter 6 follows the development of *Docu-soap*, bringing the casting principles and narrative complexities of soap opera to documentary subjects, and the appropriation of documentary techniques by filmmakers making 'mockumentaries'. Chapter 7 is called *Extreme television: flashing lights and freak shows*, referring to the recent development of extreme subject matter, from patients with severe medical conditions to people pushed to their limits. It also looks at the apparently insatiable thirst for documentary series chasing the sensations of crime, fires and accidents dealt with by the emergency services.

Part 3 is entitled *Change the mind*, referring to film's potential as a tool for education, propaganda and polemic. Chapter 8 looks at the many different fields of *Education* that documentary has been put to in Britain and the USA, from children to adults, history and science to health hints. Chapter 9 is all about *Propaganda* and the various filmic forms employed by different nations and ideologies, particularly in times of conflict. Chapter 10 expands into *Polemic* and the use of film as argument, particularly in service of contemporary single issue concerns. Chapter 11 is called *Liberation*, in the sense that it is principally about the ways in which documentary film liberates the voice of subject peoples, the oppressed and others generally denied a voice.

Part 4 is *Entertainment for all*, exploring the different avenues down which documentary has moved to bring entertainment to a mass audience. Chapter 12 covers *Formats and reality TV*, the key drivers of television schedules that attract both young audiences and the advertising revenue chasing them. Chapter 13 looks at the many formulae of *Lifestyle and makeover*, which also reflect the consumerist tendencies and tastes of today's audiences. Chapter 14 covers the broad field of *Performance*, from classic rock documentary to archive-driven sports documentary. Chapter 15 is all about *Drama-doc* and the current tendency to dramatise or re-enact everything, where once this was deemed anathema by documentarists. Chapter 16 enters the outfield of *Art and anarchy*, looking at the ways documentary has invaded the art galleries and come to play an integral part of performance art.

Part 5 is called *Watch the figures*, and looks at three of the most profitable areas of documentary film. Chapter 17 assesses the much-commented revival of documentary as cinema *Box office* and, with it, the notion that documentaries have rediscovered their original ambition to be historical documents, lasting testimony to their time rather than fleeting moments to pass the time. Chapter 18 looks at *Biopics*, recognising the porous and increasingly redundant barrier between fact and fiction, as television rewrites history and cinema discovers healthy returns in the heroic lives of sports and music stars, even of presidents and terrorists. Chapter 19 explores the global phenomena of *Wildlife* and environment films, through a case study of the world's most successful wildlife film production house, the BBC's Natural History Unit in Bristol. It also finds that even this department is not immune to the impact of economic cycles and vagaries of popular taste, and reflects on how evolving concerns about the environment have politicised the natural world.

Any such pigeon-holing of creative forms into square boxes throws up anomalies and examples that either fit none, or belong equally in more than one. Where this occurs, the cross-references will be made explicit. The aim is not so much to categorise programmes as to delineate pathways down which the documentary form has developed and fields in which aspirant programme-makers may be expected to perform. It weaves together the historical, industrial and cultural context in which these forms evolve, and recognises that the mutation continues. There is deliberately no concluding chapter, because this is a fluid medium in permanent motion.

As Don DeLillo enquires, 'is there anything more important than that we are constantly on film, constantly watching ourselves'? This book suggests that yes, there is: that this obsession with the process has obscured the importance of its effects, that documentary has, often unwittingly, charted the evolution of society from a hierarchical, moralistic one to a commercial, hedonistic and relativist culture. It is no surprise that traditional documentary, with its liberal social view – often 'giving voice to the voiceless', as Rushdie has it – was in retreat in the Thatcherite world in which she declared 'there is no such thing as society'. The self-seeking, self-regarding individualism that has largely supplanted communal ethics has naturally spawned television forms that reflect that change, such as the so-called 'reality TV' shows that pitch individuals into a latter-day gladiatorial arena for our entertainment. Their proponents argue that these 'hold a mirror up to society', even empowering the audience, as its votes determine the outcome. That the elements of society so reflected are rarely the most inspiring or aspirational is inevitable because the audience is generated by its entertainment value, not its educational merit. Producers and broadcasters claim that the purest fulfilment of their mission is to give the public what it wants, distancing themselves from the past in which their 'elitist' predecessors dared to determine what was good for their audience. Today's arbiters of taste often act as if this exempts them from responsibility for the results.

It is the contention of this book that it is possible to make a good TV show without having a critical lobotomy first, and that an awareness of the culture and traditions of docu-mentary are a useful grounding when surfing the flood tide of change in the industry. The many different genres of work and platforms of delivery did not develop accidentally; they are mutations driven by a mixture of creative innovation and commercial demand, many embodying the techniques and sensibility of documentary. Some are good, some are bad, many are indifferent, but it is a fatal error to imagine that the people making them are definable by those products, as equally good, bad or indifferent. Chance has a large part to play in most people's employment opportunities, especially in the early stages of a career, where people are often scrabbling for one short-term contract after another. The finest of filmmakers may serve time in reality television, the most original of minds may learn their craft on a long-running soap. As long as their critical intelligence is kept alert, these experiences can only be beneficial. These are high volume shows targeted at audiences of a young age, so they are ideal training grounds and industry entrants help refresh those genres, but it is hard to make an acute contribution if the individual is ignorant of the cultural context. So this book charts the way in which many of the key factual genres have developed, the creative and commercial impulses that have driven them, and the surrounding forces that mould and manipulate them.

Each chapter resolves with an 'expert briefing' on a particular technique or filmic approach. Impatient students may be inclined to cut to the chase, grab the kit and run. But these notional instructions should clearly be perceived as the tools needed once the filmmaker is apprised of a project, its place and purpose in the wider world. The National Rifle Association of America are wont to invoke the God-given right to bear arms, in the face of continued gun-crime and slaughter, on the grounds that it is not the gun that kills but the person who pulls the trigger. The same might be said of the camera. The technique is strictly subservient to the programme objective and – while producers may hide behind technical innovation or apparent audience demand – they are complicit in a process that decides what is good or bad, what is seen or not seen, what is on the public's mind or banished from their thoughts. Documentary is regularly misconstrued as a neutral mirror to life, but this book will show that it has never been that nor can be, and that the constructions it has spawned are freighted with meaning and impact on our vision of, and relationship to, the world. As a sage producer of the old school once said: 'The camera is a lethal weapon: handle it with care.'

Part I

Talk to the camera

Whereas most film drama plays out in front of the camera, much televisual non-fiction adopts the full frontal approach of addressing the camera directly. The epithet 'non-fiction' is a hostage to fortune wherever its broad brush stroke is applied, from written biographies that speculate about the subject's feelings and motivations to films that pretend to deliver unmediated truth. Television's reliance on the real world – real people, real places, real tragedies – does not reduce its many fictions; programmes and the people that appear in them are directed and produced much as they are in drama. The screen presenter merely puts a friendly face to the controlling hand.

The original meaning of the word fiction, from the Latin *fictio*, is a forming or shaping of things, be they events or elemental truths. That is what television does – organises features of the messy world for popular and mostly easy consumption. Every aspect of the technical process is a construction based upon a series of selective judgements, i.e. a fiction. 'The camera doesn't lie' is itself a fiction, or half-truth, not least because what it tells you by definition excludes everything it doesn't tell you. What subject matter you choose to film, where and whom you film, which bits you eventually use and how you put them together are all subjective choices, made for reasons variously good, bad and indifferent. Coming to terms with this authorial process, and exercising its powers effectively and responsibly, is the central core of factual television – and of this book.

In the past, people turned to storytellers and priests to construct a narrative for their lives, explaining the wider context in which their trials and tribulations had meaning and, in some cases, may be rewarded in a future life. Television has largely taken over that role, shaping the vast array of facts and figures, images and experiences it has access to into a set of recognisable and digestible narratives. At the birth of the mass medium some 60 years ago, the world was still organised along traditionally hierarchical lines with supporting moral verities. So the worldview widely presented was largely non-contentious, and often supported by an avuncular intermediary: the white, middle-class, middle-aged male that is still the commonest image of broadcast authority on Western television. As he stepped in front of the camera to speak directly to us, catching our eye and easing our understanding of the world, he defined the standard, reassuring presentational form of this latter-day priesthood. This is defined as 'the expository mode' in Bill Nichols's influential *Introduction to Documentary*:

> The expository mode addresses the viewer directly, with titles or voices that propose
> a perspective, advance an argument, or recount history. Expository films adopt either a
> voice-of-God commentary (the speaker is heard but never seen) . . . or utilize a voice-of-

authority commentary (the speaker is heard and also seen), such as we find in television newscasts . . . The commentary . . . is presumed to be of a higher order than the accompanying images. It comes from some place that remains unspecified but associated with objectivity or omniscience. The commentary, in fact, represents the perspective or argument of the film.[1]

That perspective is rarely of divine inspiration, the god's voice being that of Mammon, or the economic interests of the channel. These may be overtly commercial or regulated by the government and legislation of the day. The expository, avuncular mode remains the staple of television worldwide, from news bulletins to most forms of factual programming, although women and ethnic minorities are now better represented, and often in virtual partnerships on-screen as couples banter their way through the business of the day. Secure in the television studio, programme 'anchors' interact with the reporters at large on the high seas of the real world, who also address the camera as if it were their 'friend' in the studio, who in turns asks them questions on our behalf, before turning back to address us directly him- or herself. Though friendliness has replaced the more severe gravitas of old, omniscience and indisputable authority remain the presumption of most television 'hosts' addressing the camera. The international uniform of suits and ties for men, professional clothes for women, underpins that authority. Even successful satirical subversions of the form, such as US Comedy Central's *The Daily Show with Jon Stewart*, rigidly adhere to those conventions – and the great and the good fight to get on the show, from White House insiders to the President of Pakistan. When Jon Stewart delivers to the camera another story about the asininity of public life and ends with a raised eyebrow, he may be mocking the mendacity and incompetence of our so-called masters, but not the system that produces them. As the next political has-been strides on to the set to publicise his memoirs, his hand is shaken, not the status quo.

Everybody trained to address the camera, whether it be rooky reporters or captains of industry, are told to address it as a friend, to talk conversationally without jargon, to engage with personality, not point-scoring. Politicians' careers depend upon their camera performance above all other talents. UK Prime Minister Tony Blair's photogenic qualities and easy glibness before the microphones kept him in power, and his less camera-friendly successor Gordon Brown waiting in the wings, for ten years, despite personal qualities, policies and problems that called for a much earlier handover. US presidential elections are largely dependent on television ads and election coverage, where the average sound bite contracted from 44 seconds in 1968 to just 7.8 seconds in 2000 and 2004, favouring the pithy vacuities of George W. Bush over the more complex thoughts of Al Gore and John Kerry.[2] Barack Obama's inspiring rhetoric further endorses that filmic tradition, with his speeches frequently framed in front of iconic images of Abraham Lincoln or the Founding Fathers, invoking American history to inform his grand narrative of aspiration.

Not all who address the camera seek to reassure the audience or sell themselves. As a potent instrument of persuasion, it is above all the favourite means for those with a tub to thump or story to tell. At the cutting edge of reportage, reporters investigate the underbelly of society, from consumer scams to state corruption, urgently advising us that we need to take notice and help purge the reported cancer from our body politic. Even those, for whom deep cover is the essence of their investigation, command the camera and reveal themselves, the emotions and dangers they put themselves through on our behalf. This apparent professional suicide is deemed a necessary sacrifice in the validation of such work.

As issues of representation came increasingly to the fore during the late twentieth century, it was not just in the traditional on-camera roles that minorities wanted to be seen. They wanted to front their own programmes in their own terms, broadening the vision as well as the voice. Forms of partial and polemical television that would have been anathema to its founding fathers became more common; meanwhile, new technology enabled newer intimacies such as the self-shot video diary and the proliferation of niche channels where every specialism could find a camera to address. While some saw liberation in these developments, many were only watched by their own kind, a kind of speaking to oneself. This progressive, fragmenting democratisation of the airwaves continues with new openings and byways on the burgeoning pathways of the internet, where anyone can go and anything does. While much of this material is like so much dust free-falling in space, some achieve a clarion voice that punches through the ether. Many still address the camera in the way they remember from children's television, and most rely on the uniqueness of their own voice or vision, the individual addressing their audience through the technological peephole of our time.

The following chapters in this part explore the evolution and practice of these different factual forms that have at their heart this essential feature: they talk to the camera.

1 Reportage

reportage n. – 1 the act or process of reporting news or other events of general interest.
2 a journalist's style of reporting[1]

The word 'reportage' tends to represent two parallel tracks – the visual and the editorial. It has been used to describe the work of photojournalists and documentary cameramen who bring a particular vision to their images of the world, from the historic Soviet newsreels compiled by Dziga Vertov to the acclaimed war photographs of Don McCullen. And it is used to credit the longer forms of narrative journalism that bring some authorial insight to bear, whether it is published works, such as those of the Polish journalist Ryszard Kapuściński, or investigative films, such as those of the campaigning Australian journalist John Pilger. Veteran current affairs producer Ed Braman describes it like this:

> I've always defined reportage as narrating and filming the moments of engagement. What I mean by that is – 'We arrived in this place and this is what happened, and this is what we discovered next'. It is the process of reporting as well as what is reported, and the spirit in which it is reported . . . Kapuściński, absolutely, a great model of reportage. Ed Murrow was a fantastic model of reportage. Fred Friendly, Tom Wolfe – for whom the process was paramount – Joan Didion, whose work on Florida, Miami is fantastic reportage. 'I engaged with this person, this is what they told me. This is what I learnt about it'. It's not people or events as fodder in some larger argument promulgated by John Lloyd or Will Hutton. It's: 'I actually care about what this person said to me and I care about what I saw, what happened to people'. That's reportage.[2]

Reportage is therefore seen as the opposite of the scorched earth journalism of the news pack, which stakes out a place or person, sucks a story dry and moves on like a swarm of locusts. The good reporter invests time, energy and some of their soul in digging deep to reveal the buried truths of a story. Some will be making long form films, others filing dispatches for news bulletins. It is not about quantity, but the quality of the work. Pilger himself quotes approvingly the American journalist T.D. Allman's tribute to *The Daily Express*'s Wilfred Burchett, who slipped the leash of Allied occupation forces in Japan to 'warn the world' of the radiation fallout from the H-bomb dropped on Hiroshima in August 1945:

> Genuinely objective journalism not only gets the facts right, it gets the meaning of events right. It is compelling not only today, but stands the test of time. It is validated not only

by 'reliable sources', but by the unfolding of history. It is journalism that ten, twenty, fifty years after the fact holds up a true and intelligent mirror to events.[3]

Pilger has made a career of stepping on toes to get those facts, and then stepping in front of camera to put his uncompromising construction on events as important as the Indonesian military suppression of East Timor and American connivance in Pol Pot's Cambodia. His is a deceptively languid style of reporting, with a lacerating lance for the corruptions and collusions of power. It has, inevitably, made him few friends in powerful places. While regularly commissioned by Independent Television (ITV) in the UK, Pilger has never been able to get American networks to show any of his 55 films, but he remains unrepentant:

There is a hunger among the public for documentaries because only documentaries, at their best, are fearless and show the unpalatable and make sense of the news. The extraordinary films of Alan Francovich achieved this. Francovich, who died in 1997, made *The Maltese Double Cross – Lockerbie*. This destroyed the official truth that Libya was responsible for the sabotage of Pan Am 103 over Lockerbie in 1988. Instead, an unwitting 'mule', with links to the CIA, was alleged to have carried the bomb on board the aircraft. (Paul Foot's parallel investigation for *Private Eye* came to a similar conclusion.) The *Maltese Double Cross – Lockerbie* has never been publicly screened in the United States. In this country [the UK], the threat of legal action from a US Government official prevented showings at the 1994 London Film Festival and the Institute of Contemporary Arts. In 1995, defying threats, Tam Dalyell showed it in the House of Commons, and Channel 4 broadcast it in May 1995.[4]

Do not be confused by this Russian dolls' nest of references. Reporters of distinction recognise the value of each others' work and celebrate it as standing head and shoulders above the sea of mediocrity, the 'churnalism' that Nick Davies (2008) writes about. The political reportage of current affairs documentary at its best challenges the orthodoxies pedalled by the establishment of the day, and routinely reported by the hacks of the day. But the stakes are high, as its history shows.

Reportage then

This important strand of television documentary originated in the post-War period as an extension of current affairs coverage, owing as much to radio as to the well-established film tradition. Early television, like radio, had lacked the ability to pre-record and edit, so news bulletins were broadcast live with just the odd still picture. Radio paved the way in recording and editing techniques and early videotape editing evolved the same process of linking actuality sequences with narration. News operations seized the opportunity of extending their reportage in this way, but inevitably enshrined the reporter in the dominant role, standing in front of the camera. Consistent with the early broadcasters' belief in their role as revealers of truth to their audience, this set one standard of television documentary in a classic narrative form: storytelling for the modern age, illustrated with moving pictures.

This reporter tradition persists today, even more strongly in the United States than in Britain, not least because of the dominant figure of Ed Murrow, dramatically revived in the George Clooney feature film *Good Night and Good Luck* (2005). Ed Murrow, with his wartime radio reporting from London, introduced Americans to the authentic sounds and experiences of war by creating the CBS radio documentary unit in 1946. This produced the original radio documentary series *Hear It Now*, which, with the arrival of producer Fred Friendly, led in 1951 to the seminal television documentary series *See It Now*. Although this initially featured several different stories in each half-hour, it had become a single issue strand by 1953.

The year 1953 was also the year that the BBC launched its long-running flagship programme *Panorama*, initially as a rather unsuccessful fortnightly magazine programme. It was not until the following year that it did its first single-issue documentary, on the hydrogen bomb, and this, along with the arrival of Richard Dimbleby as presenter and Grace Wyndham-Goldie as producer in 1955, established it as the premier current affairs programme, featuring extended documentary reportage. As former reporter and *Panorama* historian Richard Lindley writes, current affairs reporting, or 'long-form journalism' as it is sometimes called, was a radical departure for Britain:

> When *Panorama* began in 1953 there was a void, darkness on the factual face of television. ITV did not yet exist, and through prejudice and inertia BBC News had failed to develop. It was left to *Panorama* to invent television journalism in Britain.[5]

Wartime necessity had ensured six years of government propaganda, widely applauded as sustaining the morale and helping win the war, so a renascent BBC television (closed down 1939–46) was reborn emasculated. Politicians did not trust the new medium. Winston Churchill thought it full of communists and never once gave a television interview, and even the then Director-General of the BBC, Sir William Haley, a former editor of *The Times*, did not think news appropriate on television. A proper television news service was not established until November 1954. So Grace Wyndham-Goldie's passionately held belief in television's public service role, mediating between politicians and public, with reporters actually questioning policy-makers and analysing the results of their policies, was quite revolutionary.

The appointment of Richard Dimbleby was a masterstroke of balance, always a critical consideration for the BBC as it struggled for independence from its political masters. Dimbleby was not only an heroic war reporter, who had been the first to enter a liberated Belsen, but had also commentated on George VI's funeral and Elizabeth II's coronation (the latter being the first major live television outside broadcast, a unique event responsible for widespread sale of television sets and therefore television's arrival as a mass medium in Britain). Freighted with establishment gravitas, Dimbleby's urbane questioning of guests live in the studio provided both the 'right of reply' balance required and the authority that licensed reporters to probe deeply into their subjects. This authority was evidenced, if not abused, when Dimbleby made a light-hearted spoof film for the 1 April 1957 edition about the 'spaghetti harvest in Italy', which many of his suggestible audience took seriously. In 1959, Robin Day joined *Panorama*, importing his fearless brand of questioning that showed television current affairs had come of age, and was no longer so subservient and reverential. The arrival of ITV, and the start of its weekly current affairs magazine *This Week* in 1956 and Granada's *World in Action* documentary strand in 1963, were further milestones on the road to establishing a rigorous practice of documentary reportage.

The American Constitution, through its First Amendment guaranteeing freedom of speech and of the press, ensured that American television documentary was made in a freer form.

While British politicians like Churchill looked askance at the more invasive lenses of American television reporters, Ed Murrow was fearlessly taking on Senator Joseph McCarthy, the racist American Legion and segregation in southern schools. His last, most famous film, *Harvest of Shame* (1960), exposed American farmers' exploitative reliance on poor migrant families, stirring up considerable controversy and emphasising the important, investigative nature of true reportage.[6]

CBS Reports had replaced *See It Now* in 1958, and for ten years was the most influential news programme in the United States, culminating in 1968 with *CBS Reports: Hunger in America*, which explored the shortcomings of government food programmes. So great was the programme's impact that more than $200 million in additional funds were voted for food programmes, and a US Senate inquiry was held.

The 1960s saw a rapid expansion of television documentary on both sides of the Atlantic. Fast-developing technology – lighter cameras that could be hand-held, faster film stock not requiring lights, the evolution of synchronous sound – and an equally dynamic social and political landscape both contributed to this boom. It was a defining moment in the United States, as American media historian Mary Ann Watson says:

1960 is a natural dividing line, a discernable breaking point in American history. The Kennedy years are this discrete period of history that are bracketed by television milestones. At the beginning you have the Great Debates and at the end, tragically, you have television's coverage of the assassination and funeral of President Kennedy. And, in the interim, television became absolutely central to American life . . . Television was really at that period what I like to call social glue, it was common currency. By 1956 television was already the most dominant mass medium, but, by 1960, television was still only 14 years old.[7]

As in America, in Britain at the time there was a strong sense that the 1960s was a turning point in history. Television was at the forefront of the cultural revolution that was transforming society, from pop music and fashion to sexual liberation and political dissent. Just as news – as its name promises – is about the shocks and surprises of change, not the everyday, so television feasts on what is novel and striking. Reporters were the town criers of their age, complete with kipper ties and bell bottom trousers. They came and stood in people's living rooms, many of which had only just acquired their first television sets, and introduced people to sights and sensations they had never experienced before. For many, these novelties were quite shocking, and the reporters became the audience's friends, interpreting the strangeness as a kindly uncle might initiate a child to the mysteries of the world. They lived in this fast and furious world, and they knew how to explain it to those who did not.

The British Broadcasting Corporation inevitably had a patrician, often patronising, attitude towards its audience. Producers and reporters were overwhelmingly white, male, middle class and mainly from Oxbridge. This did not mean that they were all conservative, socially or politically, any more than they were the communists of Churchillian myth. Many had grown up with a cinema that featured the social documentaries of Edgar Anstey, Humphrey Jennings and others, and were the first generation to enjoy the fruits of the Labour Welfare State. They were passionate about taking their cameras where they had not been before, exploring the old and the new equally avidly. It was more their masters' metropolitan egocentricity and their own naivety that led some such documentaries to start at London's

Euston station, with the reporter announcing that he was heading north into the unknown to investigate some subject or community.

Granada Television, which had won the weekday franchise for the northern region of England at the inception of the UK's Independent Television network (ITV) in 1954, saw itself as a proletarian corrective to the effete southern BBC. It specialised in hard-hitting documentaries and gritty dramas. The weekly *World in Action* series launched in 1963, under the editorship of former *Daily Express* reporter Tim Hewat. It abandoned the studio presenter and magazine format of *Panorama* and reported a single issue in documentary form from the appropriate location. From the outset, Hewat wanted the programme entirely shot on portable 16 mm film cameras with mobile sound, whereas the BBC was only making limited use of what the engineers still felt was sub-standard gear for short news and newsreel sequences. The BBC did not set up its own in-house 16 mm film unit until 1964. The stranglehold that engineers and systems regularly had on creativity at the BBC is a theme that I shall return to at various stages throughout this book.

According to the Institute of Commonwealth Studies at the University of London, which preserves some of their key transcripts and research materials, '*World in Action* was the first weekly current affairs programme in Britain to pioneer pictorial journalism on film and to risk taking an independent editorial stance'.[8] *World in Action*'s very first edition, in January 1963, raised hackles as it drew attention to Khrushchev and Kennedy's squabble over the arms race. *World in Action* took even more flak over an exposé of the miserable living conditions of South African and Angolan blacks. The countries' ambassadors protested, and the ruling body of Independent Television, the ITA, decided that the programme was not sufficiently impartial and decreed that the authority should in future vet editions, which many saw as an intolerable intrusion on journalistic independence. This experience only served to stimulate a tradition of fiercely independent reporting that embraced some of the most distinguished reporters of their generation, from David Leigh, now Investigations Editor of *The Observer*, and John Ware, until recently chief investigative reporter on *Panorama*, to undercover reporter Donald MacIntyre and filmmaker John Pilger.

Such reporters build substantial bodies of knowledge and reputation that in turn earns them a particular licence to address the camera with authority and a significant degree of independence. Pilger's 1970 *World in Action* on the imminent end of the war in Vietnam took a typically challenging line, asserting that the war was ending because of what he called *The Quiet Mutiny*:

> The war is ending not because of the Paris [peace] talks or the demonstrations at home. It is ending because the largest, wealthiest, most powerful organisation on Earth is being challenged from within, from the very cellars of the pyramid, from the most forgotten, most brutalised and certainly the bravest of its members. The war is ending because the grunt is taking no more bullshit.[9]

This is a tone of voice, not to mention an analysis, that would have been found in no BBC programme of the time, let alone in a US broadcast. Pilger's supporting cast of serving grunts (G.I.s = general infantrymen), admitting their disenchantment and casually discussing the killing of unpopular officers, would also have been unlikely to feature unchallenged elsewhere. But Pilger's quiet anger follows in the honourable Ed Murrow tradition of challenging the audience to care. When reporters of this kind address the camera, it is difficult to remain neutral or unmoved. As Pilger commented:

I suppose some of you watching this film will say it's peddling the anti-American line yet again. Well, perhaps another kind of person could make another kind of film. But I have lived in America and I have been in the mud of America's war in Vietnam and I do know that thousands of young American soldiers . . . are fighting an enemy that isn't called 'gook'. It's called the US Army – and that takes guts.[10]

World in Action increasingly moved away from on-screen reporters towards the narrated documentary that became another gold standard of British television, and to which we shall return in Part 2. Screen reporters continued to be used for most BBC current affairs programmes, making extended film reports about the big issues of the day that then led on to the politicians and powerful answering questions raised live in the studio by the programme's chief inquisitor, such as *Panorama*'s unforgiving Robin Day. The tradition is continued by Jeremy Paxman, himself a former *Panorama* reporter, on BBC2's *Newsnight*, whose world-weary scepticism about the evasions of government ministers is a challenge many seek to avoid. Media-savvy performers, such as Margaret Thatcher and Tony Blair, knew they could reach a larger audience with much less risk or challenge on a radio or television chat show, such as *The Jimmy Young Show* on BBC Radio 2 or Channel 4's *Richard and Judy*, rather than being savaged by licensed rottweilers like Paxman or BBC Radio 4 *Today* programme's John Humphreys. But it remains undeniable that the strength and rigour with which the powerful are called to account in this way is a measure of the health of a democracy, of its freedom of speech and of the independence of its broadcasters.

The power of personality

Far from the hard-hitting reportage that distinguished *Panorama* in its heyday, its producers' earliest ambitions were for an altogether softer magazine programme, with a little bit of something for everyone. In some ways presciently, they placed much of their hope in a strong host who could master a wide range of subjects and interviews, commanding an equally diverse audience. Those producers wrote in a memo to their bosses:

> The programme would be built around a central figure who, besides being a genial and acceptable personality, should be catholic in his interests and possess a lively and enquiring mind. He should be capable of talking to experts in many subjects on their own ground.[11]

It is a job description that could equally apply today but, as any experienced producer knows, the missing element is the less quantifiable performance ability, where all those desirable talents are not fazed by the lights, cameras and multiple distractions of a television studio, but only reach their full potential in that unforgiving glare. Recognition of the rarity and value of that quality has led to its being increasingly highly valued. The BBC's highest-paid presenter in 2009, Jonathan Ross, was originally a researcher who was parachuted in front of the camera in his producer's hour of need. Taking to this environment as if born to it, he never looked back, with his ego expanding to fill the proffered panorama of opportunity, along with his reported £6 million annual pay-packet. This unfettered sense of self-worth took a fall in 2008, when a guest slot on fellow Radio 2 host Russell Brand's show went too far and provoked a national outrage, which resulted in Ross being suspended for three months without pay.[12] However, the BBC stood by its commitment to pay top rates for such top talent, although it has since announced across-the-board cuts of around 25 per cent.

Panorama's first presenter was an amiable and voluble Irish Fleet Street reporter called Pat Murphy who got forty guineas (£42) and made such a hash of it he was sacked after his first disastrous appearance. Over 50 years on, *Panorama* was relaunched in 2007 with a new presenter in whom great hopes were vested to save the programme's flagging fortunes and audiences. Jeremy Vine is a BBC lifer whose jobs have included stints as a Radio 4 *Today* reporter, Africa correspondent, BBC *Newsnight* presenter and Radio 2 lunchtime show host. Another amiable and voluble man, hopes that he would bring some of his large radio audience to the ailing TV current affairs flagship – relocated to a year-round prime-time slot, but truncated to half an hour – have been largely fulfilled but, as some BBC journalists lament, at the cost of 'dumbing down'. Sceptics feel that programmes suffer less from the time loss than a ratings-chasing populist agenda that fights shy of the hard stories that were once *Panorama*'s staple. This is denied by former *Panorama* Editor George Entwhistle, but then somewhat contradicted when he says:

> We don't do subjects, we do stories. We look for entry points and storytelling devices that help draw an audience into subject matters they may not be familiar with or want to engage with. [A programme about] Northern Ireland could be the story of . . . a family's quest for answers. It might begin with digging for bodies in a field; hooks and incentives for viewers to stay watching. People won't watch 'Northern Ireland' just because we tell them it's important.[13]

For 30 years, the sectarian conflict that amounted to an undeclared civil war gave Northern Ireland an undisputed prominence on the public agenda, however boringly repetitive and hopelessly bleak the story may have sometimes seemed. Peter Taylor was a *Panorama* reporter whose meticulous research and wide-ranging contacts have earned him a well-deserved reputation as the most knowledgeable television reporter on Northern Irish affairs. His successive series on the three key groups involved in the conflicts, *Provos*, *Loyalists* and *Brits*,[14] and the books[15] that followed, are part of an impressive body of work that started in 1972. He doesn't feel that a story's importance can merely be gauged by public taste, and in all his work, latterly largely on terrorism, reveals how most reporting, by comparison, is reductive, simplistic and two-dimensional. He never takes sides, but talks to everyone, disproving the naive presumption – notoriously leading to the censorship of such work under the Thatcher government – that talking to terrorists advances their cause by giving them 'the oxygen of publicity'.[16] Peace was only achieved in Northern Ireland by the Blair government talking to the various factions. It is a stance that has always been adopted by the best reporters, notably by the late, great Charles Wheeler, as celebrated by many obituarists:

> Sir Charles Wheeler was once described as 'the reporters' reporter', someone who believed there was no substitute for being on the spot and talking to the people involved. Some critics accused him of editorialising, but he believed it was wrong to remain dispassionate about issues that were truly shocking.[17]

Wheeler also became disenchanted with a BBC management that was increasingly controlling and apparently fearful of government. When presenting *Newsnight* in 1987, he had a famous spat with the then Deputy Director-General, John Birt, over his arrogant assertion that *Newsnight* should do more analysis, without defining why or what he meant. Although this took place at a private meeting of the Current Affairs department, this was recorded for posterity and available for viewing on the internet.[18] Wheeler carried on reporting into his 80s, continuing to criticise what he saw as a loss of direction of the BBC News, with its 24-hour rolling news and tabloid agenda. Unlike the current generation of reporters, big beasts like Wheeler and Taylor were not on short-term contracts, not fearful of unemployment if they rebelled, and not afraid to question how such editorial shibboleths as 'impartiality' or 'balance' are applied.

The scrupulous fairness, the search for balance that was always the BBC's central principle, has been tested over time. For many of us working for the BBC during the 1970s, the very notion of 'balance' was ludicrously simplistic. An unchallenged assumption of British broadcasting, it suggested the reducibility of all issues to a two-dimensional, oppositional model, as if fairness and insight could be achieved by sitting opposing viewpoints on either end of a notional see-saw. As any primary school child knows, balance is then achieved by where you choose to insert the fulcrum: the judgement remains firmly in the constructor's, or producer's, hands. Producers know how much, or how little, licence they have in exercising that judgement. Rarely written down, this latitude reflects the received opinions of the time, the political position of the organisation *vis-à-vis* the government and its licence renewal, and corresponding economic and commercial pressures on the channel. Over time, all broadcasters are called to account on how they exercise that judgement and, in anticipation of that reckoning, sometimes fight shy of supporting their reporters' independence.

James Mossman was one of the great reporters of *Panorama* in the 1960s, something of a matinee idol at a time when as many as 20 million people watched the programme. Generally considered one of the best and brightest stars of his generation, Mossman incurred the wrath of his then masters by his hard interviewing of Prime Minister Harold Wilson, and later for taking the Prime Minister of Singapore to task for his tendency to incarcerate his political opponents. He angered even Hugh Carleton Greene, the BBC's normally easy-going Director-General (1960–9), who said of the Mossman–Wilson interview that he 'had shown too much personal emotion. He had not been justified in appearing personally involved'. Following the Singapore PM questioning, when Mossman chaired a discussion at a meeting of Commonwealth leaders, Greene felt enough was enough. He circulated a furious memo, saying:

> Mossman's handling of the discussion last night was absolutely deplorable . . . He was opinionated and rude . . . Has the time come when we should decide once and for all that Mossman should not be used any more in roles to which he is unsuited?[19]

A National Theatre play in 2007, *The Reporter* by Nicholas Wright, explores how Mossman's career took a downward turn after this and ended in his suicide in 1971. His suicide note was enigmatic: 'I can't bear it any more, though I don't know what "it" is'.[20] An extreme reaction to rejection, but that is the precipitate downside of stardom in any world. Reporters are not immune to the blandishments of fame, and need support in their difficult work in front of the camera.

Constant pressures

Many reporters have found their licence revoked, as a result of their independence of mind embarrassing the powers that be. The UK media are very keen on systems of self-regulation, in which companies are encouraged to police and censor their own, under threat of more severe sanctions. This sometimes puts managements in the position of backing good reportage only at cost to their own future. Thames TV paid the ultimate price when a *This Week* film in 1988, in which Julian Manyon reported on alleged SAS executions of IRA suspects in Gibraltar,[21] so infuriated the Thatcher government that the rules governing Independent Television contracts due for renewal in 1991 were changed. This led to Thames losing its long-running, lucrative franchise to supply London and southeast England with its weekday independent television. *This Week* editor Roger Bolton was no stranger to such controversy over Ireland stories, having already had run-ins with the government when editing the BBC's *Tonight* and *Panorama* programmes, but the scale of the reaction orchestrated in the right-wing press made sure that the fallout was far greater this time.[22] The story and its political impact is told at length in Pat Holland's *Angry Buzz*:

> Margaret Thatcher was deeply outraged by the audacity of *This Week*'s journalism. For her it was, quite literally, treachery to question the actions of the security services. An eminent Conservative peer told Roger Bolton that he hoped the experience of the Inquiry 'would put us and other television teams off making such programmes'. He was also told by a vocal critic of the programme, 'Of course there was a shoot to kill policy in Gibraltar, just as there was in the Far East and Aden . . . But it is none of your business. There are certain areas of the British national interest you shouldn't get involved in.'
>
> (*Observer*, 4 March 1990)[23]

Political pressures have constrained editorial freedoms on both sides of the Atlantic. Award-winning investigations producer Charles Lewis left his well-paid job at CBS's *60 Minutes* in 1989, to set up the Center for Public Integrity in his back room. We shall return to his subsequent successes in the next chapter, but the need he felt at the end of the Reagan era (1981–9) to escape an increasingly stifling corporate world more than justified the financial sacrifice. 'My colleagues thought me mad,' he says, 'but it was the sanest thing I ever did.'[24] Other reporters at that time found the political climate and its tentacles harder to escape. Five leading UK environment correspondents, in both newspapers and broadcast, lost their portfolios within one year during the Major era (1990–7). Some believe undue government pressure was exerted on all the major news organisations to reconsider their commitment to what the Tories thought their Achilles heel – the environment – and which they cynically denigrated as 'muck-raking' journalism. As a result of that pressure those leading environment correspondent portfolios were largely subsumed within more anodyne responsibilities and 'difficult' reporters were paid off. It is not a story that has ever been pursued, not least because it reflects so badly on the very organisations that might be expected to resist such pressure. A generation later, the environment has become the story of the era and every organisation and politician is scrambling to establish their environmental credentials.

The other key pressure to impact upon serious reportage is commercial: the broadcasters' constant fight for audience share in an increasingly fragmented marketplace and, for many, a corresponding dependence on dwindling advertising revenues. Commissioners are under constant demand to refresh their product in every genre, even where news and current affairs are central planks in their public service licence obligations. Many serious reporters feel that they have been squeezed out in favour of younger, more attractive, less challenging television models. *Panorama*'s downsizing and rebranding is only the latest in a long line of BBC efforts to bring a younger, hipper audience to current affairs. They sent rock bassist Alex James, of Blur fame, to Colombia to investigate the local effects of the cocaine trade of which he had once been such an enthusiastic consumer.[25] Unequipped with the critical detachment of a good reporter, he interviewed the country's right-wing, CIA-supported President Uribe as if he was a global guru in the 'war on drugs', leaving this viewer wondering whether the BBC had finally mislaid its marbles. The programme even persisted in captioning the country as 'Columbia'.

Reportage was the name given to the first attempt to produce a current affairs magazine for a young audience, running on BBC2 from 1988 to 1994 under the aegis of the then Head of Youth Programming, Janet Street-Porter. Stylish young presenters, such as Sanka Guha and Magenta Devine, fronted fast-moving programmes about youth-friendly topics such as music and investigative exposés of issues like football hooliganism. It was all a bit amateurish, and famous for cutting off interviewees before they had said anything, but it did introduce an early sense of interactivity by running phone-ins and conducting phone polls. Guha and Devine became most closely associated with the long-running *Rough Guide* travel shows, which inserted some cultural and political awareness into the travel genre, but youth current affairs fell by the wayside, to be occasionally resuscitated in increasingly short-lived shows such as 2003's *Weekend with Rod Liddle and Katie Silverton*. Then producer Ben Rich set out his stall on the BBC website:

> We want to cover politics and current affairs in the way we talk about it amongst ourselves (most of our team scrape in under 45 too), sometimes serious, sometimes passionate and sometimes mocking. For whatever reason, people in our age group watch less television news and current affairs than older people, and we want to see if it is the style that is putting many of us off. Our presenters, former *Today* programme editor, Rod Liddle, and Kate Silverton, presenter of numerous BBC current affairs documentaries, and host of Sky News' 3D programme, will, we hope, offer a sharp and occasionally humorous take on the week's events.[26]

Apart from the inadvisability of attempting to attract a young audience by assuring them that the programme-makers mostly 'scrape in under 45 too', airing this show at 9 am on a Saturday morning, when most of the target audience would be safely in bed nursing the hangover or conquest of the night before, raises questions about the sanity of those BBC chiefs. This traditionally is a programme slot reserved for children's programmes aimed at entertaining the kids while their parents sleep it off. Yet this was not some casual decision, but the outcome of a £100,000 year-long review to find out why the under-45s were not watching political programmes. It was a review undertaken because the BBC was approaching another of its regular jousts with the government over its licence fee renewal, and politicians were increasingly unhappy at their fall from favour in the public eye, instanced by collapsing electoral turnouts. So it was an important attempt to reinvigorate the democratic process. Bizarrely, it chose to scrap relatively successful shows such as BBC1's *On the Record*, with the authoritative, if silver-haired, John Humphreys at the helm, and introduce embarrassments like *Weekend*, with the curly-haired maverick Rod Liddle, 43, strangely at sea. Stephen Pile in *The Daily Telegraph* enthusiastically skewered this effort:

> What has changed is that the firm but liberal Dimbleby-style interview has been replaced by the truculent, retarded adolescent, Liddle-style. In last week's programme they did an

item examining why British youth lead the world in sexually transmitted diseases. Liddle was on absolutely top form. Always keen to advance his youth credentials, he said: 'Young people have become more and more promiscuous, which on the face of it seems like a good thing to me.' Cool, Rod . . . they are pretending to be hip, but the mask keeps slipping. Why does the BBC not just employ a bona fide young person?[27]

Rod Liddle, it should be acknowledged, had been a successful editor of the flagship BBC Radio 4 *Today* programme, deft at behind-the-scenes manipulation of reporters and stories to keep this establishment water-pump refreshingly novel and challenging. But the skills of a good editor are very different from a good reporter, just as you wouldn't expect a top notch football manager to return to the pitch as a promising striker. Exposing him in this way left Liddle 'pouting at the camera like a moody teenager',[28] in Pile's phrase, and the show faced an early bath.

I have run this story at length not just for its entertainment value but for the light it throws on the snakepit in which reporters are trying to practise and hone their craft. The snares of the celebrity culture that has come to dominate so much of popular discourse in the twenty-first century make it all the harder for a good reporter to go about their serious business undistracted by the bright lights and blandishments on offer. Reporters such as Rageh Omaar have the very double-edged success of being catapulted from the relative obscurity of the newsroom to international celebrity overnight. The man they dubbed the 'Scud Stud' for his frontline Iraq war despatches was delivering the Huw Wheldon lecture within a few weeks and now shows up as one of the subjects on photographer Samir Hussein's 'Celebrities' website, just below Tom Cruise.[29] In terms of the BBC's diversity objectives, having a black reporter who is also a practising Muslim certainly helps diminish the perception of the corporation as being, in Greg Dyke's words, 'hideously white'. But it is a lot of pressure to place on one man's shoulders, especially as his Baghdad dispatches inevitably attracted charges of bias from right-wing politicians and pundits. Rapidly headhunted by the nascent Al-Jazeera English channel in 2006, Omaar continues to front major documentaries for the BBC, but often I feel for the appeal of his name rather than the depth of his knowledge. His *This World: Child Slavery* (BBC2, March 2007) took him on an epic journey around a gigantic subject, involving an estimated 8.4 million children worldwide, but failed to mount a more effective critique than saying this was a bad thing. This was not reportage in depth.

Reportage today

Change is an inevitable aspect of the commercially competitive landscape of television, but there needs to be protection afforded to the fine craft of reportage, all the more so in times and areas of public disinterest, just as there is to endangered animal species. Former *Panorama* producer Kevin Sutcliffe, now responsible for the award-winning *Dispatches* and *Unreported World* strands at the UK Channel 4, feels that change and protection are perfectly compatible. Whereas he feels that while BBC current affairs is still struggling to move on from its past lost authoritative pre-eminence, Channel 4's more diverse, individualistic approach has enabled it to weather change better:

Since the invasion of Iraq in 2003, I think people have become aware that the world is a much more dangerous place, and that's the sensibility we cater to. They want to know more about that dangerous world and that's what brings them to serious current affairs ... *Dispatches* has become much clearer what its priorities are, and currently it is Afghanistan, Iraq and the War on Terror, which we may return to at least six times in a year. It means I can't do the subjects I might have found quite interesting in the past but, because we have a clear proposition, we can punch above our weight ... *Dispatches* is on air 40 weeks a year at 8.00 pm on Monday – up from 32 last year – and that's a serious commitment to hard investigative journalism in a prime spot ... Where else [in the UK] can you find an hour of in-depth current affairs television every week on prime-time terrestrial television? It should be happening on the BBC, but it's not.[30]

This chapter has largely concentrated on high-end reporting, the laudable aim of the best not just to make a name but to make a difference. But the increasingly transitory nature of broadcast commissions puts more and more reporters and producers in the fingernail club of the freelance world. The desire to rock the boat is more than offset by the imminent capsizing of a career. And a combination of increasingly determinist forms of editorial control and tighter deadlines makes it all the less likely that the reporter has the freedom or the time to evolve an independent line of inquiry. In the same way that the face that addresses the camera is often no more than the mouthpiece of the unseen producer behind, the rise and fall of programmes and their messages is also determined by the ebb and flow of the powerful but often unremarked tides of media politics. As James Curran and Jean Seaton suggest, in their seminal study of media politics, *Power Without Responsibility*, the regulatory framework of British broadcasting keeps the broadcasters in a role of uneasy subservience to the state:

Broadcasters have come to see the state as their enemy. Yet broadcasting institutions ultimately depend on the state for their legitimisation. This authority cannot be replaced by a pluralist ideal of reflecting social and cultural variety. Indeed the adoption of this principle has left broadcasters peculiarly vulnerable to the more general attack on public service broadcasting.[31]

The stakes are high precisely because reportage at the highest level reveals flaws at the highest level. The best reporters have not only paid their dues but been to places and seen things denied to most of us. The doyen of news presenters in the UK, the main host of *Channel 4 News*, Jon Snow earned his authority from over three decades of tramping the world as a foreign reporter, and he still leaves the studio to report big events, conferences and disasters from the front line. He is a genial and intensely fair-minded man, but is not wedded to old school ideas of balance, as he writes in the postscript to his book, *Shooting History:*

I am a politically motivated journalist, but not in the party-political sense. I even argue that we are the best kind of journalists, we who are fuelled by passion and determination to alert our fellow human beings to the truth.

I suppose the central truth that I have arrived at ... is that in our immediate age, the war without end that is the 'war on terror' is proving a dangerous and wrongheaded strategy that is driving communities apart at home and abroad. It threatens to fracture our world. The contorting of events to fit an ideologically-based global analysis is proving more dangerous by the day.[32]

A very different kind of television reporter has grown from other traditions, the video diary (Chapter 4) and the travelogue (Chapter 13). In the way that earlier masters of written reportage made extended pen portraits of distant parts of the world and their experiences in them, lightweight video and DV cameras have empowered a new wave of travellers with sound and vision. Many operate at the cheap and light end of the market, investigating various aspects of hedonism and youth culture, from clubbing to extreme sports. For instance, Ashley Haynes became very well known for his exploits exploring the *Sin Cities* of the world in two 15-part series for UK satellite channel Bravo, bravely sampling countless sexual delights and perversions for the audience while maintaining a quizzical, self-deprecating eye for the camera. His personality and humour rise above the often tawdry nature of his subject matter.

Sean Langan, operating at the other end of the journalistic spectrum where few would like or dare to go, brings a very twenty-first century take to on-camera reporting. He has perfected the use of the hand-held camera to record intimate details in dangerous regions such as Iraq and Afghanistan and his own reactions and thoughts at the same time. His camera captures his own responses in every eventuality from fear to fun, interview to personal reflection. He achieves a unique insight to situations beyond the reach of conventional cameras, chatting with the Taliban or with Shia women, and bringing a much-needed humanity and understanding to arenas of conflict. Films made for *Dispatches* in 2006[33] saw Langan dodging bullets in a firefight and penetrating deep into a Taliban mountain stronghold. Consistent with his confessional camera style is the honesty with which he reveals the terror that such moments can produce, and the wish that he hadn't come this far. Not for him the traditional machismo of the war reporter: this is a very modern response to the problems reporters face.

Sean Langan fell into television by accident – as a features journalist heading for Kashmir and asked to take a camera along to make a video diary (about which series, more in Chapter 4). So technically inexpert was he then that Langan says the BBC technicians taped up all the controls on his Hi-8 video camera save the on–off button, yet so extraordinary was the material that he shot following up the trail of Kashmir kidnappers and their victims that it launched him on an award-winning career:

> Because I wasn't a there making a TV programme, I was there as a journalist and I got so carried away with the story and I got to know the family of the hostage and it became genuinely a very personal journey I was just filming and, as a result, I think it's definitely

Figure 1.1
Sean Langan displays his trademark hand-held camera technique

the best TV I've ever done, compared to all my other stuff. Two reasons: I got very involved in it, passionately involved, I got caught up in the whole thing, looking for these hostages. I wasn't there thinking: 'I'm a TV guy making a documentary', and yet I did religiously film everything and that helped it; but that whole thing that I was genuinely there for six months . . . Even then I realised that this was the way I wanted to make documentaries, find something you're passionately interested in and find the time to follow it through and, if you've got the time, that will compensate for a million other faults. At the same time I realised that, having found the way I wanted to work, there lies a zero career because, to wait until you find a story close to your heart, and then take as long as it takes, in today's television you won't have a career.[34]

Sean Langan's trademark style is the way he holds his camera at arm's length, enabling him to swivel the lens to capture his own comments, reactions and laconic asides, whether interviewing Taliban insurgents or dodging bullets with a British army in a firefight. He finds it unnerving to be asked learned questions about this method at documentary conferences because he admits the style emerged from him being too lazy to carry the tripod he was originally sent out with to do his reflective diary pieces on.

The flouting of conventions undoubtedly helped reinvigorate the documentary form, and many people feel that Current Affairs departments would be stronger if more had taken a more robust and innovative approach to their programme-making, keeping abreast of audiences' changing needs and perceptions. As Langan says, there was and maybe still is a view that serious stuff should be like 'eating your greens', something not very pleasant but good for you. He sees no reason why all forms of television shouldn't try equally hard to entertain and his view is that his best work comes from those natural, revealing human moments that emerge unprompted, whereas his least successful is when it is freighted with a preordained thesis or the pressures of a commissioner hungry for a timely result. Ed Braman, who edits the *Unreported World* strand for Channel 4, agrees:

The only options in current affairs were either to be pointy-headed or to be vulgar . . . We spent so much time pretending we were the elite, that current affairs was the television equivalent of Latin, it was only to be dealt with like Oxford Greats by a certain esoteric bunch of people who could speak seven different languages and knew the calibre of the Taliban's weapons . . . We developed a belief, that was shared across all current affairs programmes, that were elite private little clubs, that it was our job to tell the stories not that people wanted to hear but the stories people ought to hear . . . Today we talk about narrative storytelling. If current affairs had done that job earlier, and understood that that was what our job was, if we had understood real lessons from documentarists, a lot of these problems would have been attenuated early on.[35]

Whereas Peter Taylor's films are the considered distillation of a large amount of research, enabling him to command a clear line by which he leads us through complex stories, Sean Langan's work uses the travails of his travels as the narrative. The viewer shares the journey and its revelations as they happen. Of course, the apparent serendipity of these journeys underplays his considerable experience and the planning and negotiations that get him into these often extraordinary situations. But Langan's films do not pretend to the commanding overview, they offer an intimate perspective from the ground, the front line. They succeed through the sheer force of personality and skill of Langan himself, largely working alone. One sofa-bound critic regretted Langan's failure to ask the Taliban more probing questions but, quite apart from the questionable sense of being difficult when guns are trained on you, that is not Langan's style. He gets up close and personal with whomever he meets, Tommies and Taliban alike. The way they respond is very much part of getting to understand these men better. In 2008, Langan paid the penalty of getting that close, being kidnapped in the Pakistan–Afghanistan border region. Because of the remoteness and Langan's lonely way of working, it was three weeks before his family and Channel 4 employers found out, and three months before they secured his release. Traumatised, and having been subjected to mock executions, he tells me that the experience has entirely wiped out his short-term memory. Such is the price of dedication to reportage.

Getting up close and personal – while hopefully affording reporters some measure of protection – is the main justification for using 'embedded' correspondents in wars, notably in the 2003 Iraqi invasion. Reporters who camped and tramped with individual military units were able to film hitherto unseen aspects of war and share its impact and hardships. 'Embedding' journalists . . . has brought warfare home to us as no war has been brought home before', says former BBC war correspondent Martin Bell. However, critics of this device argue that this is a very effective way of controlling the media by getting them focused on the minutiae, all seen from one side and too closely bonded to their units to take a critically detached view. Reporters from across the political spectrum have also attacked the abuse of the Green Book in Afghanistan – a contract drawn up between the UK Ministry of Defence and media organisations to guarantee maximum press freedom while preserving operational security (Opsec) – which was actually invoked to support reporters who toe the MOD line, a subject we shall return to in Chapter 9. Research undertaken by the Cardiff University School of Journalism for the BBC after the Iraq invasion found elements of truth in both positions. Professor Justin Lewis, deputy director of the Cardiff journalism school, said at the NewsXchange conference in Budapest in November 2003:

> The criticisms that were made at the time, that the embedded reporters were more likely to give a pro-war spin, do not hold up. But we do have some reservations, particularly about the narrative that is created by embedded reports, where the only discussion is about who's winning and who's losing, with little of the wider picture.[36]

The study also found that television reports produced by embedded correspondents during the conflict in Iraq gave a 'sanitised' picture of war. Those who were concerned about that sanitising effect and refused the stifling embrace of the military minders in Iraq were more liable to pay the ultimate price, as did the ITN's experienced war reporter, Terry Lloyd, who was killed by that worst of all euphemisms, 'friendly fire'. The inquest in October 2006 found that Lloyd had been unlawfully killed by US troops firing on the minibus in which the already injured Lloyd was being evacuated from the battlefield. The Oxford coroner said: 'I have no doubt that it was an unlawful act to fire on this minibus.' Lloyd's cameraman and translator were also killed, but absolved of any mistake or lack of preparation in this assign-ment. The General Secretary of the UK National Union of Journalists, Jeremy Dear added:

> The killing of journalists with impunity must never, ever go unpunished. Any attempt to silence journalists in this way must never succeed. The inquest verdict has confirmed what

we always suspected: that Terry's death was not an accident in the theatre of war but a callous act of murder.[37]

These are the very real risks that reporters who work in the front line face. The Committee for the Protection of Journalists lists 66 confirmed deaths of journalists in the line of duty during 2007, 32 of them in Iraq, and a further 22 yet to be confirmed.[38] Most reporters choose not to work in such lethal zones, but the same key qualities distinguish all good reporters: passion, preparation and precision. They bring to their craft an uncompromising dedication and determination that not many people associate with work. They undertake meticulous research and planning as to how best to capture and frame their story. And they have a real respect for detail, knowing that every word and picture can make the difference to the credibility and to the effect of its final form.

Reportage on camera

Americans have a disrespectful term for presenters chosen for their looks rather than their journalistic skills: 'eye candy'. The camera clearly flatters certain kinds of good looks, but the potential love affair is often truncated as soon as the mouth is opened. The faces that last are not necessarily the prettiest, but those whose personality and intelligence best fits the job in hand. Neither Andrew Marr, the BBC's former Political Editor, nor Evan Davis, the BBC's former Economics Editor, are quite in the running to be the next James Bond, but their luminous enthusiasm for and verbal mastery of their briefs make them great, natural communicators. As former ITN chief Stewart Purvis says:

> You can't teach it. You can't define it. You can't fake it. You'll know it when you see it . . . An ability to trot out facts isn't enough. Pick away at the seams of those facts to get at things that really matter, be genuinely interested in ordinary people – if you're too detached from their hopes and fears you're an academic, not a journalist. If you're jaded by the work after thirty days or even thirty years, get out of the job. One golden rule? Have something to say.[39]

There is another golden rule, easier stated than observed: keep it simple. A news reporter has on average about 90 seconds to voice a report on a UK television. At an optimum of 3 words a second that is a maximum of 270 words, without pause and allowing no inserted interview or actuality, which would in most cases be unacceptable. On a live link to the studio he or she may have the opportunity of supplementary questions from the news anchor, but either way these are colossal constraints when trying to impart the context and complexity of a story. During the Bosnian war in the early 1990s, the BBC's East European correspondent was Mischa Glenny, also a respected historian of the Balkans. He found the persistent and growing demands from his editors in London for ever shorter bulletins summarising the former Yugoslavia's immensely complex ancient, multifaceted tribalisms in two-dimensional bite-sized packages increasingly intolerable.[40] He eventually resigned rather than travesty his knowledge.

Other reporters will say that there is always a way to say something meaningful, however briefly, without trivialising the subject. Each has their own way of immersing themselves in mounds of detail, and then emerging with a clear line through it. The best reporters have an inordinate respect for words, their power and dramatic effect. John Simpson, himself an Oxford English graduate, but better known as the BBC's World Affairs Editor, is an admirer of his fellow wordsmiths, like BBC News special correspondent Jeremy Bowen. In Simpson's third volume of autobiography, *News from No Man's Land: Reporting the World*, he quotes a Bowen 1999 dispatch from Kosovo, in which he 'rounds out the details the camera can't':

> The flat stank of urine and decay. Something was very badly wrong. She said her name; she is seventy years old, and a Serb in a place where Serbs are no longer welcome. She was weak and confused. Her front door had been kicked in, the neighbours said, by Albanian fighters from the KLA.
>
> Her photo album was open: the family in better times. A young Serb paramilitary, perhaps a grandson with a machine gun, and her husband with the Yugoslav army in the Second World War.
>
> She kept looking back. Then we realised the decomposing body of her husband was in there with her. He'd been dead for six days.
>
> In normal countries, you'd call the police. But in Kosovo there are no police. NATO smashed their buildings and forced the policemen, all Serbs, to leave. NATO's armoured columns provide overall security, not social services. Twenty-four hours later, she was still there.

> This is reporting of the highest order it seems to me . . . It moves from the life of a single disregarded individual to the level of international politics in a few terse, underwritten sentences. And it is deeply discomforting. As you watch the pictures and listen to the words, you are forced to consider what happened to the old woman and why; and about our own involvement in this entire campaign. And yet Bowen doesn't tell you what to think: he just presents you with the painful facts, then leaves it up to you to decide.[41]

That eye for the telling detail, with the visual pictures augmented by the spoken ones, is a particular skill. It is the opposite of the obvious: the reporter doesn't need to tell you what you can already see, but the things that you cannot, whether it is the smell or the unseen significance of the scene. Instinctively identifying that significance requires more than judgement, it needs both nerve and knowledge. The number of specialist portfolios in television news has not just grown to fulfil reporters' career prospects. They are necessary so that more reporters have the time to acquire specialist skills and knowledge with which to counter the increasingly sophisticated massaging of messages from governments, corporations and other lobbying groups. However, when they get too close to the trail, as the environment correspondents did in the 1990s, the hunt itself is in danger of being abolished. The other danger is that specialists become too close to and cosy with the fields and interests on which they report. As Curran and Seaton observe:

> The popular image of journalists (elaborated in many movies) as intrepid hunters after hidden truths is hardly realistic. Specialist reporters in particular are closely involved with, and indeed dependent upon, their sources. Thus crime reporters identify with the police, defence correspondents with the services, and industrial relations experts with the trade unions. But, in addition, journalists who are better seen as bureaucrats than as buccaneers,

begin their work from a stock of plausible, well-defined and largely unconscious assumptions. Part of their job is to translate untidy reality into neat stories with beginnings, middles and denouements.[42]

Despite the overnight stardom of BBC Business Editor Robert Peston for breaking the Northern Rock collapse in 2008 and Treasury stories about the ensuing economic recession, there are many who believe that it was the failure of economics correspondents to maintain an adequate distance from their sources that left society so poorly forewarned about that recession, and its inevitability in hindsight. Yet Curran and Seaton's dystopian view need not be the only outcome of such 'swimming with the sharks'. A generation of reporters educated to interrogate those 'unconscious assumptions' and resist the freemasonry of professional association can yet be expected to hold the Machiavellian princes to account. It is not just a mechanical fact-checking skill that is required. It is the dogged digging of individuals with a particular understanding of their chosen field, the rugged individuality of the reporter who will not easily be misguided or scared off. It is a characteristic that translates as honesty and reliability on screen. As Andrew Marr writes in *My Trade: A Short History of British Journalism*:

> Journalism needs the unexpected. It needs the unpredictability and oddness of real life. That means it needs real reporters. There is no better protection against the special pleading and salesmanship of the PR machines than decently paid and experienced journalists, trusted inside their organisations to use their judgement.[43]

Conclusion

Screen reporting is a tough job, requiring reporters to always have their wits about them, even while looking good and always knowing which camera is on them. While some hang up their safari suits and settle to a life recycling all they know in fictional form, others migrate to the safer environs of the television studio and become the key newscasters. Their experience in the field is palpable in the authority they bring to news announcement, even when reading other people's words, though not all transplant successfully. Their experience can show in interview, particularly when confronting evasive politicians, but not all survive the migration from field to studio desk, where they become more part of a production machine. And some never entirely give up the front-line work. Jon Snow frequently quits the gleam of the Channel 4 newsroom for the glare of the real world at some key summit or disaster. BBC Foreign Correspondent Ben Brown has taken to the studio, presenting on the BBC News Channel and sometimes on prime-time News on BBC1, but he has no intention of permanently escaping the field, the real world of the reporter, where their eye is our window on the world.

That said, the world of reportage is moving on apace with the advances of the internet and online journalism. In 2003, the number of people in the world consuming their news first online overtook broadcast figures; in the United States over 80 per cent get their news online first.[44] The journalist, photographer and online guru Ben Hammersley – progenitor of the influential *Guardian* newspaper *Comment is free* weblog site and originator of the term 'podcasting' – claims that more Americans read British newspapers online than watch CNN, Fox News and MSN News combined. He believes that the combined skills of print and audio-visual journalism is just reaching a tipping point, where the new forms of web storytelling will render both hard copy and broadcast obsolete, or at least secondary. What he calls the traditional 'dead tree' newspaper edition will be no more than a daily printout of a 24-hour rolling news operation, but an operation that will supplant what he dismisses as 'the wallpaper of broadcast news', such as Sky News and the BBC News Channel:

> Web news is massively more popular than broadcast news now. I think that the big winners will be the newspapers and the big losers will be the broadcasters. . . . Bloke in suit behind desk talking to camera with prettier girl sitting next to him is not going to work. People don't watch it, with its logo and its theme tune for the war. But if we use it to just tell stories: fantastic![45]

News executives beg to differ, and the remodelling of Channel Five News in 2008, with the arrival on its red sofa of the comely Natasha Kaplinski at a reported £1 million annual salary, doubled its audience figures, according to head of news Chris Shaw.[46] This bucks the trend of diminished audiences elsewhere in the broadcast news spectrum, but may explain what one BBC journalist calls 'eye candy rampant', with the number of blondes hired recently. Concerned at the constant erosion of their audience, especially among the younger demographic, BBC News – newly restyled as a multimedia operation – is also experimenting with alternative delivery platforms they hope will appeal more, from their well-established website to mobile phones. Reporters and editors are encouraged to reveal a more human profile by regular blogging, but it is unlikely that the Wheelers and Taylors of this world will find a new outlet for their serious reportage on what the techies like to call 'the 4th screen'. The mobile phone may well have an expanding role as an information tool, but it is an inadequate device for communicating considered analysis or striking pictorial impressions. Furthermore, the undifferentiated mass of information and opinion – good, bad and indifferent – that is the internet is the antithesis of authoritative form. Even some of its gurus admit that its promiscuous torrent underlines the need for expert analysis that recipients can trust. Self-styled web apostate Andrew Keen says 'the internet is killing our culture:'

> Web 3.0 will be where the smart people seize back control and get rid of all this 'social media' fetishizing innocence, amateurs, the child in us. I am not against the internet, but I am for curating it by experts . . . The challenge for professional newspeople is: you have to learn to emancipate yourself from all this mass humility.[47]

While news organisations and industry experts cannot agree on what the digital future holds, it is best for the reporter to concentrate on perfecting the established verities of their craft. Stories that combine the dramatic elements of conflict, jeopardy and a satisfying denouement will always be in demand, as will those who can write and present those stories compellingly. An inquiring mind, that may sometimes find compliance with editorial or management dictate difficult, is also a prerequisite. Originality and freshness score highly, so investigations, particularly those involving the cloak and dagger of undercover work, are at a premium.

Expert briefing – presenting to camera

The presented documentary is usually one that has been largely researched and written in advance. Pieces to camera are normally constructed in the knowledge of where they will probably come in the final film, what information they must therefore include, and so tend to commit the filmmaker to a particular style and narrative arc. This is as true of a live linked news package as it is of meticulously researched, long-form documentary series. The process is just one aspect of well-planned filmmaking:

1 **Serving the story**: Good research not only distils a complex subject into a simple narrative, ensuring the essential information is drip-fed to the audience in comprehensible sequence and form, but also finds the pictures, people and places to support and augment that story. The reporter's job is to synthesise those elements and lead the audience by the hand down that preordained path. Pieces to camera are not essential, and each should be justified in context. How frequently presenters address the camera directly, if at all, is both an aesthetic and editorial decision, requiring answers to several questions, e.g.:
    - Will camera links clarify the story and be the most efficient means of imparting the necessary information?
    - Does the audience need a human 'interpreter' to negotiate difficult material, or will their presence stand in the way of sympathy with the subject?
    - Is the reporter one whose face and voice work well within this film, and have the right tone for and reputation with the target audience?
    - Do the locations for the film and the mode of shooting allow for engagingly framed pieces to camera that match and augment the content?

2 **Ownership**: These questions presume that the film is being made for a known programme slot and assumed audience, as most television commissions are. Reporters and presenters are generally selected as being appropriate to their audience, but their ego and professional desire to spend as much time as possible in front of the camera must be tempered by producers' and directors' consideration of the needs of the film. They also need to adjust their performance for the particular audience and context, such as time of day, in which the film will be viewed. But the best reportage is where all these elements cohere organically around the reporter and he or she has undisputed 'ownership' of the film, by virtue of having clearly conceived the film's message and imprinting their own character on every aspect of it.

3 **Setting out your stall**: The most widely-used piece to camera is the opening 'situationer', in which the reporter sets the scene in the most compelling location, telling the audience what the film is about and where it is headed. This is rarely the opening scene of a film, which commissioners prefer to be some visually or viscerally exciting sequence that will engage the audience to stay with you. But this is the moment your film's purpose and reporter's personality reveal themselves, so it needs to be perfectly pitched. Unless the documentary is necessarily shot in chronological order, as in a voyage of discovery, it is advisable to leave the shooting of this sequence to nearer the end, when the film's feel and everybody's performance is better bedded in and the scope is better known. Even the best-researched and prepared documentaries can take you down unexpected paths, often to the film's benefit. If, for instance, your reporter set out to film the story of a country's agrarian revolution,

but ended up recording the outbreak of civil war, your opening link would need to be changed.

4 **Wrapping it up**: The second most obvious link, though less popular these days except in news – because of its tendency to be glibly conclusive – is the tailpiece. In a world short on absolute certainties, reporters are discouraged from being too prescriptive, but there are occasions where a summary is useful and enumerating the questions left unanswered can suit the moral relativities of the day. Elsewhere links may act as bridges to new locations or themes within the film, or may describe things the reporter witnessed but could not film or show. Increasingly, this personalised use of the reporter to share the sensations and emotions of 'being there' is what such pieces are used for. This often requires the link to be delivered in some telling, active environment – a military firefight or a hospital ER – which contemporary digital technology has made increasingly feasible, but which are normally delivered extempore, i.e. on the hoof and unscripted.

5 **Keep it simple**: Whenever and wherever written and performed, pieces to camera should be short and pithy, delivered in the present tense and addressed directly to the camera as if in conversation to an equal. They should not preach or patronise, nor presuppose much prior knowledge of the subject: they should avoid technical terms and jargon, facts and figures as much as possible. Where figures are unavoidable, they should usually be rounded up or down to make them easily speakable. £4,859,976 is 'just under five million pounds'; 'nearly one in four children live in lone-parent families' (actually 22.9 per cent or 2,672,000 dependent children). But when it comes to politically contentious statistics, such as the numbers of asylum-seekers and prisoners in jail, or the rate of inflation, it pays to be precise. Of course, all facts must be accurate and checked before committing to film, or the resulting piece to camera will have to be binned. The penalties of reporters ad-libbing vital information, albeit on BBC Radio 4's *Today* programme, were dramatically proven in the head-rolling fallout of the Hutton Report on Andrew Gilligan's broadcast about the 'dodgy dossier' on Iraq's presumed Weapons of Mass Destruction.

6 **Know what you are saying**: While pieces to camera may well be written in advance, they should never be read on camera. Most seasoned reporters do not work from a verbatim script, but have a very clear idea of what they have to say and how long they have to say it. The most common form they work from are written as bullet points – the three or four facts or thoughts they have to communicate – buttressed by essential details and names. They will have worked out a few well-chosen phrases, and that's as much rehearsal as most will undertake, in order to avoid becoming unnatural and wooden. None of this is easy, especially if the shot has other live elements or shot development within it. Then, even when picture and performance are perfect, the requirements of sustained, uninterrupted sound often occasion another run. On documentary location, pieces to camera are the shots requiring the most retakes. You will frequently see screen reporters' flailing fists conducting themselves through what was probably the frustrating umpteenth take. In case the creative demands prove over-ambitious, it often pays to do a safety take in a less fractious environment.

7 **Know how it will fit**: Increasing use of freer form, improvised documentary incurs less constructive angst, but even chirpy asides to camera in observational documentary mode still have to fulfil all of the above strictures. They need to convey the right level of accurate information in useable sound bites. Witty repartee with travelling companions on a long journey rarely translates into pithy extracts when edited. The important

context is the final film, not the moment of recording, and the astute reporter always knows how such links might fit with the other sequences being shot. The freer the form, the clearer the reporter or producer should be about the balance of the material being shot.

8 **Sense and celebrity**: The increasing use of celebrities undertaking what have been called 'immersive' documentaries – where they share their voyages of discovery on camera – inevitably use a subjective presentational form that frequently has them speaking to others, i.e. not to camera. This liberates them to personalise and editorialise, but often necessitates a second, anonymous voiceover commentary presenting the facts and reinforcing the message. This is a documentary appropriation from formatted factual entertainment shows, where such emphatic narrative reinforcement is used to build suspense.

9 **Look the part**: It may seem obvious but, if the presenter is seen regularly on camera, their appearance is as important as their words. Consistency in clothing, condition and facial fuzz is essential if you do not want your audience distracted. Film presenter Barry Norman was so famous earlier in his career for wearing different shirts in shots for the same scene that it became a running gag in a comedy sketch show. If not shooting in narrative sequence, it is advisable to keep your presenter wearing similar clothing throughout. Many carry several identical shirts to avoid the problem. Similarly, it is a good idea to keep the same hair style throughout a shoot, and ensure males shave consistently throughout. Such considerations can seem trivial on a long shoot in difficult circumstances but, when you spend time in an edit trying to make a serious presenter look less like a quick-changing impressionist, you will wish you had been more meticulous.

10 **Film speaks for itself**: Documentary film is about revealing stories through pictures and experience; and the danger of allowing an inexperienced reporter free rein is that the only editorial content ends up in the pieces to camera, and all the pictures are no more than animated postcards of the reporter's travels, which amount to nothing without his or her constant commentary. This is the making of a home movie, not true reportage like that of Sean Langan. A good reporter, however large and characterful a presence, should always be serving the story, helping bring it to life. This can be through voicing their experience to camera, but that voice should never be at the cost of letting the pictures and people filmed speak for themselves.

2 Exposé: investigations, undercover and the so-jo

exposé n. – the act or an instance of bringing a scandal, crime, etc. to public notice

The linear arrangements of a chapter can make for arbitrary distinctions that do not adequately reflect the complexity of life, and it is abundantly clear that some reporters featured in the previous chapter – Murrow, Pilger, Taylor, etc. – are investigative journalists *par excellence*. But they ply their craft in the field of mainstream current affairs, alongside which has grown, on the one hand, a specialist field of investigative journalism and, on the other, a field of television that started in the UK in the 1980s with a large reporter called Roger Cook, who specialised in doorstepping crooks, literally putting his foot inside their doors, frequently suffering abrasions and even bone fractures as a result.[1] The growing demand for investigations and exposés is part of television's wider search for sensation and excitement to keep audiences from slipping away. Most US stations now have a unit dedicated to investigations of one kind or another, frequently investigating consumer concerns close to home, such as Los Angeles NBC affiliate Channel 4's *Investigative Reports* featuring shows like *Contaminated: Restaurant Food Investigation* , where 'award-winning Joel Grover goes undercover and exposes dangerous problems with food that ends up in popular SoCal restaurants'.[2] January 2007 saw the launch of *CNN: Special Investigations Unit* , a new long-form investigative series, airing Saturdays and Sundays at 8 pm Eastern Time, that features CNN's top correspondents delivering in-depth reports on pressing issues currently in the news'.[3] More of what current (in America, public) affairs does routinely, you might think, but given that extra filip with the buzz-word 'investigation'.

In the UK, Channel 4's premier current affairs programme, *Dispatches*, set a new standard for investigative reporting week in and week out. It also runs an occasional sub-strand deploying another buzz-word, 'undercover', where reporters infiltrate institutions, using miniature cameras, microphones and recorders so that, posing as nurses or air stewards, they can secretly film their co-workers slacking on the job. Undercover exposés between July 2005 and January 2007 included *Undercover Teacher* (revealing 'the depressing conditions at three of the country's most troubled secondary schools', July 2005), *Undercover in the Secret State* ('the cruel realities of daily life in North Korea, presenting powerful undercover footage and interviews with defectors fleeing the regime', October 2005), *Undercover Angels* ('a damning catalogue of inefficiency, neglect and sub-standard treatment that clearly compromises patient care' in two NHS hospitals, 2006) and *Undercover Mosque* ('preachers condemning integration into British society, condemning democracy and praising the Taliban for killing

Figure 2.1
Undercover Mosque proves the
value of covert filming
technology

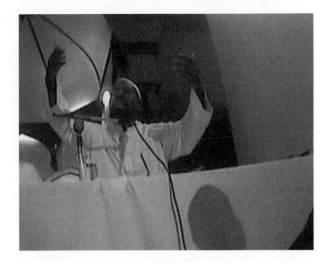

British soldiers', Birmingham, January 2007), not to mention *Ryanair: Caught Napping* ('what really takes place behind the scenes: inadequate safety and security checks, dirty planes, exhausted cabin crew and pilots complaining about the number of hours they have to fly', February 2006).[4]

These cautionary tales all purport to bring a scandal, if not a crime, to public notice and are only officially sanctioned if there is circumstantial evidence that some wrongdoing is taking place, *and* the only way to record actual evidence is by going undercover. In a legal climate where libel proceedings are an ever-present threat, British broadcasters have very explicit and increasingly stringent guidelines governing the commissioning of secret filming, and meticulous compliance with those guidelines is a first test in any consequent legal proceedings. So-called 'fishing expeditions' – where you go undercover hoping to find a story – are explicitly banned and Channel 4, like the BBC, have clearly laid out procedures, involving legal checks and eventual reference to the very senior Director of Programmes level before any such filming can take place:

> Secret filming and recording are powerful journalistic tools. Material obtained covertly may be the only independent account of the wrongdoing it captures. In the past, secretly filmed or recorded exposés have led to the revision of working practices, changes of the law, the closure of institutions and can even send criminals to prison.
>
> But with power comes responsibility. Covert filming should never be considered just another programming technique and must not be abused. Law-abiding individuals who have done nothing wrong are entitled to have their privacy respected. The right to privacy can only be overridden where the public interest outweighs it.
>
> (*Channel 4 Compliance Manual*, p. 98)

High stakes

The legal fallout can be substantial. Former *World in Action* investigative reporter Donald MacIntyre kick-started the current trend for undercover with his series *MacIntyre Undercover* for the BBC in 1999. It was allegedly then the most expensive current affairs series ever made, and was a largely successful attempt to find a contemporary frame for a programme genre in popular decline. In the four programmes of this series, MacIntyre infiltrated: a gang of football hooligans; the model girl demi-monde and their 'fashion victims'; a bunch of Nigerian con men; and an old people's care home in Kent where inmates were prey to abuse. One of the hooligans was subsequently jailed and the care home was closed, with two people cautioned by the police for five incidences of assault on their elderly charges. Despite this, the police made unsubstantiated defamatory allegations about the programme being selectively edited, which were duly printed in *The Sunday Telegraph*. In a reversal of the usual roles, it was then MacIntyre who sued the police for libel, and who eventually won their apology and substantial damages in court. It was an important vindication for the journalist and the credibility of undercover investigations. MacIntyre had been clear about this when undertaking the action, with the BBC's full support:

> In making these allegations, they have both damaged my personal reputation as a journalist and brought the reputation of the BBC's journalism into question. It is a funda-mental purpose of journalism to give voice to those who, because of their circum-stances, are unable to speak for themselves. It would not serve the public interest if our findings were diminished by totally unfounded and defamatory comments made by Kent Police.[5]

These are laudable motives and MacIntyre already had a substantial reputation to defend. He had won two Royal Television Society journalism awards for his 1996 investigations for ITV's *World In Action*, into the links between drug dealers and the private security firms who control nightclub doors. But, as the BBC programme's title suggests, he was also protecting a brand, the MacIntyre name. This raises more difficult issues regarding the whole practice of undercover investigation, which logically requires anonymity. Even in the making of the series *MacIntyre Undercover*, the reporter regularly risked blowing his cover and endangering his safety by recording pieces to camera *in situ*, such as in the bar where the fashion world bigwigs were secretly filmed taking advantage of their young models.[6] It might be argued that these pieces added nothing to the investigations, and could have jeopardised them, but added substantially to the brand MacIntyre. It did however make a second series of *MacIntyre Undercover* impossible, because his face was now very well known. MacIntyre himself was under no illusions about the service he was there to perform:

> Journalism is too small or too distant a word to cover it. It is theatre; there are no second takes. It is drama – it is improvisation, infiltration and psychological warfare.[7]

There is a small handful of investigative video-journalists working for broadcast in the UK, whose operation relies upon their anonymity, and who not only will not allow their face to be seen on screen but never allow their real name to appear in the credits. For them, the self-serving antics of a MacIntyre would be an anathema, and professional suicide. MacIntyre himself has gone on to present television programmes on other subjects, such as weather phenomena and wildlife, for BBC1 and UK Channel Five. He returned to something of the criminal world with another series for Five called *MacIntyre's Underworld*, and another form of undercover in *MacIntyre's Big Sting*.[8] In the latter he turns the table on criminals and con men by conning them, inviting fraudsters on to stage only to be arrested, or leaving a television set in the back of a car so that a local thief would steal it. The technology involved, such as the bug inside the set, add a frisson for the audience but, as MacIntyre beards the gull who bought the stolen TV set in his local pub and humiliates him and his family for our self-righteous entertainment, we wonder what greater good is served. Director of the London Centre for Investigative Journalism, Gavin MacFadyen, feels the whole 'undercover' genre is grossly overplayed, and can demean the work of serious investigative journalism:

> Anyone who puts 'Undercover' in the title is doing it just for sensation. An investigative journalist uses undercover techniques because there is no other way of getting the story. They can be useful and important, but they are a method of last resort.[9]

Undercover brings other problems, not least with repetition, as one success is often hard to repeat, irrespective of the familiarity or otherwise of the reporter. One of the BBC's most lauded undercover investigations was into a police training college in northern England. *The Secret Policeman* featured a young reporter, Mark Daly, enlisting as a police recruit and going through basic training.[10] His hidden cameras and microphones revealed a subculture of rampant racism among his fellow recruits, and the film's broadcast caused a storm of outrage, not least from the police, still bruised by having been branded 'institutionally racist' by the Stephen Lawrence inquiry in 1999.[11] The most bigoted of the police recruits filmed, PC Rob Pulling, was heard saying that Lawrence 'deserved to die' and his parents were 'spongers', as well as saying Hitler 'had the right idea' and he would kill an Asian 'if I could get away with burying the fucker under a train track'. Pulling and 11 others resigned or were sacked by the police, but Daly, whose cover was blown before transmission, was arrested on suspicion of 'obtaining a pecuniary advantage by deception and damaging police property'.[12] He had apparently adapted his bullet proof vest to take the hidden camera lens. The charges were eventually dropped, but were indicative of a culture of suppression of the truth, rather than its confrontation, in the police hierarchy. The BBC's then chief legal officer Glen del Medico revealed that the Greater Manchester police made strenuous efforts at the highest level to stop the film being transmitted:

> There were very hairy meetings between senior levels of Greater Manchester police and senior levels of the BBC. It's a bit of a commentary on the way in which the police do not necessarily have a great deal of interest in fighting racism.[13]

Del Medico and other BBC executives rightly consider this one of the best exposés the BBC has ever made, but were all too aware of the dangers they faced. Although they had sufficient circumstantial information to justify the investigation, had Daly been caught before he had recorded any of the damning evidence, he and the BBC would have been vulnerable to the most savage retaliation from police and government. As it was, the then Home Secretary, David Blunkett, initially accused the BBC of 'a covert stunt', acting as an agent provocateur, creating not reporting the story,[14] though on hearing the film he was persuaded to recant, calling the evidence 'horrendous'. Following the impact of *The Secret Policeman*, producer Simon Ford was under pressure to repeat its successful undercover formula. For this he needed a new target and a new reporter. The result was *The Secret Agent*, in which reporter Jason Gwynne infiltrated the British National Party, proving they enjoy racist views.[15] One unsympathetic reviewer commented that this was as revelatory as finding

Catholicism in the Vatican.[16] The film did lead to BNP leader Nick Griffin being charged with incitement to racial hatred, but he was eventually found not guilty in 2006. Since the film showed Griffin saying at a public meeting that Islam was a 'wicked religion' and that Muslims were turning Britain into 'a multiracial hell-hole', it suggests that Britain's race and religious hate laws are inadequate, arguably leaving the BNP strengthened, rather than diminished by the film. One of the obvious limitations of undercover, observational documentary is that this form militates against comment and analysis, whereas investigative work presupposes a sabre-toothed moral.

Investigative beginnings

So what exactly is investigative journalism? The UK Centre for Investigative Journalism says it is 'journalism in defence of the public interest'.[17] Hugo de Burgh writes: 'An investigative journalist is a man or woman whose profession it is to discover the truth and to identify lapses from it in whatever media may be available.'[18] The Center for Public Integrity says it 'is dedicated to producing original investigative journalism about significant public issues to make institutional power more transparent and accountable'.[19] The Berkeley School of Journalism's Center for Investigative Reporting says it 'is working to ensure that high-quality, credible, unique journalism does not die, but flourishes',[20] making more explicit the context of need that it serves:

> We are living in an age of upheaval, institutional collapse, and historic unforeseen change. And journalism is not immune. The only 'business' protected by the Constitution, the business of informing the public, has been eviscerated in recent years. The role that journalism plays in a functioning democracy – informing the public and holding the powerful accountable – is at serious risk. Major issues affecting the very fabric of this nation and the world go uninvestigated.[21]

So one might infer that the term 'investigative journalism' is an unintentionally ironic comment on the standard of journalism generally, implying all too accurately that government and corporate statements are routinely reported without too many difficult questions being asked, as Nick Davies (2008) confirms. The form was identified in the United States as early as 1880, with Henry Demarest Lloyd's articles on corruption in business and politics for the *Atlantic Monthly*. One of the first undercover reporters was the 18-year-old Nellie Bly, who first worked in a Pittsburgh factory to expose the appalling conditions of child labourers at the time for the *Pittsburgh Dispatch* and, from 1887, did many such exposés for Joseph Pulitzer's *New York World*, including feigning insanity to reveal the physical and mental abuses in an asylum on Blackwell's Island. By 1906, ten magazines concentrating on investigative journalism had a combined circulation of three million. Even President Theodore T. Roosevelt had taken note of this Zeitgeist and, on reading in Upton Sinclair's *The Jungle*, which described in lurid detail the filthy conditions in the meat packing industry[22] – where rats, putrid meat and poisoned rat bait were routinely ground up into sausages – he introduced the popular Meat Inspection Act and the Pure Food and Drug Act of 1906.[23] However, when a writer called David Graham Phillips wrote a series of articles called 'The Treason in the Senate' for *Cosmopolitan* magazine, Roosevelt took exception to its attacks on his political allies. He compared Phillips to the muckraker in Bunyan's *Pilgrim's*

Progress: 'the man who could look no way but downward with the muckrake in his hands; who would neither look up nor regard the crown he was offered, but continued to rake to himself the filth on the floor.'[24] Roosevelt saw the developing power of the media and set the twentieth-century presidential standard for using it to communicate with people, while attempting to constrain its tendency to ask difficult questions.

The apotheosis of investigative journalism in the United States was the Watergate investigation by the *Washington Post's* Bob Woodward and Carl Bernstein. Exposing a break-in to the Democrats' Watergate offices by agents of the Committee to Re-Elect the President (CREEP), this investigation so incriminated Richard Nixon that he was eventually forced to resign the presidency. Results – or scalps – do not come bigger than that and, although this inspired a generation of investigative reporters, it has also been blamed for arrogance and complacency in some of them. Woodward and Bernstein's book of their investigation, *All the President's Men*[25] – and much more, the Hollywood film of the same name[26] – became the lodestone for the ambitious reporter, but their luck and opportunity was not easily replicated. Daniel writes that the 1998 media feeding frenzy that surrounded the Clinton–Lewinsky scandal was an attempt to repeat that journalistic high, which reflected worse on the pursuers than on the pursued. 'Even truth could not rescue bad journalism':[27]

In most ways, the climate in which investigative reporting functioned in the 25 years that followed Watergate was not unlike that which preceded the event. Newspapers published and television aired excellent stories that revealed problems in government, business and society at large. Similarly, editors and reporters erred in ways that damaged their credibility and questioned the motives and methods of the profession . . . Most important, significant segments of the public perceived the press, with its penchant for invading privacy and using methods that seemed unfair at best, as contributing to the nation's problems rather, than helping to find its solutions.[28]

Hard times

So the 'muckraker' label has continued to stick to investigative journalists who dare to question the establishment and the status quo, and has helped discourage many proprietors from continuing to support work that they see as biting the hand that feeds them. London's *Sunday Times* had the world-renowned investigative *Insight* team – producing definitive reports into the issues of the day, such as the Northern Ireland Troubles[29] – until media mogul Rupert Murdoch bought the paper in 1986 and closed their investigations down. This was at the peak of the Thatcher decade, when business was in the ascendancy and media deregulation was the order of the day. As Murdoch's Fox news operation in the United States confirms, his empire is not in the business of asking awkward questions at cost to those imperial interests. Barnett (2005) further comments that the vital role investigative journalism plays in an informed and accountable democracy is now under serious threat from corporatisation, competition and cost-cutting.[30] While mounting a robust defence of BBC journalism – which he feels has been unfairly accused of going soft after the Hutton report judged the BBC harshly over its critical reporting of the intelligence dossier that justified the government's commitment to the Iraq war – Barnett argues that the forces and sophistication of the PR industry are stifling journalism. He quotes the BBC's Ian Hargreaves:

The fear among journalists is that they no longer have the resources to counter the increasingly sophisticated munitions of their traditional enemy, that journalism is being hung out to dry by the not-so-hidden persuaders.[31]

On the other side of the Atlantic, the Reagan era (1981–8) had also been assiduously business-friendly, keen on media deregulation and political devolution. Muckrakers were having an exceptionally hard time. Even CBS' *60 Minutes*, which had replaced *CBS Reports* in 1968 and which still runs – the only current affairs show to ever top the ratings and the most award-garlanded TV show in history – had lost its edge as the often boat-rocking barnstormer it had been. Chief investigative reporter Mike Wallace's producer of seven years, Charles Lewis, felt his talents and potential were being wasted there. He recalls that his colleagues thought him mad when he resigned to set up the Center for Public Integrity in his own back room:

> I felt that on a good number of the most important public service corruption issues of our time, the media was asleep, and most of the federal government wasn't being covered at all, frankly. And so, there were lots of records, millions of records, I realized, that no one was reading. In the very first center report, we found that 47 per cent of all the White House trade officials over a 20-year period, both Republican and Democratic presidents, had left government and gone to work for foreign governments and foreign corporations – people they were negotiating against in trade deals – they would then go to work for, after they left government. You know, there was just never any coverage of what I just described. And so the model, in a way, was born.[32]

That model, involving the meticulous combing of sources and painstaking collation of data, has led to 275 CPI investigative reports and 14 books, with a host of awards for scoops on business scandals with oil, water and the Pentagon outsourcing gravy train. Charles Lewis has written three bestselling books on *The Selling of the President*, the Center for Public Integrity has become the largest non-profit making journalistic organisation in the world, and Lewis is unrepentant for having turned his back on television and the increasingly celebrity-driven, commercially compromised journalism he sees it having embraced. The non-profit, independently-funded way of doing investigative work was first developed by the Berkeley-based Center for Investigative Reporting – 'Journalism dedicated to revealing injustice since 1977' – which happily subverts the negative with its 'Muckrakers' Blog'.[33] The launch in 2007 of ProPublica – with a $10 million endowment and run by former *Wall Street Journal* managing editor Paul Steiger – confirmed the move of investigative journalism away from news organisations dependent on advertising and distribution to an independence sustained by endowment funding, which is tax-free.[34] It prompted a *New York Times* op-ed to consider whether this should not be the future for all journalism:

> By endowing our most valued sources of news we would free them from the strictures of an obsolete business model and offer them a permanent place in society, like that of America's colleges and universities. Endowments would transform newspapers into unshakable fixtures of American life, with greater stability and enhanced independence that would allow them to serve the public good more effectively.[35]

Veteran investigative journalist Gavin MacFadyen, Director of the Centre for Investigative Journalism at London's City University, has been equally gloomy at the way things have gone in British television since the heyday of programmes like the *World in Action*, which he worked on. But he detected the green shoots of recovery in the economic crisis of 2008/9. 'The climate is improving,' he says, 'because society is in such crisis that many more people want to find out what is going on.'[36] While the media had fallen behind, servicing the trivial obsessions of the hedonistic 1990s and the corporate bottom line, MacFadyen sees a more serious and sceptical generation of journalists emerging from their forced eye-opening with the 'war on terror' and the credit crunch. 'They realise most of what they had been told was wrong', he says. Even then, of the generation of business and economics journalists whose closeness to the markets they reported on made them largely blind to the coming crisis, he points out, few diverge from the orthodox line that there is no alternative to pouring huge sums into the banks and businesses that created the problem in the first place. MacFadyen is, if not optimistic, 'encouraged' by the outrage of the generation that will have to shoulder these debts, and he feels that the television stations will come to feed that need if it is commercially useful to them.

MacFadyen hopes this is part of a wider culture of journalistic challenge that started with investigative journalist Nick Davies's *Flat Earth News* (2008), which turned the tools of investigation on journalism itself, finding it seriously wanting. Davies found print and broadcast journalists spread perilously thin over an ever more demanding spread of bulletins and platforms, restricting time and resource for original reporting and forcing an increasing reliance on recycled PR material, what he calls 'churnalism'.[37] He believes it is this that has contributed to declining circulation and trust in serious journalism:

> There is a ready supply of overpaid media executives sucking on cigars and concluding that readers are deserting their newspapers because they don't care about what's happening in the world, don't particularly want the truth about anything and are happy to be spoonfed trivia and entertaining falsehood. The reverse is true. There is a mass of people out there who know very well that they can't believe everything they read, but who precisely are not willing to abandon the idea that it is the job of news media to tell them the truth.[38]

Prospects

The essence of investigative journalism is documentary, in the literal sense of documented facts. Its practitioners are obsessive diggers of facts and compilers of information, relentlessly seeking out the lines that join up the dots. As one said to me: 'You have to think the whole time: What if this comes to court?' It is time-consuming and therefore expensive and, if that is not enough to deter proprietors and their accountants, it sometimes fails to find adequate evidence to publish, thereby writing off that investment. Because the burden of proof needed to satisfy media lawyers that an investigative story is worth publishing – to the anger of the powerful figures fingered and with the likelihood of expensive suit following – palpable evidence is required and incontrovertible video and audio is a powerful tool in any journalist's box. For some years, tabloid stings as practised by *The News of the World* have been captured on undercover video, to protect against legal action. As broadsheet papers have begun to extend their web operations into video, more journalists have taken this approach. *The Sunday Times* investigation in 2009, which revealed that at least four peers in the House of Lords were prepared to sell influence for substantial sums, was also recorded on video. The story was published first in the paper, causing a huge political storm, but when some people began to question just how true it was that the lords were really corrupt, the video was released on *The Times* website to confirm it.[39]

To many of these obsessive seekers after truth, the form it emerges on is secondary to getting the story right, and both the tools of evidence and the converging means of distribution are moving its practitioners towards shared ways of work and multimedia outputs. Award-winning documentary producer Sharon Tiller is Producer for Special Projects at the syndicated Public Broadcasting Service (PBS) investigative programme *Frontline:*

> *Frontline World* began in 2000 as an idea to develop an international news magazine, covering all the stories we couldn't do on air. In 2005, we decided we are an online series – all our creativity and experimentation is going into the Web, and for *Frontline* it is a sort of pilot or experimental project for the TV series.[40]

Steve Talbot, Director of the Berkeley Graduate School of Journalism sees that 'the future of journalism and investigative journalism is online'.[41] The Center for Public Integrity's Charles Lewis agrees:

> I don't see this as a despairing time. I see this is as an absolutely, beyond words, thrilling time, because this is where television news was in the late 1940s. Except this is larger than television – that was just one medium. So I actually think this is far larger and far more relentless than that. And that was huge. It opened up an entire new world to the masses, a mass audience around the world . . . The good news is you have a global reach, potentially, in breathtaking ways, and you will be able to gain access to expertise that most journalists do not gain expertise to, no matter how hard they try.[42]

Tiller talks of this, her multimedia world, being heavily dependent upon a new generation of young entrants who are at least dual-skilled, enabling them to service both the filmic and the written aspects of investigative journalism, though, as she honestly admits, it is in part because 'that's what we can afford'.[43] Yet, while there is heavy investment by both broadcasters and newspapers in this form of multimedia online journalism, which many see as the future dominant platform, none have so far found a commercial model for making it pay. Even as the conventional print and broadcast news media contract, their existing forms subsidise the journalism and the production of what appears on their websites. What would replace that support, if conventional media whither and die, is exercising many minds in the media and academia (Fenton 2009). In the United States, MacFadyen says, most serious investigative journalism is now funded by trusts and charitable foundations and there are prospects of this happening in the UK, despite the economic meltdown. This returns the initiative to the investigative journalist, ensuring the work is undertaken, before it finds its appropriate platform for distribution. As proprietors and broadcasters continue to cut costs, serious work is generally the first to suffer, but there may yet be the revived demand, MacFadyen predicts, if the work is already being undertaken.

Flying solo

In the interim, there are many who hymn the potential of the video-journalist, not just the lonely vigil of the undercover reporter, but the self-sufficient individual who is equipped to meet all challenges and platform deadlines, essentially equipped with just a digital camera and a laptop that enables him to write, edit and file. We have already met Sean Langan, whose brave odysseys into enemy strongholds in places like Afghanistan not only give a unique insight into those alien cultures, but nearly cost him his life. As I record, Langan came to this role as a photographer drafted in to do one of the early BBC *Video Diaries*, but others have moved in the opposite direction, from conventional mainstream camerawork to the more personal and reflective video-journalism that enables a deeper understanding of the world. Little of this work is yet formally investigative, but its ethics, aesthetics and techniques show potential for what might be achieved. Kevin Sites was a seasoned war reporter covering the war in Iraq as a freelance for NBC, when one event propelled him into a different orbit. Sites was embedded with the US Marines in Fallujah, when he happened to film a Marine illegally executing some wounded prisoners in a mosque. All footage at the time was pooled, meaning it was offered to every news outlet internationally. These graphic shots of a war crime were used in their entirety throughout the world, except in the United States, where – if used at all – stations censored the actual shooting. Sites was branded 'unpatriotic' and 'un-American' but, as he says, 'ultimately your loyalty has to be to the truth'.[44] Had he not also been blogging from Iraq, he says, he would not have had the chance to explain the full story, its context, his feelings and the journalistic rules of engagement, not least in an 'Open Letter to Devil Dogs of the 3.1'. It was the kind of multidimensional reporting denied him by the conventional news media and was a kind of epiphany, allowing him to realise the power of the internet:

> I felt like this, potentially, saved my career. It allowed me to tell the story that I hadn't told on network news. It was a 'do-over'. You don't get many chances at do-overs.[45]

So, when Sites returned home, he changed his way of work and became an online video-journalist, spending a year getting behind the news stories in twenty of the world's major conflict zones, as Yahoo!'s first news correspondent. *Kevin Sites in the Hot Zone* (2006) produced a stream of blogs, reports, stills and videos from the 20 most dangerous places on Earth, from Chechnya to the Congo, Burma to the Middle East. Sites's year of war zone travels are now repackaged as a documentary: *A World of Conflict*, released as a series of 15 online chapters, which concentrate on the human victims of war.[46] These play as a conventional documentary, rather than as a piece of investigative journalism, but the ethical posture and the solo technique are subtly subversive of conventional war coverage and do point one multimedia way forward for such work. A growing body of documentary work is being shared in segments like this, via YouTube and other sites.

Former BBC and ITN reporter David Dunkley Gyimah – who actually started his career on the *Reportage* series mentioned in Chapter 1 – is equally passionate about the technical and independent possibilities of multimedia journalism on the net. His solo-produced online *View Magazine* also deploys original journalism and comment, with writing, video, audio and stills, and an increasingly sophisticated array of technological devices that make the potential of the multidimensionality described by Sites more immediate. The site proclaims itself 'A different style and form of storytelling':[47]

If you could combine the art of motion graphics and photography, the mis-en-scene and arcing of the cinema, the language of television, the skill of radio with users' behaviour online, I believe we would be closer to understanding the power of video journalism.[48]

Gyimah is developing video hyperlinking, allowing intertextual video reference to function in the same way as meta-tagging verbal links, and talks of cameras with face recognition technology that will allow this intuitively. He not only wants the off-cuts of extracted interviews and material normally discarded in editing to be available, but linkable in and out of at any point in the cut video. He talks of 'second shift aesthetics', by which he means picking up and developing topics that mainstream television has raised but failed to satisfy its audience, either by reasons of brevity or misrepresentation.[49] Gyimah's is a fertile imagination, excited by technology and delighted to exploit the escape from the narrative linearity of traditional television and the straitjacket of news agenda and timescale. His conception of video-journalism stands in stark contrast to the newspapers and broadcasters who see VJs as a cheap alternative to crews and traditional work practices. Gyimah sees himself primarily as a filmmaker, and there is a distinctive filmic aesthetic to much of what he does. 'I shoot what I call dirty', he says, referring to his hand-held, unsettled, roving eye approach to cinematography. But his shooting, and its editing, are all in service of a new democratic ideal of what this medium offers. 'The idea of actually using a camera in itself, while not revolutionary, is part of an attempt to kind of push the agenda back, and get into a whole debate about news'.[50]

Others express this as replacing the old hierarchies of information – such as that which denied Americans the truth about the Fallujah shooting – with a 'blueberry pancake' model of information sharing, in which all blueberries exist at the same level. Even the traditional news media have embraced interactivity with their audiences, and eagerly trawl for 'user-generated content' (UGC). Investigative journalists speak of 'crowd-sourcing', where communities of interest can supply huge resources of raw data, which once would have taken ages of phone-bashing or yards of shoe leather, very quickly. But there remain widespread doubts about how much these inputs can – or will be allowed to – fundamentally shift the hierarchy of values implicit in the news agenda (Lee-Wright 2009). Similarly, the widely-trumpeted 'citizen journalist' is still a relatively powerless blueberry. The Center for Public Integrity has published a book called *Citizen Muckraking: Stories and Tools for Defeating the Goliaths of Our Day* (2000), showing how the qualities of curiosity and persistence that can make a difference are now open to all, but Charles Lewis strikes a cautionary note:

The other side of it, one that I worry about in social networking, is all investigative reporting is potentially actionable . . . the quality control, vetting, chain of custody. The internal kind of sausage-making by which newsroom assumptions are made by editors and reporters – there is no model that I'm aware of yet for social networking . . . But the challenge is you still have to have an internal quality control mechanism in a centralized way at some place before you publish.[51]

American journalists are well acclimatised to the corporate damage-limitation exercise known as 'fact-checking', and many of us have met the withering contempt of lawyers demanding justification of an assertion if all we can say is: 'it is true'. Brant Houston, executive director of the US non-profit organisation Investigative Reporters and Editors, believes that libel insurance and pro bono legal support can be found for individual investigative journalists willing to go the extra mile on stories for the internet.[52] Houston feels that economics have largely seen off the old teams of investigative reporters, but thinks that 'in-depth niche-topic reporting has the potential to be particularly lucrative online'.[53] The only alternative being widely discussed is more inter-media 'partnering'. Sharon Tiller points to successful collaborations with *The New York Times*, *The Christian Science Monitor* and the *Chicago Tribune*.[54] Whoever is picking up the tab and however the bills and outputs are being shared, video documentary evidence will continue to be more and more important.

One in the eye

One man who thinks he has this field originally covered, is Rob Spence. The Canadian documentary filmmaker lost his eye in a shotgun accident when he was a child, and has come up with an intriguing way to make a benefit of this tragedy:

> I am in development with the National Film Board in Canada to make a documentary called *Eye 4 an Eye*. By retrofitting my prosthetic eye into a wireless and web connected video camera I become a symbolic 'Little Brother' media virus who goes on a cybernetic journey literally from my point of view.[55]

Spence calls on Orwell's dystopian vision in *1984* rather more knowingly than the better-known *Big Brother* show (for more about which, see Chapter 12). *Eye 4 an Eye* aims to reveal the ubiquitous technology and tyranny of the surveillance society by this ultimate subversion of undercover recording. Allegedly the mini-optics, recording and transmission technology are well advanced and the final challenge to conquer is the precise form of the fuel cell, with technologists looking into the possibility of using the renewable resource of liquid from the tear duct. If this seems like science fiction, it originally was, being essentially the conceit of a novel *The Continuous Katherine Mortenhoe, or The Unsleeping Eye* written by David Compton in 1974[56] and subsequently filmed by Bernard Tavernier as *Le Mort en direct* (1980), with Harvey Keitel as the documentary cameraman with a camera implanted in his brain. Still a gleam in the eye of Rob Spence at the time of writing, it is clearly going to be a reality before long. Not that there will be many cameramen willing to lose an eye for the new technology. But the story does act as a reminder of the true value of investigative journalism, of bringing an original eye to bear on issues and systems that we take for granted, or have partially filtered through the lenses of vested interests.

Cutting through the commercial and political thickets in search of the truth remains a central tenet of documentary, from its earliest proponents to today's Oscar-winning tyros. It is notable that the first film of one of the great social documentarists was also an exposé of abuse in a psychiatric hospital – Frederick Wiseman's *Titicut Follies* (1969).[57] Using what became his trademark long take, hand-held, unlit black-and-white, 16 mm film shooting style, Wiseman revealed the unthinking cruelty of the institution – and by implication the institutionalised brutality of American society – so unaware of its unpleasantness that it welcomed the camera in. Robert Coles writes:

> After a showing of *Titicut Follies* the mind does not dwell on the hospital's ancient and even laughable physical plant, or its pitiable social atmosphere. What sticks, what really

hurts is the sight of human life made cheap and betrayed. We see men needlessly stripped bare, insulted, herded about callously, mocked, taunted. We see them ignored or locked interminably in cells. We hear the craziness in the air, the sudden outbursts, the quieter but stronger undertow of irrational noise that any doctor who has worked under such circumstances can only take for so long. But much more significantly, we see the 'professionals', the doctors and workers who hold the fort in the Bridgewaters of this nation, and they are all over . . . *Titicut Follies* is a brilliant work of art . . .[58]

Exposing the abuse of those unable to fend for themselves remains one of the key objectives of investigative journalism, with the elderly particularly vulnerable, as MacIntyre showed. In July 2005, BBC1's *Panorama* programme showed a film called *Undercover Nurses*, revealing a catalogue of failures at the Royal Sussex Hospital in Brighton. Shot on hidden cameras, it showed an acute medical ward with blood stains on curtains, faeces on floors, food for patients too ill to feed themselves left lying on bedside tables, old people abandoned without pain relief to die alone.

This material had been shot undercover by a nurse called Margaret Haywood. It was so effective it not only forced improvements at the hospital, but prompted a national debate about care of the elderly. A job well done, you might think. But, nearly four years later, Margaret Haywood was struck off by the Nursing and Midwifery Council for a 'major breach of the code of conduct', in invading the privacy of the patients she was hired to serve.[59] That their consent was subsequently obtained before transmission was not deemed adequate mitigation. The NMC decided:

> Only in the most exceptional circumstances should the cardinal principle of patient confidentiality be breached. Based upon the evidence it heard, the panel did not believe that this was the case and although the conditions on the ward were serious, it was not necessary to breach confidentiality to seek to improve them by the method chosen.[60]

Haywood had unsuccessfully raised her concerns with management, and the conditions had been failing at the hospital for some time, as NHS inspections had made clear. It raises the question just how 'exceptional' circumstances would have to be before whistle-blowing was justified. A qualified science teacher, Alex Dolan, who filmed chaotic classrooms in four secondary school classrooms as a supply teacher over six months for *Dispatches Undercover Teacher*,[61] was similarly rewarded for her public-spirited revelation of the ill-disciplined conditions under which teachers now routinely work. She was suspended from teaching for a year by the General Teaching Council for 'unacceptable professional conduct', on the now familiar grounds that she invaded her pupils' privacy and there were other ways she could have raised her concerns.[62] As Kevin Sutcliffe, the Editor of *Dispatches*, who commissioned the film for Channel 4, said, 'It is disappointing that the GTC chose to pursue Alex as the "messenger" rather than address the issues the film raised.'[63]

Conclusion

One of the first laws enacted under the then New Labour government was the Public Interest Disclosure Act, commonly known as the 'Whistleblowers' Charter', which came into force in January 1999. This was designed to give protection to employees who, in the public interest, revealed systematic failings in their workplace. Both Dolan and Haywood might reasonably have supposed their actions were protected under this act, specifically section 'D' on 'Disclosures qualifying for protection', specifying 'that the health or safety of any individual has been, is being or is likely to be endangered'.[64] Privacy issues are being paraded as the catch-all justification for keeping the veil firmly drawn over systemic professional misconduct. Such films are vilified for daring to challenge the authority of professional establishments whose vested interests still outweigh the clear public interests involved. And the invocation of legal and professional hearings is intended to discourage such investigations as being too costly to justify in straitened times.

Journalism, television and the internet are all, severally and collectively, at an epochal crossroads. While some investigative journalists like Nick Davies, and the 'cigar-chewing executives' he blames, may well regret the passing of twentieth-century systems of work that served them well, other investigative journalists – from Charles Lewis to Kevin Sites – find the new ways of work that the internet offers the most exciting development imaginable. The technology has enabled access to material formerly impenetrable, and to the means of processing the resulting data that did not exist before. Equally importantly, it has put the tools of recording and editing such material within reach of many; and it provides a global transmission platform accessible to each and every one of them, depriving the corporations of their exclusive door-keeper role. American technology analyst Clay Shirky sees this time to be as historic and as chaotic as the fifteenth century, when Gutenberg's printing press was in the process of putting the monastic scribes out of work, eventually leading to the Reformation as it put the Bible within everyone's reach by printing it in their own language, thus undermining the Church's role as divine gatekeeper.[65] Whether or not the broadcasters will be dissolved – their lands seized and their graven images desecrated – Shirky is right in emphasising that the crucial filter is not now at the points of production or distribution, but in consumption, the choice the consumer makes from the plethora of products on offer.

Chaos is apparent in the collapse of the old economic order and the failure of clear new business models yet to emerge. Certainly the idealistic 'blueberry pancake' model fails to offer the clear pathways that consumers need to navigate the morass and some internet gurus, such as Andrew Keen, argue that the media need to liberate themselves from the 'mass humility' and false modesty that has embraced new technology and social media without knowing what to do with it.

While the experts thrash around in uncertainty, it is a good time for innovators to show their stuff. As MacFadyen says, there is a largely unmet need for serious, relevant journalism that begins to explain the systemic failures that surround us, making all expertise suspect. 'At no time since the 1960s [the time of the Vietnam War] has there been such a young generation – sceptical, filled with radical outrage and a passion for justice', he says.[66] It is that underlying ethic that binds the disparate threads in this argument, from the core investigative issues of public interest and accountability to the new forms of video storytelling that David Gyimah champions. Confronted by the apogee, then humiliating failure, of the neo-liberal project that was the Bush regime, there emerged a shared recognition of a need for change. Combining a journalistic imperative to ask deep questions with new means of communicating the answers, filmic investigative journalism meets that need, whether self-generating or in new media partnerships to share costs. But the overriding feature that will distinguish effective work in the visual medium is a good eye and an original approach. It is that documentary filmmaking sensibility that is the common thread running through all the sub-genres in these chapters.

3   **Search engines**: As Dick comments, it is impossible to be precisely prescriptive since search engine features and options develop faster than the printed word. Google's Advanced functions make it possible to refine your search either to academic or NGO domains, as does Yahoo!; Technorati is the leading blog search engine; Twitter is evolving as a key social networking and news site. But, just as BBC researchers before the advent of the internet had to be reminded of the phone directory, bureaucracy's tendency to gather and list information makes everything from people to fact-finding intrinsically easier today. '192.com is the *de facto* standard search engine for finding people, business and places across the UK', but 'since most personal profiles, public records and other people-related documents are stored in databases and not on static web pages, most of the higher-quality information about people is simply "invisible" to a regular search engine'. www.pipl.com offers access to what is known as 'the deep web', 'estimated at 500 times that of the surface web, yet has remained mostly untapped due to the limitations of traditional search engines'.[68]

4   **Freedom of information**: While the USA have had a Freedom of Information Act since 1966, allowing access to government information and documents, the UK had to wait for its own FOIA Until 2000, only finally coming into force in 2005. Although with more exemptions than the US FOIA and subject to ministerial veto, this is an important tool for journalists, setting terms and time limits for their attempts to extract information from reluctant government departments, police, armed forces and the NHS. While *The Times*'s '59 things that would have stayed secret' enjoyed the eccentric indulgences of the powerful,[69] it was the dogged work of FOI campaigner Heather Brooke that led to the revelations of Westminster parliamentarians' systemic abuse of their allowances arrangements, despite their repeated attempts to block disclosure.[70] The Campaign for Freedom of Information publishes a useful online user's guide to the processes, protocols, costs and rights to appeal – all of which are relatively simple and straightforward – at www.cfoi.org.uk/pdf/foi_guide.pdf.

3 From lectures to landmarks: history and ideas

....

lecture n. 1 a discourse on a particular subject given or read to an audience
. . . 4 a lengthy reprimand or scolding

The single most widespread change in the presentation of British television in recent years has been the desire of broadcasters not to be seen to be lecturing their audience, for fear of driving away even more than are already migrating to other entertainment sources. The liberal, inclusive nature of modern society discourages broadcasters from their traditional role of advising audiences what is good for them. A largely anti-intellectual consensus reads in 'lecture' its pejorative 'reprimand or scolding' definition. Yet one whole strand of television grew out of this modern take on the lantern-slide lecture and there are still survivors of that tradition, ones that clearly contradict the apparent all-encompassing demand for a dumbed-down television mostly presented by people who are no challenge to the average mind but proof that everybody deserves a chance. Despite everything, there is one area of lecturing that has survived the intellectual cull and even produced some unpredictable audience successes. The unlikely hero of this hour is the academic historian.

The art of history and the history of art
....

Academia has had a love–hate relationship with the vulgar tool that is television, a box many professors profess they watch only rarely. The first 'TV don' was Alan J.P. Taylor, initially the token intellectual on a BBC panel discussion show *In The News* from 1950 to 1954, when he was fired for being too argumentative. ITV picked him up for their rival discussion programme *Free Speech*, where he remained until the series was cancelled in 1961, but by then he had established himself as the unrivalled master of half-hour lectures delivered direct to the camera, without notes or recording breaks. These programmes, mostly on twentieth-century subjects such as Russia's October Revolution and the Great War, were popular and established A.J.P. Taylor as the best-known British historian of the time. His colleagues in university common rooms around the country were vociferous in their condemnation of this 'prostitution' of his talent, while many were privately turning green with envy.

Most of the general public are blissfully unaware how differences between academics are as deep, and often more deeply felt, than those routinely expressed by politicians of opposing parties; such differences can lead to feuds that last a lifetime. A.J.P. Taylor was an unstinting controversialist who enjoyed the battle as much as the limelight, and spent most of his life popularity. He was mobbed and cheered at one public showing and was forced to hide in the lavatory for a while, weeping at the unexpected show of public affection.

Secondly, although Clark had been the youngest ever Director of the National Gallery, then Keeper of the King's Pictures and Slade Professor of Fine Art at Oxford, he had also been Chairman of the Independent Television Authority when Taylor made his regular appearances, so Clark knew something about television. He knew the camera favoured the personal and passionate presenter, but he also saw that it could explore the riches of art with a detail most people would not have seen before. It was that combination – of authoritative enthusiasm and privileged insight – that set the tone for this kind of television.

Thirdly, when it was successfully broadcast on PBS stations in the USA in 1969, *Civilisation* made a key contribution to the evolution of such factual programming as a world leader, earning Britain overseas income and influence, and leading to co-production with other broadcasters, particularly in the United States.

On the other hand, the conditional subtitle *'A Personal View'* rarely featured in any review or consideration, and has long been lost in translation. The heaping of so many eggs in one man's basket obliges the broadcaster and its audience to endorse a particular take on the subject, in this case Clark's belief that the Renaissance was the apogee of Western civilisation and that modern art was largely worthless. Not only did this enrage the modernists, but the sheer scale of *Civilisation* made it improbable that another series on art would be commissioned in the near future to air an alternative view. This unwanted skewing of issues earns television many detractors, who see undue weight given to individual historical interpretations they disagree with.

Today, Clark's unitary view of civilisation and fetishisation of individual artists is seen as naive. Furthermore, no specialist subject can exist free of philosophical and political implications, and television's taste for the personal can make that all the more explicit. Making his films during the seismic student revolts of 1968, the patrician Clark could not resist observations more popular with the establishment than with students:

> I can see them still through the University of the Sorbonne, impatient to change the world, vivid in hope, although what precisely they hope for, or believe in, I don't know . . . It is lack of confidence, more than anything else, that kills a civilisation. We can destroy ourselves by cynicism and disillusion, just as effectively as by bombs.[12]

Clark, who died in 1983, would be appalled at the cynicism widespread today, but consoled by the continuation of art history on television. In fact, the debate engendered by the reactionary aspects of his series eventually did help liberate some more adventurous commissions, such as the novelist, painter and art historian John Berger's influential series *Ways of Seeing* in 1972.[13] Made for a fraction of the cost of *Civilisation* by the BBC's Further Education department, *Ways of Seeing* tracked the commodification of the image from the Renaissance to the present. Whereas Clark had celebrated the aestheticisation of *The Nude*,[14] Berger deconstructed the images of women in art and their impact on modern advertising. As he explores, with rivetingly chosen illustrations, 'the essential way of seeing women, the essential use to which their images are put, has not changed:'[15]

> One might simplify this by saying: men act and women appear. Men look at women. Women watch themselves being looked at. This determines not only most relations between men and women but also the relation of women to themselves. The surveyor of women in herself is male: the surveyed female. Thus she turns herself into an object – and most particularly an object of vision: a sight.[16]

Ways of Seeing had an impact out of all proportion to its relatively modest audience numbers. It gave credence and graphic substance to the evolving social thinking central to the 1960s movements snubbed by Clark, and particularly to feminism and that movement's central tenet, that 'the personal is political'. Berger showed that television can deal with ideas in concrete and visually stimulating ways. It gave hope to young producers of that 1960s generation that ideas could still find a place in the television firmament. And it inspired others to take a more holistic approach to art history.

The Australian art critic Robert Hughes's 1980 BBC series on modern art was the obvious successor. *The Shock of the New: Art and the Century of Change* explored how art emerged from social and cultural change, and built its programmes thematically around the impact of technology, politics, secularism and evolving consciousness on modern art movements.[17] It also used an array of visual techniques to suggest how new ways of seeing evolved, such as mixing from the refraction of a car's headlights to the early Cubist fractures of Braque's vision:

> Television does not lend itself to abstract argument or lengthy categorisation. If the making of the series had one repeated phrase that still echoes in my head, it was not heard on the soundtrack; the inexorable voice of Lorna Pegram, the producer, muttering: 'It's a clever argument, Bob dear, but what are we supposed to be looking at?'. What the Box can do is show things, and tell . . . the great virtue of TV is its power to communicate enthusiasm, and that is why I like it. I am not a philosopher, but a journalist who has the good luck never to be bored by his subject.[18]

Bored Hughes may not be, but bullishly angry certainly. In 2004, nearly 25 years on from the first series – and now, as *Time* art critic, arguably the most influential in the world – the BBC invited Hughes to make a new episode of *The New Shock of the New*. The passion he communicated in 1980 seemed to have curdled into something like hatred for the contemporary art scene. Some uncharitably blamed Hughes's 1999 near-fatal car crash while making a television series following his 1987 Australian history, *The Fatal Shore*, the resulting legal actions against him and his subsequent depression. But his disenchantment with art as 'investment capital' or 'bullion' was explicit even in the first *The Shock of the New*.[19] What his coruscating critique addressed in 2004 was how this had come to dominate the art world, peddling conceptual art and gimmicks that impressionable people paid millions for, but he felt had no lasting value. He wrote at the time of the later film:

> Styles come and go, movements briefly coalesce (or fail to, more likely), but there has been one huge and dominant reality overshadowing Anglo-Euro-American art in the past 25 years, and *The Shock of the New* came out too early to take account of its full effects. This is the growing and tyrannous power of the market itself, which has its ups and downs but has so hugely distorted nearly everyone's relationship with aesthetics. That's why we decided to put Jeff Koons in the new programme: not because his work is beautiful or means anything much, but because it is such an extreme and self-satisfied manifestation of the sanctimony that attaches to big bucks. Koons really does think he's Michelangelo and is not shy to say so. The significant thing is that there are collectors, especially in America, who believe it. He has the slimy assurance, the gross patter about transcendence through art, of a blow-dried Baptist selling swamp acres in Florida. And the result is that

you can't imagine America's singularly depraved culture without him. He fits into Bush's America the way Warhol fitted into Reagan's.[20]

Ideas

This shocking conflation of images and ideas is, as he says, what 'the Box' – and Hughes in particular – can do well. You don't have to agree with everything such a telly-lecturer asserts, but you find it difficult to ignore. Even if such programmes make you angry, they have done their job, by exciting you to think. That active engagement was a feature of other groundbreaking series from the 1970s onwards. The mathematician Jacob Bronowski, a polymath who had written about subjects as diverse as William Blake and violence, Leonardo and Hegel, was invited to use his considerable knowledge and passion to make a series that would be seen as the scientific story of civilisation, *The Ascent of Man* (1973).[21] Another 13-part 'landmark', covering the cultural and ethical evolution of mankind, and science from Newton and Darwin to cloning and eugenics, it spanned the world and benefited from co-production funding by Time Warner. Bronowski's apparently omniscient engagement with the universe made a profound impact on his audience, nowhere more so than in the episode when he waded into the waters of Auschwitz and let the ashes of his ancestors run through his fingers. The suffering was central to the soul of the piece, the humility an important counter to Clark's patrician assurance, as commentators noted:

> In some ways, *The Ascent of Man* stands diametrically opposed to the patrician elegance of Clark's *Civilisation*. The elegy to Josiah Wedgewood [sic], for example, is based not on his aristocratic commissions but on the simple cream ware which transformed the kitchens of the emergent working classes. For all his praise of genius, from Galileo to von Neuman, Bronowski remains committed to what he calls a democracy of the intellect, the responsibility which knowledge brings, and which cannot be assigned unmonitored into the hands of the rich and powerful. Such a commitment, and such a faith in the future, may today ring hollow, especially given Bronowski's time-bound blindness to the contributions of women and land-based cultures. Yet it still offers, in the accents of joy and decency, an inspiration which a less optimistic and more authoritarian society needs perhaps more than ever.[22]

Ideas continued to be a concern of television and its makers up to the 1980s. Indeed, the broadcaster, philosopher and sometime Labour MP Bryan Magee had a surprise hit with a programme which simply featured him sitting in a studio with one of the leading philosophers of the time. *Men of Ideas* (1978) saw Isaiah Berlin, Herbert Marcuse, Noam Chomsky, Bernard Williams and 11 more leading thinkers sitting on its sofa and securing an audience keen to have its brains challenged.[23] To show how different television was 30 years ago, consider how likely you would be today to find a presenter posing this 'question' during prime time on BBC2. Yet Bryan Magee put it to Ernest Gellner, then Professor of Philosophy, Logic and Scientific Method at the London School of Economics:

> For a long time after confidence in the stable theistic premises of knowledge had been undermined, what people were looking for was a substitute for them. That is to say, there had for so long been a single category in terms of what everything was ultimately to be

explained, namely God, that for a long time people went on looking for some other such single category in terms of which everything was ultimately to be explained. At first they thought they had found it in Science. Then, with the neo-Kantians, History becomes the all-explaining category. Then you get Marxism, which tries to integrate History and Science into a single framework of ultimate explanation. It isn't till we get to distinctively modern thought – to, shall we say, Nietzsche – that people start to say: 'Perhaps there is no single category in terms of which everything is ultimately to be explained. Perhaps reality is, right to the very end of the road, pluralistic. Perhaps it just consists of a lot of different, separate things, and the only way to understand it is to investigate them severally. In this case any single, all-encompassing explanatory theory will be a delusion, a dream, and will prevent us from seeing reality as it is.' Bertrand Russell, just to take a single example, was very insistent on this approach. It deeply permeates the whole of modern Empiricism.[24]

The thought and its terms of expression could not appear on television today. Yet not only did this series score a resounding success, but Magee was invited to front a new series for the BBC in 1987, *The Great Philosophers*.[25] During the same time, the physician, opera director and sometime comedian Jonathan Miller had made a landmark medical series called *The Body in Question* (1978), David Attenborough fronted his first blockbuster series *Life on Earth: A Natural History* (1979) and American astronomer and astrobiologist Carl Sagan presented *Cosmos: A Personal Voyage* (1980, made by Los Angeles PBS affiliate KCET in co-production with the BBC, and one of the most widely seen PBS series of all time). It seemed at the time that the realm of ideas and the big series sprawling across the schedules for three months was here to stay, offering wonderful employment opportunities for the starrier academics.

Part of the promise of television at that time was the new vistas it also opened for professional journalists who had first made their name in print, then migrated to the more glamorous and better-paid reaches of television. Becoming familiar and well-trusted faces presenting regular current affairs programmes, some of these were then offered the opportunity to indulge their real interests, many of which were historical. Thus the reporters became the lecturers. Magnus Magnusson was chief feature writer at *The Scotsman* when he became co-presenter of *Tonight*. He went on to present programmes for the archaeological series *Chronicle*, and to write and front series on *BC: The Archaeology of the Bible Lands* (1977) and *Vikings!* (1980). Robert Kee had been tutored at Oxford by A.J.P. Taylor and became his friend. Kee's journalistic career included *Picture Post*, *The Sunday Times*, *The Observer* and a stint as literary editor of the *Spectator* before moving to television and presenting *Panorama* for the BBC, *First Report* for ITN and *This Week* for ITV. A prolific writer, Kee published *The Green Flag*, a timely history of Ireland in 1972, in the early stages of what euphemistically came to be called 'the Troubles'. After considerable prevarication – coverage of the Troubles caused great nervousness in broadcasters and many major spats with government – a BBC series was commissioned, which appeared in 1980. *Ireland: A History* was co-produced by the BBC and the Irish state broadcaster RTE, and shown to great acclaim on both sides of the Atlantic. It proved what contemporary conflicts always throw into sharp relief: it is hard to understand and command the present without a clear purchase on the past. As Robert Kee wrote in the book accompanying his series:

When trouble started in Northern Ireland in the late 1960s it took most people in the world by surprise. It has bewildered them ever since. This is largely because, for most people who don't live there, the late 1960s seemed to be the beginning. But the years of violence and suffering which Northern Ireland has been experiencing are simply the latest events in an old story which began long ago.[26]

What's the story?

The television audience's undying passion for history is precisely because it puts things in perspective, gives us that story that locates present troubles in a grander narrative. All television is at root storytelling and the presenter with the gift for luminous prose that enlightens its subject matter is inevitably our storyteller of choice. From costly experience, producers know that the first and most important question they are asked when pitching an idea to commissioners is: 'What's the story?' If they cannot reduce their putative programme to simple narrative, they are not in business. And it helps if the proposed storyteller, the presenter, has a name, a face and a voice that chimes with the intended audience.

One such historian who enjoyed an ascendancy during the 1980s and 1990s was Michael Wood. Blessed with good looks and an easy camera manner, his charm was described by the British press as 'the thinking woman's crumpet'. But it was less the long blonde hair and buttock-hugging jeans that made Wood a star; it was his extraordinary gift for storytelling. He would address the camera as he might a besotted student and effortlessly expound on the significance of the place he had brought them to. That engaging natural enthusiasm was expressed in making his series quests, journeys in search of the revealing moments and truths. His early programmes were called *In Search of the Dark Ages* (1981), *In Search of the Trojan War* (1985), and *Domesday: A Search for the Roots of England* (1988). *Legacy: A Search for the Origins of Civilization* (1992) compounded his popularity in the United States, where it plays regularly on PBS and cable channels. Wood describes himself as a filmmaker and has continued to make series *In Search of Shakespeare* (2003) and *In Search of Myths and Heroes* (2005), but feels oppressed by the increasingly prescriptive and restrictive demands of commissioners:

> TV is a simple medium driven by narrative to the exclusion of all else; it is not very good at analysis, argument or complexity, or representing the chaos of interacting connections of even one person's life, let alone of great events. TV likes a simple line – but history is not like that. If you reduce history to a simple line, to tableaux and simple stories, there is a danger that you will take the life out of history. I sometimes think that when TV history shows get poor ratings, it is because the audience feels cheated by the shallowness of the programme. But putting ambiguity and shades of meaning into TV programmes, without just plonking in two experts who disagree, is a task for the filmmaker, not the telly don.[27]

Wood goes on to hymn the values of history as *the* humane subject that teaches people to value other cultures and beliefs, past and present, and suggests that the government is belatedly awaking to history's value in shaping the cohesive awareness of citizenship. But he would be the first to oppose history's hijacking for ideological purpose, as has been attempted in other cultures. What he recommends is finding new ways to reflect the rich complexity of different experiences and attitudes that is the true interest of the historian. This is what falls foul of the commissioner demanding a simple storyline of the Hans Christian Andersen type, with a clear beginning ('Once upon a time . . .') and end (they all lived happily ever after, or not'). History isn't like that and, as Wood suggests, audiences are more intelligent and aware of that than such patronising assumptions allow.

The arrival of the fourth UK channel in 1982 seemed a new dawn for new ideas, and the biggest expansion of opportunity for creative programme-makers since the launch of BBC2 in 1965. Channel 4 had been the brainchild of producers desperate for an escape from the duopoly of the BBC and ITV. They should have been more wary of the support their movement for so-called 'independent production' secured from Thatcher's government. She also resented the critical power these two great institutions had and was keen to introduce the restraining realities of the market to their activities. With masterly *legerdemain*, the creative mavericks that had formerly kept a healthy dialectic disturbing the big corporations were transformed into small businessmen increasingly distracted by the harsh financial realities of where the next commission was coming from. But before the cold wind kicked in, the heat of the moment produced a spate of programmes that called to mind the heady intellectual freedoms of early television. As David Herman, lamenting the passing of that time in the *Guardian*, wrote: 'The first few years of Channel 4 produced probably the most esoteric programming ever shown in Britain.'[28] He mentions the open-ended late night discussion programme *After Dark*, Susan Sontag's TV lecture on Pina Bausch, Claude Lanzmann's film *Shoah*[29] and 'a heated discussion programme in which George Steiner and Lanzmann almost came to blows'. He also notes *Voices* and *Opinions* from those heady early days.

Opinions revived the A.J.P. Taylor model of an individual addressing the camera on a subject of their choice and included such distinguished, if controversial, figures as the novelist Salman Rushdie (yet to receive a fatwa for writing *The Satanic Verses*), the physicist Edward Teller ('father of the hydrogen bomb' and prototype for Kubrick's *Dr Strangelove*) and the socialist historian E.P. Thompson (a leading light in the CND). None of these were chosen because of their popular celebrity or cosy calming capacity. They were collectively an earnest of Channel 4's faith and mission to bring edgy, alternative fare to the public and to excite reaction. *Voices* continued in that academic vein, presented by the historian Michael Ignatieff, who became a television presenter for a number of years in Britain, before returning to his native Canada to become a Liberal politician. Leading thinkers of the twentieth century came into the *Voices* studio to debate philosophical issues such as bioethics. Umberto Eco, Nadine Gordimer, Edward Said, Bruno Bettelheim, Anthony Giddens, Susan Sontag, Joseph Brodsky, Günter Grass, Saul Bellow, Kurt Vonnegut and E.P. Thompson again were among the stellar cast of intellects whose voices were heard over the programme's six series. A seventh series was planned, with Jacques Derrida, Claude Lévi-Strauss and Noam Chomsky booked, but the channel's inexorable withdrawal from the field of ideas had started and the series was cancelled. A strand of controversialist, revisionist documentaries did emerge later at Channel 4, to which we shall return in Chapter 10.

The first chief executive of Channel 4 was the legendary history producer Jeremy Isaacs (*The World at War* (1973) and *Cold War* (1998)), and it was very much his initiative that sponsored those unashamedly highbrow programmes. When that scion of the entertainment dynasty Michael Grade took over Channel 4 in 1988, Isaacs threatened him with bodily harm if he dismantled his legacy, but the retreat from the wilder shores had already commenced, as Channel 4 settled down to business within a rapidly evolving industry. In his ten years in the job, Grade secured the channel's financial independence from ITV and built the channel's UK audience share from 8.4 per cent to 10.6 per cent, repositioning it in the mainstream of the evolving multichannel firmament. Isaacs's threat of violence was never fulfilled, though his relatively mild critique of Channel 4's increasingly crass commercialism, published in the magazine *Prospect* in December 2006, was seen as something of an overdue rebuke:

> Channel 4 set out to offer an alternative viewing experience, with the arts, current affairs and documentary prominent, and diversity at the heart of its output. Today, commercial ambitions are taking C4 down different paths. Is it still doing enough of what it was established to achieve? ... Public service broadcasters used to aim at universality, offering something to all ages and educational levels. But C4's prime marketing concept is the appeal to a 16–34 audience. This has some strange consequences – a series explaining Islam, for example, is entrusted to Peaches Geldof. There's an obsession with adolescent transgression and sex. Gordon Ramsay is hired to make a series called *The F Word*; *Designer Vaginas* is followed by *The World's Biggest Penis*. Earlier this autumn, unless I dreamed it, we were subject to a 'wank week'.[30]

Lecture series today

Isaacs fairly admits that some of the channel's output – such as *Channel 4 News* and the current affairs strand *Dispatches* – remain outstanding, but it is not just Channel 4 that has said goodbye to the philosophers. What is more surprising is that they have not said goodbye to the historians. Apart from David Starkey's golden handcuffs – and the sea of white hair that is the venerable archaeological series *Time Team* – Channel 4 had also sponsored the development of another television historian, Bettany Hughes. Her specialism is ancient history and she has managed to bring an audience to an awareness of other histories than that of the Roman Empire. She has introduced *The Spartans* (2002), *The Minoans* (2004), *The Moors* (2005), *Helen of Troy* (2005) and *Athens – the Trouble with Democracy* (2007). Slightly wooden in her first television outings, she has become an increasingly assured telly lecturer and her striking looks have made a change from the white-haired man that is still the commonest historical archetype. The comparative rarity of a young female historian on television has led to some predictably salivating reviews about 'a Helen of Troy in jeans',[31] 'making history glamorous',[32] 'full of facts and beauty, and we're not just talking about Hughes herself'[33] clearly written by tired, middle-aged men. In fact, it took a woman to call into question whether the looks were getting in the way of the facts, and not surprisingly one from the famously factious arena of archaeology itself. This is how the magazine *British Archaeology* reacted to Hughes's *Seven Ages of Britain* series in 2003:

> As we watched frequent long shots of Hughes against an impressive landscape, her wistful face, dark hair and coat tails whipped by the wind, it became increasingly difficult to read her as a popular historian. She narrated and delivered to camera confidently, though the tilt of her head and under-the-breath delivery reminded us of *Nigella's Kitchen*. The production was accomplished, but episodes lacked creative spark. The interviews felt awkward as Hughes listened all but silently to experts. The treatment feminised the past: it is veiled and mysterious, but might be available to us with the right chat-up line.[34]

Figure 3.1
Bettany Hughes stands against a
backdrop of classical ruins

Not only is the history feminised, but this series in particular related history through the experience of ordinary lives, a social perspective that gained currency in the late twentieth century, but has tended to recede on television in the face of revisionist strains keen to capitalise on familiar names and events. Like Michael Wood, Bettany Hughes commands the camera with the easy authority of genuine enthusiasm and knowledge. The camera not only likes the handsome face, it also appreciates radiant honesty. In fact, the feminisation of the past has proved a valuable field for Hughes and undoubtedly contributes to her growing appeal. It is an appeal that the waspish Starkey chose to attack in publicising his 2009 series, *Henry VIII: Mind of a Tyrant*.[35] He told the *Radio Times*:

One of the great problems has been that Henry, in a sense, has been absorbed by his wives. Which is bizarre. But it's what you expect from feminised history, the fact that so many of the writers who write about this are women and so much of their audience is a female audience. Unhappy marriages are big box office.[36]

But, as we have seen, Starkey himself scored a major hit with his 2002 series *The Six Wives of Henry VIII*, presumably revealing his feminine side. It puts a different complexion on Starkey's coincidental appearance in drag – along with fellow Channel 4 faces Jon Snow, Kevin McCloud and Tony Robinson – in a trailer promoting the channel's factual programmes. It is all just publicity, but maybe detracts from the genuine worth of the programmes. Starkey's new *Henry VIII* is both informative and riveting, pulling off the difficult task of putting the historian's vital analysis of documents visually at the heart of the documentary, without boring or losing the viewer. Starkey is not alone in bringing original historical work to the screen. Bettany Hughes's book[37] – accompanying her television investigation of whether Helen of Troy really existed – garnered very positive reviews from the classics community. Paul Cartledge, Professor of Greek History at Cambridge University's Faculty of Classics, was one of many leading academics that welcomed the book:

Bettany Hughes, already highly and widely acclaimed for her outstanding television histories of the *Spartans* and many others, now bids fair to prove that the female of the species is more readable than the male historian. Her multifaceted, multi-hued, and multi-period portrait of la Belle Helene will capture the imagination of professional scholars and general readers alike. I cannot recommend it too strongly.[38]

Classics, which had been seen as a dead subject and has disappeared from most state secondary schools, has had something of a renaissance in the twenty-first century, particularly in the person of young women like Hughes, and this new breed of classicist is happy to acknowledge the impact of television and the revival of swords-and-sandals cinema epics that started with Ridley Scott's *Gladiator* in 2000. The public need that has saved historians from the general cull of intellectuals on television is the unquenchable thirst for a meaningful narrative. The failure of religions and ideologies to continue supplying most people with a *raison d'être* or sense of purpose, and the commensurate loss of community and extended family, has left history to supply the missing links. The BBC series *Who Do You Think You Are?* – documentaries in which celebrities explore their own genealogy – has been a huge hit and tapped into people's demand to know more about their personal past. When the UK National Archives first put the results of the 1901 population census online in 2002, the site collapsed with the unexpected impact of a million hits within three hours. But there are penalties attached to carrying such a weight of expectation. As Michael Wood says, it makes it increasingly difficult to accommodate complexity and argument. This demand for history is also a demand for certainty, a story in which people can see their place and be reassured by the statement of eternal verities.

Television responds happily to this demand, for it also favours primary colours and simple nostra. The Oxford historian John Roberts's 1985 BBC series *The Triumph of the West* carried precisely the kind of unified worldview that gave audiences the required reassurance, not least in its synthesising of world history into a singular perspective of the onward and upward march of Western values. The American historian Francis Fukiyama continued this tradition of opportunistically celebrating the triumph of the West and of liberal capitalism by dubbing the end of the Cold War *The End of History*.[39] This simplification was widely and rightly rubbished, but television does like the simple line. And despite a continuing growth in the breadth and depth of academic history, with a more complex understanding of the cultural richness of social history, television has supplied a revisionist taste for narrative history reverting to the simple images of kings and queens, battles and castles. Thus the Victorian urban historian Tristram Hunt presents a BBC series on *The English Civil War* (2002)[40] and the medieval historian Marc Morris presents a Channel 4 series on *Castles* (2003).[41] Neither were merely heritage travel, but the packaging is clearly constructed for easy consumption.

The apotheosis of the lecture series was the history of Britain made for the BBC, which put its celebrity historian's name above the title: *Simon Schama's History of Britain*,[42] a breathless gallop through 5,000 years of British history, was drip-fed to the audience in three separate series. Unlike Roberts, Schama's specialty is not syncretism, so the early stages were much less satisfactory than the seventeenth and eighteenth centuries that he knows well, and which were duly accorded rather more screen time. But this is to underestimate Schama's success, which was marked by consistently high audiences for the programmes, good sales for the tie-in books and one of the BBC's highest sales at that time for the DVD of the series. Schama's wry, unassuming manner perfectly captured the Zeitgeist, while delivering the demand for a narrative approach to history. His producers had correctly surmised from the storytelling skills he had shown in his popular academic works

– such as the 1989 *Citizens: A Chronicle of the French Revolution*[43] and *Dead Certainties: Unwarranted Speculations* (1991)[44] – that his was the right voice for the age.

David Starkey did something similar in his three series for Channel 4: *Henry VIII of England*, *Elizabeth I of England* and *The Six Wives of Henry VIII*, although these were all subjects securely within his academic area of expertise, the Tudors. His multimillion pound, multi-series commitment *Monarchy* aims to cover the same millennial span as Schama's history, but opening him to the same complaint that he is entering waters for which he is less well qualified than many other academic swimmers. This is where the celebrity takes over from the specialty. This is a familiar face and a waspish voice that an audience will trust to follow Starkey into those waters. The gainsayers say that these inevitably become shallows, rather than deep, but at least these are serious historians lecturing us, not the gossip column denizens of celebrity culture like Peaches Geldof.[45]

Schama meanwhile trumped Starkey with an even more lucrative multi-series and book deal. In 2003, Schama signed a new contract with the BBC and HarperCollins to produce three new books and two accompanying TV series for £3 million (then around $5.3m), a million more than Starkey's deal the previous year. The first result of the deal was a book and TV film entitled *Rough Crossings*, dealing with stories of migration and slavery across the Atlantic Ocean and including episodes on Pocahontas, freed slaves and the Irish famine.[46] The online encyclopaedia, Wikipedia, announces this deal makes Schama a 'Superdon': 'an academic who repeatedly appears in television documentaries. The term is a portmanteau combining *Superman* and *University Don*. The term is a Briticism (sic), and has no exact analogue in American English. The Teledon is a closely allied phenomenon.'[47] Which cultural reification rather neatly summarises the phenomenon, despite its unfortunate similarity to the extinct mastodon.

In 2006, Schama presented *Simon Schama's Power of Art*, an eight-part exploration of the turning points of art, accessed through eight great masterpieces. At the time, Schama was Professor of Art History and History at Columbia University, as well as being art and culture critic for *The New Yorker*, so his credentials are impeccable. That has not stopped the other demand, that we will explore in future chapters, for all factual forms to be so studded with pictorial invention and dramatised sequences that the telly-lecturer, or 'teledon', disappears behind the pictures. Taking to the *Broadcast Now* blog site, television development researcher Andrew Wilson made exactly this point:

> This self-satisfying need to make the simplest of formats, the educational lecture, into televisual art is reaching the point of self-defeat. The *Power of Art* was so concerned with dramatising Turner's inner torment that it almost entirely forgot to show any paintings. If you truly believe your audience is sophisticated, they don't need a man wearing a fake moustache giving them an impression of what an Impressionist may have looked like.[48]

Now a seasoned television performer, Schama himself is not insensitive to this charge. In the introduction to the accompanying art book, he writes:

> The power of art is the power of unsettling surprise. Even when it seems imitative, art doesn't so much duplicate the familiarity of the seen world as replace it with a reality of its own. Its mission, beyond the delivery of beauty, is the disruption of the banal.[49]

He even invokes the same image as Hughes, the shock that artistic revelation gives us, but then goes on to reveal the banality that television production involves, inimical to the artistic shock:

Television doesn't like to be inconvenienced by the unanticipated. Filming needs careful planning. Each of our programmes turned on a crisis in the life and career of an artist, a moment of trouble in the creation of a particular painting or sculpture. En route to that climactic moment, though, we looked at other works, and lurking among them would often be something that threw me completely off balance. A picture I'd blithely thought of as a warm-up act for the big number, seen at first hand rather than through the wan medium of a printed reproduction or a dim memory, suddenly threatened, unnervingly, to be the main feature. Chastened, re-educated, I'd throw a small tantrum, want the programme turned inside out to make room for the epiphany. Directors would hear me out and try not to roll their eyes. Sometimes room would be made for this usurper, sometimes not.[50]

Atlantic crossings

One of the key values of landmark series is that they travel around the world, not least to the United States, and not just earning critical kudos and secondary income, but often being partly funded by co-production with other countries that cannot afford or are unable to make them. In 1992, the BBC signed a multimillion pound development deal with Discovery Communications Inc., giving their channels such as *Animal Planet* and *People+Arts* first refusal on upcoming series and bringing welcome cash to the BBC table. Despite the concerns of producers that this accelerated the restriction of commissions to ever more familiar subjects, so commercially successful has this deal been that it was renewed for a second ten-year period in 2002. Meanwhile, the BBC's commercial arm, BBC Worldwide, brings in well over £200 million a year in international sales and distribution, a third of it from the United States, though its reach in other territories is growing fast.[51]

The major wildlife productions we explore further in Chapter 19 can raise as much as 90 per cent of their extravagant production costs through co-production and pre-sales. British history has not quite the same mass appeal, but most of the Schama series are taken by *The History Channel* in the States, while both Starkey's and Hughes's work regularly appears on the PBS network. History made in the United States tends to be domestic and yet can be of an even more epic quality. What is termed a 'mini-series' there can run to 12 or more hour-long episodes, a length not preferred in the UK for a generation. Schama's *A History of Britain* comprised fifteen one-hour episodes, but was eked out in three five-part series over three years. The doyen of US blockbuster television history filmmakers is Ken Burns, so famous that he has a filmic device named after him (see p. 185). Unlike the classic British 'lecture' tradition, Burns eschews the on-screen presenter in favour of a meticulously researched narration, normally by a well-known voice, and an artful assemblage of interviews and archive materials, with readings of contemporary sources by leading actors and actresses. The late, best-selling historian Stephen E. Ambrose worked with Burns on his film about the legendary American explorers Lewis and Clark,[52] the subject of Ambrose's own first bestseller, and recognised the achievement of a fellow 'storyteller'. He said: 'More Americans get their history from Ken Burns than any other source.'[53]

The history they get is brilliantly researched and executed, but rarely departs far from the Stars and Stripes. Burns has made a series of one-off documentaries about American heroes and institutions, from *Brooklyn Bridge* (1981), *Statue of Liberty* (1985) and *The Congress* (1989) to *Huey Long* (1985), *Thomas Jefferson* (1996) and *Mark Twain* (2002), among others. A selection of these are released in a DVD boxed set as 'Ken Burns' America', which neatly captures Burns's role as national historian.[54] His chief claims to fame are his landmark series on *The Civil War* (1990), *Baseball* (1994), *The West* (1996) and *Jazz* (2000). *The Civil War* – the American one, of course – was a nine-part eleven-and-a-half hour blockbuster that attracted a record 40 million audience to PBS for its first showing and rare critical plaudits like 'masterpiece . . . the most accomplished documentary filmmaker of his generation' (*New York Times*) and 'this is heroic television' (*Washington Post*). The 18-part *Baseball* did even better, with a 45 million audience and raves such as 'resonates like a Mozart symphony' (*New York Daily News*) and 'rich in drama, irresistible as nostalgia . . . and an instructive window into our national psychology' (*Time* magazine).

The West and *Jazz* enjoyed equal success, and Burns is award-garlanded and very wealthy as a result. But the national psychology revealed is not to everyone's taste; some critics do not buy into Burns's rich, lush heritage approach. In *The Middle Mind: Why Americans Don't Think for Themselves* (2004), Curtis White attacks the 'blandly informative' style of these documentaries and their ability to transform the epic, violent turn of events into something resembling 'comforting Hallmark card pathos'.[55] Burns is no old school patriot, in that he was a graduate of the anti-Vietnam War generation and his films favour the individual testimony of ordinary people, echoing the social history preference of that generation. But there is something of facile Hollywood liberalism about this kind of book-ending of history, bludgeoning you with its weight and, like too many Hollywood features, neatly wrapping it all up in the final reel. As White observes, 'history is mostly just the version told by the victors'.[56] Burns managed to cause even more controversy in *War* (2007), his series on the Second World War, to which I will return in Chapter 10.

Something to say

Burns's *War* – although resulting from a similar four-year trawl for original material and interviews – is very different from the magisterial even-handedness of the previous landmark series on the Second World War, Jeremy Isaac's *The World at War* (1973), a 26-part epic that has stood the test of time as one of the greatest history series ever made.[57] In 2007, the same year that the Burns series was broadcast, the eminent British historian Richard Holmes saw fit to publish a compilation of the unused interviews recorded for the previous series nearly 40 years before.[58] With nearly all those witnesses to war now dead, this archive was re-evaluated as even more valuable than the original extracts in the edited series. Most film-makers regret the priceless material they discard in editing, often better but less easily extractable and neatly containable within the narrative arc and the tyranny of running time. Few imagine that those offcuts may prove valuable and so few are retained, but the potential offered by the internet may prompt reconsideration.

The equally meticulously researched and comprehensive oral history projects undertaken by Brian Lapping Associates have been wisely cognisant of their collateral archive value. *The Second Russian Revolution* (1991) profited the British Library of Political and Economic Science, proud possessors of 22 boxes of production files, including all interviews – audio and video – with other papers residing in the archives of the London School of Economics library; and *The Fifty Years War: Israel and the Arabs* (1998) programme and interview transcripts are archived in the Middle East Centre at St Anthony's College, Oxford. It is not just the extensive interviews with all the key players that distinguish these Lapping documentaries, but extraordinary found footage unearthed by the finest film researchers in the business. The result gives as clear a window on recent history as it is possible to achieve in this linear medium, earning plaudits from players from the world stage, such as former US Defense Secretary Robert J. McNamara:

> *The Fifty Years War* is often a tale of mistrust and betrayal, but this production strives to present a balanced view of history, and is not only impressive for its command of the facts but for its skillful and often dramatic presentation of history.[59]

The Lapping series *Death of Apartheid* (1995)[60] and *Death of Yugoslavia* (1995)[61] also are original works of historical documentary importance that outlive the ephemeral demands of the television schedule.

Standing diametrically opposed to this late flowering of the inclusive, balanced documentary form, is the latter-day Marcuse[62] that is Adam Curtis. A former Oxford politics teacher, he did not come into television as a 'telly-don', but as a researcher on the consumer show *That's Life*, more remembered for its obscenely shaped vegetables and gags than its big ideas. But Curtis credits this baptism as initiating the comic lift he brings to his documentaries, among the few left on television that unashamedly deal with the field of ideas. Each of his series starts with a short lecture enshrining the thesis of the show, often lasting over two minutes, apparently defying the executive anxiety that demands the biggest bangs in a programme's first minute and nothing too difficult to frighten the audience off. But these narrations are accompanied by Curtis's trademark barrage of edited archive, irreverently intercutting political figures and speech with popular culture icons and sounds. The conflation of images and ideas is very much the Curtis USP, instantly in tune with the MTV and YouTube generation, and is matched by the unorthodox arguments that Curtis presents.

In *The Century of the Self* (2002), Curtis announces that 'This is a series about how those in power have used [Sigmund] Freud's theories to control the dangerous crowd in an age of democracy'.[63] He charts how the development of public relations and advertising designed the model of self-centred consumerism that sponsored neo-conservatism and the breakdown of society. In *The Power of Nightmares* (2004), he claims that radical Islamists and American neo-conservatives have effectively conspired to seize power by fuelling popular fears:

> Together they created today's nightmare vision, of a secret organised evil that threatened the world, a fantasy that politicians found restored their authority in a disillusioned age. And those with the darkest fears became the most powerful.[64]

In *The Trap: What Happened to Our Dream of Freedom* (2007), Curtis further extends the argument that the proclaimed worldwide battle for democracy has had the opposite effect, of promoting terrorism and leading to the loss of age-old liberties. He explores what he terms 'a dark and distrustful vision' of human nature that has led to 'a new and revolutionary system of social control. It would use the language of freedom, but in reality it would come to entrap us and our leaders in a narrow and empty world'.[65] Quoted out of context like this, this sounds like the 'miserabilist' worldview that many television executives had vowed to eradicate from the airwaves, but that does not do justice to the endlessly innovative choice of image and juxtaposition of thought that makes Curtis's films such a joy to watch. In Britain, their iconoclastic and sceptical take on the motives and methods of the powerful are part of an honoured tradition that goes back to the eighteenth-century satire of Swift and Hogarth. In America, they are deemed so far beyond the acceptable pale that none of them have ever been shown on any television channel.

If that fact reflects badly on the self-styled 'land of the free', Curtis reflects sharply on the television landscape in which he works:

> The media class grew up during a period of certainty which was the Cold War. All those famous reporters bestrode the world and told us what was what because everything was simple. We knew who was wrong and who was right.
>
> But now they don't know anything. They know nothing! . . . But above all they know that they don't really know. And what that leads to is a terrible sense of insecurity . . . But these people are paid a large amount of money, actually, to be clever and to tell us about the world – and they're failing. It's not their fault, but they are failing at it.[66]

Clearly not a view supported by many still working in television, but one that might be addressed by examining the level of expertise documentary series now offer in presenting the world. Although the historians have managed to survive the loss of intellectual confidence Curtis refers to, there is also a growing reliance on celebrity presenters, who bring to a subject not expertise, but an audience. It was the chance involvement in 1980 of a world-famous comedian in a series otherwise presented by conventional television presenters and historians that really set this ball rolling. Michael Palin, famous as one of the Pythons,[67] was an ardent train fan who was asked to front one of the films in the first series of *Great Railway Journeys of the World*.[68] The series ran for several years, employing more comedians and personalities, from Alexei Sayle and Victoria Wood to Ian Hislop and Danny Glover. Palin went on to become the Phileas Fogg of the BBC, fronting a modern *Round the World in Eighty Days* (1989)[69] and several other very popular landmark globetrotting series, confirming the man's charm as the ultimate travelling companion, the archetypal innocent abroad, up to every challenge – not one of those clever clogs who presume to know everything. Funnily enough, Palin's fellow Python Terry Jones has also become a documentary presenter, with series ranging from *The Crusades* (1985) to *Terry Jones' Barbarians* (2006), but he bucks the trend by actually being a medieval historian.

The ascendancy of celebrity over knowledge has become the norm and it is likely that the choice of star often precedes the choice of subject. Having landed the big name, one can imagine the grateful commissioner asking: 'Where would you like to go?' Comedian Billy Connolly took a documentary crew with him on his *World Tour of Scotland* (1994), combining idiosyncratic travelogue with performance extracts, a trick repeated in *Billy Connolly's World Tour of Australia* (1996), . . . *of England, Ireland and Wales* (2002) and . . . *of New Zealand* (2004). Connolly's latest venture, *Journey to the Edge of the World* (2009), documents a 10-week trip returning to the Arctic, to which his previous visit was chiefly memorable for his naked dance in the snow. Comedian Paul Merton brings a different, more diffident approach to his travels for Channel 5, most notable for keeping his hat on in China and India.[70] The polymath Stephen Fry joined the celebrity charabanc with his London taxi drive across all 50 states of the USA in *Stephen Fry in America* (2008),[71] following a widely praised two-part documentary on his bipolarity in *The Secret Life of the Manic Depressive* (2006) and the following *HIV and Me* (2007). The BBC's Richard Klein sees this as a logical development of documentary:

> Now documentary embraces using character, more 'immersive', which gives it an authored feel. Stephen Fry decides to go out and find out about manic depression and it becomes a film about manic depression. We see Stephen Fry as a character in it while he explores the world around him.[72]

Connolly, Fry and Merton are among many whose celebrity give them free passage to travel on behalf of an apparently grateful audience. However, there are times when there is an uneasy relationship between the comedy and character of the star and the needs of the subject. Caroline Aherne and Craig Cash are largely known for the characters they write and play so well in the sitcom *The Royle Family*, but their trip to India to visit a remote children's eye hospital made for uncomfortable viewing. In *Back Passage to India* (2000) – a title that indicates the problem – they seem ill at ease and the audience is left unsure whether they are performing or genuinely unhappy to be there. It was unfortunately repeated in a BBC season of programmes celebrating the 60th anniversary of Indian independence in August 2007, which had no Indian presenters other than the English comedian Sanjeev Baskhar and no programmes commissioned from Indian producers. The 'immersive' has supplanted the authentic. The other series that has revealed the potency of the star persona is in the personal histories of *Who Do You Think You Are?* mentioned earlier. Justified as good business, this is the triumph of the personal over the political.

Conclusion

Ideas are naturally subversive and their proponents always problematic to those who are ruled by the bottom line. Commissioners sitting in their glass and ivory towers, contemplating the coffee-table book sales of another series on art, do not anticipate libel actions from insulted painters, nor escalating costs caused by academic epiphanies on location. The primary job of these series is to give intellectual credibility to the channel's schedules and disprove allegations of dumbing down. The more that the lecturer is a genuine expert sharing their original research and enthusiasm, the more that brief is fulfilled, but the harder they are to control. Similarly, rising celebrity and its increasingly astronomic evaluation also empower the presenter in their tantrums and demands. The producer can be caught between the siren voices of the superdon, assured by his 'golden handcuffs' deal to have divine right, and the channel executives, with one eye on the programme budget and the other on the 'overnights' (the overnight ratings published by BARB, the Broadcasters' Audience Research Board).[73]

Adam Curtis keeps working because his ideas are challenging and timely, and he has found a filmic form that attracts the audience. Indeed, he contradicts assumptions by delivering the younger demographic that the executives are so desperate to retain. It is possible that this attracts the same sensibility that Gavin MacFadyen speaks of rediscovering investigative journalism in Chapter 2. Thirty years ago, philosophers on a sofa could intrigue an audience, most of whom would not have been to university. Today, there seems to be a growing demand for coherent analysis from a generation that has been to university, but discovers economic and political verities collapsing before their eyes. As Curtis says, those that are supposed to know, know they know nothing, so those with a compelling thesis are shooting at an open goal, if given the chance. It is instructive that the BBC continues to support this maverick filmmaker, whereas not even public service television dare show his work in the USA. As we discover in Chapter 17, this vacuum has been responded to by the revival of cinema documentary; and, on both sides of the Atlantic, the growth of secondary distribution via DVD and the internet favours documentaries of substance. While the coffee table books turn up the following year in the remainder stacks, the web is awash with clips from meaty series like *The Power of Nightmares*. The simple, if inconvenient, truth is: it is preferable that those addressing the camera have something to say.

Expert briefing – the scripted documentary

Documentary commissioners not only seek assurance that they are buying 'a good story', but also stipulate elements that are required by a particular strand. Thus Channel 4's *Cutting Edge* wants 'important films that, increasingly, are enjoyable and funny in tone', while Discovery Europe wants factual formats that appeal to 'Phil', an emblematic 30-something family man 'interested in motors'.[74] Other Channel 4 documentary demands are for 'highly provocative polemical films', 'emotionally charged first person narratives', 'surprising and popular films about family life', 'docu-soaps and presenter-led programmes'.[75] BBC2 is looking for 'intelligent blending of constructed formats with top documentary filmmaking that deliver high-impact series', [76] while BBC4 is 'eager to increase the number of landmark specialist factual series'. None of these objectives encourage free-form 'following and shooting' observational documentaries, just to see what you turn up. They all require designing and focusing, casting and planning, creative collaboration – and scripting in some form. So here are some guidelines for the scripted documentary:

1 **What is the story?**: Hollywood established the tradition of the 'log-line', literally one sentence that encapsulates the storyline and the style in which it will be told. The discipline ensures the filmmaker has a clear handle on what they are about. The assumption is that a concept too muddy to be reducible to one clear line is unready for production. The clearer the concept, the shorter the line can be. My favourite was Nick Park's apocryphal pitch for his first feature, *Chicken Run*: 'The Great Escape – but with chickens'. The documentary line needs to be just as revelatory, whether it is *Life Story*'s 'Watson and Crick's race to find the structure of DNA' or *Air Force Afghanistan* 'chronicling life for British servicemen stationed at Kandahar air base'.

2 **Titles**: Good titles help clarify the complex and define the promise, from *The Shock of the New* to *The Power of Nightmares*. These are 'hard-bite' phrases that attract attention and promise strong sensations. Long-running series titles quickly achieve iconic status, with their literal meaning subsumed in the programme brief, whether it is *Panorama* or *Big Brother*. The choice of words in titles conveys not just meaning, whether literal or literary, but the show's aspirational level. You do not approach a programme called *Cops* or *Extreme Bodies* in search of subtlety, nor *The Daily Politics* for a laugh. Landmark series have to speak to many nations, so must rise above culture specifics to talk to the universal: *Life on Earth* and *The War*. As they said in the days of film, 'it must do what it says on the can'.

3 **Narrative arc**: Whether it is a history of a war or a country, the genesis of an idea or an invention, a metaphorical journey through time or an actual railway journey, the narrative paradigm will normally apply, because film – at least in the way that most people consume it in the cinema or on television – is a linear medium. French filmmaker Jean-Luc Godard observed that all film stories should have a beginning, middle and end, 'but not necessarily in that order'. The narrative arc is the line that connects those three, alternatively defined as 'proposition, conflict and resolution'. So dramatic storytelling requires a (preferably sympathetic) protagonist setting out on a journey; events, if not antagonists, that jeopardise the course of travel; and some sort of resolution. Screenwriting schools call this 'The Three-Act Structure'. Even an eminent historian's personal odyssey through his or her special subject can be organised in this way, with the exposition simplified for the audience and the revelations staged in satisfying, edifying sequence, arriving at the anticipated conclusion.

4 **Voice**: Most landmark series are built around a given presenter, who will normally be responsible for the original script. It then falls to the producer and/or director to establish how that will be visualised, how much will be voiced in vision, how much in commentary, whether this will call for a secondary commentary voice and/or readers for written extracts, and how many complementary speakers will be called on in the course of the programme. Too many can make the pace frenetic and programme superficial; too few may make it slow and monotonous. How strong is your presenter's voice, especially in voiceover? Can they manage long pieces to camera, enabling developing shots, or will their takes have to be cut around, line for line? Can they write conversationally, or must the script be completely re-imagined for the untutored viewer?

5 **Resources**: Even the most lavish productions will be constrained by budget, not least in how many locations can be afforded. This is not the academic's area of speciality, so you have to advise roughly how much travelling is feasible before their first draft, then plan a schedule of how much on the page can be achieved. With music, art and archive, there are also major copyright considerations, which will restrict how much secondarily sourced screen time can be afforded. Location and picture research will help flesh out the script and reveal more accurate figures on costs, but the level of ambition of the series will have been set by the commissioner and the budget given. What they will require is more bangs for their bucks; leisurely strolls through castles or galleries are rarely acceptable, unless that is the point. But they will want pictures of those castles, and getting to each costs money, as do the aerials or crane shots that achieve the stunning panoramas. There may also be the requirement for dramatised reconstruction, which I cover in more detail in Chapter 15.

6 **Pictures**: Scripts need to be realistically prescriptive in shot needs. With a visual demand that has doubled cut rates in recent years – few shots lasting more than three seconds and sound bites, PTCs or interviews, rarely exceeding ten seconds – picture starvation is a prominent problem in edit suites. Unless the requisite number and variety of shots have been acquired on location, the film will fail to sustain its visual richness and dynamic tempo as the filmmaker is reduced to repeating or eking out shots. This voracious demand for material would be reason enough to justify at least elementary scripting, but it also serves equally pressing demands to evolve a distinctive stylistic signature.

7 **Style**: Commissioners increasingly fetishise 'talent', and that not only means the on-screen talent, but the director. S/he may well be instrumental in getting a project green-lit, and their style will be integral to that decision, albeit their reputation and past success is the real key. Building that style and reputation, even the most serious filmmaker needs a stylistic reference to kick-start the creative conceptualisation of a film. It may be one scene that s/he knows is indispensable from the start, and which everything else leads up to or evolves from. It can be a pictorial reference – a work of art, the style of a photographer, a particular way of shooting the landscape. It can even be a speech or a piece of music. Adam Curtis, scripting *The Power of Nightmares*, had his personal epiphany conflating the image of the puritan Islamic fundamentalist Sayyid Qutb watching young Americans on the dance floor with the sound of the 1944 Frank Loesser pop classic 'Baby It's Cold Outside'. 'That song was what really made me want to make the film', he says.[77] It is a perfect insight to the style fellow filmmaker Errol Morris calls 'expressionistic . . . never literal'.[78]

8 **Music**: Music becomes ever more important to providing the emotional tempo and timbre of film. Whereas for Curtis it conjures up the popular cultural milieu of the time, when that is unavailable – as for ancient history – original music can conjure up the spirit of the past in a place that is now just deserted ruins, without the need for actors in antique costumes. Drama-documentary director Peter Kosminsky works closely with a composer to find themes for his characters, such as the conflicted government weapons inspector Dr. David Kelly, who committed suicide.[79] He then listens to the music on location prior to shooting a scene, so that performance and music will chime in the edit.[80] Although this is more common in drama, it is an approach that can release resonances in documentary, particularly with scripted material, and make for more richly textured film. Sounds and sound effects can also be orchestrated to create an aural landscape and mood, such as the sounds of battle or riot.

9 **Prepare for the unexpected**: However well planned and scripted a documentary is, Sod's Law applies, i.e. if something can go wrong, it will. Flexibility – from wet weather alternatives to standby interviews – can make use of time otherwise wasted. Scripting should never be a straitjacket, merely a plan of action. Spontaneity and improvisation should remain essential elements in the director's armoury. Events, people, opportunities arise during filming that a smart director can seize and use to enhance the film. If each scene or sequence is well planned to work in one ideal sequence, you will always have a set of building blocks from which a workable film can be constructed, even if not in the original order envisaged.

10 **Script form**: Do not use screenwriting software packages such as Final Draft; these are only appropriate for drama. The most useful script layout for documentary is the classic television dual column layout, sequence by sequence. The left-hand column carries all the visual information – shots defined and enumerated, with graphics where appropriate – while the right-hand column carries the aural information – script, whether in or out of vision, music and sound effects, including their ins and outs. Thus the first page of a notional script looks something like the example shown on page 72.

VISION	SOUND
1 Fast cut montage of CUs Gaudi building details	MUSIC: Federico Mompou Música Callada SFX: Street sounds of Barcelona
2 WS Barcelona	HISTORIAN (to camera):
3 Top shot La Rambla	The crazy paving of Antonio Gaudi's building ornamentation – using shards of
4 LS Historian walking towards camera	mirror, tile and bottle – was a riotous expression of Barcelona's Islamic and Gothic heritage. Architects say this makes Gaudi the last authentic practitioner of the
5 L/A CU Historian, track as he walks throw focus as he leaves frame to	Baroque in the 20th Century. Who were the wealthy burgers of Barcelona who patronized Gaudi and lived in these
6 LS Palau Guell	extraordinary buildings?
7 Animated title graphic GAUDI PEOPLE	MUSIC SWELLS and FADES UNDER:
8 MLS Historian on roof of Palau Guell	HISTORIAN (to camera): Gaudi's first and foremost patron was the wealthy Catalan industrialist Count Eusebi Güell, whose palace this is.
9 L/A WS Palau Guell	Gaudi said to Guell: GAUDI VOICE (OOV):
10 MS Photograph of Gaudi Z/I on mouth	Sometimes I think we are the only people who like this architecture
11 MS Photograph of Guell Z/I on eyes	GUELL VOICE (OOV): I don't like your architecture – I respect it.

4 *Vox populi*: the voice of the people

vox pop n. interviews with members of the public
on a radio or television programme

Arguably, the single most transformational feature of television in the early 21st century has been the emergence of members of the public as stars in their favourite shows. This has been principally through the agency of so-called 'Reality TV' – to which we shall return in detail in Chapter 12 – and also through the technological advances that have allowed increased interactivity and the growing deployment of 'user-generated content' (UGC). These mechanisms have helped generate a profound recalibration of the relationship between broadcasters and audiences, with the latter apparently taking a more active role in evaluating and forming programme content. It could be argued that these changes were forced by increased competition and the audience fragmentation caused by multichannel TV and new media platforms. But there was no obvious corollary between those market pressures and the newly discovered delight in the quotidian experience. Indeed, much of television is still driven by the exotic and extreme, and an insatiable appetite for celebrity culture. But what is new is the widespread hunger for the validation of normal life by the passing spotlight of TV – the fulfilment of Andy Warhol's 1968 prediction that 'In the future, everyone will be world-famous for 15 minutes.'[1]

The questions to address are how valuable those fifteen minutes are and just how much the voice of the people has really been taken to the heart of broadcasting, redefining the tastes, values and agendas of the day. People love to see their faces on the big screen at football matches, and youths routinely wave at the camera when passing behind reporters doing live links. It could be argued that these instances hardly amount to seizing control of the airwaves; nor does selling clips of carefully staged family daftness to video clip shows like *You've Been Framed*[2] and *America's Funniest Home Videos.*[3] News programmes, desperate to retain disappearing 'eyeballs', particularly among the young, have espoused a new relationship with their audience. But does any of this significantly affect the long-established hierarchy of values reflected on our television screens, where professionals command the camera and the lower classes provide the subjects, victims and the light relief?

Voices from the past

From its very beginnings, film has been fascinated by aspects of everyday life. The first film was the Lumière brothers' short of 'Workers Leaving the Factory' (1895) and the new

Figure 4.1
Still taken from the Lumière brothers' short, *Workers Leaving the Lumière Factory* (1895)

medium was soon seized upon by workers' and nationalist movements around the world as the ideal vehicle for expressing their messages and aspirations. Mexico's 1911 uprising gave rise to the first Latin American revolutionary cinema.[4] In the Soviet Union, Lenin identified the cinema as the most important art form for addressing the masses and newsreel became the key form for celebrating the 1917 Revolution's achievements.[5] Following Czechoslovakia's independence in 1918, documentary films celebrated the patriots' struggles.[6]

In the United States it was characteristically capitalism – a mineral prospector financed by a fur trader – that came to define the American documentary tradition. Robert Flaherty's first film, shot among the Inuits on the Belcher Islands in the Arctic, went up in flames when he dropped a cigarette on the inflammable nitrate stock in 1916. It was not until 1922 that the eventually re-shot *Nanook of the North* was released, making Flaherty's reputation. It was in describing Flaherty's subsequent film *Moana* (1926) that a young Scottish postgraduate called John Grierson, studying in the USA, coined the term 'documentary'.[7] On returning to Britain, Grierson joined the Empire Marketing Board and it was they who sponsored his own first documentary, *Drifters* (1929), commissioned ostensibly to promote the herring industry. Along with Nanook, this film's concentration on the heroic role of the fishermen defined the human focus of this genre of film.

However, it was only with the arrival of sound that the people could have a voice. Grierson's Empire Marketing Board Film Unit moved to the General Post Office in 1933 and one of their first films there, *Cable Ship* (1933), directed by Stuart Legg and Alexander Shaw, used the voices of the workers to explain their jobs. Two years later, a film made for The British Commercial Gas Association (aka the Gas Board) had Stepney slum dwellers address the camera directly. Edgar Anstey and Arthur Elton's *Housing Problems* (1935) was groundbreaking in allowing its working class subjects to command the screen in that way, speaking somewhat stiltedly as if they had equally improbably been asked to address a public meeting. Indeed, at the public showing of the film, its subjects could not believe the results, so distant was it from their everyday existence. As Edgar Anstey recalled:

> Nobody had been able to bring these poor, suffering characters to an audience before, and the woman in Housing Problems, the woman who jabs at the rat with a broom, was absolutely astonished. I got her to Stepney Town Hall (I think it was) to see the film. They were all there, the people who appeared in the film, and you couldn't hear a word because

of the roars and shouts as soon as a neighbour came on the screen. So we had to run it again, and this woman who killed the rat was absolutely astonished. I don't think she'd ever seen a photograph of herself before. She didn't recognise herself, didn't identify. She had to be told, and she gradually accepted it the second time through. But she had never been to the centre of London. She was a woman of, I suppose, forty-five or fifty, and she had never been further than this two and a half miles from her slum house . . .[8]

Over 50 years later, I had a similar experience interviewing child labourers in Asia, whose harsh and limited lives ill-prepared them for their moment on television. As I wrote at the time, 'in many cases, I was the first person to ask them their opinion, and it was often difficult for them to realise they had one'.[9] In the days before television, mass travel and information technology, state utilities saw it as their public responsibility to fund social, educational films of this kind, and many young filmmakers were passionate about their commitment to social justice and reforms. Grierson's younger sister, Ruby, was credited as an assistant on the film, but has variously been credited with giving it a feminist sensibility and its human voice.

The great documentary filmmaker Paul Rotha wrote that she and her sister Marion 'handled their characters with greater sympathy than is found in other documentaries of the Grierson group . . . [The] ability to win people's confidence gave a spontaneity and an honesty to the "interviews" that contrasted sharply with the previous, romantic method of handling people'.[10] Grierson himself admitted that Ruby had accused him of looking at life as if in a goldfish bowl, a bowl she was determined to break. She had told the Stepney slum-dwellers: 'The camera is yours. The microphone is yours. Now tell the bastards exactly what it's like to live in the slums.'[11]

In the United States, a similar socially motivated tradition sprang from the evolving photojournalist tradition, with Walker Evans's dust bowl pictures of poor sharecroppers in the Depression remaining the outstanding example. Pare Lorentz's *The Plow That Broke The Plains* (1936) and *The River* (1937) were documentaries funded by government agencies (just like Grierson's), promoting government initiatives such as the Tennessee Valley Administration, but were firmly grounded in the same sensibility of being on the side of the working man. As the American documentary historian A. William Bluem writes, 'they wished that viewers might share the adventure and despair of other men's lives, and commiserate with the downtrodden and underprivileged'.[12] These were principles arguably more in keeping with the US's republican egalitarian culture than Britain – where the middle classes had seen it as their patriotic duty in 1926 to rally together to break the General Strike – yet the iconoclastic voice of a Ruby Grierson did not emerge in the United States.

However, the kind of anger that might have seized workers' control of film did crop up in parts of Europe during the 1930s, and is captured in certain key films. In 1937, Joris Ivens's *The Spanish Earth* took a powerfully partisan approach to the republican cause in the Spanish Civil war, but the voice we remember (at least in the English version) is not that of the Spanish-speaking fighters, but of the narrator Ernest Hemingway, who was also one of the film's funders. Earlier, in 1934, Ivens had made an equally passionate film with Belgian filmmaker Henri Storck on behalf of striking coal miners in Belgium. *Misère au Borinage* established a tradition of films shot during the dramatic conflict of industrial dispute, which ran through to the 1980s and the war that the then Tory UK government waged on the unions that Margaret Thatcher dubbed 'the enemy within'.[13] Bill Nichols (2001) sees *Misère au Borinage* as important for its gritty realism, its participatory use of re-enactment, and its contributory effect on the cause.

Unlike Leni Riefenstahl's collaboration with the Nazi Party to film the Nuremberg rally of 1934, Ivens and Storck collaborated not with the government, or the police, but with the very people whose misery no government had yet addressed, let alone eliminated. Their participatory involvement helped generate the very qualities they sought to document not as spectacle to fascinate aesthetically and subdue politically but as activism to engage aesthetically and transform politically. A cinema of oratory made in collaboration with the 'wretched of the earth' claimed a solid foundation that would go on to support numerous other examples of politically engaged filmmaking from the other side of the barricades.[14]

In 1939, the Second World War intervened in that socialist, utopian course of documentary – and claimed the life of Ruby Grierson while filming a naval convoy, as she and her fellow filmmakers had selflessly joined the war effort. After the War, that cause was subsumed in the post-War Labour landslide election victory. Television had inherited the documentary mantle, and not a little of its social awareness, but was compromised by the Reithian demands for balance in all things. The camera and the microphone remained in the safe hands of the producer and above all the viewpoint was invariably the received wisdom of the establishment. It would be another generation before working people were again encouraged to seize control of the camera.

Early television tended to reflect the social hierarchy, with the dominant voice being that of the educated middle classes, their received English instructing people accordingly. Regional accents were seen as 'a bit difficult' and rarely used as more than 'colour', often deployed in the edited extract form known as vox pops. In the 1960s, a new generation of filmmakers emerged, who were as exercised as Ruby Grierson by the inequalities in society. Granada's *World in Action* was one strand of programmes that had a clear commitment to working people, and nurtured filmmakers of equal commitment. Mike Grigsby, in particular, gave lengthy screen time to the workers featured in his films about life in the dockyards and on the land, allowing them to talk at length on camera in way that gave status to their thoughts and experience. As the farm labourer sits slowly and haltingly telling his story in *Working the Land*,[15] the audience is privileged to have a novel insight, not just into a different way of life but a different means of expressing it. The camera lingers on the face, leaving the audience to consider what is being said, rather than being told what to think by a commentator.

This investment in the demotic voice was also a central part of the workshop movement that grew up in the late 1960s and early 1970s, and had a significant say in the original formation of Channel 4. The Amber Film Collective, formed in London in 1968, but settled in Newcastle since 1969, is the longest surviving group from the workshop movement, whose 'work is rooted in social documentary, built around long term engagements with working class and marginalized communities in the North of England'.[16] From their first 10-minute film about the North Shields ferry across the Tyne, *Maybe*[17] – refused transmission by the BBC because they would not compromise on its tone – through the film about the huge council estate *Byker*,[18] that 'attracted condemnation by some city councillors, outraged at the promotion of working class culture',[19] theirs has been a principled, if increasingly isolated, commitment to the popular voice.

The 1960s and the arrival of BBC2 in 1964 had seen some liberalisation of television, but had still largely failed to shake its bourgeois norms. Even the now legendary and long lost cultural anarchy of BBC2's *Late Night Line-Up* was seen as exclusive by the majority of the audience. Seeking public responses to the newly published autumn television schedules in 1971, a *Line-Up* team hung around the gates of the large Guinness brewery in London's Park Royal industrial estate to record some vox pops with the workers. It was raining, so they were invited in to the works canteen. There they were surprised to be subjected to an articulate and largely unanimous condemnation of television, its programmes and their perspectives. Responding to these criticisms, the then *Late Night Line-Up* Editor Rowan Ayers sought funding to set up the Community Programme Unit. For some 30 years, this small department was the main production house for 'access broadcasting' in Britain, charged with giving a voice to individuals, communities and experiences under- or unrepresented elsewhere in the media. It specifically excluded political groups but, by the definition of its constitution, it tended to favour the powerless over the powerful. Workers whose traditional industries were collapsing in the 1970s and 1980s were inevitably featured; the super-rich, although antagonised by Labour's super-tax, were not.

Seizing control

In *Misère au Borinage*, the strikers re-enact – with emotional intensity – a march that had happened before the filmmakers arrived, establishing a common, if controversial, way of communicating 'truth' in documentary. This technique of reconstruction continues to divide documentarists and policy-makers over 70 years later, but Nichols's important point is that it was the very mechanism that truly engaged the subjects of the film and gave them not just a measure of ownership of the resulting production but a regenerative impulse in their struggle.[20]

Some 40 years later, a group of London workers who had taken on the government – for depriving them of work and unemployment benefit during the imposed three-day week in 1973, and who had represented themselves successfully in an industrial relations tribunal – also re-enacted their experience for the BBC's cameras. They wrote their own script, from the hearing transcripts, and took all the parts, including the officials and their boss opponents, demonstrating an impressive command of the form and function of the television medium. *Tribunal* was one of the Community Programme Unit's first series, *Open Door*. Mike Fentiman was its producer:

> It came from a dramatically written letter one of them sent in and I thought, this guy can write. I met him and persuaded him that he could do it. He wrote the whole show, he wrote his friends' parts for them and then they adjusted it – 'I wouldn't have said that', 'I didn't do that' and so on – so it was an original script that was then improvised from. It was shot in four days. They played themselves and, because the bureaucrats wouldn't play themselves, they played them too . . . At the end he makes this impassioned speech: 'You keep fighting or you die. If you stop fighting, you sleep and rigor mortis sets in' . . . They won but it was a phyrric victory. Only around 200 people got paid out of the many thousands and thousands who had lost money through the three-day week.[21]

It seems impossibly quaint now that BBC television shows were once made with such ideological fervour, even encouraged by an establishment that did not share their views. It was part of a high-minded conception of public service broadcasting that constructed public service as serving disparate social needs and views above servicing consumer tastes.

Open Door was a low-budget, low-audience show that gave individuals and, more frequently, groups a producer and limited resources to make a programme that promoted their views. The most notable aspect of the deal was that these unlikely programme-makers were granted editorial control of their programmes, the BBC officially ceding final say in what could be broadcast. In some respects, this was a chimera, because programmes were still bound by guidelines regarding issues such as taste and decency, and the BBC was incapable of relieving itself of ultimate legal, ethical and political control of what it broadcast, under the terms of its charter. But the important principle was established that there could and should be other editorial views expressed than that of the centre, or political orthodoxy. And, as *Open Door* metamorphosed into the more professionally made *Open Space* in the 80s – making partial films with groups such as striking miners, Irish republicans and campaigners against the arms trade – clashes with BBC management inevitably occurred. But, to the BBC's credit, most of those disputes were successfully resolved and no programme banned. Hundreds, if not thousands, of voices denied a hearing elsewhere on television were heard, a precursor of today's understanding that the audience is composed of sentient beings with many different views, most deserving to be heard. The difference was that the government and the BBC then believed it possible to hold an accepted line on any issue and marginalise dissidents and dissent. Now, political and media fragmentation have made such unitary consensus rare, and the consumer culture has empowered the individual successfully to clamour to be heard.

Technology and change

The changes that this cultural revolution has wrought on programme-making forms has extended into every genre and not just been confined to television. The arrival of new media – web broadcasting, mobile phone transmission, etc. – has also so extended the possibilities that producers have struggled to keep up with technological evolution. For conventional broadcasters – the BBC, ITV, Channel 4 – this has meant the erosion of their audience base and their authority, leaving them to chase ever more desperately their shrinking audience share, particularly among the fickle 18- to 35-year-old demographic that the advertisers prioritise and pay premium rates to reach. Digital channels and web-sites allow much more accurate targeting of consumer groups, or 'communities of interest', and their proliferation spreads the funding resources ever thinner. This has challenged the conventional broadcasters to find new, better targeted ways of addressing their target audience.

One direct result is that the role of the presenter standing in front of the camera is less frequently the authoritative uncle doling out useful information and advice, more often the 'best mate' retelling entertaining stories that rely heavily on social recognition. It is no surprise that ITV's highest-paid presenters are the former children's presenters Ant and Dec, with whom a significant share of their audience have grown up, and who still maintain that cheeky, cheery chappie role, unencumbered by knowledge or gravitas.[22] No surprise also that the BBC's highest-paid presenter, the 48-year-old Jonathan Ross, had to be suspended for three months for a childish prank that outraged older listeners, but was all too consistent with the risqué 'naughty boy' persona the multimillionaire likes to maintain.[23] Meanwhile, the 'content providers' – as producers of factual material including documentary have now become – have also been forced to frame their material in less serious, more engaging ways. Put crudely, if the programme seems to be speaking in an intimate tone of voice about a recognisable subject or issue, the supposition is that people will much prefer this to being lectured. It is this commercially-driven imperative that has licensed a much broader range of voice and popular argot than previously, allegedly rendering the Community Programme Unit's access philosophy largely redundant. The Unit was closed down in 2000.

At a time of fast technological change, it also seems as if it is the technology that is driving the changing worldviews it conveys. But technology is neutral, amoral, merely the apparatus for conveying messages, and we need to pay greater attention to the messengers that seize these means, who they are and what messages they bring.

Three examples serve to underline the way in which the technological advances that succeed are those that fit purposes for which the context is ready.

(i) Video diaries – the triumph of the will

Arguably, Community Programme Unit's key contribution to factual forms was the video diary. Now an accepted part of the programme-maker's arsenal, the personal-confessional mode of one person travelling with their camera – and talking to it like a friend was a video revolution when it first appeared in 1991. Until then, programmes had always been shot by professional film crews, mostly on film, necessarily with separate sound. The relatively recent introduction of Beta SP had allowed the recording of sound on the same videotape, but at the operational disadvantage of having the sound recordist umbilically connected to the camera. With the arrival on the market of home video, the possibility occurred of a do-it-yourself approach, one that was initially fiercely opposed by BBC engineers, keen to keep up their high technical standards. However, the series launch producer, Jeremy Gibson, managed to overcome their objections with a heavy commitment to lengthy post-production, and a new form was born. *Video Diaries* was a raging success, perfectly capturing the Zeitgeist. It put the programme-maker in the centre of the frame and spoke in the first person, legitimising the individual, experiential approach to life and filmmaking. It was the apotheosis of the personal over the political, of form over message. It has been blamed for being a contributor to the decline of authoritative, argumentative and analytical documentary, but it also has had some notable benefits, one of which was the bringing to the screen of Sean Langan (see Chapter 1). As Langan admits, he was lucky to get his initial Video Diary assignment, because the whole Community Programme Unit ethos was not to employ fellow media types but to offer the screen to the dispossessed. But what distinguished him was being equally ignorant of the form's conventions.

> What worked about it was because I didn't understand the form. I wasn't shackled. I didn't come from News, I was a Features writer, and I hadn't been in TV. I was dealing with a very serious subject that would only normally have been covered by Current Affairs or News – human rights abuses in Kashmir, insurgents – and because, coming from Features, I didn't know the rules, and I was hopeless at filing quickly.[24]

It is the quirky, random and above all personal that is the chief legacy of the *Video Diaries* phenomenon in modern television. Quite a few formatted documentaries deploy the video diary as one element in their format, but it more regularly crops up on websites such as YouTube and Facebook (see below). The real resulting documentary revolution is that 'up close and personal' style that Richard Klein codifies as 'immersive'. More and more documentaries are fronted by a 'personality' whose experience is being apparently captured, warts and all, for sharing with the audience, often with the vicarious enjoyment of their pain and problems.

Few of these are video diaries – with celebrities the crews may be quite big and the experiences as carefully constructed as drama – but the aim is to give that sense of personal journey to documentary travel and investigation, with the talent playing up for – and to – the camera. It may be *Paul Merton in China*, or the celebrity posse climbing Mount Kiliminjaro for Comic Relief (2009), but the stress of their confected travels is mitigated by the knowledge of a large crew and, in the latter, an even larger team of bearers supporting their travails.

(ii) Web broadcasts – a community of fools?

The exponential growth of the web in the last few years, both in sites and bandwidth, has developed an even more voracious appetite for content than digital television. Where initially it was little more than a succession of sites for people to share their home videos and favourite clips, the advances of web technology have opened up a brand new industry of web broad-casters, covering a whole alternative universe of subjects and genres. Some are conventional broadcasters, led by the BBC, exploring new ways of recycling their current and past content. A lot of other media, particularly print and radio, have seen this as a new way of securing distribution profile in a fast-evolving landscape where no one is sure what the future will look like. Most importantly, many individuals and groups have seen this as the ultimate democratic vehicle for getting their message out and finding people of like mind. Just as some music acts have managed to secure a fan-base and distribution without the commercial compromises demanded by a record company deal, web production evades the television gatekeepers, the barons of whimsy that are the commissioners. Without their quality controls, this ensures a veritable tsunami of indifferent and bad material, but the increasing sophistication of insert tagging, web search engines and consumer use, ensures that good material is identifiable from within the morass, bringing many new voices to the media firmament.

It is this extraordinary opportunity – seized by millions as their views are presented to cameras around the world for the first time – that is the real revolution, more than the marvellous technology that enables it. At a *Televisual* magazine conference celebrating 'Intelligent Factual Television' at the British Academy of Film and Television Arts in London in May 2007, then Controller of BBC2, now Director of BBC Archive Content, Roly Keating said:

> I think we are at the most exciting point in the media in my career, not least because it is so unpredictable. People wanting to find ways of addressing the world and telling them about their lives is a perfect fit for the internet.[25]

Many of the best and brightest of these new sites are likely to dazzle momentarily and burn out fast, like comets, since few are economically viable prospects. Just as poetry magazines, particularly in the 1920s and 1930s, sprang up in moments of youthful creativity, but disappeared equally quickly, so will these; and the alternative, experienced by many of the first wave of web entrepreneurs, is that their brainchild has real business prospects, so is bought out making the progenitors fabulously wealthy, but honing the creative enterprise to the reductive corporatist goal of maximising profit. *Friends Reunited* was the prototype social networking site when it launched in 2000, and its founders sold it to ITV plc in 2005 for £120 million, but its star was on the wane, soon to be superseded by other networking sites, like Bebo and Facebook. The video sharing website YouTube was only born in February 2005, and sold to Google 21 months later for $1.65 billion. So successful is the phenomenon that the BBC and CBS distribute some of their product on the site.

Anthony Lilley writes about these issues and is well-placed to identify which comes first, the technical chicken – or the curate's egg she delivers. He is the Managing Director of Magic Lantern and also executive producer of Channel 4's venture into online broadcasting, 4docs. Most significantly, in September 2007 he was chosen to deliver the prestigious Huw Weldon Memorial Lecture at the Royal Television Society's Cambridge Convention, which reflects a burgeoning demand among the great and good of the UK television industry to better understand new media and its impact on their world. Lilley's talk was entitled: 'The Me in Media: participation, interactivity and the rise of the people formerly known as the audience':

> Unfortunately TV has been drawing some of the wrong lessons from new media. It's dangerous, for instance, to believe that TV is so important that every other medium aspires to be just like it. Interactive media isn't TV with clicks. [Broadcasters] have, by and large, underinvested in the creative potential of social media. They have, by and large, and I include the BBC in this, taken some short-sighted decisions to use new technologies defensively – to protect TV income or to provide new means of distribution . . .TV's obsession with channel thinking is part of the problem. If you think – as many broadcasters do – that the name of the game is battling other broadcasters for audience share and advertising – and that channels are the best tools to use to do this – then you're fighting the last war.[26]

As Lilley says, the contemporary obsession with new media is only an expensive way of misunderstanding that, while delivery platforms will continue to change and evolve, the only core constant is good content, programmes that people want to watch, however it is delivered. 'There are seeds of survival for those traditional media players who are deft, creative and ambitious enough to seize the opportunity. We still need shared stories to bond us together and those stories can still be commercially successful, make no mistake'.[27] There is, however, a view that some big broadcasters are making big mistakes.

(iii) User-generated content – but is it news?

In some ways, the BBC has been traumatised by the digital revolution. The founder of UK national and public service broadcasting (and the figurehead of world broadcasting), it has had to adapt increasingly fast to the rapidly changing styles, systems and substance of the broadcast landscape. Its recent history has been marked by desperate and costly attempts to master the new media platforms it finds itself competing in. Its digital television channels, BBC3 and BBC4, following troubled births, have been critical successes and its website a world-leader, but these have to be funded from the same long-established funding base that was constructed to resource the terrestrial services that pre-date this digital age: the licence fee. This arcane tax on television set ownership – always a bugbear to commercial rivals – is spread ever thinner to fund new services, at inevitable cost to the core services it was set up to deliver. As the BBC spends hundreds of millions of pounds on new initiatives under the rubric of 'Future Media and Technology', such as the long-delayed iPlayer, which enables web-watchers to catch up on recent television programmes – and which will eventually deliver a free archive service – thousands of production staff are being made redundant. Like the loss-making websites of most leading newspapers, no satisfactory means of monetising these new services has been found, so the old services bear the brunt of the costs.

Many BBC personnel privately feel that the technological beast has been engorged at the cost of the BBC's core function and value, as programme-maker. They see its 80-year experience and esteem being eviscerated to fund a doomed attempt to control means of delivery in a global landscape dominated by the likes of Google and their cyber-cities. One former holy cow that now feels more like a sacrificial victim is BBC News. Despite rationalising the news-gathering that services both the rolling news operation the News Channel and the bulletins on the main channels, it has not been spared the axe that has fallen across the corporation.

The ways in which the Facebook generation communicate with each other do not sit easily with a tradition of news presentation that relies on a silver-haired gent in a suit and tie, normally accompanied by a younger, more fetching woman, delivering the tablets from the broadcast Mount of Zion. Techno-zealots argue UGC (user-generated content) – people sending personal accounts and pictures of events they have witnessed at first hand, such as the London 7/7 tube bombings, or the unsuccessful follow-on attempts two weeks later – will transform news coverage and put the punter in the picture in a role other than that of victim. They may not yet be fronting their own reports, but the extension of perspective that UGC brings and the dialogue that is opening up between news organisations and their audiences is beginning to suggest the possibility of a more nuanced kind of news. Belatedly, news broadcasters are beginning to see the potential, not least in cheap sourcing to them. The expense of flying correspondents and satellite technology into remote regions is not worth it if they add no value to the picture – better a local with some unique insight should address the camera. (In the January 2009 Israeli military assault on Gaza, that was what Palestinian reporters did, as Western correspondents were forcibly excluded and left to stand impotently on the sidelines.) The underlying analysis here is that the BBC has been slow to recognise the editorial changes that the technological revolution has not only made possible, but increasingly demands. One senior BBC news executive, who prefers to remain anonymous, has this to say.

I think interactivity is about user generated content, it's about listening, it's about not treating a piece of journalism as a finished product. If you're going to be successful, your journalism is a product of a constant to and fro, constant interaction with the audience . . . In the initial coverage of Virginia Tech there were eye-witness accounts from inside Norris Hall, which were given to the BBC, by people emailing the BBC because they had been surfing the web to try to find out what the hell was going on.[28]

In the past, before electronic communication, correspondents – usually by mail – would have been dismissed as 'the green ink brigade', the kind of obsessive viewer who always wrote in, often to complain, often in green ink. Now the news organisations are delighted to have the human contact with their shrinking audiences, and recognise that their divergent views and experiences can enrich their output. It has also called into question their unitary news values, the largely unquestioned professional 'rightness' of news priority and approach. One of the leading Britons in world news, Chris Cramer (former head of news-gathering at the BBC and then chief executive of CNN for ten years) challenged those values in an interview he did with the UK newspaper *The Independent*, when retiring from CNN in 2007.

In his vision for the future, Cramer sees a role for more opinion-based journalism in television news. 'There is a school of thought, not just in the US but elsewhere, that says opinion television is somehow a bad thing. In other words, that television networks doing what newspapers have done for a couple of centuries is somehow a bad thing. I think it's only a bad thing if it's not clearly labelled.' More stories, he is convinced, will be generated by the public. 'The Saddam executions demonstrated how much this complements journalism. It's real journalism and richer journalism. How would we have known about the dissent in the execution chamber without user generated content?'[29]

There are, however, contrary views expressed among professional journalists' ranks. Chief foreign correspondent and sometime BBC TV newscaster Ben Brown represents the more dystopian view. 'During the Buncefield oil depot fire[30] we had some good helicopter shots of the refinery burning but preferred to run some wobbly mobile phone pictures instead, to add this spurious sense of UGC excitement.'[31] Other sources report that children in the neighbourhood would approach reporters with their mobile phone pictures of the fire, only to be told that the shots were too distant. The last that would be seen of these young aspiring citizen journalists would be their backs as they ran towards the fire to get the closer pictures. No casualties resulted but it is possible to see the downside of this unlicensed flow and, while BBC News (at least at the time of going to press) does not pay for UGC, there are websites that offer cash for useable news pictures of this kind, possibly threatening the free flow of such material. And many do file elsewhere, branding themselves citizen journalists and filing on websites edited and graded by popular user response.

Your news

Television news organisations (essentially the BBC and ITN) used to have the resources, experience and authority to broadcast exclusively what they believed the audience needed to know to function in an informed democracy. Now our changed culture demands that they listen to the audience and gives them what they want, when they want and how they want it, moving towards the aggregation of news around personal predilection that is already supplied by web-sites like slashdot[32] and digg[33] and delivered through whichever portal is current. But although news content through the web is up, it does not offset the loss in broadcast figures. News chiefs are all too aware that while people are Twittering,[34] they are not watching television news. There are concerted efforts to meet those lost audiences' needs, by everything from broad-casting news via mobile phones to introducing an 'entertainment hub' in the BBC newsroom, not least to keep up on the celebrity culture that used to be beneath their consideration. Former BBC Head of News Peter Horrocks had already pressed for his journalists and editors to take 'an unembarrassed embrace of subject areas that have too often been looked down on as too pavement-level or parish-pump'.[35] The BBC News website duly proclaims:

> News can happen anywhere at any time and we want you to be our eyes. If you capture a news event on a camera or mobile phone, either as a photograph or video, then please send it to BBC News.[36]

But even if there is a shift in editorial judgement, and a new openness to audience input, there is very little sign of 'ordinary people' taking over the camera and setting the agenda. Those initiatives that have made it to the screen seem tokenist at best. BBC News has a *Your News* programme which is like a local letters page on air – coming each week from a different town like a latterday *Down Your Way*[37] – and Channel 5 News also has a *Your News* segment at the end of its main evening bulletin, but neither have broken a story of any moment. When the ultra-serious BBC *Newsnight* programme attempted to canvas viewer material, they ended up with more home movies about drowning cats than exclusives; and subsequent suggestions that viewers determine story selection on a Friday night, elicited the response that that was what the producers were being paid to do – and they should get on and do it. Horrocks admits that they may have dropped the bar a bit far, and not to expect any more UGC on *Newsnight* soon. As a critical news executive says:

> What underlies all these problems is that we are in a twilight zone, a changeover period between the old model and the new model and it is true at the moment that we do still need to do both, because not everybody at the moment is going to get their news delivered by some clever piece of software that aggregates stuff and gives you 'My News' now. So you have to do both and think the problem for the BBC is that it has not thought very clearly about this and what it has tended to do is just add bits on, trying to reach new groups as it has seen markets splinter.[38]

Al Gore, the former US Vice-President turned environment campaigner (see Chapter 17) has been instrumental in setting up a model that may show the future. Current TV, launched in the USA in October 2006 and in the UK in April 2007, is a digital TV channel fuelled by a website to which mostly young filmmakers contribute 'pods' – productions in the region of five to seven minutes.[39] These are web broadcast and voted on by their audience and those that make the grade get shown on the TV channel and the makers then get paid. The pay (somewhere about £200 a pod for all rights) is only a fraction of television rates, and would not fund a fulltime career, but Current TV are looking to establish continuing relationships with their best suppliers, and it is one way of encouraging the new and maverick minds to address the camera, which is largely unfeasible in mainstream television today.

Conclusion

It is interesting to reflect that one of the very first pieces of UGC now has an astronomic value – Jeb Zapruder's grainy 8mm shots of President John F. Kennedy's assassination in Dallas, 1963. George Holliday's 1991 video recording of Los Angeles savagely police beating Afro-American driver Rodney King ultimately led to the LA riots, when police were acquitted, despite the visual evidence already widely broadcast. If we are a still a way off Ruby Grierson's revolutionary demand to seize control of the camera and microphone and 'tell the bastards what it's really like', we have progressed some distance in that direction. These changes and their drivers have done much to affect every sub-genre of documentary and factual programming, as future chapters will explore. But, while most people can now grab a camera, talk to it and broadcast the results on the web, few capture that attention that makes them a viral hit with millions of views. When they do, it is more frequently showing off than revealing truths, but there have been developments that elevate these shards of the personal to a composite view of the wider polis.

On 1 April 2009, the newly expanded group of world leaders, known as the G20, met in London to discuss concerted action to stem the global economic recession. Thousands of demonstrators descended on the city to exercise their legal right to protest the systemic failures

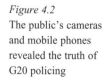

Figure 4.2
The public's cameras
and mobile phones
revealed the truth of
G20 policing

of the government and its banker friends in the City. The Metropolitan police drafted in thousands of officers to clamp down on these demonstrators, deploying powers and arguments that have been greatly enhanced in the heightened security climate caused by terrorist attacks. One of the controversial tactics used is 'kettling', where military-style force is used to corral demonstrators in particular streets, denying anyone the right to leave or join the group for some hours. No exemption is made, even for passers-by innocently caught up, or those taken short or ill. Deliberately confrontational, this excites tempers on both sides, and encourages officers to consider all demonstrators as de facto law-breakers. News photographs on the following day depicted officers snarling more fearsomely than their dogs, while others' faces were unidentifiable beneath helmets and balaclavas.

One middle-aged man, attempting to find his way home from his job on a newspaper stand, dropped dead. The police, with an autopsy conducted by a friendly pathologist, announced that he had died of a heart attack. At that point, people who now routinely use the still and video capabilities of their mobile phones, started to supply the media with pictures that revealed Ian Tomlinson had been the subject of a violent, unprovoked attack by an officer whose face was covered and badge number missing. As a second post-mortem proved that Tomlinson had died from internal bleeding, probably caused by the assault, the police had to change their story, suspend the officer, and institute an enquiry. With this evidence that personal pictures can make a difference, the trickle became a flood, showing other assaults and illegal acts by a force that clearly saw itself as above the law and at war with the public it is supposed to defend. As community activists who have attended demonstrations over a number of years now claimed, these attitudes and assaults were routine, but previously ignored by a pliant media disposed to believe the police version of such events, usually leading to tabloid headlines like 'anarchist thugs on the rampage'. The UGC in the hands of people who were there this time told a different story, hard to deny, causing senior officers to distance themselves from the behaviour recorded. In a society surrounded by surveillance cameras controlled by the powers that be, it is a small but significant adjustment in the balance of power. New technology has given a new life to the *vox populi*.

Expert briefing – dealing with the public

The arrogance that characterised much of early television can still taint producers' relations with the public, whether through abuse of trust in interactive vehicles such as premium phone-line voting, or in individuals' unhappy experiences with rapacious film crews. Broadcasters' guidelines have become increasingly prescriptive about operational standards and successive faults have led broadcast staff to undertake retraining on everything from health and safety to not lying to the public. Every filmmaker should recognise their ethical responsibilities and the implications of their behaviour. It should be a professional objective of every production and every member of its staff to leave members of the public it has dealings with feeling better, rather than worse, for the experience. Consideration need not be costly, but can benefit future working for one and all. These are some guidelines that can ease that pathway.

1   **Honesty**: Honesty is (usually) the best policy. People should be told what kind of programme their contribution is intended for, how it and how much is likely to be used, and where and when it is expected to be aired. Most guidelines for the producers for the different channels require straight dealing with people that are being filmed and their written consent,[40] which can be invalid if fair notice of context is not given. This does not mean naively revealing all the arguments and objectives, especially if this will compromise the contribution. Commonsense should prevail. In the case of investigations, particularly with covert filming, prior waiver of these conditions has to be agreed through reference to a senior programme executive. No one is licensed to play fast and loose with public confidence.

2   **Courtesy**: Courtesy and politeness should also be the norm, from the framing of demands in the first instance to managing the expectations of contributors on transmission. Even if the filming has gone well and written thanks sent, the pressures of post-production often cause production staff to fail to alert their contributors to the date and time of transmission and, worse, to the reduction or exclusion of their contribution. It should not be beyond the imaginative capacity of creative people to understand the hurt and humiliation a contributor feels when they have gathered their friends and relatives to watch their debut on television, only to find it has been cut out. This happens regularly: the possibility should be flagged from the outset and the facts and reasons communicated beforehand, in time to mitigate the disappointment.

3   **Consideration**: Despite an ever-growing popular sophistication in reading the visual media, potential contributors tend to fall into two camps: those who imagine they will be celebrated for their appearance and those who fear they will be vilified. Unless hubris or paranoia fit the programme's requirements, a significant part of production is to mitigate these reactions and put the contributor naturally at their ease, especially when technical demands predominate and problems cause delays. The skill is to understand how the contributor is thinking and reassure them sufficiently to ensure the performance required. Explanation of the programme processes, such as the non-contentious aspects of filming so far and the difficulties involved, can be a good way to engage the contributor and help them feel more part of the proceedings.

4   **Cut approval**: Where the contributor is involved from the inception of a project, either as progenitor or principal subject, the terms of that involvement need to be clearly spelt out, preferably in contractual form. Even then, those terms need to be translated into

practical lay terms, such as the amount of time and availability required of them, as well as crucial issues regarding the limits of editorial input. Many factual genres cannot accommodate any contributor input after recording, but most documentary formats and schedules can allow main contributors a privileged preview. Where possible, this is a useful fact checker for the production as well as an important reassurance for someone whose life or work is about to be exposed. Irrespective of whether they have any editorial say – and most broadcast contracts will have ensured that all rights have been signed away – reasonable contributors rarely demand changes unless they have been misrepresented or errors made.

5 **Clearance**: Working with members of the public used to be seen by television grandees as restrictive of their editorial freedom, but is now recognised as a rich and bottomless pit of diverse and largely free content. Terrestrial and web broadcasters are keen to acquire and show this material. Though few are inclined to pay for it, some still demand the level of copyright clearance and indemnity that is traditionally expected in fully paid broadcast commission compliance. This is unreasonable and a reassertion of the exploitative relationship between broadcaster and public that new media was believed to be instrumental in ending. As alternative distribution platforms develop and proliferate, the new gatekeepers will introduce standards and processes that will define the relationship with the consumer. Issues of trust and confidence, especially where profits from exploitation are or are not shared, may come to characterise that relationship.

6 **Rights**: Rights issues are already coming to dominate web business. Whereas YouTube was initially a free site where people shared favourite clips from television and film, the capitalisation of that site called into question the validity of its free use of others' copyright material. To members of the public, it is another means of sharing material, just as they may lend a friend a book or a video, but to the copyright owners it as seen as big an infringement as video piracy or illicit copying. The content provider, professional or otherwise, needs to cover themselves against future claims for such infringement. The best option currently available is to use the assertion of public domain copyright that is best codified at www.creativecommons.org and enacted by leading British broadcasters in the Creative Archive Licence Group (see: http://creativearchive.bbc.co.uk). This allows for non-commercial, non-derogatory use of copyright material within the UK, on a share-alike and attributive basis.

7 **Waivers**: Under the 1988 Copyright Act, everyone has copyright in their performance, however minimal, and unless this has been explicitly signed over, they may sue over its use. Derived from the French *droit morale* (moral right), it was supposed to recalibrate the unequal sense of power and ownership between the public and the producer, but the universally enforced all-rights sign off undermines this right, all the more forcefully enshrining the broadcaster dominance. The producer has to work doubly hard to justify the contributor's trust, when asking them to sign away all their rights, even for an unpaid vox pop grabbed on the street.

8 **Humanity**: In that the larger part of television production is about man management skills, a producer's reputation is to some degree determined by how they treat people, both creative collaborators and members of the public. The manipulation needed to achieve difficult programme ends should never be at cost to human decency, i.e. treatment producers would not be prepared to tolerate themselves. Whether being

put through difficult or humiliating routines for reality television or factual entertainment formats, or revisiting harrowing personal experiences for documentary interview, the impact on the subject's feelings and welfare should be paramount in the producer's mind.

9 **Multicultural sensitivity**: Where different cultural sensitivities are involved, such as the social and dietary observances of particular religious groups, the producer needs to be fully informed and accommodate the impact on schedules and requirements. A member of the production from the community in question is the surest way to represent such needs, but this is not always practicable. At least filming in community homes or places of worship should be properly recce'd (the universal contraction for 'reconnoitred') to ensure that all crew members are properly advised as to the dress and behavioural requirements that will not cause offence.

10 **Responsibility**: Ignorance is no excuse in law, and it should not be in television either. To enter other people's lives, homes and workplaces is a privilege that should be approached with respect and courtesy. Too many television employees are casually indifferent to the needs and feelings of their contributors, and have left a trail of damage and distrust in their wake. This has contributed to the wider perception of television as a rapacious monster not to be trusted, and although rudeness is not in the same ballpark as fraud, it is the human exchanges that people remember most. If they feel they have been treated well and fairly, that knowledge is communicated to others and the collective stock of television rises. If the experiences of individuals are routinely negative, that reputation grows and is hard to reverse. Broadcasters have producers' guidelines that must be adhered to, but they cannot prescribe every public interaction. The simpler prescription: 'Do as you would be done by' covers most eventualities.

Part II

Observe the people

We have seen how specific genres grew out of journalistic and lecturing traditions, and other forms that are primarily concerned with the voice to be heard. This section concerns itself more with the ways of seeing, the experience to be viewed, which is primarily a filmic tradition. Everyone concerned with cameras knows that they constantly redefine what passes for the objective, making the plasticity of perception palpable. As John Berger writes, 'The invention of the camera changed the way men saw'. Whereas before, Berger observes, perspective drawing and painting proposed to the spectator that he was 'the unique centre of the world. The camera – and particularly the movie camera – demonstrated that there was no centre'.[1] He quotes (in translation) the seminal Soviet filmmaker Dziga Vertov: 'I'm an eye. A mechanical eye. I, the machine, show you a world the way only I can see it.'[2] For him, that subjectivity was not a limitation, but a strength.

While Vertov developed lenses and methods to 'catch life unawares' – and saw the camera as a kind of microscope revealing the processes of everyday life – his mission to show life 'how it is' was to impose order on the chaos, not least through juxtaposition of images and even camera tricks to make his point. Thus his *Kino-Glas/Cinema-Eye* newsreel (1924) reverses film, apparently showing cattle resurrected from the butcher's slab, to prove that the meat comes fresh from the countryside. It is a ringing endorsement of the co-operative endeavours of the early Soviet era – which had rescued people from the serfdom of Tsarist rule – and which Vertov believed in. The name of his earlier newsreel series *Kino-Pravda/Cinema-Truth* (1922) consciously echoed the state newspaper's name, *Pravda/Truth*. Whose truth – and what is truth? – are questions that have always plagued documentarists and will stalk this part of the book.

Soviet 'truth' went largely unquestioned up to the Second World War, where the USSR played a vital part in the Allied war effort, and only became excoriated as lies in the West as a part of Cold War propaganda, albeit heavily aided by revelations of Stalin's pogroms. The building of a nation and the experimental evolution of the documentary form had been natural partners in opening people's eyes to the possibilities the future held and the role they had in it. Vertov was a profound influence on filmmaking traditions as distinct as the Grierson school of social documentary and Chris Marker's more idiosyncratic experiments with the observational form. Soviet documentaries of the twentieth century are a powerful evocation of the collective will, charting massive programmes of work, from the building of the first railroad from Turkestan to Siberia in the 1920s to the construction of the giant hydro-electric dam at Bratsk on the River Angara in Siberia in the 1960s. For every *Turksib* (Victor Turin 1929), there are hundreds of forgotten films that celebrate these real popular achievements in libraries and museums across the breadth of the former empire, now mouldering away thanks to the collapse of the Soviet Union and commensurate loss of funding.

Following the breakup of the Soviet Union in 1991, most of the country's valuable assets and resources were seized by a small group of opportunists who rapidly became some of the richest men in the world. Western politicians – and historians who should have known better – welcomed this 'end of history' and 'triumph of capitalism', without attending to the concomitant, less savoury truths that resulted. The single statistic that I find most resonant is that, within ten years, the life expectancy of the average Russian male fell by nearly ten years – five years between 1991 and 1994 – thanks to the rape and destruction of the economy and the erosion of regular employment, health and welfare services. Researchers Stuckler, King and MacKee lay this epidemiological tragedy squarely at the door of privatisation, the global ideology that had transferred power and wealth from the public to the private sector.[3] They say that it was responsible for an increase of the death rate in the former Communist bloc by 13 per cent in the 1990s. But this staggering fact and privatisation's impact on many millions of people – not just here but throughout the world – has not been documented on television because it does not fit the dominant narrative.

The toxic and corrupting effect on Russian life of *The Russian Godfathers* was eventually documented in an award-winning 2005 BBC series of that name,[4] these unpleasant truths having now been established, not least since the despairing Russian people had voted for a return to the centralisation of power that had once at least meant stability, in the person of the former KGB officer, Vladimir Putin.[5] But television makes less of these analytical pieces now, and they are considerably harder to get commissioned if they do not echo a received wisdom and a perceived relevance to the audience. If the Russian oligarchs had not been buying up Britain,[6] there would not have been the interest, just as the everyday concerns of ordinary people rarely justify observation without 'added value' to excite the audience's interest.

The social conscience of the pre-war Grierson school helped give rise to both the Free Cinema movement in Britain and the public service broadcasting ethics of the British Broadcasting Corporation, but those elevated principles have quietly receded in the face of commercial competition, with audiences dissipated and distracted by other attractions. Direct Cinema, or *cinéma vérité* in the French, had never had any presence on American television, but when documentary developed formulaic constructs, these proved popular and commercially viable on both sides of the Atlantic. The following chapters chart that progression, from observational documentaries of family life in the UK and the USA, through the adoption of dramatic characterisation and plot lines in docu-soap, to factual formats that replicate the thrill factor of nineteenth-century freak shows.

One thing that ties this 80 years of documentary development together is the search for the 'kino-eye' that sees things the way the audience wants to see it. Vertov was ahead of the curve because he worked in a revolutionary context that foregrounded the popular perspective and experience. Britain's socialists were as often as not public school poets easily drafted to the war effort and the post-war BBC, progressively neutralising potentially subversive perspectives and evolving a patrician view of social need. This was the BBC eye, which sometimes commenced documentaries with the presenter leaving London to visit the subjects of his gaze. As the need for ever more extreme iterations of the public condition were demanded to sustain audience share, the observational eye becomes increasingly voyeuristic.

The prosthetic eye camera being developed by Rob Spence (Chapter 2) may be the most objective, unmediated observational device yet, in that it seeks exactly to replicate the human eye, the literal rendition of Vertov's 'I'm an eye'. From which we can readily recognise that there is no such thing as an objective view, an unselective eye. Blink and you miss it. Change reel and the same thing happens. Look one way and miss the moment, as camera operators regularly do. Frame up on one action or group and you miss the others. This is what documentaries do and have always done; what has changed and continues to change is who decides what is observed, why and to what end. It was once the producers; then it was the managers, influenced by the accountants; it may now be the people themselves, but is that an advance?

5 Real life

....

real adj. based on fact, observation or experience, so undisputed[1]

The single most persistent argument about documentary is how truthful it is, or should aspire to be. 'Cinema is truth twenty-four times a second', says Bruno Forestier, a character in French film director Jean-Luc Godard's *Le Petit Soldat* (1963), asserting what we might call the creative absolute. Much misquoted and predictably disavowed – by directors such as Brian de Palma and Errol Morris, both of whom have retorted 'Cinema is lies twenty-four times a second' – one filmmaker's truth is another's poison. Television – which actually operates at a standard of 25 frames per second – has an uneasy relationship with the truth, preferring to categorise its product by labels such as fact or fiction, real or reality. Documentary traditionally stood at the apex of the factual pyramid, the fully filmically realised statement of the actual. But the interventions and selections involved in documentary realisation are what challenge its claim to be truthful. The viewfinder finds the view that the director or cinematographer wants; the final film is the artful juxtaposition of such shots to achieve the narrative, mood, argument and style of the filmmaker. As we have seen in the previous chapter, there are occasions when the objectives of the filmmaker are designed to be coterminous with that of the film's subjects, but these are rare and no less of a construction.

The ease with which truth is compromised by the everyday actions of editors in edit suites was well illustrated by an event in June 2007. The BBC had commissioned a documentary from one of its biggest independent production company suppliers, RDF Media, which would enjoy exceptional access to film the Queen going about her regal duties for several weeks. Though not the only such privileged insight – the Queen had first allowed BBC cameras in for *The Royal Family* in 1972,[2] thereby earning credit for modernising and popularising the monarchy in the public view – the access was sufficiently rare, and the public taste for royal affairs apparently boundless, that this was an important commission justifying its inclusion in the BBC1 Controller Peter Fincham's autumn preview press conference. The clip shown featured the Queen sitting for celebrity photographer Annie Leibowitz, who suggests the Queen lose her 'crown' (actually a tiara) so as to look 'less dressy'. The Queen clearly disagrees with the suggestion and, in the next shot, is seen stomping out in high dudgeon, saying she has done enough of these things. 'Her Majesty's throne a wobbler'[3] was an obvious headline that would make the PR men's day, but it turned into the Controller's worst nightmare. For it transpired that the scene in which the Queen was stomping along had happened on the way *to* this – apparently yet another tiresome photo shoot – and she had not walked out at all. The reality had been rearranged to make a more entertaining drama, but at the high cost of a diplomatic incident with Buckingham Palace and the abrupt suspension of future RDF contracts with the BBC. Suspicions that this may have been the error of a young, inexperienced editor were confounded when the company's creative director Stephen Lambert – a former BBC programme executive – admitted responsibility for the dodgy edit, though claiming this was not intended for public consumption.[4]

Cynics might say that truth is the first casualty of ratings wars, as channels fight to retain their audience share, but this story came hard on the heels of other embarrassments for the BBC. Along with other channels, they had been found to have misled viewers with regard to use of phone lines for quizzes and prizes, and the BBC had just been fined for the first time by the media regulator Ofcom for a blatant deception on the children's show *Blue Peter*. In an act of corporate contrition, the BBC initiated an internal inquisition to extirpate other acts of public deception and, having found a few, announced that all staff would have to be re-educated in matters of Truth and Honesty. That Britain's leading broadcaster should feel the need to instruct its staff that it mustn't lie to the public suggests a deeper moral malaise than one slip-up in an edit suite. Attention to – and understanding of – the truth is clearly a cultural relativity that shifts over time. In reviewing the evolution of documentary it is essential to consider the context that gave rise to its many flexible forms.

Cinéma vérité

Although coined by the Russian innovator Dziga Vertov as *kinopravda* in the 1920s – and more to express the hidden truth revealed by clever editing – the French term for 'film truth' has come to describe the tradition of observational documentary that grew up in the late 1950s and early 1960s. Several filmmakers in this tradition were trained as anthropologists, which discipline helps define the patiently watchful eye for detail and the non-invasive techniques which characterise the form at its best. Pierre Perrault's *Pour la suite du Monde* (aka *The Moontrap*) and Michel Brault and Gilles Groulx's *Les Raquetteurs* (1958) were early examples of *cinéma vérité*, but also reveal the French concern for their hidden messages about truth. This concern with textual complexity, largely absent in Anglo-Saxon documentary of the time, in part represents the French intellectual tradition but more importantly reflects France's post-War reaction against propaganda and, in particular, the incompatible truths of collaboration and resistance.

Jean Rouch and Edgar Morin were anthropologists but manage a subversion of the cinematic process in *Chronique d'un été* (*Chronicle of a Summer*) (1960), by starting with a scene in which they discuss this film study of happiness in Paris, then send their female subjects out onto the streets with microphone in hand and end by discussing on camera what they have learned. This is an anthropological vision that is as concerned about the ways it will be seen as the ways in which it is shot. As Edgar Morin wrote in an introduction to a conference on *cinéma vérité* at the Pompidou Centre:

There are two ways to conceive of the cinema of the Real: the first is to pretend that you can present reality to be seen; the second is to pose the problem of reality. In the same way, there were two ways to conceive *cinéma vérité*. The first was to pretend that you brought truth. The second was to pose the problem of truth.

(Il y a deux façons de concevoir le cinéma du réel: la première est de prétendre donner à voir le réel; la seconde est de se poser le problème du réel. De même, il y avait deux façons de concevoir le cinéma-vérité. La première était de prétendre apporter la vérité. La seconde était de se poser le problème de la vérité.)

This is far from the more popular vision of *cinéma vérité*, which concentrates on the simple, or simplistic, idea of unmediated reality made possible by the advances in lightweight, hand-held camera and sound recording technology, and faster film stock. As Stella Bruzzi records, these led to 'a less formal, more passive and responsive style of filmmaking and a concomitant adherence to an ideological belief in the possibility of accurate representation'.[5] She goes on to quote the American critic Stephen Mamber:

> At its very simplest, *cinéma vérité* can be described as a method of filming employing hand-held camera and live, synchronous sound. This is a base description, however, for *cinéma vérité* should imply a way of looking at the world as much as a means of recording . . . The essential element of *cinéma vérité* . . . is the use of real people in undirected situations.[6]

At this stage it is worth spelling out the most obvious counter to the presumptions of *vérité*: the frequency with which the presence of the camera alters the reality. Whether it is aboriginal peoples allegedly fearful it will steal their soul or would-be reality television applicants playing up to the camera, few people's behaviour is uninfluenced by its presence. Even dogs and cows tend to nuzzle the lens. And that in turn influences how the shot is framed, what and when it records. Filming street scenes in India, documentary crews have to employ people to distract the crowds that would otherwise hog the lens. When a young volunteer went to work with Mother Teresa in Calcutta, her *Video Diary*'s street scenes were distinguished by the frame of heads that she had no one to help disperse. It was a kind of video truth, about the relentless press of humanity encountered there, that more conventional documentary carefully avoids.

Although Jean Rouch is credited with a seminal impact on French *cinéma vérité*, and is claimed by the *nouvelle vague* as one of their own, his real life's work was in Africa. After the Second World War, Jean Rouch returned to Niger, where he had worked as a civil engineer in 1941. He became an ethnographer and, over a career spanning nearly 60 years, made more than 70 films of African life, culture and ritual in Niger, Ghana, Mali and Upper Volta. Working closely with the Sorka traditional healer Damouré Zika, he gained access to aspects of tribal culture he would not otherwise have been able to film. In *Petit a Petit/Little By Little* (1971), Rouch turned the camera on his own culture, with Zika – who had come to feature in most of his films – as a businessman visiting Paris to observe the natives, their quaint rituals and behaviour. By this time he had moved beyond straight *cinéma vérité*, observing that the camera always transformed the circumstances in which it was used, and that people often felt able to act more naturally if engaged in some form of play-acting, the ritual of cinema itself:

> The presence of the camera is a kind of passport that opens all doors and makes every kind of scandal possible. The camera deforms, but not from the moment that it becomes an accomplice. At that point it has the possibility of doing something I couldn't do if the

camera wasn't there: it becomes a kind of psychoanalytic stimulant, which lets people do things they wouldn't otherwise do.[7]

Despite being acclaimed as 'the father of Nigerian cinema', and working to help indigenous filmmakers, Rouch was predictably charged with neo-colonialism by many. His unique blend of observational ethnography with art film aesthetics undoubtedly fuelled that critique, but it is unlikely that any approach to filming alien cultures would have absolved a European, however sympathetic, from such charges at a time when these countries were struggling with new-found independence. It is a poignant reminder of the relativities of truth, and the limitations of the term *cinéma vérité*.

Direct Cinema

Although the term *cinéma vérité* is frequently used of mid-twentieth-century American documentary, the correct term is Direct Cinema, pioneered by the likes of Robert Drew and Richard Leacock. They had an ideological, almost messianic commitment to the notion that they could produce a kind of pure, unmediated reality film that would not carry the imprint of its maker. Robert Drew wrote an article entitled 'Narration can be a killer',[8] arguing that voiceover was what you do when you fail, and elsewhere claiming that 'the filmmaker's personality is in no way directly involved in directing the action'.[9] But, as we have seen, just because a director does not tell people what to do and say, it does not mean their presence has no influence on the outcome, nor that the resulting film will not construct a particular perspective on its subject.

Drew Associates' film of the American presidential *Primary* in 1960 had unprecedented access to the eventually successful Democrat candidate, John F. Kennedy, and Leacock claimed improbably that so unobtrusive were their methods that Kennedy occasionally forgot they were there. In truth, Kennedy proved his astute skill in playing naturally for the camera unlike his opponent Hubert Humphrey, but the camerawork subtly underlines this difference between the natural and the formal. That sympathy deficit is more forcefully developed in Drew Associates' follow-up film of 1963, *Crisis: Behind a Presidential Commitment*. About the forced integration of the University of Alabama, it pits the family-loving, cool-in-a-crisis Attorney-General Robert Kennedy against the stiffly formal, segregationist Alabama Governor George Wallace. While these films reveal that the Kennedys were the avatars of cinematic *realpolitik*, the predecessors of performer politicians such as Bill Clinton and Tony Blair, it is naive to claim that the camera is a passive observer here – it is clearly seduced by the Kennedy aura and plays up to it, while remaining distant and detached from the less loveable Wallace.

When Leacock left Drew and joined forces with D.A. Pennebaker, to make music performance films such as *Don't Look Back* (1966) and *Monterey Pop* (1968) (Chapter 14), the Direct Cinema banner effectively passed to the Maysles brothers. An exceptional cameraman, Albert had co-shot *Primary* but had declined to join Drew Associates. He worked with his younger brother, who recorded sound and edited, and together they produced commercials and promos to finance their documentaries. *Salesman* (1968) was one of the first Direct Cinema films screened theatrically, and remains a classic of the form. It follows four door-to-door Bible salesman in Boston, profiting from the brothers' knowledge of the area in which they grew up, and of working as salesmen to pay their way through university.

That knowledge, allied to their craft, is what makes the film so successful, not the pretence to have no constructivist input. As Bruzzi writes:

> There is a certain evangelical quality about many of the comments, such as Al Maysles' statement 'I regard our films as the purest form of cinema' or his brother David's belief that 'we don't impose anything on the people we film. We are the servants of our subjects rather than the other way round' (Kolker 1971: 185). Absent entirely from this description of their methods is any fundamental acknowledgement of the filmmaking process itself being the intervention that invariably makes all the difference, and this is how American *cinéma vérité* has been defined: as naive, simplistic and misguidedly idealistic.[10]

Bruzzi also quotes eminent American filmmakers who take this line, such as Errol Morris – '*cinéma vérité* set back documentary filmmaking twenty or thirty years' – and Emile de Antonio:

> *Cinéma vérité* is first of all a lie, and secondly a childish assumption about the nature of film. *Cinéma vérité* is a joke. Only people without feelings or convictions could even think of making *cinéma vérité*. I happen to have strong feelings and some dreams and my prejudice is under and in everything I do.[11]

Most modern makers of documentary film would accept that the filmmaker's hand is controlling and most aim for a signature style that distinguishes their work. Arguably the most distinguished, consistently successful and prolific American filmmaker associated with the *vérité* approach to filmmaking also wisely keeps his distance from the term. Frederick Wiseman has said:

> *Cinéma vérité* is just a pompous French term that has absolutely no meaning as far as I am concerned. The effort is to be selective about your observations and organize them into a dramatic structure.[12]

This, from a man who has always eschewed lights, music and filmic effects and, until recently, only used black-and-white film stock, is a frank admission of the filmic craft. Wiseman was a lawyer teaching at Boston University's Institute of Law and Medicine, and an amateur filmmaker, when he first felt compelled to film the life of inmates at the Bridgewater State Hospital for the Criminally Insane. *Titicut Follies* (1967) was named after a musical revue put on there by guards and patients, but the title also embodies the casual systemic cruelty that the film captures. So graphic are the scenes of abuse of the patients and their privacy that the Massachusetts State Court banned it from being shown, thereby helping launch Wiseman on a career of over 30 films, many set in institutions such as *High School* (1969), *Hospital* (1970) and *Juvenile Court* (1973). Wiseman has argued that if an institution receives support from public taxes, citizens should be entitled to observe how it works. This is as good a definition of the purposive directness of Direct Cinema as any.

Free Cinema

Free Cinema, the earlier movement in England in the late 1950s, had taken a different approach to the capture of the real. While the subjects were generally the unsung corners of working life, there was a much more consciously 'arty' imperative, and the key figures went on to become the leading British feature filmmakers of their generation. Lindsay Anderson, who started life as a film critic, made *O Dreamland* in 1953, an examination of popular culture through the prism of the Margate amusement park of that name. Karel Reisz and Tony Richardson made a film about a jazz club, *Momma Don't Allow* (1956). These and Lorenza Mazzetti's *Together* (1953) made up the programme at London's National Film Theatre on 5 February 1956, for which Anderson coined the term Free Cinema. Happily for them, it was a surprise hit. 'Queues of cinema enthusiasts, even longer than during the Festival of Britain, stood in the drizzle for hours in the hope of seeing three short films [that] in four days have become the talk of the town', reported the *Evening News*.[13] Such was the success that a total of six programmes of Free Cinema ran for three years, feeding a new taste for real life that television had yet to satisfy:

> The films were 'free' in the sense that they were made outside the framework of the film industry, and that their statements were entirely personal. They had in common not only the conditions of their production (shoestring budget, unpaid crew) and the equipment they employed (usually hand-held 16 mm Bolex cameras), but also a style and attitude and an experimental approach to sound. Mostly funded by the BFI's Experimental Film Fund, they featured ordinary, mostly working-class people at work and play, displaying a rare sympathy and respect, and a self-consciously poetic style.[14]

Free Cinema followed in the footsteps of the poet-filmmaker Humphrey Jennings, whose wartime films, particularly *Listen to Britain* (1941), were revered by Anderson, who called him 'the only real poet the British cinema has yet produced'.[15] In an article for *Sight and Sound* in 1954, Anderson had placed emphasis on Jennings's 'continuous sensitivity of human regard' and the fact that his films transcend their propagandist purpose and outlast their time 'because the depth of feeling in them can never fail to communicate itself'.[16] While working with everyday subjects, the Free Cinematographers also aspired to make films that would last. Writing in the June 1957 Free Cinema programme, Anderson said:

> With a 16 millimetre camera, and minimal resources, and no payment for your technicians, you cannot achieve very much in commercial terms. But you can use your eyes and ears. You can give indications. You can make poetry.[17]

Equally importantly, these young filmmakers emerged at a turning point in British history, with old verities retiring with Winston Churchill and the collapse of the British Empire, most dramatically instanced in the Suez Crisis of 1956. This was also the year of cultural eruption in which youth came to the fore for the first time, with the emergence of the hip-shaking Elvis Presley in the United States[18] and the naked Brigitte Bardot in France.[19] 1956 also saw the Royal Court Theatre opening of John Osborne's *Look Back in Anger*, the play which epitomised a generation of angry young men looking to reclaim their future after the long period of austerity that followed the Second World War. Free Cinema was part of that emerging sensibility which made art from first-hand experience, leading to the youth-dominated cultural revolution of the 1960s.

The Free Cinema documentary aesthetic was to have a profound influence on British television drama and feature film. The social realism of Britain's New Cinema in the 1960s was a direct product of Free Cinema, with its grainy black-and-white pictures about working-class protagonists in the industrial Midlands or North of England. Tony Richardson's *A Taste of Honey* (1961) and *The Loneliness of the Long Distance Runner* (1962), John Schlesinger's *A Kind of Loving* (1962) and *Billy Liar* (1963), Lindsay Anderson's *This Sporting Life* (1963), and Karel Reisz's *Morgan: A Suitable Case for Treatment* (1966) all deploy the documentary techniques their makers developed in the 1950s. Sadly, it had less impact on television documentary than might have been anticipated and, as Armstrong notes, the movement became history surprisingly quickly:

> By 1959 the impulse was already congealing. Whilst there is still something fresh about *March to Aldermaston* (1959), shot by a committee under the auspices of the Campaign for Nuclear Disarmament to protest the development of Britain's hydrogen bomb, Richard Burton's didactic voiceover sees Free Cinema losing its beautiful energies and ambiguities to the sound bite. What is fascinating about *vérité* filmmaking is its spectre of a piece of their past in our present. Like ghosts, these traders breaking for tea, mill workers enjoying a summer outing and duffel-coated beatniks in deepest Berkshire are all that is left of these lives. I kept wondering what became of the people they were that day.[20]

Observational documentary

As British filmmakers moved into drama, taking their audience with them, the big screen documentary fell into a long period of decline, leaving the form to be developed by television. BBC chiefs, many of them former journalists, probably would not have recognised Nichols's formal distinctions between poetic, expository, observational, participatory and reflexive modes,[21] but their didactic purposes certainly favoured exposition. So, with a strong public information ethos, the poetic mode was kept in check and the expository mode took over. Despite its honourable antecedents, nor did *vérité* filmmaking have much place in early British television. Grierson talked of documentary as 'the creative treatment of actuality'; producers spoke of 'actuality' as the illustrative bits of real life they used to trick out their reports.

Thus it was a notable breakthrough when Paul Watson's *The Family* (1974) spent 12 weeks in a high-rise flat in Reading observing the Wilkins family. Its warts-and-all portrait of the trials and tribulations of everyday family life, without the usual filter of explanatory commentary and contextual interviews, was a filmic breath of real fresh air. It was also being shot and edited as the series was transmitted, so the family reflected the experience of becoming known as it progressed. They were also vilified in the tabloid press for arguing and swearing in a now quite familiar way, but not then commonly seen on television. The Wilkins were, as Watson said at the time, 'the kind of people who never got on to television'. Today, they are the kind of people who are on television all the time and the observational style is established as one of the key forms of documentary.

What is less frequently acknowledged is that *The Family* followed the extraordinary success of a WNET series broadcast in the United States on their PBS (Public Broadcasting Service) network in 1973. *An American Family* was also a 12-part observational documentary series, largely without commentary, shot in the Loud family home in Santa Barbara and dramatically retailing family life, including the impending divorce of the parents. Unlike Watson's *Family*, the Louds were a relatively wealthy middle-class family, with a large house and four cars. Unlike the BBC version, the American series was shot well in advance and took a year to edit, before airing to massive acclaim in early 1973. The eldest son, Lance, was the first gay to be open about his sexuality on American public television, becoming something of a gay icon, and the whole family became national celebrities, appearing on mainstream network chat shows and on the front of *Time* and *Newsweek* magazines.

Despite the importance of the cinema documentarists, US television had much less of a tradition of documentary film than Britain, and a much more invasive tradition of personality presentation. So this largely uncommented observational form had no precedents in the public mind and critics tended to compare it to drama rather than documentary. This may have been intentional, as producer Craig Gilbert was clearly involved in masterminding the publicity campaign, and had his friend, the famous anthropologist Margaret Mead, pen a three-page article in the *TV Guide*, which flagged up the significance of the series:

I do not think *An American Family* should be called a documentary. I think we need a new name for it, a name that would contrast it not only with fiction, but with what we have been exposed to up until now on TV. [The series] may be as important for our time as were the invention of drama and the novel for earlier generations: a new way to help people understand themselves.[22]

Its first transmission, on Thursday 11 January 1973, was on the same evening as the long-running hit soap *The Waltons*, which presented an idealised portrait of poor but happy Virginian farm life, against which *An American Family* was seen as an iconoclastic attack on the American dream. Although the series itself avoided prescription on how the audience should react to the family and their foibles, the publicity had invoked the American dream in suggesting how relevant the subject matter was, and certainly helped crystallise the family as the central avatar of American society, the barometer by which we gauge the pressures of modern life. Critics seized upon this referential reading, and the advertising played up to it. WNET's advertisement in the *New York Times* ran, 'Newsweek described this series as "a starkly intimate portrait of one family struggling to survive a private civil war". See for yourself.'[23] The American film historian Geoffrey Ruoff has gone so far as to see in *An American Family* the seeds of subsequent American television staples as confessional chat shows and reality TV.[24] Whereas the reporting of the real had previously been the serious stuff the public watched before getting down to the entertainment, the real had now become the entertainment. Ruoff calls it 'narrative non-fiction', and writes about how it confused viewers' sense of the real:

The significance of the real was paramount, even for critics who compared the series to fictional works . . . The notion of liveness, an important dimension of television viewing, cropped up in many of the reviews. These reviewers failed to acknowledge any distinctions between representation and reality. An article in *Newsweek* 'The Divorce of the Year', announced, 'This week, in the presence of 10 million Americans, Pat Loud will tell her husband of twenty years to move out of their house in Santa Barbara, Calif.' (*Newsweek*, March 1973). By the time episode 9 was aired, in which this scene occurred, Pat and Bill Loud had already been divorced for six months. The review, like many others, collapsed the difference between story time and broadcast time, implying that viewers saw the events not as they happened, but as they were happening . . .[25]

The discourse *An American Family* provoked at the time was to resonate well beyond the moment, keeping the family sufficiently in the limelight to warrant a return in *An American Family Revisited: The Louds 10 Years Later* (1983), which concentrated on how the family had been lionised, criticised and packaged. They had, as Ruoff writes, come under sustained criticism for revealing the less flattering truths some would like to keep behind closed doors:

> A further indication of the role of television in the reception concerned the relationship between entertainment, reality and broadcasting. Some critics saw the Louds' willingness to share their private lives in a television series as an indication of a therapeutic society that thrived on the 'compulsion to confess' . . . With this in mind, reviewers attacked the Louds for simply taking part in the documentary (*The Nation*, 1973). The accusation of exhibitionism, on the part of the Louds, and invasion of privacy, on the part of the producers, led to a denunciation of television in American life.[26]

Watson's *The Family* came under similar attack, with the UK's leading anti-television campaigner of the day, Mary Whitehouse, calling for the programme to be banned. This self-appointed heroine of middle England had originally taken up the cudgels against the BBC because of what she saw as licentious coverage of the Christine Keeler affair, but had broadened her attack on all that she saw as 'poison being poured into millions of homes through television'. That she felt it even conceivable to suppress the honest vulgarity of the Wilkins family reminds us how distant from such everyday reality many viewers were at the time, and how much of an eye-opener observational documentary can be.

The trusty sword of truth

As we have seen, observational documentary's truth-seeking antecedents proposed a *modus operandi* in which the camera crew is ideally invisible, neither directing nor influencing the actions they record. This led to the widespread use of the term 'fly-on-the-wall', to describe the broad genre of work that observed everyday life and, particularly, institutions. But, just as Wiseman is drawn to his institutional subjects by a desire to reveal issues of public concern, there are few documentary filmmakers who are not driven by the hope of making a difference through their work. Critics say that eschewing commentary and interview removes the documentary's analytic power and political potential, but practitioners point to powerful effects achieved by the precision of observations recorded and the shrewd juxtaposition of those images. However dispassionate the observational eye may seem to be, there is always a controlling intelligence and agenda at work, and that is how it should be. The novelty of the work and the views it explores may be what excites the most comment, but the more profound objective – and reward – is to change the way your subject is viewed. One of Britain's most distinguished documentarists, Roger Graef, is a criminologist, and many of his films concentrate on the country's police and judicial system. 'Roger Graef's approach to documentary-making is to change social policy by providing evidence' writes one of his collaborators.[27]

Roger Graef's *Police* (1982) is regularly cited as the single most effective use of the form. An observational documentary series for the BBC, with unique access to film the work of Thames Valley police, it included an episode called *An Allegation of Rape*, in which three policemen are seen robustly questioning a 24-year-old woman who has come in to the police station to report a rape. They reveal an institutionalised insensitivity that ignores the effect their words will have on a public audience as they badger the woman to 'test' her story, accusing her of making it up. 'Have you ever been on the game? How many times have you had sex? How many men have you had sex with? Can you count them on the fingers of one hand?' and 'This is the biggest bollocks I've ever heard'.[28] It caused such a public revulsion that the police were forced to accept a country-wide change in the way they handled rape. Even so, 25 years on, rape convictions are at an all-time low[29] and a woman police officer was so disgusted with the way that her colleagues in Leicestershire behaved that she made an under-cover film, shown by Channel 4's *Dispatches*, even though this compelled her resignation from the force. In *Undercover Copper*, she reveals a continuing male culture of disrespect for rape victims and records a fellow WPC admitting that, were she raped, even she wouldn't report it to the police.[30] This is not to gainsay Graef's work, merely to recognise the limitations of power and influence sometimes attributed to the documentary film. And not all filmmakers are as purist in their approach, as John Corner noted in his *Art of Record*:

> The 'purist' form of observationalism practised by Graef was always hard to sustain and many television series of the 1980s, though they followed the general approach and projected themselves as 'fly on the wall', also used interview and occasionally voiceover to provide a continuity of information throughput and to provide an additional means of obtaining coherence and structure.[31]

Whereas the policemen in Graef's rape interrogation seemed blithely unaware of the camera and their impact upon it, other observed subjects are all too aware. In another early BBC1 observational series, which spent an academic year inside *Queens': A Cambridge College* (1984),[32] two academics in the senior common room are closely observed in a confidence 'strictly between you and me', when clearly they know there is a camera and microphone hovering behind them. The form has produced many such risible moments. In an allegedly observational film about Dartmoor prison, an absconding prisoner returned by the police is seen explaining that he had not returned from Christmas home leave because a family member was ill and 'us Eastenders stick together', to which Cockney bullshit the wing governor delivers an even more improbable rejoinder, politely inviting him to return to his cell and complete his sentence 'without any further trouble'. Too often such amateur dramatics have been staged to produce narrative coherence for an 'observational' film in which the camera crew were not present at a critical moment or not recording for one reason or another.

Not so true

Channel 4's long-running flagship documentary series *Cutting Edge* – which promises 'distinctive, compelling films that offer a snapshot of life in Britain'[33] – has had a few such moments in its generally illustrious career. In 1998, *Cutting Edge* had to pull a show about girls who were unusually close to their fathers after the subject Victoria Greetham's real father came forward to point out that the man on the show was, in fact, her fiancé. Another *Cutting Edge* film, *Too Much Too Young – Chickens* used members of the production team to 'reconstruct' scenes of rent boys being picked up in Glasgow. These came after an earlier

Cutting Edge documentary, *Rogue Males*, faked key criminal and black-market dealing scenes, leading to a chastening comment in the Programme Regulation section of that year's ITC Annual Report:

> A Channel 4 programme in the *Cutting Edge* documentary strand, *Rogue Males* (about young petty criminals in an inner city environment), faced allegations that some of the scenes presented as authentic were staged. Channel 4 published a statement admitting that to avoid the actual commission of crimes some scenes were 'constructed' but that in every case they were true to the spirit of the individuals' lives depicted. However, insofar as some viewers had been misled, in the view of both Channel 4 and the ITC, these scenes should not have been included. The Code position on this point is quite clear: the use of dramatised 'reconstructions' in factual programmes is a legitimate means of obtaining greater authenticity or verisimilitude, so long as it does not distort reality. Whenever a reconstruction is used in a documentary, current affairs or news programme, it should be labelled so that the viewer is not misled.[34]

This judgement ushered in a period in which compliance lawyers wanted the word 'reconstruction' imposed on any shot that had been set up outside the narrative flow of events and helped create a public climate of distrust about the very process of filmmaking.

The ITC were even more draconian over an earlier Channel 4 film, made in 1996 by Carlton TV about the Colombian drug trade. *The Connection* became the subject of a six-month *Guardian* newspaper investigation which revealed in May 1998 that much of the film had been faked, from the Colombian drug boss actually being a bank teller, through heroin that was probably only sugar, to 'couriers' catching flights that did not take place.[35] The ITC came to the conclusion that the company had infringed their Production Code – on which the broadcaster's licence is based – in 16 separate ways and hit them with a punitive £2 million fine. The media academic Brian Winston was one of the informed commentators at the time that felt the regulatory body was being over-zealous and ill-informed:

> The Code, and press coverage, totally failed to take account of the fact that some of these supposed infringements represented fictions which nobody could defend as documentary, while others were common to documentary practice and meant little if anything. Thus the *Guardian* was apparently as shocked by the constructed flight as it was by the use of sugar. This is the price the triumph of Direct Cinema's untenable, un-Griersonian claim to be able to present unvarnished truth is now exacting in Britain.[36]

Elsewhere, Winston has written that: 'The concept of fakery has been so broadly construed that, in its naïveté, it echoes the old error – "the camera cannot lie".'[37] Bruzzi explores the plasticity of the truths exposed through observational documentary and the resurgence of the form in 1995 with the BBC's *The House* and *HMS Brilliant*.[38] *The House* (like the Queen's Cambridge series, directed by Michael Waldman) was the result of a nine-month shoot in the Royal Opera House, Covent Garden, revealing the backstage tears, tantrums and managerial ineptitudes of the great opera house. Contrary to Direct Cinema principles, it had a viperish commentary from Jancis Robinson, better known for her precise palate as a wine critic, and may have discouraged other institutions from throwing open their doors to the BBC. *HMS Brilliant* (1995) was a series set on the eponymous warship and entirely eschews commentary. Its maker, Chris Terrill, is a master at inserting himself into communities and gaining his subjects' trust and he is firmly committed to being non-judgemental, both in the shooting and the editing of his films. Bruzzi recommends his 'new honesty', and quotes him on the subject:

> Our stock in trade [in documentaries] has to be honesty; not necessarily truth, whatever truth is – truth is a construct. We deal in perceptual truth, personal truth, not absolute truth. Who deals in absolute truth? Nobody does. It's continually an interpretation, a relating of events as we see them to our audience.[39]

It may be significant that Chris Terrill, like Jean Rouch, was an anthropologist, for this is a science with its own professional ethics that do not support disruptive invasions of communities studied. The problem for television is that its ethics have evolved in a more piecemeal way, necessarily reflective of constantly shifting standards in society, and more predicated on the outcome of what audiences believe than on the incidental impact on people filmed.

As we know, generally perceived truths can turn out somewhat differently – for instance, public belief in the justification and prognosis given for the war in Iraq – and programmes made in good faith under one public dispensation may be overtaken by events and a change in the received view. A libel case in 1998, brought by Marks & Spencer against Granada TV Limited,[40] established an important precedent further weighting the law against the broadcaster because it moved settlement in the plaintiff's interest by allowing the jury to draw an inference and effectively settle the case before the defence could put its argument of justification. Such cases fuel the perception of an unreliable medium, while restricting its freedoms. Similarly, the unfortunate coincidence of several stories about fakery, as in 1998, or other dishonesties, as in 2007, allow a head of steam to be raised, chiefly by the tabloid press, in which every television producer is branded a liar, thus requiring mass re-education. Yet, as BBC Director-General Mark Thompson argues,[41] these are a handful of mistakes identified in many thousands of hours broadcast and it is easy to lose perspective. However, it is not difficult to see how – in a climate of political and legal constraint and increased competition for audiences – documentary's central concern for real lives has been increasingly shoehorned into so-called 'reality TV' formats where participants and audiences alike have no conceivable doubt that the 'reality' is an artificial construct.

The importance of the real

Despite this, real life remains the key concern of committed documentarists, albeit that the work is harder to get commissioned and shown. Brian Woods is an award-winning filmmaker who has made important films about children, including an internationally successful exposé of China's scandalous state orphanages (*Dying Rooms*, Channel 4 1995) and a film about juvenile prisoners and punishment (*Kids Behind Bars*, BBC1 2005). His 2006 film about the children of homeless families, *Evicted*,[42] won the BAFTA for best single documentary in that year and the Royal Television Society award for best educational feature in mainstream television, despite having aired to a small audience at the relatively late hour of 10.40 pm on BBC1. Introducing the BAFTA award, the broadcaster and journalist Janet Street-Porter made an impassioned plea for more such single documentaries to be commissioned, a plea echoed in Brian Woods's acceptance speech.

Woods beat fellow nominee Paul Watson to that BAFTA award. Watson's film *Rain in My Heart* was a harrowing film about alcoholism, widely written of as his best film to date. It also introduced the novel feature of Watson ruminating to camera about the value and ethics of what he was filming – 'What right do I have to film Kath's grief and why am I asking you to watch Nigel die?',[43] he self-consciously asks. It is a cleverly contemporary device to preclude the charges of voyeurism and exploitation that have dogged Watson's career. Most critics feel that, at least in this film, the invasions of privacy were justified:

> Watson refuses to compromise with anything that remotely resembles a 'feel-good' moment – they are notable only by their absence – and his unflinching portrayal reveals a world that many may find difficult to watch. Two of the film's subjects die during the filming – one of them on camera. Harrowing images of another downing red wine and battling against panic attacks, depression and a desire to self-harm are equally, if not more, excruciating. Watson also lays bare the devastating effects that alcoholism can have on a sufferer's closest relationships, and the repulsive physical symptoms that the disease can cause. The film's remarkable intimacy is testament to Watson's skills and experience as a filmmaker, and certainly to his decision to self-shoot, something he has chosen to do now for six or seven years. He quickly becomes close to his subjects and is able to elicit the most revealing and insightful of responses, challenging our own preconceptions of what alcoholism is, and who alcoholics are.[44]

That closeness to the lives he films is Paul Watson's signature, one he shares with many of the great documentary filmmakers. In a world where decreasing budgets often only allow a few days of filming, Watson takes as long as it takes. His 2007 film *Malcolm and Barbara: Love's Farewell* was 11 years in the making, including the earlier *Malcolm and Barbara: A Love Story*, broadcast in 1999. It took that long to chart the deterioration of Malcolm Pointon, a musician struck down by Alzheimer's disease, and the effect on his life with his wife Barbara, to the time of his death. It is another painstaking and uncompromising piece of work, compassionate and important. But Watson inadvertently walked into a firestorm of controversy because the ITV publicity for the film concentrated on the apparent moment of death happening on film, whereas it had taken place three days later. At a time when British television was being rocked by successive tales of fakery and dishonesty, this small error

Figure 5.1
Malcolm and Barbara granted
access to Paul Watson's
camera for 11 years

was blown into another scandal of epic proportions. Watson was forced to trek around the radio and TV stations defending himself against a largely confected charge of dishonesty. He told BBC Radio 4's *Today* programme that he had been made 'a scapegoat':

> I offered ITV a way of resolving this issue straight and clean, and they turned it down. I asked to put in five words to explain absolutely that the picture you are looking at, at this moment, is not of Malcolm's death; he did not regain consciousness and died some days later. They turned it down at that instant and came back to me much later and said 'maybe it is a good idea and we lost time' . . . I agree that ITV should look at itself and old farts like me, but the fact is in the end I did not set out to deceive and I will know that to my dying day . . . A trust that I have had for 11 years to film two very, very nice people enduring one of fate's worst illnesses – that will get wrecked.[45]

'Trust' and 'truth' apparently stem from the same Old English word *treowe*, and they remain inextricably linked in British television today. But, as Chris Terrill says, truth is a construct and each filmmaker finds his own truth in the world he records. One only gets close when time is invested and the subjects' trust won. That becomes vital to the filming of real life and when that trust is broken the truth becomes harder to get at. Filmmakers such as Paul Watson place great importance on the continued good relations with their subjects after the films have been transmitted, because that indicates whether their trust has been respected. He says that only one of his 300 films has led to an absolute fracture of relations with its subjects: the Hooray Henrys of *The Fishing Party* (1985), a notorious exposure of young Thatcherite Tory hopefuls seen drinking and behaving disgracefully. The aggrieved toffs hijacked his appearance at the 2006 Sheffield Documentary Festival to complain that Watson had wrecked their lives.

Conclusion

Observational documentary cannot only observe the things and people of which we approve. Some truths are unpalatable and some realities regrettable, but nothing should be beyond the film camera's unremitting gaze. Watson speaks of documentary as a 'subversive' medium and, while that can only be one function of such films, it is vital that all real life be documented, not just the realities sanctioned by the powers that be. Filmmakers will always bring a particular perspective to bear on the things they show, and a visually literate audience is at ease with that. Occasional attempts by pressure groups or political interests to filter or censor reality and its champions need to be resisted by producers, well versed in the worlds they film and the implications of their being filmed. Just as Vertov did in the early days of the Soviet Union, Watson, Wiseman and Woods have all knowingly engaged with social realities they regret and hope to change. Wherever they shoot, they are frequently criticised for showing their subjects and societies in a bad light – Watson in Australia (for *Sylvania Waters*[46]), Wiseman in the United States, Woods in China – but there is a shared belief that the world is better for knowing, even if there is little will or way for those societies to effect change.

There is a contrary view that serious documentary has declined from its pole position on television a generation ago, not least because of its tendency to produce 'miserabilist' fare. It is true that films are generally made about situations where something has gone wrong, rather than gone right. We dispatch directors and crews to disasters, not to oases of tranquillity. I once received a letter from an elderly lady in Huddersfield, complaining that we only filmed the bleak parts of her home town, never the nice suburb where she lived. She agreed it was 'not Harrogate' – apparently the acme of northern loveliness – but she felt Huddersfield certainly deserved a better image. Sadly there is little public taste for nice normality, unless it is being satirised by comedies such as *Keeping Up Appearances*.[47] A series of screen shorts, *Video Nation*,[48] a successor of *Video Diaries*, did for a time offer self-shot snapshots of ordinary life on BBC2, but this project, along with most such material, has now naturally migrated to the web, leaving television to consistently 'up the ante' and emphasise the extreme to attract its dwindling audience. Cautionary continuity announcements demanded by nervous broadcasters and regulators – casually referred to by producers as 'public health warnings' – are frequently welcomed by the makers for actually recruiting an audience. Just as teenagers prefer to see an '18' or 'Restricted' film, warnings about bad language, sex and violence attract more viewers than they discourage. It was hard not to read that same excited prurience in Mary Whitehouse's and her National Viewers' and Listeners' Association's shrill pronouncements.

The bigger challenge to the *vérité* tradition is not the contractions of subject, but the constructions of format, programme formulae that determine an audience's expectations and notionally ensure their return week after week. As the next chapter explores, when television evolved from a producer's medium to a production industry, bankable properties came to supplant the freer forms of old. Television production companies can now make more money exploiting the rights to a successful format than from its original production. In some ways, this has extended and secured the documentary, but at some cost to the higher principles of social purpose and independence the traditional purists felt animated their work. Purists versus populists remains a live argument within the industry but, as the following chapters reveal, documentary remains a live culture consistently reinventing itself to spawn new ways of observing people.

Expert briefing – shooting in observational mode

Whatever mode you are shooting in, whether or not you are the camera operator, you should to know what material you are likely to need, how it will be edited and where and by whom it will be seen. Some of the most inept footage shot is observational documentary shot without that forward planning, focus and knowledge. Whether you have an hour or a month, you should strategise your time and work out how to get the best shots in the time available. Here is a checklist of points on observational shooting:

1 **Location access**: If you are following a subject, s/he may enter a building or take transport where you need to accompany them, but for which you may need prior permission and/or documentation. If this has not been possible to arrange in advance, a mobile phone call while in transit may solve the problem. Even where you have permission, you want to ensure that doors are not opened by people reacting to the camera, positively or negatively, unless that is germane to your story. And you ideally do not want to always be following behind the subject, thus only seeing their back. So the more you can run ahead and see them arrive, enter the lobby, climb the stairs, etc. the better. The essence of observational shooting is that you do not ask the subject to walk through the door again, or any of the other directorial interventions in

the flow of their life, and you normally cannot afford to make the problematic logistics of shooting part of the on-screen record.

2 **Ins and outs**: When it comes to the edit, you will hopefully not be dependent on all the travel shots that get you into and out of places and frequently pad films otherwise short of material. Always have in mind the need to acquire static location shots – wide shots of buildings entered, name plates on doors, general views of hotel lobbies, train stations, etc. – to use as a short-hand 'situationer' that can drop you into a scene. These are all the more vital in fast-cut films that have no time for travelling or seeing scenes to their natural completion. Other shots can help you get out of scenes: audiences clapping at meetings, handshakes and doors shutting after meetings, phones being replaced or mobiles shut at the end of calls.

3 **Point of view**: Following action and dialogue, you need to insert yourself into positions that give you regular intercuttable points, which ideally match the points of view of the participants. If your subject meets another person in a passageway, you should keep shooting for sound while ensuring you have at least two contrasting points of view and shots that can be used non-sync to mask cuts. If it's a meeting or presentation, you ideally need the views from both the stage or top table and from the floor, with cutaways of people listening and wide shots – again to cover the selected cuts in recorded speech. Traditionally, observational shooting eschews any recognition of the camera, discouraging subjects from acknowledging or addressing it. Today's more visually sophisticated populace understands that that is itself a conceit and is rarely confused by films that show their slips in *vérité*, with people talking to the camera, or the camera catching its own reflection. But it remains sensible practice to be consistent in the camera's role within the film, be it passive observer or active actor.

4 **Hand-held**: Styles of camerawork change with fashion, like every other aesthetic, and everyone is familiar with Hollywood's appropriation of hand-held documentary techniques to impart spurious jeopardy to carefully planned drama. It is a frequent mistake to use this opportunistically to justify constantly jerky camerawork. While you will probably be operating hand-held, the wobbly rush of camerawork on the hoof can only be justified if the camera reflects the filmmaker as an active participant in the film's journey, be it news camera literally chasing a story or paranoid fugitive, as in *The Blair Witch Project*. Even when justified, such movement can make audiences nauseous, especially when relentless. The wider the angle of lens you are operating with, the easier it is to damp the movement, but the preferred option for the film and its audience is regularly to establish operational stasis, letting action happen within a static frame. Find walls against which you can steady yourself, tables or chairs to help support the camera, anything to damp the movement and not draw attention to the camera's operation. The camera should reflect the eye of the privileged observer, and our eyes like to settle. They also do not zoom, so the use of the zoom in vision is often unsettling and needs to be justified by a change in content or emotion, as in the clichéd zoom in on eyes when they well up.

5 **Camera movement**: Panning between speakers or subjects requires not just good technical operational skills, but good editorial comprehension. Listen to speech so that you anticipate the next intervention, or watch the game so that you are following the action, not always lagging behind it. Covering music requires an intrinsic feel for it, both in knowing which instrument is playing and getting the tempo right for cuts and camera moves. If you have the opportunity, familiarise yourself with the work you are covering,

so that, for instance, you know when to come off the singer for the guitar solo, or arrive on the choir as they burst into song. Poorly executed pans fail to find their end shot and focus: you should always know where such a shot is going to end before you start. Tracking and craning shots can give a filmic effect and are easier to do than some think. Few can afford specialist mounts, but use whatever is to hand: cars in the open and wheelchairs indoors, escalators in shopping centres and glass elevators in office buildings. Even semi-abstract close-ups of wheels speeding or hair blowing can be invaluable for suggesting movement, just as planes passing far overhead or the tracery they leave behind can be useful for conveying narrative movement and time passing. Conversely, top shots are useful for giving a sense of place and perspective, and it's well worth blagging a porter to let you onto a roof.

6 **Sound**: Sound problems are the most common cause of documentary shoot failures. Observational documentary presumes sync sound, so it is vital to ensure that whatever you want is also covered adequately. On-camera microphones are rarely good enough to give comprehensible speech: they are normally of low quality and have a wide angle of pick-up that tends to pick up unwanted background sounds, obviously worse the further you are from the speaker. In a lively sound ambience, where different types of event and encounter need to be recorded, a directional mic on a gun or pole mount, pointed and ideally monitored by a separate team member, is the preferred alternative. A radio mic with a transmitter wired on the subject is the other regularly used sound source and usually the best bet, but can give poor balance in dialogue and is easily swamped in noisy environments. Although the UHF signal is more reliable than the old VHF spectrum, it can suffer from transmission interference and is subject to battery failure if in constant use. Sound overlaps and buzz tracks should be standard for anyone recording for documentary, invaluable in editing and sound mixing to cover internal cuts. Covering more complex sound, such as music, requires significant forward planning and proper multichannel cover, but a feed can often be accessed through a band's sound desk.

7 **The unexpected**: The more these operational standards become routine, the better equipped you are to go with the flow, which is the essence of obs. doc. No plans involving, for example, people, weather and public transport are likely to progress smoothly; the successful shooter is an improviser. However well planned a shoot is, some anticipated things will not happen and some unexpected things will. But this can sometimes offer you gems that you had no reason to expect. Unless the camera is clearly the cause of violence or criminality, it is generally advisable to keep shooting, whatever happens. It is surprising how often the unwanted incident yields unexpected bonuses when in the edit suite, but there is no obligation to use such material. If, however, you have stopped recording, that option is unavailable.

8 **The narrative**: While few people now stick or aspire to the purist *vérité* view that commentary is an admission of failure, it is not enough to imagine that the story can be constructed in the edit and explained in voiceover. Yet that is what many do, especially without the stock constraints that film traditionally brought. Tape is relatively cheap, encouraging the inexperienced to defer judgement to the edit. The good filmmaker has an in-built intelligence that is critically aware of the likely use and value of anything being shot, and of the elements s/he needs to maximise that effect. Each scene needs to advance the story in some way, and observational documentary requires that most of the information the audience needs be conveyed in context, normally through natural dialogue, though the thinking camera should always be on

the lookout for the pictures that tell you what you need to know – the family photograph, the wedding invitation, the gravestone or the street sign. The camera is the extension of the inquiring mind, recording the minutiae that, when distilled and conflated, will construct an original portrait of the subject.

9   **Think about the edit**: Not only should you be constructing editable scenes as you go, and checking that a comprehensible narrative is emerging from those scenes, but you should also be collecting images, sound and information that may be useful in the edit. Observational documentary should not mean the camera is constrained by the equivalent of a packhorse's blinkers. It should be constantly on the lookout for images that not only augment the scene being shot but also reflect the wider environment and subject of the film. Cultural signifiers like flags and slogans, street furniture and consumer goods, people's taste in furnishings and decoration can all add to a film's resonance. In the same way, sound should be recording ambient noises, from birdsong and wind noise to traffic passing, footfalls and people laughing. But also remember that there is a contemporary reaction against conventional editing shortcuts. 'Noddies' and cutaways have been banned by some nervous news organisations and other purists are opposed to non-diegetic sound. Non-sequential editing is another ground of controversy. You will have decided where you stand in this contested field, but you still need sufficient material to give you real choices in the final cut.

10 **Think about the audience**: All the above is about finding a natural style and approach to communicating some experience or understanding to an audience. Films shot on commission are targeted on a particular programme slot and audience, so none of these decisions will be made in a vacuum. All such decisions should be predicated on whatever prior knowledge and interest the audience can be expected to bring to their viewing. Commissioners desperate to maximise their audience tend to underestimate its intelligence, hence the increasing tendency to statements of the blindingly obvious and overemphatic narrative repetition, particularly around ad breaks. The clearer the original shooting and editing are, the less justification there is for this over-literal intervention and the more chance a film will be allowed to speak for itself. Narrative coherence is constructed from a clear vision and the technical skills to realise the elements it calls for. The hardest thing for a filmmaker deeply immersed in their project is to find the critical detachment to assess whether their efforts and intentions are clear to a first-time viewer. In the industry, that is what executive viewings are for, but it always pays to have a fresh view from someone that has not been involved and brings no preconceptions to bear. All the effort and hope can be wasted by refusing to accept that the audience usually only gets one chance to take it all in.

6 Docu-soap and mocu-soap

soap opera n. a serialized drama, usually dealing with domestic themes, broadcast on radio or television. Often shortened to soap[1]

As Sky satellite television began to take off in Britain in the mid-1990s and then Channel 5 arrived in 1997, British broadcasters had to start seriously facing the challenges of fragmenting and diminishing audiences. The traditional warhorses of drama, sitcom and light entertainment were becoming ever more expensive while proving less attractive to many of the audience. Soap opera was the one entertainment form that seemed impervious to the ravages of time and changing tastes, as ITV's *Coronation Street* and BBC1's *Eastenders* continued to battle for the top spot in the viewers' affections. This long-running fascination with the fictional everyday life of ordinary people was what stimulated a new interest in factual versions, and observational documentary metamorphosed into the so-called 'docu-soap'. There is no hard and fast definition of this form, what Bruzzi dubbed the 'New British observational documentary',[2] but what was new was its knowing construction of cast and character for that ongoing human interest. It borrowed the conventions and sensibilities of drama to invest the unruliness of ordinary life with a narrative arc and, most importantly, the spur of interest to return an audience week after week.

The heyday of docu-soap

The crossover moment, arguably, was the BBC series *Children's Hospital* in 1993, a series that excited equal amounts of public interest and critical opprobrium. Using the conventions of 'fly-on-the-wall' filming, it followed in the classical observational documentarist's footsteps of Frederick Wiseman and invaded the Birmingham Children's Hospital.[3] But where it departed from a conventional focus, which would have been more on the medicine being practised, was in its concentration on the human dramas being played out in the children's wards. The pain of the children *in extremis* and their parents' emotional rollercoaster rides made for gripping television. Critics called it exploitative and voyeuristic, but over 8 million people tuned into that first series.[4] As a result, the series was to be recommissioned over many more years, continuing to attract audiences and criticism alike. Rupert Smith's 2000 *Guardian* review captures the almost incomprehensible fatal fascination, and deserves quotation at length:

> One of the greatest mysteries of modern broadcasting deepened last night as *Children's Hospital* (BBC1) strode into its umpteenth series with another collection of sick and

injured kids and their shell-shocked parents. It's easy to sneer at the show's success, but impossible to dismiss it: the last series drew audiences of 7 million. This is no mean feat when you consider that most of us would do almost anything to avoid the circumstances depicted in the programme.

It was business as usual at Birmingham Children's Hospital: 7-year-old Nicole had sustained head injuries in a motorway accident, 12-year-old Lisa was waiting for a hole-in-the-heart operation, and tiny 3-hour-old Sam had been born with his innards hanging out of a hole in his stomach, a knotty, livid mass. The surgeons got to work, the distraught parents wept, and the patients (at least those who were conscious) showed almost unbelievable pluck. As the programme wore on, one could only wonder why 7 million people would voluntarily subject themselves to such harrowing viewing. This isn't, after all, a kid-glove handling of the subject, despite what the syrupy title music may suggest: the images of tiny children strapped into terrifying machines, with gloved hands manipulating their intestines, are the stuff of nightmare. The fact that this material is shown pre-watershed[5] simply compounds the mystery.

It's impossible not to get caught up in so much suffering humanity, nor to fail to admire the health professionals who deal with this stuff every day of their working lives – but to watch it for enjoyment? Hopefully the hospital benefits from the publicity that a prime-time BBC1 slot generates, but other than that it's difficult to understand the show's *raison d'être*. The success of *Children's Hospital*, *Animal Hospital*, *Pet Rescue* and any show in which vulnerable creatures suffer and die suggests that the nation is in the grip of a mass outbreak of Munchausen's syndrome by proxy.[6]

The *raison d'être* is, of course, that whopping audience – and what the *Guardian* is grappling with here is that unaccountable human appetite for other people's suffering. That is something we shall return to in the next chapter, but the more general point is that this gave rise to a whole welter of docu-soaps, some of which also ran for years.

Animal Hospital ran from 1994 to 2004 on BBC1, starting and ending at the RSPCA Harmsworth Memorial Animal Hospital, but also filming tales of animal woe and human grief in various different animal hospitals. The famously unquenchable thirst of British people for all things animal was further served in 1996 by *Vets' School* and its sequel the following year, 20 episodes of *Vets in Practice*.[7] This had the additional value of doing what long-running drama regularly does to refresh audience interest: move the characters into new places with new challenges, but which real life does not always deliver to schedule. It also made stars of two of the graduates of the Bristol University Veterinary School, Trude Mostue and Steve Leonard, who went on to host *Vets in the Wild* (1997) and become full-time television wildlife presenters. In this way in particular, it was the precursor of twenty-first-century reality television, driven as so much of it is by the quest for fame and fortune, not formerly a major concern of documentary.

The apotheosis of this kind of fame vehicle was BBC1's 1997 *Driving School* and its nemesis, Maureen Rees, a Welsh cleaner who had spectacularly failed her driving test several times.[8] Although only one of the learner drivers featured, her stomach-churning inability to control a car safely turned her into a national figure, who even went on to make a hit record (a cover of Madness's *Driving in My Car*) and who is still revisited by journalists and broadcasters. *Clampers* attempted to recapture the entertainment potential the following year, with a singing wheel clamper called Ray Brown standing out among his mates.[9] They even made a *Clampers Christmas Special,* in which Ray Brown performed set piece songs just as in conventional seasonal entertainment spectaculars. At this point, the entertainment has superseded any documentary value, giving credence to those who argue that a growing number of incidents in this kind of docu-soap were being engineered by the production to make a more entertaining show. This was probably an inevitable outcome of the explosion of the form as a result of its popularity. There were four docu-soaps made in Britain in 1995. There were 22 in 1998. A trickle had turned to a flood and, in the increasingly competitive television market, imitation had become the sincerest form of flattery. As commissioners rushed to repeat each others' success, respect for the facts was not their top priority.

In 1995, the BBC had launched the long-running *Airport,* featuring stories of life at London's Heathrow, the world's busiest airport.[10] Three years later, ITV countered with *Airline,* whose first series gave us the personal stories of some of Britain's largest charter airline, Britannia Airways' staff and crews.[11] While *Airport* pulled an astonishing peak audience of 10.7 million (a 44 per cent share) in 1998, *Airline* beat it with 11.4 million and a full 50 per cent share. A nation increasingly familiar with the trials and tribulations of air travel were transfixed with the minutiae of life behind the check-in desk. A certain entrepreneur, Stelios Haji-Ioannou, had launched the low-cost airline EasyJet in 1995, with one eye on the use of the developing internet as a cheap and efficient booking tool, and the other on television as a great brand enforcer. From 1999, *Airline* featured the staff and workings of EasyJet, and thus its orange livery became a familiar icon. Given that the broadcasters could not legally cede editorial control of these institutional docu-soaps, it is interesting to see what those that were prepared to reveal their staff's true nature, warts and all, stood to gain. Easyjet Managing Director Ray Webster penned a piece for *The Observer* newspaper in 2000:

> We took a big but calculated risk when we opted to give LWT's television cameras almost total access to Easyjet staff and passengers in mid-1998. As a rapidly growing young airline there were obviously going to be certain things that we didn't want to be shown on prime-time ITV . . . The business rationale is simple: we don't sell through travel agents, so all our customers have to come to us – 70 per cent to our website and the rest to our call centre. Therefore we have to find as many ways as possible of keeping the Easyjet brand name in front of the consumer. We spend millions of pounds on press and poster advertising each year but nothing on television, so the *Airline* series provides us with a useful way of getting ourselves onto the screens . . . We do not always agree with LWT over what constitutes good television, but our expertise is in running an airline – not in programme-making. And the number of people who regularly tune in to watch the series is a testament to the fact they know what they're doing.[12]

What they were doing was making Stelios Haji-Ioannou rich. Seven and a half million people watched *Airline* at 9 pm on Friday nights in 1999 (a 37 per cent share), the kind of advertising which a low-cost airline would never have been able to buy. EasyJet also got to see every episode before transmission and could challenge sequences they saw as potentially threatening safety or security. They claim not to have been enabled to get embarrassing footage removed, but they were secure in research which told them that 85 per cent of the audience only remember the name, if anything, so the business benefit was secure. Furthermore, the relationship between producers and company over ten years was too well-established and valuable to both parties for either to do anything to threaten it.

So lucrative is the franchise that ITV started another docu-soap based around *Luton Airport*[13] in 2005. It could be argued that this kind of practice allows of no more critical detachment than correspondents can achieve when covering war embedded with troops, and the job is emphatically not to uncover wrongdoing or analyse the implications of the stories told. Thus *Children's Hospital* celebrated Birmingham Children's Hospital's move into its spanking new premises in 1999, but did not interrogate the controversial PFI scheme that had financed it, nor go into the £3.5 million shortfall in the budget. The argument is that ratings chasing had been prioritised over editorial impartiality. But even, or especially, if that was not always the case, institutions and corporations with anything to hide were unlikely to allow the cameras in. Programmes such as *The House* (Chapter 5) had exposed their subjects, the Royal Opera House and its management, to such public evisceration and ridicule that other companies were much more nervous about assuming the EasyJet benefit.

Docu-soaps wane and wax

However, factual programmes that secured huge audiences for a fraction of the costs of the genres they displaced, and did not rock the increasingly unsteady broadcast boat, triggered something of a docu-soap gold rush in British television, largely unmirrored in the USA. However, very rapidly, overkill did for the goose that laid this golden egg. By 2000, the sheer number of docu-soaps had led to television reviewers referring to them as 'yet another docu-soap' with clearly pejorative intent. The form had come to be defined by its lowest common denominator. As television producer Joe Houlihan bemoaned in *The Independent* in 2000, his documentary series about a comprehensive *School Days* had been picked by several newspapers, but disparagingly dubbed a docu-soap:

> Rarely can a word have passed so quickly from celebrity to notoriety as that little word 'docu-soap'. Barely two years ago, the word was a proud banner to hang on your documentary series. It had friends in high places and great prospects ahead of it. With successes such as *Driving School*, *Airline* and *The Cruise*, it was hailed as the saviour of flagging peak-time schedules and a shot in the arm for factual programmes – a genre which had long been in retreat. Now look at it. Even its erstwhile friends will not be seen in its company and every producer knows that to offer a commissioning editor any new programme proposal labelled 'docu-soap' is a form of televisual hara-kiri. 'Docu-soap', in short, has become a dirty word.[14]

That same year, the BBC announced that it would be making many less cheap factual programmes and other channels followed suit. The gold rush was over. The amount of docu-soaps hours on the BBC fell from 48 in 2001 to an estimated 26 hours in 2002.[15] As we shall see in future chapters, other factual genres would take the docu-soap's place in the commissioners' affections, but notices of its complete demise were premature. As Houlihan writes, while television professionals tended to confuse the terms 'docu-soap', 'fly-on-the-wall' and observational documentary, the public had no such problem. He refers to a focus group of viewers who clearly discerned the difference between the emotional and factual imperatives. 'The words they associated with documentary were "real, true, revelations", while they associated "accessible, people, relationships and drama" with soap.'[16] One might add that in the docu-soap the producer or director's hand reveals itself more clearly as the moulder of the material, as stories are shaped and interwoven, and edited to produce a cliffhanger to ensure the audience's return for the following episode – the story-lining that is at the heart of successful soap opera.

The audience knows and accepts that this is an artful construct for their entertainment, and subjects like Maureen Rees in *Driving School* knowingly play up to the camera and willingly accede to the 'set-ups' that will enhance the story. Whether the drama is built up for the camera, or accentuated in the editing, this is rarely the conspiracy the puritan tendency would have it to be, more a compact with viewers who share a sophisticated reading of the potential and limits of a two-dimensional medium that necessarily compresses experience for easy consumption. Just as music has its highs and lows, fasts and slows, harmonies and counterpoint, a well-constructed piece of film, factual or fictional, requires a similar range of peaks and contrasts. Bruzzi (2000: 85) writes of the 'crisis structure' that came to dominate docu-soap in the late 1990s, quoting *The House*'s series director Michael Waldman saying that 'getting narrative from observational documentary is hard. We had to impose a structure [during editing] and that is what took time'. She goes on to detail the dependence of a later docu-soap,[17] *Hotel*, set in the Adelphi Hotel in Liverpool, whose editing concentrated on the structuring of 'a *Fawlty Towers*-like[18] farcical tension . . . almost to the exclusion of any other tangential matters'.[19]

The growing demand for more dramatic spikes in television series led even to BBC business series focusing on *Trouble at the Top*[20] and *Blood on the Carpet*,[21] albeit that each episode focused on a different 'troubled' business, so were not strictly docu-soaps. The promise of 'crisis' continues to permeate titles, such as BBC4's *Crisis at the Castle* (2007), where:

> This trio of observational documentaries follows three aristocratic families as they struggle to hang on to their historic homes. Though their lifestyle is assumed to be idyllic, a constant battle with roof leaks, falling visitor numbers and mounting debts all put pressure on their personal relationships and their peace of mind.[22]

Crisis and characters were the essence of docu-soap. Reality TV – discussed at length in Chapter 12 – re-emphasised the public desire for such personal narratives, and docu-soap has bubbled back into the schedules. As Richard Klein, then BBC TV Commissioning Editor for Documentaries, said in 2007:

> This year March 07–March 08, I will have had seven docu-soaps and three stripped docu-soaps, so ten in all, on BBC1. There's a decent market for it. It's very valuable for the channels, they're flexible, audiences enjoy them, younger audiences like them and the word 'docu-soap' is quite a good one. They're very drama-orientated the way we write them, the way they're created – I think they're a fantastic reflection on modern society . . . Why documentaries work is because we're a mirror. People have always liked to see themselves. What's the first drawings you saw on cave walls? Ourselves. That's what documentary does. So docu-soaps reflect ourselves, they reflect ordinary people, characters bigger, sometimes, than the ones we know at the office or our workplace. Docu-soaps will always be with us, they're a fantastic thing, they're great, I'm a big fan.[23]

'The way we write them' is the hostage to fortune that has the would-be purists like Paul Watson reaching for their machine guns, concerned that the impositions of dramatic construction inevitably distort the realities being reflected. It remains an argument central to the documentary community, but long since passed beyond by television. The slavish demand that the word 'reconstruction' be superimposed on any scene in a documentary that had been significantly constructed for the camera has largely disappeared with the rash of dramatised inserts and genre-busting that has occurred in the last decade. Recent discourse about specific instances of fakery has destabilised the broadcasters, but the final judgement will, as always, rest with the viewers. If they buy the compromises and confections programme-makers come up with to entertain them, then the market has given that form validity. If they perceive they are being exploited or hoodwinked, and change channels, then the market has proclaimed the sentence of death for that particular form. Even the regulatory body Ofcom has recently been noticeably less prescriptive in matters of form, tacitly accepting the ascendancy of the market in such matters.

Mockumentary-rockumentary

The breakdown in formal distinctions and characteristics is, ironically, one of the outcomes of documentary's success. Progressively since the 1980s, documentary techniques have invaded every audio-visual field, from feature film to fine art, from comedy to costume drama. High-end American television drama in the 1990s aspired to Hollywood feature film values and was shot on 35 mm film stock, but began to inject the feel of news and documentary shooting to give their dramas a sense of edgy reality. The ABC series *NYPD Blue*[24] was the style-leader here, with the activities of the fictional 15th police precinct in Manhattan shot with whip-pans, crash zooms and jump cuts that belied their careful rehearsal. Camera work that defies the smooth operation and moves of conventional cinematography has now become the filmic default setting for police and crime drama, and high octane action movies. It is no accident that the director of the hugely successful Hollywood features *The Bourne Supremacy* (2004), *United 93* (2006) and *The Bourne Ultimatum* (2007), Paul Greengrass, is a former British documentary film director who built his career through writing and directing television docu-dramas such as *The Murder of Stephen Lawrence* (1999) and *Bloody Sunday* (2002). Documentary has provided the visual grammar that is read as authenticity.

The first generation brought up on television – the 'baby boomers', so-called because they were the results of the procreation of the post-War reassertion of normal family life – uses shared visual references to frame much of their work. Comedy, formerly immured in the three-set studio sitcom or the sketch show, typically broke out of these formal straitjackets, only to create new ones of their own. The young comedians who had made their name on the comedy club circuit, notably the Comedy Strip in London, teamed up to make a series of comedy drama films for the new Channel 4 in 1982. *Comic Strip Presents* . . . made 39 films over the next 20 years, all to a degree based on parodying various filmic forms.[25] Arguably the best and the most influential was their *Bad News Tour* (1983) and its sequel *More Bad News* (1987), parodying the 'rockumentary', which purports to be an observational documentary following a band on tour but is usually more of a hagiography, designed as a marketing tool. The eponymous Bad News are a spoof heavy metal band, fifth-raters on the way to a disastrous gig in Grantham (far from coincidentally the hometown of the then Prime Minister Margaret Thatcher), accompanied by an equally useless documentary film crew. Because the contemptuous director and crew fail to flatter the musicians' egos they assault him and steal the gear in an attempt to seize control of the film and their image, a predictable enough narrative for media students.

By real coincidence, or the synchronicity of ideas whose time has come, American director Rob Reiner was shooting the much more famous feature *This is Spinal Tap* at the same time, though it was not released until the following year (1984). It also follows an inept British heavy metal band on a doomed tour to promote an album, *Smell the Glove*, albeit with some bigger gigs in the States and eventually ending up in Japan. A riot of black humour, which is now recognised as a classic, the film was not that successful initially because many audiences were confused, thinking it a genuine documentary, while many musicians felt it had all too accurately captured their lives. Rob Reiner played the documentary director himself and the success of the film is largely due to the way he made it. The actors sang and played their own instruments and ad libbed most of the lines, leading to several dozen hours of rushes from which the final cut was made, though there is also a four and a half hour bootleg being traded by aficionados. Spinal Tap reformed to make a follow-up album, *Break Like the Wind*, and perform a reunion concert at London's Royal Albert Hall, where they played to a 5,000+ capacity audience.[26] The event forms the main part of the film released the following year *The Return of Spinal Tap* (1993), but the sheer circular referentiality and commercialisation of the brand in this way effectively undermines its satirical impact.[27]

Nonetheless, Spinal Tap remains a touchstone for the whole sub-genre of 'mocu-rockumentary', despite having been beaten to the pass by *Bad News Tour* and Eric Idle's much earlier Beatles spoof *All You Need is Cash* (1978). This affectionate send-up of the Fab Four, reborn as The Rutles, with 19 original pastiches of Beatles songs by Neil Innes, is admitted by Rob Reiner to have been an inspiration for Spinal Tap. Not all Americans got the joke: it was the lowest rated show of the week when it premiered on NBC, on 22 March 1978, but did rather better the following week in the UK on BBC2.[28]

Other mocu-rockumentaries made since include the 1996 Canadian *Hard Core Logo*, about a superannuated punk band, the 1998 comedy *Still Crazy*, about the reunion of a 1970s rock band and *Sons of Provo*, a 2004 satire on a Mormon boy band called Everclean. The religious subtext often so close to the American rock world also underscores the latest incarnation of actors Jack Black and Kyle Gass's spoof rock band *Tenacious D in: The Pick of Destiny* (2006). The black sheep son of a Christian fundamentalist family, whose father is played by Meatloaf, Black's story is a kind of Wagnerian spoof in which the pair seek out the guitar pick 'of Destiny', carved long ago from one of Satan's teeth. The relative failure of this feature is unlikely to lay the genre to rest yet. As the *New York Times* capsule review had it:

> As it wobbles from one episode to the next, this rock 'n' roll comedy starring Jack Black is a garish mess, and some of it feels padded. But it has enough jokes to keep you smiling, and Mr. Black brings to it a fervent affection for the music he spoofs but obviously adores.[29]

That affection is what ultimately deprives this musical genre of its bite: Satan's teeth fail to draw blood. Other strands of mockumentary spare fewer blushes, though few rise to the vicious heights common in the eighteenth century (and revisited in Chapter 10 on *Polemic*).

Celebrity and current affairs

The only twenty-first-century television show to match the satirical spleen of the eighteenth century is Armando Ianucci's *The Thick of It*, a well-informed send-up of the black arts of spin practised inside the New Labour Number Ten.[30] With a gloriously foul-tempered, foul-mouthed portrayal of the Downing Street Director of Communications (a thinly veiled portrait of Alastair Campbell) at the centre of the web of a wonderfully dysfunctional government, this timely satire is shot documentary style, as if caught on the hoof. The team went on to make the equally successful feature film version, *In the Loop* (2008), which happily used its bigger budget to take the cast to the United States to show how the Brits were flattered into joining the Bush crusade in Iraq.[31] The same cinematographer, James Cairney, continues to make good use of the whip pans following conversations and jump cuts that convey the authenticity of documentary. It opened to rave reviews in the UK, but American notices were much more guarded, remarking that 'its exuberant, boundless cynicism will test the demand for political satire in an Obama-infatuated America'.[32] Some British cynics asked, what demand?

Celebrity culture has been a fertile ground for mocumentarists since the start of *The Norman Gunston Show* on Australian Broadcasting Corporation in 1975. Played by the comic actor Garry McDonald, as a gormless chat show host prone to gaffes, Gunston got to interview unsuspecting visiting celebrities such as Paul McCartney and his then wife Linda. 'That's funny: you don't look Japanese', he said to her, alluding to John Lennon's wife, Yoko Ono. As the show prospered, the budgets enabled him to travel abroad, subjecting the likes of Muhammed Ali, Mick Jagger and Charlton Heston to his toe-curlingly embarrassing cack-handed interview techniques. He did three series for ABC and a special for BBC2, before moving to Australia's commercial station Channel 7 in 1978 and making series that later aired on UK Channel 4.

The idea of a disguised comic harassing celebrities was given a guerrilla twist in 1995 by English comic Paul Kaye, who invented ginger-haired American geek Dennis Pennis to snatch one line exchanges with celebrities at events such as movie premieres. A typical line to Demi Moore was: 'If the part really demanded it, would you consider doing a film that required you to keep your clothes on?' The only quip he claims to regret was his line to Steve Martin: 'How come you're not funny any more?', which led to Martin cancelling all his scheduled press interviews on that tour. Although originally conceived for BBC2's *The Sunday Show*, Dennis Pennis was one of the first comic acts to enjoy more success in its three video forms.[33] Kaye killed the character off after a couple of years because of the long wet nights spent hanging around outside events in the hopes of making a minute of shot footage if he was lucky. It did not pay as well as the tabloid pics that make such door-stepping so worthwhile for the paparazzi.

The man who has made the most from the faut naïf interviewer schtick is Sacha Baron Cohen. His comic character Ali G first appeared on Channel 4's *The Eleven O'Clock Show* as the 'voice of da yoof' in 1998, which won him a British Comedy Award as Best Newcomer and his own *Da Ali G Show*.[34] Despite being an upper middle-class Jew educated at Cambridge University, Baron Cohen presents as a deluded youth believing himself Jamaican, albeit from the unlikely 'ghetto' of Staines, a featureless dormitory town to the west of London. From deep within the character he so fully inhabits, he confronts the great and the good with all the deep-seated nervousness they feel in acting correctly within a multicultural society. 'Is it 'coz I is black?' he asks them, voicing the unease, while appearing to misapprehend their name, job or orientation, casually throwing in misogyny and homophobia to further unsettle his guests. Having blown his cover in the UK, the second series was *Ali G in da USA*,[35] where he was able to sandbag a rich collection of the unsuspecting American establishment, from former UN Secretary-General Boutros-Boutros Ghali and billionaire Donald Trump to presidential candidates Ralph Nader and John Cain. He affected to confuse Gore Vidal with Vidal Sassoon, and he called Buzz Aldrin 'Buzz Lightyear'. He went on to make a feature film, *Ali G Indahouse*,[36] where he improbably gets elected to the British parliament, and to present the MTV awards, but the problem is that the heat of success rapidly burns the joke out, so Cohen has had to move on.

He had also developed two other characters in *Da Ali G Show*: Bruno, a flamboyantly gay Austrian fashion reporter, and Borat Sagdiyev, a journalist from Kazakhstan. Borat contributed brief inserts on such issues as Etiquette and Hunting to both the UK and the US shows, before being elevated to the star of his very own road movie, *Borat: Cultural Learnings of America for Make Benefit Glorious Nation of Kazakhstan* (2006).[37] In this feature film, supposedly in New York with his producer to do a documentary for Kazakh TV, Borat falls in love with the image of *Baywatch*'s Pamela Anderson and persuades his producer to travel across the States to find her in California, driving an ice cream van accompanied by a pet bear.

The story is deliberately absurd, a McGuffin that enables a rich set of exchanges with middle America. Invited to a polite dinner party in a Southern mansion, he apparently mistakes a man who says he is 'retired' to say he is a retard, then asks to be excused and returns to the table with his shit in a plastic bag – on the pretence that he doesn't understand the workings of the WC. At a rodeo, his jingoistic support for the troops in Iraq is well received, but the applause withers as each injunction ratchets up his xenophobia until he's shouting 'Kill all Jews', and turns to boos when he starts singing (and deliberately murdering) the US national anthem. At that point, with perfect metaphorical timing, the white horse carrying the Confederate flag and its rider fall over behind him and the film cuts to the next scene. It left this viewer wondering how Baron Cohen and his crew escaped with their lives, and unsurprised that the police were allegedly called 91 times during filming. Subsequently, many of the film's unwitting subjects sued for misrepresentation and the insult to their dignity, not least because the film has taken a lot of money. This was a critical and commercial hit from its opening weekends in both the USA and the UK, massively aided by negative reaction from the Kazakh government, which gave the film such acres of free press that the Kazakhs have now reversed their policy and invited Baron Cohen to Kazakhstan, an obscure country that he has helped to put on the map.

At the time of writing, *Borat* had taken a worldwide box office gross of $128.5 million, and Baron Cohen's latest film seemed set to repeat the trick. His gay Austrian fashionista has acquired an umlaut and another publicity fuelling round of abuse. *Brüno* (2009) premiered in London, with Baron Cohen as usual in character, complete with hot pants, boots and busby, claiming to be 'the most famous Austrian since Hitler'.[38] Austrians, not best known for their sense of fun, have complained about the revival of Nazi stereotypes, and some gay and lesbian organisations also seem to have misunderstood Baron Cohen's satirical portrayal of homophobia. The film's stunts include Brüno crashing (in more ways than one) a Milan fashion show in a velcro suit and appearing on an American TV chat show nursing an 'adopted black baby' he claims to have given 'a traditional African name: OJ'. The studio audience erupts in outrage, and the delighted shock of laughter these moments prompt is in recognition of the absurdity of our celebrity culture and its egocentric behaviour. While creative minds like Baron Cohen continue to mock these risible realities, Swift's spirit lives on.

Hoaxes

Whereas filmmaker–performers from Chris Morris to Baron Cohen may hoax their subjects for audience amusement, some of their predecessors were keen to hoax the audiences themselves. The Holy Grail in this respect was the panic engendered by Orson Welles's 1938 radio adaptation of H.G. Wells's *War of the Worlds*, which managed to convince many gullible Americans that their planet was being attacked by aliens from outer space. Beside this, the British propensity for practical jokes on 1 April – April Fools' Day – is mild, best represented by BBC *Panorama*'s spoof 1957 report on the spaghetti harvest in Switzerland. The success of this hoax was due to the authority of the programme and its eminent presenter Richard Dimbleby, and that in turn led to charges of abuse of trust. The context in which it is seen is critical to the success of hoax mocumentaries, and inevitably leads to complaints from those who have been gulled.

One of the more successful hoaxes was executed in his native New Zealand by *Lord of the Rings* director Peter Jackson and co-director Costa Botes. *Forgotten Silver* (1995) is a sophisticated documentary purporting to have discovered the work and charted the life of Colin McKenzie, a long-forgotten pioneer of New Zealand filmmaking. It uses the full panoply of arts history technique, from trotting out interviews with experts and McKenzie's 'widow', to contemporary stills and extracts of footage from his 'reportage' of Gallipoli and his 'masterwork' *Salome*. Although being shown in a NZTV quality drama slot, the story had previously been 'broken' in the New Zealand *Listener*, a well-regarded arts magazine, which created a context of credibility. As the New Zealand academics Jane Roscoe and Craig Hight explore, *Forgotten Silver* worked because it played on the fragile sensibilities of a still young culture concerned to build and protect its national myths:

> A central part of the effectiveness of the programme with New Zealand audiences is the subtlety and variety of ways in which its filmmakers exploited cultural stereotypes and accepted notions concerning the nature of New Zealand history and society. This is combined with the more general conventions of documentary-making, forms of representation which . . . draw upon naturalised myths concerning notions of 'objectivity' and 'truth'. Outside of the use of outside experts (such as film historian Leonard Maltin) and scientific knowledge to validate the claims made by witnesses and the historical record, a second and more interesting feature, in terms of myth, has Jackson as a reporter performing the roles of both detective and tourist for an audience.[39]

The filmmakers claimed that they had intended the audience to realise gradually that this was a hoax, though were pleased at how successful they were at creating the illusion, and argued that their film was better researched and more 'true' than most products of the 'infotainment' industry. As Jackson said:

> We never seriously thought that people would believe it because we kept putting in more and more outrageous gags – custard pies in the Prime Minister's face, making films out of eggs, and the Tahitian colour film.[40]

The irony is that it worked not just because it was very well made but because people wanted to believe it: it was a valuable contribution to New Zealand's limited cultural history.

So people were not just angry to be made fools of, but to be deprived of this cultural gain. Other hoaxes also trade on their public's wilful delusion, not least in the fantastic world of extra-terrestrial aliens and abduction.

Americans have an apparently inexhaustible appetite for all things alien, which seemed to peak in the 1990s, in the vacuum caused by the end of the Cold War. In 1995, Fox TV screened what has been called 'one of the most controversial TV documentary specials ever aired in prime time'. *Alien Autopsy: Fact or Fiction?*[41] contained graphic black-and-white film of the apparent autopsy of an alien reportedly killed in the infamous 1947 Roswell incident, when the story has it that a UFO crashed and the US government hushed it up. The autopsy footage was said to have been sold to a London-based film producer called Ray Santilli for $100,000 by the original cameraman, flown into the USAF base under great security nearly 50 years before. Ten million people watched the first transmission and the film has been seen by many millions more around the world since. It was only in 2006 that the English sculptor and film special effects maker John Humphreys finally admitted to having made the dummy used in the hoax autopsy. He also said that he appeared in the film as the chief surgeon and helped Santinilli shoot the footage. The latex models were filled with sheep brains, chicken entrails and knuckle joints bought from Smithfield meat market.[42] UFO watchers everywhere preferred the original story, which had been presented by Star Trek actor Jonathan Frakes, and who encouraged viewers to decide for themselves the validity of the autopsy footage, as he regularly did in his Fox TV show *Beyond Belief: Fact or Fiction*, which mixed fake and true stories.

A similar hoax film appeared in 1998: *Alien Abduction: Incident in Lake County*.[43] Shown as a one-hour special on UPN in the United States, their advance publicity announced: 'The recently acquired videotape is the sole testament to the fate of the McPherson family, missing since last Thanksgiving Day'. Purporting to be a home video shot by the McPherson's 16-year-old son Tommy, the footage is intercut with various 'experts' and 'Ufologists', who discuss the 'evidence'. Recognising public scepticism, these different approaches were given chapter headings such as 'hoax theory', 'cover-up theory' and 'reality theory' to suggest that this was a forensic investigation. The careful construction of the material leading up to the climax of the alien encounter, and a subsequent discussion accepting this as authentic, leave the suggestible viewer in no doubt. Like all good drama, it has managed the conflict and given voice to the doubts and dissenters before laying them to rest and letting the protagonist triumph. That said, the cast list on the end of the show should be all a sentient audience needs to know, so, when it was aired in New Zealand, NZTV-2 saw fit to cut the credits off, lamely arguing that it was required to make the transition to the next show and anyway, people could see it was a spoof. As Roscoe and Hight write, hoaxes work due to contextual factors, 'not least of which was the attitude of network broadcasters who appeared willing to participate in promotions which encouraged a confusion of these programmes' ontological status'.[44]

One such programme deliberately grossed people out, but in a good cause. In 2007, Dutch TV station BNN announced a new reality TV show in which a terminally ill woman would decide during a live show which of three patients would receive her kidneys and thus save their life. Dutch politicians including Prime Minister Jan Peter Balkenende, church leaders, media commentators and medical experts fell over each other to condemn the appalling taste of *De Grote Donor Show/The Big Donor Show* before it was transmitted on 1 June.[45] But an hour into the 80-minute programme, it was revealed to be a hoax and the 'dying woman' was an actress, although the kidney patients were for real. They had agreed to participate knowingly in the stunt to raise awareness of the serious shortage of kidney donors in the Netherlands, causing people like them to wait over four years for a transplant, with 200 a year dying on the waiting list. The TV station had taken up the cause because their former director of programmes, Bart de Graaf, was one of those who had died, aged 35. Dutch Education and Culture Minister Ronald Plasterk – a molecular biologist and former Head of the Dutch Cancer Institute – who had days before called the show 'inappropriate and unethical'[46] recanted and called it 'a fantastic stunt'.[47]

The new millennium has seen continued borrowing and porous boundaries between genres, that reflects the audience's ease with reading form. Two examples serve to illustrate the point. In 1999, the writer and executive producer of the enormously successful *Seinfeld* sit-com, Larry David, made a mockumentary about himself: *Larry David: Curb Your Enthusiasm*. In it, he mocks the conventions of civility that rule his affluent, Jewish, Los Angeles life and reconstructs himself as a man who gives vent to the thoughts and feelings that we routinely suppress. So successful was this device for puncturing the artifice of polite society, that this comedy of exquisite embarrassment went to series and has become a beacon in the alternative comedy pantheon. Shot in documentary mode, Larry David continues to play his alter ego with a devastating tendency to say what's on his mind, and the supporting cast all use their own first names in this subversive take on social truth.[48]

In 2000, a trainee producer on a BBC TV course asked a mate to help him out with a filmmaking exercise, and a delusional office manager called David Brent made his screen

Figure 6.1
Larry David's *Curb Your Enthusiasm*
documents the embarrassments of life

Figure 6.2
The Armstrongs was a docu-
soap whose characters and
storylines strained credibility

debut. Ricky Gervais and Stephen Merchant's *The Office* is a sit-com that takes the form of a docu-soap. Set in a paper wholesaler's office in the unlovable town of Slough – which the poet John Betjeman once invited enemy aircraft to bomb[49] – the show purports to be a documentary about the bored office staff and their boss, who fancies himself as an inspirational leader and natural comic. This acute observation of urban angst, set in the kind of dead-end office milieu where many of its audience now work, struck a chord with them, though some were allegedly convinced it was a documentary. Most responded to the comedy of embarrassment and *The Office* went on to make a clean sweep of the BAFTA awards for 2001. The show has subsequently won many other awards, sold container-loads of DVDs, and been remade in various languages, including French, German and American. The American version, made by NBC and first aired in 2005, has also been an award-winning success but makes the characters kinder and more aspirational, as required by the American audience. As *The New Yorker* wrote: 'The BBC and NBC are two offices separated by a common language':[50]

> The challenge that faced the American 'Office' was to honor the spirit of the original while tweaking the workplace dynamics so that audiences would want to watch more than twelve episodes . . . The British 'Office' was a pitiless meditation on rules and class. The American 'Office' doesn't care about class . . . In the British 'Office', we never learned most people's names; the American version lovingly anatomizes everyone and takes advantage of the long-take documentary format to reveal the full complexity of everyone's feelings . . . The American show is much more willing to bend reality in the service of a joke . . . The workers at [the British] Wernham Hogg wear muted blues and grays and seem to be drowning in queasy fluorescence; they never see the sun. The show's format compounded the gloom, because our emotions weren't being cued with pop-song hooks or jolted by a laugh track; yet, by placing the cameras right up in the action and interspersing one-on-one interviews, the show allowed us to discover the characters for ourselves. The documentary verisimilitude also allowed scenes to peter out with a blank look or a sigh rather than build up to the American joke-joke-joke crescendo, known as the 'blow', a structure that usually involves someone bellowing at a freshly slammed door, 'Does this mean we're not getting married?'.[51]

To complete the circle, a BBC2 series in 2006, *The Armstrongs*,[52] featured the eponymous couple who we learn run U-Fit, Coventry's third largest double glazing company. As this unlikely pair struggle to run their company and recruit a sales force that might actually be able to sell something, their language becomes racier and funnier. 'I won't shit on anyone's head unless I have to, but if I do, it will be from a very great height' says Ann. 'We could get rid of Sally and make the others think "shit". It'll be like taking dynamite to a naked flame festival,' says John. If there was any doubt that this was another sit-com in *The Office* mode, Ann then hires a white Zimbabwean motivational guru called Basil Mienie, also with a taste for one-liners: 'They are all dead. They just haven't fallen over yet.' Except that this was a docu-soap and these were all real people going about their real business. The Armstrongs clearly have a sophisticated understanding of the plastic form they are performing in, and play to the camera in a subtly knowing way. Despite revealing their ineptitude and their catastrophic staff, the series has helped their business prosper. This is life imitating art imitating life in a modern cycle of referentiality. It is, above all, entertainment.

Conclusion

Where once the importance of the issue was paramount in deciding documentary imperatives, as I have already stated, the question that came to dominate pitching and commissioning sessions is 'What's the story?' If the answer wasn't crystal clear, and preferably couched in the narrative paradigm of Hans Christian Andersen, the programme did not get made. Films did not have to start with 'Once upon a time . . .' and end with '. . . they all lived happily ever after', but commissioners had learned the basics of screenwriting and were looking for narrative arcs, jeopardy and resolution. Docu-soaps delivered real life organised according to those dramatic principles. They sought out characters that would engage an audience and contrived storylines that would keep them returning from one week to the next. Above all, they had learned that the stories that people found most compelling were about everyday issues close to home.

Drama soaps may collapse the timescales of event – moving couples quicker through the cycle of love, marriage and divorce faster than the national average – but they reflect the self-obsession of the times and carefully eschew involvement with the wider world. Terrorism and the arts, politics and economic issues tend not to taint these hermetically-sealed interior worlds. Docu-soaps seek out similar bubbles of experience, and also tend to edit out the exterior forces that threaten the dramatic cogency of the narrative. Mobile phone calls, for instance – that we all know interrupt everything from safe driving and social events to professional meetings and nights at the theatre – only ring when they advance the story. There is considerable nervousness about the extent to which this misleads the audience, but every survey that has been done suggests the audience is generally sophisticated enough to perceive the relative levels of intervention and artifice, and makes its mind up accordingly.

Mockumentary builds on this shared understanding, the audience's knowing apprehension of visual styles and constructions; and the outrage engendered by some hoaxes is often just a cynical opportunity to attack television broadcasters for the power they wield. Comedy, at its best, is always subversive and the subjection of the famous and their values to ridicule is bound to attract powerful responses. It is, however, a perfectly valid use of film: to question shibboleths and call the powerful to account. As the alien abduction films suggested: let the audience make up their own minds. It is arguable that this engenders a more mature and democratic relationship with the audience than subjecting all material to a state-approved filter of rectitude.

Expert briefing – directing like drama

Docu-soap and mockumentary require many of the skills and oversight of drama, normally without the large support crew those can command. The further away from unmediated observational documentary you move, the more these skills may be called upon. Docu-soap's dramatic structure can largely be constructed in post-production, but the execution of set-piece encounters and events does require careful planning and some, if not all, of the crafts undertaken by specialist departments in drama. The formats we cover in Chapter 12 require even more of drama's sensibilities and logistics, as clearly do any forms of documentary reconstruction. Even a solo filmmaker can enrich his or her approach by reviewing a project through the lenses of drama's many specialities. So this is a checklist of the different perspectives that need to be considered in those different roles:

1 **Screenwriter**: American television has always invested proportionally more in writing talent than Britain does, and not just in the high end drama series such as *The Sopranos*. Factual TV commissions are predicated on exactly what each episode will deliver, not just in its elements, but its narrative arc and resolution. This calls not just on incisive and detailed research, but the ability to arrange the resulting information into a coherent and cogent package. Just as Hollywood feature films regularly go through successive drafts and writers, successful TV shows will have progressively built and refined the combination of characters and plots, locations and events to make a telling story. Depending on how volatile the environment being filmed, eventuality may affect the planned shoot, and editing can always add or subtract elements, but no shoot should be undertaken without a well-considered plan. If an outline script works, constructed from well-crafted scenes, then the film can probably only get better in the execution, often with the building blocks rearranged. This is not to suggest that the director should be planning every subject's move and feeding them every line, but research should have established what they do and what they say, and have identified those moves and words which will serve the story you are trying to tell. You are normally not inventing the reality, but artfully framing it to make an entertaining picture. That's what the screenwriter does with the story, particularly when adapting someone else's work, as in the adaptation of a novel.

2 **Casting director**: Whereas in drama the script needs to be complete – and usually greenlit – before casting, in documentary the casting will largely be consonant with the development and writing, as the real-life characters usually deliver the story. But the principles of casting will help select characters that will gel to give a satisfactorily dramatic result. There need to be contrasts and the promise of conflict. It is pointless to cast people who look and sound the same, and say the same things; it is useful to have opposed experiences and points of view. Even while forging the close relationship with individuals that will ensure their unguarded performance, you need to have the critical detachment to know how they will play on screen: will they be strong or weak, sympathetic or liable to put the audience off? Which will be your lead players and who else do you need to round out the picture? If you have to have experts, can they speak well enough to sustain the audience's interest and not turn off?

3 **Design**: One of the key people in drama is the production designer, who is responsible for the look of the show. Documentaries are generally set in the subjects' own homes or workplaces, and the selection of your subjects needs to place equal emphasis on their built environment. If your film is built around a factory, say, but you expect to

follow your key characters home, then those homes need to be checked for filming practicalities and visual consistency. A class warrior shop steward may turn out to live in an unexpectedly bourgeois suburb, which you can only use if your intention is to undermine his or her credibility. The same goes for a lord who lives in a bed-sit. This is not to endorse the sloppy equations that much location choice entails – e.g. high rise = sink estate = poverty + crime – but to remind you that such readings are hard-wired into audience perception and, if you want to subvert them, you have to embed that revised reading in your narrative. You cannot site an office sequence with a successful businessman in a student hall and expect an audience to take it seriously.

4 **Location manager**: The location manager in drama will normally find the locations for the designer – even if s/he dresses them differently for the needs of the story – and is responsible for both the contractual arrangements and the logistics of the shoot. Translated into documentary terms, this encompasses some key considerations. When a person agrees to be filmed, you need to be explicit about where and when. Their daily routine may involve several locations and other people, so many different permissions will need to be sought. When that is secured, physical access, security clearing and parking, power and light where necessary, interference in the work of others, all need to be agreed, and preferably signed off by the manager responsible. Even with all this in place, the schedule may need to be changed through events beyond your control – weather, illness, etc. – so flexibility also has to be built in.

5 **Production manager**: The person who sits at the centre of this increasingly complex web is the production manager, who may well also feature in a documentary production, while subsuming some of these other roles. S/he works for the producer, ensuring the smooth running of the production, its office, budget and paperwork, managing contracts and staff. In a small production, this role may be taken by a production assistant or the producer, but it is essential that one person knows and controls everything, with appropriate fiscal oversight. It does not matter if the budget is one hundred or one million, the schedule one day or one year, the organisation needs to be centralised and clear. Collective management can rarely work, because of the many competing strands to consider, the need for clear communication, and the fact that sequential decision-making is slow and inefficient.

6 **Costume and make-up**: Unless working in period drama, even low-budget features often leave this to the actors to sort, but sourcing specialist needs, such as police uniforms and prosthetic make-up, such as for wounds, can be time-consuming and costly. Few documentaries will have need of these elements, but mocumentaries regularly do. Even docs can run into trouble, when people cast for their working credentials turn up in their Sunday best, or a presenter wears a different shirt in every shot. Things that you fail to notice on location then become the most obvious in the edit, when it is too late to remedy without re-shooting. It is just another area to think through in advance, discuss with contributors and ensure consistency and continuity.

7 **1st AD/Schedule**: Drama rarely shoots in chronological sequence, requiring meticulous continuity note-taking and shot listing. The first assistant director's job is to break down the script against the location list and work out the most efficient scheduling of the cast, crew and other resources. Most documentaries don't have that luxury and are necessarily shot in sequence, but similar logistical problems regularly occur. If your subject is a train journey, do you need passing shots of the train, and its departure and arrival? How are you going to get those if your camera is on the train?

Various possibilities exist, from a second camera to shooting the same train on different days; but all of this needs thinking through, as does how you get the crew back from Crewe, or wherever.

8 **2nd AD/cast movement**: Also, you do not need to be a big star to get very frustrated if kept hanging around in the cold while the camera is set or some problem sorted. Good logistics – particularly regarding transport, accommodation and food – can transform a shoot; bad organisation can ruin it. It would normally be the second assistant director's job to look after the cast, give them their calls and arrange for their transport. A documentary director will probably be doing all this, but making unreasonable or inconsiderate demands of people can be catastrophic, whereas thoughtful arrangement of transport and meals may make all the difference. Ninety per cent of this kind of filming is people management, and how well you manage them will determine how well they perform.

9 **Production assistant/logs**: Traditionally in documentaries, the production assistant would look after the contributors, but budgets rarely run to their being on location these days. In drama, they are more concerned with the tracking of the script, its changes and the sequences shot. Continuity is a vital part of this. In the absence of a PA, you have to do all this yourself, which can mean logging rushes at night when others are asleep. It is difficult when struggling to get through the day, but essential, to keep a running tally of the shots taken and those dropped and/or needing re-shooting. Whatever form the shooting script takes, you have to take time out to check you are recording all the bits you need, not relying on optimism.

10 **Editor/lab reports**: In drama, the editor would be working during the shoot, screening and logging the rushes and giving the cinematographer and director detailed feedback. This is more normally the thing you have to do for yourself in your hotel room at night, which at least tape allows where film needing processing does not. Leaving a location without confirming that you have the footage you think you have and need is so obviously stupid, it is amazing how often it occurs. Fatigue and delusion are all too common causes.

11 **Post-production co-ordinator**: Faults caused by failure in any of the previous ten departments, it is always fondly imagined, can be sorted in the edit. Normally something can be done to salvage a bad shoot, but inevitably at reduction of the ambition of the project, and usually at greater cost in time and resource than shooting it adequately in the first place. In drama, a post-production co-ordinator should cover their fee by the deals they strike with the technical post-production houses needed, and good scheduling of those resources. Poorly planned or executed post-production always takes longer than anticipated and, with often expensive hourly rates, can quickly blow a budget. Production accountants may identify a cheaper editor or grader, but a bad one will always cost more in the end, taking longer to deliver a less good job.

12 **Sound editor/dubbing mixer**: Knowing how important sound is – 50 per cent of the audience experience and rather more of the resulting information – drama hives off sound completion to separate sound editors (and Foley editors to source the non-diagetic sound) before spending hours mixing the final down in a multi-track studio. The tendency in cheaper documentary has been to neglect the sound, crashing tracks together on Avid and hoping the urgency of the cutting will cover the bumps. This is another false economy that is failing to get the most out of the material, and which

people watching at home with their 5.1 cinema surround sound tend to notice. Clever sound mixes, leading sound, focusing up appropriate ambient sound and, where you are using it, well-recorded commentary, can transform a film.

13 **Music**: One feature film director said that the most important member of the creative team after him was the composer, because he did the one job that the director could not do: compose music. Some documentarists loathe the way that music is used to accentuate emotion and audience reaction, but it is there because it works. Music directs the ear the way that the camera directs the eye. While documentaries can rarely afford an orchestral score, musical mates have often added a whole creative layer to friends' documentary films. Engaging them early in the creative cycle can make this a more rewarding experience for both, though in reality many composers work to click tracks made after the film has been locked off. Even the use of pre-recorded music can change the way a film is read by its audience, as long as it is well chosen.

14 **Press and publicity**: A significant part of feature film economics is the print distribution and marketing costs, often more than the cost of production. Television subsumes these costs, so producers frequently forget to prioritise them, only to discover that the broadcaster has misrepresented the film in press releases, or blown the surprise ending in the on-air trailer. Whether or not a producer has an interest in the back-end – the secondary returns on markets beyond the first transmission – it is wise to collect useable publicity stills throughout the shoot, and attempt to control publicity on release, particularly to retain PR copy approval. In this way you attempt to manage the context in which your film is received and appraised. It is not just your film whose integrity you are attempting to save, but your own and the reputation that will affect your future work opportunities.

7 Extreme television: flashing lights and freak shows

extreme adj. 1 being of a high or the highest degree or intensity . . .
2 exceeding what is usual or reasonable; immoderate

Just as health and safety departments have contrived to take the risk out of work and public places, so television has had to become increasingly careful not to upset its audiences with unexpected scenes or effects. Stroboscopic lighting may cause epileptic attacks, and sexual activity or bad language may offend vocal minorities, so these things are carefully flagged in the programme introductions. Channel 4 even experimented for a while with a little on-screen icon indicating explicit content, but withdrew it in the face of widespread ridicule. In fact, as mentioned in the previous chapter, any producer with challenging content, and keen to have maximum impact, is glad to have what is dismissively referred to as a 'public health warning' before their programme. It attracts more viewers than it loses, adding a frisson of dangerous promise that helps a programme stand out in the sea of less distinct competition. The other powerful marketing tool is the programme title. Out have gone the clever titles and subtle *doubles entendres* of the past, in have come titles which explicitly say 'what's in the tin'. By 2007, the single most attractive word to set a prospective audience's heart racing was apparently 'extreme'. On Sunday 23 September 2007, the multi-channel satellite broadcaster Sky listed 106 programmes on its UK channels that day carrying the word 'extreme' in their title, from *Extreme Hollywood* and *Extreme Skinny Celebrities* to *Ray Mears' Extreme Survival* and *Jeremy Clarkson's Extreme Machines*.[1]

Historian Eric Hobsbawm dubbed the twentieth century the *Age of Extremes*[2] in his history of 'The Short Twentieth Century, 1914–1991', contrasting the cultural revolution of the *avant garde* and the social revolution of democratisation with the horrors of the Holocaust and conflicts from the Great War to Bosnia. In the twenty-first century, despite 9/11 and the 'war on terror', most people's lives are so routine that they crave the frisson of danger and are inevitably seduced by the promise of something 'extreme' to enliven their normality. Just as rubbernecks cause chaos on motorways, slowing down to gawp at an accident in the other carriageway in the hopes of spotting a dead body, the television schedules have been clogged for some 20 years with shows offering similar vicarious thrills. One sub-genre is referred to as 'ambulance chasers' – an American phrase coined to describe lawyers who chased ambulances to secure the lucrative business representing accident victims – as it chases emergency services around in search of scenes grim and graphic. Originating in the 1930s United States with the photo-journalism of Weegee – who got his crime and accident picture scoops through monitoring New York police shortband radio – it has become a source of cheap, voyeuristic television on both sides of the Atlantic.

Cop shows

The Fox TV show *Cops* is the longest-running series of its kind, having first aired in March 1989. Hitting its 700th programme in November 2007, it has followed police forces in action all over the United States and in Hong Kong, London, Latin America and Russia. Each episode lasts just 22 minutes and comprises 3 self-contained segments about unrelated incidents, all in classic *vérité* form without music or commentary, letting the police officers involved explain what's going on. The series also runs on cable channels such as FX and Zone Reality TV, where they run current programmes and past *Classic Cops*. These channels are living tributes to the popularity of the form, carrying a host of spin-offs and imitator series, such as *LA Cops*, *Mardi Gras Cops*, *Reno Cops*, *Vegas Cops*, *Honolulu PD* and *Eyes in the Sky* (with the LA police helicopter). In case the sensation rate is not high enough for the home thrill-seeker, series are also made where material is grouped by type. Hence *High Speed Pursuits* and *Future Cops: Hot Pursuit*, which emphasises the public interest dimension: 'Since 1980, over 5,300 people have died in the United States as a result of police pursuits and one-third of the people who die are innocent bystanders'.[3] They do not promise 'live deaths', but the hope is instilled.

By comparison, UK series seem tame, because British 'bobbies' are rather more reticent on camera and the police are rather more reserved about the numbers killed in car chases.[4] British police generally do not carry weapons – although more do so now in security roles

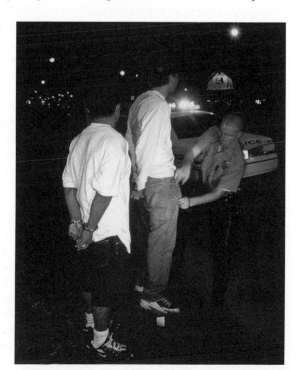

Figure 7.1
Cops go about their business, assuring the public they have crime in hand

– so the excitement of the shoot-out tends not to occur. Nonetheless, the BBC has made many series of police in action. *Rail Cops* was a series about the British Transport Police, which had the macabre feature of people who throw themselves in front of trains, but refrained from focusing on the dismembered body parts.[5] *Sky Cops* had the fun of South Yorkshire Police's Air Support Unit chasing fugitives from justice from on high, whether they were on foot traced by infra-red night sights, or in 4x4s careering across farmers' fields.[6] *Girl Cops*[7] was about the lives and work of a group of female police officers in Manchester, which included firearms training but failed to produce the body count sought by audiences of this genre, and was further discredited in thrill-seekers' estimation when recommended as 'motivational' by the UK Women and Work Commission.[8]

Such observational series are generally honourable and honest, but rarely hit the heights or expose the extremes an increasingly demanding audience wants. One problem is that a series shot by a crew is limited by the number of shooting hours affordable, and budgets have tended to get tighter, further restricting the time available to wait for something 'good' to happen. Producers of this kind of documentary material are familiar with the immutable rule – known as Sod's Law in the UK, Murphy's Law in the US – whereby, on the days you commit resources to shoot the emergency services, few or no emergencies take place, whereas on the days you rest your exhausted crew, all hell breaks loose and you are not there to film it. One cheap option is to use police footage, which an increasing number of forces routinely shoot now. An early example of this variant was ITV's *Police, Camera, Action!*,[9] which grouped particular types of criminal activity, often motoring offences, under a rather schoolmasterly public information style commentary delivered by the newsreader Alastair Stewart. Using CCTV and police car on-board cameras, often of poor quality without sound, these pictures had to be dubbed and edited as excitingly as possible to sustain interest. This cheap and cheerful series ran for eight years, until Stewart was convicted of drink-driving and a nervous broadcaster pulled the show.

The American equivalent was Fox TV's *World's Wildest Police Videos*,[10] which first aired in 1998 and whose name indicates that this would be even more entertainment-driven. The show was pulled for a while in 1999, because of advertiser nervousness about the unsignalled staging of some events in the show. The series was toned down, and for a while its name reduced to just *Police Videos*, before the *World's Wildest* title was reinstated to recapture the audience it was aimed at. Each hour-long episode averages 13 segments and most conform to the age-old narrative of the chase, obviously shot from the police perspective and uncritically supportive of that perspective. As the University of Southern California media academics Ted Prosise and Ann Johnson write: 'All of the excitement that the show produces is attributed to the desperation of the suspect.'[11]

> Viewers are no doubt aware that what they are seeing is a carefully packaged product. But the package produces a consistent message: the police always make good decisions and the suspects are always guilty. The program functions as excellent PR for police institutions. Police work appears as a high-speed, high-tech adventure. The narration provides the officer's side of the story on controversial police practices that have drawn public criticism, such as prolonged high-speed pursuits, ramming fleeing cars in such chases, and unwarranted searches of automobiles. These actions are depicted as consistently effective and safe forms of law enforcement. In the world of WWPV no one is hurt and all the suspects are blatantly guilty.[12]

With a competitive industry chasing audiences as assiduously as the police chase suspects, questions about the responsibility of producing such uncritical footage rarely trouble producers. Camera technology meanwhile has improved and is both smaller and more easily operated by amateurs, so the next phase was to give the police their own cameras. Confusingly sharing a title with a 1994 movie and a more recent CBS TV drama series, *Protect and Serve* was another series that served the American audience's insatiable appetite for reassurance that the boys in blue are out there protecting them – and getting the shots. 'From drunk drivers to naked girls to riots, our nation's police force sees it all and then has to deal with it. Using cameras they capture all of these incidents on film for the rest of us,' Zone Reality TV assured its prospective audience.[13]

In Britain, ITV did something similar in 2007 with *Cops with Cameras*.[14] They gave miniature cameras to various police forces around the country and then cherry-picked the best for their prime-time television show. This featured the usual variety of high-speed car chases and drug busts, but even with all this footage to choose from, viewers were left less than thrilled. As the *Guardian* pointed out, they presumably only got the footage that the police were willing to hand over, and this was less than impressive: 'Crikey, if this is the stuff they're happy for us to see, God knows what their less proud moments are like'.[15] Fellow police officers were equally withering. One blogging custody sergeant called it: 'The Laurel and Hardy show'.[16] Another PC posted his comment on the same blog:

> The major problem is its difficult to police with a camera strapped to you or worse some fool in the back of the car. I watched a bit but like you pc south west spent most of the time telling my other half thats not how i run my Q unit.
>
> But I suppose its a excuse for those PC's we know well who would perform for CCTV never mind a real camera crew. I'll keep my head down and if necessary book annual leave to avoid a film crew.[17]

This semi-literate but heartfelt posting confirms the Johnson and Prosise thesis that, however apparently 'real' such footage is, these are highly selective and massaged accounts, with which many police officers would not be associated. In Britain more than America, reticence still plays a part, but the overriding reason everywhere is that police officers see such constant filming as potentially offering hostages to fortune. Just as user-generated content (UGC) is revealing dubious policing of protest, CCTV footage has undermined police accounts in the past, and the amateur footage of the police beating of Rodney King led to the 1992 Los Angeles riots. For every individual police officer fancying stardom, there is a whole squad who would prefer to go about their difficult business without the accountability of filmic scrutiny. Once the cameras have been let in, and the footage allowed to go out, an alert viewer might reasonably ask just how real and representative the result is.

Heroes and villains

The critical issue for programme-makers should be the effect their programmes have on the public and their perception of reality. News programmes tend to feature bad news more than good news, and factual programmes increasingly seek out the sensations that will capture an audience. This necessarily problematises our worldview and, particularly with the area of crime, instills a distorted view of the prevalence of crime. Sociologists such as David Altheide have written extensively on the media's 'problem frame' and the 'discourse of fear' it promotes.[18] While we all share the understanding that were the murder rate of the *Inspector Morse* drama series to happen for real, Oxford would be the Murder Capital of Europe, emphasis on crime in factual programming cannot produce the same comfort zone. The BBC's long-running *Crimewatch* programme – having convincingly dramatised some of the worst, unsolved crimes of the month – traditionally ended with the long-running presenter Nick Ross's avuncular homily to trust the police and: 'Don't have nightmares, do sleep well.'

Nick Ross first used that line on 7 June 1984 and personally signed off for the last time on 2 July 2007. *Crimewatch UK*[19] was originally based on a German series of the 1970s – *Aktenzeichen XY . . . Ungelöst (File XY . . . Unsolved)*[20] – which sought the public's help in cracking unsolved crime. Initially, the British police were suspicious of working with television producers and only a few forces agreed to co-operate. The show was only given an initial run of three programmes, and it was not until the third that they got a breakthrough, with a member of the public helping solve a rape in the New Forest. As the show then prospered, police awoke to the possibilities of using the BBC as a PR window and have since fought to get on the show. Running only once a month, police officers take an active role in the studio from which the show is broadcast, presenting evidence and taking phone calls from the public. Three or four cases are dramatically reconstructed in the original crime sites with actors closely resembling the victims, which is where the public's memories are prompted – and their nightmares begin. After its first 13 years featuring 1,632 cases, *Crimewatch UK* was able to boast of 514 arrests as a direct result of audience intervention, 42 of them having been sentenced to life imprisonment.[21] After 23 years and 2,900 cases, they were only claiming a success rate of 1 in 6, but their audience had also halved since their heyday of 9 million.

Crimewatch UK is seen by the BBC as a pinnacle of its public service broadcast remit, melding its entertainment and public information roles with a powerful interactive element involving the audience, all to a great social benefit: the solving of serious crime. Seen through that prism, the programme is an ineffable good. Its detractors don't see it as social glue, but the opposite, instilling a paranoid culture that overemphasises serious crime and encourages in us a suspicious mindset about our fellow citizens. There is, for instance, a view that *Crimewatch*'s understandable adoption of the sensational case of the murder in 1999 of one of its own presenters, Jill Dando, contributed to the public frenzy that has incarcerated the wrong man. Barry George went to the Appeals Court twice before his conviction was quashed in 2007, whereafter he was acquitted at his retrial on 1 August 2008, having spent over seven years in jail for a crime he did not commit. The perception is that our armchair atavism, our feral bloodlust for criminal scapegoats, has not just spawned a culture of fear, but allowed a creeping authoritarianism. As stars of their own successful show, the police effectively determine priorities and perception. The producer is more concerned with shaping the material and keeping the audience interested.

In her book *Crimewatching*, the film academic Deborah Jermyn records the programme's series producer Kate Thompson acknowledging the difficult juggling act she has between ethical and entertainment considerations. 'We need people who watch to be witnesses. It's a constant concern. You have to make it interesting enough for people to watch without ever becoming gratuitous. And it's hard to get that balance right sometimes.'[22] While admiring the professionalism of the show, Jermyn's view is that the media's constant emphasis on crime and its prosecution is a cause of anxiety for society, and particularly for women. 'This practice perpetuates a culture of fear among women which is not representative of actual crime figures. The proliferation of stranger crime feeds a "culture of peril".'[23] That in turn is what feeds an unquestioning demand for law and order, with emphasis on the order.

America's Most Wanted, the US variant which has run on Saturday nights on Fox TV since 1988, spreads its net wider, covering emergency response stories, missing persons and fugitive finding as well as encouraging the audience to help solve crime. That wider ambit is fuelled with Fox's gung-ho spirit, supercharged since 9/11 with a righteous mission to celebrate the men in blue. The *AMW* website runs a memorial site called 'In the Line of Duty' – emblazoned: 'RESPECT. HONOR. REMEMBER.' – which seeks to ally its audience to the same uncritical support as President Bush's infamous charge 'You're either with us or against us' over the 'war on terror'. The site starts with the grim statistics:

> More than 1,600 law enforcement officers have died in the line of duty during the past 10 years, an average of one death every 53 hours or 166 per year. There were 154 law enforcement officers killed in 2004.[24]

Brief biogs of those dead officers follow, most of whom were 'shot and killed' doing their duty, which sad feature should command respect, but also evades such issues as the gun culture responsible for this roll call. The *AMW* site also identifies its 'Dirty Dozen – the worst of the worst – the 12 fugitives [presenter/host] John Walsh wants to take off the streets the most'.[25]

It is inconceivable in contemporary British culture that a television presenter would presume to be the authority that defined this public need, but that presentational difference disguises a syncretism of object, a shared goal to eradicate evil in society without delving too deeply into its causes or definition. That vengeful culture imprisons one in every 2,000 Americans, the highest rate in the developed world, 8 times as many Hispanic and 32 as many of them African-Americans as white.[26] Because of their extraordinary rate of incarceration, one in every 20 American black men over the age of 18 is in a state or federal prison, compared to one in every 180 whites. In certain states, the incarceration of black men reaches devastating levels: in Oklahoma and Iowa one in every 13 black men is in state prison; in Rhode Island, Texas and Wisconsin, the figure is one in every 14.[27] But these are not issues that bother *America's Most Wanted*; they might correctly argue that all races are represented in both their fugitives and police victim lists. It could also be argued that their overriding aim is to increase those incarceration figures.

While these shows are television's right-wing tabloid troubadours, the United States has moved into higher production quality documentary series, which employ the full panoply of drama in the pursuit of latter-day morality tales. The New York-based Hybrid Films has developed a particular run of programming that reflects the real-life characters and storylines more familiar from successful drama series such as ABC's *NYPD Blue* and HBO's *Six Feet Under*. Their first, *Talk to Me: Hostage Negotiators of the NYPD* (1999), was quickly followed by *NYPD: Emergency Service Unit* (2000), both aired on the US Arts and Entertainment cable channel. The Emergency Service Unit they followed into action is an elite force that combines technologically sophisticated rescue teams with SWAT squads, with the improbable motto of 'Anytime Baby!'. The strap line for the series ran 'When a citizen needs help, they call the police. When the police need help, they call ESU'. Giving a flavour of the dramatic heroics involved, the company's promotional material tells you what to expect:

> These urban cowboys can do it all – from rescuing people from car and subway accidents or talking down suicidal jumpers from bridges, to SWAT-style raids on guntotting [sic] drug dealers.[28]

The moulding of heroic roles and narratives around serving police officers fitted the Zeitgeist of the period following the events of 9/11. Fourteen of the 23 serving NYPD killed in the collapse of the Twin Towers were members of the ESU, and their names are memorialised in the iconography of the NYPD Emergency Services Guardian Angel.[29] Considerably more firefighters were killed, 343 of them, and they became the heroes of the hour for New Yorkers and their then Mayor, Rudi Giuliani, and for the world's media as the story reverberated around the globe. The French filmmakers, the Naudet brothers, were shooting a documentary about a probationer fireman on the day and captured one of the only two known live action shots of the first plane hitting the World Trade Centre. They went on to make a definitive feature documentary, *9/11* (2002), shown initially on CBS and essentially made from the firefighters' perspective. The elevation of firefighters to being the folk heroes of their day has prompted other work, such as Lilibet Foster's *Brotherhood – Life in the FDNY* (2004), which also allows the firefighters to construct their own heroic narrative. The instructor announces portentously to the new recruits:

> Look at these faces. Somebody in this room is going to die. This is a life and death job. Your life and your brother's life depend upon it . . . This is the New York City Fire Department. We do things our way.[30]

Britain does not celebrate its firefighters in the same way, despite a long-running and very popular LWT television drama series, *London's Burning* (ITV 1988–2002). In the absence of the grand narrative that 9/11 supplied, Brits have to go back to the Second World War to find anything comparable in the documentary world and, even then, Humphrey Jennings's *Fires Were Started* (1943), about London firemen tackling the Blitz, was a dramatised documentary, albeit enacted by the firemen themselves. Britain's comparatively shy firefighters have only been celebrated recently in Northern Ireland, in a 6-part regional documentary series about the fire services of Belfast, Ballymoney, Armagh and Londonderry. BBC1's *Fire Watch* first aired in Northern Ireland in April 2002, but failed to set the nation alight.

UK ambulance services have been slightly better served by documentary television, though normally in a supporting role in series focused more on medicine and the medics. They emerged more on their own terms in three series of *Trauma* on BBC1 (2004–7) and its even more provocatively entitled sister show, *Trauma Uncut* on BBC3. The first two series were set around the Royal London Hospital in Whitechapel and the London Air Ambulance Service, literally and metaphorically taking off with the excitement of airborne medicine flying to save lives. The third series came down to earth with the Royal Liverpool Hospital and the Merseyside Regional Ambulance Service, probably more accurately reflecting everyday medicine, but without the high-flying drama that sustained the previous series.

British action men and women are generally less inclined to strike the heroic pose that comes so naturally to their American counterparts, and television that merely records their routines regularly fails to excite. Only when the producer steps in and accentuates the drama does the work apparently secure its due recognition. Thus a series effectively spawned by *Crimewatch* called *999* – in which gripping tales of emergency services in action were dramatically restaged with factual testimony from the survivors – came closer to putting them on a public pedestal more normally occupied by the police. Fronted since its launch in 1992 by the award-winning newsreader Michael Buerk, he initially failed to see that this, unlike the news, was a modern form of myth-making:

> Originally, in my simplistic way, I felt a lot hinged on suspense – would the person get out of this ghastly predicament? – and that was lost if every item ended with survival, even if there was a reasonable amount of damage. The powers that be were against me and proved entirely right. The stories operate on the same basis as fairytales for children – climb behind the sofa and close your eyes – where the great thing is kids can engage their deepest fears and know everyone lives safely ever after.[31]

While Buerk is absolutely correct in his identification of children's fiction's age-old role in exploring and validating fears, applying that to their parents' factual information needs is intrinsically more problematic. As we know, in reality people don't all live safely or happily ever after. But in a television world where reality is not enough, those distinctions between fact and fiction frequently dissolve. Reviewing another well-made documentary series by Hybrid Films for *The New York Times* in 2000, Caryn James wrote about what she headlined 'Real Detectives, Real Crimes, Real Voyeurism'. She felt that in Hybrid's *Brooklyn North Homicide Squad* for US Court TV 'the line between reality and fiction all but disappears'.

> Brilliantly edited and paced, it is as slick and compelling as any police drama on television, which is exactly the problem. From the swift montage of characters and New York streets in the opening credits to the thumping music between scenes, the series applies the techniques of dramas like *NYPD Blue* and *Homicide* to gruesome reality. The series's energetic storytelling engages us even when its voyeurism is repellent.
>
> *Brooklyn North* carries a frisson of the forbidden. We have no right to be here; murder shouldn't be replayed as entertainment; yet this insidiously effective drama makes it hard to turn away.[32]

Other extremes

Making it hard to turn away is the prime objective of television commissioners, an objective ratcheted up as the number of available channels grows exponentially, making it easier for the audiences to do just that: turn away. The alternative to hitching a ride with the emergency services as a way of cruising human distress is for the producer to cut out the middle man and organise the metaphorical car crash. The rise of the daytime chat shows, where people confront their errant spouses and violent exchanges are confected for the braying audience in the studio and at home, is not the subject of this book, but is a significant contributor to the demands for ever more extreme encounter. There has always been a voyeuristic element central to documentary, but it has become more important in the competition for the distracted audience. The late producer and editor of the BBC's *Man Alive*, Desmond Wilcox, had a simple device when interviewing someone *in extremis* about their harrowing life events. When the tears began to well, you would hear Desmond's quiet, concerned voice say: 'If this is upsetting you too much, we can always stop'. The brave interviewee would normally choke back a sob and go on, and the camera would zoom in – and that was the point. It was a coded instruction to the cameraman to focus on the tears. Today, everybody cries and tears are two a penny. As Paul Watson's brush with the ITV press office over *Malcolm and Barbara: Love's Farewell* demonstrated,[33] you now need a death on camera to pull the punters.

So far, death has largely been treated with care and responsibility on British television. The first death actually recorded and transmitted in the UK was in the BBC science series *The Human Body*,[34] in 1998. The series was presented by Professor Robert Winston and used contemporary techniques to investigate the human lifecycle through the body, ending with the peaceful death on camera of a cancer sufferer. Death has become a taboo in a culture both physically healthy and socially isolated enough for most people now to reach middle age without experiencing death at first hand. Demythologising the process is an appropriate public service objective, but inevitably excites extreme reactions.

Channel 4 typically pushed the boundaries further in 2002 with the live transmission of an autopsy as it was performed for the cameras by the Austrian Dr. Gunther Von Hagens. The Channel 4 website proclaimed:

> In Channel 4's *Anatomy for Beginners* you can see a real and spontaneous demonstration of human anatomy. The beauty and intricacy of the human body is laid bare in a sophisticated modern version of a tradition that extends back to the middle ages and beyond.[35]

Channel 4 placed emphasis on the fact that postmortems used to be held in public – just as had surgery on live patients, hence the term operating theatre – but not for 170 years, and they still had 130 complaints made to the Independent Television Commission. The complaints were dismissed because, in the ITC judgement:

> although the subject matter and content of the programme approached the limits of what is allowed by the programme code, those limits were not exceeded and the images were no more explicit than those already seen on UK television.[36]

The ITC was in its last year of existence, before being subsumed within Ofcom, but it is interesting to note its relativist position on matters of taste: we've seen it all before, so that's all right.

Shock docs

There is a long-established tradition of television producers pushing at the boundaries of taste, to see how much they can get away with, and the extent to which they are responsible for the changing limits of public acceptance is clearly significant, if difficult to determine.

The recent appetite for the extremes of human misery feeds a jaded palate sated on more common problems. The documentary series *Extraordinary Lives* is one of the few undisputed successes on the UK Channel 5, regularly attracting an audience larger than much of their entertainment fare. The year 2007 saw the launch of the seventh run of this series that attempts to find freakily unique human conditions or, as their website says: 'Sometimes heartbreaking, sometimes inspiring, each thought-provoking film tells the story of a person whose unusual condition, ability or power challenges scientific understanding.'[37] The titles tell you what to expect: *The Boy Who Sees Without Eyes* – the 14-year-old blind American boy who navigates by sound; *The Twin Within the Twin* – the 36-year-old Bengali who carries his foetal twin inside his abdomen; and *The Twins Who Share a Body* – Abby and Brittany Hensel, the world's only known dicephalus conjoined twins, i.e. two heads on one body. Sue Davidson commissioned the strand for Five:

> *Extraordinary People* grew out of the Science brief and Justin Kershaw, who created it, was fascinated by the whole area of the Sachs books – *The Man Who Mistook His Wife For a Hat* and so on – and saw the titles of all our programmes in somewhat similar vein. It started off what has become a bit of a genre now, looking at the most extreme variations in human bodies, human abilities, disabilities, whatever, but within the umbrella of Science. Although a lot of them could be described in the 'shock doc' genre, I don't think they are if you look at the tone of programme: it's the fact that they are rooted in science that gives them a kind of rigour and stops them becoming completely gratuitous and exploitative, because you feel there's a real journey there.

This is a fine, though important, distinction. The pejorative label 'shock doc' is invited by the Channel 4 series more challengingly entitled *BodyShock*, which has run since 2003. The titles seem similar: *The Boy Who Gave Birth to His Twin*, *Born with Two Heads*, *World's Biggest Boy* and *Half Ton Man*. The subject matter is virtually identical, but Channel 4 is more direct in its appeal to the prurient in its audience. Sample the gleeful tabloid tone of their online write-up of the *Half Ton Man:*

> Weighing the same as five baby elephants and a shade less than a Mini Cooper, Patrick Deuel is one of the heaviest men ever and a medical miracle. His heart and other organs should have collapsed long before he reached his record-breaking weight of 76 stone 8 lbs. A wall has to be knocked out of his house so he can be taken to hospital – in a reinforced ambulance – where he is kept on a strict diet and loses a staggering 30 stone. After a gastric by-pass operation he is sent home. It is now up to him to decide if he wants to live or carry on eating himself to death.
>
> One of Patrick's supporters has been Rosalie Bradford, who was one of the world's fattest women. She was eight feet wide and could not leave the house. It was only when she realised her addiction to food was a response to being abandoned as a child that she lost an incredible 900 pounds. Through the remarkable stories of Patrick and Rosalie, *BodyShock* anatomises the science of extreme weight loss and the bewildering lives of the growing number of people who seem intent on eating themselves to death.[38]

Science makes a relatively late, light entry to the picture here, and the sign-off 'eating themselves to death' is indicative of a harder-nosed programme agenda. ITV followed up with a whole Brooklyn hospital full of subjects in *Half Ton Hospital* where 'patients carry an incredible average weight of 50 stones each.'[39] Sue Davidson is convinced that is what distinguishes her commissions from the opposition. 'We're not like *BodyShock*, we only do uplifting stories, so there is a feel-good factor to them, which is very Five'. This is not a broad attack on another channel. Channel 4's contribution to public service documentary is universally acknowledged, and its best known contribution to this arena, *The Boy Whose Skin Fell Off*,[40] garnered worldwide praise and Davidson's unstinting admiration:

> We would have done because that was a very uplifting tale. We would have had a lot more science in it, so you would have learnt more about the condition, but we would have done it because he was uplifting about his death. It wasn't dark.

The eponymous 'boy' was actually a man of 36 called Jonny Kennedy. He had a genetic condition called Dystrophic Epidermolysis Bullosa (EB) – which meant that his skin literally fell off at the slightest touch, leaving his body covered in agonising sores. The deal he struck with filmmaker Patrick Collerton was that he would review his life while filming his final fight against skin cancer. Jonny's extraordinary character and wit shone through his grim tale and untimely death, even embellishing the customised coffin he was interred in, and his tale reached an extraordinary 5 million viewers' hearts, raising £500,000 for DebRA, the charity working on behalf of people with this hitherto unsung condition. This, most commentators agreed, is what the public service remit of British television is for, and the grabby title was more than justified by the results. Mark Lawson in the *Guardian* had anticipated that this was another huckstering title 'designed to entrap channel-flickers' but concluded: 'Few television programmes in history have managed simultaneously to be so hard to watch and so rewarding.'[41] Jonny's mother and carer Edna, had made a moving contribution to the original film, and added her assessment to an update made in the aftermath of the film's success:

> Jonny wanted to do the film to get EB and DebRA better known, but it has been so much more than that; the film seems to have touched so many people . . . Jonny has achieved something amazing and I know that, wherever he is now, he will be jumping with joy at the response the film has had.[42]

Not all films can aspire to these heights or win an International Emmy, as this one did, but this level of sympathy and engagement with the subjects and their condition could rescue programmes from the charges of unsavoury exploitation. However, their very prevalence suggests a return to the days of the fairground freak show, and disability activists have begun to mount a critical challenge to them. Laurence Clark writes for the BBC disability website *Ouch! (It's a disability thing)* and mounts a robust case:

> During these programmes I often find myself screaming at the TV: 'Where the hell do they find these people?!' I suspect that someone somewhere has set up an agency called Rent-a-Freak, specifically to supply the most bizarre, eccentric disabled people they can find to budding documentary makers. But unlike today's documentary subjects, the freaks of old were at least paid to take part – and had some say over their performances.[43]

The final curtain

Before the internet made available images of anything that anyone can conceive, there was some attempt to regulate the flow of pictures and perversity. Television was heavily regulated; film and videotape were overseen by the British Board of Film Classification, as they still are. It was film compilations, distributed commercially as VHS tapes, that first identified the market for the voyeuristic forms this chapter has covered. The breakthrough release was a video produced by EduVision Films Ltd, which featured high speed car chases and crashes. *Police Stop!* grossed £3.5 million in 1994. *Police, Camera, Action* started on ITV the same year. *Caught In the Act!* (1995) intercut villains caught committing crimes with closed circuit television footage of sexual acts, and *Road Rage* delivered liberal dollops of what it said on the tin. The 1996 tape *Everyday Operations* offered graphic footage from hospital operating theatres, which caused something of a row over its poor taste. But where EduVision encountered some particularly negative publicity, thus generating even greater income, was in its 1995 compilation of *Executions*. This featured 21 'live' killings from around the world, while laying claim to an educational motive:

> State-sponsored murder or justice? More than 26 million people have been executed since 1900. But less than 10% have committed any real crime, other than belonging to the 'wrong' religion, race or political party. An objective look at the cultural, social and historical context of the death penalty, 'Executions' offers a rare insight into the rights and wrongs of the ultimate act of retribution.
>
> It chronicles the tools of the executioner's grim trade. It questions so-called 'humane' execution and in so doing indicts the mass murderers of barbarous regimes. The images of death, drawn from around the world, are as shocking as they are tragic. But only by witnessing them and understanding their background can you hope to decide for yourself when, if ever, execution is the punishment that fits the crime.[44]

It is arguable just how educational or influential *Executions* was, but today YouTube and similar sites list executions as one of the plethora of entertainment options on offer, indiscriminately mixing the historical and the contemporary, the real and the faked. You can thrill to the amputations and beheadings allegedly meted out under Sharia law and other extreme belief systems, and watch the hanging of Saddam Hussein and adulterous adolescents. By this technology, the world has become a giant peep show and the more responsible and regulated media are struggling to keep up, fearful that the audiences they are losing are actually being seduced by this more extreme fare. There is a concern that television producers will feel obliged to continue to raise the bar to compete, and filmmakers' motives will continue to become more suspect, disgusting many while others flock to the spectacle. There is an historical echo of the ancient Colosseum, where the Roman emperors had to increase the violence of their gladiatorial productions and up the body count to appease the bloodlust of an ever more jaded public.

In 2004, 24 people jumped to their death from the Golden Gate Bridge in San Francisco. It is apparently the most popular suicide spot in the world. There have been more than 1,200 deaths there since it opened in 1937, yet the authorities have repeatedly refused to put up the kind of safety net that has cut the death toll elsewhere, such as at England's equally jumper-popular Clifton Suspension Bridge in the Avon Gorge at Bristol. Now the debate has been reignited by the very effective means of film. Filmmaker Eric Steel filmed 23 of the 24 suicides in 2004 and made a feature documentary that has been seen all over the world and forced the Bridge Authority to reconsider their aesthetic and economic objections to putting in place a suicide barrier.[45] A triumph for the humane value of film, one might suppose, but there is another view.

To get permission to film the bridge for a whole year, Steel had to lie to the Bridge Authority about his plans and objectives. He said he was filming 'the powerful and spectacular interaction between the monument and nature' and that his work was to be the first in a series of such documentaries about national monuments such as the St Louis Arch and the Statue of Liberty. Then he had to watch people die to make his point, though he says he had his crews equipped with cell phones set to speed dial the bridge patrol should anyone be spotted about to jump. They apparently did save six lives this way, one person more than once. But had they been excessively zealous in this regard, they would not have had a film and Steel admitted that when filming, it was his inevitable instinct to continue filming. 'I realized that this girl was about to jump. But when I was behind the camera it was almost like it wasn't real because I was looking through the lens.'[46]

The Bridge Authority were furious at the deception and, no doubt, in now being forced to spend $2 million on an engineering study of the best way to build a safety barrier. But they also point out that the film may well have the effect of highlighting the current ease of suicide there and encouraging copycats. Suicide prevention experts support this view, with Anne Haas, research director for the American Foundation for Suicide Prevention, saying: 'Studies show that, particularly with vulnerable people and youth, seeing pictures of suicidal acts results in an increase in suicides.'[47] Columbia University epidemiologist Madeleine Gould says that 'It's a pity Mr. Steel didn't make the deaths more unattractive, jumping in this beautiful setting'.[48] Details they feel may have had a more powerful disincentive effect include the excruciating pain a body endures hitting the water at 75 miles per hour, the shattering of bones and organs that precede a slow, agonising death, before the corpse is swept out to sea to be eaten by sharks and crustaceans.

Of course, the voyeurs would have enjoyed such details, but the relatives and friends of the victims that Steel subsequently interviewed would not. And this is another charge against Steel. He did not tell those bereaved he approached that he had already filmed their loved ones' deaths. He claims he did not because he 'didn't want the word to get out and possibly encourage people to kill themselves who saw a chance to be in the film'.[49] There are those who feel that the reason was more pressing and pragmatic: if they had known what he was up to, they may well have not co-operated. In the light of these caveats, *The Bridge* has sharply divided people. While Tribeca and San Francisco film festivals showed and praised it, Sundance and Berlin refused it for being exploitative. Critics ranged from the hyperbolic to the apoplectic. Stephen Holden of *The New York Times* called it: 'One of the most moving and brutally honest films about suicide ever made . . . remarkably free of religious cant and of cozy New Age bromides. Eerie and indelible'.[50] *The Daily Telegraph*'s Benjamin Secher called it 'this voyeuristic, vacuous film'.[51]

Conclusion

Film, or, to be more precise, tape, is an amoral medium. The plastic itself has no principles and is equally at ease recording the extremes of existence as it is the everyday event.

The questions every camera operator and filmmaker has to face, sooner or later, is whether to keep filming or not, whether to intercede in the events they are witnessing, and what are the implications of these decisions. Paul Watson, addressing film students at Goldsmiths College, talked of the issues he faced daily in filming in Sarajevo during the Bosnian War. He posed to them his dilemma as a documentarist, filming a woman and child trying to make it through barbed wire and across open ground under sniper fire. Carry on filming, or not? Rush out into the lethal fire zone to lend a hand, or do something else? Various decisions were proffered by these unblooded filmmakers. Watson said they were nice people, but that the filmmaker carries on filming. 'It's what we do. We are witnesses. Without us people won't know what's going on.'[52]

If the plastic is unexposed to the tragedy unfolding, the message is stillborn, the dilemma a private thing rather than a public statement. If it is exposed, the subsequent use of that footage, its context and interpretation, will define the value and morality of the decision. With no film, there is no discourse, no potential for remedy and, in Watson's view, no benefit from the opportunity and sacred duty of witness. The truth is buried with the body. That is the reasoning that sustains documentarists, war reporters and others operating in hazardous zones. It is often extended to encompass all extremes, and justify all excess. So the dilemma remains: when does that decision fail the public interest test and fall back to a level we might reasonably brand 'exploitative, vacuous, voyeuristic'?

When a highly regulated television industry laid claim to the moral high ground and unselfconsciously presumed to dictate to its public on matters of taste and public interest, it was possible to mount a consensus on what was right and wrong in what are essentially operational decisions. But with the elevation of the market – which has no more intrinsic morality than plastic or the gun – as the key determinant, programme-makers have drifted into a state of moral relativism which often leaves them filming as the ground shifts beneath their feet.

The Bridge neatly encapsulates the contemporary paradox. Where once, not so long ago, it would have been inconceivable to film and show people plunging to their death – and clearly many people still find that repulsive – it demonstrably has forced a cynically cash-conscious authority to revise its plans, which could lead to saving countless lives. Others had to die – though none were pushed and others saved as a result of the filmmakers being there – and lies were told to achieve that end. Steel's supporters would chalk this up as a moral victory. Others feel it a bridge too far. Filmmakers operating at the extremes have to face these philosophical questions and be prepared to defend their answers. Where they are at their most exposed, they feel that the broadcasters and distributors only support them if the market does. Good audience figures retroactively justify dodgy decisions, bad ones or a bad press consign the filmmaker to exile beyond the pale. That is what Paul Watson felt happened to him, as he was left to use his own money hiring lawyers to defend his reputation. He feels abused by the criticism, but vindicated by the continued support of his bereaved subject Barbara and her family, whose trust he has retained.

Where filmed subjects concur in their depiction and can accept the final film, charges of exploitation are hard to sustain. Voyeuristic they undoubtedly often are and, as Laurence Clark complains, there is an unhealthy obsession with the freak show, but there is no evidence of people being coerced into appearing. Films of *The World's Biggest Boy*[53] or *The Woman With Half A Body*[54] may offend the sensitivities of some, or indeed many, but the claims for their social education values have to be recognised, along with the subjects' desire for validation

have an unexpected bearing on the story. This requires extra research effort on the interviewer's part, like any work that is going to stand out, and may not always yield a result. But a doctor with an interesting medical history, say, or a business correspondent with a failed former business, would give your investigation an extra edge. Even in the least contentious interviews, with the best of interview subjects, anything that makes the exchange more novel and interesting for them is likely to generate more fruitful responses.

8 **Ask open questions**: To achieve the self-contained extract, questions have to be carefully designed as open, not closed ones that can be answered 'Yes' or 'No'. Prepositions normally yield questions that give the evaluative answers required: 'What do you think about . . .?'; 'How much can this change . . .?'; 'Where will this leave us . . .?' Not: 'Are you worried?'; 'Is this good?' Do not jump in when the subject starts to waffle or is clearly going on too long to be useable. Let them finish and then ask them to summarise, as in 'Could you just highlight what you think are the most important points there?' Not only do these points tend to yield the required structure of response, but they imply a human conversation rather than an interrogation.

9 **Record clean tracks**: You also need to ensure that the answers are clean, clear of your question, and that you don't talk over them or interrupt. Clear sound pauses not only allow clean cuts in editing but, where needed, enable reordering of answers. You should also record a buzz track of the room with no one talking, to lay over any cuts that you do have to make. This is particularly important where there is intrusive ambient sound, though hopefully you will have chosen the quietest location possible. Fridges, TVs, mobile phones and any other machinery causing background hum should be switched off. Stop recording when aircraft or other loud noise intrudes, and only start again when it has fully disappeared.

10 **Cover your tracks**: Some crews can become blasé about entering people's homes or offices, reorganising the furniture to get their shots, and then leaving the room unrestored and the interviewee feeling abused. There is no benefit in causing unnecessarily bad feeling and no cost in consideration and fully expressed gratitude. Even the atmosphere generated by a combative interview can usually be ameliorated by sincere thanks and the explanation that editorial imperatives demanded the questions asked. Written thanks, by letter or email, should also follow, along with details of transmission. 'Professionals' frequently fail to do this, making a return visit unwelcome, particularly when they have decided not to use the interview. There may well be good reasons for dropping them, but these should be communicated to the interviewee, so that they are not left humiliatingly to find out on the night, in the company of family or friends. Poor protocols and bad behaviour sit uneasily on those who lay claim to the moral high ground.

Part III

Change the mind

As the two previous parts have shown, the central tension in documentary is between the veracity of the subject matter and the objective of the filmmaker. This cannot resolve as a simple binary – are we getting a clear picture or being spun a particular line? – as popular discourse about bias and objectivity would have us believe. The constant evolution of new forms and genres renders obsolete simplistic distinctions between 'fact' and 'fiction' and, I would aver, between 'truth' and distortion. Whose truth and why we are being told it enables us to read the work accordingly. The party political broadcasts that UK public service broadcasters are obliged to carry are, at one level, the most honest films on television, in that we know who paid for them and why they are made and broadcast: to try and persuade us to vote for the particular party. By that same token, we largely ignore them and use them as an excuse to change channel or make the tea. Yet we choose a particular newspaper precisely because it reflects everything from our reading age to our personal prejudices.

The subdivisions of documentary covered in this part are all, to a greater or lesser degree, unashamedly keen on changing our minds, for good or ill. Education – one of the Reithian triptych of values – is largely deemed to be a good thing, whether it is the schooling of children or the introduction of adults to new interests. But education is an intensely political arena, from broad policy differences about how prescriptive curricula should be to hard fault lines about the teaching of religion in schools, or Creationism in science classes. Charged with finding a broadly acceptable path through these minefields, both the BBC and independent television have found their schools offerings increasingly marginalised and under attack from commercial interests. Adult education also reflects the cultural needs of the time, from benign social intervention such as adult literacy schemes to feel-good phenomena like cookery shows. Open University programmes, once late-night corduroy in tone, are now flashy shop window models with splashes of education lite. In a country still given to use of the phrase 'too clever by half', television education has become a stealth operation.

Propaganda, like the party political broadcast, is generally clearly targeted and visible for what it is, unless you happen to live in a country where there is no alternative with which to compare it, or you happen to agree with the message. It is easy to see the heroic images of Soviet film, like Victor Turin's *Turksib*, and the Nazi myth-making of Leni Riefenstahl's *Triumph of the Will*, for what they are. But Londoners facing the Blitz would not have regarded Humphrey Jennings's *Britain Can Take It* in the same light, any more than patriotic Americans would have criticised *Protect and Survive* films during the Cold War, or Israelis home news coverage of the 2009 Gaza incursion. In a world riven by ideological differences, but dominated by the free market, the medium is the message and its control is power.

Polemic is an important weapon for diverse expression in a free democracy, just as anyone has been allowed to speak on any subject on a soapbox at Speakers' Corner in London's Hyde Park since 1872. It challenges the traditional orthodoxy that any issue can be reduced to a simple two-dimensional dualist opposition, treats audiences as critically astute adults and invites them to make up their own minds. At its most creative, it uses the withering wit of satire to explode the pomposity of the powerful, and reveal the absurdity of received opinions and dominant systems. Yet, at a time when the Western economy is on the point of collapse, satire that should have helped puncture this South Sea bubble of the digital age has been unaccountably absent, and polemic is largely restricted to contrived controversialism. In part, this may be due to the atomisation of society and fragmentation of audiences, noted statistically in declining exercise of the vote and participation in religion and other communal activities. Increasingly people's activities have moved into elective niches, notably online. Social networking sites and the opportunities for artistic expression online are seen as empowering people previously excluded from media hierarchies, but can corral people with their own kind.

We end this part with a chapter on the liberation that film and video has allowed to the disenfranchised, from women's groups in different cultures to emerging nations and nascent democracies. This cannot hope to be a comprehensive survey, but is indicative of the documentary form's extraordinary power to transform lives and give voice to the voiceless. Whereas that was the role of the Community Programme Unit in Britain during the 1980s and 1990s (Chapter 4) – now disbanded on the questionable grounds that the need has gone – the visible contribution to emerging democracy in China, and to popular expression from Africa to Latin America, celebrates documentary's role in the transference of power.

8 Education

....

education n. 1 the act or process of acquiring knowledge . . . 2 the act or process of imparting knowledge

Educational programming is a particular case study in how television has evolved from a monochrome, didactic message board to a media-rich multi-platform experience, in which broadcast material is only one part. Documentary has featured throughout that history, but has also been forced to adapt to meet changing needs. Television's involvement with education has been a complex one, determined by the changing politics and culture of the time, and reflective of its audiences' often conflicted views of education's values. When Lord Reith formulated his mantra of the BBC's mission 'to inform, educate and entertain' in the 1920s, Britain was still a profoundly hierarchical and deferential society, where everyone knew their place and accepted that the majority should do what they were told. Radio was seen as an extension of that unquestioning system, so Reith surprised the establishment by coming into conflict with the Conservative government of the day during the General Strike of 1926, when he insisted on reporting on all sides. The then Chancellor of the Exchequer, Winston Churchill, wanted to commandeer the BBC, as politicians have frequently aspired to do, and this threat was enough to pressure Reith to ban from the airwaves trade union representatives, Labour politicians and even the emollient voice of the Archbishop of Canterbury. This was the moment at which the BBC's reputation for impartiality – and its compromised relationship with government – was forged. It is also an appropriate background against which to read the licence and limitations placed upon its educational role.

Taking reality to school
....

Education is a two-way street and can only commence with the willing participation of the people on the receiving end. Television's early days in Britain followed the implementation of the 1944 Education Act, which made secondary education universally and freely available for the first time. Servicemen and women returning from war demanded a fairer distribution of the spoils and elected a Labour government to deliver. Education was seen as a necessary part of the package, the means by which working-class boys and girls could seize new opportunities. Television in due course evolved schools production departments to support this endeavour, and a whole generation fondly remember the school television set – there was normally only one – being wheeled out to give the class welcome relief from teachers scribbling on blackboards. So iconic were such programmes – and the countdown clock that preceded them to alert teachers to how long they had to settle their pupils – that they were parodied in a recent BBC TV comedy series, *Look Around You*.[1]

Both the BBC and Independent Television for Schools and Colleges started schools broadcasts in 1957. Early schools programmes set out to support the subject syllabuses, and many were not much more visually interesting than the blackboards they replaced. Grappling with science subjects, ITV's *Experiment* concentrated on science experiments being undertaken by anonymous hands, while the disembodied voice of producer Jack Smith explained what was going on. These, like the BBC's *Chemistry/Biology/Physics in Action*, were shot in the television studio, but Jack Smith also took the class out on location with his 16 mm camera, to experience at first hand the dangers living creatures faced in hostile environments like building sites, in *A Place to Live*, and in *Pond Life*. This was classic wildlife documentary footage, with an unashamed educational agenda. The aim was to bring to life those topics that too often seemed moribund on the page.

Educational programmes were not as well-funded as mainstream programming and, in those halcyon days before internal costing controls, the main constraints were actual cash costs, such as travel and accommodation on location, and film stock and processing. For this reason, most programmes were confined to the studio, and those that did occasionally escape its confines were severely limited in how far they could go and how much they could shoot. These programmes often stole the styles – and sometimes the presenters – of the more mainstream children's programmes. The BBC 1980s middle school *Science Workshop* was an unashamed copy of the long-running *Blue Peter* format – three contrasting characters in the studio introducing items, some of which would involve a degree of jeopardy filming in the real world. *Science Workshop*'s action man on film location was Malcolm MacFee, whose role was really something of a clown, as fondly remembered by the television history website TV Cream:

> Children settled down in front of the bouncing cartoon elephant titles safe in the knowledge that at some point Our Malcolm would be guaranteed to fall in a canal, get covered in paint, or have some other humiliation heaped on him. A simple enough bit of 'jazzing up', really, but when it comes to the notoriously 'difficult' subjects of maths and science, anything that'll keep a fidgety kid looking at the screen long enough to grasp the concept of areas and gravity is desirable to say the least. Perhaps that's why it's these subjects that have produced some of the oddest schools' programmes of all . . .[2]

TV Cream goes on to list various returning devices, such as the spaceman falling to Earth and so requiring concepts explained very simply (BBC's *Maths-in-a-Box*), the dumb detective needing his assistant to help unravel the clues (BBC's *Maths File*) and the astronaut unravelling mathematical conundra in space with the help of a robot (*Wondermaths*).[3] These all represent a move towards the imaginative landscape of drama, though no format or genre was theoretically beyond the Schools remit. Their job was to find ways of keeping the young minds engaged and, budgetary limitations aside, they were for a while enormously successful. As TV Cream notes:

> The 1970s and early 1980s were the heyday of ITV and BBC schools' television . . . By 1980 each channel was making around 50 series for schools and colleges a year. Eighty-four per cent of primary schools and 69 per cent of secondary schools were making use of daytime TV programmes in lessons.

They ranged from the long-running primary school favourite *Look and Read* (BBC 1967–2005) to the seminal 'Sixth Form' show *Scene* (BBC 1971–9), which mixed gritty dramas by leading playwrights with documentaries, both exploring themes close to the teenage experience. Well before the teen soaps of today, education was documenting young lives in recognisable and refreshing ways. A significant number of schools programmes were documentary – for example, ATV's *Starting Science* and Granada's geography show *A Place to Grow* – but a different kind of realism was beginning to encroach on the Schools patch.

In September 1983, BBC schools programmes were moved from BBC1 to BBC2, making way for daytime television, though that did not happen for another three years. For the same competitive reason, ITV moved their schools programmes over to Channel 4 in 1987. As the multichannel environment rapidly developed along with the internet, both departments began to feel the bite. BBC hours were squeezed ever shorter and eventually moved to the early hours of the morning, on the assumption that all schools had recording facilities and could make better use in scheduling programmes to suit themselves. From October 1997, the BBC dubbed this nocturnal transmission *The Learning Zone*, and used it to cover all its educational commitments. Channel 4 evolved a different strategy, gradually withdrawing from primary and curricular based programming, and concentrating on the social needs of teenagers, which its version of the BBC *Scene* programme – *Off Limits* – had served from the start. Channel 4's Director of Television Kevin Lygo's Statement of Policy for 2007 defines it thus:

> Our strategy in schools programmes is to focus on 14–19-year-olds. We will continue to work with the DfES, education experts and teachers to define our key areas, to ensure they have the greatest relevance to the curriculum.
>
> Programmes in 2007 will focus on media literacy, careers advice and gay teen sexuality, with additional series on globalisation, science, philosophy – and also on parents. We will also extend our distribution on different platforms; in particular, Channel 4's Education programmes will increasingly be available through our new video-on demand service, to make them as accessible as possible. We will also continue to provide CD Roms, Broadband and online services for schools and colleges, and digitised clips for teachers will be available through Clip Bank, the service for secondary and FE teachers. Channel 4's Education schedule in the morning will continue to be supported by programme notes, available free online at www.channel4.com/learning.[4]

The cynic might see in this focus the careful building of a brand loyalty among the notoriously intractable young, just as they are about to enter the age demographic most prized by advertisers and seen as Channel 4's core audience. *Greg Dyke's Get Me the Producer, Let's Talk Sex with Davina McCall* and *My Big Gay Prom* all played to the well-established Channel 4 reputation for provocative celebrity and sex talk.

Initially less controversial was the slow secession of schools airtime. Migration onto the net was the inevitable move for education, as its bandwidth rapidly expanded to allow transmission of more video material. Channel 4 announced the diversion of its entire education budget to internet output in December 2007. Out would go those typical Channel 4 shows and in with the New Year would come multimedia plans such as *City of Vice* – an online game based on a new prime-time drama series exploring Georgian London; *Insiders* – a new spin on traditional careers advice, with a network of blogs based on real-life contributors; and *4Pioneers* – a social networking service for teenagers who have considered starting their own business. The only show to survive the platform jump is an observational documentary series following 21 teenagers over the course of a year. Participants will try to gather support from around the internet to achieve their goals, through social networking and video sharing services. One teenager attempts to regain custody of her child, while another sets out to win the Eurovision Song Contest. Documentary is seen as one form that not only survives the change from TV to web, but can gain from its interactive possibilities.

The BBC's first major move online was *Bitesize*, a multimedia curriculum revision service for school students, which launched as early as 1998, with predigested revision materials online, supported by books and tapes. Some five years before the rollout of broadband, this put the BBC ahead of the game and was duly successful as students seized on the list of things they needed to know to pass exams. Building on this success, the BBC took the decision to re-brand its Schools programmes online as BBC Jam, which it had licensed in 2003 and launched on trial in January 2006. Something in the region of £150 million was committed to the service, £60 million for the technology, of which about half went to Microsoft, who had won a competitive tender to develop a new content management system that allowed children to keep a record of the learning modules they completed on the site. The platform was also built to be secure so that children could not be tracked when online. Frank Flynn, then BBC Head of Education, felt that the key development was the way in which Jam was pupil-centred:

> The BBC has always created mediated resources targeted for teachers to use in classrooms. But with the advent of [the internet] we saw the potential for an online service that would create a direct dialogue with learners while supporting the school's curriculum. So the idea was that we would create a service that would form a bridge between home and school. It would support the curriculum and enrich it. But it would be targeted directly at learners.[5]

One of the specialist production companies in the new world of multimedia education production is Illumina Digital Ltd, who had a big contract to develop a multimedia project around the new school subject of citizenship for BBC Jam. Their Director of Education and Broadband, Mike Flood Page, sees the new multimedia approach as a fundamental change in the nature and focus of educational media:

> The old broadcast model was: We make great stuff and we send it to you. Be grateful. The new model is: What would you like? When would you like it? Where would you like it? How would you like it? The teacher and the learner are in the driving seat, not the broadcaster . . . At the core of everything we do is research . . . It is true that we are using the insights of marketing, focus groups, etc., for trying out ideas. We also do user testing, which is rather more forensic . . . You don't just ask them: Would you like this? You observe what they do when faced with the resource. If what we do doesn't work for them, it's dead in the water . . . Television has got more like this because, when you have one or two channels, you could do what you like, but when you have 500 channels, each fighting for a niche, they have to be very targeted on their audiences.[6]

Illumina's *Be in the Mix* online world for BBC Jam, with narrative elements, video, activities all designed around citizenship, was developed with the help of 21 focus groups across the whole of the UK. It cost £850,000 but, like the rest of the alleged £80 million spent on BBC Jam programming, it will not be seen. As the BBC became more market-oriented in this way, it enraged the commercial educational publishers and resource providers, who argued that they were being undercut by unfair commercial competition from the cash-rich public broadcaster. They took their argument to the EU Commission in Brussels and, for the first time in such an attempt to invoke states rights legislation against the BBC, won. The new BBC Trust ordered the immediate suspension of BBC Jam in March 2007, depriving schools of the service they had been offered, not to mention suppliers and 200 people of their jobs. Chitra Bharucha, then Acting BBC Chairman, said:

> Promoting education and learning is one of the BBC's six Public Purposes and a core part of the Corporation's public service remit. A decision on how the BBC delivers this purpose must, under the terms of the Charter, be based on the interests of the public after considering the effect on the market.[7]

Emboldened by this victory, the complainants are now reported to be setting their sights on *Bitesize* and other would-be profitable sectors of the BBC's service. In a triumph for the privateering spirit of Mrs Thatcher, who recognised no value without profit, public interest in this arena is now deemed subservient to market forces. So others' commercial imperatives supersede the needs of the young. Of course, cash-strapped schools would prefer to acquire their educational support materials for free, especially from so reliable a source as the BBC, but the idea that the BBC must withdraw from the field so as not to damage the profiteering of others seems a sad retreat from the Reithian heights. It only goes to show how politically charged the field of educational broadcasting is.

Knowledge is power

Since the early days of the trade union movement, a compelling slogan had been 'Knowledge is Power'. The motto of the *Lancashire and Yorkshire Co-Operator* spelt it out in the 1830s:

> Numbers without Union are Powerless
> And Union without Knowledge is Useless[8]

So, after long hours on the factory floor, working people took themselves off to Mutual Improvement Societies to acquire the knowledge that would in due course enable them to better their lot. In 1899, the trade union movement set up Ruskin College in the heart of Oxford, to offer degree-level education to workers without the formal qualifications for a university place, and it has transformed lives and opportunities ever since, including those of the former Deputy Prime Minister, John Prescott.

Prescott was also one of the belated beneficiaries of the education revolution initiated by the Wilson Labour government of 1964, which identified adult education as a critical component in the 'white heat of technological advance' that they saw themselves spear-heading. There was some jockeying for position between government departments and the BBC over the direction of adult education delivery, but the BBC seemed to have won the day when Don Grattan was made Editor of Further Education Television in October 1964, charged with making 'five liberal adult education programmes a week'.[9] Within a few years,

Further Education evolved into a sizeable department making many hours of television a week over a range of subjects from politics and moral philosophy to history and psychology.

Languages formed one of the cornerstones of the department, as a growing number of people were taking foreign holidays and fancied learning a bit of French or Spanish. These were mildly entertaining shows, mostly shot on location with a Pierre or a Pedro engaged in arch 'real life' linguistic encounters that enabled would-be tourists to know how to order a loaf or a lunch in the local tongue. BBC Publications did a brisk business in the accompanying workbooks and language tapes, which enabled people to practise in the peace of their own home, or in their cars on the way to work. Although the central programmes were documentaries, these were multimedia propositions before the term had been coined.

History programmes were also popular, and tended to come from a more populist perspective than the A.J.P. Taylor lectures. *Milestones in Working Class History*[10] (1975) and *The Past at Work*[11] (1980) pretty much capture the flavour. *Milestones* tracked trade union history from the Luddites to the 'Red Clydeside' shipyard workers of the day. It took an explicitly socialist approach to the values of organised labour at a time when mainstream treatment of these subjects with such sympathy attracted widespread odium, as did Ken Loach's *Days of Hope* mentioned in Chapter 15. Further Education, consigned to less prominent transmission times at the end of the evening, did not need to satisfy the same political sensitivities. It even managed a latter-day version of those Mutual Improvement Societies in the series *Trade Union Studies*.

This series appealed directly to trade unionists wanting to learn about better means of industrial bargaining and organisation, but many such FE series fitted within the wider definition of 'social action broadcasting'. This meant that programmes were intended to stimulate some form of social action in their audiences, from taking further classes to volunteering, but also implied an activist agenda on the part of their producers. Some attended meetings of the social action broadcasting network with fellow broadcasters and like-minded academics, to discuss how better to effect social change through broadcasting. This level of commitment would be seen as diversionary today, if not downright dangerous. But the objectives were not all political, and few interpretable as party-political. The animating spirit of the producers and directors working in the department, which changed its name to Continuing Education in 1978, was a desire to find novel ways of sharing enthusiasms across every conceivable field, much of it achieved by documentaries shot with people already enthused by the subject.

Some quite happily espoused government policy objectives, such as the major adult literacy campaign *On the Move*[12] – which showed inspirational stories of people empowered by learning to read and write – and the attempt to persuade Asian housewives to take courses in English as a Second Language, *Parosi*[13] – which used Hindustani soap opera to build an audience, but also featured success stories from the communities. Others merely aimed to address a shortfall in home crafts and, in so doing, made stars of their presenters. *Delia Smith's Cookery Course*[14] ran from 1978 to 1980 and made its unassuming Catholic presenter the best-known cook of her generation – long before the later rash of celebrity chefs. The American Kaffe Fossett brought a whole new dimension to knitting and got himself elected the 'UK's King of Colour and Design'. And the academic botanist David Bellamy delighted and entranced audiences with his cheeky wit and cheery speech impediment, making him Britain's favourite environmentalist, at least until he became embroiled with corporate advocacy and global warming denial.[15]

Arguably the most important and influential FE show was made relatively early in the department's history. John Berger's *Ways of Seeing* (1972)[16] radicalised art history and promoted cultural studies with its original screen essays on aesthetics and perception. Berger's original take on the uses and abuses of publicity, reproduction and images of women was intensely political and seemed a world away from the more conventional ways of seeing invoked in Kenneth Clark's *Civilisation* just three years before. Berger's aim was to educate the public in the awareness that everyday imagery had been subverted to manipulate the masses in much the same way as Marx had identified religion as 'the opium of the masses':

> Publicity exerts an enormous influence and is a political phenomenon of great importance. But its offer is as narrow as its references are wide. It recognises nothing except the power to acquire. All other human faculties or needs are made subsidiary to this power. All hopes are gathered together, made homogenous, simplified, so that they become the intense yet vague, magical yet repeatable promise offered in every purchase. No other kind of hope or satisfaction or pleasure can any longer be envisaged within the culture of capitalism.[17]

Berger went on to win that year's Booker Prize for his novel *G*, and scandalised literary London by dedicating half the prize money to the Black Panthers, the British branch of a radical black organisation. Not all FE programmes aspired to these iconoclastic heights, but the freedom to think outside the envelope was a given of this work, and a freedom no longer apparent in contemporary television.

Figure 8.1
Front cover of *Ways of Seeing*
by John Berger

Open University

Television opened the possibility of making the life changing opportunity afforded the few at Ruskin College available to many. Since the beginning of broadcasting, the idea of a 'university of the air' had been a socialist dream but, under Harold Wilson's Labour premiership, it became a reality. Wilson rated the creation of the Open University the most important achievement of his political life. Stewarded into existence by his Minister of Arts, Jenny Lee, the Open University started teaching its first students in 1971, using mail correspondence, radio and television teaching to communicate with its far-flung, mostly working students. Its night-time transmissions on BBC2 were noted for long-haired, bearded professors squinting into cameras before turning to chalkboards that gave television comedy a rich vein for parody. But the dedicated BBC production department that existed at the Milton Keynes university campus for a quarter of a century did a lot more than that. At their best, they married cutting edge academic expertise to television techniques in a way which enriched television's documentary language. And not just to the University's current 180,000 students benefit.

The much-mocked OU lectures ceased broadcast on television on 16 December 2006. For some time they had been concentrating on DVD and internet delivery for course support. But, in the meantime, the OU had moved to take over the role of the now defunct FE department, investing its resources and expertise in mainstream programming that had incremental value to its viewership. One of the first of this new crop of crossover programmes was *Rough Science*, which dumped a team of scientists in a remote environment and challenged them to make things work from naturally available resources. The ingenuity these intrepid explorers showed in devising everything from insect repellent and toothpaste from natural sources to a low-tech camera and radio made from things like old saucepans kept an audience sufficiently entranced for the show to run for six series.[18] The combination of intelligent enterprise, based on practical scientific knowledge, and a well-documented sense of *esprit de corps* made a format that was a thinking person's reality TV show – a sort of *I'm A Scientist, Get Me Out of Here!*.

The same sense of adventure has enlivened other Open University co-productions, such as *Renaissance Secrets*[19] and *Coast*.[20] *Renaissance Secrets* took a detective genre approach to history, for instance questioning Johannes Gutenberg's posthumous claim to be the inventor of the printing press and reconvicting Roderigo Lopez, who was hung, drawn and quartered in 1594 for trying to poison Queen Elizabeth I. *Coast* offers a voyage around the coastline of Britain, exploring the intersections between human geography and history, between marine life and geology, and making those inter-disciplinary connections that film can do so well. It was one of the first products of a new system of programme development at the BBC, which itself took a forensic approach to understanding its audience's attitudes and needs. This led to the multi-disciplinary, many-presentered aspect that had formally been thought too confusing. This in turn prompted the rich online site that developed the various different specialist interests stimulated, from history and geography to marine and environmental sciences. While not everybody would sign up for an OU degree as a result – though undoubtedly some did – there was a range of possible levels of engagement that made use of the interactive possibilities new media now offer, from an online eco-quiz to sight specific information. The series was so successful it was recommissioned several times.

Global education

What unites all these educational programme productions is the desire to enrich the experience of their audiences, whether tiny tots or tottering elderly, and ideally stimulate further thought and activity. The threat to the broadcaster is that this may entail the loss of the newly stimulated audience, at cost to their figures. There once was a show called something like *Why Don't You Turn Off the Box and Go Do Something Else?* In an increasingly competitive world, no such hostages to fortune are likely to emerge. While in Britain, educational objectives have been quietly marginalised, the conflict between educational broadcasting and commerce was played out more graphically in the United States.

National Educational Television was a network that existed in the USA from 1952 to 1970. Initially the distributors of educational shows between local radio and television stations, it slowly grew into the makers of a five-hour daily package of hour-long interviews with leading artists and historians, noted for its dry, academic approach that earned it the nickname 'The University of the Air'. When it moved to New York in 1958, subsequently spinning off its radio operation and adopting a 'NET' brand that jockeyed for position as 'the fourth network', conflict with the existing three networks and the powerful economic interests they represented was inevitable. Their flagship programme *NET Journal* made and broadcast hard-hitting documentaries about the key issues of the day, such as poverty and racism, which aggravated some affiliate stations, both because they did not play well with their business funders and advertisers, and because they resented the growing power of NET as both producer and broadcaster. The Ford Foundation was persuaded to reduce their funding of NET in 1966 and, although the government stepped in to support it through creating a Corporation for Public Broadcasting in 1967, this was eventually to supplant NET with the Public Broadcasting System in 1970. NET merged with the Newark station WNDT-TV and *NET Journal* struggled on as PBS for a couple of years, but its teeth had been drawn and PBS continues as more of a creature of its affiliates.

The NET acronym briefly re-emerged in the 1990s as National Empowerment Television, with a right-wing bias reflecting the tenor of the times, the liberal 'education' replaced with the libertarian 'empowerment'. PBS' current schedules are an equally accurate reflection of contemporary American views. History is framed under the *American Experience* rubric, featuring such titles as *American Experience: D-Day* or *The Perilous Fight: America's WWII in Color*, taking the Americo-centric viewpoint best characterised by their naming a domestic baseball series 'The World Series'. The 25-year-old *Nature* programme does feature wildlife from all over the world, and the 35-year-old drama showcase *Masterpiece Theatre* is largely dependent upon British television drama, from *The First Churchills* and *I, Claudius* to *Prime Suspect* and *Bleak House*. Such quality brands are cherished much longer in the United States than in the UK, where series come and go in ever shorter runs.

What Britain calls current affairs, the Americans call public affairs, and arguably the most important programme on PBS is the public affairs documentary strand *Frontline*. When it started in 1983, the days of Ed Murrow and *See It Now* were long gone and it fell to WGBH to pick up the baton and reinvest in the investigative and challenging tradition. They do a lot on controversial subjects from abortion and the American criminal justice system to the war on terror and extraordinary rendition, and have been called by *Newsday* 'television's last fully serious bastion of journalism'. They claim to do more hours of serious investigations than the three commercial networks together, but, though award-garlanded, it is a difficult task to maintain in the face of critiques of 'liberalism' from a neoconservative America. More of their work is now done online, as we found in Chapter 2. As a balance, PBS' long-running news flagship, the *News Hour with Jim Lehrer*, is heavily corporately funded and notably more establishment-friendly. But funding for the PBS network remains under a permanent threat.

Education remains a key feature of the PBS network, both in its attempt to broaden the knowledge and imagination of the American public, and in its commitment to the school system. Like its British counterparts, it makes a number of programmes and teacher support materials across the age range from Kindergarten to Grade 12, now available online as well as on air. Many surveys have endorsed the value of this resource. A national teacher training institute report in 2002 found that:

> Eighty-six per cent [of participants] reported that their students are more engaged when electronic media are used in the classroom, 81 per cent reported that their students learn more, and 75 per cent reported that students retain more information.[21]

A Centre for Public Broadcasting report in 2004 went further. *Television Goes to School: The Impact of Video on Student Learning in Formal Education* reviewed all the literature and found widespread support for the maintenance of this kind of educational broadcasting. It reported:

> Shephard (2003)[22] predicts that streaming video technology may soon afford teachers the opportunity to download clips to their computers where they can then be used in conjunction with other learning technologies to form a comprehensive educational experience. Minkel (2003) suggests that DVD is more likely in the short run to have a significant impact on the classroom, while noting the challenge school librarians face in accommodating yet another format change in their media purchasing plans.
>
> A new control-group study by Cometrika however may drive faster adoption of streaming technology (Reed 2003).[23] The report, which was industry-funded and therefore invested in a favorable outcome, cites dramatic learning gains from the use of on-demand standards-based video clips, based on findings involving over 1,400 students in three Virginia school districts (Boser 2003).[24] Third- and eighth-grade students using the video clips showed improvements of 12.6 per cent greater than students in the control group in the two studied content areas of science and social studies.
>
> As the long history of research clearly shows, the educational value of visual media is positive and significant. While the format, delivery channels, and storage options may change, video is now and will continue to be an effective, engaging, and essential tool in our nation's classrooms.[25]

The use of video to bring enlightenment and education to the world has been around since the British brought film shows to remote Indian villages in the days of empire. Satellite television now penetrates every corner of the globe, offering not just the opportunity to educate people but to subvert them, as Berger warned, to capitalist ways of seeing. But where educational television works best seems to be in societies that are already tele-literate, but educationally deprived. Two successful experiments in Latin America serve to illustrate the point, in the two countries most addicted to the soap opera called the 'tele-novella'. Telesecundaria is an initiative started in 1968 by the Mexican Ministry of Education to supplement the shortage of secondary school teachers in rural areas. It is aimed at schools, broadcast during school hours, and is still posited on classroom take-up with a live teacher present, who teaches after the programmes. It is so successful that not only are a million students dependent upon this input to their education, but complementary programmes have now been started throughout central America, in Honduras, Panama, El Salvador, Costa Rica and Guatemala.

In Brazil, the giant Globo television network started a Telecurso distance learning project for schools in the 1970s, which led in the 1990s to the Telecurso 2000 project. This offers a comprehensive set of television education to the army of Brazilian workers who, for one reason or another, failed to complete their education. So this is a form of remedial education for adults, which covers the entire secondary school syllabus, from Portuguese to science. The programmes are broadcast from six in the morning, but the key feature is that many factories and other workplaces make arrangements for their workers to take time out for classes during the day. One reason for the project's success is that the education is all based around life skills and delivered in dramatic form, employing actors in recognisable real-life environments: home, work, hospital, etc., but this also contributes to high production costs. Those costs are currently born by the Globo network, only partially offset by the sale of course books and videos, but the numbers of participants are now numbered in their millions.

Education today

While educational television affords developmental fuel to a hungry audience around the world, in Britain, as we have seen, it is migrating to different platforms in an increasingly fragmented digital universe. This does not mean it is in decline, far from it. In 2005, the UK government launched a whole education service on digital television and online called Teachers' TV. Costing the Department for Education and Skills £20 million a year, but granted full editorial independence, this channel not only makes programmes for teachers, heads and school governors, and support materials for key stage curricular needs, but debates and documentaries around the key issues of the day. One documentary strand – *What's Going On?* – sees the world and its problems through the eyes of children in the front line. *Indigenous Children in Australia*, *Child Refugees in Tanzania*, *Street Children in Mongolia* and *Child Soldiers in Sierra Leone* are just some of its many pertinent titles. *What in the World?* is another series of documentary human stories from countries such as Malawi, Ecuador, Guatemala and India. *Ingenious Africa* is a series that 'highlights the strengths of African innovation', attempting to subvert the frequently negative images of Africa by celebrating its ingenuity in everything from agriculture to astronomy, engineering to sustainable development models. An African project manager, Melanie Naidoo, sets the tone:

> Africa is the place that you will find some of the solutions for the globe, because conditions in some of our African countries are so dire. The solutions are equally exciting for me, the solutions that are generated here need to be shared universe-wide. I believe the perseverance of our people will lead to a total transformation for Africa and it will inspire the rest of the world.[26]

Other documentaries take on the hard subjects mainstream channels are increasingly shy of: the brutalities of war, gang warfare, refugees and asylum, and the veil in Saudi Arabia.

With some 2,500 programmes freely available to download from the internet, Teachers' TV is a valuable resource keeping the internationalist, liberal conscience of education alive and well replenished with original material. It is a significant user of documentary techniques and sensibilities. But it is also part of the wider renaissance of educational programme-making at the forefront of the multimedia universe.

Since 1997, the Royal Television Society has run a separate Educational Awards ceremony, celebrating a rich panoply of categories from specialist pre-school and primary programmes to educational impact in mainstream television and multimedia awards. In the first year, it was largely a head-to-head between BBC Education and Channel 4 Schools, with largely predictably worthy programmes winning. Perhaps the most prescient was that year's Multimedia award, which saw off the then conventional CD-Roms also nominated:

> In January, viewers of BBC2's *The Net* were invited to get online after the programme ended and take part in a project called 'The Mirror'. This was an exercise in 'shared spaces' – whereby a large group of people can come together to create a community based on mutual interests in a virtual (shared) environment. It was also a major piece of research between BT, the BBC, Illuminations (the production company behind *The Net*) and Sony for the future hybrid of TV and online communications . . . More than 600 successful registrations were logged within an hour of the programme finishing, and over the project's 7 weeks, 2,250 people from as far afield as South Africa and Australia joined 'The Mirror'.[27]

In a world of millions networking through Facebook and interacting in the virtual world of Second Life, this may seem like small beer but, at the time, it was breakthrough stuff that helped put the BBC and educational television in the driving seat of multimedia development. Ten years on, the BBC was still in that driving seat, securing all four nominations for the multimedia award and the winner being what has been heralded as 'the world's first broadband interactive film'.[28] Based on the HBO costume drama series *Rome*, *CDX* was a mystery video game built around a notional BBC drama executive who goes out to the Cinecitta film studios in Rome, using documentary footage especially shot in Rome. The RTS Jury said:

> This is a beautifully designed and delivered piece of educational material, which effectively blurs the line between learning and entertainment, making a truly compelling experience. The combination of video, gameplay and links to programme resources demonstrates an extremely high level of integration between content and format.[29]

The 2006 primary school interactive award was won by one of the commercial education companies who had just successfully scuppered the BBC Jam project, Espresso Education.

Conclusion

What all this reflects is not just the possibilities of the evolving technology, but the fundamental shift in education practice and learner perception. Schools no longer wanted long form narrative programmes that wrapped everything up, nor had the time to accommodate those slabs in their lessons, so uptake was fast declining. Students brought up in a channel-hopping environment, with the dexterity of gaming and the associative elisions of the internet, were bored with the linear, passive paradigm. What these new multimedia approaches do is offer a media-rich experience which puts the learner, as Mike Flood Page says, 'in the driving seat'. As opposed to offering the definitive take on a subject in a virtual lecture, however well filmed, they develop ideas with what they call 'user case scenarios':

> We'll go and say: 'Who are the audiences you are trying to reach with this? What do they want?' We will then go and research them and we will come up with something. It is not rocket science. If this is your proposition and this is your audience: What is it they want? What is their daily life style? How are they going to use this? And we work from there. That underlying approach works through all the resources we develop.[30]

And Flood Page's company, Illumina Digital, do not just make educational programmes. Their approach to development is increasingly common throughout television, inverting the traditional approach whereby programme-makers decide what to offer the public. In an attempt to retain audiences, the audiences get to help define what they want. Where once a subject of public importance would have been identified and a documentary commissioned, now the research is commissioned to identify the importance and then the approach that will sustain it. Old forms and approaches are merely some of the options on offer. As Flood Page says, 'Video has a crucial part in a lot of it, but it's not what you'd call documentary any more'. He cites one project, *Breaking the News*, as a good example, which employs documentary techniques and sensibilities – and a whole lot more:

> Channel 4 came to us and said: Let's have kids make the News. What you have on that site[31] is a very good example of a cross-platform project. You have a straightforward course that tells you how to broadcast news, for 14–19-year-olds, across the board. You have a 'behind the scenes' look at Channel 4 News, a whole day you can inter-rogate, from before the morning News conference to the debrief after the evening show's gone out, with four strands. You follow the News Editor, who's obviously critical; you follow the presenter, Jon Snow; you follow a producer-reporter making a package; and you follow the people making the News belt. You see the editorial process in close-up, and there are some master classes as well. But the third thing is: there are some tools there. There's an online video editor. ITN has provided some rushes and you can edit your own material . . . You've got great content, great learning resources and the capacity to generate your own content . . . That's a total education resource of a new kind with good video in there.[32]

As a part of the project, ten schools submitted young journalists who spent a day at ITN making and presenting their own news programme, which was transmitted along with the documentary that charted their experience.[33] So linear programming and documentary have not disappeared, but just become part of a wider, richer mix; and the internet ensures that programmes and projects have a longer shelf-life, Teachers' TV being a good example. On their website,[34] as seen at the RTS Educational Television Awards, are many fine examples of the documentary form, consistent with the form's established traditions, but all with the focus on getting a message across. The next chapters concentrate on particular uses of such focus.

Figure 8.2
Channel 4's *Breaking the News* got kids making the news

Expert briefing – multimedia project management

Although those who have grown up familiar with multimedia platforms and interactivity do not find multi-platform approaches alien, they do require more sophisticated planning and management processes than conventional documentary. The BBC breaks the process into five stages: Planning, Design, Production, Validation and Maintenance, which I have adapted here to laying out the basic process. This, and the software programmes available, tend to change rapidly:

A. PLANNING

1 **Shared skills**: Television is essentially teamwork. Even the lonely video-journalist needs someone to buy his work and technicians to distribute it, but most projects are much more collaborative – and multimedia work has elevated these synergies to a new high. There are three core skills areas involved, which may mean as few as three people, or three teams:

(i) *Editorial and content*: These are the more conventional programme-making skills of conception, writing and shooting, which would normally deliver the finished product, but now only becomes one prong of the trident. This includes the newly expanded role of the (creative) director/project manager, who has to interpret the brief and manage the team, as well as liaise with the client, although the business side may well have been taken care of by an executive producer.

(ii) *Design*: Much under-used in factual television, maybe only thought of for graphics, here design becomes a key player in conceiving the look of the multifaceted project and the experience it offers. This will probably incorporate animation, modelling, photographic and art direction roles.

(iii) *Technical*: Again banished to the back room in television, here taking a lead role in the functionality of the project, particularly in its interactive elements and delivering the tools to enhance the experience. Not only does this include the key role of programmer, but also network manager, ensuring the hosting, support and interactive services work.

2 **Team building**: Ideally, all three skills areas are represented on project teams from inception, so as to extend the possibilities, but in realisable terms. Each should know what is feasible in their area, within the constraints of time and budget available, so that development of ideas remains focused on the practicable. The ergonomics are arguably even more vital than the open-plan offices of conventional television production, allowing creative collaboration across sophisticated technological platforms. Modes of work and forms of communication are necessarily less hierarchical – see Silicon Valley and the triumph of the techno-garagistes – as the work culture helps define the creative parameters.

3 **Costs and constraints**: Just as television commissions are driven by the tariff available for the slot, the money justifiable for any given programme output, multimedia projects have to work within cost parameters. One rule of thumb for computer-based training materials is a development ratio of 100:1, i.e. 100 man hours' development for each computer-based hour of user experience,[35] but complex demands can easily compound that and the limits of 'blue sky thinking' trial and error have to be agreed. Project briefs, resource limits, product licences and progress reports need to be meticulously documented if teams and clients are to continue in harmony. It takes time to get things right, and even more time to get them simple. Creatives have to learn to compromise.

B. DESIGN

4 **End user and market research**: The key determinant is the project brief: not so much the subject, but the object. Who is this to serve, to what end? This requires a 'user needs analysis'. Programme-makers used to doing things in their own 'auteurist' way find this the hardest paradigm shift. The most valuable experience for them is to get involved in the market research themselves. Having been set a goal, the first stage is to get to know their target audience. The conventional marketing tool of focus groups, carefully selected to represent the demographic cross-section of desired audience, give first-hand knowledge of tastes, desires, knowledge base and skills. Such groups need to continue to play a part in development if the product is to be user-friendly.

5 **User dynamics**: End-use modelling builds up a profile of the audience's character, behaviour and likely usage. Brainstorming among team members uses research knowledge to identify approaches that should meet that user's needs and interests. These can be defined by linear features – narrative arcs, learning progressions, targeted outcomes – and by lateral elements – interactive tools, parallel information paths, knowledge reinforcement – all designed to give a constructive, active learning model, as opposed to the passive paths of old. They can be expressed in flowcharts that can fill whole walls of the production office, or interactive storyboards, for which there are software packages.

6 **Component design**: This is the stage at which content is refined and defined, and secondary sources (such as pictures, text and music) are researched, copyright is cleared and acquired. Not only should the pictorial and graphic representation, the script and interactive features be designed to cohere practically and aesthetically, but the conversion rates, file storage and delivery platforms all need managing to ensure seamless delivery.

C. PRODUCTION

7 **Prototyping and road testing**: Having planned the overall reach of the project and how its elements will interact, the team then sets out to build the parts. However well conceived, the key test is when those parts are brought together, as a prototype, with strains emerging at the points of intersection. These issues require flexibility and mutual understanding of the difficulties encountered by other team members in fulfilling their contributions. Once there is a working model, this is the time to road-test it, before all the budget has been spent on final passes on the film material, graphics, etc. User testing has to be sufficiently rigorous to test every aspect of the user journey, how it meets or conflicts with their expectations, how easily and successfully they manipulate the elements, how they rate the experience and outcome. It is important that this stage is forensically observational, not overridden by maker interrogation.

8 **Revision, integration and mastering**: Revision is the application of the information gleaned from testing and internal trialling, ironing out faults and fine-tuning the project. The more data acquired at this stage, the greater the chance of the project's successful uptake. It requires considerable humility in creative teams to accept criticism and the loss of cherished elements to the greater good of the team effort and ultimate goal, and this in turn necessitates good team management. Integration ties the elements or 'assets' together in that final form, which is then mastered.

D. VALIDATION

9 **Market test**: With the mastering done and the final embellishments made, the project is ready to air but, unlike television, this is time for final test runs because this is a product that will hopefully have an infinite life, rather than a brief moment of broadcast glory. These final tests should prove to both makers and the project's commissioners that it meets the brief and will last the course.

Formal trialling essentially involves environmental testing, working how well the programme works in actual real user environments, observing the user's own interaction with the material as well as the delivery efficacy, bandwidth performance, etc.

E. MAINTENANCE

10 **Constant monitoring**: Once up and running, the smart multimedia producer not only monitors the uptake data – page impressions and video downloads – but also keeps a qualitative evaluation running, which input data will be used to enrich team skills and future projects. Unlike the television programme, rarely viewed more than once, the multimedia project is a transparent machine inviting competitors to take it apart and improve upon the model. Informed self-criticism is the best chance the producer has to remain ahead of the game and, unlike conventional TV production, it is written into the culture of this work. As one BBC multimedia producer says: 'It either helps further development of the product or it breaks it'.

9 Propaganda

....

propaganda n. the organized dissemination of information, allegations, etc. to assist or damage the cause of a government, movement, etc.

The internet has been welcomed as the ultimate releaser of information and enabler of free speech but governments have moved as best they can to regulate the flow and exclude what they deem unacceptable, whether it is child pornography in the West or political dissidence in the East. Media mogul Rupert Murdoch has said that 'all forms of government ultimately are not going to succeed in trying to control or censor the Internet', but many are making a significant attempt so to do. China, with the fastest-growing media industry in the world, employs over 30,000 people to police the net and eradicate any mention of forbidden subjects such as Taiwanese independence, the Dalai Lama's campaign to free Tibet or the 1989 student massacre in Tiananmen Square. President Clinton famously once said that trying to control the net was 'like nailing Jello to the wall'. The Open Net Initiative, based at the Harvard Law School, produced a comprehensive survey of China's mastery of the art of Jello-nailing in *Internet Filtering in China in 2004–2005: A Country Study*:

> China's Internet filtering regime is the most sophisticated effort of its kind in the world. Compared to similar efforts in other states, China's filtering regime is pervasive, sophisticated, and effective. It comprises multiple levels of legal regulation and technical control. It involves numerous state agencies and thousands of public and private personnel. It censors content transmitted through multiple methods, including Web pages, Web logs, online discussion forums, university bulletin board systems, and email messages.[1]

Western media companies such as Google and Skype have been routinely condemned for going along with these restrictions to secure a foothold in this lucrative market, but the pragmatism of capitalism argues that if they don't, someone else will, and their prime obligation is to their shareholders. In December 2005, Microsoft shut down a Chinese blogger's site at the Chinese government's request. More seriously, Yahoo! handed over email records of Chinese journalists to the authorities that resulted in Wang Xiaoning and Shi Tao now serving ten-year prison sentences for 'incitement to subvert state power'. The World Organisation for Human Rights USA took the company to court in Washington in 2007 and a Congressional hearing roundly condemned the company, with Tom Lantos, chairman of the congressional foreign affairs committee saying to Yahoo!: 'While technologically and financially you are giants, morally you are pygmies'.[2] The journalists had emailed electronic journals advocating democratic reform and establishment of a multi-party system to replace the present authoritarian state. Yahoo! claimed that they had no alternative to compliance in handing over the information, and admitted no fault, but did apologise to the journalists' families and agree to pay their court costs and an undisclosed settlement.

Western commentators have sarcastically dubbed China's efforts 'The Great Firewall of China' but, as Nicholas Bequelin of Human Rights Watch in Hong Kong says, 'China would not have succeeded in censoring the Net without the support and co-operation of foreign IT companies'.[3] This critique is a continuation of the argument that surrounded Rupert Murdoch's decision to exclude the BBC from his Star TV satellite service in 1993, as a result of Chinese displeasure over an unsympathetic BBC documentary on Mao Zedong. For all its subsequent economic liberalisation and booming trade with the West, China is determined to suppress the emergence of a critically free media. The internet has become the new battleground and censorship the primary weapon, but that is merely the negative side of propaganda, the propaganda of omission rather than commission.

If governments cannot control what is said, they move to suppress anything they don't like being said. With the declaration of emergency in Pakistan on 3 November 2007, as President Musharraf desperately tried to hold on to power with an imminent election, the four independent news broadcasters were closed down and several journalists imprisoned. Two companies, Geo TV and the ARY network, continued broadcasting by satellite from Dubai, so Pakistan banned the import of satellite dishes and pressurised the United Arab Emirates to close the stations down, which the UAE duly did on 16 November. The UAE, despite having a much higher GDP, life expectancy and standard of living than Pakistan, shares its propensity for controlling its people. The Open Net Initiative records: 'Controls on Internet content in the UAE, actualized through filtering and other forms of enforcement, are geared toward safeguarding political, moral, and religious values'.[4] Under a new ordinance, Pakistani television journalists also face up to three years in jail for broadcasting 'anything which defames or brings into ridicule the head of state'. As Niccolò Machiavelli observed in *Il Principe* (The Prince) a mere 500 years ago, a successful ruler has to control his image:

> One prince of the present time, whom it is not well to name, never preaches anything else but peace and good faith, and to both he is most hostile, and either, if he had kept it, would have deprived him of reputation and kingdom many a time.[5]

Revolutionary use of film

Controlling the mind of the people is one, if not the principal, aim of any government, for from it is derived the power to do anything they may wish. One of the earliest, most sophisticated and most successful users of film for propaganda purposes was the Soviet Union. From the October 1917 Revolution onwards, Lenin and the *politburo* recognised the cinema as the most effective means of engaging the vast and disparate people to engage in common goals and thought. The Editor of *Kino-nedeyia/Cinema-week* was Dziga Vertov, whose newsreels and written manifestos came to embody the transformative potential of film. He borrowed Marx's denigration of religion as 'the opium of the people' and applied it to what fiction film had become. The series of monthly newsreels he produced he called *Kino-*

pravda/Cinema Truth (1922–5). He called his approach to filmmaking *Kino-Eye* and his followers *kinoki*: their role was to elevate the film form from entertainment to a key element of popular political analysis:

I am cinema-eye – I am mechanical eye. I show you a world such as only I can see . . . Freed from the tyranny of 16–17 images per second, freed from the framework of space and time, I co-ordinate any and all points of the universe, wherever I may record them. My mission is a new perception of the world. Thus I decipher in a new way a world unknown to you.[6]

Revered to this day as a great pioneer, Vertov was too original and troublesome to be an effective long-term propagandist and was not patronised by Stalin but, in part thanks to Vertov, Soviet cinema produced two important genres of propagandist film, the historic and the epic. The first was the revisionist history, which reached an early apogee in the work of Esfir Shub (1894–1959), a former film editor who stumbled across the home movies of Tsar Nicholas II, which became the basis for her epic documentary, *Padeniye dinastij Romanovykh/The Fall of the Romanov Dynasty* (1927). She went on to make a sequel covering the years 1917 to 1927: *Velikij put/The Great Road* (1927) and then a prequel covering 1896 to 1912: *Rossiya Nikolaya II i Lev Tolstoy/The Russia of Nicholas II and Leo Tolstoy* (1928). In this trilogy, Shub emerges as a sophisticated and effective propagandist. While the still image communicates a specific truth, or lie, film can stimulate an intellectual exchange with its audience. It is widely known that Russia under Stalin exiled or executed former leaders such as Leon Trotsky, and retrospectively and crudely airbrushing them out of historic photographs. Shub's enormously influential approach to historical compilation filmmaking was in the subtle juxtaposition of image that leads an audience to believe it is drawing its own conclusions. An overt dialectic between the home movies of the Romanovs and the lives of the poor sets up the potential for a range of critical readings of subsequent images. As Burke quotes Shub:

To assemble a documentary film you only have to think clearly. The spectator has to manage not only to see people and events properly, but to memorise them. Let the lovers of cheap montage effects remember that to edit simply and with a clear sense is not at all easy, but very difficult.

(Shub, 1972: 18)[7]

. . . Her legacy remains in that form of political documentary cinema where archive material is used dialectically or against the grain as part of a historical argument or debate.[8]

The other classic legacy was in the even more archetypal Soviet documentary celebrating the great public works that dragged the feudal Russian economy into the modern age. The seminal work here is Victor Turin's film about the building of a railway linking Siberia and Turkestan, *Turksib* (1929). Whereas Vertov and his *kinoki* believed in 'life caught unawares', Turin had worked in Hollywood for ten years before the Revolution and had no compunctions about re-enacting or setting up scenes to tell a more compelling story. But he also used extended subtitles which prefigure the use of grandiloquent spoken commentary in service of the bigger theme. That tone of voice is also clearly discernible in Mikhail Kalatozishvili's *Jim Shvante (marili svanets)/Salt for Svanetia* (1930), in which a backward community starved of salt is saved by the Soviet construction of a new road. Stalin felt that Kalatozishvili was too obsessed with the backwardness of Svanetia and too propagandistic in the socialist message and his next film was banned. Although many miles of extraordinary footage of Soviet engineering and enterprise were shot, such as that of enthusiastic Komsomol youth braving a Siberian winter in a canvas city to help build the vast Bratsk hydro-electric dam on the River Angara,[9] the increasingly paranoid Stalin regime crushed Russia's documentary tradition, even as it gave a language and ambition to world documentary filmmaking.

Propaganda remains a primary use of the powerful medium of film. The justification will usually be of the highest kind – such as preserving security or democracy – but one key means will be through restricting the flow of information and controlling its interpretation. At times of war, a population may well acquiesce to the need for such controls. Britain first understood the power of propaganda in the First World War (1914–18), though only setting up a Ministry of Information in 1917. The same year it took over the newsreel company Topical Budget, to make morale-boosting films on the home front, even though the generals were loathe to let cameras anywhere near the slaughter on the frontline. India was the powerhouse of the British Empire and the supplier of thousands of troops and – as it had already begun to evolve its cultural love affair with film – plans were made to bring heroic images of that contribution into the Indian hinterland, reinforcing support and recruitment. But difficulties between London and the British-run Government of India delayed orders for a fleet of cinema trucks until it was too late and the war was over.

Although the British government had belatedly understood the potential of film propaganda, there was a waning taste for it once peace came. 'In wartime, propaganda was seen as a necessary evil, but in peace-time it was believed that Government standards should return to normal as soon as possible.'[10] It was only later, in the 1930s, as the clamour for Indian independence grew, that a more concerted use of peacetime propaganda grew with the distribution of films, both factual and fictional, that propounded the British line. Alexander Korda's unashamedly jingoistic 'Empire films' were intended to hold that line, but their arrogance probably did more to fan the flames. The 1935 *Sanders of the River*'s opening dedication – 'to the handful of white men whose everyday work is an unsung saga of courage and efficiency' – is all too typical. As Indian film historian Prem Chowdhry writes:

> The Indian media condemned the propagation of empire films as British propaganda. In Film India's opinion 'the imperialist propaganda was the crudest and most vulgar sort' in which Indians were depicted as nothing better than 'sadistic barbarians' . . . The Hindu took it as 'vilification of India through screen, which lowers us in the estimation of the world and these films shown in India inflame us'. In their critical attacks, the Indian media highlighted how the screen portrayal of Muslims in Western films was ridiculing Muslim practices. For example, a film like *Real Glory*[11] was severely criticised for scenes in which the hides of pigs were flaunted in front of members of an Arab tribe before the Muslims were made to bury their face in them.[12]

Seventy years on, such filmic portrayals of Islam enjoy renewed power to inflame outrage and lethal reaction. Dutch filmmaker Theo van Gogh was stabbed and shot to death in Amsterdam in November 2004 following the TV transmission of his film *Submission*,[13] which explored violence against women in Islamic society and offended some through its provocative use of Koranic texts superimposed on naked female bodies. In Britain, even the documentary exposure of extreme preachers in mosques excites investigation by a nervous police force.[14] Neither of these were propaganda works but they excited the same degree of reaction. Strictly they belong more in the following chapter on Polemic. But they illustrate the fact that the battle for hearts and minds that propagandists engage in is a constant one, with many different fronts and faces. Wartime produces the most extreme need and offers the broadest canvas for controlling media.

Making war

In the Second World War, the Germans had their Ministry for Public Enlightenment and Propaganda, commonly known as the *Propagandaministerium*, while the British had a Ministry of Information. They were both engaged in a range of activities to put the best possible gloss on all stories relating to their own country's war efforts and to demean their opponents. Both recognised that documentary film was one of the most effective forms of propaganda.

The Nazi propaganda minister, Joseph Goebbels, not only commissioned propaganda newsreels and Nazi epics, but kept up the production of comedies and romances that attracted the German masses to the cinema in the first place. He also introduced mobile cinemas to

Figure 9.1
Leni Riefenstahl runs up the flag
for the Nazis in *Triumph of the Will*
(1934)

ensure the rural poor were not excluded from the message, and resisted a move to ban all foreign films, though kept a tight control on those that were allowed. The undoubted propaganda triumph of the pre-war phase was Leni Riefenstahl's film of the Sixth Nationalist Socialist Party Rally held in Nuremberg in September 1934. An admirer of Hitler, who in turn admired her earlier fictional films, Riefenstahl had already made a short film (*Sieg des Glaubens/Victory of Faith*) in 1933, the year that Hitler had come to power. But the elegiac epic *Triumph des Willens/Triumph of the Will* was to become the most famous propaganda film epic of all time. Its symphonic structure and use of music and iconography are extraordinary. One American critic writes about its 'masterful blend of the four basic elements of cinema – light, darkness, sound and silence – but it is not just an achievement in cinematic form, for it has other essential elements – thematic, psychological, mythological, narrative and visual interest – and it is in the working of these elements that Riefenstahl transcends the limitations of the documentary film and the propaganda film genres'.[15] Riefenstahl went on to do an equally impressive job filming the propaganda triumph that was the Berlin Olympics of 1936. Her two-part documentary, the first great sports film – *Olympia: Fest Der Völker/Olympia: Festival of the People* and *Olympia: Fest Der Schoenheit/ Olympia: Festival of Beauty* (1938) – extends the fascist aesthetic, underpinning the self-styled 1,000-year Reich's claim to historic supremacy by mixing from classical statues to modern athletes.

The balletic qualities Riefenstahl brings to her filmmaking may be ascribed to her first career, as a dancer, which may have also helped her evade prosecution after the War, eventually de-Nazified and classified as a 'fellow traveller', not a war criminal. She found it virtually impossible to get financed as a director thereafter and turned to still photography, but the enduring argument about whether she was culpable or merely naive is central to all filmmaking in the service of a system or idea. How far the filmmaker goes to placate their government or financier reflects either how fortunately synchronous they are in their objectives or how malleable they are, more often the latter. Of course, if the filmmaker or production house can convince themselves they are right, on the side of the angels, then the sense of compromise involved in bending the truth is supplanted by the higher goal. Some of Britain's wartime filmmakers, such as Humphrey Jennings, saw themselves as socialists, surrealists and poets – but in no way compromised by their nationalist fervour. Jennings was no jingoist, but found his range in war, as Williams writes:

> World War II's extraordinary conditions restored Jennings's professional fortunes and inspired his visual lyricism. Because of newly available Ministry of Information funding, to boost civilian morale and to promote Britain's cause to undecided neutrals, Jennings found a focus for his disparate talents and influences as the GPO was reformed as the Crown Film Unit. Jennings's output is regarded as among the best records of this 'people's War' in any national cinema. His films are driven by creative tension between affection for traditions and a symbolist's eye for the telling details of a people under the stress of modern war. Initially, Jennings's Home Front documentaries were unashamedly and (given the crisis of the time) justifiably propagandist.[16]

The indomitability of the plucky Brit under the bombardment of the Luftwaffe during the Blitz was the subject of films such as *Britain Can Take It* (1940), *Listen to Britain* (1942) and *Fires Were Started* (1943), and transformed Jennings's involvement with the Mass Observation movement into a more insightful construction of the popular experience *in extremis*. He was unashamed about the propagandist elements of what he was doing, because he believed in the justice of the cause, but it did not discourage him from extending the licence he was granted when the opportunity arose.

When the Nazis massacred the Czech village of Lidice in reprisal for the 1942 assassination of Reinhard Heydrich, the self-styled 'Protector' of Bohemia, a Czech poet wrote to Jennings suggesting a film. Jennings came up with the idea of re-enacting it in – and with active involvement of the people of – a Welsh coal-mining village, Cwmgiedd. The Ministry of Information was happy to finance this film, though probably not consulted about the choice of a village of pacifists, none of whom had volunteered for service, and where the use of the Welsh language and sense of oppression by the English would be used to stand for the Czech sense of being under the German jackboot. *The Silent Village* (1943) is not Jennings's best film but – perhaps because – it was one that got closest to what he was trying to say about people in film, 'far more important to me than the Fire one'.[17] He found the honesty, courage and support he got from the coal miners an illuminating contrast to the self-serving elites he was more familiar with. He was particularly dismissive of the fellow travellers he came into conflict with when trying to finish films, having a singularly bruising run-in with producers wanting radical cuts during post-production of *Fires Were Started* at Pinewood. 'Of course, one expects that from spineless well-known modern novelists and poets who have somehow got into the propaganda business – who have no technical knowledge and no sense of solidarity or moral courage', he wrote.[18]

While Jennings's work was largely on the Home Front, a lot of the Crown Film Unit's work was on the field of battle. Roy Boulting's *Desert Victory* (1943) was one of the finest war-zone documentaries, winning that year's Oscar for Best Documentary. Following the Eighth Army's punishing push across North Africa against the Afrika Korps, from the battle of El Alamein to their final victory at Tripoli, the unit's losses all too accurately reflected the costs of war. Four cameramen were killed, six more wounded, and seven captured by the Germans. *Desert Victory* was a great popular and critical success, creating an appetite for feature-length combat documentaries on both sides of the Atlantic:

> *Desert Victory* is incisive, lucid, and complete in its handling of actual, close-range combat footage, some of it captured from the Germans in their retreat. The shots of night-time artillery attack are spectacular. *Desert Victory* contrasts the immediate strategy of battle with the lives of individual fighting men, from the general in command to the infantry-men in the trench; this technique was also used in such later American films as *With the Marines at Tarawa* and *To the Shores of Iwo Jima*. The narration here is much less strident than that of American combat films, and, for the most part, the sound was recorded directly at the scene.[19]

The Crown Film Unit had been in production for over two years before the United States entered the war in December 1941. While the Unit worked with largely young, in-house talent, the American propaganda machine naturally turned to Hollywood, and established feature film directors such as Frank Capra and John Ford. Ford had over 100 director credits to his name before he shot the first widely distributed US combat documentary of the war. He was on leave from Hollywood as head of the Field Photographic branch of the Office of the

Co-ordinator of Information, and got himself assigned to film the defence of the US Naval Station at the Pacific atoll of Midway.

The Battle of Midway is only 18 minutes long, but packs a powerful punch in its graphic representation of the 3-day battle, capturing the percussive effects of heavy artillery, one of which explosions rendered Ford unconscious and wounded, so earning him a Purple Heart as well as an Oscar for his pains. The battle footage only fills the middle third of the film, the other parts given to characterisation and flag-waving imagery, overlaid with martial music – from *Yankee Doodle Dandy* to *Onward Christian Soldiers* – and some arch dialogue from the likes of Henry Fonda, all of which heavily underlines its morale-rallying propagandist purpose.[20]

Some of the same heavy-handedness marks the seven highly effective propaganda films made by Frank Capra and Anatole Litvak in the *Why We Fight* series, the first three of which set out to chart the history that had brought America to war: *Prelude to War*, *The Nazis Strike* and *Divide and Conquer* (all 1943). Subsequent instalments were vital in uniting the American people to the destinies of allies of which they had little knowledge.

The Battle of Britain (1943) opens in Calais with the visit of the all-conquering Fuehrer. The commentary, punctuated by martial music, sets the mood for the epic struggle:

> Now Adolf Hitler stood, just as Napoleon had stood more than a hundred years before, and looked across the English Channel at the one fighting obstacle that stood between him and world domination. The chalk cliffs of England stood sheer and white, out of the choppy waters, and beyond: a little island, smaller than the state of Wyoming. Crush that little island and its stubborn people, and the way was open for world conquest.[21]

Evincing sympathy for the plucky island breed was relatively easy in a nation where many still sentimentalised their British roots. *The Battle of China* (1944) had a tougher job to do, getting Americans to make a distinction between the orientals who had attacked Pearl Harbour unprovoked, and those with whom the Japanese had previously been at war. The commentary adopts a much more basic tone:

> To understand China, three facts must never be forgotten. China is history. [Pause] China is land. [Pause] China is people. Chinese history goes back for more than 4,000 years. That's a long time. It was only 168 years ago that Washington crossed the Delaware . . .[22]

Having set this primary school tone, the film goes on to paint a picture in primary colours between the Chinese and Japanese as the ultimate disparity between civilization and barbarism, good and evil. That simplistic rhetorical device reducing everything to black and white – 'you're either with us or against us' – is not just the inevitable effect of war, but remains a popular but limiting factor in many a documentary film, as well as in political rhetoric and reportage up to this day.

By the time Capra and Litvak got to the two instalments of *The Battle of Russia* (1944), they had decided to pep up the epic mix, both with uncredited footage from features like Eisenstein's *Alexander Nevsky*, to sketch in Russia's heroic history, and with celebrity endorsements from the leading US military men of the day, which increase in hyperbole until the roll-call ends with MacArthur:

The SCALE AND GRANDEUR of the (Russian) effort mark it as the GREATEST ACHIEVEMENT IN ALL MILITARY HISTORY.

(General Douglas Macarthur, Commander-in-Chief, Southwest Pacific Area)[23]

These films compress a complex history into a clear narrative, with a comprehensible, if incessant, commentary delivered by Walter Huston. As historical compilation films, they would have stood the test of time, if it were not for their convenient and contrived failure to mention the Soviet Union's communist system, which feature would not have played well in eliciting sympathy in the States, but which was to dominate American polity from 1945 onwards. So the propaganda goal of 1944 – the Alliance   was reversed in the propaganda role that followed – the Cold War, where the Russians were recast as the enemy and Communism vilified as the deadly contagion that threatened the world. The other great wartime ally, China, was also shortly to join this demonology of the great Red Menace, when Mao Zedong took over in 1949. Most of Western propaganda for the next 40 years was dominated by this realisation of the mythic enemy that Orwell saw being developed and warned of in *1984* – the construction of fear that helps enslave a populace to its government's will:

A new poster had suddenly appeared all over London. It had no caption, and represented simply the monstrous figure of a Eurasian soldier, three or four metres high, striding forward with expressionless Mongolian face and enormous boots, a sub-machine gun pointed from his hip. From whatever angle you looked at the poster, the muzzle of the gun, magnified by the foreshortening, seemed to be pointed straight at you.[24]

The Cold War

This personification of evil is one of the most persistent functions of propaganda, and by definition one that the visual media serves particularly well. The character of the enemy, the personalized threat, changes with the time – Nazi, Commie, IRA bomber, Muslim terrorist. But one overarching function remains the same: to cow the populace into subservience and acquiescence. Terrorism, and particularly the attack on the World Trade Centre in September 2001, has emboldened governments, particularly in the US and the UK, to enact ever more oppressive legislation under the guise of security. The UK Labour government had already extended the extension of detention permitted without charge to 28 days, and was narrowly thwarted by the House of Lords in its attempt to extend it to 42 days in October 2008, despite this not being sought by the police or security services, or justified by precedent. The international human rights organisation Amnesty had already reported on what it called the UK's 'Broken Promise':

Since the early 1970s, when the UK authorities began introducing emergency measures in the context of the conflict in Northern Ireland, human rights have been sacrificed in the name of security. Among the serious abuses facilitated by emergency measures have been torture or other ill-treatment and unfair trials.[25]

The filmmaker is frequently co-opted in the vanguard of this propagandist role and the contribution has traditionally been framed as 'public information', what the post-War Labour

Prime Minister Clement Attlee called 'an important and permanent part in the machinery of government' when he set up the Central Office of Information in 1946. He said that 'the public should be adequately informed about the many matters in which Government action directly impinges on their daily lives'.[26] Initially, with the upbeat hope instilled by a new welfare state, the COI produced one-minute films showing people how to use a handkerchief when combating the cold (*Coughs and Sneezes*, 1945 and *Don't Spread Germs*, 1948), but the Cold War soon came to predominate. *The Berlin Airlift* (1949) – 'the story of a great achievement',[27] when the West combined to defeat the Soviet blockade of Berlin – and *Operation Hurricane* (1953) – the building and testing of Britain's first hydrogen bomb on an Australian island – were more indicative of the nuclear build-up that was becoming the dominant concern of the age. The final commentary, by Chester Wilmot, of *Operation Hurricane* captures the quite philosophical official British voice of the day:

> That lethal cloud rising above Montebello marks the achievement of British science and industry in the development of atomic power, but it leaves unanswered the question of how shall this new-found power be used – for good or evil, for peace or war, for progress or destruction. The answer doesn't lie with Britain alone, but we may have a greater voice in this great decision if we have the strength to defend ourselves and to deter aggression with complete commitment to the cause.[28]

Nonetheless, the object of the propaganda was to help deliver that complete commitment.

American propaganda of the time was less nuanced. Coronet Instructional Films's *Communism* (1952) kicks off with the observation that 'Russia today is regarded as a grave threat to our nation, to our freedom, to the peace of the world',[29] and goes on to paint a very different picture of Russia from that seen in *The Battle of Russia* eight years earlier. A constant supply of films warning of communism's implacable campaign for world domination, such as the US Navy's *Red Chinese Battle Plan* (*c*. 1964), kept the US public in the fearful state of mind necessary to support massive military spending and eventually the Vietnam War. The sense that this was not some distant conflict, but one that threatened every American homestead, was constantly reinforced by Civil Defense Administration films about the imminent nuclear threat and how to cope with nuclear fallout. *A New Look at the H-Bomb* (1957) has the awkward-looking Federal Civil Defense Administrator, Val Peterson, standing in an office set, giving the public instruction on the threat of nuclear fallout:

> Now I'm not here to frighten you. As a matter of fact, Americans just don't scare easily anyway – and it's a good thing that they don't in this atomic age. But it's a part of my job, as Civil Defense Administrator, to give you the facts.[30]

The facts are, of course, incredibly grim, but soft pedalled here to suggest that a bit of pluck and preparation will see people through. The most famous of these film essays was the Civil Defense Administration's *Duck and Cover* (1951), which showed schoolchildren how they could learn from the animated Bert the Turtle, who popped inside his shell to avoid explosions:

> We all know the atomic bomb is very dangerous, and since it may be used against us, we must get ready for it . . . If you are not ready for it, it could hurt you in different ways.

It could knock you down hard, or throw you against a tree or a wall. It is such a big explosion it can smash in buildings and knock sign-boards over and break windows all over town! But, if you duck and cover like Bert, you will be much safer.[31]

So children were assured that slipping under their school desk or kitchen table, or crouching against a wall or even under a picnic cloth or newspaper, would help them survive the Bomb. Such palpable nonsense was merely one way of wedding children early to the cause – probably its most important line is 'we must remember to obey the civil defense worker' – and its association of nuclear defence with the fire service and traffic control is all part of an attempt to normalise the nuclear arms race. The Cuban missile crisis, in 1962, when the USA went head to head with the USSR over the presence of nuclear missiles pointing at America from nearby Cuba, was the nearest the world came to nuclear war and was apparently narrowly averted when the Russians agreed to withdraw. It gave a massive fillip to the nuclear arms industry and to the doom-mongers on either side of the Atlantic. In Britain, as late as 1980, the UK civil defence programme produced a series of 20 short public information films and accompanying booklets under the umbrella title *Protect and Survive*, which also pedalled plans and provisions for a domestic nuclear fallout shelter underneath the table in your own home. Fortunately, no one has as yet had to try one out, so the policy of Mutually Assured Destruction (MAD for short) is deemed by some to have worked – because we are still here. To what extent that is attributable to propaganda remains a moot point but, at the time of writing in 2009, NATO generals are still arguing for a 'grand strategy' to include a nuclear 'first strike' to pre-empt threats from rogue nations with nuclear arms.[32]

No doubt films will be made which support this new instigation of fear, but much of traditional propaganda has foundered in the face of irony, as a more visually literate populace has learned to recognise when it is being sold a line. In 1982, a film that had taken five painstaking years to make, effectively eviscerated US Cold War propaganda. *The Atomic Café* drew on a wide range of such footage to reveal the manipulation and lies at its heart. As Stella Bruzzi writes:

Out of propaganda, *The Atomic Café* constructs ironic counter-propaganda; Out of compiled images from various sources it constructs a straightforward dialectic between the past and present. *The Atomic Café* operates a similar duality to that found in the majority of politically motivated compilation films, that the archive documents are respected on their own terms as 'evidence' at the same time as they are being reviewed and contradicted by their recontextualisation.[33]

This should remind us that the term 'propaganda' is relative; it is easy to spot propaganda for what it is when standing outside the time and culture for which it was made. Londoners dodging the bombs of the Blitz and taking mutual comfort in the cinema would not look at the patriotic films of the Crown Film Unit as attempts to manipulate their minds, but as stirring hymns to the common cause. As the documentary film historian Erik Barnouw writes: 'The irony is that the term is invoked precisely when the film has failed as propaganda. When the choices please us we do not invoke it.'[34] Barnouw also points out that at one level, all documentary is propaganda, in that it presents evidence and testimony in the service of an idea, and yet, on another level, it is not a very effective medium for propaganda:

Documentary should be seen as a very difficult medium for propaganda, precisely because it confronts its subject matter openly. It announces its topic. It alerts our critical faculties. A more potent and persuasive form of propaganda is popular fiction, precisely because it is received as something else – entertainment, a word associated with relaxation.[35]

Propaganda today

Propaganda works best in a pliant population with common goals, hence its impact in wartime and need for a common enemy. But the more disparate the audience, the less likely it is to be effective. The BBC World Service was always more effective during the Cold War than its American counterpart, the Voice of America, because of the stridency of the latter and the much more nuanced voice of Britain. Whereas the Voice of America spoke from the self-evident assurance of right, with everything framed metaphorically by the star-spangled banner, the BBC gave an apparent range of opinion and experience, normally in the voice of people from the respective regions. They were frequently exiles, from the Iron Curtain countries or other regimes, so not entirely impartial, but nor did they appear to be mouthpieces for the British government. There was an apparent commitment to truth and objectivity. The subtlety is in which truths and positions were most valued and frequently expressed. This is known as the propaganda of omission, rather than commission. The former, like a polite relative at a family do, merely avoids talking about things that are uncomfortable and that don't serve their worldview. The latter brashly asserts whatever their beliefs are, irrespective of their impact on or unacceptability to the recipients. The BBC World Service is financed through a grant in aid from the Foreign Office, and has to be seen to serve British interests, through concentrating on issues and areas that serve that purpose. Thus, during the Cold War, stories about the Soviet Union and Eastern bloc were of paramount importance and their respective language services well-endowed. Now that the government's priority has shifted to the Middle East, most of those language services have been closed to fund the BBC Arabic Television Service[36] and BBC Persian.[37] This is not about the propagation of lies, more evidence that 'he who pays the piper calls the tune'.

There was a gleam in Western governments' eyes when the Al-Qaeda attacks of 9/11 offered the promise that 'everything was changed', giving them the chance to take actions hard to justify before, from suspending civil liberties to taking pre-emptive strikes against sovereign states. The so-called 'Bush doctrine' was based on the President's bellicose announcement that 'Every nation in every region now has a decision to make. Either you are with us, or you are with the terrorists'[38] – and so justifying facing the full weight of American military might if they believe you are a threat, as nation or individual. Cashing in the vast credit of human sympathy in the world for America's loss with the Twin Towers, Bush sought to suppress opposition and criticism, and for some considerable time achieved it on the US front. But, as the whole 'war on terror' and its strategies unravelled, an opposition eventually found its voice and began to interrogate the propaganda machine that had whirred into action so effectively. One documentary film among many charts 40 years of US government use of propaganda during wars from Vietnam to Iraq. In his book of the same name, Norman Soloman's *War Made Easy: How Presidents and Pundits Keep Spinning Us to Death* quotes approvingly Voltaire's maxim: 'As long as people believe in absurdities they will continue to commit atrocities.'

When the huge news outlets swing behind warfare, the dissent propelled by conscience is not deemed to be very newsworthy. The mass media are filled with bright lights and sizzle, with high production values and lower human values, boosting the war effort. And for many Americans, the gap between what they believe and what's on their TV sets is the distance between their truer selves and their fearful passivity.

Conscience is not on the military's radar screen, and it's not on our television screen. But government officials and media messages do not define the limits and possibilities of conscience. We do.[39]

The pictures that soldiers took in Abu Ghraib helped undo the Operation Iraqi Freedom myths so carefully built with the co-operation of a servile media and its embedded correspondents. It is a truth widely held that a reporter in bed with his subject is unlikely to retain an absolutely uncompromised objectivity in his coverage. But, as we have discovered, reporters were offered the freedom of that relatively comfortable compromise or risk the kind of 'friendly fire' that killed ITN's Terry Lloyd in March 2003. A 2006 inquest found that Lloyd was unlawfully killed by American fire that targeted the makeshift ambulance taking him to hospital, after he had already been wounded in crossfire.[40] With modern telecommunications, it is not possible to control and censor all communications, as the British Ministry of Defence had managed to do in the remote and isolated terrain of the Falklands War in 1982. It is easier to control access to the story, influencing the circumstances in which it is assessed and how it is received. After the PR disaster of the Lebanon war in 2006, the Israelis mounted a highly effective propaganda machine to justify their violent incursion in Gaza in January 2009, banning all correspondents from Gaza and lining up a well-briefed team of apologists to fill the hole thus created.

In Afghanistan – a conflict that has become more bitter, protracted and hopeless even than Iraq – there has been a growing resentment among the press corps at the way the British Ministry of Defence attempts to massage the message. Reporters talk of a 'devastating breakdown of relations' between reporters and the MOD. 'Dealing with the Ministry of Defence is genuinely more stressful than coming under fire,' says *The Daily Telegraph's* defence correspondent, Thomas Harding. 'We have been lied to and we have been censored.'[41] Because the war in Helmand province is so dangerous and inaccessible, the only viable access is as 'embeds' on army helicopters, and the reporters claim these trips are severely rationed to suit the anticipated spin, favouring uncritical coverage from TV stars like Ross Kemp or flag-waving tabloids over more critical correspondents like Harding. 'They manipulate the parcelling-out of embeds to suit their own ends' he says. 'They use it as a form of punishment to journalists who are off-message or critical of strategy or tactics.'[42]

The *Guardian's* James Meek says: 'I was told quite candidly that the priority was the tabloids and television because it was important for recruitment'.[43] That not only requires a positive spin on stories, but the softening of negative stories, especially the mounting death toll. A voluntary agreement drawn up between the MOD and news editors, the Green Book, obliges reporters to email their copy to the Army to ensure their 'press freedoms' do not compromise Opsec (operational security). We are supposed to understand that this is neither censorship nor propaganda, merely an attempt to save lives. Yet, by May 2008 Afghanistan was claiming more US servicemen's lives than Iraq and, in July 2009, 22 UK servicemen died there, with British military deaths in action in Afghanistan long having exceeded the total Iraq war. These are stories barely reported in the UK press, because the reporters cannot get there. Can this be an unintended, accidental outcome?

Conclusion

In some ways, a government does attempt to define the limits and possibilities of conscience. It is for the reporter and filmmaker to resist the blandishments of power and interrogate the spinners of tales who would recruit us to their propaganda purposes. The rise of government news agencies supplying news packages to cash-strapped radio and television in both the UK and the USA is a dangerous extension of political influence that may not be made clear to its audience. Labelling – of increasing interest to consumers keen to find where their food comes from and what it contains – should equally be demanded of information sources. The internet has given us a plethora of sources but created a logarithmic problem in identifying the wheat from the chaff, the truth from the spin. It is no surprise that it is government departments that make some of the most extensive use of this informational shop window but, Freedom of Information Acts notwithstanding, there are still powerful forces at work filtering the latter-day version of 'all the news that's fit to print'.[44]

That said, there are propagandist ends that one can agree with – health education for example. The word 'propaganda' literally means 'propagating' – more familiarly used by gardeners about plant reproduction – and comes from the Roman Catholic *Sacra Congregatio de Propaganda Fide* (Sacred Congregation for Propagating the Faith).

At least that origin indicates the sense of dogmatic persuasion, but the use is secularised in Spanish-speaking South America, where it simply means 'advertising' and carries no pejorative overtones. In fact, *Propaganda* is also the name of a successful contemporary British advertising agency, which appropriates the powerful associations of its name in the service of its new branding business:

> Propaganda's BrandLab team knows how to talk to consumers to get the truth, and not just focus-group answers. We believe in asking 'why' till we cannot ask 'why' anymore. Only then can we get a true brand insight. And only then can we develop an insight-rich marketing and advertising campaign brief that will influence your consumers in the way you want.[45]

So propaganda would appear to be emerging from the dark shadows associated with its use in the twentieth century, to find a morally relativist role in the twenty-first century. Brands are the new allegiances, their messages the new mantra. Call it influence, or persuasion, propaganda has always had the potential to be benign, and is clearly seen to be by those who share its ideological goals, just as the deeply religious feel compelled to share their 'enlightenment'. Tele-evangelism, long a mainstay of US television, is only a recent arrival in the UK, and Ofcom rules forbidding it to appeal for money on air were only relaxed in 2006,[46] presaging a new phase of propagandising television in the digital age.

At the start of the Cold War, with equal and opposite ideologies apparently tooling up for a Third World War, George Orwell naturally imagined an extreme dystopia controlled absolutely by propaganda. 'If you want a picture of the future, imagine a boot stamping on a human face – for ever.' In fact, the (Western) human face is being flooded by media moisturiser, massaging away human wrinkles, cares and thought in a deluge of consumer indulgence. And the dread unseen tyranny of *1984*'s Big Brother has been expropriated as the most successful international television brand of the twenty-first century, where the world's wannabes subject themselves to the glare of 24/7 screened humiliation in pursuit of transient fame. Orwell would no doubt be appalled, but not necessarily surprised by this ironically dumbed-down outcome. He had long been exercised by what he saw as the decadence of language and yet believed that its decline could be arrested, and he derided the liberal position that 'language merely reflects existing social conditions'.[47] For *1984*, he invented the idea of Newspeak, where language is progressively sanitised by the state, history and literature rewritten, and dissidence finally deprived of the truth, references and words to exist. He reckoned it might take until 2050 to achieve that:

> The whole climate of thought will be different. In fact there will be no thought, as we understand it now. Orthodoxy means not thinking – not needing to think. Orthodoxy is unconsciousness.[48]

Expert briefing – psychological filmmaking: going for effect

The vast majority of documentary films are commissioned and financed to serve a purpose other than the filmmaker's desire to make that film. It may be to meet a particular channel objective or social need, to celebrate an event or idea, to expose wrongdoing or sell a product. The filmmaker should enter a deal in the full knowledge of the financier's objectives and only sign a contract with the will and ability to deliver on those goals. Few projects announce themselves as propagandistic, but many are to some degree and it pays the filmmaker to understand that expectation and examine their conscience at the outset. Film is a psychological weapon and can be turned to many effects:

1   **Raising the temperature**: Many of the highest-regarded films are those which expose some social ill and sufficiently disturb their audience so that there is some resultant pressure for change. This involves the often harrowing revelation of individual stories of emotional upheaval in such a way that individual members of the audience empathise strongly. That in turn requires the filmmaker not only to understand what aspects of the story can be made to have that resonance, finding the points of common connection, but also encouraging the subject to reveal their innermost trials and tribulations. This means employing emotional intelligence to recognise which aspects of the story and its impact on the subject will connect directly with the hearts of the audience. Having someone break down on camera is one of the more commonly contrived devices, but not necessarily exploitative if the subject is fully apprised of, and sympathetic with, the objects of the film and agrees with the use of that material. For many people, the interest of others represented by the camera can provide a form of catharsis; many use the interview as a form of confession, a washing away of sins, including those visited upon them. So a sensitive handling of such moments need not just be revelatory, but can bring closure. As long as they are well shot and handled, an audience reads such moments as privileged insights and reacts as to a personal exchange.

2   **Feeling the pulse**: Political and wartime propaganda is the kind that requires a mass reaction, welding the many to a single purpose. Traditionally it is the drum that accompanies troops to war, and music still remains the most potent tool for marrying an emotional reaction to a particular idea, as in a national anthem or football stadium chant. The instillation of a shared sensation is obviously easier with a crowd, as in the

theatre, but television still has the power and the tools to bring a nation together, as for Diana's funeral. The beat of the music not only drives the tempo of the narrative but conveys its aim: hence the use of martial music at train termini in the morning rush hour and soft jazz in hotel elevators. The timbre and key are equally important: major key for engendering positive and upbeat response, changing to minor key for setbacks and contemplative moments. Suspense we all know comes either with those sharp, high notes on the strings or deep bass notes echoing a pounding heart. A film's music score can take its audience through an emotional rollercoaster ride, depositing them in exactly the state of mind required, which in American film is almost invariably with everything neatly resolved, jeopardy, tension and fear packed away. But propaganda may want those rabble-rousing emotions allied to their cause, the soundtrack delivering the required sensation.

3   **Checking the eyes**: As hypnotists prove, the eyes are susceptible to suggestion up to a level that can make people do anything. Even the notionally conscious can be persuaded to perceive things that are not there, from faces in the clouds to threats that do not exist. Long before the wonders of CGI (computer generated images), the camera could frame, focus and contrast images so as to heavily freight their meaning. From heroic images of Soviet workers to the monumental group of soldiers raising the Stars and Stripes at Iwo Jima, some pictures have the power to sear the retina and carry a complex ideology without words. Totems like flags, like the swastika, act as detonators for the explosive mixtures of idea and emotion that characterise belief systems, be they political or religious. This is the same mechanism that advertising seeks to trigger, by defining the brand and its packaging so well that instant recognition conveys meaning and desire. The pack shot at the end of an ad has to draw together the threads of information that precede it in one memorable frame, just as the single inanimate relic of a human tragedy can be the most eloquent memory of a complex life wasted.

4   **Powering the lungs**: While images may be worth a thousand words, that worth has probably been built through the words that preceded it. Words chosen as carefully as by a poet, and delivered with the power of the orator, can resonate long beyond the moment. Think of Martin Luther King's 'I have a dream' speech, with its classically rising rhetorical triplets culminating in the aspirational 'free at last, free at last, thank God almighty, free at last'.[49] No words are wasted, but every one counts and their repetition has the cumulative, emotional effect of the greatest music. The words carry more meaning in their shared experience and hope than any image could, and nothing could serve their purpose better. Barack Obama drank deeply and spoke passionately from this cup of knowledge. Words fulfilled human needs for many thousands of years before the birth of film, and national leaders such as Hitler and Churchill owed their popular standing to their powers of oratory. Television demands a different kind of performance from today's leaders, the appearance of normality and sincerity that Clinton and Blair practised, and the word use is very different, emphasising popular argot, evading verbs and commitments. A well-chosen word can define the meaning of the moment, a bad one can wreck it.

5   **Reflexes and movement**: All of these parts are subservient to their impact as a whole entity, a film whose editing has marshalled its orchestral forces to deliver a symphonic effect. The juxtaposition of sounds and images, the use of light and shade both visual and metaphorical, and the narrative journey through a range of landscapes and emotions to the desired conclusion are all master-minded in the post-production

process. An awareness of the state of mind of the audience, its prior knowledge, interests and sympathy, will help fine-tune the mix – hence television's obsession with ratings, audience research and focus groups – but the elemental forces film can muster reach beyond the everyday, consumerist consciousness to a visceral connection with the human psyche. The extremes of human emotion and experience are the natural preserve of film and, used to creative ends, constructive or destructive, have the power to change not just minds but lives.

6   **Agitating the viscera**: Jamaican sound systems are so loud, the DJs can target resonances on specific organs of the body, one chord palpitating the lungs while another vibrates the liver.[50] Filmmakers have always sought to make the heart pump through romance or excitement, while horror films concentrate on unsettling the bowels. The instillation of fear is arguably the most potent of film's visceral effects, and is the one most used by propagandists to hymn their cause, whether it is exaggerating the external threat of invading hordes, or warning society of 'the enemy within', as Margaret Thatcher dubbed the miners fighting for their jobs in 1984. Fear unites the crowd like no other emotion. As the philosopher Elias Canetti writes in his seminal work on *Crowds and Power*: 'There is nothing that man fears more than the touch of the unknown',[51] and the casting of oppositional forces as 'the Other' is what binds the individual to the group, producing the motive force to achieve whatever goal the propagandist has in mind. Moral panics about deviant groups in society have exercised people in every age, from cut-purses in the sixteenth century to paedophiles and asylum seekers today, exciting the mob to action, such as the Welsh illiterates who drove a paediatrician from her home in Gwent.[52] The essential feature here is to target the primeval responses of the mind, removing intelligence and rationality from the picture.

Rewriting history

While, as we have seen in Chapter 3, history is an area that has survived changes in fashion, not least through the presentation of charismatic academics, it is also a fertile field for challenging, revisionist views. One historian who has helped Channel 4 keep its controversialist flag flying has been the Oxford historian and *The Sunday Telegraph* columnist Niall Ferguson, now a Professor at Harvard. He first burst upon our television screens in 2003 with a revisionist view of *Empire*.[15] At a time when Western leaders were apologising for the imperial and racist transgressions of previous generations, Ferguson argued forcefully for recognition of the great strengths and contributions of the British Empire:

> The British enslaved millions, expropriated millions and looked on as millions starved. But, there were also really quite remarkable achievements, which people today tend to forget. In 19th and 20th centuries the British presided over an empire which encouraged free trade, invested billions in the developing world and spread the legal norms, which are indispensable for economic development. And of course in 1940 the British Empire was the only thing standing between Nazi Germany and her allies and world domination. So I ultimately argue that the benefits outweighed the costs, although those costs were undeniably very high. What we need to do is to compare the empire, not with some utopian ideal, but with the real historical alternatives that contemporaries faced.[16]

The series excited the divisions of opinion for which it was designed, with another prominent right-wing television historian, Andrew Roberts, hailing Ferguson as 'the Errol Flynn of British historians',[17] while the liberal press decried this 'neoconservative ideologue'.[18] The general view is that Ferguson's genius for self-promotion through contrarianism matched Channel 4's profile perfectly. 'It's not about being a contrarian for its own sake; it's about being willing to test all hypotheses in the way that Karl Popper said scientific inquiry should be conducted,' Ferguson protests.[19] The venerated science philosopher might have been piqued to find his critique of historicism being invoked to justify Ferguson's morally relativist approval of empire, but it helped neutralise the liberal press's response to the series.

As a result of this successful debut, Ferguson went on to make a television series on the American empire, *Colossus*,[20] and the bloody conflicts that dominated the twentieth century, *The War of the World*.[21] *Colossus*, written in the immediate aftermath of the invasion of Iraq, is full of the conflicted views that British intellectuals who have been seduced by the status and money on offer in the United States hold. He admits to America's weakness and overreach, but 'unlike most European critics of the United States, I believe the world needs an effective liberal empire and that the United States is the best candidate for the job':[22]

> The American Empire sure ain't perfect. Power has corrupted it, as power corrupts all Empires, even those established by democracies. And yet the alternative to Empire is never Utopia. More often than not, it's either bitter ethnic conflict – or another, much nastier Empire.[23]

Such blithe pragmatism did not play well in America, where Ferguson was about to take up his post at Harvard. In May 2006 he addressed the prestigious Council on Foreign Relations in Washington, anxious in the immediate aftermath of the publication of the Abu Ghraib torture pictures to hear how this neo-con historian, who had been one of the siren voices cheer-leading the Iraq war, might help extricate them. They were not well pleased to hear that instead the US should be there for 40 years and live up to its destiny as the global imperial power. Even one of Ferguson's admirers, the editor of *The Washington Monthly*, Benjamin Wallace-Wells, had to comment: 'In less than 10 minutes, Ferguson had pulled off that rarest of Washington double plays, alienating liberals and conservatives alike.'[24] More seriously, Wallace-Wells points out that, though a brilliant archival historian, Ferguson had only got into the study of empire five years earlier, as a result of the invitation from Channel 4. His prominence had come as much through the accident of history that rapidly propelled him to consult with governments desperate to bring intellectual credibility to their imperial adventure.

> Ferguson knows just enough about empire and America to make an argument which is on its face convincing, but not nearly enough to be right. The attempt at empire-building he pushed America towards in Iraq is clearly failing. But rather than question his own thinking, he now argues that a bigger, better version of American empire would have worked and still could. In this, he resembles the American Communist Party of mid-century: The problem with Stalin's Soviets, they said, was that they weren't Communist enough.[25]

It is interesting to contrast this over promoted historian, with his undue influence in Washington due at least in part to his television career, with Ken Burns, the American television documentary filmmaker who has found himself labelled 'the most recognizable and influential historian of his generation'.[26] The eleven hours of Burns's undisputed masterpiece *The American Civil War* were watched by 40 million viewers on its first transmission, in September 1990, making it then the most watched PBS show to date. Its epic sweep across the historic landscape that redefined America also refined the style that characterises Burns's work – a measured, poetic commentary underscored by music, relatively few interviews, with readings of contemporary sources by leading actors, and above all 17,000 contemporary photographs lovingly explored by the rostrum camera. Whole scenes are constructed from one still, and the way the camera zooms and pans across the print is so powerful and recognizable that it has been named 'the Ken Burns effect'.

While Burns's success is an application of this style to a consensual view of American history, he is regularly castigated as being a polemicist, not least due to his liberal take on race and the Afro-American as being central to the American identity, hence his key central trilogy of work being on the Civil War, Baseball and Jazz. In *The American Civil War*, the leading role of blacks in the struggle is foregrounded from the beginning of the first episode. A single, sustained, beautiful aerial shot over a riverscape – drenched blood red by the setting sun – is the perfect visual corollary for a seminal quote from the leading black abolitionist Frederick Douglass, voiced in the rich baritone of Morgan Freeman:

> In thinking of America, I sometimes find myself admiring her bright blue sky, her grand old woods, her fertile fields, her beautiful rivers, her mighty lakes and star-crowned mountains. But my rapture is soon checked when I remember that all is cursed with the infernal spirit of slave-holding and wrong; when I remember that, with the water of her noblest rivers, the tears of my brothers are borne to the ocean, disregarded and forgotten;

that her most fertile fields drink daily of the warm blood of my outraged sisters: I am filled with unutterable loathing.[27]

While the tone could hardly be further removed from hectoring, the epic scale of Ken Burns's series has the effect of rewriting popular perception of history, revealing some of the less heroic aspects of the national psyche through its obsession with baseball, or confronting the alternative cultures it slaughtered in *The West* (1996). In this way, it fulfils the role of polemic, not in the literal translation from the Greek *polemikos*, warlike, but in the cultural sense of being likely to stimulate discussion or controversy.

While there are those on the left who find Burns's reverence for American history and heroes too soft and sentimental, it is not just those who wear the white cowls of the Ku Klux Klan that find his placing native American and African-American experience so centrally a challenge to their own sense of American identity. Thus there was a strong hint of *schadenfreude* when his 2007 opus *The War*, a fairly exhaustive, if not exhausting, series on the Second World War, caused a vocal outcry because of its failure to include mention of the half million Hispanics who fought in it. The offence was compounded by the initial scheduling of the transmission of the first episode on Mexican Independence Day, the start of Hispanic Heritage Month. Transmission was delayed by a week and a Latino filmmaker, Hector Golan, was hired to add a couple of Hispanic interviews and other additional footage. *The New Yorker* was typical of comments:

> You have to work very hard, and take yourself very seriously as the keeper of the keys to America, to make a tedious documentary about the Second World War. But that is what Ken Burns and Lynn Novick have done . . . At fifteen hours, 'The War' is too much of a not good enough thing. A spark is missing – a spark that you almost always find in even the most unassuming documentary on the History Channel.[28]

A waspish delight in a fall from the heights of success more commonly associated with British comment, but Ken Burns has little to fear. He had just signed a new 15-year contract with PBS, keeping him making his multimillion dollar projects until 2022, when he will be nearly 70, a level of job security afforded no British documentarian, polemicist or otherwise.

Iconoclasm

While Burns's polemic builds heroic figures up, another tradition would tear them down. During its heyday in the early 1990s, when its UK audience share topped 10 per cent, Channel 4 ran an occasional series called *J'Accuse*, referencing the Zola letter in the Dreyfus case, itself one of the great polemical pieces of all time.[29] Screened as part of the *Without Walls* arts strand, *J'Accuse* had its own title sequence – a chisel desecrating a stone slab engraved with cultural icons' names, scratching over them the title *J'Accuse!* Each film offered a protagonist, normally a journalist, half an hour to mount an attack on a cultural icon, either a famous writer or artist, or a more general popular cultural phenomenon, such as Manchester United or the television news. Some successfully hit their targets with forensic deconstruction of their subject's multiple failings, others were little more than rants. Janet Street-Porter's *J'Accuse: Technonerds* was among the latter, broadcast in March 1996.

Street-Porter had only recently parted company with L!VE TV, the short-lived cable channel she had been joint Managing Director of and where she had spectacularly fallen out with former Sun editor Kelvin MacKenzie, leaving after four months. His populist gambits – topless darts and the News Bunny giving thumbs up or down on news stories – failed to save the unwatched channel. She had had her own revenge in her McTaggart lecture at the 1995 Edinburgh Television Festival. There she laid in to all the men who she felt had impeded her career at the BBC and elsewhere. 'A terminal blight has hit the British TV industry . . . this blight is management – the dreaded four Ms: male, middle-class, middle-aged and mediocre'.[30] She also accused Channel 4 of being stuck in a 1960s time-warp, so it was kind of them to offer her the canvas to vent her Luddite vitriol on another pet hate, the internet and all who patronised it: 'Every culture needs some kind of blotting paper to soak up the socially challenged.'[31] This ill-conceived and not very far-sighted polemic served its purpose, exciting an army of enraged nerds in what was to become known as the blogosphere. The internet has prospered rather better than Street-Porter.

The more predictable targets of J'Accuse were such formerly unchallenged icons as Vincent Van Gogh, Philip Larkin, Sigmund Freud and Virginia Woolf. The latter 'feminist icon' was one of the first to get the treatment, with the poet Tom Paulin calling her 'one of the most overrated literary figures of the 20th century'.[32] This set the more reasoned standard for the polemical strand, where cultural figures have been expropriated to represent meaning beyond their artistic value and deserve being critically cut down to size. Writers people regularly invoke without ever having read are an obvious candidate for this service, which has the estimable objective of getting people to think. Some of the more successful programmes were ones that extended the critique to pop culture shibboleths and created an ensuing argument among the public and in the press. Hunter Davies's J'Accuse: Manchester United (1995) raised the issue of the corporatisation of football and exploitation of fan-bases with their regularly changing strips, which kids pester parents to buy. Davies accused Manchester United and other clubs of corrupting and perverting the course of English football by 'cutting itself off from its cultural and geographical roots'.[33]

Alison Pearson took on the might of BBC News and ITN in J'Accuse: The News (1994), criticising the form and function that TV news had come to adopt. From pompous theme tunes 'suggesting the imposition of martial law' to male presenters with female sidekicks, 'literally a bit on the side – the perfect trophy wife',[34] Pearson picks away at both the presentation and formulation of the news. She effectively itemises the lack of senior women and the preference for reports from 'identikit pretty boys' with lantern jaws, the ascendancy of pictures over content, and the pressure for human interest (or, as she says, 'inhumane interest') over common sense. She decries the 'yoking of the mawkish and macabre', instancing the invasive coverage of the then recent funeral of the murdered toddler Jamie Bulger. 'Parents crying because their child is dead isn't news.'[35] Veteran reporters, from Francis Wheen to Mark Tully, are rolled out to confirm that the growing demand is for drama and disaster, at cost to context and comprehension. This is not a ranting piece, far from it, but a reasoned critique supported by evidence and testimony that makes a compelling argument.

The presentation may look a little dated today, but the argument largely holds true, despite the competitive evolution in the meantime of rolling news and online news. What has fallen out of fashion is not the false worldview promoted by TV news that Pearson rails against, but the opportunity to mount such an argument. J'Accuse disappeared in the mid-1990s, though it was briefly resurrected with a pair of films covering the Iraq war. In *J'Accuse: Jacques*, war-supporter William Shawcross mounted a hatchet job on Jacques Chirac, the President of France, for his failure to join the 'coalition of the willing' and his alleged long record of cosying up to Saddam Hussein.[36] In *J'Accuse: Uncle Sam*, the *Guardian*'s New York correspondent Gary Younge explored the American media's uncritical support for the war and the accompanying sense of a resurgent McCarthyism in the United States.[37] Both are valid positions, but reflective of great swathes of current opinion, and the very symmetry of these equal and opposite views more closely correlates to the conventional 'balance' of current affairs – everything reduced to two sides.

Questions of faith

True polemic does not require such checks and balances; it comes from, and sometimes aims at, the nature of belief. One of Channel 4's more effective essays in the medium, disproportionately remarked and remembered considering its 30-minute running time, was Chris Hitchens's attack on the late latter-day saint, Mother Teresa. As an Irish bishop intones at the beginning of *Hell's Angel: Mother Teresa of Calcutta* (1994), 'Of all the women of recent history, no one has captured the public imagination more than Teresa of Calcutta'.[38] Hitchens repaints the portrait of the saintly Nobel Peace prize recipient as a self-serving confidante of fraudsters and dictators, reminding viewers of her stand against contraception and abortion and her preference for saving souls over saving lives. He points out that her relentless globe-trotting has made her 'a missionary multinational with turnover in the tens of millions', which would fund a fine hospital in Calcutta, if she did not spread herself and her resources so thinly around the world. But 'the Convent and the Catechism matter more than the Clinic':[39]

> Mother Teresa's cult of death and suffering depends for its effect on the most vulnerable and helpless – abandoned babies, say, or the terminally ill – who supply the occasions for charity and the raw material for demonstrations of compassion . . . In the subliminal appeal that she generates, there is something of the mission to the heathen, something of the colonial outpost and something of the Florence Nightingale. While, in the silent and abject demeanour of her patients, there is something of the deserving poor. The great white hope, in this iconography, takes on the big black hole.[40]

Polemic does require strong writing, which Hitchens practises widely, for many publications including *Vanity Fair* and *The Atlantic*. A dedicated controversialist and atheist, Hitchens returns to the field of dogma time and again. His book *God Is Not Great: How Religion Poisons Everything*[41] ensures his regular involvement in heated television debate in his adoptive United States, but it is his fellow atheist, the former Oxford Professor for the Understanding of Science, Richard Dawkins, who made the most potent television polemic for atheism in his two-part documentary, *The Root of All Evil?*.[42] The programmes explore the connection between religious fundamentalism and lethal ideology, and the way religion spreads like a virus and warps morality:

> For many people, part of growing up is killing off the virus of faith with a good strong dose of rational thinking. But if an individual doesn't succeed in shaking it off, his mind

is stuck in a permanent state of infancy, and there is a real danger that he will infect the next generation.[43]

Dawkins told Jeremy Vine that he wanted the series to have the same name as his subsequent book, *The God Delusion*,[44] but Channel 4 insisted on the *Root of all Evil?* title to create controversy.[45] He expanded further in the *New Statesman*:

Of course religion is not the root of all evil. No single thing is the root of all anything. The question mark was supposed to turn an indefensible title into a debatable topic. Gratifyingly, title notwithstanding, the emails, letters and telephone calls to Channel 4 have been running two-to-one in favour. The pros mostly praise Channel 4's courage in finally saying what many people have been thinking for years. The antis complain that I failed to do justice to 'both sides', and that I interviewed fundamentalist extremists rather than the Archbishop of Canterbury . . . The point is that faith, even moderate faith, is pernicious because it teaches that believing something without evidence is a virtue.[46]

For the purposes of compression (and so as hopefully not to bore) I have had to extract lines from a longer article, in the same way that film routinely extracts useable chunks from longer interviews. Dawkins's producer skilfully managed to chart a compelling course through the hours of recorded conversation, but inevitably attracted complaints from those who felt their position was as a result oversimplified. An Oxford academic who had already crossed swords with Dawkins in print,[47] Professor of Historical Theology Alister McGrath, was interviewed for the programme but his contribution was excluded because it did not fit in the final film. McGrath has gone on record as saying that he had made Dawkins 'uncomfortable' and was excluded because he did not perform the role assigned by Dawkins and his producer.[48] He accuses him of being both journalistically and intellectually disreputable:

Dawkins seems to think that saying something more loudly and confidently, while ignoring or trivializing counter-evidence, will persuade the open-minded that religious belief is a type of delusion. For the gullible and credulous, it is the confidence with which something is said that persuades, rather than the evidence offered in its support. Dawkins' astonishingly superficial and inaccurate portrayal of Christianity will simply lead Christians to conclude that he does not know what he is talking about – and that his atheism may therefore rest on a series of errors and misunderstandings.[49]

In a variation on those 'behind the scenes/in the making of' DVD extras, Dawkins has produced a 3-DVD set of 8 uncut long interviews recorded for the programme, including the McGrath interview.[50] It is easy to see in these unedited rushes why the lengthy, carefully considered answers were not easily extractable, and did not measure up against the more extreme statements that did make the cut and make Dawkins's argument more succinctly. That is the nature of polemic.

The spat has also kept McGrath busy, trotting around Britain and the United States arguing that it is Dawkins that is deluded, and McGrath has rushed out another book in rebuttal of the million-selling *God Delusion* called *The Dawkins Delusion? Atheist Fundamentalism and the Denial of the Divine*.[51] He has yet to be asked to make a television programme, but Dawkins's polemic remains correct that, on both sides of the Atlantic, religion is still given reverential status on television and the atheist argument as such is rarely heard. The relative success of this battle of ideas suggests that polemical programming has great potential value and audiences can be engaged by such thoughtful issues. But it is television's failure to engage sufficiently frequently with anything that is deemed too challenging that has helped drive the audiences to rediscover cinema documentary, particularly in the United States. This revival is the subject of Chapter 17, but there is a strand within it that belongs here.

The American dream?

With *Fahrenheit 9/11*, *Sicko*, and *Bowling for Columbine*, film polemicist Michael Moore has made three of the top five highest-grossing documentaries of all time. He first sprung to fame with a film odyssey trying to bring General Motors CEO Roger Smith to account for the 30,000 jobs lost through plant closure in Moore's hometown of Flint, Michigan. In *Roger and Me* (1989), Moore developed his screen persona of the shambling bear in a baseball cap being endlessly rebuffed by a cruel and unaccountable corporate establishment, even as he ironically uncovers its multiple failings. This became the basis for two television series investigating the unsavoury underbelly of America, *TV Nation* and *The Awful Truth*. *TV Nation* was a co-production between BBC2 and NBC, the latter having commissioned the pilot but uncertain whether to go ahead until the BBC came on board. It was a satirical news magazine show hosted by Moore, employing a raft of young reporters to front reports from the whackier reaches of American life and corporate excess. Louis Theroux and Janeane Garofalo were among those who made their name on this show. The synopsis of the first show gives a neat indicator of the topics and approaches the show would take:

NAFTA
TV Nation travels to Mexico to take advantage of the North American Free Trade Agreement and make the show with cheaper labor and maximize profits – just like GM and Converse.

Taxi
New Yorkers know cabs may be difficult to get at rush hour or during a rainstorm. Black New Yorkers know another reason a cab may be hard to get – drivers refuse to stop for

Figure 10.1
Michael Moore takes on the American gun lobby in *Bowling for Columbine* (2002)

them. *TV Nation* goes to the streets to find out who is more likely to get a cab in New York City – Yaphet Kotto, a distinguished black actor, or Louis Bruno, a convicted white felon.

Appleton

Appleton, Minnesota has hit hard times lately. So what did they do to improve the economy? They built a prison, of course, using private and public funds. *TV Nation* goes to Appleton to discuss with the community the only thing missing to make their dreams come true – inmates.

Love Canal

Remember Love Canal, the small town near Niagara Falls? You may only remember the evacuation that occurred there due to the leakage of toxic waste into homes. But now, some industrious realtors are trying to convince people to move back to the new, less toxic Love Canal.

Mike's Missiles

Remember the Cold War? And threats of nuclear weapons being aimed at us? These weapons are not still a threat, are they? *TV Nation* creator Michael Moore travels to Russia to find the missile still aimed at his hometown, Flint, Michigan and convince the Russians to redirect it.[52]

Showing Yaphet Kotto not being able to get a New York cab set the style for a series of stunts designed to reveal the worst of human nature in humorous ways. This has been Moore's approach with remarkable success, though not a few setbacks. *TV Nation* got better critical notice than audiences and NBC dropped it after one season. Fox TV picked it up and in its second season (1995) it won an Emmy for 'Outstanding Informational Series', but they too then dropped it. Plans for a third series were eventually reconceived as a new show, *The Awful Truth*, made for UK Channel 4 and played out in front of a live studio audience.[53] The targets became harder, from attacks on right-wing politicians to the staging of a mock funeral outside a health insurance company, Humana, that was denying a policyholder a life-saving pancreas transplant. This segment not only forced the company to relent, but eventually led to Moore's 2007 feature-length assault on the inequities of American healthcare, *Sicko*. But *The Awful Truth* only lasted two series.

The twenty-first century has not generally been a good time for dissidence: 9/11 killed off any public taste for it in the United States and ironic commentary was quarantined as unpatriotic. If Osama bin Laden was Public Enemy Number One, Michael Moore was arguably Number Two, the enemy within, the traitor willing to give succour to the terrorist by finding fault with the President. His 2002 book, *Stupid White Men . . . and Other Sorry Excuses for the State of the Nation!*,[54] laid out his conspiratorial view of the neo-con Bush White House. He identifies the 2000 election as the conclusion of a coup that had started with the deliberate deregistration of thousands of African-Americans and relied on the stupidity of the American majority. Moore's publisher, Rupert Murdoch's HarperCollins, attempted to get him to tone down his criticism of Bush and change the title, but Moore's appeal to librarians over this challenge to free speech forced the publisher's hand and, despite little promotion, the book became the top non-fiction seller of 2002.

Moore's *Bowling for Columbine* documentary feature the same year – anatomising America's pathological attachment to guns following the Columbine high school massacre – and his Bush-baiting speech at the Oscars when it won, helped fuel the Moore hate profile. His subsequent film, *Fahrenheit 9/11*,[55] which explored the madness that had gripped America and its search for 'homeland security' since 9/11, drove right-wing commentators to distraction. Websites sprung up attacking Moore[56] and two of their progenitors combined to write a book with the subtle title *Michael Moore is a Big Fat Stupid White Man*, opportunistically published by Moore's own publisher. 'Postwar documentaries gave us the documentary, Rob Reiner gave us the mockumentary, and Moore initiated a third genre, the crockumentary',[57] it announces, going on to attempt to refute many of Moore's claims. While it contributes to a growing sense that Moore is a narcissist with at best a selective approach to the truth, it fails to undermine the overarching value of the mirror that Moore holds up to America, or reach the heights of entertainment that have made him such a commercial success. Documentary films that attack him – Alan Peterson's *Fahrenhype 9/11*,[58] Michael Wilson's *Michael Moore Hates America*[59] and Rick Caine and Debbie Melnyk's *Manufacturing Dissent*[60] – only serve to build up the hype surrounding this larger than life polemicist. They are tributes to the power of his message, which must have had some part, however unquantifiable, in awakening America from its somnolent thrall eventually to turn against Bush's imperial adventure in Iraq. There are many who feel that this end alone justifies any means.

Satirical shortcomings

Britain's own stuntsman polemicist, the comedian Mark Thomas, was once on the same television chat show as Michael Moore and said: 'I pick on receptionists too', satirising the tendency of them both to make their point by regularly being rebuffed at corporate front desks. Moore was not amused, revealing Thomas as the smarter of the two, perhaps not least because he has not enjoyed the level of stellar success that always seems to deprive people of their senses of perspective and humour. *The Mark Thomas Comedy Product* employed stunts to embarrass the powerful, as does Moore, but had a more serious investigative edge, a feature that eventually led to Channel 4 cancelling the show.[61] Thomas is now occasionally employed as a reporter on the current affairs strand *Dispatches*, where he has covered such issues as the arms trade and Coca Cola in his own inimitable style.[62] Reviewing his 2006 book,[63] James Hawes in *The Daily Telegraph* takes the very British approach to spiking Thomas's guns, condemning through faint praise:

> Thomas's investigations are gripping. We can all cheer the public debagging of lying politicians, corporate bagmen and shifty arms dealers. Thomas is driven by a simple, old-fashioned desire to tell the truth in the hope that this might change things . . . He is, in fact, a public-school meta-patriot who would have been thoroughly at home in Gladstone's Liberal Party, stealing the show (and the limelight) like a young Lloyd George, with fulminations against immoral arms manufacturers 'suckled on the fatty milk of government defence contracts'. To him, Britain can never be just another country trying to pay her way by fair means or dodgy: she can and must have higher moral standards than the rest of the world – and if she does, that chastened world will surely listen.[64]

Hawes – the novelist, not the television director of the same name – has established a reputation as a 'snappy satirist', a laconic wit more in tune with the Zeitgeist than Thomas's liberal outrage. Satire was *the* British form for skewering the powerful 250 years ago, but it has latterly suffered in a world of consumerist moral relativity. It can, however, still be the most potent polemical weapon. *The Day Today* was a surreal parody of a news show on British television, which aired for just six episodes on BBC2 at the start of 1994. Like a lot of British TV comedy, it grew out of a radio show, *On the Hour* (BBC Radio 4 1991/2), that had proved anchor Chris Morris's cynical view that people would believe anything, as long as it was delivered emphatically enough in the over-modulated cadences of news-speak – many viewers subsequently rang in to complain of the presenter's rudeness to his 'guests'. The television show added a rich mix of visual pastiches to the verbal parody of news speech patterns and Morris's aggressive presenter posture. It showed 'clips' from a fictitious documentary series set in swimming pool, a spoof soap opera set in a bureau de change, a mock MTV channel 'Rok TV' (featuring the psychotically violent rapper Ferk-U) and a parody of the real-life rescue show *999*, where a sheepdog is seen to avert a helicopter disaster. The storylines were frequently absurd, but the satire bit deep into the self-important hype of the news machine and the establishment values it holds. Politicians in the then Tory government were regularly lampooned and, although Morris won the 1994 British Comedy Award for Best Newcomer, it was unsurprising that the show was not recommissioned by the BBC.

The more risk-taking Channel 4 eventually allowed Morris to make a series called *Brass Eye* (1997), but the then Chief Executive Michael Grade repeatedly interfered, demanding cuts and rescheduling shows until an exasperated Morris inserted a single frame subliminal message in the transmission print of the final show: 'Grade is a cunt'. The reason for the channel's loss of nerve was twofold: Morris had identified all the issues on which public sensitivities were at their most raw: drugs, sex, animals, crime and so on, and then invented scandalous storylines which celebrities and politicians were invited to condemn, uncritically accepting the most improbable lines fed by Morris and his team. The most successful episode was on drugs, where celebrity TV presenters Noel Edmonds and Rolf Harris, and Mrs. Thatcher's former Press Secretary Sir Bernard Ingham, were all seen holding a yellow tablet and condemning the fictional drug 'Cake'. The late Northern comedian Bernard Manning says:

> One kiddy on Cake cried all the water out of his body. Just imagine how his mother felt ... You can puke yourself to death on this stuff – one girl threw up her own pelvis-bone ... What a fucking disgrace![65]

Tory MP David Amess not only contributed an elaborate condemnation of the fictitious substance, but raised it in a parliamentary question in the House of Commons.[66] The hubris of those in the public eye was exposed to the audience's hysterical ridicule, a slight difficulty for a broadcaster reliant on such people's goodwill. Morris knew he wouldn't be making a second series:

> Watch this programme now, because it will never be allowed a repeat. British law prohibits a video release and I'm too puked out to consider a second series. *Brass Eye* should put an end to the recent spate of feeble, under-realised faux-prankster drivel. It won't of course. It will just spawn another host of second-rate imitators. So top this, you quisling fucks.

The whole of the media is a deception, everything that happens is a deception, cloaked in coded statements – a pay rise, a sacking, whatever. I can't stand that high-handed attitude that there's a proper way to behave. Everyone's fucking about. I'm just displaying it. You can dupe people till the cows come home as far as I'm concerned.[67]

This appears to be a scatological version of the classic anarchist text of the Situationist International, which sees society as a spectacle, a commodified set of images like a screen that the appropriate revolutionary act would be to destroy, to which I return in Chapter 16.[68] What it makes clear is the seriousness of Morris's intent, though that is apparent in any intelligent reading of the programmes, but just as people fell over each other to appear, they also rushed to condemn with equally ill-considered judgement.

Despite all this, Morris got his repeat. Long after Grade had left Channel 4, the channel chose to schedule a rerun of *Brass Eye*, and commission an additional episode. 'Paedogeddon'[69] was an even more controversial exploration of the contemporary moral panic about paedophilia, engaging other celebrities – who had clearly not seen the first run – to make fools of themselves, including endorsing the spoof charity 'Nonce Sense'. 'Nonce' is the term prisoners give those convicted of sexual crimes, because they are a 'nonsense crime'. Seeing internationally renowned rock musician Phil Collins seriously assure us 'I am talking Nonce-Sense' perfectly captures Morris's comic intent, but 2,000 people complained about the programme while politicians and tabloid press competed to condemn Morris in a perfect orgy of the sentimentality and hypocrisy that Morris set out to send up. In a sympathetic *Observer* profile, Euan Ferguson captured the mania:

> The *Mail* went loco, calling it 'The Sickest TV Show Ever'. The red-tops followed, as 'outrage' mounted . . . Then it got sillier. Government Ministers condemned the programme, only to admit they hadn't watched it. The papers which were frothing most exuberantly began quietly shooting themselves in the feet. One *Mail* splurge on the programme (headed 'Unspeakably sick', the words of one of the Ministers who hadn't watched it) was preceded by close-ups of Princesses Beatrice (13) and Eugenie (11) in their bikinis; in the *Star*, beside a 'shock-horror-sicko' Morris story, sat a picture of singer Charlotte Church in a tight top ('She's a big girl now . . . chest swell!'). Church is 15.[70]

'You couldn't make it up!', as the hacks (who regularly did) used to say; but is not so much the blatant hypocrisy that beggars belief as the widespread, unsophisticated inability to recognise and appreciate satire and its polemical purpose. Over 250 years after the satirical heights of the eighteenth century – works such as Jonathan Swift's *Gullivers Travels* (1726), John Gay's *The Beggar's Opera* (1729) and William Hogarth's *The Four Stages of Cruelty* (1751) – the self-appointed arbiters of taste would not recognise genius if it were to walk in the door. In 1729, Swift published *A Modest Proposal for Preventing the Children of Poor People in Ireland Being a Burden to Their Parents or Country, and for Making Them Beneficial to the Public*, in which he recommends that Ireland's poor escape famine by selling their children as food to the rich:

> A young healthy child well nursed, is, at a year old, a most delicious nourishing and wholesome food, whether stewed, roasted, baked, or boiled; and I make no doubt that it will equally serve in a fricassée, or a ragout.[71]

It is a meticulous exposure of the grinding poverty of his fellow Irish, and is a wonderfully sustained piece of irony about the patronising ignorance of the powerful, with their simplistic schemes for eradicating social ills. It would not be difficult to conceive an updated polemic about poverty and government social policy today, though it would be difficult to get it commissioned. One can easily imagine the disingenuous vitriolic froth from tabloid reviews if it were televised.

Morris has only been involved in sitcoms since *Brass Eye*, neither his co-writing *Nathan Barley*[72] nor his appearance in *The IT Crowd*[73] fulfilling the promise of that earlier hit. Now Morris has announced that he is making a film for Channel 4 satirising terrorists. He told *The Sunday Times* Arts Editor Richard Brooks: 'the film will seek to do for Islamic terrorism what *Dad's Army*, the classic BBC comedy, did for the Nazis by showing them as "scary but also ridiculous".'[74]

Conclusion

If it ever sees the light of day, Morris's terrorist satire will be fulfilling both what Channel 4 and Chris Morris should be doing – drawing attention to the absurdities and excesses of the world in which television is at best the modern court jester: a licensed critic and privileged polemicist. These qualities can only be nurtured in systems with confidence, by broadcasters with broad shoulders, able to weather the sabre thrust of the satirists and the stormy reactions they provoke when they find their targets. As the most barbed newspaper cartoonists – artists such as Steve Bell and Martin Rowson – know, the most ruthlessly portrayed politicians are often their biggest fans, quite often paying for the original drawings to decorate their homes. Politicians have thick skins and a pathological need to be noticed and cartoons serve that need, capturing for eternity their fleeting moment of fame on the national stage. Yet craven producers and enervated broadcasters are fearful of the political backlash that may further undermine their shrunken power base, and rarely dare anything as dangerous as was commonplace 250 years ago.

There is another force at play here, which has different names but amounts to the same influence: multiculturalism, diversity, political correctness. In academic circles, Michel Foucault demonised the polemic as intellectually reductive and two-dimensional[75] and a whole new culture of 'uncritical reading'[76] has grown up. This and parallel social discourses of inclusion have arisen as a direct response to the largely unquestioned moral verities that had sustained society through two world wars and produced a culture of what George Orwell called 'political quietism'. When writing for the first edition of the short-lived post-War magazine *Polemic*, Orwell identified particular brands of nationalism and the unitary values that they would hold.[77] He defined the predictable myopia that accompanies nationalist sentiment, and its affinity to classicism, racism, anti-semitism, etc., finding intellectuals particularly at fault for not resisting the degeneration of their critical faculties by such crude associations:

If you hate and fear Russia, if you are jealous of the wealth and power of America, if you despise Jews, if you have a sentiment of inferiority towards the British ruling class, you cannot get rid of those feelings simply by taking thought. But you can at least recognise that you have them, and prevent them from contaminating your mental processes. The emotional urges which are inescapable, and are perhaps even necessary to political action,

9   **Grading**: Wipes and visual effects are generally considered toys not for serious use, but the sophisticated possibilities of grading in the digital universe can transform the look and feel of the final film. Inordinate time and expense is spent trying to give videotape productions the texture of film, but there are many other subtle facilities within the grader's palette. Colour correction is not just there to achieve pictorial accuracy, but can enhance mood and emotion, literally illuminating the underlying text and symphonic structure of the film. The rollout of HD as industry standard format will make ever greater demands on this important aspect of postproduction.

10 **Graphics**: Just as with music and commentary, graphics should be designed to integrate with the piece from the start, whether as full-frame information source or chest captions crediting contributors. Caption placing should determine shot size – for instance, difficult to place over a BCU of a talking head, or in a fast cut sequence. Graphic sequences should be designed to fit with the visual and informational style of the surrounding film, but can stand out if too cartoonish or complicated. They should also be clearly compatible with the intended voiceover, in both the precise information and the way that is formulated.

11 **Process and paperwork**: Although it can seem obsessive and time-wasting, a well-organised edit, with bins and cuts appropriately labelled and all sources archived, can save time and grief later. Original sources should be retained as back-up against loss or disc corruption until the production is completed. Just as the log identifies the raw material source, all secondary sources should be logged, not just for possible re-laying or extensions, but for compliance documentation necessary to ensure copyright is cleared. Without this process being undertaken and meticulously recorded, a production may not be transmittable and final payments may not be made by the commissioner.

12 **Edit suite diplomacy**: A filmmaker working alone in a darkened suite is a prime candidate for lunacy and needs ways of retaining a sense of perspective. Two minds are better than one but, when working with an editor, it is sensible to look for complementary experience, intelligence and skills, not complimentary subservience that will only echo your weaknesses and endorse your mistakes. Be prepared to listen to advice and adapt to accommodate it; no film cannot be improved. This also goes for the visiting executive or commissioner. They may be importing the unwanted reality check from the commercial coal face or audience ratings war, but they may have a point and they probably have the final say. Better to negotiate and retain as much control as possible, rather than to immolate yourself and your project in a pyre of righteous anger. Many filmmakers have; it is the unwanted madness of the post-production process. A well-ordered edit and a well-ordered mind is the best defence.

11 Liberation

....

liberation n. 2 the seeking of equal status or just treatment for or on behalf of any group believed to be discriminated against: women's liberation; animal liberation

It is in the nature and name of broadcasting that it reflects and plays to the broad consensus. It finds it very difficult to let spirits roam free, for fear of scaring off the great majority that attract the advertising or pay the licence fee. Television may, from time to time, seek to stoke controversy and even innovate, but only as far as the audience will support it. As soon as a programme series fails to meet its anticipated ratings, it is liable to change, demotion to a later, less exposed slot, or more likely cancellation. This is not just true of ITV, like the American networks dependent upon the advertising revenue that follows the audience. It can happen at the BBC, where interpretation of the public broadcast charter responsibilities places emphasis on reaching all the audience and thus the heights of popularity, at least on its main channels. Before the internet, outraged sensibilities had little recourse other than to write to the television executives to complain at the majoritarian exclusion of different and dissident voices. The new media have liberated a veritable tsunami of opportunity and opinion, forcing at least a token recognition by the mainstream media. Facing the fragmentation of their audience in the multichannel digital universe and the possibly permanent loss of younger audiences to the internet and other new media, the broadcasters have belatedly adopted such contemporary ideas as 'diversity' and 'inclusion'. Programme-makers are charged with finding ways of extending their programme propositions so that interactivity may involve the audience, and newsmen are encouraged to engage their viewers in the news-gathering process by running 'user-generated content' such as mobile phone pictures. There is, as yet, little evidence that any of this will or can fundamentally transform broadcast editorial values or behaviour.

What the new media have done is to open up new possibilities for communication that circumvent the television. The laptop and the video camera are all people need to make films on their own, and there is a quiet revolution unfolding that has opened many doors. Distribution ranges from the local and personal to the megalithic. At one end of the spectrum, video sharers are showing and discussing home-grown documentaries in pubs; at the other, equally amateur footage is going around the world. YouTube launched in February 2005, with the trademarked tag line: 'Broadcast Yourself'. Within 18 months it was hosting over 6 million videos and had registered 1.73 billion hits.[1] In November 2006, Google bought YouTube for $1.65 billion.[2] Not to be outdone by this explosion of DIY clips, first the BBC and then ITN have jumped on the bandwagon and now post their own clips of broadcast material on YouTube that they feel will capture the younger demographic they have lost to the internet. Both concentrate on celebrity culture and reality TV moments, and ITN also runs a weekly compilation of their 'wierdest videos of the week', *This is Genius*.[3]

It could be easily argued that this misses the point. There are some who feel that what we are witnessing is an emerging independence movement, shaking off the stranglehold of the media empires and their imposed orthodoxies. One South London man, John Yates, until recently ran a regular event called Unreported World: 'Indy Film Nights offering free screenings of documentaries made by a wide range of individuals not attached to media empires'.[4] The films reflect dystopian views on such subjects as the international banking system, the oil business, US interests in the Middle East and the war on terror, and reveal a burgeoning alternative world of filmmaking largely excluded by contemporary television. One film shown here and elsewhere on a flourishing alternative circuit is Katie Barlow's *Visit Palestine*,[5] a documentary about a Western volunteer in Jenin, Caoimhe Butterly, who is seen living and working with the women and children, confronting Israeli tanks and being shot. The *Guardian*'s Peter Bradshaw called it 'raw, urgent movie-making' and emphasised how this kind of film reveals an experience normally airbrushed from television screens:

> The director makes no apology for showing some of the everyday shocking reality that doesn't get on the mainstream news – shattered corpses, children with bullet wounds – along with arias of desolation and defiance from the widows left behind.[6]

Fellow filmmaker Ken Loach, no stranger to political filmmaking, nor to broadcasters' resistance, agreed:

> Katie Barlow's film *Visit Palestine* is both a devastating account of daily life for Palestinians and a fine portrait of a brave and selfless Irish woman who lives with them. No one talks politics yet it is a deeply political film. You are left with a burning anger on behalf of those who bear the occupation of their land and appalling military oppression with such fortitude. Israel, the US and their apologists stand indicted and, on this evidence, convicted.[7]

Visit Palestine is not the only film about the Palestinian experience that has failed to find a place on British television. Yet, as broadcasters shy away from the difficult and challenging in case they further alienate their dwindling audience, they have inadvertently helped promote this alternative voice, and not just in urban areas. When *Visit Palestine* played for one night in the Regal Picture House in the Tory heartland of Henley-on-Thames, it sold out to a unanimously enthusiastic, exclusively middle-aged audience. It is, however, a voice that is better developed in the United States, longer starved of intellectual fare on television, and where it is frequently associated with the anti-globalisation movement. A typical case in point is the film about Argentina that the world-renowned author of *No Logo: Taking Aim at the Brand Bullies*,[8] Naomi Klein, co-produced with fellow Canadian Avi Lewis. *The Take* (2004)[9] chronicles the expropriation of an auto-parts factory in Buenos Aires, idle since the economic collapse of 2001. Set against the turbulence of a presidential election, it charts the workers' struggle to regain control of their lives and reassert the dignity of work in the face of a remote and failing economy. It is a voice that finds resonances around the world, and a means that has helped liberation movements everywhere.

Women's liberation

Naomi Klein follows in a family tradition. Her mother, Bonnie Sherr Klein, was also a filmmaker and best-known for one of the most successful anti-pornography films to come out of the women's liberation movement. *Not A Love Story* (1981) was also one of the most commercially successful films to have been made by the National Film Board of Canada. It follows stripper Lindalee Tracy on a graphic journey through the adult entertainment business. Touring the pornography district of New York's Times Square, Klein's voiceover states:

> Pornography is an eight billion dollar business, now larger than the music and film industries combined . . . There are four times more pornography outlets than McDonalds restaurants in the US.[10]

Through the revelation of the pornography business's techniques, and interviews with leading radical feminists of the day such as Kate Millett and Robin Morgan, Tracy is persuaded of the abusive nature of pornography, as Klein hopes the audience will be. However, this liberating insight was challenged by many feminist critics for its failure to set pornography within the wider context of patriarchy and gender violence, suggesting that:

> *Not A Love Story* is a film about pornography which is itself pornographic . . . Having leading feminists talk about pornography was not strong enough to offset the interspersal between these interviews and progressively more offensive pornographic material.[11]

The eternal argument about symptom and cause – whether the visual representation of pornography or violence gives rise to social ills or merely reflects them[12] – should not detain us here, but the stimulative role that film has in bringing these issues out into the open, provoking debate and liberating the individual is very much the point. The essential selectivity of film, the fragments of opinion and experience that make the final cut, give emerging views shape and focus.

Sometimes the filmmaker may suggest the frame that best communicates the life, such as in a film about Guatemalan prostitutes, *Estrellas de la Lineas/Stars of the Tracks* (2006). Filmmakers Jose Maria Rodriguez and Jesus Velasco were trying to make a film about a poor area of Guatemala City, named La Linea after the railway line that used to run through it. Many of the women who live there are sex workers and wanted to know how to improve their lives in a society where many are routinely murdered. The filmmakers suggested that they form a football team to participate in a local league run by the football academy Futeca. Their first game, against the local elite Collegio Americano, was abandoned when that team's appalled parents realised who their daughters were mixing with, insisting on the prostitutes' expulsion and the hosing down of the benches for fear of their contracting AIDS from the sweat. A local journalist helping with the project, Andreas Cepeda, says that the film conceived this as a deliberate stunt: 'An intentional, confrontational act to provoke two polar opposites within society, without violence, to experience and observe their reaction'.[13] Some commentators have complained that this was exploitative of the women. Nonetheless, the team has continued to play, other teams have been formed – such as the Tigers of Desire from the Flores brothel – and the film has been fêted internationally, from the Berlin Film

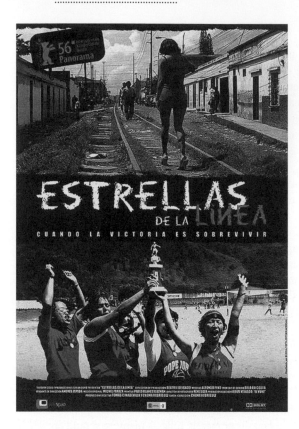

Figure 11.1
Guatemalan prostitutes kick balls in
*Estrellus de la Lineas/Stars of the
Tracks* (2006)

Festival in 2006 to the Human Rights Watch International Film Festival in New York in 2007. As such it has raised the profile of the prostitutes and their problems, and, equally importantly, their self esteem. Susy Sica is a 43-year-old Mayan, illiterate and a single mother of seven, who feels that football has liberated her life: 'When I'm on the field practising, even though I'm only a few blocks away from the tracks, I forget I work there. I feel like I'm someone else.'[14]

The fragmenting factions of the women's movement and their more arcane arguments may have been difficult to capture on film, but the validation of women's lives around the world has been one of the triumphs of the feminist film movement. The New York-based distributor and production assistance facilitator Women Make Movies has been in operation since 1972 and promotes films made by and about women from all over the world. Their catalogue of over 500 films[15] is an indicator of the health of this sector, even if it still struggles to be heard in the masculine mainstream. WMM is a big educational distributor and helpfully groups their films in categories such as 'Run Women Run: Women in Leadership and Politics', 'Globalization, Labor and Women's Lives' and 'Going Green: Women and the Environment', but this does not adequately capture the range of perspective and pain, humanity and hope this filmography includes. Some reveal the systems that oppress women in certain cultures. Anat Zuria's *Sentenced to Marriage* (2004) follows three Israeli women pursuing a divorce through the rabbinical courts, the only recourse available to them in this patriarchal, theocratic society. The film starts with a graphic line from an ancient rabbinical text:

A woman is bought in three ways and buys herself in two ways. She is bought with money, with wit and with intercourse and buys herself with divorce and with the death of the husband.[16]

It takes two women four and five years respectively to secure their divorces; the third fails altogether. In Mystelle Brabbee's *Highway Courtesans* (2005), she follows the fortunes of 16-year-old Guddi Chauhan in the Bachara community of India, which traditionally forces their daughters into prostitution. Filmed over seven years, we see the young girl's evolution through prostitution and self-poisoning to a failed relationship and sterility, before she escapes prostitution for a low-paid but rewarding life as a teacher. If not exactly liberated from their oppression, both films show the strength individual women develop in adversity, as the Offscreen.com website comments:

In *Sentenced to Marriage* and *Highway Courtesans* women of vastly different social, cultural, racial and economic background similarly suffer hardship under unjust and archaic patriarchal social custom and law. Neither film lessens the pain these women feel, or attempts to gloss over the complexities of their respective social realities. However, the approach taken by both filmmakers is to foreground the good that can come from the strength of character of the participants, no matter how difficult or long the struggle.[17]

Some people advance the argument that intruders from other cultures, however sympathetic and skilled they are as filmmakers, can never capture the true reality of the subjects. Not only is this patently untrue, but the needs served frequently outweigh such niceties. American filmmaker Liz Jackson gives voice to the women of the Congo in a film that aims to unlock an ashamed silence that has helped mask the impact of a decade of civil war. *The Greatest Silence: Rape in the Congo* commences with what has become a feature of this kind of documentary: the revival of intertitles, more familiar from the days of silent film, now deployed in place of commentary so that the subjects' voices are not made secondary to the filmmaker's narration. Intercut with women's eyes and words paying eloquent testimony to their victimhood, the titles give you the stark facts:

Since 1997 a brutal civil war has been raging in the Democratic Republic of Congo . . . It is the deadliest conflict since World War II: almost 4 million people have died . . . And there are the invisible casualties: tens of thousands of women and girls who have been systematically kidnapped, enslaved, raped and tortured.[18]

As the women begin to tell their story – and the militia men boast of what they have done to them – UN officers and aid workers confirm the atrocious scale of this largely unreported humanitarian disaster:

Ces femmes ne parlent pas et ce silence tue milles des femmes dans les forêts du Congo. / These women don't speak out and silence kills thousands of women in the forests of the Congo.[19]

This film has been shown on HBO in the United States, not least due to the reputation of its maker. Some other well-established directors do work in the same spirit of sisterly collaboration, using their professional position to liberate other voices. The English director

Most would-be Iraqi filmmakers had no equipment. One young Iraqi had completed a postgraduate programme at the Baghdad School of Fine Arts before the invasion, where he had had to make do with a 35 mm stills camera in the absence of any film or video cameras. Following the invasion, Hayder Mousa Daffar was working as a cashier at the Palestine Hotel, and offering his services as a translator and fixer free to visiting journalists and diplomats, as long as they promised to tell any American producers they might know that Daffar was 'The Iraqi filmmaker with No Camera'. An American producer called Aaron Raskin heard about him, got in touch and the eventual result was a film made by Daffar and a group of Iraqi filmmakers, *The Dreams of Sparrows* (2005). It charts their attempt to reconcile the conflicting points of view among Iraqis regarding the war, Saddam Hussein and the occupation. The film shows how these events, and the experience of recording them, change the filmmakers' minds and characters. People who embraced the Americans on their arrival and the fall of Saddam have had to think twice as the killings continue and things deteriorate. The filmmakers address their own camera and reveal their own thoughts in reaction to the death of a friend, killed by Americans, who riddled his car with over a hundred bullets:

He was the first one to be happy at the fall of Saddam's regime . . . Baghdad, Baghdad is hell, really is hell. US troops and government of USA is very dirty here. In start, when Baghdad is fall, when Saddam is gone, I am very happy. Not just me. Believe me. All Iraqi people . . . US troops is very hardhearted.[23]

The film is dedicated to Saad Fakher, an Associate Producer, who was killed during the production. Hayder Mousa Daffar went on an epic tour of the United States promoting the film and set up the Iraq Eye Group with Aaron Raskin. This organisation's aim is 'sustainable media self-empowerment within Iraq and increased media exposure for these issues internationally'[24] and, in 2006, the Soros Foundation's Open Society Institute awarded them a significant grant to pursue their goals of human rights and freedom of speech. Although *Dreams of Sparrows* has been seen around the world, their primary distribution window is now a site on YouTube, making their work more widely available.[25]

Black voices

As Hayder Mousa Daffar found, limited access to both the means of production and the means of distribution severely limits the opportunities for filmmakers working outside conventional structures. In the wealthy United States of the 1960s and 1970s, the civil rights movement's exclusion from power and equality was matched by their relative invisibility in film discourse. The short-lived Black Arts movement (1965–75), which flourished with the parallel Black Power movement, stimulated a flowering of poets and writers, but no filmmakers. Despite the grand narrative that Martin Luther King and Malcolm X had to impart, their image was still largely mediated by the white media. The more notable black presence on screens at the time was the then commercial vogue for blaxploitation features such as the original *Shaft* (1971). It was not until 1987 that the full story of the epic struggle from 1954 to 1965 was told, in the award-garlanded six-part documentary series *Eyes on the Prize*, which gave fresh impetus to black people, not just in the United States but in the UK too. Its maker was Henry Hampton, whose Blackside Productions was the largest independent African-American-owned documentary production company. In the light of its success, he was able to make a second series of *Eyes on the Prize*, charting subsequent developments up to the 1980s, and other films charting the African-American experience, such as *Malcolm X: Make It Plain* (1994) and *I'll Make Me a World: A Century of African-American Arts* (1999). Hampton died of lung cancer in 1998, widely revered for his contribution to African-American arts, but he has hardly blazed a trail that many have been able to emulate.

Just as Barack Obama found, the United States is still conflicted in its views on race, ready to embrace the African-American only as long as he subsumes his voice within the major key of the Star Spangled Banner. Hollywood has been similarly slow to promote the African-American director. With the honourable exception of Spike Lee, no African-American director is internationally known who has not first become famous as an actor in mainstream movies – proving themselves first 'one of us'. This limited liberation is what helps shield the American public from the deeper fault lines that run through their society, only occasionally erupting to the surface, as during the 2008 presidential race. Directors who work with this as their primary palette are marginalised, such as the filmmaker Charles Burnett. The prolific film critic of the *Chicago Reader*, Jonathan Rosenbaum has long championed Burnett's work in the face of widespread indifference:

> I think a strong case can be made that Charles Burnett is the most gifted and important black filmmaker this country has ever had . . . Given the difficulties he had in the 70s and 80s getting films made, [he] seemed in danger of becoming the Carl Dreyer of the black independent cinema – the consummate master who makes a film a decade, known only to a small band of film lovers.[26]

Writing on the thirtieth anniversary re-release of Burnett's debut feature, *Killer of Sheep* (1977), about a weary black abattoir worker in the Los Angeles ghetto of Watts, Rosenbaum recognises that it is partly because Burnett does not pursue a predictable commercial path that he is hard to pigeon-hole. 'I think it has more to do with Burnett's resistance to hustling and branding, which is in fact an important part of his greatness',[27] he writes, instancing his oeuvre's mixture of drama and documentary, from the contemporary folktale *To Sleep With Anger* (1990) to *America Becoming* (1991), a feature-length documentary on the immigrant diversity of America's evolving multicultural society. On the re-release of *Killer of Sheep*, Burnett emphasised that this experience is his primary subject, clearly superseding the filmic form it appears in:

> The middle class is shrinking for whites and blacks, there's a lot of outsourcing, people are losing their jobs, and a lot of people are homeless. There's a lot more fear and concern for the future than there was in the 1960s and the 1970s. The reasons we made the film, *Killer of Sheep*, [were] it seems like a lot more innocent. Iraq has drained a lot of resources away from America. And the people affected by this the most are people of colour.[28]

Such covertly political use of film may be one of the reasons that commercial interests shy away from Burnett's work. For the most part, they feel safer with the work of Bill Miles, the only African-American independent producer based at WNET/Thirteen in New York, one of the leading PBS stations. Over the last quarter century, Bill Miles has produced some

15 PBS 'specials' on African-American history, such as *I Remember Harlem* in 1981. This meticulously-researched history of the New York black community's 350-year history followed his 1977 debut *Men of Bronze*, about the all-black 369th Infantry Regiment that fought under the French flag during World War I, and which set the style for Miles's particular form of oral history.

Miles frequently returns to the unrecognised contribution of black soldiers, from *The Different Drummer: Blacks in the Military* (1983) to *Liberators: Fighting on Two Fronts in World War II* (1992), which he co-directed and co-produced with Nina Rosenblum. *Liberators* was nominated for an Oscar, but fell foul of Jewish and veteran groups' complaints about its inclusion of claims that two all-black battalions liberated the Buchenwald and Dachau concentration camps. A seven-month inquiry by WNET found the film and its research 'seriously flawed' for allowing the testimony to go unchallenged and uncorroborated, but the producers riposted that such oral testimony was 'an essential way to inform the historic record, especially in light of the omissions concerning the contributions of African-Americans to the military in World War II'. Because such testimony is often impossible to verify, they argued: 'that is the reason for collecting oral testimony which must be included, not censored, in the historic record'.[29] WNET chose not to repeat the film and to tighten its documentary practices, but *Liberators* remains available on DVD and a testimony not just to black military history but to the problems that such voices have in getting heard.

Third Cinema

If the United States is still nervous about the discourse unleashed by the civil rights movement in the early 1960s, it was even more fearful of the world's liberation movements that followed on in the late 1960s. National independence movements gave rise to a broader critique of capitalism and students around the world manned the barricades with threats to the established order, from the Sorbonne to the campuses of California. Though quickly suppressed, from among their number came a new breed of filmmaker, who saw the power of the weapon they held in their hands: the camera. Seizing on the internationalist spirit of the times, it was the movers and shakers of Latin American cinema that conceived the idea that there could be a tri-continental response to the economic and cultural dominance of America. *Grupo Cine Liberacion* (Cinema of Liberation Group) represented the solidarity of Latin American filmmakers embarking on this battle, and it was the writing of the Argentinian filmmakers Fernando Solanas and Octavio Getino, in their film journal *Tricontinental*, that gave the movement the name 'Third Cinema'. The First Cinema was defined as the passive, escapist consumerism of Hollywood; the Second Cinema was the individualist auteurism of European arthouse; and the Third Cinema was to be a democratic, inclusive counter-culture, freeing up the means of production and distribution to liberate the individual and the world:

> The anti-imperialist struggle of the peoples of the Third World and of their equivalents inside the imperialist countries constitutes today the axis of the world revolution. Third Cinema is, in our opinion, the cinema that recognizes in that struggle the most gigantic cultural, scientific and artistic manifestation of our time, the great possibility of constructing a liberated personality with each people as the starting point – in a word, the decolonization of culture . . .

What determines Third Cinema is the conception of the world, and not the genre or any explicitly political approach. Any story, any subject can be taken up by Third Cinema. In the dependent countries, Third Cinema is a cinema of decolonisation, which expresses the will to national liberation, anti-mythic, anti-racist, anti-bourgeois, and popular.[30]

Solanas and Getino formulated the theory of Third Cinema only after they had shot and released their three-part, four-hour documentary *La Hora de los Hornos/Hour of the Furnaces* (1968), which combines many of the elements they see as central to the liberation project. A dramatic, dynamic denunciation of the violence of neo-colonialist ambitions in Latin America, the film contrasts the life of the wealthy with the misery of the poor. The first part is constructed as a film essay on 'Neocolonialism and Violence'. The second part, 'Act for Liberation', is more observational and is split into two sections: 'Chronicle of Peronism' and 'Chronicle of Resistance'. The final part, 'Violence and Liberation', dedicated to 'the new man being born out of this process of liberation', is a threnody on violence. The film also combines most documentary elements, from newsreel, archive and stills, to interviews, observational footage and reconstruction, from Dziga Vertov-style intertitles to didactic commentary. This 'anything goes' approach to ramming home its political message owes much to Solanas's previous career in advertising, but also makes the film 'an unforgettable experience':[31]

The film establishes a close relationship between form and content, seeking to sensitise its ideas and varying each section according to the topic dealt with. The political-ideological perspective, in a strongly Manichean register typical of the period, mainly combined a historiographic revisionism which contested the liberal version of Argentine history – the main issues discussed in the Havana Tricontinental Conference and an uncompromising Fanonian-rooted 'thirdworldism'. Fritz Fanon's influence was certainly remarkable; in every exhibition, a sign with his motto 'Every spectator is either a coward or a traitor' hung below the screen.[32]

Third Cinema was essentially the filmic voice of the revolution and embraced any of the movements within film which could be seen as 'revolutionary', such as the work of the leading Cuban filmmaker, Tomás Gutiérrez Alea. His *Memorias del Subdesarrollo/Memories of Underdevelopment* (1968) is taken from Edmundo Desnoes's novella *Inconsolable Memories*, the memoir of a morally ambiguous bourgeois intellectual living in Havana in the period of time between the Bay of Pigs Invasion and the Cuban Missile Crisis. The first feature to be shown in the United States since the Castro revolution, this was a mixture of drama and documentary, 'a collage . . . with a little bit of everything' as Gutiérrez said. *Memories of Underdevelopment* uses documentary techniques from long unbroken hand-held shots to fast-cut montage sequences, from observational footage to stills, archive and newsreel. The use of Hollywood film clips, and recorded speeches by Fidel Castro and John F. Kennedy, add the Third Cinema effect of being an expropriation of every element as a direct challenge to the linear stylistic straitjackets of Hollywood.

Third Cinema also retrospectively embraced Gillo Pontecorvo's *La battaglia di Algeri/The Battle of Algiers* (1966), a black-and-white film of the long, bloody independence war between the French army and the Algerian Liberation Front. Its quasi-documentary treatment and unflinching representation of the viciousness of guerilla war have made it the most influential film reference on terrorist insurgency to this day, being used for practical information by Irish republicans, Palestinians and even the American military planning the 2003 Iraq invasion. *The Battle of Algiers'* even-handed portrayal of atrocities committed by both sides have led to it being criticised by both left and right for being insufficiently moralistic, but its evasion of such propagandistic simplicities are what have made it so powerful. The film historian Peter Matthews writes:

> The director and his screenwriter, Franco Solinas, wanted to commemorate the popular uprising that had succeeded in ousting the French from Algeria in July 1962. That event triggered a seismic wave of anti-colonial movements across the Third World, serving both as a millennial image of freedom and a more practical lesson in the violent means deemed necessary to win it. Algiers would itself help to galvanize those struggles by uniting the revolutionary prerequisites of a cool head and a blazing heart. No other political movie in the last fifty years bears the same power to lift you from your seat with the incandescent fervor of its commitment. And none before or since has anchored that passion in so lucid a diagnosis of the fault lines separating exploiter and exploited. Pontecorvo's work can now be recognized as an absolute pinnacle of counter-cinema – a *ne plus ultra* of a mode that seeks to intervene strategically in the war for social change.[33]

But, as Williams observes, few so highly lauded films have had so few significant imitators. He feels it is precisely the bleak representation of the Frantz Fanon view[34] it adopts, that the violence endemic to colonialism reduces its resistors to that level, was too intransigent for most tastes. He suggests that the Greek political filmmaker Costa Gavras was the key beneficiary of Pontecorvo's legacy, but that he typically siphoned his quasi-documentary techniques into notionally political conspiracy thrillers, such as *Z* (1969) and *State of Siege* (1973). 'But the true heirs of *Algiers* have been numberless filmmakers from Brazil, Argentina, Bolivia, Cuba, Senegal, Mali, Tunisia, Morocco, Palestine, and Algeria itself – inspired by Pontecorvo's supreme empathy to tell their own stories of nationalist striving.'[35] The prescriptive nature of Third Cinema ideology, while using disparate techniques, may have made it more influential than it seems and yet less visible. Many Third World film voices were emerging in the postcolonial world, though not all conforming to the revolutionary ideology propounded by Solanas and Getino. While the Senegalese filmmaker Ousman Sembene was inventing African film drama, Kidlat Tahimik was taking on the American-influenced Filipino film industry with his semi-autobiographical fable *Mabagangbong bangungot/Perfumed Nightmare* (1977). As filmmakers evolved their own nation-specific crafts, from Satyajit Ray's Bengali masterpieces to Ken Loach's brand of English social realism, they have all been retrospectively welcomed to the pantheon of Third Cinema greats. In the 1980s, the Ethiopian film writer Teshome Gabriel attempted to give a new formulation to the by then largely redundant term:

> Third Cinema includes an infinity of subjects and styles as varied as the lives of the people it portrays . . . [Its] principle characteristic is really not so much where it is made, or even who makes it, but, rather, the ideology it espouses and the consciousness it displays.[36]

As the film academic Chris Berry comments: 'In so doing, Gabriel transforms Third Cinema from a prescriptive line into a descriptive field.'[37]

Liberation is not the inevitable outcome of history, any more than progress is. Much of Latin American film was crushed by dictatorships in the 1970s, with the US-backed *coup d'état* in Chile in 1973 and the military coup in Argentina in 1976 joining the Brazilian military dictatorship (1964–85).

China

Whereas Bangladeshi documentary reflected the needs of a nation liberated from subsidiarity, China's so-called New Documentary Movement tends to celebrate the individual emerging from the conformity of the Maoist years and the 'Cultural revolution' that suppressed free cinema. Although still airbrushed from official and popular discourse, the massacre of students in Tiananmen Square in 1989 is clearly *the* event that marks a turning point in the sensibilities that inform documentary. Prior to this time, Chinese documentary was made for state-controlled television and still largely consisted of the illustrated lecture that characterised early television everywhere, authorised narratives on big themes intended to improve and impose orthodoxy. Called *zhuanti pian*, 'special topic films', to distinguish them from shorter newsreels, *xinwen pian*, they were essentially propagandist. But the contacts that economic liberalization had opened, and the exposure to Western archetypes notably through the internet (despite China's massive attempts at cyber-control), helped sponsor a documentary awakening. A combination of more widely available and utilisable DV camera gear and a much less rigorous system of censorship than that imposed upon feature film have also enabled documentary filmmaking.

Many filmmakers have started working for Chinese television in the daytime and making films on their own time. Some went on to find work as independent artists, such as Wu Wenguang, whose *Liulang Beijing – Zuihou De Mengxiangzhe/Bumming in Beijing – The Last Dreamers* (1990) was the first observational documentary, breaking with the commentary tradition. Following five fellow artists – a writer, two painters, a photographer and a theatre director – Wu 'felt a strong urge to record this rapidly changing China and this group of artists because I sensed it would be changed or even disappear very soon'.[38] His hand-held camera follows them in their work and living spaces and gives them time to live within the frame, amounting to a two and a half hour running time. As the writer, filmmaker and critic Ernest Larsen writes:

> Wu is not afraid to show us 'nothing' – someone cleaning a flat, for example, or making a painting . . . It is tempting to see this figure of style as distinctively 'Chinese' – but the temptation is worth resisting. Furthermore, Wu's long takes and emphasis on duration serve as a kind of counterpoint to the suddenness with which Tiananmen was crushed . . . The prolonged moments of near silence in Bumming in Beijing produce the aesthetic effect of outlasting the remembered roar of government tanks.[39]

Wu caught up with his five artists for a second film five years later, *Shihai Weijia/At Home in the World* (1995), as their lives and aspirations had changed, and most had settled in other countries with varying degree of success. This encapsulates the 'political in the personal' that is at the heart of these films from China's New Documentary Movement. Shi Jian and Chen Jue's *I Graduated!* (1990) features eight students who graduated in the year of Tiananmen and who discuss their personal lives, hopes and fears, with the constant nagging question of whether they should leave for a life of freedom, but perhaps menial employment, in the West or stay to fill the preordained roles their good degrees destine them for in China, though even these certainties are now in question. Li Hong's *Hui Dao Fenghuang Qiao/Out of Phoenix-Bridge* (1997) finds four young girls who have come from a remote village in Hunan province to work as noodle vendors. Chen Weijun's *Hao Si Bu Ru Lai Huo Zhe/To Live is Better than to Die* (2002) is a harrowing portrait of the Ma family in another poor provincial village, where 60 per cent of the population have AIDs as a result of having sold their blood to a company using contaminated equipment. All these films deploy the sympathy of the personal moment to communicate their subtle critique of the wider world. It is what documentary does best and what has clearly liberated Chinese filmmakers to seize their role as contemporary commentators. The California film academic Bérénice Reynaud sees a pattern emerging in all these films:

> Peasant life was always full of hardship and misery, but never before had they to sell their blood or send their wives away, by the thousands, to be able to offset the poor return of the harvest. Never before were they snatched, by the hundreds of thousands, to fulfill the needs of industrial development or work on high-rise building construction sites, only to be spit out when they are no longer needed, losing their jobs to modernisation, their homes to urban development, their sanity to drugs or homelessness, their children to delinquency . . . These different documentaries are also quite specific about the way globalisation affects various categories of the population – from peasants to peasants-turned-industrial workers, from men to women (who experience different forms of displacement and internal migration, as the jobs offered to them are dissimilar), from adults to children, who may be the first generation of Chinese to come from a mass phenomenon of dislocated families, drug-addicted parents, runaway mothers, homeless relatives . . .[40]

One phenomenon that led to a more explicit politicisation of Chinese documentary was the number of young television producers sent to Tibet, where they experienced not just a different culture but one suffused with a sense of grievance and desire for liberation. Learning to see life through others' eyes was an important development for filmmakers and the independent Chinese documentary as a whole. Widely regarded as one of the best of the resulting films is *Ba kuo nan jie shi liu hao/No 16 Barkhor South Street* (1996), Duan Jinchan's sly take on the *ju wei hui*, the neighbourhood committees through which the Chinese administration not only administers local law and order, but everything from marital affairs to political education. Duan's lovingly filmed observation of one such committee in Lhasa, as Tibetans are instructed on how to celebrate China's takeover of their country, needs no commentary to make its message clear. This film also marked a step change in technique, using superior sound and more careful editing. This, and the fact of it winning the prestigious *Grand Prix du Festival du Réel* in Paris in 1996, seems to have made this and the films that followed more acceptable to the Chinese authorities.

As Duan Jinchang and his fellow filmmakers enjoy the plaudits of the international festivals, the real liberation that is occurring is the growing availability of new means of production and distribution. Wu Wenguang speaks of the liberating opportunities afforded by DV, a medium that he feels has transformed his and others' work. He even executive produced the first Chinese underground feature shot on DV, Zhu Wan's *Haixan/Seafood*

(2001), instancing a creative dialogue that has opened up between documentary and independent feature filmmakers. But the more important evolution is the work that Wenguang has been doing training villagers to film their own lives. The China Village Self-Governance Project, co-funded by China and the EU, could easily have deteriorated into a government PR stunt, but the training at his studio in Beijing that Wenguang and his colleagues gave ten villagers selected from all over China resulted in some delightful vignettes of everyday life now being shown all over the world. The villagers were not involved in editing the ten-minute shorts that each shot, but Wenguang says that the training for that is the next stage in the project, a project that seeks to reduce the yawning gap between industrialised urban China and the rural poor.

The other Chinese development, more in tune with the rest of the word, is what they call 'cellflix', short films made on their mobile, or cell, phones. Normally only a few shots lasting no more than a minute. Since January 2006, the Shanghai-based magazine *Metroer* has run an online competition for these, where they are freely downloadable. Online video apparently manages to evade the draconian proscriptions placed upon online text in China, but in any case the tendency is towards irony and satire, referencing film and other cultural phenomena. *Zai XizanIn Tibet* parodies Tibetan movies while *Shanghai Freak* shows artful images of the city, cut to the sound of Carla Bruni (Sarkozy)'s *La Dernière Minute*. As the American film academic Paola Voci writes:

> In China, as elsewhere, new locations and new media have redefined the experience of watching a moving image, beyond the cinematic experience . . . Self-reflectivity and irony have also been recurrent traits of online movies. Unlike their feature-film counterparts, which can only be downloaded either illegally or at a cost, *cellflix* (mobile phone movies) and *e gao* (spoofs) are mostly legal and free . . . The relevance of 'non-feature film' independent movies does not lie in their technological novelty *per se*, but rather in how they are contributing to redefine the visual in China, while also de-intellectualising the discourse on dissent and avant-garde. Their most provoking feature is not the use of new means of production and distribution, but their deployment of lightness and their exploration of mockery, sarcasm, paradox and insincerity as evocative and disobedient visual pleasures.[41]

Conclusion

For those of us for whom dissent is the norm, where sarcasm and disbelief in the governing system is endemic, such freedoms are taken for granted. That does not necessarily mean they are used well. While the Chinese are seizing these newfound opportunities with both creative hands, much of the video posted on Western sites is derivative and self-regarding, a form of showing off in a world where consumer choice has apparently diminished the need or demand for thoughtful critique. YouTube is better known for performing animals than probing analysis. As we have seen, mainstream television has banished more demanding material to the margins at best, while it struggles to cope with a fragmenting market and the incursions of the upstart internet. The latter offers unfettered opportunity to liberate each and every voice, but finding the correct form and context is not as easy, nor as free as it would appear. The internet is still expanding fast and a stable market model is yet to emerge, but the fantastic sums paid for social networking sites indicate that someone expects to make a great deal of money from all this activity. Advertising is currently the main income generator, which may ally some inappropriate messages with your statements of principle. But there are other compromises. Few people posting their private details on Facebook realise that they are signing over copyright ownership, so that – if they become the victim of a crime, say – those details can be sold to tabloids and other news machines keen to exploit their bad news. Sites routinely expect to take all rights in your material if they pay for your work, as Current TV do, or if not, they still want rigorous clearances pre-arranged, such as the dormant ITV Local.

Better to construct your own site and post your own video log, as the ground-breaking video-journalist David Dunkley Gyimah introduced in Chapter 2 does. As he says: 'People would like to make the news, but they believe it is the exclusive preserve of the big corp-orations, like the BBC and ITN. But they can do it.'[42] The Israeli human rights organisation B'Tselem have proved that point with their video camera distribution project, which won the One World Media Trust special prize in June 2009.[43] Over three years they distributed 160 cameras to Palestinians on the West Bank, and then in the Gaza Strip, to record their experiences. Video footage such as the beating of Palestinian shepherds by masked settlers in Khirbet Susiya, a settler firing from short-range and wounding three Palestinians in Hebron, and soldiers harming Palestinians or refraining from enforcing the law on violent settlers have been broadcast widely by Israeli and international media.[44] Footage is passed to the police, such as the Hebron incident, and there have been convictions, though not in this case. More important is the opportunity for Palestinians to seize some control and redefine themselves as other than helpless victims. As the 29-year-old Palestinian project co-ordinator Issa Amro says, 'It's a very good kind of reaction to the violence. Instead of throwing stones back, they go to the camera and start filming'.[45]

The impact goes beyond that, as intended by the project's founder, Israeli filmmaker Oren Yakobovich, who had served in the Israeli Army in the West Bank, where he had realised how different the Palestinian reality was to the image perpetuated in Israel. As the One World international award recognised, there is something vitally resonant in the liberation won with a camera:

> I realised something was wrong with the narrative I knew. For Israelis there is a conspiracy of silence. Nobody wants to know what is happening there . . . For the Israeli public it was the first time they really managed to feel what it means to be Palestinian. For the first time Israelis are identifying with the Palestinians.[46]

At the same time, the millions of Iranians who took to the streets to protest what they saw as the rigged presidential election of 2009, filmed these attempts at liberation on their mobile phones. The shocking images of people shot by Iranian forces – most graphically the 19-year-old student Neda Agha Soltan bleeding to death in her father's arms – reverberated around the world, making it impossible for the repressed not to share their pain. But the speed and breadth of that image transmission may also be responsible for the equally speedy dissipation of its impact. Similar dissemination of the violent repression of Burmese monks in 2007 did nothing to ease their lot, and Iran continues to mine political energy from the West's outrage. Liberation, as women and African-Americans eloquently attest, is not won so easily. The camera is merely one weapon in the war.

Expert briefing – shooting for the net

Think of the internet as a work in progress, with the fast links of broadband still only in their infancy. Within the life of this book, widely available speeds of 12 megabytes/second should make internet connections equivalent to television signals. As this and the home equipment move us rapidly towards multimedia convergence, with everything sent and received through the same screen and interface, distinctions between broadcasting and online will gradually disappear. Equipping yourself to shoot for the web and self-publish there merely puts you in poll position, as the resourcing and support available to traditional television producers tend to shrink:

A. CAPTURE

The kit and connections required are surprisingly simple:

1 **A camcorder** ideally capable of providing HD in full 1080 line resolution. Sony's HVR-Z1U is a professional favourite, but the cheaper and ultra-compact HVR-A1E is adequate. There is a movement towards tapeless operation as memory cards become cheaper and support more material (see p. 48), but tape and tape cameras still remain cheaper at the moment.

2 **Additional sound capacity**: a professional shotgun (directional) microphone, such as a Sennheiser ME66, for good clean sound and a radio lapel microphone with camera-mounted receiver, such as the Sennheiser Freeport, for interviews and other speech inputs. Don't forget headphones to keep constantly monitoring sound, the usual feature of disappointing results.

3 **Robust kit bag** with, among other things, a lens cloth for keeping the lens clean, a pen for labelling tapes, spare batteries and charger. Most solo operators dispense with tripods, though a few favour the lighter benefits of the monopod, to give stability when operating in difficult conditions. At the heart of operations should be an efficient system of logging tapes, contributor details and rights clearances where necessary.

4 **Laptop** with sufficient processing capacity and memory, ideally a minimum of 2.4 GHz and 2 GB RAM, respectively. The industry standard is an Apple MacBook or PowerBook, not least because only Macs support journalists' most widely used editing software, Final Cut Pro (or the cheaper version Final Cut Express: iMovie is not really adequate for more than the simpler functions).

5 **Flash motion graphics** enable you to complete films in a manner that has that extra sense of professional finish, not just embedding information more effectively but giving your product a gloss.

6 **The latest version of Adobe Dreamweaver**, the web development application. This supports the quick and easy design and maintenance of your website, though you should have knowledge of HMTL, metatagging and SEO (Search Engine Organisation). Tagging allows the subject specific connections with your site and equivalent video hyperlinks are only just around the corner.

7 **A web hosting contract** can be very cheap, with a plethora of propositions competing in the market to service every need, from simple site maintenance to complex domain content management supporting sophisticated interactive applications.

B. CONTEXT

Thus equipped, you have all you need to service your own online site. This is an infinitesimal fraction of the capitalisation of a television channel, and you need only address the subjects and audience of your choice. Your audience will find you, as long as you follow the basic rules of engagement:

8 **Style**: For the moment at least, Web films need to be conceived to suit their user and likely context of use. They will probably be seen on a small screen with limited sound by a lone viewer, not on the home cinema environment television is now aiming for with HD production. Shooting gonzo, or 'dirty' as Gyimah calls it, recognises that close and personal viewing experience, with films cut fast and tight, with punchy sound and music.

9 **Brevity**: Most video pods run three to six minutes, rarely more than 10 minutes. Full-length can be run non-stop, as long as the user's broadband rate supports it, but anything more than 20 megabytes is difficult for many. Furthermore, whether seeking information or illustration, the web browser's lateral, associative approach prefers a concentrated experience.

10 **Metadata**: SEO (search engine organisation) is currently word-driven, so key words need to be embedded in headline and supporting text to ensure that your film is found by appropriate searches. While the formal textual meta-tagging is no longer the established protocol, video hyperlinking is still in an early stage of development.

11 **Distinctiveness**: As text bloggers have discovered, the key to internet success is having something original to say. Video loggers, or 'vloggers', equally need to have a distinctive voice and message. They need to bring a novel insight and approach to bear, expanding stories and making connections that mainstream journalists and filmmakers cannot or dare not.

12 **3-6-9**: David Gyimah recommends a standard approach to shooting on the hoof, whereby you shoot a wide-shot or contextual opener for three seconds, possibly over an opening question or introductory line, then move into a mid-shot of interviewee or subject for six seconds, before going in close for nine seconds. This works uncut, but also reflects the likely useable segments if you are going to edit and extract. Most shots last no longer than three seconds on screen, and you rarely see an interview clip lasting longer than ten seconds these days.

Part IV

Entertainment for all

A fter a year in which television had been rocked by scandals and all the terrestrial broadcasters had been chastised and fined for various failings in their duty of care to the public, the highest profile victim of the period bounced back to say 'it's all entertainment'. Peter Fincham lost his job as Controller of BBC1 in 2007 over the editing of a documentary about the Queen but, after a few short months reacquainting himself with his family, he had been hired by an ailing ITV to help arrest the company's decline. To emphasise how quickly reputations are redeemed, he had also been offered the opportunity to deliver the prestigious McTaggart lecture at the August 2008 Edinburgh International Television Festival. The previous year in Edinburgh, the lugubrious Jeremy Paxman had caught the humbled mood of the industry and delivered an ethical broadside against its plummeting standards. Fincham embodied a newly buoyant mood that signalled the end of the hair shirt era and a return to the core business, which he defined as entertainment, albeit in the various forms of drama and sport, comedy and factual, news and current affairs:

> Television is a broad church, but it does not want empty pews. At ITV entertaining our audience is part of our DNA. So is our commitment to providing our services free to the consumer.[1]

The consumer, you note, has replaced the viewer, indicating the commercial nature of the relationship. The political subtext of the speech was an attack on Ofcom, the industry regulator whose job it is to see that ITV fulfils its public service broadcasting (PSB) responsibilities in return for its broadcast wavelength spectrum and the licence to broadcast. These duties they argue, from religion to regional news, are the most costly relative to their returns on the balance sheet. They argue that they should be freed from these shackles to enable them to make more money 'providing what people want', i.e. entertainment for all. Minorities, whose interests PSB is there to help preserve, are now served they argue by other means: cable channels and the internet. Free the broadcasters to cast their nets as broadly as possible, they say. They were only allowed to turn the former regional federation of ITV into a corporate monolith in 2002 on the strict undertaking that they maintain those PSB duties, but they argue that is no longer relevant. 'Things change', Melvin Bragg plaintively argued, clearly concerned that his share options were a shadow of their former glory.[2]

Television has always been about broadcasting reach – reaching as many people as possible and carefully counting the audience figures on which to base future programme and advertising spend, where appropriate. But its progressive industrialisation in the 'late nineties' and 'early noughties' has created a seismic shift in values and processes. It is not just ITV that has seen a radical clearing of the less profitable elements of the programme prospectus. With increased competition and a reduced licence fee, the BBC has had to make successive cuts over several years, with the former flagship departments of Documentaries and Current Affairs taking some of the biggest hits. Documentaries have been completely subsumed within a reorganised factual department; Current Affairs is now a much reduced subdivision of the News empire, it also having taken significant cuts. But where these mighty oaks have been felled, new growths have taken root.

Fertilised by the demand for new ways of reaching the audience – particularly the young with money to spend and brand loyalties yet to form – forms and formats have emerged to rekindle the excitement of broadcasting and re-engage the public, not least through the new opportunities of interactivity and online bolt-ons. These are the new arenas for creative energies and occupation, many demanding the new media understanding of how programmes can have presence and staying power across the multiple platforms available – '360 degree commissioning' in the BBC's short-lived jargon of a previous (2007) moment – but most obviously dealing in the currencies of contemporary popular culture: celebrity and personal aspiration. While celebrity gilds the lily, giving form to aspirations, the real star of twenty-first-century television is the individual, freed from the passive sofa of the spectator to strut the stage for a moment, as reality television contestant or makeover subject. These chapters chart the evolution of these forms and the parallel breakdown between the genres of drama, documentary and art.

12 Formats and reality TV

....

reality n. the state of things as they are or appear to be, rather than as one might wish them to be

In the twenty-first century, the classic documentary has been under assault from many other competitive genres. In 2000, the British Film Institute compiled a list of 'The Hundred Greatest Television Programmes'[1] ever, as chosen by a poll of the television industry's good and great. Only nine of the hundred were documentaries, mostly long-running series, reflecting the importance placed upon a large body of work, from Granada's current affairs flagship *World in Action* (1963–98) to the BBC arts strand *Arena* (1975–present). Others were key genre pieces in history – *Civilisation* (1969), *The World at War* (1973–4) and natural history – *Life on Earth* (1979), *Walking with Dinosaurs* (1999). *The Death of Yugoslavia* (1995) and *The Nazis – A Warning from History* (1997) were other landmark series, also mentioned in Chapter 3. That leaves just one stand-alone documentary that made the top 100 television programmes, *28 Up* (1985), which came in at a creditable number 26 in the chart.

28 Up was not actually a one-off documentary, insofar that it was the fourth in an occasional series initiated in 1964 with a cast found by the then young documentary researcher Michael Apted. *7 Up*[2] followed a group of children from different backgrounds who were then seven and since then, every seven years, Apted – the subsequently successful Hollywood director – has returned to Britain to look his characters up and film their progress through life. Of the 14 original participants, only 3 eventually withdrew in adult life and most were still featured in the *49 Up* episode in 2005. *7 Up* was made for *World in Action*, just another documentary finding the political in the personal, and was never intended to become the recurrent phenomenon it has. The original idea was a classic one-off, to illustrate the extent to which class defined children's aspirations and expectations, and referenced the Jesuit founder Francis Xavier's line: 'Give me a child until he is seven and I will give you the man'. But it struck a chord, and the return to the same group seven years later[3] set in train the pattern that has emerged as a prototype format, with the inevitability of the cycle defining the audience's relationship with the content. But it is much more than a satisfying frame. The intimacy that these people have evolved with Apted's camera, and the reflexivity it has allowed over the unusual canvas of a whole lifetime, have given the series a unique position in documentary history. When Channel 4 decided to celebrate the *50 Greatest Documentaries* in 2005, the *Up* series took the number one spot. The influential American film critic Roger Ebert affirmed the choice: 'It is an inspired, almost noble use of film. It helps us understand what it is to be alive'.[4] The series has spawned many copies around the world, from America and Australia to Russia, South Africa and Japan, and the BBC celebrated the new millennium by commissioning a new series with a new set of 7-year-olds from the original production company, Granada, starting with *7 Up 2000*.[5] All this pays tribute to the significance that this series has had on the documentary form. It unconsciously laid the template for a formalised structure that has gradually become dominant, but which has simultaneously allowed a more unpredictable and incomplete narrative. As Bruzzi writes:

> The premise . . . is to follow subjects with no definite end in mind, as no one can exactly know how the lives of the individuals featured will turn out; the films are poised between certainty (surety of intention and motivation) and uncertainty (the unpredictability inevitably caused by the individual subjects), and the trajectory or conclusion of either is the result of a combination of imposed formal structure and unexpected changes in direction.[6]

People tune in for the seven-yearly update precisely because they are curious to know what has happened to these people in the intervening years. That their largely unwanted fame has clearly influenced how these lives have turned out, thus making the documentary value of their experiences strictly limited, does not seem to matter to the audience. It is the entertainment value of watching real people engage with the dramas of life that makes these films so seminal. That Apted's characters largely fulfilled his original determinist thesis, by following the life paths anticipated by their class and schooling, is now deemed secondary to the minutiae of their observed lives. The randomness of individual behaviour was what was at the heart of docu-soaps. The formatted, or constructed, documentary added a framework for that randomness to flower within, and a narrative arc that gave a programme a clear audience proposition. Reality television formats took the framing mechanism to new heights – and depths.

Documentary formats

An early pinnacle of the documentary format was *Faking It*. Its simple premise was to take a member of the public and train them over four weeks to pass themselves off as something they were not in a public test, where experts would have to try and spot the faker among the genuine contestants. The first show featured a softly-spoken, young Oxford-educated gay, Alex Geike, who managed to pass himself off as a bouncer at London's Hippodrome club. *Faking It* was devised by RDF Media's Stephen Lambert, who referred to it as 'a modern-day *Pygmalion*'; and the second show followed the Shaw play's plot by trying to turn a working-class Northern woman, Lisa Dickinson-Gray, into someone who could pass as a lady. Unfortunately she did not transform into My Fair Lady, but these first two programmes had shown an audience taste for the concept and it went to series for the next three years. Among the most successful transformations achieved were cellist Sian Evans becoming a club DJ and former naval petty officer Spencer Bowdler triumphing as a drag artist. The more improbable the journey, the more compelling the viewing was, but only if the central character won at the end. Where they were spotted in the final test, audience appreciation plummeted, as they felt cheated. Of course, the real documentary point of the show is the journey of self-discovery, but this is where the format becomes more important than the substance.

Annette Hill dissects this phenomenon in her book, *Reality TV: Audiences and Popular Factual Television*:

The narrative drive is one of transformation, and as such the transformation from, say a classical cello player is only really complete when the end result is success as a nightclub DJ. When the transformation is not a success, the programme ends on a flat note. As viewers, we know the chances of a classical cello player successfully becoming a nightclub DJ are slim, especially in a short timeframe, but nevertheless we want to see the story as life affirming. If this means the programme-makers have to work hard to ensure a likely positive outcome by pre-selecting someone who has a high chance of succeeding, then many viewers would accept this constructed element of the programme in return for a successful outcome.[7]

What viewers want and will, or will not, wear has become the key determinant to television commissioning, and the main reason for the relative demise of traditional documentary in the face of formats and other more user-friendly forms of factual television. RDF Media followed up their BAFTA award-winning success in *Faking It* with *Wife Swap*, an even more successful format. It debuted in 2003 with an audience of 6 million – *Faking It* had previously been judged a relative success with just 2 million – and has been constantly recommissioned ever since. *Wife Swap*'s premise is even simpler – take two families and switch the wives for ten days, and watch the sparks fly. The incoming wife has to abide by the rules of the house, left in written form by the departed wife, who is simultaneously learning how her replacement's life is organised. After the first week, they can introduce their own rules, explaining what benefits this will bring to their adoptive family. At the end of ten days, the two couples reunite and meet to discuss the lessons of their swap. Because the show is cast for conflict, with couples from radically opposed backgrounds and cultures, the swapped wives don't always last the course and those final bull sessions often turn into bovine recrimination. It is this that attracts the audience, but it also attracts condemnation.

Feminists decry the whole sexist assumption the *Wife Swap* programme is based upon, that the woman is the domestic goddess/nester–nurturer, as opposed to the hunter–gatherer man. As Natasha Forrest's critique argues, the central premise is that 'a woman's place is in the home' and the series struggles to accommodate the reality that most women work and have identities outside the home. She points out that the simplified oppositional framework allows no serious social or structural analysis, leaving it inevitable that the individual woman is blamed for any failings the programme's producers knowingly flush out:

Wife Swap managed to pitch the women against each other so successfully that each episode ended with the poor confused husbands looking on in wide-eyed innocence as their wives laid into each other, attacking each other's lifestyle choices and angrily defending their own. As one housewife bitterly told her career-focused opponent, 'for a woman to fail as a housewife is ridiculous'.[8]

Pitting poor working-class against wealthy professionals, blacks against racists, is not the subtlest or most illuminating way to reveal the fault lines in contemporary society, but it has proved a ratings and format sales winner for RDF. The company has an American subsidiary that has been making an American version since 2004, and there are franchised versions playing in Croatia, Sweden, Norway, Denmark, Estonia, Latvia, Lithuania, Serbia, Germany, the Netherlands and in Belgium, where it's called *De Nieuwe Mama/The New Mum*. That title draws attention to the innocents collaterally damaged in the crossfire, the children. While the parents, as adults, are free to make the misguided decision to open their lives to this level of prurient intervention, the children are drawn in by default, and many episodes concentrate on their emotional resistance to changes foisted by the surrogate standing in for their real mum. Current child protection legislation relies on the parents to safeguard their children against exploitation, but when the parents are instrumental in that exploitation the only, draconian sanction is the intervention of the state. Annette Hill raises the issue:

> In one episode of the first series in the UK (Channel 4, 2003), a working-class white family swapped lives with a working-class black family. The 'white wife', who confessed her fears that the other family might be non-white, openly argued with her adoptive husband, and her eldest daughter openly argued with her adoptive mother, at one point calling her a 'black bitch'. Whilst the parents will have given consent for themselves and their children to participate in the programme, did the children know the type of experience they were letting themselves in for, and did they have recourse to complain about how they were represented in the programme once the programme had been aired?[9]

Clearly not, but many of the adult participants also feel aggrieved that they did not read the small print on their contracts before signing up. One vegan businesswoman – a former TV presenter who might have been expected to know better – felt that she had been misled when sent to a rotting hulk, home to a carnivorous 'New Age' family whose life and food she could not stomach, but then discovered that she was liable to reimburse all production costs if she pulled out.[10] An Oklahoma Christian tried to sue ABC for $10 million when his American 'wife swap' turned out to be a gay man. He alleges that the producers threatened not to reveal where his wife was or pay to send her home if he left the show, suggesting she might leave him, which allegedly made him mentally ill.[11] RDF Media refute all these charges, but there is a premium on the amount of discomfiture they manage to engineer. Manipulation and misrepresentation have always been occupational hazards in documentary, but some feel they have become production devices in these factual formats.

Others argue that there are genuine resonances that go beyond an audience appetite for car crash television. The leading lights in the field are people who started in straight documentary departments, making one-off documentaries, and have now discovered richer returns in this field. Stephen Lambert, the RDF Media director of programmes responsible for *Faking It* and *Wife Swap*, had first been a documentary filmmaker on the BBC documentary strands *Forty Minutes* and *Inside Story*. Helen Veale, Creative Director of Outline Productions, which makes series such as *The House of Tiny Tearaways* and *Dumped*, formerly worked in current affairs at the BBC and produced *The Goldring Audit*. Both are ardent proselytes for formats that bring a bigger audience to subjects previously the preserve of a serious minority. Richard Klein, the BBC's former Head of Independent Commissioning for Knowledge and Commissioning Editor for Documentaries, prefers the term 'constructed documentary', and feels it has a valuable role within the broad church of documentary television:

Constructed documentary ranges across a wide spectrum ... *Faking It* is a more redemptive, early model, I thought rather brilliant actually. *Wife Swap* is more aggressive, if you like ... *Wife Swap* does take the view – and Stephen Lambert is a really brilliant man in this area, I think he understands a lot about television, he thinks a lot about society, and *Wife Swap* says that we are tribal and, if you put different tribes in the same kitchen, you get a row, you will be able to expose the differences between those tribes; that's what *Wife Swap* does.[12]

Although there is a view that the creative invention of these formats have revived a popular taste for factual programming that conventional documentary had long since failed to satisfy, if ever it had, there remains a strong body of opinion that sees television irredeemably dumbing down. In 2007, Channel 4 decided to initiate a new attraction by kicking off each series with a *Celebrity Wife Swap*. The announcement that Vanessa Feltz had been despatched to magician Paul Daniels's house, prompted the *Guardian*'s Stuart Jeffries to write a leading article bemoaning the sound of Channel 4 'scraping the barrel'.[13] Stephen Lambert resorted to the *Guardian*'s *Comment is Free* blogsite to rebut some of his charges:

It's true that the reality and lifestyle programmes are the popular genres that fund the rest of the schedule. As a middle-aged man myself, I find that these aren't always the programmes I want to watch; but far from being cynical ground bait (what Reithians at the DDC still called light entertainment programmes as late as the 1970s), Channel 4's reality and lifestyle output has consistently redefined public service broadcasting for a younger, contemporary audience. Like many independent producers, my company has been encouraged to find popular, entertaining formats that inform and educate viewers about the complex diversity of modern British life. *Wife Swap* reveals the different values that families live by; *Faking It* demonstrates people's extraordinary ability to learn and change given the right support; and, most recently, *The Secret Millionaire* takes large numbers of viewers into the lives of some of Britain's most deprived communities.[14]

The Secret Millionaire[15] was the third of the factual formats Stephen Lambert initiated for RDF Media. It parachutes a wealthy business person into a poor community to work as a volunteer for a couple of weeks before revealing their true identity and surprising deserving people and projects with some unexpected largesse. Against the charge that this was patronising, and the revival of a rather Victorian approach to philanthropy, is the incontrovertible evidence of a large audience that may have otherwise found documentaries about the social issues involved resistible – and the award of the Rose d'Or in Lucerne in 2007, to add to the ones won by stablemates *Faking It* and *Wife Swap*. In fact, *Faking It*'s 2003 gong had been the last Golden Rose awarded in Montreux, up to which time only one programme won each year, and it had normally gone to a light entertainment show or, if a documentary, a showcase for a major musician such as Itzhak Perlman or Yo-Yo Ma. So Lambert and RDF Media have surfed a wave that is recognised internationally.

One seed had been sown nearly a decade before. In 1994, Lambert became the founder editor of the BBC2 strand *Modern Times*, a series that gave considerable freedom to its filmmakers, but was increasingly concerned about form. One notable form to emerge from that stable was the poetic-musical documentary invented by the creative partnership of filmmaker Brian Hill and poet Simon Armitage.

Docu-musical

Brian Hill had pitched a film about what ordinary people do on a Saturday night to Lambert for the first series of *Modern Times* and, having settled on Leeds and interviewed 150 people, was struggling for a frame to pull it all together. He wanted to characterise the city, much in the way Dylan Thomas had framed place in *Under Milk Wood*, so he turned to the Lancashire poet Simon Armitage. What emerges in *Saturday Night* (1996) is a portrait of a city and four contrasting characters going through their Saturday night, all woven artfully together with music and a poetry that adds a note of magical realism, for instance seeing an ordinary cat through a boy's eyes as a Bengal tiger. Armitage voiced his own poetic narrative:

> Leeds on a Saturday afternoon, beginning to cool
> Leeds in a different light
> A Leeds of the mind.
> Where a woman drags a kid up the north face of a great pyramid
> And a Bengal tiger disappears into the foliage
> And a boy trains dogs for the Chinese state circus
> A motorcade speeds down the Avenue of the Americas
> And a boy rides a bike through the goal posts and out of the known universe.[16]

The film was well received, allowing another to be made, where this time the participants would themselves speak Armitage's poems and sing the songs he had written especially for them. This was doubly risky, since the subject was alcohol dependence. Intriguingly, Armitage chose not to meet the alcoholics Hill's team had chosen, but listened to their recorded interviews 'for speech rhythms, phrasing and cadenzas',[17] which he used to find the right tone and timbre for each contribution. They only moved into song because one of the characters, a young man called Duncan, turned out to be a singer from a musical family, two of his brothers being members of the pop group UB40. He is seen strolling through a pub, singing as if in a rock video with none of the other drinkers noticing:

> I'm a drinking man, I like a good drink
> I'm a thinking man, I like a good think.[18]

Although most people only sing in the privacy of their own bath, getting them to do so on film unlocks a much more revealing intimacy than usually achieved through interview. Maxine Baker is one of many who have hailed this as the birth of 'a whole new sub-genre of documentary',[19] recognising that there is something that goes beyond the usual demands of self-validation that drive marginalised people to reveal themselves on camera. The sub-genre not only recognises their existence, but elevates their issues to the status of an art form. Hill chooses to call this 'musical documentary', but the Australian academic and television executive Jane Roscoe prefers 'docu-musical', which she calls 'seriously playful – playful in form; serious in content'.[20] There is a striking sense that, through that play, people feel more able to reveal themselves than they would through conventional discourse, finding something of the reward in release that professional performers do. Roscoe continues:

> The *Drinking for England* participants do not seem to us to turn away from themselves, but rather to be 'self-fashioners' through the extension of their conventional pieces-to-

camera into verse and song. Like Irvine Welsh's junkies in the 1996 novel *Trainspotting*, their troublesome identities do not fit socially approved stereotypes, and they celebrate this. Also like Welsh's characters, they reveal a more complex identity through their idiolect – the 'voice' that characterizes them with its tones, word-choices and distinctive phraseology. Verse and song take the idiolect beyond their 'normal' speaking voice. Conventional modalities of voice are thus extended and expanded. Within these developed modalities of voice, new levels of character are revealed (rather in the way soliloquy in drama and aria in opera halt narrative in order to progress character).[21]

This aspect was best developed in the fourth of the five Hill–Armitage films, the multiple award-winning *Feltham Sings* (2003),[22] where inmates of the Feltham Young Offenders Institution in London perform songs about their lives and crimes. Armitage followed the same practice, writing songs inspired by their recorded speech patterns and all were performed, save two Jamaican cellmates who rejected his 'naff' work and wrote raps of their own. Baker comments 'their performance is arguably the best in the whole film',[23] but Roscoe and Paget write:

> Good as both their songs are, however, they do close Linden and Cass off. The two of them reveal more of themselves in interview than in their self-penned songs. Their lyrics comprise a relatively commonplace lexicon of hip-hop/rap.[24]

Nonetheless the process, despite all the difficulties of filming and recording inside the security of the prison, does liberate the prisoners and restore their humanity in a valuable way. Hill repeated the exercise in Downview Women's Prison in Sutton for *Songbirds* (2005),[25] with composer Simon Boswell, who had first joined the team for the less well-received *Pornography: The Musical* (2003).[26] While Hill and Armitage had a long-established non-judgemental detachment that enabled them to negotiate the emotional and ethical minefields involved in this work, Boswell brought a fresh understanding to the 'recovery' or 'healing' Armitage argues the films can bring their incarcerated subjects:

> These women have been put in prison and denied a voice, so giving them a song is a process of giving them self-esteem. I've worked with and watched a lot of professional singers, and what strikes me is that if they're any good they are both confident in what they're doing and at the same time vulnerable . . . These [docu-musical] performers are amateurs and you've got to help to shore up their vulnerability. The song is about them, an endorsement of their lives. If they can do it – if they can sing it – it gives them self-belief . . . Being given a song . . . is a short cut to the real emotional hub of what you're about. I think the audience get this, because of that combination in singing of being vulnerable and showing bravery.[27]

The performative mode was used by filmmaker Joe Bullman in a subtly different way in *The Seven Sins of England* (2007).[28] In response to the then Prime Minister Tony Blair's assault on the binge drinking and general incivility of young Britain today, Bullman set out to prove that Blair's hearkening back to a Golden Age was a misguided myth – Britain had always been beset by violent, drunken hooligans. He found that England's first law against binge drinking was passed in 616 AD, and there was plenty of textual evidence from every generation that people had always bewailed the violence and vomit of their young. Bullman's innovation was to get latter-day louts to perform those texts to camera, showing how little things had changed. As Channel 4's website proudly proclaimed:

> In *The Seven Sins of England*, real-life hoodies, binge-drinkers and chavs deliver the authentic words of 11th-century binge-drinkers, Edwardian yobs, Elizabethan xenophobes and 17th-century hooligans in this recreation of historical 'chavvery'.[29]

What was striking was how well these often drunken performers from Bullman's native Essex actually performed those words. As *The Independent* commented:

> His subjects give surprisingly eloquent renditions while downing vodka shots, taking part in post-pub brawls or just hanging around menacingly in an underpass . . . the most refreshing aspect of *The Seven Sins of England* is the voice it gives to those normally denied one.[30]

Reality television

It may seem a contradiction that people can discover their voice through others' words, be they Simon Armitage's or culled from ancient texts, but this understanding is at the heart of much that has been – often retrospectively – branded 'reality television'. It is, ironically, in the virtual reality of television formats that people feel most free to play themselves, a process not dissimilar to the idealised avatars people choose for themselves in the *Second Life* website. As long as the rules are clear, they can play the game and many feel more empowered than they do in the passive role of submission to an observational documentarist, however sympathetic. Daytime talk shows, such as *Kilroy*[31] and *The Jeremy Kyle Show*[32] in the UK and *The Jerry Springer Show*[33] and *Ricki Lake*[34] in the US, have long traded on people's will to fight their relationship battles in public, often literally if not honestly. Such is the appeal of the limelight, transforming personal trivia into what they delude themselves to imagine is epic drama, that would-be participants often have agents and the shows' producers employ armies of researchers trying to weed out the fakers and serial appearers. So-called 'reality television' has taken that popular thirst, in both participants and spectators, and turned it into a gigantic money-spinner around the world.

2000 was the break-out year for reality TV. Whereas most change in UK television had been gradual, the reality phenomenon seemed to change everything, irrevocably, overnight.

Figure 12.1
Big Brother, freak show or not, remains the most successful reality TV format of the 2000s

In the UK, it was *Big Brother* which broke the mould, giving Channel 4 its highest ever ratings and, vitally, with disproportionately high audiences in the difficult to attract 18–34-year-old demographic most desired by advertisers. In the USA, it was *Survivor* that earned CBS the number one slot that year, a show that was originated by Brits, initially unsellable in the UK and deemed a failure, but then it was commissioned for a couple of seasons following its American success. *Survivor* was a team-(tribe-)based game show set in an exotic location, with good-looking contestants vying for a big, $1 million prize pot. While its production used more conventional documentary techniques than *Big Brother*, the latter's success can be put down to new ways of pursuing the documentary objective of observing the minutiae of human behaviour, albeit in pursuit of a relatively modest £70,000 win. Set in the claustrophobic confines of the 'Big Brother house', and watched by dozens of cameras 24–7, the decidedly unglamorous 'housemates' thrilled Britain as their relationships evolved and their personalities unravelled. These two seminal formats, which sold around the world, transformed television in a number of ways, defining two sub-genres within the burgeoning reality TV landscape. But it is important to recognise that, innovative though they were, they drew upon some well-established features of the popular media, an industry that is constantly under pressure to reinvent itself. Annett Hill synthesises the elements that led to this particular point in television history:

> Popular factual television has developed during a period of cross fertilisation with tabloid journalism, documentary television and popular entertainment. The late 1980s and 1990s were a period of increased commercialisation and deregulation within the media industries. As audiences have shopped around, channel surfing between terrestrial, satellite/cable and digital channels, broadcasters (and narrow casters) have looked to produce cheap, often locally made, factual programming which is attractive to general (and niche) viewers. The development of reality programming is an example of how television cannibalises itself in order to survive, drawing on existing genres to create successful hybrid programmes, which in turn generate a 'new' television genre.[35]

The competitive imperative is understandable, but the persistent arguments about reality television being a commercially-driven 'dumbing down' fails to engage with precisely why these formats are so attractive and successful. The reasons are many, and synthesise public needs in much the way that the genre synthesises forms. One feature services the viewer's natural inquisitiveness about other lives and behaviour – previously the preserve of documentary – with the familiar technology of surveillance. When *Big Brother* was conceived in the Netherlands in the late 1990s, the Dutch parliament was very exercised with the fast-growing number of CCTV surveillance cameras and their threat to privacy.[36] The regulatory instruments of the Dutch Personal Data Protection Act of 2000 and the Hidden Camera Surveillance Act 2003 followed, but not before the show – whose very title *Big Brother* knowingly references the draconian surveillance systems of George Orwell's dystopian fantasy, *1984* – had made prurient prying a worldwide trend. In Britain, the number of CCTV cameras had topped one and a half million, with the average Londoner apparently caught on one some 300 times a day, a virtual intimacy in place of real contact. *Big Brother* caught the Zeitgeist of this deracinated, constantly-monitored community perfectly.

Another phenomenon was the distribution pattern, a form of saturation bombing that had never been tried with any other programming, save major sporting tournaments such as the

Olympics. As satellite television had begun a fresh assault on audiences, with the introduction of digital broadcasting in 1998, the mainstream broadcasters had tended to hedge their bets with ever shorter runs, of both documentary and drama series, so that embarrassing failures could be quickly buried. The commitment to nightly broadcasts for nine weeks was a brave departure, which aimed to build soap-style engagement with characters, and proved it could sustain this over a long period of time. With *Big Brother* having achieved a record Friday night audience for Channel 4 in the finale of the first series – with 9 million watching, constituting a 46.5 per cent share of the available audience[37] – broadcasters knew they could flood the airwaves with this kind of product and the audience apparently would not tire. In fact, the success of *Big Brother* drew attention to the relative under-performance of the surrounding shows – characteristically the venerable white-haired archaeologists of *Time Team* – which failed to retain that audience the advertisers craved. It led to a flood of hastily commissioned late-evening series with 'Sex' in the title, which mostly did not attract the discerning young any more than *Time Team*. From series 2, the new digital channel E4 (E for entertainment – aimed at 18–35-year-olds) was able to run live feeds from the house and offer interactive users alternative camera angles. The subsidiary series, *Big Brother's Little Brother*, a magazine of related trivia fronted by Dermot O'Leary, also ran on E4, and was joined in 2004 by Russell Brand's live chat show, *Big Brother's Big Mouth*.

This multichannel proposition is one part of the *Big Brother* multimedia strategy. So, a third key feature was the evolving technology that enabled the live web-streaming of activities in the *Big Brother* house 24 hours a day. Liable to freeze with low bandwidth availability in the first years, it still enshrined the show as being at the cutting edge of new multi-platform delivery, which is now standard with widely available broadband and post-broadcast downloads. Despite Channel 4's ill-advised and short-lived decision to charge £9.99 a month for the facility during series 3 – due to a cash crisis following the advertising slump of 2001 – this contemporary extension of the proposition is a still-underrated innovation that transformed the nature of the television audience's relationship with the programme's content. The selection, and censorship, of material that was then selected for the nightly digests also helped fuel the growing online community of bloggers debating the show and its interpretation. All this fed back and is now a staple of multimedia consideration, but is arguably as important a function of interactivity as the weekly vote to decide which of the nominated housemates should be evicted. Nonetheless, the burgeoning use of texts, mobile phones and the interactive 'red button' facility on the growing number of digital sets has kept the audience involved and the production companies enriched.

Arguably, the overarching achievement of twenty-first century reality television is the apotheosis of the Warhol prophecy: 'In the future, everyone will be world-famous for 15 minutes'.[38] Being on television is its own reward. One of the most significant factors in the majority of reality television shows is self-promotion and self-referral: people put themselves forward to be chosen and to be judged. In the past, this was largely only true of game shows and quiz shows, though *Who Wants to be a Millionaire?* had significantly upped the ante. Documentaries and factual programmes generally went out and found their own subjects for whatever the objective was. Now, significant numbers of the audience beat a path to the producer's door, desperate for their moment in the spotlight and willing to do just about anything for it. The word 'wannabe' was coined for surfers in 1981, but has found new currency in the world of reality television, where millions of applicants worldwide apply for the few hundred opportunities offering passing fame and, rarely, fortune. There is even a strand of self-help books specifically for American wannabes trying to get onto reality TV shows. They recommend how to develop a 'character' that will get you cast by producers and adopted by the audience:

> Those who play strong and loud at the outset generally become known as 'the first one eliminated', so enter the game carefully. Create alliances early, but stay under the radar for the first few days so you can observe and connect with your teammates. Once the game is underway, manipulation is the key. Whether you're playing your competitors by displaying emotion on cue, using alcohol to gain information from your fellow reality stars, or working to eliminate your enemies, you have got to be quick on your feet if you want to pull the strings quietly. The true puppet-masters are, of course, the producers and other professionals who are working to create a ratings-worthy story – and as a result, you'll know how to play them too.[39]

American reality shows slotted more easily into the long-running series pattern, whose consistent ratings drive television schedules. *Survivor* is typical of such series, lavishly shot on location and then subjected to slick post production before earning its place in the prime-time schedule. In summer 2000, *Survivor* gave CBS its biggest ever summer hit with audiences of just under 52 million, only exceeded by the Superbowl. That was a 44 per cent audience share but, more importantly, rising to 60 per cent among 18–34 year-olds.[40] The viewers loved the scheming between the contestants and the challenges they were subjected to, like eating insects and rats, walking on hot coals and standing for hours under the sun on a tree stump. The BBC reported: 'Many say part of the programme's appeal was that it mirrored the office politics of corporate America',[41] and *The New York Times* concurred, saying that the show's message, won by a ruthlessly strategic corporate trainer, was 'trust no one'. But, 'just as murder mysteries transform our fear of death into a playful entertainment, *Survivor* turns the competitive nightmare of contemporary life into a benign game'.[42] *The Times* critic also noted the sophisticated editing, and the use of contestants talking directly to camera, as key contributions to the format's success.

These filmic techniques – and an extraordinary fan base sustained by the blogosphere – have helped build a *Survivor* subculture that other reality television shows have struggled to emulate. From 2001, the series has run twice a year, meaning it is on US television six months a year, always based in a different exotic location. Knowingly, series 16 pitted a team of the show's most ardent fans against a team of past favourite contestants. The long-running show host, Jeff Probst, draws attention to the narrative arc that is at the core of most good drama or documentary, or hybrids like this:

> As far as the show goes, I think the reason that *Survivor* is still on the air and why it's endured is, great storytelling. I've always felt that *Survivor* is Joseph Campbell[43] at its best. It's unscripted, real life drama. Everybody in this game is on their own journey. They leave their ordinary life behind and they embark on this adventure that will forever change their life. Anybody who comes onto this game, whether they last 3 days or 39, their lives are forever changed. They almost always experience a spiritual death whether it's being voted out, which is a death in this game, or whether it's finding yourself so low you don't know how you're ever going to make it and you think about quitting. Then you dig deep and you revert and you're a new person.[44]

Celebrity

Another factor that soon became attached to the reality TV bandwagon was the fading star – actors, singers, so-called celebrities whose agents were having increasing difficulty getting them the bookings. Suddenly there was this phenomenon that offered the opportunity of weeks of prime-time exposure, initially to members of the public. All that was needed was for reality television to retrospectively embrace those whom the phenomenon had helped dislodge from the pantheon of light entertainment. *Celebrity Big Brother* was originally conceived as a short (eight-day) contribution to the BBC's multi-platform charity fund-raiser *Comic Relief*, but it rapidly became an annual fixture for Channel 4, growing to 26 days by 2007, when its ratings began to plummet. In desperation, the producers parachuted into the Big Brother house someone who had only become a celebrity thanks to her own appearance on an earlier *Big Brother* – Jade Goody – and her family. An abrasive, ill-educated cockney – who had nonetheless gone on to make a reported £3 million from television appearances, book deals and a perfume line – Goody could be relied on to inject some conflictual heat into the house, not least because one of the more prominent contestants was a Bollywood star, Shilpa Shetty.[45] The racist comments and racial bullying that ensued led to the predicted rise in audience figures,[46] albeit at the cost of a record 44,500 complaints, the loss of Carphone Warehouse's sponsorship and a stinging rebuke from the regulator Ofcom. The Channel appeared regretful, announcing that *Celebrity Big Brother* would be discontinued; but this would have been commercial suicide. It reappeared, reconceived as *Big Brother Celebrity Hijack*, on the digital channel E4 in January 2008, with the admission that *Celebrity Big Brother* would resurface in 2009, which it did.

I'm A Celebrity . . . Get Me Out of Here! first transplanted a bunch of Z-list celebrities for two weeks in what purported to be the Australian outback in August 2002. The show documents the campers' activities over 24 hours, and then the edited highlights are presented live by ITV's star double act, the Geordie hobbits Ant and Dec. Its nightly 90-minute broadcasts proved an immediate ratings success in the UK, despite an unsuccessful attempt by CBS to sue for infringement of copyright, as recognisable faces were put through similar trials to contestants in *Survivor*, not least the Bushtucker Trials, normally involving snakes, spiders or other creepy crawlies. But the jungle was not as remote as the cameras contrived to show, it being near a luxury hotel and 30 minutes from the Gold Coast, New South Wales, and much of the 'jungle' set was covered by plastic sheets. Largely unconcerned by the artifice, the British audience continues to enjoy the closely filmed discomfiture of the so-called celebrities. They vote by phone, text or digital interactive button for those they want to take the trials or be evicted – but the show tanked in its American, French and Dutch versions. From the UK Series 2, there has been a companion, 'behind the scenes' show on the digital channel ITV2: *I'm A Celebrity . . . Get Me Out of Here! Now*, presented as an insider's view by Mark Durden-Smith and one of the previous contestants. This parasitic programming had previously been piloted by ITV in the two seasons of *Survivor*, where the nightly *Survivor: Raw* offshoot had saved ITV2 from a ratings black hole. Although the main show was a limited success, the spin-off showed the way that the big broadcasters would go, spread their investment and diminishing audience returns laterally, rather than focusing exclusively on the prime-time shows.

Serious realities

Celebrity did not merely appear in reality television as ritual humiliation. There were some larger than life figures who would add a kind of gravitas to the genre. The billionaire real estate entrepreneur Donald Trump, whose skyscraper in Manhattan is modestly named the Trump Tower and was used as the base for the first five series of the show he hosts, *The Apprentice*. This series, billed as 'the ultimate job interview', pits about 16–18 aspiring businessmen and women against each other in a series of weekly challenges, which are reviewed in the Trump boardroom, leading to one of the hapless contestants being fired. The ultimate goal is a highly paid year's apprenticeship to the great man. The first series in 2004 helped NBC out of a ratings hole caused by the end of two of its long-running hit drama series, *Friends* and *Frazier*. Although the series audience has shrunk year on year, NBC has continued to commission it twice yearly and schedule it in the key Thursday prime-time slot, against big hitting drama such as *Desperate Housewives* and *Cold Case*. This is because it continues to attract a disproportionately high share of the all-important 18–49 audience demographic, where factual programmes routinely out-perform drama. The same phenomenon has been noted in the UK, where the British version is fronted by the businessman Sir Alan Sugar. Here the show airs on BBC1 (although the first two series in 2005 and 2006 were on BBC2) and the fired candidate – actually despatched several weeks before – then faces a live studio audience in the BBC2 (formerly BBC3) show *The Apprentice· You're Fired!*, hosted by Brummie man of the people Adrian Chiles.

One of the features that distinguished *The Apprentice* UK was its beautiful aerial shots of London, floating over the city to give it a contemporary grandeur and make the show look like a New York-based feature film. It had other aspects of drama, such as the fact that although those overhead shots implied the contestants were being called to Sugar's boardroom in Canary Wharf, his actual office headquarters were in unlovely Brentwood, Essex, and the 'boardroom' was actually a film set in Shepherd's Bush. Continuing the drama, the 'walk of shame' the evictees took were shot in advance, and the suitcases they touted were empty. Nonetheless, the series certainly demonstrated the best of documentary craft skills, both in the way the tests and resulting testiness were captured and in the artful editing of the different elements. *The Apprentice* was hailed by some as a new maturity in the reality medium, also answering former BBC Director-General Greg Dyke's lament that a liberal arts-led BBC did too little on business and industry. Roly Keating, Controller of BBC2, proclaimed: 'Intelligent reality is back with a gripping insight into the machinations of the business world.'[47] The series brought a young audience to a business show, which in turn garnered a host of awards, including the BAFTA for Best Feature in 2006, and Best Reality Show Rose d'Or at Lucerne the same year. Yet it had its detractors, like the *Guardian* commentator Jonathan Freedland, who found in it everything he detested about a foul-mouthed, aggressive, hierarchical Blair's Britain:

> What this suggests is that deference is far from dead, it's just that now there is a new class to be deferred to – the aristocracy of wealth. And in this new nobility, Alan Sugar's blood is purest blue. The programme buys into that notion in a deeper way. For it rests on, and reinforces, the ideological assumption that has underpinned politics since the 1980s – that the only goal that really matters is profit. The tasks set by Surrallan may be varied, ranging from fashion shows on cruise ships to selling petrol cans, but they only ever have one

Angus Macqueen, when Head of Documentaries at Channel 4, said of the *Celebrity Big Brother* racism row:

I'm one of those people who in January thought the channel had forgotten quite how iconic *Big Brother* is. I personally don't like it very much but, year in and year out, it tickles something in British society that's at the heart of what British society is talking about.[60]

The *Celebrity Big Brother* spat was an engineered car crash, but it certainly got people talking. As Macqueen said, it surprised him. 'I think more clearly than any documentary's ever done for me, I think I knew what it was to be Asian or black in Britain'.[61]

That is quite a claim for someone who has made some of the finest documentaries in Britain, but it cuts to the heart of the reality television achievement. Because it is principally a vehicle for the individual ego, and normally cast from the ranks of the audience, it speaks directly to the experience and sensibility of the general viewer. Thus, when it stumbles across matters of moment, it does hold a remarkably revealing mirror up to that audience. It is not always an edifying spectacle, as Goody and her mates proved. But although the specific text there was about race, it has been suggested that most British popular discourse, most UK television, and certainly most of its reality television, is about class. Even in the celebrity variants, reality television carefully casts people with a strongly proletarian appeal, with the odd toff thrown in for light relief. Its mass appeal is predicated on the notion that we, the people, are for once commanding popular attention, and the elitist assumptions of broadcasters who thought they knew what was good for us have been trounced. It is, of course, an illusion. Allowing the punters free reign in these carefully constructed bear gardens is fine if that's what they want to watch. But there is no sign that this will lead to them reading the news or taking over the boardrooms, Sir Alan Sugar notwithstanding.

At the time of writing, the most recent format to go into production in the USA enters the workplace with a very different focus, the millions losing their jobs due to the recession. *Someone's Gotta Go* features small firms struggling to survive and gives the whole workforce the chance to decide who gets fired at the end of the show. *Variety* announced that Fox TV had picked up this latest idea from Endemol USA, the American arm of the company that made *Big Brother*.[62] 'It's *Survivor* meets *The Office*', announced Fox reality chief Mike Darnell, saying it would be shot in documentary style like *The Office* and arguing that it would empower workers, who normally see their bosses making the wrong decision. In this show they get to examine the books and see how much each of them makes before deciding who's 'gotta go'. Endemol USA's David Greenberg goes further:

We're always trying to find the next thing that is topical and timely in the Zeitgeist. What could be more current than the financial crisis and dealing with the realities of losing jobs? This is an extension of that real-life experience. For a lot of people, it takes the pressure off them. As a boss myself, I don't want to have to make those decisions. It's safe to say that it hasn't been difficult to find companies willing to participate.[63]

A cynic might say that it would not be difficult to find participants in a Russian roulette show, if the prize pot was big enough, but there should be other standards to consider before going lethally to air. One of the most successful formats worldwide is *The Moment of Truth*, where increasingly invasive and embarrassing personal questions are asked of contestants on air until they answer untruthfully (as determined by a previously taken polygraph test). The show's creator, US television executive Howard Schulz, first trialled the show in Colombia as *Nada más que la verdad*, where it was a success until contestant Rosa Maria Solano was asked, 'Did you pay a hit man to kill your husband?' and she duly answered 'Yes', to secure her $25,000 prize. The husband had fortunately been tipped off by the hitman, but the show was killed off. Nonetheless, the format has been sold to 44 other countries, with the jackpot ranging from 25,000 euros in Germany to $500,000 in the United States, where it plays on Fox. In Greece, the show has been banned by the regulator after several warnings for questions considered too risqué. The Antenna channel that showed it, and the production company Shine Reveille, who owns the format, were reportedly considering appeal to the European court of human rights. Howard Schultz appealed to the Greek regulator, invoking the Bible: 'The truth sets people free, as John the Apostle states in the New Testament'.[64]

Great have been the claims for reality television, from empowerment to enrichment, but it is generally the producers who have been enriched, and few human rights have been extended. Reality television may have held up a refreshing new array of mirrors to contemporary society, extending inclusivity, but the audience vote hardly makes such shows less judgemental than their patrician predecessors. They are all constructs, all driven by commercial considerations and need, above all, to entertain. The feature filmmaker Brian de Palma may yet have been prescient in his 1974 rock musical re-imagining of *The Phantom of the Opera*, *The Phantom of the Paradise*, with its immortal line: 'Execution, live, coast-to-coast, now that's entertainment!'[65]

Expert briefing – multi-camera shoots

Many formatted and reality TV shoots require multiple camera set-ups, either with several cameras trained on the same arena of action, or multiple shoots occurring simultaneously in different locations. Conventional outside broadcasts are major engineering events, cabling centrally balanced cameras into a mixing desk, effectively replicating the studio experience on location. An increasing number of cameras are remotely controlled, as in the Big Brother house. But this briefing is concerned more specifically with organising documentary shoots, where more than one cameraperson is iso-recording at the same time:

1 **Style counsel**: The director has to conceive the overall look and feel of the show, from the way in which landscapes and people are framed to the colour temperature and use of camera movements. *Big Brother*'s magisterial aerial shots would not work so well if the ground shooting did not complement them, with its shiny glass corporate surfaces and glossy black MPV motorcade. Similarly, the intercut between the increasingly frenetic competing teams works because both are shot in the same urgent, hand-held style that helps accentuate the tension. In *Survivor*, the camera fulfils a more voyeuristic role, eavesdropping conversations and panning around to find other contestants listening in, emphasising the conspiratorial and paranoid aspects of the show. Such series and complex shoots normally work with a 'style bible', which codifies all the stylistic aspects to ensure conformity.

2 **Clean briefs**: None of this can be made to work unless the entire team knows the score and has a clear understanding of what is being sought and how it must be captured. The style bible can help agree the conventions, but only a shared sensibility

will ensure that the right moments are grabbed. These are usually moments of conflict and emotion but, if two or more cameras are operating, the operators also need to know who is getting the whites of the eyes, who is getting the context, and how to avoid shooting each other. Establishing a strong team dynamic and ethic, with mutual understanding of procedural principles and programme goals, underscores the objective and welds an effective filmic force.

3   **Floor plan and shooting script**: Whether it is a two-camera interview shoot or a multi-camera event, it pays to have a drawn-up plan where camera positions and shot cover are planned for the edit. This can be as basic as establishing a line that the cameras don't cross – so as to ensure talking heads can be intercut – or as complex as an orchestral shoot, pre-planned to the note. For music and other scripted events, from lectures to plays, the director should be totally familiar with the text and have devised a shoot plan that can be easily communicated to, and assimilated by, the camera team.

4   **Largely logistics**: It is tough enough for one camera crew chasing a single subject, but it can become a dysfunctional circus with several crews in circulation. Two things can mitigate this: detailed location planning and effective telecommunications. Good location management will not only co-ordinate the most efficient use of crew resources but also identify access routes, parking, power sources and any other likely demands, from food and drink to lavatories and wet-weather shelter. Mobile phones are normally sufficient for most occasions, until overuse empties the battery, or you hit a signal-free dead zone. Walkie-talkies were once a production staple and can still be a useful back-up for local communications and cueing on large locations. It is also in these fraught situations where a runner earns their name.

5   **That's entertainment**: Formats and reality shows are conceived and commissioned for their mass appeal, so the shooting and the overall narrative arc needs to be coherent as an entertaining narrative. This traditionally involves:

(i)   *the set-up* – where the proposition is laid out graphically and the cast introduced, often truncated as the series becomes more familiar and can carry last week's best moments, but rarely dispensed with;

(ii)   *the challenge* – this week/episode's particular storyline, usually explained by the show's host;

(iii) *the planning* – where the teams discuss, allot roles and strategise;

(iv)   *the chase* – where those strategies are played out, and conflicts arise;

(v)   *the resolution* – where the challenge is completed;

(vi)   *the reckoning* – where the tallies are taken and someone pays the price. Some shows also tack on the reflection – a team review, before trailing the next week's highlights at the end. A director's cover and editing will subtly vary the timbre and tempo of each segment, just like a symphony, conducting the audience through the highs and lows of the characters' journey.

6   **Crafty characterisation**: At the conceptual stage, the range of characters required to make the concept work will have been carefully considered. These are not left to whoever turns up, among the wannabes desperate for their 15 minutes. The good producer casts archetypes that will best serve the proposition and challenges involved. The show will be designed to reveal the talents and flaws of these people, and the shooting will favour the richest returns from the resulting moments of conflict and triumph. It is no accident that shows invariably concentrate on certain characters and

certain traits more than others. Some anticipated moments work better than others but little is left to chance, and editing can often redeem and clarify less successful exchanges.

7 **Playing by the rules**: Just as no competent sportsman enters the competitive arena without a plan to win, no contestant participates in reality television without a strategy. The audience expects this in any such game, but they also expect fair and equable application of the rules. Given that each reality format invents its own rules, these have to be conceived and enacted to make the most compelling viewing. In the first UK *Big Brother*, Nasty Nick was expelled for illegal plotting to manage the eviction of other contestants. In the first US *Survivor*, the eventual winner set the standard for Machiavellian gamesmanship that just managed not to break the rules. Clearly the all-seeing eye of the show's cameras cannot be allowed to capture wrongdoing, without this being addressed by the production's rule-keeper.

8 **It's all ritual**: As we have seen, each reality show is largely a kit of parts cleverly constructed from previous television models. The innovation is in how those parts are synthesised, which is usually through months of trial and error. But 'reality' also trawls deeper social needs and resonances, about tribalism and class, and comes up with formats and formulae that sometimes mimic the rituals of religion. The best proponents of the form may seem to be those most willing to push the limits and release the wilder currents of determination and self-belief. But, in the final analysis, the most successful shows have the well-established cultus of a religious liturgy, with the contestants having to prostate themselves at the well-rehearsed stations of the cross, before being crucified or transfigured.

13 Lifestyle: house and garden, makeover and motors, food and travel

....

lifestyle n. 1 a set of attitudes, habits or possessions associated with a particular person or group. 2 such attitudes, etc., regarded as fashionable or desirable

A t the dawn of the new millennium, no one would have imagined that one of the most enduringly successful television programmes in Britain would be a petrol-head show, which had been around since 1977, with a presenter whose hair-style was of a similar vintage. Yet *Top Gear* was BBC2's top-rated programme of 2007, with the episode on which Britain's new Formula One driver-hero Lewis Hamilton appeared garnering an extraordinary 8.4 million viewers, just shy of Channel 4's highest-rated *Celebrity Big Brother*.[1] Jeremy Clarkson and his two sidekicks, James May and Richard Hammond, are regularly castigated for being macho throwbacks, grown-up schoolboys with an irresponsible taste for speed and disregard for road safety and the environment. Yet their programme also won the Royal Television Society award in the Best Features and Lifestyle Series category for 2007. The citation read: 'This series has continually reinvented itself, and the three presenters really are *Three Men in a Boat* for the 21st Century.'[2]

The *Three Men in a Boat* analogy is well-chosen, for one of the key components of the show is a range of stunts involving the intrepid three in daft escapades such as turning cars into boats, driving 4x4s to the North Pole, or racing cars across Europe or America. All of these stunts are scripted and shot like drama, nothing left to chance, with the trio fulfilling their characters' roles: May – misanthropic upper-class fop doomed to fail; Hammond – boyish enthusiast who has bounced back from a near-death experience; Clarkson – alpha male up for anything, as long as he wins. If it were presented as documentary, *Top Gear* would drown in a sea of complaints of fakery. But, as factual entertainment, it is exempt from such charges, even if the illusion is maintained for the audience. Despite the sophistication of the contemporary viewer, it is doubtful whether this is universally understood. Like *The Apprentice*, it raises issues about the credibility of some of the newer, reinvented uses of documentary techniques.

Reinvention is at the heart of the show's success. The long-running *Top Gear* location-based magazine programme had become increasingly tired and had been cancelled in 2001, only for its producer and presenters (without Clarkson and May) to decamp to Channel 5, to make a similar series called *Fifth Gear*.[3] This had prompted the BBC to reconsider *Top Gear* and reinvent it in 2002 as a bigger, studio-based show, more in keeping with the shiny-floor entertainment shows that were making a comeback. The programme is still full of beautifully shot location footage of gleaming performance vehicles – as well as road-tests of production-line cars the audience might actually buy – but augmented with celebrities undertaking time trials in a 'reasonably priced car' for a place on the 'leader board', as well as the afore-mentioned stunts. The programme has an armoury of signature shots, from the dashboard-mounted mini-cam – which captures the commentary and gurning of the presenters as they put vehicles through their paces – to the tarmac-level wide shot through which the vehicles speed. All these documentary inserts are dissected in the studio with a lot of laughter and the baying approval of a standing crowd of fans. Far from turning viewers off, Clarkson's liberal-taunting, politically incorrect views are very much part of the attraction, though only because imparted with a humour and deft lightness of tone. The former informational content has been wrapped in entertaining packaging that is hard to resist, and plays to a huge audience that is keen to join the club. You may not want to imitate Clarkson's hairstyle, but you would not mind sharing something of his lifestyle.

Homes and gardens

The appeal of the unruly grab-bag that is lumped together as 'lifestyle programming' is widely understood to be predicated on the audience's voracious needs in an atomised culture. Since Michel Foucault's seminal work on *The Care of the Self*,[4] there has been a growing academic discourse that sees in these programmes a viewer's search for the style and taste that will define their identity. No longer defined in their choices and behaviour by the communities they were born into and the roles dictated by that birth, people have to find themselves and select the trappings for their life from the consumer riches on offer. Television is more than a virtual mail-order catalogue; it takes the role of a mate that gives informed and privileged insights into the implications and benefits of making certain choices, thereby affecting the quality and value of people's aspirations. 'There is hardly a desire more widespread in the West today than to lead "a life of your own",' writes the German sociologist Ulrich Beck,[5] but there is a terrible anxiety about how best to fulfil that.

> If globalisation, detraditionalisation and individualisation are analysed together, it becomes clear that the life of one's own is an experimental life. Inherited recipes for living and role stereotypes fail to function. There are no historical models for the conduct of life. Individual and social life – in marriage and parenthood as well as in politics, public activity and paid work – have to be brought back into harmony with each other. The restlessness of the age, of the Zeitgeist, is also due to the fact that no one knows how or whether this can be achieved.[6]

Television comes to the rescue and assures us it can help, and so has moved on from the age of instruction to the age of aspiration. Whereas early programmes such as DIY shows featuring the once-famous Barry Bucknell[7] offered a buffer's guide full of practical tips, today's equivalents are about the fulfilment of dreams. The first format to trade on the home as an expression of personality was *Changing Rooms* (1996),[8] even though the counter-intuitive idea here was to have friends and neighbours do up each other's rooms, with the help of designers Laurence Llewellyn-Bowen and Linda Barker. The prevalence of bold colours and use of MDF may not have been to everyone's taste – and the classic show climax, when the new rooms were revealed to the nervous home-owners, often led to sulks or tantrums – but the show provoked a wave of programmes that encouraged people to lavish time and money on their homes as an expression of their individuality. *Home Front*[9] ditched the neighbour conflict for developing tensions between the home-owners and the designers making over their home – Llewellyn-Bowen again – and garden – Diarmuid Gavin. Since both have fairly *outré* views of good design – Llewellyn-Bowen's camp dandy favours a latter-day rococo aesthetic while Gavin's gardens tend to be ultra-modern 'outdoor rooms' notable for their architectural installations – a conflictual narrative was assured. But it is important to note that this process does confer a narrative, a concrete way for people to organise this 'life of their own'. As the influential social scientist Anthony Giddens – best known as the author of Tony Blair's 'Third Way' for New Labour – writes:

> A person's identity is not to be found in behaviour, nor – important though this is – in the reactions of others, but in the capacity to keep a particular narrative going. The individual's biography, if she is to maintain regular interaction with others in the day-to-day world, cannot be wholly fictive. It must continually integrate events which occur in the external world, and sort them into the ongoing 'story' about the self.[10]

Television seized upon this role, to stage those events and help people find their plot.

Various channels of activity present themselves as ways of self-discovery, and each spawns bodies of programming that document other people's attempts to transform their lives, successful or not. The BBC's Lifestyle web pages[11] group these programmes under seven headings: Consumer, Food, Gardening, Health, Homes, Lifestyle and Parenting, all with antecedents that pre-date the currency of the word 'lifestyle'. Gardening shows, for instance, have been around since the beginning of broadcasting. The first television gardening programme was broadcast live from Alexandra Palace in London in 1936. *In Your Garden with Mr. Middleton* built on the success of Mr. Middleton's radio programme, which 3.5 million people listened to on the BBC's Home Service on a Sunday afternoon. *Gardeners' Question Time* has run on BBC radio since 1947 and *Gardeners' World* has run on BBC TV since 1968.

Gardeners' World has gone through successive reinventions, from its initial outside broadcasts from the Oxford Botanical Gardens to its current garden site in central Birmingham, under the watchful eye of Tony Buckland. While the show's success is celebrated in its also spawning the UK's most successful garden magazine,[12] an informational website[13] and an annual show,[14] there is a narrative that fulfils a contemporary need. The previous head gardener, Monty Don, was the first presenter of *Gardeners' World* not to be a trained gardener, seeing himself principally as a writer. He has written at some length about his recurring depression and seasonal affective disorder, which has been offset by his passion for gardening. While the horticultural establishment lived up to their homophone by being offended at an amateur taking the leading role, the public responded well to this human narrative, capturing as it does the story of gardens as redemption beyond mere propagation. With the website and magazine better suited to carrying the information, the filmed show can concentrate on the inspiration, and the almost magical connection between dirty digging and beautiful flowers. This is a show that contrasts the wide-shot of busy context with the big close-ups of muddy fingers handling these life forms and the plant world's almost abstract hues. Monty Don also parlayed his experience of the redemptive power of gardening into a project attempting to rehabilitate drug addicts through working on the land. *Growing Out of Trouble* was a five-part documentary series that charted the inspirational progress of a group of young heroin addicts working on a small-holding, and the effect it had on their lives.[15]

Lifestyle programmes are a kind of a drug in themselves, selling a host of seductive ways in which people may escape the drudgery of their existing lives for something better.

What used to be called 'homes' are now routinely referred to as 'property', freighted with speculative expectation. Not only has this become most people's chief asset but one which they hope will continue to appreciate, thereby enriching and liberating them. Reversals in the housing market may have dampened some enthusiasm, but the first decade of the twenty-first century has been notable for a spate of property shows, particularly on the UK Channel 4. The first of these is the least typical, in that it is a classic documentary format charting individuals' attempts to build or transform their ideal property over a matter of months or, in some cases, years. *Grand Designs*[16] is presented by the designer Kevin McCloud, who brings an engaging enthusiasm to every project he visits, even as he trudges through a muddy building site that shows little signs of evolving into the palace of its progenitor's dreams. The programme patiently records the key moments of a project's development, and its setbacks, over as long as it takes to reach completion. McCloud's visits and sympathetic interviews are contrasted with close-ups of the special techniques being deployed, or rainwater dripping into some unfinished space. This requires the production to invest considerable patience and a healthy budget, since many projects fall behind schedule and determined property owners 'face a second winter in the caravan' or whatever. But the eventual completion is a satisfying conclusion to the narrative and always applauded by McCloud, even when he clearly has reservations about some of its elements.

The *Grand Designs* series has charted about six new builds and house transformations a year since 1999, though returns to update stories previously featured now increase the series run to 12. McCloud has become something of a popular icon and his show a successful brand. The series has spawned its own monthly *Grand Designs* magazine and an annual trade fair, *Grand Designs Live*, now spreading over nine days at one of London's top exhibition halls, from where a nightly live show of the same name is beamed.[17] This incorporates the annual *Grand Designs* Awards for best new build, eco-home, conversion, restoration, remodelling and redesign and, in a 2008 recorded video on the website, McCloud invited the public to cast their votes:

> *Grand Designs* tries, wherever possible, to celebrate what is truly exemplary in the built environment, and that's what we are looking for: stuff that takes the breath away, that is a joy and a delight and, in a way, moves architecture forward.[18]

Figure 13.1
Suave designer Kevin McCloud's *Grand Designs* is the ultimate home makeover show

Many would-be participants do not get on to *Grand Designs* because their plans are unimpressive or unrealistic, or because they will not make good screen performers. As McCloud told *The Observer*, the series celebrates people committed to a life-transforming experience:

> It's as though it's a lifetime's worth of pent-up ambition focused into one project. I just find it extraordinary that people are prepared to take that risk: their house, their future, their money, their investments, their sanity. It's not dissimilar to the kind of emotions which drive people to other extremes, like war and family tragedy. It's probably why the films are so watchable. People go through a big adventure. Like selling up the house, buying a yacht and sailing around the world, or trekking to the North Pole with your children, or climbing a mountain in the Himalayas. It is something that takes you to another place. It expands and stretches you. You get to the point where you have kids and you're settling down, and you think: there has to be more to life than 2.1 kids and a nice car and a nice job. There has to be some way of making a mark, of expressing yourself, in a way that is different.[19]

So *Grand Designs* embodies a grand narrative of the self. *Grand Designs* was Channel 4's second most successful programme brand in 2007, only beaten by the *Big Brother* stable.[20] But McCloud is really only interested when the programmes promote good design. He is also increasingly concerned with sustainable architecture. Another project had McCloud involved in the construction of an ecological housing estate near Swindon, filmed for Channel 4 as *Regeneration: The Castleford Project*. This was conceived as a prototype for local regeneration being driven by residents themselves, encouraging other communities to take ownership of their built environment and 'Regenerate your own town!'[21] However, McCloud's elevated aims are not shared by the other successful series in the Channel 4 property portfolio.

Property Ladder[22] features the more prosaic concerns of people trying to make a profit by doing up their property. During a period of fast-growing house prices, this became a popular way of maximising savings. But, as the show's presenter Sarah Beeny frequently finds, people are rarely smart at designing saleable refurbishment, taking advice, or managing projects efficiently and economically. Unlike *Grand Designs*, *Property Ladder* is more of a cautionary tale about what not to do, but it remains a hugely popular programme feeding audience fantasies of taking a masterful hand and getting rich quick. Local versions of the series also play in New Zealand, Australia and the United States, where it is made by The Learning Channel.

Location, Location, Location is a format show in which presenters Kirstie Allsopp and Phil Spencer take instructions from a couple looking to relocate to a new area.[23] They find and show them three properties, explaining the pros and cons of each, and then ask the punters to choose which they prefer. They comment on their clients' thinking, many of whom make what appears to be the wrong choice, and frequently the sale does not go ahead. Allsopp and Spencer know what they are talking about; he used to run a successful agency, Garrington Home Finders, and Allsopp is an aristocrat with a Conservative's antipathy to government regulation, particularly vocal on the recently introduced Home Information Packs (HIPs). She was announced in October 2007 to be undertaking a review of property sales policy for the Conservative party:

An Englishman's home may once have been his castle, but under Labour you have to get the state's permission and pay a state-sponsored inspector, before a prospective buyer can cross the threshold. Hopes and dreams are tied up in bricks and mortar. Yet the Government, in their inability to admit they are wrong, appear determined to play politics with property.[24]

Apart from the solecism – where 'playing politics' is always what the other side does – it is interesting to note that these shows, in which audiences invest a lot of credence, are increasingly part of a wider commercial interest, where presenters and production companies have a vested interest in the buoyancy of the market they are promoting.

To celebrate her political brief, Allsopp was invited on to BBC1's *Question Time* programme on 13 December 2007, where she assured viewers the London housing market was too resilient to be facing a property price fall. That same day the Royal Institute of Chartered Surveyors had released a report saying that, throughout England, house prices were falling faster than at any time since 1998, and even in London they had declined for the second successive month and at double the rate.[25] As that downward trajectory continued into 2008, Beeny and Allsopp were asked if their shows were sustainable, and they both blithely assured the reporter that 'there's always going to be a market for these programmes' (Beeny) and 'the advice we give in a falling market – if, again, the market really is falling, which I strongly doubt – is even more valuable than in a rising market' (Allsopp).[26] Spencer's Garrington Home Finders went into administration in February 2009, the month the Land Registry House Price Index recorded a continuing annual house price fall of 16.5 per cent.[27] Channel 4's publicity material for the show in 2009 recognised the implications for the housing market of the credit crunch, though carried Spencer's prophecy that price falls would bottom out in autumn 2009. It also continued to refer to his 'highly successful Property Search company, Garrington Home Finders'.[28] It is not the property market that is resilient, but the lifestyle programming it has spawned, feeding as it does on people's dreams.

Channel 4's fourth property franchise serves the desire of people to buy somewhere nice abroad, mostly in the Mediterranean. Since 2000, *A Place in the Sun*[29] and its various offshoots have found holiday homes or helped people relocate, not just in France, Spain and Greece, but in countries as diverse as Romania, Canada, the Caribbean and South Africa. The programmes are the shop window for a burgeoning business empire, selling books for would-be purchasers, the biggest-selling magazine in the market, and *A Place in the Sun* trade fairs around the country – four in different locations in 2008. The latest attempt to exploit the brand was announced by Channel 4 in April 2008:

CHANNEL 4 AND BROOKLANDS GROUP JOIN FORCES TO LAUNCH
APLACEINTHESUN.COM

A Place in the Sun goes digital with summer website launch, featuring an online classifieds portal to follow magazine and exhibition success. This is a unique joint venture bringing together brand management expertise, in-depth new media knowledge and extensive overseas property experience . . . At the heart of the *A Place in the Sun* website will be a comprehensive overseas property sales database, driven by a sophisticated multiple-layer search tool including the latest geographical map-based search technology.

Says Paul Whitehead, Head of Corporate and Business Development, Channel 4: 'With tens of thousands of people investing in overseas property each year, the *A Place in the*

Sun brand, with its tremendous consumer interest built through the TV series, magazine and live events, really lends itself to a dedicated website. This is Channel 4's first entry into the rapidly growing space of online classified advertising and a great example of the channel working with programme brands, production companies and partners to explore new business models and ways of working in the digital landscape.'[30]

It is at least arguable that this is a commercial extension too far for a public service broadcaster with a responsibility to the audience whose lifestyle aspirations it so zealously feeds. There was already a growing concern about the numbers of people, often in retirement, that these programmes had encouraged to sell up and move abroad when that decision was not always well-advised. Nearly 200,000 moved abroad from the UK in 2006.[31] As some of the films show, many moved without speaking the language of their new home, let alone having any understanding of the different culture and customs in which they were to live. Countries such as Spain and France have become less enamoured of the hundreds of thousands of Britons arriving and, in September 2007, France withdrew free healthcare from UK retirees under 65. Spain also does not offer free healthcare to younger pensioners, and Greece does not treat any foreign retiree for free.[32] Since most Britons' pensions are paid in sterling, those in the euro zone have found their real worth significantly reduced since 2007, yet unable to reverse their decision to emigrate. The lifestyle dream can turn into a nightmare, but such uncomfortable truths rarely cloud *A Place in the Sun*.

There are some television series that take a consumerist or cautionary approach, from BBC1's venerable consumer magazine *Watchdog* to ITV's occasional . . . *from Hell* series – as in *Builders from Hell*, *Holidays from Hell*, *Restaurants from Hell*, etc. But the general impetus of lifestyle programming is promotional rather than critical, which is why their commercial brands are so exploitable. Broadcasters routinely argue that all their programmes observe guidelines and do not let ancillary commercial activities influence editorial decisions. But it is a specious argument when the revenue stream from those activities outstrips the relatively low margins on programme production, and would be threatened if the programmes began to bite the hands that fed them. Travel shows that routinely take freebies from travel operators and hotels are inevitably less keen to criticise those offerings; and, whether or not they pay, they will inevitably have been given the unrepresentative experience of the best rooms and service.

Food for thought

Food programmes can also stumble into areas of conflict of interest, just as food writers regularly note that the appearance of a notebook can transform the service in any restaurant. Then there is the 'Delia effect', named after the extraordinarily influential television cook Delia Smith, which relates to the run on certain ingredients as a result of their promotion in televised recipes. Delia was responsible, at different times, for nationwide runs on cranberries, eggs, glycerine and capers. Although a multimillionaire from the global sales of her books, Delia is also food editor of Sainsbury's in-house magazine. Now before a series she consults widely with supermarkets and suppliers, to warn them of the items she will be promoting. Her 2008 series excited criticism for its retrograde embracing of convenience foods and her outspoken dismissal of organic food. *How to Cheat at Cooking*[33] contradicted the aspirational nature of most screen cooking, and returned to the basics of fast family fuelling, using readily available supermarket wares, from tinned meat to instant mash. She shows the easy way to do it, knowing that there are more families strapped for time and cash than there are nascent Gordon Ramsays, but those who have fought long and hard to improve norms of nutrition and food knowledge wonder whether this is a cynical commercial ploy. However, the producers of products subject to the Delia effect are happy.

The excitable TV chef Jamie Oliver found himself caught in the cross-fire between criticism and commerce, when he took up the cudgels against factory farming. This front page slash in *The Daily Mirror* set the fox among the chickens:

Jamie Oliver's chicken crusade

Angry Jamie Oliver last night blasted his Sainsbury's paymasters for ducking out of his hard-hitting TV investigation into factory farming. Telly chef Jamie, 32, who is paid £1.2 million to front Sainsbury's advertising campaigns, is furious because the store's bosses snubbed an invitation to take part in a public debate about the gruesome way factory-farmed chickens are treated.[34]

Jamie's Fowl Dinners was part of *Big Food Fight*, a slew of programmes taking a combative approach to the process of factory farming chickens. It was clearly incompatible with supermarket interests. On the day the programme was scheduled, *The Daily Telegraph* reported: 'Celebrity chef Jamie Oliver has written an open letter to all 150,000 staff at J. Sainsbury in an attempt to distance himself from negative comments he reportedly made about the chain.'[35] The letter, addressed to Sainsbury's chief Justin King was duly published on the web.

Dear Justin,

It was great to talk to you this morning although I wish it was in different circumstances.

I am incredibly upset as I feel that today's *Mirror* article misrepresents the programme as a whole. As I explained, it must have been the journalist's intention to focus on the issue of Sainsbury's non-participation in the studio debate. I feel my words were taken out of context. My positive comments about Sainsbury's, and there were many, have all been ignored somewhat.

I am happy to confirm what I have said on several occasions: that Sainsbury's have the most to be proud of on this important animal welfare issue. I am proud of my longstanding relationship with Sainsbury's but it certainly wouldn't be right if I couldn't be seen questioning any of the supermarket's standards.[36]

With that sorted out, Jamie Oliver's future income was apparently secured, but it was obviously an unhappy episode for all concerned. Oliver had left the BBC after his first series, *The Naked Chef*[37] – which had built his screen reputation and fortune – because the BBC felt that the Sainsbury's contract impaired his independence. Nonetheless, he had gone on to do socially valuable work, training unemployed youth in *Jamie's Kitchen*[38] and improving *Jamie's School Dinners*,[39] proving to many that corporate riches were not incompatible with good work. But the BBC has stuck to its editorial guidelines, which are very specific about the potential conflicts of interest in lifestyle programmes:

Increasingly advertisers and manufacturers are seeking to employ presenters to endorse products. Although the BBC does not seek to place unnecessary constraints on talent, it is essential that promotional activities do not constitute a conflict of interest and do not undermine the editorial integrity of presenters or the programmes they present . . .

Sometimes lifestyle programmes give a degree of consumer advice and this will affect the presenter's ability to undertake promotional activities. Lifestyle presenters who give advice on what branded products to buy or use should not undertake any advertising in any medium for products or retailers associated with the subject matter of their programmes . . .

Television cooks or chefs should not undertake any radio or television advertising for any product or retailer associated with the subject matter of their programmes . . . Producers should ensure that the retailer's products are not used, shown or referred to in their programmes.[40]

It is hard to imagine, but only a generation ago the BBC had a blanket ban on the use of trade names in programmes, so that not only were cornflakes and cars only mentionable as generics, but the Kellogg's label and Ford insignia had to be obscured on camera. It was the irresistible clout of sports sponsorship that broke that increasingly unworkable prohibition, and now television is one great supermarket for the senses. The BBC is trying hard to hold the levées against the commercial hurricane, but commercial channels take a more relativist approach, unconcerned as long as their audience is not worried. Product placement companies supply cars and branded goods for free to dramas and any other shows where their use can benefit their makers, and people are drowning in a sea of consumer longing. Companies pay for that privilege legally in the USA, and are about to get the same privilege in the UK when, in 2010, the government is expected to allow it for commercial broadcasters to offset lost advertising revenues.[41]

Academic discourse is more concerned with the desires and sense of identity that such conspicuous consumption endorses. Kirsty Fairclough organised the first international conference on Lifestyle TV at Salford University in April 2007 to address these issues:

Millions of people watch these programmes every day and they have a huge social effect. In many ways they encourage people to look at their lives as projects – the perfect house, the perfect looks and the perfect meals. The shows also reflect society's attitudes to class and taste by providing aspirational models and the expertise to emulate them.[42]

The celebrity chef Heston Blumenthal even called his 2007 BBC series *In Search of Perfection*, although this referred to his scientific approach to perfecting the cooking of iconic dishes, from chicken tikka masala and risotto to hamburgers and Christmas lunch.[43] There is a huge audience for cookery programmes, but most people's aspirations fall short of the laboratory standards that Blumenthal brings to his 'molecular gastronomy', a term he has now repudiated.[44] By 2008, the Delia backlash more accurately captured the Zeitgeist, with her cheap and cheerful approach. *How to Cheat at Cooking* also included documentary inserts about Delia's other passions, most notably Roman Catholicism and Norwich Football Club, as an earnest of how time spent in the kitchen has to be balanced with the other important things in life. Lifestyle programming has become increasingly holistic in this way.

The other food hit of the spring 2008 season was *Come Dine With Me*, a Channel 4 show in which four people take it in turns to cook for each other and criticise the food they eat.[45]

This started as a daytime show in 2005, with each contestant's dinner on successive days and a new group each week. Now the whole cycle is shoe-horned into one weekly episode, but the reality television appeal of ordinary people trying to cook to impress, often failing, and the *Wife Swap*-style catty competitiveness it spawns has found a faithful following. It also set the food fad firmly within the arriviste agenda – a calling card for those who wanted to flaunt their bourgeois pretensions – but has since developed as another class battle-field, in which people happily parade their ignorance and rejection of certain foods, and conspire to undermine the most aspirational among them, like ganging up on the class swot in the playground. As such, *Come Dine With Me* not only deploys documentary techniques but typical documentary sensibilities, finding the telling details within the wider frame.

Make me perfect

If food, homes and gardens are the outward symbols of a person's achievement and purpose, the most revealing aspects of their identity are their clothes and looks. Or so another strand of lifestyle programming would have us believe. Personal makeover shows are big business, not least due to the value they have to the fashion and beauty businesses. *What Not to Wear* was the prototype show here, with a format in which a typically dowdy woman would be set up by her friends or relatives, secretly filmed and then browbeaten into improving her wardrobe and looks with the bossy help of fashionistas Trinny Woodall and Susannah Constantine.[46] They would go through her wardrobe, contemptuously throwing out much, and give some key pointers. The participant would then be given £1,000 to go shopping, not always taking all the advice, before a second round of advice finally fixed on the new clothes and image. *What Not to Wear*'s founder producer Vicki Barrass had previously worked in current affairs and traditional documentary and sees the show's success as 'Reflecting society and its belief that their individuality should be expressed and people thinking they should be able to indulge their psyches and can afford to do so'.[47] When promoted, after three seasons, from a half-hour on BBC2 to an hour on BBC1, Barrass included two intercut storylines in each *What Not to Wear*, normally women sharing some life-affecting event, such as illness or divorce. This tended to give the programmes added depth and poignancy, where the reasons for people's low self-esteem and poor body image were shared, and the audience had longer to share their journey to the inevitable life-affirming transformation. This usually takes place at a party of friends and family, where the subject reveals his or her new look to the jolly throng. Barrass is keen to play down the wider themes touched upon:

> When it can work, fine, but it's not always better. Concentration on the individual and their story is equally fine. Other times people are interested in the wider ramifications. In a special *What Not to Wear as a Sportswoman* – one of the women is black, talking about growing up as 1 of just 3 black families in Eastbourne, wanting to shower herself white. It's a really moving interview and it gets that experience over to a BBC1 peak-time audience that would never have watched a one-off doc on racism in Britain. But any political or societal message is very much a subtext.[48]

Having doubled the audience with the move to BBC1, Trinny and Susannah were eventually made an offer they could not refuse by ITV. While *What Not to Wear* got a new couple of presenters, *Trinny and Susannah Undress . . .* moved the focus to couples and the difficulties they were having in their relationships.[49] This show inevitably delved more into the home background in typical documentary fashion, but also served a growing popular prurience by emphasising the nudity that is such a nightmare for the physically insecure. *The Naked Truth* is a key moment in the show, where the problem couple are obliged to undress behind a back-lit screen and use a cabled live spy-cam to reveal segments of each other's bodies, at the instruction of Trinny and Susannah. The nudity feature of the format was sold hard by an ITV billboard campaign, depicting Trinny and Susannah concealing naked people's modesty with just their artfully placed hands. This upset the notoriously touchy London Underground taste censors, requiring some artful air-brushing while generating the desired publicity. Despite that, *Trinny and Susannah Undress . . .* fared slightly less well in the all-important audience ratings than *What Not to Wear* – with its new more laid-back presenters Lisa Butcher and Mica Paris – and only nine episodes have been made in two years. Some criticisms have been levelled at Trinny and Susannah for straying into areas of therapy in which they are not qualified, so there is clearly an audience discrimination about what they will wear.

Debuting the same year was Channel 4's similar show, *How to Look Good Naked*, with male fashion stylist Gok Wan.[50] Situated halfway between *What Not to Wear* and *Trinny and Susannah Undress . . .*, this show combines the solid clothes and make-up tips of the first with the naked self-assessment of the latter. Participants have to place themselves by body size in a line-up of differently sized women in their underwear – they always imagine themselves several sizes larger than they are – disrobe for a naked photo-shoot, and appear in public on a catwalk. It is a tall order for people overcoming low self esteem. But in Gok Wan, a stylish, effervescent gay man who once weighed 21 stone, *How to Look Good Naked* has a presenter who radiates empathy and personal understanding. He knows how to get people to become comfortable with their bodies and dress to make the most of their shape. There is never an attempt to make people lose weight and there is some universal message of hope in the remarkable transformations he manages to achieve in people's self-image. It is a lifestyle show that adds more than style to life, but the same format failed to work when made for an American audience.

Stars and stripes

The American *How to Look Good Naked*'s [51] presenter, Carson Kressley, was already famous as one of the five presenters of *Queer Eye for the Straight Guy*,[52] a makeover show for men, and this association and his flamboyance could not create the same chemistry as Gok Wan. *Queer Eye* had deployed five gay men ('The Fab Five') with different specialisms, from food to fashion, home design to hair, to prepare a man for some special event. The five arrived in an SUV with a Swat Squad approach to making over the man, passing bitchy remarks on his existing style and grooming. Nothing could be further from the careful and compassionate esteem-building that worked in *How to Look Good Naked*, and Americans are generally less forgiving of the personal failure that is at the root of this particular makeover show. Despite a big marketing lift-off, *How to Look Good Naked* was cancelled after its first seven-week run on Lifetime because of poor audience ratings. Abigail Harvey, whose job running the BBC production office in New York was largely to remake successful UK formats for the American market, endorses that cultural difference:

What I find interesting here is that subtlety doesn't count for much . . . The Americans use an expression: they want characters that 'pop' and by that they mean they want loud, larger than life characters. Now that slightly flies in the face of Britain, where a character doesn't have to be loud and larger than life to be interesting, and they don't even have to be liked to be interesting. In fact, I'd say that the British sensibility is to have characters that are often rather ghastly, who you enjoy seeing them hang themselves, and enjoy their awfulness in their journey on screen. Americans don't like to have unattractive characters. I don't mean physically, but they like all their characters to be likeable.[53]

While lifestyle programming is huge in the United States, with whole channels dedicated to it, the demand is for programmes that are relentlessly life-affirming. As Harvey says, the subtlety, ambiguity and nuance that documentary sensibility brings to such programmes in the UK have no place in the US. While such shows may play well in New York and Los Angeles, the heartland audience is in the so-called 'fly-over states'.

It is the housewives in Kansas who are the mainstay of these programmes that we make, and while the channel wants to think it is really hip and fashionable – it wants to be NY and LA – it doesn't want to alienate. There is a sense that people in the mid-West aspire to the lifestyle of those who live along the coast but can't have that, and they [the channels] don't want to alienate them by pushing that in their face. So there is a bit of a conundrum and the sense that you are playing to the lowest common denominator,[54]

This manifests itself in fast-cut programmes aimed at people with attention deficit disorder, requiring endless reiteration of the programme concept and what has just happened or is about to happen. *What Not to Wear* has been successfully remodelled for the American market, but Vicki Barrass says it is a cheaper, simpler make with a budget, like all American shows, ruthlessly tied to its audience ratings:

Ratings are everything. There are many differences about an American audience. Definitely everything has to move that much faster and I always liked making programmes pretty snappy. You always feel you're just watching highlights. It doesn't ever feel that you are going through the experience, unlike a good doc or *Grand Designs*. It's just snapshots . . .
  In fact they are rerunning cut-down 10-minute versions of *Changing Rooms*, where you just get the set-up and the reveal, the resolution, cutting out all that boring stuff of how they got there. It's the way things are going.[55]

The emerging form of internet video pods running at most five or six minutes may further shrink the normal programme span, but even the existing television hours and half-hours are broken up into bite-sized morsels. Frequent commercial breaks, already taking 17 minutes out of a programme hour, mean constant recapitulation which, says Harvey, effectively allows just half an hour's original material. She says that the key elements of documentary technique are denied by the mechanistic demands of the American channels, not allowing observational material to unfold naturally and dramatically, without the imposition of characters' voiceovers or programme commentary. And the commentary has to be couched in the most prosaic terms, not the sometimes witty crafted use of language that characterises the best of English written narration. 'It's very straight, so literal, and it is so frustrating because you're not exploring this richness of language that could elevate a show':

What the Americans tend to do is, rather than just letting reality to play out – for the audience to make their own minds up about what's going on there and what the filmmaker wants to convey – you're bludgeoned over the head with it because the person themselves tells you what they want you to think . . . Nothing is made for the audience to be intelligent, to fill in the gaps; your hand has to be held through the process.[56]

Nip and tuck

The outer boundaries of American lifestyle programming might make you want your hand held, if not your stomach. Leading the putsch for the extreme, noted in Chapter 7, was the 2002 ABC show *Extreme Makeover*, which added plastic surgery to the more conventional makeover options of clothes, hair and make-up.[57] As the surgeon's scalpel joined the cutting words, a new level of self-reinvention went mainstream. What had formerly been the preserve of Hollywood stars and the terminally rich now became the new aspiration for those determined to change their image. In the very first episode of *Extreme Makeover*, two women were comprehensively remodelled by plastic surgeons and cosmetic dentists keen to extend their skills to a lucrative new popular market. Kine had an upper and lower lip reduction and a breast lift. She had liposuction around her abdomen, losing ten pounds and two inches from her waist. Her teeth were whitened and straightened. She also had Lasik eye surgery so she no longer needed to wear glasses. Tammy had a brow lift, upper and lower eye lifts, a nose job, collagen injections for fuller lips, and porcelain veneers put on her teeth. Both were welcomed back into the bosom of astonished families and both reported improved self-confidence and relationships. It was a formula which proved popularly replicable for several seasons, some involving tummy tucks and face lifts for men as well, but a tragedy that became widely publicised in 2005 may have been responsible for the subsequent downturn in viewing figures that eventually had the show cancelled.

Following the show's initial success, many people applied for the possibility of an 'extreme makeover' at ABC's expense. A few days before Christmas 2003, a 28-year-old Texan, Deleese Williams, was in the studio audience for an *Extreme Makeover* recording, when the spotlight turned on her and her selection for the show was announced. Deleese had always been bullied for the way she looked, and wanted the show to lift her breasts, remove her stretch marks and 'redo my jaw so I don't look like a freak'. Deleese's family was soon to learn that nothing was cost-free, when the production crew descended on their town of Conroe, Texas and extracted some very critical comments from them, particularly from Deleese's husband and sister Kellie, who was also her business partner. Deleese felt bruised, but all the more determined to be reconstructed to change their minds. However, when she arrived in Hollywood for the filming, two weeks of preparation led the maxillofacial surgeon to recommend that the facial reconstruction required would take too long for the show's tight production schedule, so Deleese was sent home to face the family unchanged. She went into hiding, her marriage went into a decline, and her sister eventually killed herself. Deleese sued ABC and the programme's producers, the unfortunately named Lighthearted Entertainment. After a protracted legal battle, an undisclosed settlement was reached. Fighting to rebuild her life and marriage, Deleese Williams's makeover was internal rather than external – wisdom at a high price:

I thought you needed to be perfect and I realize that you don't. You can be who you are, and that's what I teach my children now. I'm older and wiser now, I guess.[58]

Production companies do attempt to weed out such problems by psychological profiling of would-be contestants, but clearly they do not test the contestants' friends and families in the same way, who yet may take collateral damage, as happened in this case.

While there is no denial that programmes have a duty of care to their subjects, there is also the duty of care to their audience, not least in the aspirational models that lifestyle programming promotes. Annette Hill writes extensively about the problematics of the 'Ethics of care' that reality television programmes create. She notes Foucault's invocation of Greek and Roman concepts of the care of the self, and their reliance on societal norms that no longer obtain. Quoting widely, from Giddens, Bonner et al., she explores the ways that the consumerist drive of such shows also imparts a whole new set of values that 'give material form to a particular narrative of self-identity':

Lifestyle and health-based reality programmes . . . are constructed in such a way that they implicitly and explicitly address viewers about good and bad ways to live their lives, and good and bad ways to care for themselves and other people . . . Viewers relate the stories of ordinary people and their experiences to their own family practices, and their own understanding of care and responsibility for the family and the family household. Thus these programmes can encourage viewers to apply an ethic of care in their everyday lives.[59]

The spate of plastic surgery shows incurs a much higher risk and level of concern than when it was only the home or wardrobe that was under threat. Dr 90210[60] – named for the zip code of Beverley Hills – features graphic footage of starlets seeking surgical enhancement and MTV's I Want a Famous Face finds individuals who feel that their future success will be assured by having their face remodelled to look like stars.[61] Britney Spears, Victoria Beckham, Brad Pitt and Arnold Schwarznegger are among those who have been gruesomely used as such role models. Fox TV's The Swan made the extreme makeovers into a contest, which used plastic surgery on two 'ugly ducklings' each week, one of whom would eventually go forward to the final pageant to decide who was the finest 'swan' of all.[62] This was widely condemned as being 'obscene', 'hurtful and repellent even by reality's constantly plummeting standards',[63] but one of the plastic surgeons on the show, Terry Dubrow, hit back with the claim that 'plastic surgery is entertaining; plastic surgery as entertainment is here to stay'.[64] American medical ethicists repudiate this line, while admitting that these shows are largely responsible for a 64 per cent increase in plastic surgery procedures between 2002 and 2005:[65]

Illustrating real-life plastic surgery experiences as a form of entertainment has trivialized the practice of cosmetic plastic surgery. While reality TV shows increase public awareness about the latest surgery options, they have created a troublesome by-product – unrealistic and unhealthy expectations in potential patients. It is crucial for patients to understand that plastic surgery is real surgery with real risks. Further, the introduction of entertainment into reality-based plastic surgery programs has tarnished the image of the profession.[66]

The Swan was cancelled at the end of its first year, less because of the criticism, more because of falling audiences, but plastic surgery has experienced a substantial boost among ordinary people. As the entertainment industry weekly magazine Variety wrote: 'There is nothing wrong conceptually with The Swan, so long as viewers embrace the rather disturbing premise that physical beauty is the overriding measure of self-worth.'[67] As The Boston Globe said of *I Want a Famous Face*, 'it's like watching people play Mr. Potato Head with their own bodies and minds'.[68] Although it may seem from what is shown on television that there are more Potato Heads in the United States, British television also finds a willing audience for this kind of material. *Cosmetic Surgery Live* was UK Channel Five's contribution to the genre, broadcasting nightly for two weeks at a time. Although linked live from Hollywood, with some procedures taking place live, much of the material was pre-recorded and the show made as much of its 'never seen-before procedures including: breast enhancement and full body liposuction, both undertaken while the patient is awake; scarless breast augmentations through the nipple; and open rhinoplasty'.[69] British television is much more graphic than the American equivalent, where nipples and areolas are still routinely airbrushed out. But American doctors seem more willing and natural screen performers. The British Association of Aesthetic Plastic Surgeons took violent exception to the circus antics of their more showbiz-oriented overseas cousins. Their President, Adam Searle, said:

> I am appalled at the voyeuristic and pornographic extravaganza of the new series of *Cosmetic Surgery Live*, and condemn it utterly. The show does not portray the 'real world' of plastic surgery, and in fact does a disservice to thousands of patients who benefit from cosmetic procedures . . . When it comes to health issues presented on television, public education and safety should come before entertainment. Despite the popularity of 'makeover' reality shows, the majority of people who would consider plastic surgery do not want to drastically change their appearance. Yet there are those who, given the opportunity, would elect to undergo an excessive amount of procedures for a complete body overhaul and never be happy with the outcome . . . There is a real danger attached to having many procedures at once, including a higher risk of infection and longer time to be spent under anaesthetic. Fortunately, although people may enjoy the voyeurism of total transformations on television – most don't want that for themselves.[70]

The definition of voyeurism in most jurisdictions involves non-consensual invasion of privacy, but in these programmes people not only consent to the exposure but fight to participate. Time-scales are collapsed by television, risks under-played unless they aid the narrative, and benefits exaggerated to give bring satisfactory closure to the programme. Whether it is old people seduced into relocating abroad or young people encouraged to have their bodies remodelled by scalpel, the risks and negatives should form an integral part of the public broadcast message. But the tendency of these programmes to become merely the shop windows for whole department stores of commercial enterprise inevitably compromise productions and constrain them from allowing too critical an edge to emerge. Uncomfortable truths would be bad for business.

Conclusion

Where Reality Television is indisputably the first factual form of the twenty-first century, lifestyle television still feels like the last hurrah of the last century. In *The Century of the Self* (2002), Adam Curtis tracks the marketing skills that turned Western culture into the consumer society of today (Chapter 3). The final triumph of the neo-conservative ascendancy in the last 20 years of that century was in the commodification of everything, not least the self. Property prices were promised to grow infinitely – 'no more boom and bust', said then Chancellor Gordon Brown – and people were encouraged to borrow excessively against that expectation, to have the lifestyle and the makeovers they wanted now. Television not only tapped that burgeoning want, but fuelled it, and expanded into commercial sectors that promised lucrative secondary revenue streams, albeit at cost to any principles of impartiality. Just as business and financial journalists were mostly too close to their sources to see the crash coming, so programmes predicated on moving people up market or to a place in the sun had many reasons to keep their eyes blinkered, milking the bubble while it lasted. Equally, as aggrieved shareholders and savers complain they had a right to expect better stewardship of their assets by the so-called experts, viewers might reasonably demand better information about the vested interests programmes represent, especially as the government until recently maintained its opposition to paid product placement.

Broadcast television guidelines (see below) are quite specific about the legal duty of care owed to their participants, and some would argue that these should be as explicit with regard to the audience as well, many of whom may be unaware of the downsides of the lifestyles being promoted. But the evolution of multichannel television and the switch to a less-regulated digital spectrum means that people are expected to approach their television fare much as they might the Shopping Channel, shopping around for whichever entertainment commodities best suit them. Ironically, the original UK Lifestyle channel (launched 1985, owned by WH Smith) was one of the early casualties of satellite television, ceasing to broadcast in 1993. It was succeeded by UK Living, then called Living from 1997, to distance itself from the UK branded channels that launched that year, such as UK Style. Arguably the most successful channel relative to its home market is Australia's Lifestyle Channel, but even their director of programming and production, Trevor Eastment, admits that the market probably peaked in 2002.[71] Now he says he cannot make a programme without significant web content attached:

> If it's a cooking show, I need to have all of the recipes, the restaurant, the chef's biography and the name of all the places he visited and how to get there.[72]

With the audience knowing that the information can be sourced there, it allows the shows to be more character-based and anecdotal. This coincides with the other development – noted by the Australian academic Tania Lewis at the time of the arrival of *Queer Eye for the Straight Guy* in 2003, as the 'ironicised' contextualisation of advice in such programmes – moving away from the straight instruction of the DIY expert to the construction of lifestyle offerings as exercises in social identity:

> As a role model for viewers and a mediator between broader community concerns and the world of TV, the makeover expert is charged with both policing and opening up to scrutiny social norms around selfhood.[73]

The reinforcement of enhanced values of style and taste broke down gender stereotypes of who did what and brought the slobbish male into the shopping mall, at enormous benefit to purveyors of everything from toiletries and clothes to the household commodities that were now matters of equal concern to both partners. As Lewis notes: 'A central feature of this refiguring of lifestyle consumption as reflexive and calculative is the focus on consumption as a form of knowledge acquisition.'[74] With television viewing reversing its decline in the first year since the economic collapse, it remains to be seen whether this form of cultural commodification remains as popular in the post-recession world.

Expert briefing – producer's guidelines

Every broadcaster has comprehensive guidelines that it is a producer's obligation to abide by. In the event of any legal action against a programme reaching the courts, one of the first judicial tests is whether the broadcaster and/or producer have observed the guidelines. If not, they lose, and ignorance of them, as of the law, is no excuse. So comprehension and compliance are vital. What follows is only a handful of the conventions that govern contemporary practice, and apply equally to internet and public performance as they do to broadcast:

1 **Copyright**: Copyright not only extends to all creative works, but to ownership of individual spoken contributions, so in every case explicit, normally written, permission is required. Programme-makers also need be aware that any copyright material incidentally caught on shot – such as pictures on people's walls or book covers on their bookcases – or recorded in passing – such as music on the street or literary quotation – are included and can lead to suit from the owners (see more detailed expert briefing in next chapter).

2 **Contempt of court**: Any case where legal proceedings are pending or in process constrains what may be broadcast about that case and all participants. Even casual comments recorded in the context of a totally different kind of show – e.g. reality TV contestants discussing a celebrity arraigned on drugs charges – can be construed as contempt because of their potential to influence the jury and thus the conduct of justice. This does not apply in non-jury trials, because judges are considered to be above such influence.

3 **Criminality**: Programmes featuring individuals subsequently caught up in court cases, either as perpetrators or victims, become *sub judice* until the trial is ended. The filming of criminal activity is not in itself illegal, although anything which could be interpreted as the commissioning, provoking, aiding or abetting of an offence is itself criminal, and failure to act responsibly will be criticised in court. The police have no right to seize 'journalistic material' but can apply to a judge to order its sequestering as evidence. Most broadcasters' guidelines specifically forbid paying criminals for interviews about their crimes.

4 **Defamation**: A statement is defamatory if, when said about a person and published to a third party, it would make ordinary people think less of that person. In the case of television programmes, that has come to be interpreted as even where a defamatory statement was not explicit, but inferred from the context 'by a reasonable person', namely a jury. Because of these unusually draconian libel laws and the international distribution of the internet, the British High Court has opened its doors to actions from anyone, anywhere who does not like what they read or hear about themselves on a website, because it can be accessed in the UK. Making a film makes you equally liable in publishing a libel, and the burden of proof, or justifying fair comment 'in the public interest', can put considerable strain on productions, encouraging caution.

5 **Errors and omissions**: Producers working in highly contentious areas, such as corporate or criminal investigations, can and should insist a reverse indemnity be inserted into their production contract, whereby they are covered against punitive

action caused through no fault of their own. The 'Errors and Omissions' clause restricts their liability where they have made every reasonable effort to check their facts and abide by both the law and the guidelines. Many corporations and other powerful bodies routinely threaten legal action to deter such investigations.

6 **Health and safety**: Producers need be aware that they are personally responsible for the wellbeing of all employees and members of the public on a production site, whether it is in the studio or on location. Programme-makers should routinely fill in risk assessment forms. This does not just matter where dangerous stunts are involved, but wherever any equipment, cables or electricity may endanger safe passage, or simply where the distraction makes people less vigilant than usual. There is also a duty of care to the audience not to promote activities that may be hazardous to health, whether tricks you tell children 'not to try at home', or diets that require medical supervision. All broadcast productions have to be checked to ensure that they do not include stroboscopic effects or other causes of photo-sensitive shock.

7 **High risk and hazardous environments**: Broadcasters keep lists of countries and areas they consider hazardous, not just war zones but areas of insurrection, criminality and terrorism, many where media personnel are increasingly the target. International guidelines were agreed in 2000 stating that only experienced journalists should be sent to war zones, and only voluntarily. News organisations now insist on appropriate training on equipment to minimise such threats, and on instilling protocols that enable producers to de-escalate dangerous situations – including preparation for being taken hostage. As with crime, particular care has to be taken not to inflame violence and disorder, further endangering production crews and their contributors. Unlike other areas of crime, the Terrorism Act enforces a duty to disclose to the police terrorists and planned acts of terror.

8 **Impartiality and neutrality**: Internet activities, such as presenter and editor blogging, have loosened the controls of conformity imposed upon broadcast production staff, but they are still banned from doing anything that may bring their employer into disrepute, which includes attacking or abusing colleagues. Particularly in news and current affairs, they are forbidden from expressing political views or joining political parties. The BBC guidelines have recently extended this proscription to explicitly include personal profiles on social networking sites. Some freelance presenters and producers are hired specifically to take a controversial line in particular programmes, but public service broadcasters still have a contractual obligation to effect impartiality through the balance of their programming.

9 **Interests and promotion**: All broadcasters forbid factual programmes giving 'undue prominence' to commercial goods and services, but this is a rule whose interpretation has changed over time. On channels sustained by advertising and programme sponsorship, the object is not to undermine their revenue stream through unpaid in-programme plugs and promotions. For the BBC, it is more an attempt to retain the editorial independence and integrity with which it justifies its licence fee. The corporation formally forbids product placement and presenter endorsement where a conflict of interest may be perceived, but government rules only forbid third parties from paying for such arrangements. Freelances, independent producers and presenters are all supposed to declare any commercial interest that may be deemed to compromise their critical freedom. But most broadcasters turn a blind eye to the widespread uptake of freebies in travel, lifestyle and consumer shows, justifying these as being 'for the purposes of review'.

10 **Privacy and fairness**: Whereas US Law explicitly excludes people in public life from laws forbidding intrusion and disclosure of people's private life, the European Human Rights Act (1998) enshrines a general right to privacy where none previously existed. Shows filming police and ambulance personnel in action now routinely conceal the features of bystanders to protect their rights, where their permission was denied or unobtainable. Invasion of that privacy can only be justified, and will only be transmitted, where the public interest served is deemed to outweigh the rights lost. Similarly, undercover filming has to be agreed at the highest level in advance of filming, and only where the material cannot be acquired by other means and the results are of sufficient public importance. Children are subject to particularly stringent protection from any filmed intrusion, without the express permission of their parents.

11 **Taste and decency**: While this is the most flexible area, it remains a battlefield for broadcasters and producers, and the area which attracts the most complaints from the public. British television applies a 'watershed' policy, ensuring nothing deemed 'too adult' is broadcast before 9 pm, when younger children are supposed to be tucked up in bed. After that time, the three shibboleths of bad language, sex and nudity, and graphic violence are all progressively more acceptable. These standards vary greatly between national cultures: mainstream American television being more permissive about violence than the UK, but considerably less explicit in sexual content. Issues of disability, race and religion have tended to become more contentious in liberal cultures, occasioning greater caution in such matters on the part of broadcasters. Being subjective, the standards for these judgements are imprecise and always in flux, more reflective of the relative confidence of the broadcaster at the time than any objective rule.

As with the law, ignorance of these guidelines is no excuse, so producers keen to work for broadcasters should familiarise themselves with them and the details of compliance required. They are all available online as follows:

BBC: www.bbc.co.uk/guidelines/editorialguidelines/
ITV: www.itv.com/AboutITV/Commissioning-Production/ProducersGuidelines/
    default.html
Channels 4 and Five: www.independentproducerhandbook.co.uk/
    370/7a-channel4-viewer-trust-guidelines/7a-channel-4-viewer-trust-
    guidelines.html

14 Performance and performers

performance n. 1 the act, process, or art of performing, 2 an artistic or dramatic production

I n playing up to the camera, inventing a persona for the passing moment of fame, reality television participants are paying homage to the celebrities whose world they yearn to enter. Just as every stumble along Amy Winehouse's troubled career pathway feeds a press frenzy, stars have always provided far more entertainment than they set out to deliver on stage and screen. From the early days of the modern entertainment industry, documentary filmmakers – not least through being of the same generation as the rock legends of the 1960s and 1970s – were quick to see the potential of performance that exceeded the staged event and its traditional broadcasts on entertainment showcases such as *The Ed Sullivan Show*[1] in the United States and *Sunday Night at the London Palladium*.[2] Audiences do not want to worship stars from afar, accepting the gilded image as constructed in the Golden Age of Hollywood: they want to get up close and personal, enjoying the quirks of human nature, warts and all. As film cameras became more mobile, they inevitably began to penetrate the process behind the performance, the performers behind the scenes. Although some genres' performers have managed reasonably well to preserve their privacy and mystique – opera singers and even some sportsmen – others have actively sought the camera's stare as a useful adjunct to their fame and fortune, however humiliating its revelations. This chapter will look at three variations on the theme: the classic rock documentary, the sports documentary and the celebrity showcase. It will show that performance documentaries are much more than mere celebrity anthropology. At their best, they chart the popular culture of their time in the most visceral and evocative manner.

Rockumentary

The prototype for the so-called 'rockumentary' is D.A. Pennebaker's film of Bob Dylan's 1965 UK tour, *Don't Look Back*.[3] Although it charts a seminal phase in Dylan's musical career, launching his electric rock to a sometimes hostile folk fan base who feel he has sold out, it only contains 35 minutes of performance, just over a third of the film. The rest is classic observational footage of the man travelling, working on songs and dealing with an insistent, but largely ignorant, press. Echoing the folk-rock evolution, it also charts the decay of his relationship with folk singer Joan Baez, who walks out in one scene, never to look back.

Although the film presumes to offer the ultimate backstage pass, an unmediated image of the man behind the ironic mask, it becomes apparent that this is a performer who is never not performing, a chameleon who plays different roles for the camera. David Baker writes:

> The opening section of the film establishes not simply the multiple character who emerges from contrast between the two songs 'Subterranean' and 'All I really want to do', it also includes one particular version of a backstage Dylan: (understandably) nervy before going onstage, but also affected – looking around for his cane. Even before the landing at Heathrow Airport the viewer has been presented with multiple and contradictory Dylans, both onstage (the songs) and backstage. Further, I suspect, the decision to begin with a backstage Dylan who then goes onstage is a signal to the audience that the Dylan of the remainder of *Don't Look Back* is a character who – as numerous commentators have pointed out – is always 'on', a kind of method-actor who is acutely aware of his perform-ance in front of the supposedly 'fly-on-the-wall' camera.[4]

The entertainers who had pioneered this permanently performing approach to the media were the Beatles. Their irreverent responses to the press and the notion that their entire life was some kind of spectacle was brilliantly captured by Dick Lester in their first feature film, *A Hard Day's Night* (1964).[5] Credited as a result by MTV as the 'father of the music video', Lester was actually using the documentary techniques that were re-energising British cinema at the time, shooting realist films about working-class life. The Beatles crested this new wave, knowingly sending it up and not taking themselves too seriously. Before they became pop legends, they were the lovable boys from next door, and it was documentary that was to best find common cause with this new demotic form.

When the Beatles topped the bill at the Palladium on 23 October 1963, London ground to a halt due to the mobs of hysterical fans, leading to the press coining the phrase 'Beatlemania'. Ed Sullivan spotted the phenomenon when he passed through Heathrow Airport, and booked the band for three shows in February 1964. Their first appearance on *The Ed Sullivan Show*, on 9 February, secured an audience of nearly 74 million, a near 50 per cent US share and the largest television audience ever recorded at that time.[6] Cleverly, Granada TV in Manchester, who had given the Beatles their first TV exposure, had hired the distinguished American documentary filmmakers Albert and David Maysles to cover this first Beatles US tour. Banned for contractual reasons from filming the television shows or the first live concert – at the Washington Coliseum on 11 February – the Maysles obsessively captured all the offstage aspects of the tour, from the moment they stepped out of the plane into an adoring throng, through the band's banter in limousines and on the train, to chilling out in their hotel rooms. David Maysles flew to Manchester with the first few days' footage, which was hastily edited and transmitted as *Yeah! Yeah! Yeah! The Beatles in New York* on 11 February 1964, while Albert continued filming for the longer *What's Happening! The Beatles in the USA*,[7] which aired later in the year. These films not only helped elevate the Beatles to legendary status, but also set the standard for performance documentary. From here on, mere passive recording of a stage show was considered a poor effort; the point of filming was to add something to the experience, ideally that privileged insight 'behind the scenes'. Pioneers of Direct Cinema in the States, the Maysles knew that they were tapping into something more than a passing commercial fad. David Maysles commented at the time of *What's Happening*'s release:

I was trying to show how they typify a great part of American youth. I feel that there is a sort of restlessness. They want to find out what's happening in town. Where are we going to go? . . . They're always looking for something – for a 'beat'.[8]

Humanising the star, identifying what they had in common with their audience, was a novel turn for entertainment moguls, who had always preferred to preserve their stars' mystique and keep the masses at arm's length. The increasing flexibility of 16 mm film operation happily coincided with the spirit of liberation that infected the time and the music. Although Elvis Presley was still labouring under the old-school management of 'Colonel' Tom Parker, who had insisted he accept his two years' drafting into the US Army, the Beatles reflected a healthy disregard for authority and orthodoxy. Yet their 'mop-top' haircuts and designer suits were still seen as square by other emergent groups, and the Rolling Stones turned down the London Palladium because they felt it would be bad for their image. As the *Stones in the Park* commentary says: 'The Beatles got the MBE, but the Stones won't get anything because they are so anti-establishment.'[9]

Better for the Stones' image was to become the subjects of French avant-garde filmmaker Jean-Luc Godard, who filmed them recording *Sympathy for the Devil* over four days in June 1968 at the Olympic Sound Studios in London. Following hot on the revolutionary events in Paris the previous month, Godard used the music as the soundtrack for a set of images reflecting his bleak Marxist perspective: black militants reading from black power texts while torturing white women in a scrap yard by the Thames; 'Eve Democracy' being interviewed about revolution; fascist texts being read in a pornographic bookshop in Soho. But the real interest of Godard's film is in the revealing footage of a band crafting a rock classic that has been credited with stimulating the whole satanic rock genre, one that gave the world bands like Black Sabbath and Venom. This obsessive observation of the details of music-making and recording was novel at the time, as was Godard's slowly tracking camera, which has now become a recording studio cliché. The film also reveals that the drug-damaged Brian Jones has become musically and physically isolated from the band that he once led but is now about to leave, shortly before his death. He sits strumming away in the corner, already en route to another place. Godard's own title for the film *One Plus One* and his final cut were superseded by the producer's more commercial version, *Sympathy for the Devil*.[10]

The Rolling Stones also had a relationship with Granada TV, since *World in Action* had screened an exclusive interview with Mick Jagger after his jail sentence for drug possession was quashed in July 1967.[11] Although on screen he was cross-examined by such pillars of the establishment as *The Times* editor William Rees-Mogg, the crew behind the camera were more of an age and sympathy with Jagger. This relationship led to the same production team shooting *Stones in the Park*, the famous free concert the Stones gave in Hyde Park in July 1969. 'An English park on a Saturday afternoon', the film announces, with shots of couples dozing on the grass and old men diving into the Serpentine, but eventually revealing the hundred thousand people who have pitched up to hear the band for free. Jagger strolls onto a small stage festooned with friends and hangers-on to sing such iconic songs as 'Midnight Rambler', 'Satisfaction', 'Jumping Jack Flash', 'Honky Tonk Women' and 'Sympathy for the Devil'. The performance is not their best; the band are ill at ease and under-rehearsed. Brian Jones had been found dead in his swimming pool just two days before and this was replacement Mick Taylor's first gig. But the film is important as a record both of the band at the crossroads and of its social context. Granada's documentary cameramen capture vignettes of the crowd and the Stones backstage to give a real sense of the event, its emotional impact and historical moment, with Jagger commenting on 'the capitalist system' and reading Shelley's 'Adonais' and releasing butterflies in tribute to the departed Jones.[12] Jagger, like Dylan, performs for the camera, but the Stones' youth and vulnerability evince audience empathy. That the stoned dream was soon to be tarnished is foreshadowed by the appearance in Hyde Park of Hell's Angels as crowd 'policemen' with swastikas on their helmets, whose kind would make a fatal reappearance at Altamont later that year.

Performance and performative

These films not only captured a particular Zeitgeist, but redrew the frame of reference for a generation, connecting the performer to the viewer in many ways. The punters crowd onto the Stones' stage, and the crowd is an intrinsic part of the film and of the performance. The language and references are explicitly part of a shared counter-culture that defined itself in opposition to 'straight' society. The music is anthemic and arousing, giving voice to the emotion and aspiration of the assembled mass, who often join in. So the better performance films are much more than a passive record of great concerts or events.

The documentary sensibility delivers a filmic reflection of the way that popular music is located at the centre of its audiences' existence, channelling its hopes and dreams. Though not what Bill Nichols had in mind when defining the 'performative mode' in documentary, performance documentaries can contain a complex reflexive element that clearly fits the definition:

> Performative documentary underscores the complexity of our knowledge of the world by emphasising its subjective and affective dimensions . . . Performative documentary restores a sense of magnitude to the local, specific and embodied. It animates the personal so that it may become our port of entry to the political.[13]

The most political effect of music of this era was to give birth to the sense of a global tribe of youth, who had more in common with each other than they did with other generations in their own societies. Even the World War of the previous generation, which had allied nations in a common purpose, had not managed to instil an internationalist sensibility among ordinary people. Quite the reverse; it had reawakened nationalism and local communities. But seeing that generation fall back into the military posturing of the cold war – and the demonisation of communism that justified the slaughter of the Vietnam War – young people around the world were ready for a voice that unified them in opposition to all this. The Beatles were the phenomenon that breached the wall – and it was John Lennon who later sang 'Give Peace a Chance' – but 1960s music was a much broader tide, embracing all voices that yearned to break out from the stifling constraints of the time. Like a global tsunami, it flooded the world and ushered in a sense of a 'global village' long before the internet was born. Ever bigger concerts and festivals were staged, bringing artists and their faithful fans together, and filmmakers with equally long hair were always there to capture the moment.

Festivals

An early apogee of this movement was the Monterey Pop Music Festival in June 1967. Planned by an emerging rock aristocracy of The Beatles, The Beach Boys and The Mamas and the Papas, this three-day event brought together an extraordinary roster of talent that was duly filmed by D.A. Pennebaker and his crews. Among many distinguished performers, *Monterey Pop*[14] included Jimi Hendrix's explosive American debut, break-out performances by The Who and Janis Joplin, and introduced the pop world to soul singer Otis Redding and Indian sitarist Ravi Shankar. It was the first major pop festival and the first big rock benefit, where everyone save Shankar appeared for free, and the beneficiary, the MIPF (Monterey International Pop Festival) Foundation, run by record producer Lou Adler, is still receiving revenues to this day. It brought bands together from different musical traditions across the States that had not formerly mixed and helped forge a sense of international brotherhood. Pennebaker's freewheeling footage captures the happy delirium of the hippy crowds and slides off the lead singers to the backing musicians in a way which cleverly echoes an intelligent viewer's scoping of such events, where being there and sharing the whole thing is an integral part of the experience. The respect the musicians show for each other is synchronous with the universal, naive hope that infused that 'Summer of Love', as the poet and American studies academic, Rod Phillips, writes:

> Throughout *Monterey Pop*, Pennebaker subtly but insistently introduces the theme of love and community. From the opening statements of audience members, in which one young woman predicts that the event would be 'a big love-in', to the serene shots of California hippies dancing, embracing and camping in communal teepees, to performers like Otis Redding referring to the audience as 'the love crowd', Pennebaker idyllically captures the 1960s Zeitgeist of peace, love and brotherhood.[15]

Ironically, it was the success of *Monterey Pop* that helped concentrate less idealistic minds on the sheer economic potential that was vested in this brotherhood. As record companies rushed to sign the acts that enraptured the festival hordes, others imagined the financial returns possible for charging festival entrance fees, running concessions and exploiting the film and recording rights. It was venture capitalists that first conceived the granddaddy of all festivals, the Woodstock Music and Art Fair of 1969. Artie Kornfeld of Woodstock Ventures offered Warner Brothers the option of making a film of the event for just $100,000, the cost of the film stock alone. He told them:

> Hey, guys, there are going to be hundreds of thousands of people out there. It's a crap shoot: spend $100,000 and you might make millions. If it turns out to be a riot, then you'll have one of the best documentaries ever made.[16]

Even without the riot, he was proven right.

Michael Wadleigh was to direct, with a pick-up crew of 100 from New York, on the now all too familiar deferral basis – they would only get paid when the movie went into profit. Wadleigh had the idea of making a latter-day Canterbury Tales, as those hundreds of thousands of hippies made their pilgrimage to upstate New York to dance to the music, make love and denounce the Vietnam War. Woodstock Ventures were still dreaming of making money. They had sold 186,000 $18 tickets in New York before the event, but 50,000 turned up at Max Yasgur's farm in upstate New York before the security fences were finished. The anarchist collective, Up Against the Wall Mother Fuckers, cut the fence down to allow it to become a free festival for the remainder of the 500,000 that eventually arrived for 'History's Biggest Happening', as the *Time* magazine cover story heralded it:

The baffling history of mankind is full of obvious turning points and significant events: battles won, treaties signed, rulers elected or disposed, and now seemingly, planets conquered. Equally important are the great groundswells of popular movements that affect the minds and values of a generation or more, not all of which can be neatly tied to a time or place. Looking back upon the America of the '60s, future historians may well search for the meaning of one such movement. It drew the public's notice on the days and nights of Aug. 15 through 17, 1969, on the 600-acre farm of Max Yasgur in Bethel, NY.[17]

Yasgur was a successful dairy farmer, who had struck a hard bargain of $75,000 for the lease of his land. The local community had tried everything from the law to intimidation to stop the festival, fearful that the vast numbers expected – thought to be more at one time in this place than had walked upon it in all previous time – was an invasion that would paralyse, if not destroy, their quiet rural community. News of those attempts merely brought more people, earlier than anticipated, blocking the New York Thruway and surrounding roads for days. The background business barely makes the film, but the quiet decency of Max Yasgur does, as he stands on the stage to address an enthusiastic multitude:

I'm a farmer [ecstatic cheers] . . . I don't know how to speak to 20 people at one time, let alone a crowd like this. This is the largest group of people ever assembled in one place at one time. You have proved something to the world: that half a million kids can get together for 3 days of fun and music, and have nothing but fun and music, and I 'God bless you' for it.[18]

The Woodstock Venture cost its four entrepreneurs $3.4 million and it was some years before they went into profit, essentially due to the film, a wide-screen celebration of those three days of fun and music. One of the earlier uses of split screen, it juxtaposed the images of crowd and performers and tried to shoehorn as much as it could into its gargantuan three-hour running time. Among the crew was one Martin Scorcese, who was to go on to make many great performance films, and it was edited by the woman who would edit all his films, Thelma Schoonmaker. She was nominated for an Oscar and the film went on to win the Best Documentary Oscar in 1971. Also nominated were the sound recordist Larry Johnson and the sound mixer Dan Wallin, for one of the most powerful soundtracks, which set a new bar for the quality and intensity of such location recording. The 64 reels of 8-track recording of all the music involved 3 non-stop recording sessions of 18 hours apiece, and brought to the screen a live aural dimension previously only associated with the careful construction of film epics. The triple vinyl soundtrack album issued at the time was also a colossus of its kind and sold around the world to all those hippies who had wished they were there. The event, the film and the album all culminate with Jimi Hendrix's legendary performance. His agonising rendition of 'Star Spangled Banner', with its triumphant chords curdled into downward spiralling shrieks on the guitar, presciently heralded the end of the dream. Thirteen months later, Hendrix was dead, and Altamont had happened.

In 1969, the Maysles Brothers were back in action, chronicling the Rolling Stones tour of the USA. *Gimme Shelter*[19] records the band at their Madison Gardens concert and recording in the Muscle Shoals studio in Alabama, but much of its observational footage concentrates on the behind-the-scenes dealing required to mount a free concert at the Altamont Speedway in California. This event provided the narrative for the film, because it was where an 18-year-old called Meredith Hunter apparently pulled a gun in front of the stage and was subsequently stabbed to death by a Hell's Angel. This was captured on film by the Maysles cameras, leading to Universal Pictures offering $1 million for the film. The poster for the film when it was released read: 'The Music that Thrilled the World . . . and the Killing that Stunned It!' It raises questions of taste and culpability: whether the Stones and their managers should take responsibility for what happened, whether they should have carried on playing, and whether the resultant profiteering from it was acceptable. The film shows Jagger's constant pleas to a restless audience to calm down, and reveals how the Angels, who had been asked to guard the stage and gear, chose to take a rather more active role in man management, leading earlier to the knocking unconscious of one of the support bands' lead singer, Marty Balin of Jefferson Airplane, when he tried to intervene to stop a fight. In the tradition of Direct Cinema, the film eschews commentary, but uses the device of the Stones reviewing the footage in the edit room, and getting David Maysles to rerun the killing in slow motion. 'It's so horrible,' Jagger says; but he is able to walk away, the questions unanswered.

Forty years on, the Rolling Stones are still together, still touring and still laying claim to be 'The Greatest Rock and Roll Band Ever'. Martin Scorcese captured this senior rock citizenry in the concert film *Shine a Light* (2008).[20] It features performances in two specially staged New York concerts tacked onto the end of their 'A Bigger Bang' US tour in 2006, and demonstrates how etiolated the performance film genre has become. Although the performances are good, the sound and camera work – employing no less than 18 top cinematographers – state of the art, the whole affair is a carefully managed promotional exercise, from the fictionalised preparations at the start, with the self-regarding screen presence of the director, to the hand-picked celebrity audience, including Bill Clinton, for whose Foundation this is notionally a benefit. As the salon.com website says: 'It's all the spontaneity of rock 'n' roll – fossilised.'[21]

No doubt the aim of hiring Scorcese to make this film was because of the epic job he had done on filming The Band's legendary final concert at the Winterland Ballroom in 1976. The Band were widely recognised as one of the most talented groups of musicians playing at the time, with a style and sound that synthesised the key roots of popular music, from folk and rock and roll to soul and blues. They had been Dylan's backing band in the days of *Don't Look Back*;[22] they had provided in 'The Weight' an iconic theme tune for the seminal hit film

Figure 14.1
No retirement age for rock stars as Martin Scorcese's *Shine a Light* (2008) proves

Easy Rider;[23] and they had worked with many of the biggest names in rock music. Charting that history, *The Last Waltz* was The Band's swansong, with arguably the greatest roster of guest appearances ever in any such event.[24] Over a dozen stars who could normally sell out a stadium on their own guested, from Eric Clapton and Van Morrison to Joni Mitchell, Muddy Waters and Bob Dylan. *The Chicago Tribune* critic is one of many who have hailed this film as 'the greatest rock concert movie ever made – and maybe the best rock movie, period'.[25]

Scorsese had orchestrated the shoot like one of his features, with a stage set borrowed from San Francisco Opera's production of *La Traviata* and a roster of cameramen who normally lit features, including Michael Chapman (*Raging Bull*), Vilmos Zsigmond (*Close Encounters of the Third Kind*) and László Kovács (*Easy Rider*, *Five Easy Pieces*). These were significant cinematographers and creative artists not used to being told what to do. The problem with film cameras is the need to reload their film magazines every few minutes,[26] and at one point Scorsese had ordered everybody to stop shooting and reload. László Kovács, fed up with Scorsese shouting through the headphones, had taken his off and so was the only camera running when Muddy Waters started singing 'Mannish Boy'. The bravura camerawork throughout the film not only captures the rhapsodic music but instills the proceedings with a sense of grandeur. This contrasts well with the intimate, unrehearsed interviews with The Band members, conducted by Scorsese himself, as they reminisce about their 16 years on the road. The mixture of guileless humanity and great stagecraft are what make *The Last Waltz* a fitting coda to what one can call the Golden Age of concert films. Concert films continue to be made, like *Shine a Light*, but most concerts are recorded by outside broadcast units, with multiple cameras directed through headphones and their output mixed live on site and often pumped live to the world, like Live Aid was in 1985, and the Glastonbury Festival most years since. OBs capture performances, but are the visual equivalent of the crowd experience, rather than the privileged individual insight to which a documentary film aspires. This is why sports performances are so dominated by event cover and relatively rarely the subject of documentary.

Sporting chances

Along with the obvious audience demand for live transmission of their club and country teams' performances, the economics of sport drive much of television. When the former first division clubs broke away from the English Football League in 1991 to form the Premiership, it was primarily to maximise revenues, which result it has spectacularly achieved, making it the richest football league in the world. It was far from coincidental that the Premiership's birth occurred at the dawn of satellite broadcasting and Rupert Murdoch's nascent BSkyB was prepared to pay a then astronomic £191 million for the first five seasons. Although it was years before the satellite broadcaster went into profit, Murdoch's global empire could wear billion pound losses to secure his near monopoly of multichannel television, and football was central to that strategy. The commodification of the game played havoc with BBC and ITV finances, depriving them of their former commanding duopoly and leaving the BBC to settle for the late evening highlights package. Sky has remained in the game. In the 2007 deal, Sky paid £2.7 billion for three years, with the new cable channel Setanta Sports taking what was supposed to be a third of the package, the monopoly broken up at the insistence of the European Commission.[27] These gigantic sums are what enrich the clubs and enable them to pay the huge fees that attract the best players in the world.

The television rights tend to come in a bundle, including documentary access that is of marginal interest to the sports entrepreneur. The financial returns on documentary are tiny compared to the live broadcast rights, and it is in nobody's interests to license individuals to poke around undermining the myths of the 'beautiful game'. So it is that sports documentary is a largely undernourished genre, frequently denied access to the fields of dreams. Documentary at its best challenges the received orthodoxy. For all the money spent on it, the conventions of football coverage have changed little in decades, with much of the play covered from a high stand camera on the half-way line, offering the wide shot that reveals the breadth of play. Touchline cameras focus on the individuals on the ball, and their histrionics as they take a dive or receive a warning from the referee. Frequently we miss moments of play, as shots at goal are replayed from various angles. It is possible to watch a whole match with some of the players on the pitch never being picked out by the coverage. For all the cameras deployed, it is a necessarily partial view. Two documentaries have confronted these limitations by the simple device of concentrating on one player for a whole match. In *Football as Never Before* (1970), the experimental German filmmaker Hellmuth Costard trained eight 16 mm cameras on the leading player of the day, George Best, during a match between Manchester United and Coventry City.[28] There are few wide shots and we only see the goal that Best scores. The other goal, which Best sets up, we only discover has been scored by Bobby Charlton when Best congratulates him. It is a fascinating study of how one man fits within the complex organism that is a football team.

When Douglas Gordon and Philippe Parreno decided to use the same technique 35 years later, training 17 synchronised video cameras on the French football star Zinedine Zidane during a Real Madrid game with Villareal in 2005, they claim not to have known about the Costard film. Gordon is a Turner Prize winning artist, whose work is frequently about getting people to look at things in the public realm differently. In *Zidane: un portrait du 21e siècle/A portrait of the 20th century*, the spectator is mesmerised by this iconic figure bestriding the pitch in a virtual cinematic bubble, eventually exploding in rage and being sent off in much the same way he would be a year later in the World Cup Final. Gordon explains how the film was an attempt to wrest the image of the footballer from the conventional manipulations of the media:[29]

Most televisual representations of football are based on a kind of theatrical convention of only shooting from one side – you have an entrance-left-exit-right type of motion. By breaking that down, you actually break up the architecture of the stadium. It's no longer rectangular; it's become circular in a way. We wanted to make a portrait of a man: a working man who happens to be Zinedine Zidane, and the work happens to be football. It wasn't a particularly good day at the office for him – he didn't score any goals, and he got red-carded. But we wanted what we did to be along the lines of a Robert Bresson picture; to capture the honesty of the everyday.[30]

American filmmaker Spike Lee was so impressed by the *Zidane* film that he used the technique to film a documentary for NBC about basketball star Kobe Bryant.[31] Although ESPN and ABC already had 22 cameras focused on the important Los Angeles Lakers NBA and San Antonio Spurs meeting in April 2008, Lee brought in 15 more, all focused on Byant and what Lee calls his 'wonderful body parts':

The *Zidane* film was a whole new level of how to do a sports film, so I've taken that to follow Kobe around. Not just on the court, but in the locker room and how he prepares for the game, what he does afterwards.[32]

Although the drama of the personal can be as compelling as the epic tournament in which it takes place, sports coverage has inevitably concentrated on the grand narrative, most notably as the embodiment of national prestige. Countries vie to host the Olympic Games, despite punitive costs to their exchequers, in the belief that their moment of glory will confer enhanced cultural and economic capital in the world thereafter. The most notorious such grandstanding was also the subject of one of the greatest sports documentaries, Leni Riefensthal's *Olympia* (1936).[33] The Berlin Olympics of that year were conceived on an epic scale, to hymn the arrival of the thousand-year Reich, and Riefensthal's innovative cinematography rose to the occasion, with breathtaking panoramas and crane shots. The stirring marriage of image and sound and the breaking of the film into two parts contribute to the epic sense of history in the making. The first part, *Fest Der Völker/Festival of the People*, sets the event within the classical tradition the Olympic Games invokes, laying overt claim to the legacy of the imperial tradition. The second part, *Fest der Schönheit/ Festival of Beauty*, concentrates more on the Nazi fetishisation of gilded youth. The fact that other nations won medals, not least the four golds won by the black American sprinter Jesse Owens, may have undermined the subtext of Aryan supremacy, but there is little doubt that this is the classic image-building the Minister of Propaganda, Josef Goebbels, was paying for. Riefensthal claimed *Olympia* was not Nazi propaganda, but, coming after *The Triumph of the Will* (1934),[34] her equally effective film about Hitler's Nuremberg rallies, also paid for by Goebbels, history finds against her.

The Nazis had also had another sporting propaganda victory earlier in the summer of 1936, when the German heavyweight Max Schmeling had knocked out the black American Joe Louis. Joe Louis's son considers that this was the most important bout of Louis's life, because it was when he woke up to the responsibilities of the role he was playing in his nation's history. It made Louis determined to take the world title and eventually win the rematch. Talking in an HBO sports documentary, *Joe Louis: America's Hero . . . Betrayed* (2008), Joe Louis Barrow Junior says:

> He got very focused, he got very driven, because he thought he hadn't only let down his camp, he had let down all of black America . . . [The rematch] was a huge propaganda and Hitler was proud of his Aryan Max Schmeling, who was going to once again defeat the black man. And all of a sudden these two fighters were not just two heavyweight fighters. Here was Joe Louis, a black man representing freedom and democracy, even though he couldn't live those freedoms and democracies. And here was Max Schmeling, who wasn't a Nazi, who was holding up the banner for the Aryan race . . . When they walked into that ring in 1938, it wasn't about the heavyweight title of the world, it was about the world. It was about: What is the symbol? Who is the strongest? Who is the most powerful race?[35]

Joe Louis won the fight for democracy in 2 minutes and 4 seconds, and went on to hold the world heavyweight title for an extraordinary 12 years. In those days, people flocked to the cinema to see the fights in the newsreels that accompanied the main feature. Today, they have to pay a premium to Sky to see live coverage. HBO showed the Joe Louis special in their Black History Month, incidentally revealing the racial fault lines that still dog the United

States in the twenty-first century. Sport and music remain the two most notable paths out of the ghetto for African-Americans, so many of the films made are freighted with meaning beyond the simple performance highs. Because boxing is so individualistic and elemental, it has produced some of the most extraordinary characters and performances on film, including Muhammed Ali's notorious 'Rumble in the Jungle' in 1974. Ali, with his name change and refusal of the draft to fight in Vietnam, had become a black hero and one of the most famous men in the world. With a title referencing the pre-colonial history of black Africa, *When We Were Kings*, Leon Gast's Oscar-winning documentary of this fight, took 22 years to make it to the screen, due to contractual and financial problems.[36] Initially, music documentarist Gast was hired to shoot a *Woodstock*-style record of the three-day 'black Woodstock' music festival staged in Zaire at the same time, to help raise the $10 million purse the dictatorial President Mobutu had put up. The concert went ahead, with the appearance of stage greats such as James Brown and B.B. King, but the bout was delayed for a month due to Foreman having an eye injury.

Gast stayed on and filmed the preparations of the increasingly frustrated camps and the fight itself. The film falls into four sections. The first part is a survey of Ali's early career, with the aim of identifying him with the Civil Rights and anti-colonial movements, and suggesting a leading role in aligning African-Americans with Africa. This resolves in the second part, with Ali arriving in Africa, serenaded by the music of the concert: 'Say it loud: I'm black and I'm proud'. The third part is the delay occasioned by the Foreman injury and the opportunity it gave Ali to forge more links with the locals. The final part is the bout, Ali's victory and its coronation of Ali as the unifying African-American hero. An aging Ali was not expected to be able to stand up to the younger, hard-hitting George Foreman, and was quoted by bookmakers at 7:1 against, but he took the fight, only the second man to regain the world heavyweight title. Retrospective comment from luminaries such as writer Norman Mailer and filmmaker Spike Lee add the perspective of years that gives the film an additional historical value. The American film academic Leger Grindon writes:

> *When We Were Kings* celebrates the optimism, fortitude and determination necessary to command one's destiny. The hero in *When We Were Kings* emerges as a crusader for social justice whose identity is drawn from his racial community. The closing 'When We Were Kings' montage does not simply valorize Ali, but inspires the audience to acknowledge the prospects for heroic action that combines physical excellence with social leadership, fervent conviction, self-sacrifice, and a commitment to others.[37]

It is unusual that a film delayed nearly a quarter of a century managed to achieve more status and impact than if it had been released at the time. Then it would have been a flash of that unique moment, with great star performances: like journalism, 'the first draft of history'. The delay benefited from Ali's metamorphosis to legendary status, and the film has become a genuine historical artefact. With some events, it may be possible to predict the record will be of future significance, but most films are made in the spirit of the time, uncertain whether it will last beyond its first showing.

When We Were Kings was not the only film that came out in the mid-1990s to capture the African-American spirit of aspiration through sport. Steve James's *Hoop Dreams* (1994) follows two African-American boys from Chicago through four years in high school basketball, charting their highs and lows, their families and friends and the games that embody their opportunity to escape the projects.[38] College talent scouts circle like vultures, and Spike Lee is seen visiting a Nike-sponsored summer camp at Princeton, giving the young hopefuls a harsh reality check:

> Nobody cares about you. You're black; you're a young male. All you're supposed to do is deal drugs and mug women. The only reason why you're here is you can make their team win. If their team wins, the school gets lots of money. This whole thing is revolving around money.

The boys get their college sports scholarships, giving a satisfactory closure to the 170-minute film, but too few sports documentaries aspire to the depth of social reading that this film does. The monetisation of those dreams that Lee mentions, and the commodification of sport not least through television, makes for a controlling hand that generally prefers the preservation of the mystique and the burnishing of star images. Stories of corruption and drug-taking will continue to exercise the tabloids and their fellows in broadcast news, but the towering edifice of contemporary sports business seeks to keep such probes at bay, and has the money to discourage and to sue when they want. In May 2007, the English Premier League initiated a class action against YouTube and its parent company Google for infringement of their rights over fans' posting of Premiership highlights. Joining with the US music publisher, Bourne Co., they seek to restrict the fastest developing distribution of performance video, the internet.[39]

Performance video

As we have seen across other genres, new technology has enabled different forms of consumption that have tended to marginalise traditional constructs and supply content in more raw forms. The demand for this kind of product was well established before broadband made web delivery universal. Cheap video cameras had made possible the capture of performances, from bootleg recordings of concerts to the obsessive charting of specialist sports fans. One of the earliest arenas to capture extraordinary performances and spawn a whole new distribution market was skateboarding. In the early 1990s, VHS compilations of grabs and grinds, fakies and flips were changing hands for significantly large shares of pocket money. Today, they are mostly available free online, complete with their obligatory fish-eye lens shots and rock music scores. A Google search for skateboard videos offers an unbelievable 8,630,000 results, second only to videos about running in the individual sports fields.[40] Football attracts even more, with YouTube hosting fan sites encouraging the upload of videos that will also attract advertising revenue, from their own diaries to treasured moments. To the legions of fans and web-surfers, the sharing of such videos and clips is the same as a conversation or pointing something out in the newspaper, but to the copyright owners it is piracy.

Copyright infringement has brought the whole file-sharing issue to a head. Clubs such as Arsenal and Manchester United are global businesses. With rights now worth a massive £2.7 billion to the Premier League, they fear that failing to stem the internet trade will lead to the eventual haemorrhaging of their profits. By making suit with American music publishers, by suing in the Southern District Court of New York, and by inviting other interested parties to join their class action, they are attempting to establish a once-and-for-all statement of principle on intellectual property rights. The defendants are equally vehement that their activities are expressly protected by the US Digital Millennium Copyright Act of 1998, enacted to protect a free internet. In its legal answer to the action, YouTube and Google state:

> Legitimate services like YouTube provide the world with free and authorized access to extraordinary libraries of information that would not be available without the DMCA – information created by users who have every right to share it. YouTube fulfils Congress's vision for the DMCA. YouTube also fulfils its end of the DMCA bargain, and indeed goes far beyond its legal obligations in assisting content owners to protect their works.[41]

Just as sampling in music can breach copyright in both the composition and the performance involved, clips from football matches are a valuable commodity whose distribution their owners want to control. Fans at football matches are no more welcome to bring their video cameras than concert goers are to record the event. But the point of sport is that it is a live event and what matters most is the instantaneous shared experience. Live football is fabulously lucrative business and its relay has reinvigorated bar earnings in Britain and throughout Europe. In music, the CD business has contracted alarmingly, but the live performance business has expanded exponentially, with big bands making more from touring than recording. The boards of the big stadia of the world are now hosts to the constant tread of rock dinosaurs' feet, as they dust off their greatest hits and pocket millions for their efforts. As IT guru Andrew Keen says:

> The smart business follows the music business. The copy is dead. The 21st century is the time of the live act. In the midst of digitisation, the only thing left is the physical.[42]

This is a rhetorical reaction to the virtual reality that has been a key contribution of new media, where the sad enjoined to 'get a life' have instead got an avatar and an imaginary existence in the online site *Second Life*. Keen believes anything truly live has seen a commensurate beneficial reaction, with passive media like television taking the hit.[43] Even theatre has confounded the jeremiahs and shown healthy profits long after its predicted demise. Since 1992 the National Video Archive of Performance has been carefully recording the best of UK theatre, under a special licence with the Federation of Entertainment Unions that waives artists' fees, and exhibits them for free in the Victoria & Albert Museum in London. However worthwhile, theatre archival is rarely a commercial purpose. But, in tune with the revival of the live act, the recording of live performances continues to be a worthwhile business for all aspects of the music business, from rock to opera. For those unable to get to the big stadia or afford the astronomic ticket prices, the DVD offers the next best thing. And leading the live revival are acts one might have supposed dead. In May 2008, Amazon's best-selling music DVDs were *Genesis – When in Rome: Live 2007*, *ZZ Top – Live from Texas* and Julien Temple's *Sex Pistols – There'll Always Be An England*.[44]

None of these live event films are complete without the privileged insights, the behind the scenes extras. As the inevitable Amazon punter review of the Sex Pistols film adds:

> What really made this DVD for me were the extras. One part is 'the knowledge', which is the band's guide to what places in London were important in the history of the Pistols, and within this is John Lydon's open-top bus trip around London – you get a taste of it from the trailer but the full segment itself is excellent. It's refreshing to let them do their

own talking given all the hype that normally surrounds the band and I think you have to give a lot of credit to Julien Temple for capturing it all.[45]

Julien Temple is a director whose life's work neatly spans the arc of this chapter. The leading filmmaker to emerge from the British punk scene, he is best known for his long association with the Sex Pistols, whose first film footage he shot for the short documentary *Sex Pistols Number One* (1976). He fell out with band members over *The Great Rock and Roll Swindle* (1980) – the feature-length fictional documentary that took former manager Malcolm MacLaren's egotistical view of the band's short and chequered history – but re-established relations to make *The Filth and the Fury* (2000), very much the band's view of their leading role in the punk movement. The title was taken from a *Daily Mirror* headline at the time of a tabloid-confected storm of rage at the Pistols' appearance on Thames Television's *Today* programme.[46] Presenter Bill Grundy goaded band member Steve Jones to 'Say something outrageous', after he had called Grundy 'a dirty old man' for propositioning fellow punk guest Siouxsie Sioux on air, so he called him 'a dirty fucker' and the tabloids had a field day, securing the Sex Pistols a notoriety and invaluable publicity for their *Anarchy in the UK* tour. Like it or loathe it, this is performance documentary that enshrines the Zeitgeist perfectly. Speaking of his subsequent film memorialising his friend *Joe Strummer: The Future is Unwritten* (2007), Julien said:

> Punk was rubbish. Other than the Pistols and the Clash, all those other bands were really awful. I couldn't listen to them. But kids should know about it, because it was the last time when this country had a youth culture uprising which said things that needed to be said.[47]

Although he has made a bigger career from directing rock videos, and has tried his hand at features (notoriously *Absolute Beginners* in 1986, the failure of which nearly brought the British film industry to its knees), Temple remains a music chronicler in the troubadour tradition. Along with the Pistols and Strummer films, his epic portmanteau documentary *Glastonbury* (2006), which *The Observer* called 'one of the most absorbing and inspiring music films ever made',[48] puts Temple in the first rank of documentarists. Asked by Glastonbury founder Michael Eavis to chronicle the extraordinary event that annually churns up his Somerset farm each predictably wet British summer, he was not satisfied with the material that he was shooting and access to all the years of BBC event cover, made available when they came on board to finance the film. In tune with both the democratic spirit of Glastonbury and the temper of television, which had developed a hunger for the dreadfully dubbed user-generated content, Temple invited festival-goers to send in their film and video of treasured moments. As over 900 hours arrived in the post, to add to the hundreds of hours he already had, Temple nearly had a nervous breakdown, but the resulting two-hour film is a magical evocation of the supreme British festival. Temple manages to capture both the environmental and political sub-currents and the sense of shared ownership that give it a particular place in British popular culture:

> I think making the film mirrored the experience of going to the festival. The rules and role-playing that exist in normal life no longer hold; you're thrown into this incredibly random and vibrant event and you sink or swim. There's certainly an element of surviving

Glastonbury as well as enjoying it . . . If you said to me in 1971 that, 30 years later, I'd be ringed in by steel and security cameras would be filming my every move, I would have just thought it was some mad Orwellian nightmare. But Glastonbury may still be considered a prequel of how we have to behave if the climate goes berserk – love the mud, forget your computer and be human again.[49]

This is the paradox of Glastonbury that the eponymous film captures so well – a revisit to the earth-loving, free-loving Sixties within a steel security cordon consuming the power and resources of a small town; 177,000 people who can afford £175 (plus £5 booking fee and £4 p&p)[50] for a weekend camping in a sea of mud; an unseemly fight among millionaire acts as to who should be on the bill to give their market credibility an upmarket summer polish.[51] As the festive campers get out their mobile phones and send the live pictures home to friends, there is no one checking whether the pictures are of their happy faces or pirated shots of the band on the distant stage.

The YouTube generation (motto 'Broadcast Yourself') increasingly sees itself as performers in its own live movie, whether waving at the camera in live events or adding to the ten hours of video uploaded to YouTube every minute.[52] Viacom are suing over the pirated use of commercial material – alleging Al Gore's *Inconvenient Truth* had alone taken 1.5 billion illegal viewers – but there are bigger fears that the internet will collapse under the sheer weight of self-regard in circulation. In 2007, YouTube alone consumed as much capacity as the entire internet did in 2000, and YouTube has only been going since 2005. The US internet data company Hitwise reported an actual decline of 9 per cent in American online video hits in the year to May 2008, but a 6 per cent increase in time spent online, with YouTube taking a dominant 75 per cent share.[53] In the UK, internet traffic to video sites increased 178 per cent in the year to February 2008, with YouTube taking over 69 per cent of it,[54] but it is the roll-out of video on demand by the major terrestrial television companies, notably the BBC's iPlayer that has caused an exponential growth in loading. In June 2009, a simmering row between the content providers and the internet service providers erupted, with BT demanding that the BBC and YouTube be forced to pay for the growing weight the ISPs are forced to carry. 'We can't give the content providers a completely free ride and continue to give customers the [service] they want at the price they expect', complained BT's managing director of retail business, John Petter. 'Everyone wants high speed broadband at low prices, but we can't do this unless content providers such as iPlayer chip in. It costs a huge amount for us to carry this content.'[55]

Downloading a DVD on demand takes the equivalent bandwidth of 16 million web page downloads, 400,000 emails, or nearly 2,000 iTunes songs – and 6 times as much if it is in high definition Blue-Ray.[56] IT gurus assure us that the technology is capable of growing with demand, and there is no need to return computer-less to the primordial mud as Julien Temple suggests. But someone is going to be forced to pay, and that will inevitably be the punter in the end. Temple's *Glastonbury* film and YouTube both suggest a continuing deterioration of a clear-cut distinction between Habermas's private and public spheres.[57]

Celebrity culture

As the performers formerly known as the audience push themselves to the front of the stage – whether madly gyrating in a Glastonbury field, amusing the country's jaded palate by being humiliated in the Big Brother house, giving a new meaning to the phrase *Britain's Got Talent*, or uploading their amateur antics onto YouTube – the demand for genuine star turns becomes ever greater. Their live performances, however long in the tooth those stars may be, have to be big to stand out from the rising tide of banality. Andrew Keen talks of the social network bubble being about to burst, and Web 3.0 being where the smart and talented seize back control of the public sphere from the talentless wannabes. He detests a world that has fetishised innocence, amateurism and the childlike, and is sure the resurgence of the live music industry presages a return to a hierarchy of valued talent and expertise.[58] Many take issue with him and what they see as a false dichotomy, and support what they believe is a newly democratised media, instancing the phenomenal revival of television talent shows. There have always been people who can dance and sing; and since the advent of cameras they have found their way onto film and video. This is not a social revolution, and the hapless gulls of reality television are not empowered in any real way. Superior technology in the capture of performance cannot disguise limited talent. But the opening of doors between the privileged and their audience may represent some small advance in social leavening.

What documentary has moved in to is the remorseless recording of public people's private lives, where celebrities pursue their audience's love by revealing all. Key examples from the popular end of the market are the docu-soap that purported to give the world the inside story on *The Osbournes* – the everyday story of a middle-aged rock star and his dysfunctional family life – and *Katie & Peter*, the televised, and doomed, relationship of a former topless model and sometime pop singer who met during another reality TV show, *I'm a Celebrity: Get Me Out of Here*. *The Osbournes* was hailed as MTV's most successful show ever and ran for four series from March 2002 to March 2005, coincidentally launching the careers of Ozzy Osbourne's wife Sharon as a talent show judge, daughter Kelly as a singer and son Jack as a 'personality'. It is perhaps most memorable for the turds that Sharon's dogs left all over their Hollywood mansion. Katie Price, aka Jordan, originally most famous for her surgically enlarged breasts, has brilliantly parlayed her celebrity into a multimillion-pound industry, which includes ghost-written books and leading her child-rearing home life on camera. Launching the third series, *Katie & Peter: The Next Chapter* exclusively on ITV2,[59] would-be regular geezer Peter Andre announced:

This new series shows what a happy and successful family we are and the love we have for each other. I think people continue to be fascinated by our lives because we are for real and we don't hold back. People relate to us and we show that we are normal, even though our jobs aren't. It's no secret that we bicker a lot, but that's totally the secret to a happy relationship! I think our friends and family would say that we, as a couple, are loved up, passionate and very good with our children. But that Katie moans a lot.[60]

On 2 July 2008, Sky News announced that sister company News Group newspapers was paying substantial undisclosed damages to Katie and Peter for allegations made by a former nanny in *The News of the World* about their being poor parents.[61] Normal people do not have access to the notoriously expensive libel courts, nor do cameras, but it is another extension of a life lived in the limelight, celebrity as performance. On 13 May 2009, the couple announced they were splitting up. Without a shred of irony, a spokesperson said: 'They have both requested that the media respect their families' privacy at this difficult time.'[62]

Documentary frequently fulfils the purposes of PR. When ex-Spice Girl Geri Haliwell was looking to reinvent herself as a solo artist, she turned to one of Britain's best-known woman documentarists, Molly Dineen. A personal voyage type of observation documentary, *Geri* (1999) is notable for an early and ongoing conflict over editorial control. 'What's the point of making a film to destroy my public image?' raves the troubled star.[63] Normally Dineen, like most contemporary filmmakers, lets her subjects see the material but cedes no editorial rights. 'When I made *Geri*, a 90-minute portrait of the pop star after she left the Spice Girls, she wanted total control. We settled on 50-50.'[64] What emerged was an overlong and somewhat indulgent film that is not without insight into the self obsession of the podium personality, but equally does no harm to her career. Commentators have contrasted this with Martin Bashir's notorious *Living with Michael Jackson* (2003), the revelations in which led to the late superstar's humiliating 4-month trial for child abuse in 2005.[65] That was the apotheosis of self revelation, leading to media crucifixion, albeit to eventual exoneration in the courts. It is believed that this, the attendant near-bankruptcy, and the 40-concert London comeback he planned to revive his reputation and fortune all contributed to his demise at the age of 50 in June 2009.

Stars are torn between the need for exposure that maximises their earnings, and the more natural human desire for peace and privacy. The mob baying at the gate, or media representatives such as the paparazzi staking out homes and holidays, seek to deny them that quiet, but will indulge their peccadilloes, as long as they share them openly. Sean Redmond writes of the constant pressure on stars to humanise themselves by using the media as a confessional:

> Stars and celebrities confess – they always have invested in the revelatory mode of self-enunciation – but in the self-reflexive, ubiquitous, highly simulated environment of 24/7 media culture today, they centrally rely on the confessional to authenticate, validate, humanize, resurrect, extend and enrich their star and celebrity identities. Stars and celebrities confess, and in so doing confirm their status as truthful, emotive, experiential beings who – as devotional fans – we can invest in.[66]

Conclusion

That is the public premise: a new world of openness and emotional honesty in which the star makes full and frank account of themselves. Where once it was enough to invite the camera backstage or to the hotel room after the performance, now it is omni-present, from bathroom to bedroom. That ultimate style-setter Madonna upped the ante with the knowing documentary film of her 1990 'Blond Ambition' tour, *Madonna: Truth or Dare*[67] (1991) aka *In Bed with Madonna*, which juxtaposes full colour performance footage with black-and-white 'personal' footage, including bedroom antics with her dance troupe. Three of the dancers subsequently sued her for misrepresentation and invasion of privacy, which may indicate just how choreographed the supposedly private moments are.

Just as the sports rights owners are unhappy with independent filmmakers poking around behind the scenes of their lucrative franchises, stars are naturally keen to preserve control of such facts and images that are shared with their public. Even if the truth does not carry the threat of the 18 years in jail Jackson faced, celebrities need to manage the media and not reveal aspects of their lives and character that undermine the carefully burnished image.

We may have moved on from the Hollywood dream machine, that managed to suppress issues such as Rock Hudson's homosexuality, but no one should believe that the current confessional mode is unmediated. As Redmond writes:

> The star or celebrity confessional is also of course a marketing and promotional technique used to brand, commodify, and profile an individual. Stars and celebrities whose fame is waning, or who have been caught in a compromising situation, or about whom a falsehood has been publically revealed, use the confession for damage limitation, and to resurrect their careers. Stars open up most when they have the most to lose.[68]

It was not always thus. The Roman emperor Marcus Aurelius enjoined his subjects to remember that 'there is a proper dignity and proportion to be observed in the performance of every act of life'.[69] He would have found that today's performance culture gives the lie to the assumption that the intervening 1,800 years should be counted progress. The mere 400-year-old Shakespearean trope 'all the world's a stage'[70] gets nearer to the way we engage today, though we should include Sean O'Casey's cynical addition '. . . and most of us are desperately unrehearsed'.[71]

The tower of Babel that is the modern media edifice encourages everyone to share the illusion that they too can be a star, if only on their own website. To stand out from that ceaseless noise, the real star has to make a bigger splash, either by the giganticism that has come to distinguish the big live stage shows, or by extreme behaviour enacted for a friendly camera. The documentary remains the best means for capturing these transient phenomena, but it is a world in which an objective and dispassionate eye is increasingly hard to find.

Expert briefing – copyright issues

In the UK, the Copyright Act 1988 introduced the French concept of the *droit morale*, the moral right everyone is assumed to own in anything they create, from their own image and words to works of art. Thus the filmmaker needs to secure written authorisation to feature any contribution, from an interviewee to a film clip, a family photograph to a piece of music. Similar rights exist in the USA and other countries, and most are signatory to international copyright conventions.

Copyright automatically exists in all written, recorded, visual and performed work. It does not apply to ideas, names or titles, though the latter can be recorded as trademarks. It is vital that clearance for all found sources is sought early in the production process, because this takes time and permission may be denied or too expensive, and once a film is built around such elements it can be equally costly to replace them:

1 **Ownership**: The copyright in a film is assumed to be vested in the named producer and director, although the director or both will usually be asked to assign their rights to the production company or financier. Such assignment of rights is a normal prerequisite of film financing, though contracts should specify the creative rights and responsibilities, such as who has final cut. Where a script or screenplay is involved, all rights will also need to be assigned.

2 **Words**: Use of extracts from published works, or their adaptation, requires the agreement of the copyright owner, normally the author, unless they have been dead

for 70 years. This can usually be negotiated via the publisher, but inquiries may then be passed on to the writer's agent. The main exception, as for all creative works, is 'for the purposes of review', the time limit for which beyond publication is not clearly defined.

3 **Stills**: Photographs, even if sourced from newspapers or magazines, are copyright protected and their use will normally attract a flash fee, however brief their flash on screen is, based upon each appearance. Thus a rostrum sequence can be prohibitively expensive, whether it flashes through a number of pictures or lingers on one.

4 **Film**: Archive sources are a vital part of the documentarist's palette, and can take a substantial part of the budget. A growing amount is accessible online, but still needs to be cleared with the current copyright holder. There is also a growth in material available under the Creative Commons licence pioneered in the United States, where material is made freely available for sharing and copying, but restricted to non-commercial use. Many universities have similar education licences for educational use, but filmmakers need be aware that these licences normally preclude public display outside the campus, i.e. screenings at international festivals and competitions. When making films under these rules, it is advisable to ascertain the feasibility and expense of future clearance, should the demand arise. Clip fees are normally calculated on rates per minute 'or part thereof', so you can pay the same for a second as a minute, and incur an additional charge for each segment discontinuously sampled.

5 **Internet**. The worldwide accessibility of material on the net has caused some people to imagine it is free to use, but copyright applies here in precisely the same way and powerful owners of music and movie rights have started to take punitive action against individual infringements. People should also be careful about the small print in boxes of Terms that you are supposed to have read before hitting the 'I Accept' button. The Terms under which personal material is posted on some sites, such as Facebook, assigns all rights to the site, so your images become their property.

6 **Music**: Music involves two sets of rights clearances: composition and performance. The MCPS (Music Copyright Protection Service) looks after the rights of the creator, whether they are a singer-songwriter or classical composer. This covers the score, whether written down or not, lyrics and any associated artwork. If published, approach the publisher, and remember that all music remains in copyright until 75 years after publication (extended in the US for another 20 years in the Copyright Term Extension Act of 1998), so 'Happy Birthday' is still copyright protected until 2030.

   If it is a recording you wish to use, your first port of call is the record label. The PRS (Performing Rights Society) looks after the interests of performers, who have a claim on any subsequent use of their recorded work, unless it has been sold. When applying for the right to use, you normally have to disclose precise context, and performers have the right to refuse if they feel that context would damage their image. Some recordings are so valuable as to be virtually unclearable. Filmmakers should be aware that this process can be slow and time-consuming, not least because the amounts of money it raises are insignificant to the companies involved. Films will normally not be shown or paid for without these agreements signed, so factor in several weeks for copyright clearance early in your production cycle. The options are to use pre-cleared commercial film music, with a small standard fee, or commission original music and acquire all rights.

7 **Public places**: Recorded music played in public places, whether in pubs or elevators, should have been licensed, but this does not cover secondary recordings where you happened to be filming. The same is true of artworks and photographs caught on film, especially if featured in shot. As a filmmaker it is your responsibility to identify the ownership of any copyrighted work you incidentally record *in situ* and clear it in the normal way.

8 **Territories**: Copyright is normally cleared by region and by platform, attracting an escalating scale of fees according to the spread of rights acquired. The three most common designations of region are: 'UK and Europe', 'North America' and 'Rest of the World'. Clearance can be for two domestic television showings only up to public display across all platforms. Commissioned work will specify what rights are required, but may also demand that the work be clearable for additional territories if and when required, as when international sales are made.

9 **Liability**: The producer is liable for all copyright claims, though the broadcaster becomes jointly liable on transmission, which is why compliance is rigorously enforced. Once lawyers become involved, these can be costly omissions. (The 'Errors and Omissions' clause mentioned in the previous expert briefing does not apply here.)

10 **Project protection**: All copyright is automatic and does not require registration, although there are commercial copyright registration services offering 'peace of mind'. Ideas cannot be copyrighted, though formats can be, and professional bodies recommend either sending registered delivery packages to yourself or deposited in bank unopened with a date stamp as insurance against intellectual theft. Broadcasters have terms of trade that require them to acknowledge receipt of ideas within a couple of weeks and give a response within a few weeks more. Their standard *pro forma* cites the likelihood of other projects being pitched and/or developed in the same area, and – so far as this author is aware – no action for theft of programme ideas has ever been successful.

15 Drama-doc and docu-drama

> **docudrama** n. a film or television programme based on true events, presented in dramatized form

During the decades when television was developing fixed genres through corporate departments, it seemed possible to define the distinction between documentary and drama. The latter employed actors to deliver scripted lines to a preordained narrative; the former used real people in the chaotic context of everyday life. Except that quite often those real people were asked to say specific things that helped clarify the storyline, one which was quite often predetermined. Some people still fondly preserve the presumption that true documentary can only be unmediated reality captured on camera and retailed with minimal post-production intervention. If that puritan definition were enforced, very few documentaries made could retain the label, maybe a few per cent of films so-called. Directors routinely ask people to do something again, from repeating what they have said to walking twice through the same door to allow shooting from a different angle. In the vast majority of cases, these basic filmic functions do not skew the intrinsic truth of what is being portrayed, but they do intrude the filmmaker's brush into the picture, normally with the intention of making the storytelling better, more dramatic. In recent years, the genre boundaries have come crashing down and the distinctions make little sense. This chapter will suggest that they never did, and documentary film has always been in the drama business, while drama has drawn regularly and fruitfully from the documentary well.

Courting controversy

'Those in power hate drama-docs, because the camera goes to places where they do not want it to go', says screenwriter Jimmy McGovern.[1] When Brazilian documentarist José Padilha wanted to follow up his first film *Ônibus 174/Bus 174* (2002) with another film about the desperate lives of Rio de Janeiro's poor, this time based on the memoirs of two military policemen, he found no one would talk on film. *Bus 174* was based on hours of footage broadcast live on Brazilian television in 2000, as slum kid Sandro do Nascimento hijacked a bus and held 11 people at gunpoint for four and a half hours. Padilha was one of 35 million people watching the real-life drama unfold, but was alone in painstakingly investigating the tragic back story that led to this standoff – his mother's murder, his escape from a police *favela* massacre, his time in prison. Padilha wanted to continue to explore these revealing undercurrents in Brazilian life from another angle. Former policeman turned writer

Rodrigo Pimentel's *Testigos ausentes/Absent Witnesses* offered a visceral insight. BOPE (Batalhão de Operações Policiais Especiais, or Special Police Operations Battalion) is the elite squad of the Rio state military police, with a reputation for incorruptibility and extreme violence, but their methods are neither filmed nor open to public debate. The book's details were authentic, but no one was willing to appear on film to confirm it, for fear of their lives.

So, with the same obsessive attention to detail that he brought to *Bus 174*, Padilha re-created the activities of BOPE in the actual *favelas*, building the dramatic narrative around one period of intense police activity. Operation Holiness was the name given to preparations made by BOPE to make the *favelas* safe for the Pope's visit in 1997. The film's details were so accurate that, when a rough cut leaked out on the internet, the police went to court to have the film stopped. They did not want their methods, such as their sneaking into the *favelas* through the open floodwater drains, revealed. 'They wanted us either not to release the film or to edit out all the torture and killing scenes', Padilha says.[2] The judge ruled in his favour, because the film was accurate. 'Once it had opened, the police launched a second suit under military law against the former BOPE cops who had helped train the actors or given us information', Padilha adds.[3] This time, the government ordered the police to desist, because public opinion supported the director. His film is all too true, and vitally important. And that can stand as a better aspiration for the filmmaker than whether the cast were actors or not. But it is just that compelling truthfulness that can often cause the controversy.

English filmmaker Peter Watkins used documentary techniques and amateur actors to recreate the Battle of Culloden in 1964. Using hand-held camera and fast cut close-ups to suggest the chaos of battle, with actors acknowledging and addressing the camera, *Culloden* uses these anachronistic devices to bring 1746 to life.[4] It was a breakthrough moment in the evolution of documentary drama and acknowledged as such. Its depiction of the brutal suppression of the Highland Scots was not a reading of history that caused much disagreement at the time. However, Watkins's use the following year of the same techniques to dramatise contemporary concerns about the potential impact of a nuclear war on Britain sent the British establishment into paroxysms of outrage. *The War Game* (1965) was based on Watkins's meticulous research – interviews, Civil Defence documents, scientific studies and accounts of the effects of the Hiroshima and Nagasaki blasts as well as the non-nuclear devastation of Dresden, Hamburg and other cities during World War II.[5] This information is conveyed graphically on screen, complemented by vox pop style interviews, and the harrowing depiction of what it would be like if 'the Bomb' – as the threat of nuclear annihilation was commonly dubbed – was to fall on Kent. The film was intended for transmission on 6 August 1966, the anniversary of the bomb dropped on Hiroshima, but, following lengthy BBC discussions with the Home Office and a private showing to the Cabinet, the film was withdrawn and not broadcast until nearly 20 years later. 'The effect of the film has been judged by the BBC to be too horrifying for the medium of broadcasting' it announced, particularly with regard to 'children, the very old or the unbalanced'.[6]

The BBC tried to dismiss the film as 'less than a masterpiece' and to this day maintains that the decision was one it made independently. However, the then Postmaster General, Tony Benn, has gone on record to say:

My recollection is that the Home Secretary – [Frank] Soskice – decided to ban *The War Game* and, as PMG [Postmaster General] and Minister for the BBC, I was told to transmit the instruction to them.[7]

The Chair of Governors at the BBC was Lord Normanbrook, a previous Head of the Civil Service who had chaired a top secret committee to advise on civil defence and war strategy in the event of a nuclear attack. One of the film's key contributions was to show how ignorant the public was and how poorly prepared for nuclear attack. The real reason for banning the film was that it was too certain to fulfil its objectives, and frighten a pliant population to react against being sleep-walked into a nuclear winter. The leading theatre critic of the day, Ken Tynan put it succinctly in *The Observer*:

It may be the most important film ever made. We are always being told that works of art cannot change history. Given wide enough dissemination, I believe this one can.[8]

Such power was not to be wielded without the agreement of the state, so broadcast dissemination was denied. But because of the huge furore raised, the BBC reluctantly agreed to a cinematic distribution through the British Film Institute, which led to their further embarrassment when *The War Game* won the Oscar for Best Documentary of 1966. What had been commissioned as a drama was recognised for its factual, documentary verity. Unlike *Culloden*, which was a dramatic reconstruction in documentary mode, *The War Game* mixes different documentary modes and the dramatic realisation of Armageddon, in a way which makes the viewer question the distinction. Phillip Drummond writes:

The War Game confuses and yet demarcates the two modes. The 'dramatic' sequences, with their highly 'documentary' look, are retained as fragmentary and discontinuous illustrations of an ongoing documentary narrative which itself disorientingly moves back and forth between statements and assumptions that this is 'really happening' before our eyes, and other types of proposition and warning that this is how it 'could be' and 'might look'.[9]

It was the function, rather than the form, that so excited censorious minds in Whitehall and it was the powerful effect of the docu-drama form – developed by others as an exasperated Watkins moved away to the more liberal environment of Sweden – that stimulated many political storms over the next couple of decades. The cry would go up that this form could confuse people, but what really worried the powers that be was that it would convince people. As the BFI's Dave Rolinson writes:

Although these productions provoked long debates on the nature of drama-documentary form in the media, academia and the industry itself, it has been suggested that such debate may mask anxieties that are more about political content than form.[10]

Ken Loach was the other key auteur in those heady days of the mid-1960s. Having cut his teeth on the cutting-edge studio drama serial of the day, the BBC's *Z Cars*,[11] he used the drama showcase of *The Wednesday Play* to evolve a new hybrid to address current issues. Working with young writers from the contemporary social realist tradition, Loach evolved a body of work that was to have as much political influence as artistic.
Up the Junction is set in the then working-class area of South London, Clapham Junction, and concerns three young working girls and the thorny issue of abortion. It combines its dramatic story, shot in documentary style on location, with documentary elements including

an interview with a doctor who encapsulates the film's moral by mentioning '35 deaths per year that we know are directly attributable to the back street abortions'.[12]

The film helped stimulate public debate in the UK that led to the legalisation of abortion in 1967. Jeremy Sandford's script for *Cathy Come Home* charts the wreckage of a young working-class family, when the family are made homeless following the man's workplace accident, and the children are forcibly taken into care by Social Services.[13] Loach's film has wrongly been credited with creating the homeless charity Shelter, but it publicised that organisation's coincidental launch, helping put housing issues on the map. In 2000, *Cathy Come Home* was voted the second most influential programme of all time in the BFI's poll of top TV. David Mercer's screenplay *In Two Minds* (1967) portrays the descent into psychosis of the daughter of a dysfunctional family.[14] Heavily influenced by R.D. Laing's *Sanity and Madness in the Family*,[15] it caused a tidal wave of reaction from the psychiatric establishment, who claimed that it misrepresented as schizophrenia more conventional hysteria and depression. Nonetheless, it put in the public domain issues of mental health that still remain difficult to intrude into popular discourse.

Loach wanted his films, in their privileged prime-time slots, to be seen as 'continuations of the news',[16] and predictably these films were attacked by pundits and politicians as misleading to an allegedly ignorant public incapable of judging whether they were fact or fiction. What made them so threatening was precisely that they were both: facts carrying the punch of fiction. Loach struggled on against constant attack with films about a docks occupation in Liverpool (*The Big Flame*, 1969) and the Pilkington glass workers' strike of 1970 (*The Rank and File*, 1971), both scripted by the socialist writer Jim Allen. But reactions came to a head when Allen and Loach collaborated on their first historical piece, *Days of Hope* (1975), a 4-part history of the Labour Movement during the critical period 1916–26.[17] Refining his documentary techniques, so that both the shooting and the sound recording have that raw edge and blurring of focus found in observational documentary, Loach's first television work in colour film brought out the beetroot faces of the establishment.

Far from the official concerns that the public would not know whether it was fact or fiction (despite the absence of colour film or television in 1916), they were deeply concerned that the public would all too clearly read the drama's allegorical critique of government and police. Again they tried to have the series banned, but this time the BBC stood firm and instead made the concession that they would make a documentary about public perceptions of reality in docu-drama. This was duly made and shown in the BBC's premier documentary strand at the time, *The Tuesday Documentary*. It commenced in the home of a family identified by Audience Research as 'typical', a married engineer and his two children in Basingstoke, as they watched *Days of Hope* on transmission. As the end titles roll, the camera pans around to ask what the archetypal audience thought. The engineer thoughtfully says he found the drama compelling, though clearly the factual narrative had to be compressed to fit the timeframe and so on, calmly giving the lie to the patrician pretence that the public cannot be trusted to make their own minds up. This is the real political discourse surrounding docu-drama, more than the undoubtedly socialist bias of many of these films and their attempt to put issues on the public agenda. As producer Tony Garnett said at the time:

> Our own anger is reserved for the phoney objectivity, the tone of balance and fairness affected by so many programmes. We deal in fiction and tell the truth as we see it. So many self-styled 'factual' programmes are full of unacknowledged bias. I suggest that you really are in danger from them and not us.[18]

An even bigger row broke out in 1980 over Anthony Thomas's drama-doc for ITV, *Death of a Princess*.[19] He wanted to make a film about the execution in 1977 of a Saudi princess and her lover for adultery. Extensive travelling in Saudi Arabia produced a wealth of material, but none that could be broadcast without exposing the contributors to the same fate. He used the transcribed interviews as the basis for a full drama, with his own role investigating the story also characterised, as 'Christopher Ryder'. Shot in Lebanon and Egypt, the film not only pieces together the circumstances of the story and opinions about it, but presents a compelling picture of a culture in which women are veiled and segregated, unable to drive or vote, and only allowed to marry with a male family member's permission. That this was true – and that the summary executions without trial had actually happened – was precisely why there was such an uproar, with the Saudi embassy trying to get the film banned, calling it 'an unprincipled attack on the religion of Islam and its 600 million people, and on the way of life of Saudi Arabia, which is at the heart of the world of Islam'.[20]

ATV and its co-producer, Boston PBS station WGBH, stood firm and both showed the film despite a flurry of diplomatic and economic threats from the Saudis. Among the sanctions that followed were restrictions on British business and visas, the expulsion of the British Ambassador from Jeddah and the withdrawal of British Airways' rights to fly Concorde over its land, thereby wiping out the profitability of its Singapore run. Various Tories fulminated in the columns of *The Times* and *The Daily Telegraph*, but normal relations were restored within a few months. Deputy Foreign Secretary Ian Gilmour was quoted in the *Financial Times* calling for the banning of the genre: 'Sir Ian said that the whole [dramatised documentary] genre was something to which the Independent Broadcasting Authority and BBC should be giving very careful attention' but his boss, Lord Carrington, remarked that though the film was 'deeply offensive' it was not the government's job to ban films.[21] Twenty-five years later, in 2005, WGBH in Boston saw fit to rerun the film and raise the question whether the status of Saudi women had improved in the meantime, generally concluding it had not, but a commercially reduced ITV saw no reason to revisit the controversy, even though docu-drama has been an ITV staple.

Dramatic truth

As Nichols says, documentary is a 'fuzzy concept', 'no more easily defined than "love" or "culture"' and definitions change over time.[22] He makes the distinction between mechanical 'reproduction' and artistic 'representation', and notes that styles and standards evolve at different times in different cultures. The British Academy of Film and Television Arts (BAFTA) Best Documentary category has, for the last 40 years, been called the Robert J. Flaherty Award, named for the man many call the 'father of documentary'. Yet it is arguable that, for many of those years, Flaherty's own films would not have been considered for the prize because of the flagrant, but unflagged, dramatisation involved.

Nanook of the North (1922) was a dramatic construct from beginning to end, with Inuit playing the roles of husband and wife, a 3-sided igloo built to accommodate the bulky camera and the light it needed, and spears used for seal and walrus hunting where guns would by then have been used. The film exaggerates the isolation of the community and the perils it faced, but Flaherty defended this as enshrining the deeper truths about Inuit life; and the film is still credited for its 'salvage ethnography', preserving cultural traditions on the point of their extinction. The equally epic *Man of Aran* (1924) is also a fiction, albeit using the Aran islanders to recreate the life of their recent past, such as hunting basking sharks to provide them with lamp-oil, which they had not done for 50 years. In the most striking scene, the fishermen of Aran battle a flood tide in their open rowing boats, to make land before the coming storm. To film this scene, Flaherty had first to persuade them to put out in these dangerous conditions, when normally they would not have risked their lives. Even if the health and safety police were not to stop such irresponsible intervention today, purists would deny its documentary value, yet the scene fulfils perfectly its aim: to capture the indomitable spirit of men whose existence was a constant battle with the elements.

The early flowering of documentary in England in the late 1930s was also reamed with dramatic devices. The iconic *Night Mail* (1936) did not just deploy the poetic commentary of W.H. Auden and the music of Benjamin Britten but, more prosaically, rebuilt the mobile sorting office in the studio and employed the night mailmen to recreate their work for the camera. Its co-director, Harry Watt, went on to develop this dramatised documentary style with *The Saving of Bill Blewitt* (1936) and *North Sea* (1938), the first dramatising the benefits to small businessmen of the Post Office Savings Bank, the second re-enacting true stories of ships caught at sea in winter storms. As Swann writes, these films:

> were not, significantly, of the straightforward pedagogical type of film, but were much more humanistic, and most important perhaps, employed narrative devices such as scripted dialogue, studio sets and conventional dramatic development and resolution, which engaged viewers like regular commercial motion pictures.[23]

Humphrey Jennings, as we have seen in Chapter 9, extended this documentary palette into a more fully realised dramatic art. *The Silent Village* (1943) had Welsh coal miners playing their Czech counterparts, and *Fires Were Started* (1943) had London firefighters playing themselves as they tackled the wartime Blitz. Lindsay Anderson wrote in 1954 that Jennings 'is the only real poet that the British cinema has yet produced'[24] and many would say that the accolade still stands. Kevin Macdonald's reverential documentary portrait, *The Man Who Listened to Britain* (2000), casts him as the filmmaker's filmmaker, whom he calls 'an avant-garde artist, a rebel outsider, but also now known as the Poet Laureate of Britain at war'.[25] As Maxine Baker writes:

> *The Silent Village* represents a turning point in British documentary history. Until the young filmmakers who worked on the documentaries which were sponsored by the state in the 1940s, the working class were rarely seen on the big screen . . . Jennings took working people, taught them how to act and made them into stars. In doing so, as Richard Attenborough claims in Kevin's film, he helped to establish the method of screen acting which continues to dominate in British fiction cinema – the 'realist' tradition.[26]

Certainly the performances Jennings elicited from the exhausted firemen in *Fires Were Started* are achingly authentic, undoubtedly helped by the innovation of involving his contributors in creating the scenes and allowing them to improvise their own lines. There is no record of audiences at the time being confused by whether what they were watching was fact or fiction. The truths implicit in those stories were far too live in the popular mind. By contrast, a generation later, when the American filmmaker Connie Field showed her documentary about wartime working women, *The Life and Times of Rosie the Riveter*

(1981),[27] to an all-male union meeting, they did not recognise that the archive newsreel featured an actress performing the iconic role of Rosie the Riveter. 'What's wrong with you women today?', one man asked. 'She had the right attitude, that one they interviewed'.[28] Although the issues – of women's work and equality – found a contemporary resonance, the documentary standards of the day did not embrace such enactment. Literalism had adversely affected the audience's ability to read the text.

Yet in both Europe and America immediately after the war the preponderance of the documentary tradition had a profound effect on cinema, spawning a wave of films that spanned the drama-documentary divide. Roberto Rossellini's *Città Aperta/Open City* (1945) and Vittorio de Sica's *Sciuscià/Shoeshine* (1946) spearheaded the 'neorealist' movement in Italy while Sydney Meyers's *The Quiet One* (1948) helped create the American tradition of street shooting, which even led to Elia Kazan's *On the Waterfront* (1954) being referred to as a 'documentary', according to Erik Barnouw.[29] Barnouw links it with the poetic film tradition that he charts developing particularly in Eastern Europe, but which he notes was economically marginal and was largely obliterated by the advance of the television documentary.

Documentary filmmakers in post-War Britain were largely employed by television, first by the BBC and then by ITV. Most came from a journalistic tradition, though many would go on to make television drama and direct feature films, often in the realist tradition. In the USA, television did not invest in documentary to the same degree, so documentary remained more an exclusively film tradition. It had its essentially *vérité* phase, as we saw in Chapter 5, but Direct Cinema was not the only product of the late twentieth century. Errol Morris – who I quoted in Chapter 5 as saying '*cinéma vérité* set back documentary filmmaking twenty or thirty years' – broke the rules that had kept dramatic reconstruction out of serious or 'straight' documentary.

The Thin Blue Line (1988) told the story of Randall Dale Adams, who had been convicted of murdering a Dallas police officer in 1976.[30] The film goes on to meticulously deconstruct the case and prove Adams innocent, leading to the extraordinary result of Adams's eventual release from death row. Billed as 'the first movie mystery to actually solve a murder', *The Thin Blue Line* is more remembered for its stylised recreations of the murder, endlessly replayed from different angles as the complex web of intrigue is unravelled by the filmmaker. Morris quipped that it was 'the first non-fiction film noir'. The *New Yorker* commented at the time:

Morris – who has a degree in philosophy, and who once worked as a private detective – seems to be investigating not just this squalid murder but the very nature of untruth . . . We watch the same actions occur over and over again, with slight but significant variations, on the same dark stretch of road – a setting that Morris endows with an unearthly vividness, composed of the piercing beams of headlights, silhouetted figures, flashes of gunfire, the revolving red light on top of the police car, and rich, enveloping night-time blackness – and we think, against all reason, that one more detail, a different angle of vision, will suddenly reveal the truth, that these reconstructions somehow have the power to take us to the heart of things.[31]

Reconstruction had until then been dismissed as trashy and untruthful by documentary purists, and *The Thin Blue Line* was denied an Oscar nomination in 1988 because it was deemed 'not a proper documentary'. But its style made it enormously influential, in both documentary and feature film, and, because it dealt so powerfully with truth, the naive belief that fact and fiction were incompatible took a fatal hit.

Television reconstructed

Despite its unpopularity at the American Academy, and at the BBC, drama-documentary had had its proponents elsewhere. One of the most distinguished worked for Granada TV and its noted journalistic strand *World in Action*. Leslie Woodhead – who directed the *Stones in the Park* film covered in Chapter 14 – had done National Service in the 1950s as a Russian translator in Berlin, intercepting Russian military radio traffic. It had given him a life-long interest in the affairs of the Eastern bloc, and a commensurate frustration with not being able to film there as freely as in the West. He says:

> It was at that time that we began to do these highly journalistic drama-documentaries, simply as a way of solving problems of access.[32]
>
> It wasn't that I'd ever met an actor and frankly I wasn't particularly interested in drama, but drama-documentary as a tool or a weapon to – as it were – to punch a hole in the Iron Curtain was really why I got involved with it. I first did a film about a Soviet dissident general (*The Man Who Wouldn't Keep Quiet*).[33] I later did a film about a dock strike in Stetin in Poland, which led to the formation of the Solidarity movement (*Strike*).[34] Then in 1980 I did *Invasion*, which was about the Soviet invasion of Czechoslovakia.[35] So there was a cluster of things there about this part of the world, which all used dramatisation out of necessity as a way of getting in here.[36]

Woodhead talks of later, in 1990, being invited to show *Invasion* to Alexander Dubček, the Czech leader the Russians deposed in 1968, and his endorsing of how accurate its dramatic representation of events was. 'It was just like that! That's right!' Woodhead remembers him repeating, a memorable and thrilling moment for a filmmaker. But, having discovered the dramatic almost by accident, he only made one more drama-documentary after *Strike*. *Why Lockerbie?* was another story difficult to visualise without reconstruction, as the plane and its passengers had been blown out of the air for reasons and by whom it was still unclear.[37] However, as photographs and footage of everything become more widespread, Woodhead has not since felt the need to recreate events for his films, though the dramatic form has undoubtedly enhanced his storytelling skills. Among the 20 films he has made since *Lockerbie*, the most award-garlanded internationally are both tales of the darker nights of the human soul. *A Cry from the Grave* (1999) recounts the tragedy of Bosnian Muslims caught in the fall of Srebreniča in 1995, drawing heavily on the civilians' and soldiers' own video material.[38] *Children of Beslan* tells the story of the 2004 Chechen siege of a Russian school, in which 171 children and 200 adults died.[39] With heartfelt personal testimony, neither film would have profited from actors impersonating the stories; but many other public stories have gained public comprehension, and some resolution, through docu-drama.

Among the many other talents originally nurtured by Granada's *World in Action*, is the Hollywood director Paul Greengrass. His first low-budget feature, for Channel 4 Films, was *Resurrected* (1989) – the true story of a soldier left for dead after the Falklands War who refuses to play the jingoistic hero when he eventually reappears – but it was not until

Greengrass started writing his own scripts that his work really took off. *The Fix* (1997) was the true story of a big football match-fixing scandal of the 1960s, uncovered by investigative journalist Mike Gabbett, a role that Greengrass could identify with, having spent 10 years on *World in Action*.[40] Next came *The Murder of Stephen Lawrence* (1999), the iconic tale of the 1993 killing of a South London teenager, whose racist attackers had never been brought to book due to an inept and corrupt police inquiry.[41] By this stage, Greengrass had refined his trademark style of edgy hand-held documentary shooting, with his then regular cameraman, Ivan Strasberg, largely working with available light. He even deployed the same sound recordist, Albert Bailey, who had recorded the original Channel 4 documentary on the case, *The Stephen Lawrence Story* (1997).[42] As Bailey recalls, there was a difficulty reconciling the demands and standards of documentary, where you grab such sound as you can on the hoof, with those of drama, where you must capture every scripted word with pristine clarity. But achieving that feel was the Greengrass goal.

Greengrass also worked with the Lawrence family and their advisors, to ensure a genuine sensitivity not just to the facts of the case, but the emotions and their effects. The style paid even bigger dividends in *Bloody Sunday* (2002), Greengrass's take on the January 1972 day in Derry, Northern Ireland, when British paratroopers shot 26 civil rights protestors, 14 of them fatally.[43] Again, he achieves an authentic composite picture of that day which is credited more than any other with escalating the Northern Ireland 'Troubles'. Greengrass's experience on *World in Action* and the worldly wisdom such journalism brings imbue what might otherwise have been an action movie with a human gravitas:

> I've seen a lot of political violence in my life. I know what it looks like, I know what it smells like, I know what motivates young men to do it. I've talked to them about it. I know what victims feel like, you know? I know the abominable effect it has on politics. I know how intractable it is.[44]

Greengrass was talking here about his equally effective recreation of the fateful flight on 9/11 where the passengers fought back against their hijackers – *United 93* (2006) – but the same sensibility applies. He sought out the victim's surviving relatives not just for their input but for their approval. It was allegedly due to Matt Damon having seen *Bloody Sunday* that Greengrass got his big Hollywood break, directing Damon in *The Bourne Supremacy* (2004), the success of which elevated Greengrass to the 'A' list and ensured the green-lighting of his personal 9/11 project:

> You can make films about these events that are not these bleak and tragic events. [*United 93* was] a different film about a different subject, but the principle is the same . . . Let's try and create a shared narrative of it, which doesn't duck the truth of what happened, but which doesn't seek to judge and condemn or caricature or marginalize. Let's try and draw together, see if we can't paint a picture of this event that we'll all look at afterward and go, 'It must have been something a bit like that'.[45]

While Greengrass comes from the Woodhead journalistic tradition, another strand of docu-drama arrives by the Loach pathway, making drama from the real. With *Bloody Sunday*, they arrived at the same spot, with Greengrass's *Bloody Sunday* being broadcast three days before Jimmy McGovern's *Sunday* on the same subject, marking its 30th anniversary.[46] McGovern was a successful television drama writer, having cut his teeth on the soap opera *Brookside* in 1986 and gone on to write the popular drama series *Cracker* (1993–5) and *The Lakes* (1997–9). A working class Liverpudlian, who had left school at the age of 16 and done manual jobs until training as a teacher at 30, he brought a personal Merseyside involvement to two important docu-dramas. *Hillsborough* dramatised the worst-ever UK sports stadium disaster, at the 1989 FA Cup semi-final between Liverpool and Nottingham Forest, where inept police crowd control and security cage fencing led to 96 deaths.[47] The dramatisation focuses on the human dimension within the catastrophe, not always easy when reporting big events that traditionally reflect big interests. Twenty years on, Hillsborough is still instanced as the ultimate failure of crowd policing, and *The Sun* is still reviled in Liverpool for its erroneous blaming at the time of Liverpool fans for the tragedy. As Rolinson writes, the film captures the event's iconic status:

> *Hillsborough*'s impact lies not in polemic but in its raw human drama. Far from airbrushing the families, *McGovern* achieves his typically strong and nuanced character-isation, showing the dissent within the families' justice campaign and the very human effects of trauma, recrimination and grief.[48]

Dockers (1999) recreated the harrowing and ultimately unsuccessful 28-month Liverpool dock strike against 500 dockers' mass sacking in 1995.[49] McGovern evolved the *Dockers* script with some of the dockers involved, through a Workers' Educational Association writers' workshop he ran with Irvine Welsh. The process was charted in a companion documentary, *Writing the Wrongs*, which was transmitted immediately before *Dockers*.[50] It demonstrates the potential of docu-drama for mining rich seams of personal experience and finding their most telling expression, with the active collaboration of those involved. Normally a writer will play the role of a vulture, as McGovern says, but:

> It is wrong to pick the brains of people who have been through hell.[51] The process of writing a drama-doc is as important as the drama-doc itself. It must empower the powerless.[52]
>
> It was hair shirt altruism that inspired *Dockers*. The process of empowerment for the real-life dockers was incredible to witness. At the end of it I felt more enriched than I'd ever been in my life. The dockers said that there was no room for a scab in the drama and I had to convince them that you must give the devil the best tunes. Drama comes alive with moral dilemmas. You have to try to get into the psyche of all your characters, including the rapists and child killers. I wrote the first speech for the scab, but the heart and soul of the scene came from a sacked docker.[53]

That negotiated collaboration between the visceral engagement of the protagonists and the knowledge of the practised storyteller is a device still rarely used. Writers, who are often also directors, like Greengrass, will spend years doing their research and investigating their subjects, but what emerges will have to carry their own unique signature, which may not reflect the true voice of those involved. Using a different technique, Paul McGuigan worked with young offenders in the North of England to get their versions of their lives through drama workshops. *Little Angels* (2002) is composed of scenes improvised by its key players in a series of exhaustive workshops, where they were encouraged to relive moments in their lives which revealed the reasons for their offending.[54] McGuigan then persuaded family and friends to play themselves, and cast other parts with local people off the streets, shooting with a documentary crew in the original locations.

The two main characters of *Little Angels* are both heroin addicts from Middlesborough. Michelle's mother died when she was ten – a scene she emotionally recreates – and her father then turned to drink, leaving her locked out of the house when she returned from school. By 13 she was having sex for money and, not long after, turning to the drugs that are central to over half of all teenage offending. Filming had to be negotiated around the anarchy of the addicts' lives – with drug-taking and court appearances taking precedence – and one shocking scene finds Michelle injecting into her neck, as the crew found her when they showed up for filming. The BBC nervously returned to its familiar concern, that the public would not be able to distinguish fact from fiction, and insisted on a complicated formula at the beginning to clarify the unusual blend of documentary and re-enactment. More importantly, leading drug agencies applauded the film for authentically capturing the real, human causes and costs of the drug and offending cycle for the first time, and use it in training their volunteers. Normally such characters are marginalised as victims or worse, so here McGuigan says, 'We wanted to give Michelle and Shaun a chance to tell their own stories because we rarely hear in detail what young drug addicts think and feel.'[55]

The docu-drama form seems to work best when it fulfils that function. Defending his *Sunday* against Greengrass's more successful *Bloody Sunday*, McGovern notes that his film 'was based on personal testimony, focused on the people on whom a drama-doc should always focus: the victims and their families'.[56] It is a laudable aim, not always easily realised, especially if there are irreconcilable differences between affected parties. When ITV made a film dramatising the 1989 *Marchioness* pleasure boat disaster – in which 51 young party-goers lost their lives in the worst ever accident on the River Thames – there was a very negative reaction from some of the victims' families. While Eileen Dallaglio, whose daughter Francesca died, thought the film 'excellent', Margaret Lockwood Croft, who lost her son Shaun, complained to ITV that it should not be shown:

> The film is distressing and insensitive because it spends a lot of time graphically depicting people drowning. The majority of the families and survivors were not consulted while the film was being made and we see nothing positive coming out of it.[57]

Nick Elliot, ITV Controller of Drama, took the decision to shelve the film because of unresolved 'creative issues', saying it was not good enough to be shown, despite the expenditure of £2 million.[58] It is arguable whether a more collaborative approach would have improved the film, but the ethics of making a drama of other people's tragedy clearly demands diplomatic skills and human sensitivity of a high order.

Eighteen years after the events the *Marchioness* film portrayed, there was also the sense that it was still 'too soon'. This is often the complaint about docu-dramas, as if their inventions are more damaging to the grieving than other forms of report and comment. Greengrass had this with *United 93*, the first mainstream feature to deal with 9/11, but of course the reaction is the same as that of those in power who would ban the genre: it is too damn effective, precisely because such films can touch us on the raw, dealing with events that sear the soul and trouble the conscience. Veteran documentary filmmaker Nick Broomfield has also moved into the genre, first with *Ghosts*, about the Chinese cockle pickers drowned in Morecambe Bay in 2004,[59] and then with *Battle for Haditha*, about a US Marine massacre of innocent Iraqis in 2005. Whereas his classic documentary style was a journey in search of a character and their story, with his own intervention prominent on camera, the drama form enables him to cover subjects that have already occurred, and gone unrecorded:

I think it's all to do with the storytelling, and it's about the best way of telling the story. *Ghosts* was made with non-actors, many of whom had been through the things portrayed in the film. So it was experimenting with genres, playing with the boundaries. With the whole subject of illegal immigration – you can't get into the workplace, except with hidden cameras – like *Whistleblower* – and lots of illegal immigrants don't want to be filmed, for fear of deportation.[60]

Despite Broomfield's privileged prominence in the industry, he says that he was 'very lucky' that Channel 4 funded what 'wasn't a very commercial proposition: a film that was 80 per cent in Mandarin with an unknown cast' and 'it's very difficult to get funding for anything that's controversial'.[61] *Ghosts* was unashamedly an attempt to evoke sympathy for the economic migrants we tend to ignore, 23 of whom died when cut off by the tide.

Battle for Haditha tells of 24 men, women and children killed following a roadside bomb that killed one Marine and injured two others. The film has a more sophisticated structure, telling the story from three distinct perspectives: the insurgent bombers'; the overreactive Marines'; and the innocent Iraqis', slaughtered in reprisal for the bomb.

'I wanted to take three points of view and understand them as well and as fully as I could', says Broomfield. For the soldiers, he used marines that had been through the battle for Falujah, where anything that moved was deemed a legitimate target, and housed them in barracks, getting them back into the same frame of mind that he believes had allowed those animalistic instincts to incubate so lethally in Haditha. Even allowing for the circumstances in which these stressed, ill-educated young soldiers operated, it is difficult to leave this film unangered by their excess and the system that sponsors it and suppresses the evidence. Although the story caused a media frenzy, leading to charges against eight Marines, at the time of writing seven have been exonerated, leaving only one facing a court martial.

Making history

To some degree, all the films in the last section are still within the journalistic purview of current affairs, so representing 'the first draft of history'. Current Affairs, as a BBC department, was the most resistant to what many saw as the unnecessary ornamentation of dramatic reconstruction. With live witnesses and abundant archive material, many felt that drama debased the currency of facts. Yet one of the most eminent and meticulous of reporters, Peter Taylor, deployed a small amount of reconstruction to heighten the drama in his *SAS: Embassy Siege*, the 2002 retelling of the occupation of the Iranian Embassy in London in April 1980. This extraordinary event, and its conclusion in an armed SAS assault, had been relayed live for six days on television, including the incendiary resolution. All but one of the hostage-takers were shot dead, but Taylor's documentary had interviews with all of the key hostages, whose mature reflections were textbook oral history. The minimal use of shots and explosions as dramatic punctuation, along with graphic representation of the negotiators' phone calls, added a stylised frame to the talking heads and gave the film a stylistic punch that helped it win Best Historical Documentary at the following year's Grierson Awards.

This is the other use of drama in documentary, and can often amount to no more than a filler for a film's gaps. History programmes have become increasingly dependent upon the device, as a kind of visual relief from the insistent presence of the presenter's face and the paucity of other sources. Thus, as the historian desperately attempts to instil some excitement and life into intransigent ruins or a long-deserted battlefield, the picture frequently zooms in on some candle or firelight, losing focus to mix back in time to an actor in the garb of the period. This is the twenty-first-century version of the Victorian taste for fanciful illustration in storybooks, when history, mythology, literature and empire were all pillaged as material for contemporary potboilers aimed at a newly literate readership, who had to be attracted by the colourful illustrations. Television today has the same demographic in its sights and commissioners in every genre are primarily concerned with the story and how compellingly it can be told, hence the invocation of drama and dramatic imagery. Yet character and conflict are at the heart of drama, and semi-detached, non-speaking actors in ancient costume rarely engage in the way producers fondly imagine. And documentary is rarely funded to the level of costume drama, which is costly to produce well.

The Writers' Guild of Great Britain has awakened to this and to their commensurate loss of income, as the Guild agreements with the industry do not extend across the increasingly porous boundary between drama and documentary:

> On the documentary side actors speaking scripted dialogue pop up everywhere, from ancient Egypt and Imperial Rome, through the wonders of Victorian engineering and the escape from Dunkirk, to Simon Schama's *The Power Of Art*. Dramatised passages within documentaries are clearly seen as adding value, attracting audiences, and therefore increasing the chances of a project being green-lit. This should be good news for writers; it makes a change from writing about cops and doctors, and any increase in job opportunities is welcome. Unfortunately not all scripted drama is commissioned on the same terms.[62]

While it is not inevitable that doing reconstructions on the cheap produces poor results, there has been something of a retreat from their ubiquity in historical documentary. The culture journalist Mark Lawson noted that *Monarchy*, the 2006 series from Channel 4's top historian, David Starkey, eschewed reconstructions for the first time, while his arch rival at the BBC, Simon Schama, used them with less successful results in *The Power of Art* (2006). 'As reviewers have been notably rude about *Power of Art*'s dramatised interludes, Starkey's avoidance seems prescient', Lawson concludes.[63] Schama has used reconstruction effectively in the past, most notably in his contribution to the historical investigation documentary, *Murder at Harvard*,[64] which dramatises various speculative scenes around the 1849 case, based on Schama's 1991 book, *Dead Certainties (Unwarranted Speculations)*.[65] Of that book, William Boyd wrote: 'Schama employs the tools of fiction boldly to go where no historian would dare to tread; into his subjects' minds . . . and it works.'[66] Some reviewers took a more critical line, arguing that history should be about truth, not myths and doubts, and that historians who fail in this noble occupation should, like the murderer at the heart of Schama's study, 'be hounded from the shelter of academe and buried in unknown graves'.[67]

Schama and his producers on *A History of Britain* were also taken to task in *History Today*, for what documentary filmmaker and historian Martin Smith calls 'the intention of deluding the public'.[68] He quotes producer Clare Beavan as saying her job was to 'hoodwink the audience', by introducing non-contemporary materials and reconstructed sequences to enhance the narrative. He points out that such sequences do not comply with the BBC guidelines on flagging reconstruction:

A reconstruction is an event explicitly staged for the cameras or microphone, and where the programme team was not present when the event originally occurred. Reconstructions should be clearly identified so that no one is misled.[69]

Smith concludes: 'The present situation demeans television, demeans historians, and most importantly insults the public, who pay for both.'[70] This appears to endorse the conservative view that the public should be protected from their own gullibility, but is also prescient, given the succession of scandals about misrepresentation that were to rock British television in 2007, leading to the BBC forcing its production staff to take re-education classes in not misleading the public. This whole period is characterised by increasingly desperate attempts to retain audiences by stimulating their jaded palates, with a corresponding loss of vision, as management took their eyes off the moral compass. For the toilers at the programme-making coalface, that they were merely trying to tell engaging stories is insufficient justification for misrepresentation. But when the terms of engagement are clear, dramatic devices can still enrich factual programme-making.

Unspeakable truths

One of the projects that Richard Klein chooses to represent his tenure as the BBC's Commissioning Editor, Documentaries, is *The Verdict* (2007),[71] which had actors playing the leads in a fictional rape trial conducted by real barristers and judicial staff. Played out over five nights, it attempted to represent the slow, painful revelation of facts over the same time period as a real trial might take. The audience's inevitably prejudiced cross-representation was reflected in a jury of celebrities, ranging from the perjured peer Lord Archer (whose conviction and peerage would normally debar him from jury service) to the former footballer Stan Collymore (equally famous for slapping then girlfriend Ulrika Jonsson and subsequently being caught dogging in a car park). The reliance on celebrities to ensure an audience seemed to me to diminish the series' attempt to reflect real-life reactions through docu-drama, but executive producer Klein was confident this was not so:

> You need to already have an interest in who they are. If it had been twelve good men and true who you'd never heard of, I can guarantee you people would have been less interested

Figure 15.1
An unlikely celebrity jury help
to make rape 'more real' in
BBC2's *The Verdict* (2007)

and it would have been less revelatory about the nature of the jury system, which involves, and is very hard to remove, prejudice – because we're all human beings.

I think what was really interesting about that particular jury was: they responded as many other people responded to the case. You should see the message boards, it was the biggest message board response we've ever had: 12,000 conversations at any one time, huge. I thought it was really interesting that their response to the evidence as it came out in dribs and drabs, as it does in a court case, reflected almost identically how many people were responding out there, in different ways, different people siding with different members of the jury.[72]

By the commissioners' herd instinct that regularly produces similar programmes at the same time – see *Bloody Sunday* above – Channel 4 had also put a drama-doc about rape out three weeks before. *Consent* was similarly an invented case performed by actors, with real barristers, expert and judge, and even filmed in the same location, Kingston Magistrates' Court.[73] One key substantial difference was that *Consent* used members of the public instead of celebrities, drawn from the electoral role as juries are. The other was that *Consent*, unlike *The Verdict*, also chose to reveal that the jury got it wrong, insofar that the fictional rape had notionally taken place, but remained unproven. Predictably, *Consent* attracted lower audience figures than *The Verdict*, but also less criticism than that programme did. Even the ever-liberal *Guardian* was moved to comment:

Isn't it a disgrace that a perfectly defensible idea for a public service TV programme, namely a drama that exposes viewers to the hitherto inscrutable deliberations of juries, has to be spiced up with a bunch of Z-listers seeking to boost their fame in one of the most degraded ways imaginable?[74]

Among many voices and organisations that condemned the programme was the End Violence Against Women campaign, whose chair Professor Liz Kelly was quoted as saying:

The Verdict is guilty of trivialising rape. This is reality television that misses much of the reality of rape – for example, the fact that most women are raped by someone they know. With rape rarely dealt with at any length by broadcasters, *The Verdict* is a missed opportunity to show the facts on rape. The bleak truth about rape is that little support or justice exists for women in this country.[75]

Both Richard Klein and Brian Hill would argue that this was exactly the message of their films, that their interest was stoked by the dispiritingly low conviction rate, of 5 per cent of cases brought to court, which their respective dramas reflected.[76]

Conclusion

This example is indicative of the unusual passion drama-docs can still arouse, when attempting to deal with difficult truths in fictional form. The hybrid has been called faction, and factional would be an apt term for its effects, but its true value is in getting the punters in, the increasingly elusive audience that wants to be entertained rather more than being informed. Richard Klein is now Controller, BBC 4, which remains the last outpost of serious documentary on the BBC, but his enthusiasm for new forms of documentary is unlikely to be diminished:

> I think documentary at the BBC, as everywhere else, has had to change to reflect the fact that we're in a multichannel environment, people have much more choice and, like every other genre, it's always in flow, it's always changing and so forth. So documentary at the BBC is like having a broader palette, it has more colours on it.[77]

The colours are what excite the general audience, while aggravating vested interests of subjects covered, who would rather things were black and white. But there are many places still denied to a documentary camera, from courtrooms to boardrooms, many where vital decisions about our lives are taken. Dry analysis is insufficient to engage our interest in the way such powers are used or abused, but drama has the palette to paint the compelling picture and focus our minds, just as it has in different forms since the days of Aeschylus, Euripides and Sophocles. Two and a half thousand years ago, 'tragedies' charted the cathartic downfall of our betters: kings, gods and heroes; while 'comedies' concerned the aspirational stories of common folk on the make. Today's dramas tend to concentrate on ordinary lives, but with a strong tendency to the tragic, with crime and war frequently the arena. Perhaps the next big thing will be comic docu-dramas, with narratives designed to be uplifting. No chapter can be comprehensive on such a large field, so I will return to this territory with the Chapter 18 on *Biopics*.

Expert briefing – writing proposals and treatments

A written proposal helps the person with the money see the point of putting it in your film (and later helps persuade others who didn't hear your passionate pitch). Commissioners say that a good idea is all it takes, but the busier they are, the more decisions they have to take, the more likely a brief, punchy written proposal will hit the mark and generate that elusive meeting. A treatment is a verbal version of the project itself:

1 **Title**: The title is most important. If and when the film is made, the title will be what people remember or forget, the label in listings that attracts or repels audiences. If it is evocative and sounds attractive, neatly encapsulating the idea without being too descriptive, it suggests your thinking is creatively focused. Some programmes were effectively commissioned on the title alone, notably *Wife Swap*.

2 **Strap line or subtitle**: Equally important, especially if the title is allusive and needs explanation. The subtitle defines in a line what it is your selling, whether it is 'The first time cameras have been allowed inside this high-security prison' or 'A series in which film stars reveal the secrets of their love lives'; and it should mention the film's length (and number of episodes when a series e.g. 6 x 60').

3 **Honesty**: A proposal should play up the strengths of the idea and play down the pitfalls, but it should not promise anything or any person the filmmaker cannot deliver. Where access to a place and/or key talent are essential to making the film, the extent to which these are secured should be made clear – and having secured them in principle is normally essential.

4 **Writing**: Like any story, the first paragraph of a proposal is the most vital, setting the scene, describing the arc and defining the spirit of the piece. This means the writing should feel like the film. Get this right and you have your reader hooked; fail and they will not finish the page. There is a general, if harsh, view that anyone who cannot express their idea concisely and compellingly cannot make a coherent film.

5 **Facts**: The proposal should be lean and direct, with as few facts as possible. The main ones should reflect the practical plans, again defining how organised your thinking is as well as indicating cost implications. Locations are key, as is the shooting and completion schedule. Promote any talent involved. If cameraman or composer are award-winning, say so.

6 **Style**: This should be implicit in your subtitle, but given explicit detail later on. If it is an observational documentary, or a stylised piece; whether it is to be presented or commentated; with conventional interviews or reconstructions; with music, effects or particular lighting: all help define the kind of film you hope to make. But do not go into great detail or attempt to tie everything down – most commissioners like an intriguing project to which they can still bring something.

7 **Illustration**: Generally a no-no, you should be able to write the pictures that stimulate the financier's mind. It is generally agreed that expensively-produced illustrated proposals are often self-defeating, tying the idea down in ways which lead to the wrong kind of critical conversation. This is not true in the case of international co-productions, where they help generate a collective understanding and override language differences. If, however, you are selling a single human subject or presenter, a photograph should be included.

8 **Additional information**: What may be beneficial depends upon the system in which you are trying to work. You should know the tastes and needs of your mark, ensuring that you are proposing a film they may want and can finance. In television, this also means knowing the slot-lengths and budgets available, and that the channel is running this kind of piece. References to that knowledge suggest a business-like and focused approach. Your covering letter (with CV where appropriate) should further clarify that awareness: in practice the whole exercise is writing for one person's known predilections and needs.

9 **Outcome**: The proposal is a selling document, normally preceding a verbal pitch, so it should ideally be constructed to secure a meeting, rather than a commission. If you are improbably lucky, this may lead directly to commission. More commonly, further development is required, following meeting and conversations. This may take the form of a treatment, which is a more detailed document – ideally describing the film scene by scene – and possibly also a budget and schedule.

10 **Treatment**: Treatments are often required as part of the development and financing process, not least because they can also help the filmmaker clarify their thinking, make better use of their time and resources, and make a better film. It's the creative equivalent of the soldiers' '7 Ps': 'Proper preparation and planning prevent piss-poor performance'. But it is also the confirmation of the practicality of the idea that you have so far successfully pitched.

A treatment is a description of the completed film – scene by scene, sequence by sequence – with all visuals and sound, couched in the historic present tense. As a virtual film on paper, the narrative, content, style and pace should all be apparent to any film-literate reader, enabling editorial and technical discussion.

11 **Presentation**: If written for a financier or as part of a development deal, you should have sought clarification of what is required. Generally, you should only write what will be seen or heard in the film, in the present tense, laid out in one paragraph per scene. Write colourfully and concisely, using verbatim quotes from your characters to bring them alive. Style should be embedded in the writing, but reliance on features such as stills, archive, reconstruction, music and visual effects should be clearly indicated.

12 **Length**: A treatment is as long as it needs to be to impart the relevant information. A complex narrative with many different locations and contributors will take several pages, whereas a single subject observational film will probably be shorter, focusing on the known facts and desired outcomes. But evasion at this stage of an unscripted film may well be seen as a filmmaker unready to do the job; even an observational documentary has known and agreed objectives, which a good filmmaker can imagine in advance.

13 **Objective**: A good treatment may well be the deal-maker that gets the film green-lit, but it should not become the straitjacket which constrains imagination. All films are organic and should grow in the making. However, everyone, from financier to film editor, needs to know there is at least one plan of action that will work, even if a better one emerges from the elements.

14 **Success**: Most development work ends in failure, in that most projects do not get made. Documentary is the most over-subscribed genre in television and thousands of ideas are pitched for every one made. Rejection is an occupational hazard, most frequently because the idea is poorly-developed or inappropriate for the slot targeted, but also because it failed to excite or meet the need at the time. Learning to refine ideas so that they are instantly recognisable and fit for the particular commissioner's purpose is part of a process that enables producers to rise to the top of the pile. Aspirant filmmakers need to continue to improve their narrative and presentational skills, so every development can still be profitable as a useful learning curve.

16 Art and anarchy

....

art n. the creation of works of beauty or other special significance

Most film or video that is shot is of, at best, of transitory interest and no special significance. The home movie shooter only sees the great sights of his travels through a 3.5 cm flip-out screen; the millions of CCTV camera images are rarely reviewed and, even when they are needed, in the solving of crime say, have frequently been lost or are too poor to be of use. Television itself sponsors a transient culture that fetishises the new and the instant hit, usually salvaging only the best comedies and dramas for repeat and DVD release. As the chapter on Lifestyle shows explored, the medium has been significantly compromised by the messages it carries, increasingly acting as a purveyor of goods. This reading was central to the revolutionary writings of Guy-Ernest Debord, the chief philosopher of the anarchist Situationist International, the movement at the heart of the Sorbonne events of 1968 and other student action. He saw the screen as the most obvious manifestation of a capitalist world that had reduced everything to an advert for itself, a subversion of all activity, art and aspiration to a unified spectacle, commodified, disempowering and alienating:

> In societies where modern conditions of production prevail, all of life presents itself as an immense accumulation of spectacles. Everything that was directly lived has moved away into a representation.[1]

Although Situationist International split in 1972, not least over differences about how violent Debord's 'emancipation from the material bases of inverted truth' should be, students of the time had read this as an invitation to lob a brick through the screen, metaphorically if not actually. 'On every occasion, by every hyper-political means, we must publicize desirable alternatives to the spectacle of the capitalist way of life, so as to destroy the bourgeois idea of happiness',[2] he had written. Sit-ins and demonstrations were popular means at the time, but their screen representations were framed to suit the dominant view, of mindless hordes spoiling for a fight, thus fuelling the view that the screen was central to the problem. The then largest ever peacetime march in London took place on 27 October 1968, organised by the Vietnam Solidarity Campaign to protest the US war in Vietnam. A previous march in March had ended in a riot in Grosvenor Square, outside the American embassy, and the organisers wanted to avoid a repeat. Well over 100,000 marched peacefully to Hyde Park for speeches, while a small splinter group headed for Grosvenor Square and a return match with the police. In so doing, they gave the TV cameras the pictures they wanted, and the greater achievement of the VSC march was largely ignored. It presaged the end of the peaceful protest movement, and encouraged the minority who favoured more violent direct action. The controlled and controlling images of television continued to reflect the processed view – and the revolutionary notion of smashing the screen was appropriated for one of the most iconic commercials of all time.

On 22 January 1984, during the third quarter of American football's Super Bowl to decide the season's NFL champions, Apple had bought a commercial slot to launch their first Macintosh personal computer. The 60-second slot cost $736,000, and the ad cost over $900,000 to make, but it was worth it to reach the 71 per cent audience share of eager football fans watching, though the Apple board had not liked the film itself. Shot by tyro Hollywood director Ridley Scott, the commercial used a George Orwell *1984* theme, showing an audience of pliant automata filing in and seated before a giant screen, from which a hectoring tyrant lectures them on 'unification of thought'. From the back of the hall runs a lithe blonde, chased by the thought police and carrying a large brass hammer, which she swings and hurls through the screen, shattering it and the tyrant's message. The film ends with the caption: 'On January 24th, Apple Computer will introduce Macintosh. And you'll see why 1984 won't be like 1984.' The commercial went on to win numerous awards, including the title of 'the greatest television commercial ever' in the trade paper *Advertising Age*.[3]

The traditional reading of this ad was plucky, funky Apple taking on the mighty IBM corporation, who had come late to computers, but was now selling similar numbers to Apple. Introducing a select preview of the ad to an autumn 1983 Apple event, the young Apple chairman Steve Jobs sent up his ancient rival and its dominating stranglehold on the computer dealerships. He claimed

> Apple as the only force that can ensure their future freedom. IBM wants it all and is aiming its guns on its last obstacle to industry control: Apple . . . Was George Orwell right about 1984?[4]

He then played the ad to massive applause. According to Adelia Cellini, writing in the Apple online mag *MacWorld* in 2004, that's not quite the way the ad's creators saw it:

> The original concept was to show the fight for the control of computer technology as a struggle of the few against the many, says [producers] TBWA/Chiat/Day's Lee Clow. Apple wanted the Mac to symbolize the idea of empowerment, with the ad showcasing the Mac as a tool for combating conformity and asserting originality. What better way to do that than have a striking blonde athlete take a sledgehammer to the face of that ultimate symbol of conformity, Big Brother?[5]

While the Big Brother figure is clearly Orwellian, no such scene occurs in *1984*. Steve Hayden is the credited writer; Debord gets no credit. Yet it is hard not to imagine that young minds schooled in the revolutionary haze of UCLA and Berkeley in the 1960s and 1970s had not been exposed to Situationist thought. That a central concept had been adapted for the promotion of a product, however hip, is the ultimate inversion of their objective, while being perfect proof of the theory. Such circularity infects much screen work, and particularly the art world that has increasingly seized video as a tool.

Film as a subversive art

Since the birth of film – when the Lumière brothers' film of a train approaching the camera had frightened audiences running from the theatre[6] – its representations of reality have had the ability to disturb and shock. Those who see themselves principally as artists have regularly sought that effect, so have frequently turned to film, whether as passive record of their artistic activities or, increasingly, as the artwork itself. Those who see themselves principally as filmmakers know they are artists, but tend not to shout about it. Most of the great movements in twentieth-century modern art were influenced by, and frequently involved with, film. Surrealism's most compelling images include Dali's collaboration with Luis Buñuel on the film *Un Chien Andalou*, with its close-up of a woman's eyeball being slit and ants emerging from a hand's wound.[7] The distorted modes of expressionism and cubism owe much, as Hughes comments (Chapter 3), to the refractions of light evinced by advancing technology. The deconstructionist rage of Dadaism – essentially a revolt against the slaughter of the First World War – found a filmic form in the films of Léger and Richter,[8] paving the way not just for surrealism but for photomontage and the revolutionary use of film in the 1960s to challenge contemporary taboos. American cineaste Amos Vogel, founder-director of the New York Film Festival, tracks this conflation of forms within a wider landscape of expanding scientific knowledge and collapsing beliefs and verities, in his seminal 1974 work, *Film as a Subversive Art*:

> It is . . . no longer possible for an artist creating within this historical period to portray reality along mimetic lines (art as the imitation of reality) or to view it as a coherent, fully intelligible construct, capable of apprehension through his sense organs and in its documentary aspects, a valid representation of the universe. In our age, as never before, truth implies the courage to face chaos.[9]

Whereas this book attempts to define documentary sub-genres, Vogel tracks an artistic explosion through the mid-twentieth century that was principally driven by the desire to explode such formulations. In this chapter, I shall concentrate as much as possible on experimental filmmakers who used documentary forms, but drawing the line here between drama and documentary is meaningless, such banal straitjackets being precisely the object of artistic subversion. Surrealism, by definition, deals in the fictions of original imagery, but Dada drew more on found images and owes as much to Dziga Vertov's expressionist use of newsreel as to Duchamp's use of a urinal as an art object. Dada's supreme legacy is the assertion 'It's art if I say it is art', freeing the artist from meeting the standards of the academy.

In this way, many art films use the lens to frame aspects of reality and express it as art. Some films are collages, often using the speed of film (24 frames per second) to give a brain-popping audio-visual experience. Bruce Connor's *Cosmic Ray* (1962) is just 4 minutes long but manages to intercut 2,000 different iconic American images, from a nude dancing girl to Mickey Mouse and the GIs raising the flag at Iwo Jima, a shocking juxtaposition for those still wreathed in the Stars and Stripes. Don McLaughlin used the same technique to showcase 3,000 years of great art, also in 4 minutes, cut at the rate of 8 per second to Beethoven's 9th, in *God is Dog Spelled Backwards* (1967). 'Theoretically, the world's greatest images, combined with the world's greatest music, should produce the world's greatest film', opined its maker.[10] Like so many of these experimental films, they are not just subverting the traditionally hierarchical ways of reflecting cultural value, but encapsulating a time when every image is commodified and, by that same process, devalued and made transitory.

Time lapse photography produces similarly intense results in Werner Koenig's *Aktion 540* (1968) with its speeded-up day in a city market, and Donald Smith's *Go Slow on the Brighton Line* (1952), the view from a steam train cab apparently doing 800 miles an hour on the run from London to Brighton. Paul F. Moss and Thelma Schnee's *Power of Plants* (1949) introduced stop-frame to reveal plants growing through obstacles like rocks and displacing metals. This once-experimental technique is now used routinely to shoot natural evolution and cityscapes morphing from day to night. Similarly, contemporary fast-cutting and the insertion of semi-abstract shots to enrich documentary texture draws unconsciously on pioneering avante-garde work such as Stan Brakhage's *Anticipation of the Night* (1958) and Richard Myers's *Akran* (1970). Brakhage, regarded as the most influential experimental filmmaker of his time in America, articulated the concept of the 'untutored eye', in which he recognised that cinema had the novel potential of revealing a world of primordial innocence, where the spectator engages actively in the process of conveying meaning and the filmmaker steps back from the imposition of conventional narrative:

> Imagine an eye unruled by man-made laws of perspective, an eye unprejudiced by compositional logic, and eye which does not respond to the name of everything but which must know each object encountered in life through an adventure of perception. How many colors are there in a field of grass to the crawling baby unaware of 'Green'? How many rainbows can light create for the untutored eye? How aware of variations in heat waves can that eye be? Imagine a world alive with incomprehensible objects and shimmering with an endless variety of movement and innumerable gradations of color. Imagine a world before the 'beginning was the word'.[11]

Brakhage's subject matter was life and death or, as Brian Frye's homage to Brakhage (who died in 2003) defines it, 'Being'.[12] From the birth of his first child in *Window, Water, Baby, Moving* (1959) to the post-mortem graphically portrayed in *The Act of Seeing With One's Own Eyes* (1971), he is not deploying these events as metaphors; they are all part of a greater metaphor: perception itself. As Frye writes:

> The key image of *The Act of Seeing With One's Own Eyes* is quite likely the bluntest statement on the human condition ever filmed. In the course of an autopsy, the skin around the scalp is slit with a scalpel, and in preparation for exposing and examining the brain, the face of each cadaver is literally peeled off, like a mask, revealing the raw meat beneath. That image, once seen, will never leave you.

That clear, unforgiving, non-didactic gaze is one aspect of Brakhage's legacy to cinema, but his poetic films are dismissed by Nichols as purely formal constructs, devoid of real meaning.[13] However, Testa argues:

> Brakhage's films also could be construed as the uncompromised pursuit of the film image as 'indexical sign', to use one of Nichols' (and other film theorists') favourite terms, and one they mistakenly use as a synonym for images that are directly referential or 'realistic' . . . Brakhage's style of filmmaking is a radical pursuit of the further implications of this indexicality'.[14]

Although this is no place to become ensnared in the semantics of semiotics, it indicates the destabilising nature of Brakhage's contribution to the film *oeuvre*, and its ongoing challenge to the norms of literalism.

While the literal dominates mainstream film, experimental film enriched the cinema's arsenal of metaphor. However, original filmic metaphors soon become overused clichés. Jean Cocteau's *Le Sang d'un Poete/The Blood of a Poet* (1930) is book-ended by the image of the dynamiting of a giant factory chimney. This then original metaphor for destruction has recurred countless times. Louis A. van Gasteren's *Het Huis/The House* (1961) compresses glimpses of three generations of a family's life, as their Dutch mansion is methodically demolished. Peter Hutton's *In Marin County* (1971) speeds up the demolition of a whole neighbourhood of suburban houses to make way for a new highway. As soon as film grammar and methods became established, it was the avant-garde's job to break the mould. Once commercial cinema and television adopted montage, it was discarded and the opposites essayed, as in Andy Warhol's unblinking six-hour gaze on a man sleeping in *Sleep* (1963–4) and his eight-hour single shot of the Empire State Building, both shot in real time. Meanwhile, Jean Luc Godard, in films like *Une Femme Mariée/A Married Woman* (1964) and *Masculin-féminine/Masculine-Feminine* (1966) was routinely deconstructing conventions of film grammar and narrative, juxtaposing over-extended uncut interviews with stylishly cut scenes, cutting into scenes in close-up without set-up. These inventions are intended to disturb the audience.

Documentary techniques, enabled by lightweight cameras, are inevitably appropriated by mainstream cinema, but as soon as they are, the avant-garde moves on. Minimal cinema eschewed all narrative or explanation, presenting an unmediated picture from which an assumedly intelligent audience could draw its own conclusions. Andy Warhol is often credited with the inception of this ill-defined movement with his montage of people kissing, *Kiss* (1962), the self-explanatory *Blow Job* (1963–4) and the aforementioned *Sleep* (1964). Stephen Dwoskin's *Asleep* (1961) preceded these, a short film concentrating on a sleeper's feet; but *Naissant* (1964) is where his most distinctive contribution emerges, with its 14 minutes concentrating on a pregnant girl's troubled face. Dwoskin invites the viewer to involve themselves 'in the moments of a person', to 'think with her'.[15] He uses the same device to more devastating effect in *Dyn Amo* (1972), a two-hour film about strippers, the first part of which is a more conventional documentary approach, but the last harrowing half hour concentrates almost exclusively on a stripper's tear-streaked face as she is violated and humiliated. Some commentators have dismissed this work as dull and pornographic, but it was an important earnest, both of all subject matter being admissible and that such film need not have a simplistic moral. Dwoskin's work has evolved into other areas since, but he still writes of this role of film as a kind of elemental witness:

Filmmaking has to (in my opinion) be honest and revealing. It has to bear witness to the subject and to the self. It has to allow the viewer to be able to engage with their own selves and their own feelings. Films, my films, have to open up to the elusive and intimate space in order to permit the viewer to enter them or reflect upon them. Filmmaking can therefore be a space where the viewer, like the filmmaker, introduces their own form of 'narrative', a 'narrative' that is not necessarily conclusive or resolved; a process that questions through its own inherent contradictions.[16]

This introspective bent was part stimulated by Dwoskin's childhood poliomyelitis – making him unusually dependent on women, who came to be his primary subject – and part by his training as an artist, first working as a graphic designer and art director for companies such as CBS Records in New York:

> For me cinema was the contemplative move from the sensibilities of painting to those of the moving picture. Conceptually this was a simple move and therefore a simple decision. Film added the element of time to an otherwise static image and I needed that element of time to extend my voice . . . Film is my language . . . and without my language I cease to be.[17]

Dwoskin co-founded the London Filmmakers' Co-op in 1966 and taught at the Royal College of Art from 1973 to 1983, where he wrote a review of independent cinema at the time, *Film Is . . . the International Free Cinema*.[18] The book covers the contemporary explosion of experimental film in that period from its origins in the 1920s, and discusses over 700 films. He charts its various strands, not least its propensity for shock, as when discussing the work of Austrian filmmaker Kurt Kren, the so-called 'father of postwar European avant-garde cinema', all of whose films were prefixed by their number and year of making:[19]

> With the making of his sixth film, *6/64: Mama and Papa*, Kren introduced subject-matter that was considered at that time to be highly revolutionary or even explosive. He began filming 'actions' and 'happenings' staged by Otto Muehl and Günter Brus, and by the Vienna Institute for Direct Art.[20]

Muehl's original artistic aim had been 'to overcome painting on canvas through staging the process of its destruction' but, along with Günter Brus, he developed a new concept of Aktion, where the body became the canvas. Muehl's 'actions' largely concerned group sex, with many bodies involved in mutual masturbation and penetration, quite often with other bodily fluids and less expected aids, such as foodstuffs. Reproducing a still from *Mama and Papa*, which features a penis and testicles arranged on a plate surrounded by eggs, Vogel comments:

> The unexpected combination of sexual taboo and food provokes both shock and laughter, not merely because of the visual pun but because organs are not often presented to us in 'tasteful' display for purposes of eating.[21]

The set-ups are usually quite arch, theatrical rather than filmic, and the editing not strictly narrative, as it jumps around the action in time and space, frequently cut to classical music from the German Romantic catalogue. In these alienating devices it could hardly be more distant from the notional narratives of the then emerging American adult film industry, with their cheesecake characters and cheesy storylines.

Kren became committed to the Aktion movement, but found conventional film labs refused to grade and print his films, so he had to resort to a backstreet blue movie lab in Vienna. In one of his most notorious films, *16/67: September 20–Gunther Brus aka, Eating, Drinking, Pissing, Shitting Film* (1967), Kren shot exactly what it said on the film can. He was quite unfazed by the material: 'It is very dirty, being about eat-drink-piss-shitting. Many friends will hate me after having seen that film. Sorry. It had to be done!'[22] Bruehl went on to found a commune committed to free love, and was eventually imprisoned for having sex with teenagers. His was just one part in a global explosion against the sexual suppression that had constrained at least Western society for the previous two centuries. Whereas Germanic versions have that heavily transgressive style clearly connected to their recent history, Scandinavian cinema reflected a less hung-up sexual culture, with a more humane approach that had, in the long run, much greater impact. Vilgot Sjoman's *I Am Curious Yellow* (1969) was widely hailed as the catalyst of the new permissive cinema, with much natural sex and genitalia, though no apparent penetration. It probably did more than any other film to break down the conventional constraint on showing sex in commercial film. But it was a Danish film, Johan Jacobsen's *A Stranger Knocks* (1963), which had already had an even more far-reaching impact on US cinema. Because its act of intercourse was so essential to the plot, and did not even feature nudity, its prohibition was appealed to the Supreme Court, which duly found the whole system of state censorship so anachronistic it abolished it. As Vogel notes: 'This development contributed significantly to the later era of sexual permissiveness in the American cinema.'[23]

God bless America

Toppling the taboos of sex and death was only the beginning for the shock troops of independent cinema, the destructive power of heavy ordinance before the brave new world could be built. Intellectuals such as Dwoskin and Brakhage saw their work as part of a greater plan, influencing not just the way the world was viewed but, as a result, how it may be improved. Two years before his death, at a retrospective of his films in Montreal in 2001, Brakhage said:

> Maybe my film will not last but it might inspire a poet to write something. In several hundred years I believe we can do away with war. Mad as that sounds. And I believe art is the only way to do away with it. I don't think it'll be done by people sitting around saying, 'I hate war.' Or, 'war is awful.' Well forget that, you might as well go into a rain dance to get the rain. You have to lodge something in the deepest human consciousness to make certain things unthinkable, like the rape of children. But it certainly isn't now. So some of the films you saw tonight are hopefully in that direction, not because they are my films but part of the whole process of affecting other artists, other people in general. We have to have something long-lasting enough to make the horrible unthinkable. That is my social task. It is on the 400-year plan.[24]

Yet his final films had taken him back from the world of the real to the abstract art world from which he had come, painting shapes onto film stock. He died still working on *Stan's Window* (2003), a self-portrait scratched in the emulsion with his fingernails. He had expressed the desire for his film to free itself from all tawdry associations with literal reality. 'That is not a film as poetry, not film as literature, not film as illustration, moving picture illustrations of literature or all the things that it mostly is as you see when you turn on the TV.'[25] Brakhage was not alone in his desire to distance himself from the Society of the Spectacle.

Jonas Mekas brought a very different sensibility to the nascent New American Cinema, which he named as the film critic of the New York Village Voice from 1958. A Lithuanian samizdat poet who had survived a wartime German labour camp, he had arrived in New York with his brother in 1949, and immediately bought a Bolex:

Let's record the dying century and the birth of another man . . . Let's surround the earth with our cameras, hand in hand, lovingly; our camera is our third eye that will lead us out and through . . . Nothing should be left unshown or unseen, dirty or clean: Let us see and go further, out of the swamps and into the sun.[26]

Despite the burgeoning immigrant culture in New York – greatly enhanced by the Jewish diaspora of the pre- and post-war periods, which produced some distinctive literary voices drawing on that experience, such as the novelist Jerzy Kosinski – Mekas's poetic voice of loss and memory is a uniquely personal idiom. He had been an obsessive 'filmer' for years before he came to realise that his métier was not the experimental drama of his debut, *Guns of the Trees* (1962), but the documentary diary. It was not until 1967 that he realised the fragments of film he had been shooting and collecting amounted to a personal testament.

Diaries, Sketches, Notes or Walden (1967) was the first of a series of documentaries that was all to be called *Diaries, Sketches, Notes*, albeit with different subtitles; confusion over labelling in the film labs forced him to drop the title, but not the plan. *Reminiscences of a Journey to Lithuania* (1972), which documents his first return since fleeing in 1945, plays with the nature of memory, as he tries to construct memories of his past from a country now a quarter of a century older. It makes Mekas consider why he chooses certain moments to film. 'And what are those moments, what makes me choose those moments? I don't know. It's my whole past memory that makes me choose the moments that I film.'[27] With *Lost Lost Lost* (1975) he returned to footage he shot in his first ten years in the United States, struggling to make sense of and make his way in this alien culture, while subsequent films chart his marriage, the arrival of his family and the inconsequential minutiae of everyday life.

Lionisation by the independent film community has made Mekas more self-analytical in recent years, with his book *Just Like a Shadow* and his film *As I Was Moving Ahead I Saw Brief Glimpses of Beauty* (both 2000). The latter is a 4 hour 48 minute review of his family life, in which he freely admits not much happens, 'no drama, no great climaxes, tension, what will happen next'. When he shows his son taking his first steps, or a cup full of berries picked in a meadow, he explains that he is composing 'a sort of masterpiece of nothing. Personal little celebrations and joy . . . miracles of everyday, little moments of Paradise'.[28] As the LA film curator Genevieve Yue observes, this object is realised beautifully in Mekas's work:

To watch a Mekas film is to experience the intimacy of someone sharing his life with you. When this is done in a theatre, it is as if the room is filled with old friends. Together – and Mekas is a master at bringing an audience together – you sit as guests at his table, watch his children grow, and even share in his unnameable sorrow. 'I drink to you, dear friends!' he calls out in *As I Was Moving Ahead* . . . and though he is speaking to the people gathered around the table onscreen, it's easy to believe he's speaking to you, the viewer.[29]

This monumental life's work significantly predates the apparently original *Video Diary* form discussed in Chapter 4, and the foregrounding of the first person noted in Chapter 12.

Other directors have turned to the diary form as the personal antithesis to big Hollywood film. And many have found the technical and economic benefits of video have allowed them to keep working in an adverse culture. The once leading English feature film director Ken Russell, now unable to get commercial features financed, is making ultra-low-budget films on video in his back garden, and the disabled Stephen Dwoskin, now largely confined to a wheelchair, says video has saved his life:

> The most poetical films, starting with *Trying to Kiss the Moon*,[30] my autobiographical diary, have reached their completion thanks to the use of video; *Intoxicated by my Illness*[31] was the starting point of it all. An unsettling film on the approach of death, shot exactly when I was taken to the hospital in intensive pneumology care. Because digital editing allows me to bring in a contrast between the lyricism of the sound track and the violence of the images, which brings about an increased effect of unreality. By also stretching extremely the sound grain and the visual grain, my work becomes more similar to the act of painting that was my first activity and also that of my dear partner Frances Turner, who died in 2002. Video has been for me a resurrection, I could no longer do without, neither technically nor financially.[32]

Dwoskin, Brakhage and Mekas are artists and poets, but see themselves as filmmakers. Subsequent artistic generations have adopted different appellations, reflecting changing approaches to their art. Bill Viola calls himself a video artist, and has been called 'the best video artist in the world'.[33] He started work in the early 1970s as technical director of production for Art/Tapes/22 in Florence, one of the first video art studios in Europe, and his early work is typically concerned with deconstructing the image-making process, playing with monitors and mirrors in *Tape 1* (1972), variable speeds of audio and vision in *Composition D* (1973) and camera movement in *Level* (1973). Most explicitly, *Cycles* (1973) comments on the television image itself. In Viola's own website's favoured description:

> A large window fan is used to interrupt the scanning process of a broadcast TV image, challenging television's one-way dominance by pitting one domestic household device against another. The fan becomes a metaphor for the process of 'blowing' information out from the screen and onto the viewer. At the same time, the varying speeds of the fan blades create optical interference patterns across the image that shift in stability as the fan speed comes in and out of phase with the fixed rate of the scanning TV picture. The fan alternately masks and reveals select frames of television, and simultaneously demonstrates the illusory nature of the image as a beam of rapidly scanning light.[34]

While this subtle assault on the Society of the Spectacle was in tune with the experimental filmmakers of the time, Viola's work has over time moved away from the political towards the mystical, attracting some criticism. While few contest his mastery of the medium, some feel the results are becoming sterile, as the online critic John Haber writes:

> With a technique rarely matched in art today, not even outside video, Viola searches nature in hope of finding his humanity. What he finds instead are cold comfort and a cartoon of childhood.[35]

On the plus side, other reviewers find much to commend in his image-making. Reviewing his 2008 exhibition in Rome, the *Financial Times*'s Rachel Spence wrote:

> It is a triumphant vindication of an artist who refuses to treat the big issues – life, death, birth, love, sex – with the flippant irony and superficial shock tactics that are the lexicon of so many of his peers.[36]

Blown away by the Renaissance riches he encountered in Florence in his youth, Viola's work seems increasingly to aspire to the grandiose imagery of the Old Masters. Nude figures stride towards camera through downwashes of light and water, or float up from deep water, their arms extended in Messianic supplication. Viola spent 18 months in Japan studying Zen Buddhism, which accounts for the mysticism, but his references remain essentially Western:

> Even though I am not a devout Christian in terms of my spiritual practice, I still am a product of that cultural system. And of course, that in turn is based on the body: the disintegration and transfiguration of the body. A huge amount of art has been generated by the image of a dying man, Christ.[37]

The Messenger, evoking the mystery of the cycle of life and death, was exhibited in Durham Cathedral; now Viola has been commissioned to produce London's first two permanent video altarpieces for St Paul's Cathedral.

Cathedrals were the highest expressions of man's art in their day, towering constructs that modern man would find hard to achieve with all the advantages of modern technology (witness the time it took to finish Gilbert Scott's Victorian Gothic Liverpool Cathedral). Their vaulted acoustic provided the hi-fi of the time; their stained glass windows the nearest they had to the colour and narratives of television. Now, with telling circularity, the technology of television will adorn the focal point of Sir Christopher Wren's masterpiece. Traditionalists may be shocked at this invasion, but in truth it is the art that has been subverted to the service of ancient gods, video as a votive offering, transient technology aspiring to the eternal.

Critical video

Viola's projections on the high altar are merely the final stage of video's acceptance as high art. For many years, it has been difficult to enter a gallery without encountering a darkened room in which video is playing on eternal loop, often to an audience of one or less. Unlike with paintings, sculptures, drawings, photographs, it is impossible to scope them first before deciding which to give your attention to; with video you have to settle down and watch a few minutes before embarrassedly shuffling out, imagining the contempt of the connoisseurs there keen to see it through. Consumers of conventional documentary, aware that different rules obtain, may struggle to find the value in watching David Beckham sleep for over an hour, or Belgian women bathed in lamplight and wreathed in smoke. But there is an elemental connection between these uses and the essence of documentary observation.

Sam Taylor-Wood's *David* is not just an homage to Warhol's 1964 film *Sleep*, but a comment on our obsession with celebrity and the homoerotic charge of this particular body seen so intimately at close range. It is using documentary technique to achieve the heroic monumentalism of portraiture, fetishing the gendered form of the masculine ideal just as

Michelangelo's *David* does. But, prone and asleep, he comes closer to the vulnerability of the female nude that has dominated Western art since the sixteenth century.[38] 'And', as the *Telegraph* noted:

> By showing Beckham from close to in bed, Taylor-Wood implies that the viewer is lying next to him, able to reach out and touch him, like a lover. It's a neat reversal of a tradition that has, for the most part, been the province of male artists, and it is to Beckham's eternal credit that he agreed to collude in Taylor-Wood's stylish updating of a tired genre.[39]

It is instructive to see how much can be achieved with a locked-off mid-shot.

The Belgian filmmaker Chantal Ackerman's *Femmes d'Anvers en Novembre/Women from Antwerp in November* (2007) comprises two contrasting projections: *The Square Black and White Portrait* – giant black-and-white screen showing shots of a beautiful woman's face as she smokes a Camel; and *The Landscape* – five smaller, mainly colour, frames watching different women in various nocturnal street scenes, standing, sitting, smoking, waiting. As French curator Dominique Païni writes:

> Face and landscape, close-up and distance shot – the basic, binary terms of filmmaking are reconstituted in the gallery. It is as if, by sparing her the duty of compliance with the demands of narrative, the space of the gallery (or museum) has once again provided Ackerman with the opportunity to get back to the essentials of cinema.[40]

While *The Square* consciously references Hitchcock's *Vertigo* (1958), *The Landscape* demonstrates the documentary camera's ability to read experience and emotion: from drunkenness and despair to concern and concentration. Akerman's work ranges across a variety of notional genres but, as she says, whereas cinema aims to make time pass without notice, she wants her viewers to be aware of the time passing, and that makes it difficult for her to get conventional documentary funding:

> No, no. It's not for me; it's because you have to ask for money. But that suits me, in fact. It's good for me. Because the minute I start writing, I like it. But for the documentaries

Figure 16.1
Shot close and personal,
an iconic footballer asleep
in Sam Taylor-Wood's *David*

now, they want it to be more and more defined, and I absolutely cannot define things. So I circle around it. I write around the film, around the hole, let's say, or around the void. Because I want to go and make a documentary without knowing what I'm doing. They always demand, 'Tell us what you're going to do'. And all I can tell you is that I just don't know. It's precisely because of this lack of knowledge that there can be a film.[41]

Traditionally, established documentary filmmakers were granted the freedom to pursue the subjects that their instincts dictated, but today every nervous commissioner wants to know what they are up to. Only the artist is free to do what he or she wants.

Miriam Rosen, interviewing Ackerman at the time of her major retrospective at the Pompidou Centre in Paris in 2004, suggested she was an inveterate 'border crosser'. Ackerman responded: 'One could say that I'm on the border between so-called experimental film and narrative film and that I travel from one to the other'. Other artists have exercised this licence to travel, both metaphorically and physically. Jeremy Deller won the 2004 Turner Prize with *Memory Bucket* (2004) – his idiosyncratic documentary about George Bush's hometown, Crawford, Texas – and *The Battle of Orgreave* (2001), his dramatic documentary restaging for cameras of one of the key events of the 1984 miners' strike. *The Battle of Orgreave* was shown on television and was a comparatively rare intrusion of contemporary art into the political sphere, but has also been defined as a 'site-specific art performance' which raises issues about our heritage culture, re-enactment within historical understanding, and the position of the artist in relation to community art works.[42]

The leading UK art prize, the Turner, is a barometer of the dominant trends in British art and, to traditionalists' fury, has for many years featured more video artists than painters among its shortlists and winners. Steve McQueen – now a successful feature film director whom we shall return to in Chapter 18 – won in 1999, and Isaac Julien, another noted filmmaker, was nominated in 2001. But the tendency for many artists is to use video as merely one method on a vastly expanded artistic canvas, either as one aspect of installation art, or as a parallel to work in other media, such as sculpture and photography. It is often the medium they choose for the most personal exploration, such as Willie Doherty's exploration of his conflicted hometown of Derry, *The Only Good One Is A Dead One* (1993), or Darren Almond's 4-screen installation featuring his widowed grandmother's return to the Blackpool of her honeymoon, *If I Had You* (2003).

Other artists use extant film or television, either as found material or focus for attack on the media of the Society of Spectacle. The 2008 Turner Prize winner Mark Leckey's films expropriate from any media – Jeff Koons's *Rabbit* (1986) in *Made in 'Eaven* (2004), Viz comic's cartoon *Drunken Bakers* (2006) and an abundance of film footage of underground music and the party scene from the previous 30 years in *Fiorucci Made Me Hardcore* (1999). Fiona Banner, whose work is largely concerned with words, either anatomising existing film texts (*The Nam*, 1997) or screenplays for imagined work, 'still films' as she calls them, such as *Arsewoman in Wonderland* (2002). This pornographic text spread across the wall of Tate Britain, as part of the 2002 Turner Prize nominees' exhibition, caused a predictable outcry and prompted the *Guardian*'s Emma Brockes to take porn director Ben Dover along to review it in a piece entitled 'It's art, but is it porn?'.[43] Not really, not commercial enough, was the verdict.

In 2002, the enterprising installation artist Phil Collins – not the famous rock star – travelled to Saddam Hussein's Iraq to film Iraqis waiting for auditions for a non-existent

Hollywood movie, featured in his video *Baghdad Screen Tests* (2002). Being an essentially exploitative exercise, it is an illuminating precursor to his installation in the Tate, when nominated for the 2006 prize. He set up a television production office in the gallery, 'shady lane productions', staffed from nine till five every day and notionally making a documentary, *the return of the real*, featuring real people whose lives had been ruined by appearing in reality TV shows.[44] In an interview filmed in the 'production office', he comments on the artifice of television, exampling the technical and directed artifice of the interview itself, and talks feelingly about the exploitative nature of the medium:

> This project is about the blind spot of television, how it betrays people, how it lets people down, how it upsets and disturbs. Some of the stories are very harrowing and, of course, at points you feel it is inhumane to film. And, at other points, you feel it is inhumane, or insensitive, to turn the camera off. It is horrifying that the camera can be a horrifying, brutalizing instrument. How can I ask you to stop filming when I know that, if I say that, that's the thing you will include . . .
>
> What we are working towards is a forum where people can address the news media, the press, about their experiences on shows, where they were sold it as a documentary and yet, halfway through, it became a tabloid story.[45]

The forum was a live press conference at the Café Royal, where nine of Collins's aggrieved subjects told their stories to representatives of the press and broadcast media, on whom Collins's cameras then turned. The film of that event then became one of the main elements in a multi-screen exhibition, which also included films of extended interviews with the subjects, conducted by media lawyer Mark Stephens, and anonymous testimony from television professionals revealing the tricks of their trade, presented as scrolling autocue texts. The press release for the exhibition announced that Collins 'investigates the post-documentary culture which reality television has come to epitomise'.[46] It is an intriguing use of the tools and techniques of documentary to expose both the mechanisms and the damaging effects of reality television while, with ironic circularity, repeating the process of exploiting people's emotional journeys as material.

Collins would argue, as documentary filmmakers do, that the ends justifies the means, that – more than the catharsis subjects may gain from expressing their pain – the message needs to be communicated. The problematic issue is that the people who need to hear that message, the television audience and the commercial interests who serve their tastes, may not be avid gallery-goers, and the numbers who do would not register on a TV audience rating. It could be argued that 'shady lane productions' would have been better occupied getting a real documentary onto television to address the relevant audience, but that would be to imagine broadcasters subsidising self-criticism. As Mark Stephens says, he was troubled at the cynicism of a television industry exploiting people for commercial gain, and keen to help give some prominence to 'voices which are so often censored by the media which has already misrepresented them'.[47] The chances of hearing this debate broadcast are slim.

Changing ways of seeing

As television has gradually receded from the philosophical and intellectual, art has expanded to film the vacuum, offering a critique of contemporary society, its media and methods. Video and documentary are inevitably primary resources in this role. The Otolith Group – Anjalika Sagar and Kodwo Eshun – are one example of an artistic sensibility working with these tools. They have been very active preserving the work and legacy of the now defunct Black Audio Film Collective, and curating exhibitions with this kind of political, community-based video. Their first film, *Otolith I* (2003), reviews our conflicted present from an imagined future in 2103. *Otolith II* (2008) expropriates Godard's notorious conversation about the validity of terrorism – between a naive young Maoist and the dissident philosopher Francis Jeanson in *La Chinoise/The Chinese* (1967) – and marries it to documentary photographs of Sagar's grandmother's visit to Mao's China. In its playing with time and culture, the art academic T.J. Demos finds a real element of promise in Otolith's work:

> The advancement of documentary film into imagined territories, as pioneered by Godard and Marker, as well as Jean Rouch and Black Audio Film Collective . . . is clearly of growing interest among contemporary artists, as demonstrated not only by the Otolith Group but also by Walid Raad's Atlas Group, Pierre Huyghe, Amar Kanwar and Steve McQueen. The significance of these renewed explorations lies in the realization that the production of documentary film without an element of fiction merely reifies its object. It appears, moreover, that only by admitting fabulation into its storytelling can documentary practice fully excavate the hidden recesses of reality that retain the possible scenarios, unrealized futures, and failed aspirations that constitute the full scope of experience. Through its engagement, the Otolith Group inspires the unlikely hope that we may still alter our fate.[48]

Widely excoriated for the interventions that he makes in his documentary work, the Dutch artist Renzo Martens is arguably the most effective of all at revealing the heart of darkness so often the goal of committed documentary. His *Episode III: Enjoy Poverty* (2008) is a savage indictment of Western involvement in the Democratic Republic of the Congo, focusing not on the conventional extractive industries but on the 'aid and development' armies of the UN and NGOs. Starting with a smug press conference at which the World Bank announces an aid package worth $1.8 billion, Martens films himself standing up to ask if this does not make poverty the Congo's premier resource. Smiling, the World Bank representative says it is not a resource, but admits that the aid is worth more than all the country's exports – from gold and diamonds to rubber and palm oil – combined.

The film then follows Martens on a Conradian journey through the country, trying to convince the Congolese people to exploit their poverty in the way that the whites do, from the press photographing dead bodies to Médecins sans Frontières, unaccountably following Western interests in the mineral-rich war zones. He erects a large neon sign reading Enjoy (Please) Poverty and encourages poor wedding photographers to turn their cameras on the more lucrative images of raped women and dying children. He then explodes their hopes by taking them to meet Médecins sans Frontières doctors, who say they would not grant them access. When Martens points out that they routinely allow Western press access to make money from such images, they first say that this is different, it's 'communications', and then say they take better pictures than the Africans. Western liberals are made uneasy, deliberately, by this apparently casual and ruthless destruction of hope, but Martens expertly defuses their sentimental reaction by pointing out: that's what the West does in Africa – 'Phantom Aid', which repays itself, through its agencies, mentors and media, 80–90 per cent of aid 'donations'. He says his 'piece of art is dictated by the politics [of inequality and inhumanity] it sets out to portray':

> This film is a problematisation of the role art can play in the world – a world that is so incredibly badly organized . . . I set out to make a representation of the status quo, where people have no agency over their own lives . . . Hope is being generated, and then cut off when larger interests are at stake.[49]

This is big, important work, a more sophisticated, internationalist version of Michael Moore's polemical canvas. But where Moore is the unsubtle giganticist, a Claes Oldenburg stuffed figure, Martens is the filmic pointillist, an incisively satirical Seurat. *Enjoy Poverty* is as angry and as iconoclastic as any work written about by Amos Vogel in *Film as a Subversive Art*, and it reveals, as Martens intends, 'the power structures that exist between people watching and people being watched'.[50]

Conclusion

The desire to alter our fate, arouse and anger us, are the constant threads that link the aspirations of art with the ultimate aims of film. It would be too simple to say that the gallery has replaced the cinema and television as the primary arena of ideas, but there are contradictory trajectories here, as television has moved to cede the moral high ground dispensing aesthetic advice and is now more inclined to instrumentalism in the marketplace with the masses, while art has extended its reach to engage with politics and philosophy. Jean Rouch said 'Simultaneously a liberation and a fulfilment, it (photography) has freed Western painting, once and for all, from its obsession with realism'.[51] Speaking in 1967, at a high point of abstraction in modern art, he did not foresee how much the camera would supplant the paintbrush as the artistic instrument of the time, nor that the discourse about realism would become so dominant.

   This could be labelled a constructivist age, following on the iconoclasm of the mid-twentieth century with which this chapter commenced. Film is a less subversive art now that it has shattered the taboos and left its audience largely immune to shock. An exhibition that attempted to embrace this new maturity in 2007, while still celebrating the explicitly erotic through the ages, fell somewhere between the opposed polls of academic rigour and popular prurience. *Seduced: Art and Sex from Antiquity to Now* made much of its R-rating, restricting entry to over-18s, and the visit from the City of London police to ensure that it did not contravene obscenity laws. 'They're completely cool. We're kosher,' announced the artistic director of the Barbican, Graham Sheffield. Co-curator Martin Kemp said: 'We are not setting out to shock, but it is certainly provoking.' Marina Wallace, another of the curators, added: 'We want London to be thinking about nothing but sex for three months.'[52]

   Replete with Warhol's *Blow Job* (1963/4) and a recent alternative homage offering the female alternative – as k.r. buxey's *Requiem* (2007) features her own face as she is being orally pleasured – plus 13 sado-masochistic homosexual portraits by the American photographer Robert Mapplethorpe – which had the Cincinatti museum director who first exhibited them in 1990 indicted for obscenity, albeit later acquitted – *Seduced: Art and Sex from Antiquity to Now* was clearly hoping to court a bit of controversy and bring in the punters. But the queues that attended the Royal Academy's *Sensation* show a decade earlier failed to materialise. As a long, thoughtful piece by *The Independent*'s Tom Lubbock noted, art has always been concerned with the erotic, not just in the less prudish times of the Greeks and Romans revisited in this exhibition, but also throughout the work of the Great Masters – Titian, Rubes, Ingres, etc. – whose explicit nudes you are encouraged to take your children to see for free at the National Gallery. There was a time, he writes, when even these were consigned to locked back rooms and used specifically, as the poet W.B. Yeats remarked, to help 'fill the cradles', but not for over a century. Even the patrician Lord Clark, whose *Civilisation* we covered in Chapter 3, wrote 'no nude, however abstract, should fail to arouse in the spectator some vestige of erotic feeling, even though it be only the faintest shadow',[53] but, when giving evidence to Lord Longford's Committee on Pornography, he drew the line at art which is 'an incentive to action'.[54] On that, he may have found himself improbably aligned with Ben Dover.

The Viennese Aktion movement was inevitably short-lived, prompted as it was in part by a sense of post-War self-loathing. Anger is a difficult emotion to sustain. Like satire, it tends to be specific to a particular space and time, whereas much of the work covered here is concerned with the plasticity of those concepts and the capacity to escape their constraints. Vogel was prescient in discarding 'mimetic' realism, and in his view that 'truth implies the courage to face chaos', but the nature of that chaos is in constant flux. At the time of writing, recession has exposed the unfettered free market as another failed human illusion, with significant impact on the attendant inflated sums paid for art works. Filmic art engaged with issues, illuminating the real through the refractions of artistic imagination, may be on the cusp of establishing a new value, a role in which conventional documentary has lost its pre-eminence. We may not be about to see the artistic destruction of Debord's Society of the Spectacle – anyway it seems to have begun the job of self-demolition from its own obesity – but there is a growing public dissatisfaction with the economic and political systems responsible for current catastrophes. Video is revealing the fissures in society, from decaying public services to overactive policing, and its constructive use may yet help address the moral vacuum of the moment, an object to challenge the finest minds.

Expert briefing – ways of seeing

Where the artist leads, society follows, and the way the camera infantry frame the world is an often unconscious reflection of that constantly shifting social vision. Ross McElwee says: 'Godard said every edit is a political statement. By extension, I think every camera movement is a political statement. You opt to zoom in because you're after something.'[55] You may not rationalise your use of the zoom in that way, but each choice, conscious or unconscious, reflects your worldview and its attendant hierarchy of values. The study of semiotics unpicks the way images are freighted with meaning,[56] but here are a few practical examples:

1   **Relative authority**: During the industrial disputes of the 1970s and 1980s, striking workers were invariably depicted on the picket lines by hand-held cameras, often randomly framed, with union representatives speaking to reporters well off camera. The shots, and therefore their subjects, often looked dodgy and unreliable. Management were usually shot behind desks or in their boardroom, surrounded by the trappings of power, on carefully framed, tripod-steady shots. These communicated

solidity and reliability. In *The Shining*, Stanley Kubrick deliberately subverts the orthodox film geometry – which sits the human subject on the lines achieved by notionally dividing the screen into thirds – to destabilise the audience and suggest more horrors are imminent.[57] So both the context and the operation of interviews convey a lot about the authority and credibility of the interviewee.

2   **Which side you are on**: In the early stages of the miners' strike of 1984, news footage was routinely shot from behind police lines, so that all conflict was framed from the police perspective and all aggression and missiles seemed to emanate from the miners. Only when an Open Space documentary was made from the miners' side of the lines was the skew of that coverage realised, and rectified. Widespread use of mobile phone video facilities has now put that option, and therefore some control, back in the hands of the public, as witnessed by the material shot in London of the policing of the G20 protests in 2009. Restricted access to war zones, and the process known as 'embedding', ensures the same controlling effect, of only seeing conflict from one side, so demanding that other sources may be found to rectify the imbalance.

3   **Point of view**: The POV is something of a film cliché, used to convey various points, from the literal to the lateral. Didactic filmmakers will insert shots of objects observed from the viewpoint of the speaker, as the much overused 'cutaway'. More imaginative filmmakers extend the POV's use as a signifier of threat or other disturbance, either from the attacker's POV or as the object of attack, as in the paranoid moving POV of the threatened subjects in *The Blair Witch Project*.[58] This enormously successful film was responsible for a host of feature films adopting faux-documentary approaches, including the use of random POV shots spuriously to indicate the absence of a conventional controlling filmmaker's hand.

4   **Point and counterpoint**: While the most conventional means of constructing a narrative argument in film is the dialectical method – thesis, intercut with antithesis, leading to synthesis – the pictorial equivalent is closer to musical counterpoint, the dominant compositional tradition in Western music since the fourteenth century. Pictures convey the principal statement of the theme – subject, place and how to read it – then the composer/filmmaker introduces harmonious, or dissonant variations on that theme – leading inexorably towards recapitulation and conclusion. Party political broadcasts frequently adopt this approach, precisely because they do not want to give equal time to their opponents, as they are obliged to do in televised debates. Classic US presidential election TV ads for Richard Nixon in 1968 set the style with dystopian visual themes of a riot-torn, crime-scarred America against which the reassuring baritone of Nixon is countered, promising 'honest talk', 'hope' and 'freedom from fear'. Each film ends with the screen legend: 'This time vote like your whole world depended on it'.[59]

5   **Height, light and lens**: Cameras conventionally frame people at their eyeline's elevation, precisely because that literally treats them as equals. Shots 'stylishly' framed looking up at people inevitably enhance their esteem within the frame, while shooting from above conveys that sense of looking down on the subject. Sam Taylor-Wood's *David* was not shot from above, the usual perspective on the vulnerable sleeper, but from his head height, the sightline of the lover. Lighting can also change what we see in the face, from the exaggerated contours, such as picked out in German expressionist horror films, to a frontal flood that magics away an old lady's wrinkles. The lens chosen can also flatter or flatten the subject, with excessive use of the wide-angle in close particularly inclined to distort. Veteran politician Tony Benn would

harangue camera crews with the semi-informed: 'I hope that's not a wide-angle lens – you're trying to make me look stupid!'

6   **Subject/object**: More problematic is the lens's impenetrable stare that can reduce every person and living thing to the status of an object. Even in the heroic documentary images of Soviet workers, there is still an implication that it is the camera, the Kino-eye, which has conveyed or endorsed that status. Today, poverty campaigners are increasingly concerned that images of the poor, the needy and the oppressed in all societies have the unintended effect of objectifying and confirming their victimhood. They are the powerful means of communication for charity fund-raising – the big-eyed starving child – but the iconography is all too appropriate to the inequality it addresses. The challenge is to find ways of depicting people as whole beings, rather than objects of pity, reflecting their self-image and, equally importantly, hearing their voice. Similarly, the propensity for over-dubbing foreign voices, rather than subtitling, may make it easier for audiences, but robs the speaker of their autonomy.

7   **The fallacy of choice**: Conscious that the first century of documentary was largely didactic, instructing a passive audience on what was important and what to think about it, broadcasters have embraced the digital 'red-button' options to allow audiences to override their decisions and choose other perspectives. The same hierarchy of values selects those options, so this digital democracy only serves to replicate the determinism of supply. What television finds harder to embrace is the genuine liberation of voice and view that the internet has nurtured. The challenge for documentary is not just to enable a thousand new filmmakers to bloom, but for their cameras to capture the myriad varieties of life, in all its peculiarity.

8   **Honesty and revelation**: As television documentary forms become increasingly constructed, the pursuit of truth that still exercises public support for documentary, seems ever more elusive. Dwoskin's claim for film that is 'honest and revealing' should remain one lodestone, enabled by Brakhage's 'untutored eye'. The possibilities of digital technology make Mekas's cinematic 'intimacy' much more achievable than ever, so the object of honest revelation and validation of every experience is a feasible goal. The liberty of the art documentary – and any self-financed film – is that it escapes subservience to imposed goals.

Part V

Watch the figures

While the greater part of this book has been concerned with the transmutation of documentary into more constructed and commercial forms, what has become of the traditional single documentary? For the most part, television had subsumed single documentaries within edited strands, such as the BBC's *40 Minutes*,[1] which not only restricted the running time but also bore a strong stamp of the editor and his or her tastes and judgement. This reflected the growing managerialisation of television production, with the imposition of notional brands on strands to deliver a particular product for a particular audience. Many filmmakers resented this restriction on their creativity, and many more were judged incompatible with specific editorial determinants. A few well-established individual directors, from Nick Broomfield and Paul Watson to Molly Dineen and Brian Woods, have managed to keep working to their own particular lights, but that is a licence largely withdrawn from the mainstream. Other well-established filmmakers, such as Roger Graef, regret the reduction of commissioner demand for single documentaries:

> There is a sense that the schedulers and marketers are making a lot of the decisions now . . . It's product not programmes, like widgets. It's a counsel of despair.[2]

There is a countervailing view, that not only has there been something of a revival of the long-form filmic documentary, but that television has had a hand in it. In 1997, BBC2 introduced *Storyville*, under the editorship of Nick Fraser, with an initial series of six single documentaries. By 2004, *Storyville* had migrated, with a lot of the serious programming, to BBC4 and Fraser was commissioning some 40 films a year. He admits the old model of BBC sole commissioning and putting up 100 per cent of the budget is long gone and that his job is 'creative brokerage', putting in some money and helping arrange co-production with other countries:

> We work a lot with Arte, the French and German broadcaster; we sometimes do things with Spain; we collaborate particularly with Scandinavian countries – Denmark has very good filmmakers and there are very good executives in Danish TV; ditto Sweden; ditto Finland. In Finland in particular, where the nights are so long or there's no day at all, they seem to watch a fabulous quantity of documentaries. We also have links with Canada, and I've piled up as many contacts as I can with American broadcasters such as PBS and HBO.[3]

Fraser feels that documentary revival has been stimulated by 'a reaction against the platitudes and stereotypes of television', particularly in America and among the young, and because of the cheap availability of the means of production. As Clay Shirky says of the internet, the gateway is now in the hands of the producer, the filter more at the point of consumption.[4] Fraser adds that the documentary has replaced the novel and the screenplay as the contemporary cultural form the young aspire to:

> People should go out and shoot them if they're in love with the subject, and that we broadcasters, if we take seriously the depiction of truth, have to act as sponsors and give encouragement.[5]

That remains the ideal, but Fraser admits that the broadcasters, including the BBC, are primarily interested in making mass-market appeal shows for the home audience, and their sponsorship of documentary is strictly secondary to that.

The complementary ground for optimism is the revival of the cinema documentary, with roughly two a week now going on release in the UK. Fortunately, the new co-production funding model allows films with television interests to also have a theatre release, and leaves the producer with the residual rights to exploit secondary markets. Thus the works of love Fraser cherishes can find backers from across a wide spectrum and can find outlets across a wide range of platforms around the world. For example, I first saw the Francis brothers, Nick and Marc's, feature documentary *Black Gold* (2007) on a transatlantic BA flight. The film's 2½-year production period illuminates the possibilities and pitfalls of starting out to make a film with global reach and ethical concerns, in this case for the Ethiopian farmers who produce the coffee consumed by the urban sophisticates of the West, and raising awareness of the economic disparities involved. They started filming in 2003, in Ethiopia and at the world trade talks in Cancun, Mexico, at their own expense:

> We put our own resources in at the beginning, and took the risk getting the original events shot, which wouldn't wait for a commissioning green light. Then we joined up with Fulcrum TV to seek funding from trusts, foundations and Norwegian co-production. We went to Screen South, the UK Film Council and then took a rough cut to the Sundance Documentary Composers Lab. Then Britdoc came in and helped unlock funds for post-production. We premiered at the Sundance Festival [2006], but we are still working hard two years on, servicing the festival demands, supported by the Docfactory.[6]

Black Gold was eventually shown on the PBS network in the United States and on More 4 in the UK,[7] and is not unusual in involving its makers in the complex demands of financing and marketing. This is what independent filmmakers do in the commercial cinema sector, and what has helped the renaissance of screen documentary that we cover in the next two chapters. There is here a sense that documentaries have rediscovered their original ambition to be historical documents, lasting testimony to their time rather than fleeting moments to pass the time.

The final chapter, *Wildlife*, is on the documentary genre that remains one of the most consistently successful in television, both as a domestic banker and a worldwide guarantee of co-production and sales. Yet not even these skilled filmmakers are entirely free from the vagaries of the market, even as their techniques continue to evolve, bringing a constantly replenished sense of wonder at the natural world. In this, and with a renewed sense of mission at a time of global warming and species threat, they seem more in tune with these other developments. By concentrating on the recent history of the BBC's Natural History Unit in Bristol, the undisputed leading natural history filmmakers in the world, we can see how all the threads explored in this book converge in one specific documentary sub-genre. From the pressures of scheduling and restrictive budgets, to the creative possibilities of new technology and multimedia platforms, with the economies of scale and benefits of worldwide distribution, the NHU's wildlife world contains all the elements of contemporary documentary practice within a frame that faces all the cross-currents of an industry consumed by the figures.

17 Box office

....

box office n. 1 an office at a theatre, cinema, etc., where tickets are sold . . .
2a the public appeal of an actor or production

t is no accident that, as the formal, traditional documentary concerned with social issues
has declined on British television – and was always a rare beast on US TV – screen
documentary has seen something of a renaissance in the twenty-first century. While UK
documentary filmmakers despair at the ratings-driven obsessions of television commissioners,
formerly their only source of funding, they rejoice at the promised possibilities of making
documentary for cinema, and the secondary and DVD markets that come with that exposure.
Whereas in the late twentieth century, a documentary would be difficult to find in a mainstream cinema, by 2009 one or two documentaries were getting a cinema release every week.
'The recent revival of cinema documentary has given the genre a huge boost', says award-
winning documentarist Marilyn Gaunt.[1] But two notes of caution need be struck here.
First, the cinema is driven by its box office receipts, a much harsher and more finite judge
than UK terrestrial television ratings; the majority of features fail to turn a profit on release,
freighted as their balance sheets are with the additional costs of publicity and distribution.
Second, the documentary renaissance is not only minimal, but essentially driven by the United
States. In the last decade, barely a handful of UK documentary productions have turned a
profit in the cinema, not producing any significant changes in the economics of or employment
in the industry. As Angus Macqueen, former Head of Documentaries at Channel 4 says:

> The feature theatrical documentary – if you want my honest opinion – I think in Britain
> still doesn't really exist. Kevin Macdonald with *Touching the Void* is I suspect the only
> one that has made any serious money. Very many of the American films are films we
> wouldn't even show on our TV. They are not well enough made – and which we have
> made in different forms less indulgently, more editorially controlled – but which in
> America speak to a very large country that has a television that doesn't serve its audience
> with that sort of material. I just don't think people are going to go to the cinema [here]
> and pay £20 for a night to watch a documentary. They might do for Al Gore . . . but very,
> very rarely.[2]

Macqueen mentions his former Channel 4 colleague Jess Search, who is arguably Britain's
leading proselyte for theatrical documentary. As the Chief Executive of the Channel Four
British Documentary Film Foundation and BRITDOC, she aims to encourage and support

Figure 17.1
Kevin Macdonald's *Touching the Void* (2003) reconstructed a tragedy and documentary's cinematic hopes

British documentary makers on the international stage. She believes that new sources of funding can be found to help regenerate the form, and cites corporations as the likeliest source:

> Film is still the most powerful medium for communicating values and emotions to people – making it a highly attractive proposition to sophisticated consumer brands. So it should come as no surprise that Eurostar produced full film financing for British filmmaker Shane Meadows' latest film *Somers Town*, which is set in the area adjacent to St Pancras station – Eurostar's London home. But Meadows is a fiction director (albeit an award-winning one) and in reality it is the documentary film format that has the most to offer brands.[3]

The obvious examples are for youth-oriented brands like Red Bull associating themselves with teen-friendly subjects such as music and sport, but it is hard to imagine hard-nosed corporations backing critical works such as Al Gore's *An Inconvenient Truth*. Search recognises that films about climate change sponsored by energy companies may well be compromised and incredible, but argues that companies and audiences are much more sophisticated these days, and cites Puma's sponsoring the Cannes Film Festival premiere of British filmmaker Jeremy Gilley's *The Day After Peace* as evidence that serious issues can be espoused by commercial concerns.[4] She points out that broadcasters, with fragmented audiences and declining advertising and sponsorship, have in any case largely stopped treating difficult and obscure subjects and impose greater and greater controls on filmmakers, whereas feature directors have traditionally been cut more creative slack. However, whether chasing profits or kudos, it is unlikely any company will invest in documentary features unless they are expected to make a splash at the box office.

War of words

The contemporary Hollywood yardstick for a hit feature is a film that takes upward of $100 million at the US box office. Some 400 made that accolade between 2000 and 2008, the period credited with the documentary renaissance. Yet just one documentary was among them, Michael Moore's 2004 counterblast to the Bush war on terror, *Fahrenheit 9/11*, which had grossed $119,194,771 by the end of 2008.[5] Documentary distributors consider themselves successful to take \$1 million at the box office, which returns they then anticipate will eventually be at least doubled by DVD sales and other secondary distribution. The more successful exceptions to that rule mostly feature subjects that strike a chord with the audience, suggesting a need inadequately met by other media. In the 2000s, these have clearly been dissenting voices on the environment, politics and religion.

The colossus bestriding the political field is the polemical filmmaker Michael Moore, whose polemical work we explored in Chapter 10, a divisive figure who excites admiration and antipathy in equal quantities. His 1985 debut, *Roger and Me*, first deployed Moore's 'honest Joe' character in search of public truth, chasing the boss of General Motors in an attempt to bring him to account for the damage he had wrought on jobs in his home town of Flint, Michigan. The success of this film gave him television opportunities to develop this schtick in a variety of stunts aimed at entertainingly revealing systemic failing and corruption within government and companies on either side of the Atlantic. The George W. Bush presidency gave him his best targets and, in 2002, his virulent cinema feature on America's gun culture and resultant high school massacres, *Bowling for Columbine*, became the top-grossing documentary up to then. Deploying rock stars such as Marilyn Manson and comedian Chris Rock, he mounted a savage attack on the American shibboleth of the so-called 'constitutional right to bear arms' and its powerful lobby, the National Rifle Association. In Moore's baiting interview with the ageing chair of the NRA, the late Charlton Heston, the Hollywood divinity who had starred in many biblical epics, Moore sets out his stall as the man righteously willing to take on any icon, in contrast to the USA's still surprisingly deferential culture. When *Columbine* went on to win the Best Documentary Oscar, Moore further outraged convention by using his acceptance speech to lambast President Bush. He invited his fellow nominees on stage 'in solidarity' and then said:

> We like non-fiction and we live in fictitious times. We live in a time where we have fictitious election results that elect a fictitious president. We live in a time where we have a man sending us to war for fictitious reasons, whether it is the fiction of duck tape or the fiction of orange alerts. We are against the war, Mr. Bush. Shame on you, Mr. Bush, shame on you. Any time you get the Dixie Chicks and the Pope against you, your time is up.[6]

The denizens of the entertainment industry, who booed Moore for intruding this harsh reality into their self-congratulatory cocoon, missed the point. However sincere Moore is – and there are many, not just of the right, who question this[7] – Moore is an astute businessman who knew that America was ready for the dissident voice, and the box office spectacularly proved him right. The film which picked up that Oscar speech's theme, *Fahrenheit 9/11* (2004), was refused distribution by Disney but went on to be by far the most profitable documentary in history. Although the film released before President Bush's re-election, it prefigures the continuing decline in support for the Iraq war and in Bush's popularity, with him finally leaving the White House as the most unpopular president of all time. Moore's subsequent attack on the inequities of the American healthcare system, *Sicko* (2007), may not have had much influence on that outcome, but again proved box office gold and reflected the popular taste for change, which was eventually to bring Barack Obama to power. In this way, the twenty-first-century cinema documentary renaissance has proved an intriguing barometer to America's political climate.

Gathering clouds

In the years before *Bowling for Columbine* in 2002, the only surefire documentary returns were to be found in escapist fare on the giant IMAX screens, to which I return below. But the Bush years – ranging as they did from the attacks on New York and Washington in September 2001 to the virtual collapse of the banking system in 2008 – produced a growing appetite for the intellectual debate clearly absent from the White House and from the television networks. Typical of this movement is the Canadian-made *The Corporation* (2003), which deploys a panoply of interviewees to make its argument that the corporation should be viewed as a psychopathic individual, given its nature as amoral, acquisitive and indifferent to the harm it causes others. Along with the predictable, compelling testimony of the likes of Noam Chomsky and Naomi Klein, *The Corporation* also finds financiers and Republicans to make its case, such as the unsuccessful Maine candidate for Senate, Robert Monks, who says: 'The corporation is an externalizing machine (moving its operating costs to external organizations and people), in the same way that a shark is a killing machine'.[8] Eschewing flashy techniques and settling for well-edited comment, even the conservative UK finance and business periodical *The Economist* was moved to comment approvingly of the film:

> Unlike much of the soggy thinking peddled by too many anti-globalisers, *The Corporation* is a surprisingly rational and coherent attack on capitalism's most important institution.[9]

US critical reception was equally good, with influential critic Roger Ebert describing how it had moved him to argument at a Chicago dinner party – until his wife had kicked him under the table. The only criticism he had was, as is often the case with the deadly serious, it was a bit long-winded:

> *The Corporation* is an impassioned polemic, filled with information sure to break up any dinner-table conversation. Its fault is that of the dinner guest who tells you something fascinating, and then tells you again, and then a third time. At 145 minutes, it overstays its welcome. The wise documentarian should treat film stock as a non-renewable commodity.[10]

Most documentaries are now shot on much less costly tape, requiring no such prudence in the shooting, and frequently leading less skilled directors to over-shoot, with often dire cost to the film's post-production schedule, if not its focus. But there is little doubt that one of the key attractions of the feature documentary is that it allows complexity and concentration no longer deemed possible on television. People committing to two hours in the dark of the cinema give their undivided attention to a film that can therefore afford to deep mine difficult subjects, which a constantly distracted home television audience will not, especially if constantly interrupted by advertising breaks. In that contemplative space, these films offer what some writers have identified as a new 'politics of documentary form',[11] an arena which dares to ask the right questions of the centres of power that the conventional news machines seem unwilling or unable to ask, whether through journalists being over-stretched, external and internal corporate pressure, or undue reporter reliance on closeness to their sources.

There are always exceptions. When the biggest corporate bankruptcy in US history occurred, it was the result of a young *Fortune* reporter, Bethany McLean, in March 2001 asking the simple question 'Is Enron over-priced?' Although tech stocks were bombing at the box office, fans couldn't get enough of Enron, whose shares returned 89 per cent she reported.[12] 'Enron now trades at roughly 55 times trailing earnings', a huge multiple of the norm. McLean established that the company was secretive about how it achieved these astronomic figures, and analysts and investors were equally in the dark about the company's activities, but content with their ignorance as the profits continued to flow. What McLean revealed was a far from healthy business model, trading in complex derivatives and futures rather than the core energy business – gas pipelines, iron and steel assets – on which the company was founded. The real had been replaced by the virtual, a trade based on faith in the company, which duly was revealed to be fraudulent. The former CEO Jeff Skilling was eventually sentenced to 24 years in jail for his role in the scandal.

Before that, the whole sorry saga had been made into an excellent film that charts this complex fraud, and reveals the systemic complicity of America's financial industry, including most of its leading investment banks, in this latter-day South Sea Bubble.[13] But no one outside Enron shouldered any blame. Their accounting firm Arthur Andersen went bust, but the accountants' conviction for obstructing justice by shredding Enron files when the scandal broke, was overturned on a technicality and – as the events of 2008 were to prove – the financial system continued to take fabulous profits on business that was largely fabulous, i.e. based on fable. Six years on, it was if Enron had never happened, as the reckless disregard for scruple or commonsense in the Gadarene rush for profit all but brought the whole financial system crashing down. Alex Gibney's *Enron: The Smartest Guys in the Room* (2005) stands as a prophetic warning, as well as evidence that feature documentary has become a potent tool for the smartest minds in the media.

The economy was one lead story of the decade; the environment was another. Ironically, it was the man who many thought had been unjustly cheated of the presidency in 2000, when the Supreme Court had ruled in Bush's favour over disputed Florida electoral returns, who led the field with the surprise hit that was *An Inconvenient Truth* (2006). Al Gore had written a best-selling book about the environment, *Earth in the Balance*, in 1992 and had helped broker the Kyoto Protocol on greenhouse emissions in 1997, only to see it unanimously rejected by the US Senate. Following his 2000 defeat, he had returned to this prior concern, stumping around the country giving an earnest illustrated lecture on the threat of global warming, an issue consistently denied by the oilmen in the White House. Quentin Tarantino's producer, Lawrence Bender, saw the lecture in New York and was inspired to make a film version, hiring TV drama director Davis Guggenheim (*NYPD Blue*, *24*, *ER*) to direct. Although they opened the talk up, and introduced some breathtaking sequences, the film is still in essence a lantern lecture, driven by the voice and passion of Al Gore. That so simple a format could become the fourth highest grossing documentary in US history, and win an Oscar, is not just a tribute to Gore's passion and eloquence, but to the craving for truth that brought in the audience. Although motivated by very real concerns for the future, Americans also strongly relate to the elemental natural world of their country's history, one endlessly referenced in Hollywood imagery from classic Westerns to contemporary road movies. Gore captures this in his elegantly simple opening comments:

You look at that river gently flowing by. You notice the leaves rustling with the wind. You hear the birds; you hear the tree frogs. In the distance you hear a cow. You feel the grass. The mud gives a little bit on the river bank. It's quiet; it's peaceful. And all of a sudden, it's a gear shift inside you. And it's like taking a deep breath and going . . . 'Oh yeah, I forgot about this'.[14]

It's a wonderful world

An Inconvenient Truth marries the personal and the political, the sense of a natural self with a political message, in a way which chimes with the new seriousness of its time. But it also builds upon a long tradition of romantic, often sentimental, nature films that have helped sustain American cinema and television, and owe as much to Walt Disney as they do to wild destiny. As we find in the chapter on wildlife films, these seem to inhabit a parallel, apolitical universe, remaining persistently popular and largely immune to shifts in fad and fashion. One technical innovation has, however, literally enlarged the genre and ensured a staggeringly large number of box office successes from a relatively small number of screens.

The IMAX format, developed in the 1970s, deploys the simple idea of running 70 mm film through the camera horizontally, rather than the conventional vertical track, thus exposing much larger frames of celluloid and capturing much greater detail. None of the film surface is used for sound track; sound first ran on a separate, synchronised 35 mm track, and is now digital. The detail in the image allows for huge screens with a steeply pitched audience rake that puts the spectator's vision inside the massive frame. This requires a vast, six-foot projector weighing one and a half tons; and the sheer unwieldiness and expense of the production equipment has made the format largely impractical for drama and other genres, but it has been a winner in capturing and communicating the natural world for captive audiences, such as school students taken to museums and other educational institutions, in documentaries which normally run about 40 to 45 minutes.

Greg MacGillivray has directed two of these awe-inspiring and highly profitable voyages into the deep, *The Living Sea* (1995) and *Dolphins* (1999), both Oscar-nominated. The first is a survey of the world's oceans, emphasising the fact that it's a single interconnected ocean, with interdependent life-forms. Its human contributors include surfers, researchers cataloguing and tracking whales, a Coast Guard rough weather rescue squad and a deep-ocean research team. The second also features scientists studying dolphins, particularly for their intelligence and sophisticated communications systems, as well as a commentary by Piers Brosnan and music by Sting. MacGillivray says:

> I grew up surfing, sailing, snorkeling and diving on southern California's beaches. The ocean is my life. I hope my films inspire people to love the ocean as much as I do and to do everything they can to ensure its lasting health.[15]

With the late Jim Freeman, MacGillivray founded MacGillivray Freeman Films in the 1960s and the company is now the world's largest producer and distributor of giant screen films. Of the dozens of films they have made, the most successful has been the first of their 'Great Adventures' series, *Everest* (1998). For shooting climbers in the unforgiving conditions of Mount Everest, MacGillivray initiated the development of the first all-weather, lightweight IMAX cameras, although, at 42 pounds, these are not most documentary cameramen's idea of 'light'. Despite *Everest* remaining the most profitable IMAX film to date – taking $125,700,000 worldwide – and third on the documentary table, not all MacGillivray Freeman Films make such big profits.

MacGillivray's surfer sang-froid has equipped him with the right attitude for the film business:

You've got to basically just sort of flow with the business cycles and not get too uptight. In the ocean, there are so many factors affecting the size and condition of the swell. The same thing is mostly true about running a business. There's ebb and flow, and a lot is beyond our control. Be confident that change will be good, and look for the bright side even in a downturn.[16]

Making a triumph from tragedy, MacGillivray was filming the loss of the Louisiana coastal wetlands when Hurricane Katrina happened. 'We wanted the original film to warn people what nature could do to New Orleans. Then we watched it happen,' he says. *Hurricane on the Bayou* (2006) captures the before and after, building the story around four Mississippi musicians and subtly showing what is lost when the ecology is not protected. It is part of a lifelong commitment to making films about the elemental value of water. With *Grand Canyon Adventure: River at Risk 3D*, MacGillivray moved relatively late into the IMAX revival of 3D, which has further enriched the giant screen experience. In hiring the legendary film star Robert Redford as narrator he found a fellow spirit; he says: 'He's a true environmentalist, loves the outdoors and the West, and has the credentials to validate the film's message.'[17]

The stated aim of all MFF films is to 'to inspire, inform and entertain people of all ages',[18] an Americanised version of the BBC's old Reithian precept, 'to inform, educate and entertain'. There is no doubting the sincerity of that aim, and MacGillivray has won environmental awards as well as film ones. But whereas the worthy Brits emphasise 'educate', the Americans lead on 'inspire', and there is no doubt that the giant IMAX screen, with its extraordinary images, grandiloquent soundtracks and Hollywood star narrations are above all awe-inspiring. That 'wow' factor has been used by American producers to sell other subject strands, not least the American space programme, from *The Dream is Alive* (1985), on the Space Shuttle, to *Space Station 3D* (2002). Other IMAX hits have featured funfair rides – *Thrill Ride: The Mechanics of Fun* (1997), archaeology – the *Mysteries of Egypt* (1999) and stock car racing – *NASCAR: the IMAX Experience 3D* (2004). But the single most popular subject area remains the natural world, especially since the development of IMAX 3D. Among the critters and habitats that have set the American box office tills jangling have been *Bugs!* (2003), *Sharks 3D* (2005), *Wild Safari 3D* (2005), *Deep Sea 3D* (2006), *Sea Monsters: A Prehistoric Adventure* (2007) and *Dolphins and Whales 3D: Tribes of the Ocean* (2008). Involving lengthy production processes and expense, as we see in Chapter 19, wildlife producers need to know their endeavours will be rewarded. According to US film industry analyst Wade Holden, of the 275 documentaries released from 2002 to 2006, only 6 were wildlife documentaries. But their combined gross of $163.1 million was a healthy 26 per cent of the $631 million all released documentaries grossed in that time.[19]

We note the way wildlife film has both fierce advocates and detractors, but one thing that can unite them is resistance to the tendency to anthropomorphise animals, applying the cute human characters of Disney fantasy to the real natural world. One producer so accused, Adam Leipzig, President of National Geographic Films, was a former Disney producer. When he saw the French film *Marche de l'Empereur* in 2005, he quickly acquired the US rights along with Warner and spent six months retrofitting a new soundtrack, with lush music and a honey-toned commentary from film star Morgan Freeman, that many feel falls into that anthropomorphic trap. But Leipzig knew what he was doing, spotting that the indomitable mating rituals of the bipedal, serially monogamous emperor penguins, fighting the icy Antarctic conditions, would work as a heart-warming metaphor for the audience and their life battles. *March of the Penguins* (2006) took $77,437,223 at the box office, making it the fifth highest-earning documentary of all time, (not allowing for inflation-adjusted figures).[20] *USA Today* declared 2006 the year of the penguin as other media and films, like *Happy Feet*, rushed to climb aboard the anthropomorphic bandwagon.[21] *The Washington Post* coined the term 'fuzzumentary' for the new breed of cute documentary, in a feature entitled 'March of the Cuddly-Wuddly Documentaries'.[22] Leipzig remains unrepentant – and rich:

> I think of our new genre as reinventing both the documentaries and the adventure movies of the past. I don't call it a documentary, I call it a 'wildlife adventure', because this is a movie you go to because it's fun and entertaining, not because it's, quote, good for you.[23]

However, Leipzig's next 'wildlife adventure', *Arctic Tale* (2007) tanked – barely making a million. Husband and wife team Adam Ravetch and Sarah Robertson had spent 15 years filming polar bears and walruses in their disappearing Arctic habitat, but were persuaded by Leipzig that to reach the lucrative family audience, they needed to cut out the predatory kills that sustain these animals, and accept a schmaltzy commentary talking as if from the animals' point of view, by Queen Latifah. One typical review commented: 'its pre-teen targeting and vague hipster posturing ultimately distracts from what might have been a more effective message movie'.[24] The general view was that the attempt to be 'cute' and avoid the 'offensive' realities of nature red in tooth and claw had fatally undermined the real story, about the effects of global warming. It seems that audiences willing to take a lecture from Al Gore are unwilling to be patronised while, if it is the Disney audience the producers want, they would be better sticking to the cute cuddly animals that don't kill for a living.

God and me

Ironically, released only a few months before *Arctic Tale* was a film which explores most graphically these contradictions at the heart of the American soul. Timothy Treadwell was a failed actor and recovering alcoholic who had discovered a personal mission, spending 13 summers camping among grizzly bears in Alaska, observing them and 'protecting' them, though it was unclear what protection he afforded them. For the last six seasons he had filmed the bears and himself talking to them and, increasingly, talking to the camera as he struggled to make sense of his life and mission. 'If there is a God, he would be very pleased with me', he muses. 'Am I a great person? I don't know – I am different'.[25] After Treadwell, and his unfortunate girlfriend, had eventually – and predictably – been attacked and eaten by one of the bears, the German filmmaker Werner Herzog took the surviving footage and interlaced it with interviews with Treadwell's friends, family and less sympathetic opinions, like the air taxi pilot who says 'He got what he deserved'.[26]

What *Grizzly Man* reveals, apart from insane bravery and some beautiful footage of the bears, is a man spinning out of control, with increasingly paranoid rants at the human race, weirdly offset by his hugely sentimental anthropomorphisation of the bears (and foxes), with names he has given them and the constant iteration of that overused phrase 'I love you'.

Werzog's brilliant editing of this material shows Treadwell's disintegrating personality all too clearly but, while distancing himself from the Disneyfication of the bears, he avoids judging him. It manages not to be voyeuristic – Herzog wisely chooses not to use the extant soundtrack of the fatal attack – but still has an epic quality that makes it some kind of contradiction of the American dream: a narcissistic ego confronts the wild frontier and is literally consumed by it. The *Guardian* called *Grizzly Man* a 'tragicomedy', commenting 'It is poignant, it is beautiful, and it is absolutely hilarious'.[27] But the *Chicago Sun-Times* probably spoke for more when it reported: '*Grizzly Man* is unlike any nature documentary I've seen; it doesn't approve of Treadwell, and it isn't sentimental about animals.'[28]

Austin comments on the way that the dual authorship – Treadwell's voice and character and Herzog's off-screen commentary – has the effect of endorsing through framing Treadwell's personality and perspective. He writes of Herzog's 'status as an auteur' and 'unmistakably physical' presence. 'Herzog's voice is privileged as a locus of authority throughout *Grizzly Man*, even while it avoids the claims of the "voice of God" by repeatedly stressing the subjectivity of the speaker.'[29] Without Herzog's intervention, it is hard to see how this inchoate mass of material could have been welded into a powerful instrument. His bleak worldview and dispassionate view of the extremes of nature focus the conflicting aspects of Treadwell's life. As Herzog himself comments, 'There is such a thing as poetic, ecstatic truth. It is mysterious and elusive and can be reached only through fabrication and imagination and stylisation'.[30] It is the frame that mitigates what Renov calls the 'healthy skepticism regarding all documentary truth claims' that he feels such autobiographical works breed.[31] He believes that 'the *very idea* of autobiography challenges the *very idea* of documentary',[32] but notes the growing popularity of what he calls 'domestic ethnography' among 'the plurality of autographic modalities'.

There are certainly a lot of 'first person' documentaries about. A supreme example is Jonathan Caouette's *Tarnation* (2004), in which the filmmaker, a gay artist in his 30s, painfully revisits his mentally ill mother and the home video he has been shooting of their disturbed lives since the age of 11. Towards the end, he confronts his inability to escape his own history in what Renov calls 'a vivid and gut-wrenching soliloquy'.[33] This is the apotheosis of the self-regarding, first person video diary film, whose confessional and self-revelatory features' currency may owe more than a little to the self-centred focus of reality television. The ascendancy of 'I' and 'me' in public discourse has mirrored the decline in abstract, thesis-driven communications and, despite the appetite we have just seen certain films feeding, it is no surprise that there is this parallel development in self-referential approaches to contemporary concerns.

Among other films that have used the form with some success in the cinema, Andrew Jarecki's *Capturing the Friedmans* (2003) deploys home video and personal testimony to reveal the damage wrought on him and his family, when their father and his elder brother were arrested for possessing child pornography and abusing boys. Perhaps the unsavoury subject kept the box office to a modest $4 million, despite very supportive reviews. Nathaniel Khan's *My Architect: A Son's Journey* (2003) is a personal voyage of discovery around the man who 'made' him but whom he barely knew, the late architect Louis Khan, who left behind several fine buildings and three families. As Megan Ratner's review observes: 'Nathaniel Kahn's somewhat ambiguous role in his father's life seems to allow him to avoid conclusions and, most admirably, to resist the modern American mania for "closure".'[34] A more conventional narrative leads to an anticipated end in Morgan Spurlock's *Super Size*

Me (2004). Spurlock uses his own body as a test vehicle for the effects of an exclusive McDonalds diet, with inevitable effects on his weight and health. In 30 days he acquires 24.5 pounds and liver damage; the film acquires nearly $30 million at the box office worldwide.

War and peace

Errol Morris's *The Fog of War: Eleven Lessons from the Life of Robert S. MacNamara* (2003) approaches the subjective in a different way – interviewing his subject for 23 hours and refusing to have any other 'balancing' testimony in his film. As John Kennedy's and Lyndon Johnson's Secretary of Defense, MacNamara had been one of the most powerful and reviled men in America during the 1960s Vietnam War, having formerly been involved in the atomic bombing of Japan that concluded the Second World War, and subsequently running the World Bank for 11 years. Morris did not want such a unique history to be diluted by alternative views, and the effect of the ruminations of this intelligent, morally compromised man is mesmeric, though he never admits to regret or error. The material is illustrated by beautifully edited archive and specially shot footage – of the kind with which Morris established his filmic signature in *The Thin Blue Line* (1989) – but the key framing device is the 11 graphic chapter heads, or 'lessons' which extrapolate the morals of the story, like latter-day commandments. These were all the more telling as the film was released in the year the US and UK invaded Iraq, another example, like Enron, of the power elite's blindness to the prophetic lessons of history. There is no evidence that George Bush ever saw the film, whose lessons would have advised him:

1   Empathize with your enemy . . .
2   Rationality will not save us . . .
3   There's something beyond oneself . . .
4   Maximize efficiency . . .
5   Proportionality should be a guideline in war . . .
6   Get the data . . .
7   Belief and seeing are often both wrong . . .
8   Be prepared to re-examine your reasoning . . .
9   In order to do good, you may have to engage in evil . . .
10   Never say never . . .
11   You can't change human nature.[35]

If he did, he was only paying attention around Lesson 9. But Morris can take cold comfort from the entry into the political phrase book of his film's title. When video footage emerged of President Bush being warned of the dangers of Hurricane Katrina, disproving claims to his not having been told, the White House's proffered excuse was about the difficulties of decision-making in 'the fog of war'.[36]

The so-called 'war on terror' has produced a spate of documentaries that talk to the conscience of America, reflecting growing public disillusionment with the war. Errol Morris's *Standard Operating Procedure* (2008) and Alex Gibney's *Taxi to the Dark Side* (2007) both deal with the same subject: the abrogation of law and morality that has allowed torture and inhumanity to characterise the American military overseas in this period. Both are devastating works that prefigure President Obama's famous inauguration pledge to reassert 'the rule of law and the rights of man'. 'We will not give them up for expedience's sake', he said, having introduced the subject with the line 'We reject as false the choice between our safety and our ideals'.[37] This false polarity had been established in 2001 by George Bush in his response to 9/11, when he had stated: 'You're either with us or against us in the fight against terror.'[38] As both films show, that simplistic reductionism led to murder and misery that debased even the norms of war, but each work takes a different approach.

The earlier *Taxi to the Dark Side* starts with idyllic images of rural Afghanistan and the story of Dilawar, an innocent young taxi driver who was caught up in an American sweep of suspected insurgents and ended up being tortured and dying in the Bagram air base prison. As was routine, the military announced that his was death 'by natural causes'; and the truth would have remained buried with him had not Seattle journalist Carlotta Goll uncovered a death certificate that had ticked the box 'Murder'. The military doctor's notes said that Diliwar's legs had been 'pulpified' and, had he lived, 'it would be necessary to amputate' them.[39] Eventually, some of the soldiers responsible were brought to trial, but only after the photographs of subsequent abuses at Abu Ghraib were publicised two years later.

Gibney interviews the men who were charged, who calmly detail their systematic abuse of prisoners, but still seem mildly affronted that they were brought to justice, when they were only doing what they were told to do, in circumstances for which they were not well prepared. They seem morally cauterised, but the real strength of the film is the weight of testimony Gibney produces to prove that the real responsibility ran all the way to the top, with no one but these frontline grunts taking the blame. The captain who was in charge of their unorthodox interrogation techniques, one Carolyn Wood, had unsurprisingly moved on to Abu Ghraib and, far from being arraigned, was eventually given a staff position. The military high command are shown in a conspiracy of official denial, and the line of culpability is drawn all the way to the Pentagon and the White House, namely Defense Secretary Donald Rumsfeld and Vice-President Dick Cheney. Rumsfeld is shown to have signed off on torture techniques, and Cheney is seen defending waterboarding and talking of 'using whatever methods are necessary'.[40] There is a mass of compelling evidence here, if slightly overwhelming at 105 minutes; but the poignant appearance over the end credits of Gibney's late father – a Second World War naval officer who died during the film's making – lamenting the loss of law and honour that had sustained his service in the darkest hours, reasserts a moral sensibility whose absence is the film's subject, the eponymous dark side that has cost countless lives.

Morris's *Standard Operating Procedure* concentrates more – and more sympathetically – on the soldiers involved in the infamous pictures from Abu Ghraib. It was the pictures that fascinated Morris, recognising that they tend to be read as the whole ugly story, when they are really only a partial window on a much more murky, complex scene, as Gibney has shown. 'Why not talk to the people who took the photographs?' he thought.[41] His favourite subject turns out to be the young soldier who took most of the pictures, Sabrina Harmon. Morris is fascinated by Harmon's naivety, allowing herself to be seen addressing the camera with a thumbs-up over a dead detainee – a gesture also used by Lynndie Englander alongside abused Iraqis – but he appears to accept her assurance that she was recording these images as a matter of responsibility:

'I was trying to expose what was being allowed . . . what the military was allowing to happen to other people,' Harman said. In other words, she wanted to expose a policy;

and by assuming the role of a documentarian she had found a way to ride out her time at Abu Ghraib without having to regard herself as an instrument of that policy.[42]

Perhaps it does not matter whether Harmon really snapped her shots with a mission, or guilelessly recorded her banal everyday experience like every other aficionado of Facebook. Certainly she failed to appreciate the iconic value of the image she took of the hooded figure on a box, his arms outstretched to electrical wires, casually remarking 'He wasn't even being tortured'. As Morris observes, this suggestive image carries more punch than the more graphic ones; and Hermon's distinction shows how far normative standards had slipped. Another female co-defendant, Megan Ambuhl, confirms that 'standard operating procedure' – the usual military code that specifies every aspect of behaviour in a given circumstance – was absent, thereby giving the troops *carte blanche*. 'They couldn't say that we broke the rules because there were no rules'.[43] Yet both her and Hermon were convicted of dereliction of duty, with Hermon sent to prison for six months for five further counts, including conspiracy and maltreating detainees.

Deploying Morris's trademark stylish reconstructions and interviews delivered direct to camera, via his own Interrotron invention, this is a threnody for the lost innocence of the soldiers – many of whom were convicted and incarcerated – and the perversion of justice, where only them and no senior officers were charged; the officers were only reprimanded. As Morris astutely comments: 'No one has ever been charged for abuses at the prison that were not photographed.'[44] One of the soldiers make the point in the film:

You can kill people off camera, you can shoot people, you can blow their heads off. As long as it is not on camera, you're OK; but, if it's on camera, you're done.[45]

Baker calls Morris a 'philosopher/filmmaker'[46] – he was a History and Philosophy college major – and it is this sense of a restless intelligence behind the lens, seeking out philosophical truths more than the prosaic facts of more conventional journalistic approaches, that distinguishes his documentaries and makes them seem so apt for the uncertain twenty-first century. He says:

I have this old-fashioned American belief that it's wrong to punish the little guys and to let the big guys get off scot-free. But it's not a film that lectures to anybody about anything. It's an attempt to take you into a strange world and an opportunity to think about it. In a way, I feel hopeless to address the war as a whole. I don't know how to do that, even. I do know how to look at individual stories in the hopes that they tell us something about the nature of this war. People may not, ultimately, be outraged by torture, but I think people are outraged by a certain level of unfairness.[47]

According to *Taxi to the Dark Side*, even after the revelations of Abu Ghraib, 35 per cent of Americans thought torture was acceptable. Presumably they believed, like the soldiers, that it was justified because it saved American lives. But, as Gibney's film reminds us, people will say anything they think the torturer wants to hear to get him to stop, so information acquired this way is rarely reliable; torture has never been proven to have saved a single life. Most tellingly, Gibney offers the statistics that, of all the men seized in Afghanistan, only 5 per cent were picked up by US troops; 93 per cent were exchanged for bounty by local warlords, and only 8 per cent proved to be Taliban.[48] Most, like the luckless Daliwar, were innocents, entitled not just to the Geneva conventions that the Bush regime repudiated, but to the due process of law. Despite President Obama's explicit re-endorsement of these commitments, questions remain how animated the American public is by those values. At the time of writing, in early 2009, both films had only taken a quarter of a million dollars at the box office, a disappointing fraction of the $5 million *Standard Operating Procedure* cost to make, funding that Morris freely admits was only made possible by his Oscar for *The Fog of War*.

Good Christians

Yet, at the heart of the War on Terror, was a righteous zeal, exemplified by the born-again Christian George Bush and the imminent Catholic convert Tony Blair. Although the United States guarantees religious freedom, not least through constitutionally separating religion from state, overt piety is a prerequisite of high office – and that means professing the Christian faith that some 75 per cent of the electorate still follow. To get elected, Barack Hussein Obama had to disprove the serious political slur that he was a Muslim. Across the Atlantic, although the United Kingdom has an established church, less than 10 per cent visit it and Prime Minister Tony Blair suppressed discussion of his faith because 'In our system people think you're a nutter'.[49] It was not least Bush's religiosity that fed deep scepticism in the British public and parliament at Blair's desire to join the American crusade in Iraq, necessitating the specious 'dodgy' dossier of so-called facts that convinced the parliamentary waverers. Although a traumatised America lapped up Bush's ringing address, when he stepped up to the lectern at the National Cathedral service of remembrance for the dead of 9/11, he gave the kind of speech more likely to strike fear in Britain:

> God's signs are not always the ones we look for. We learn in tragedy that His purposes are not always our own. Yet the prayers of private suffering, death in our homes, or in this great cathedral, are known and heard and understood . . . This world He created is of moral design.[50]

The words were undoubtedly framed to give comfort to the substantial forces of Christian fundamentalism who have been fighting, with some success, to introduce 'intelligent design', aka Creationism, onto school curricula and into public discourse. All this is necessary background for an international audience trying to understand why the two top box office documentaries in the USA during the election year of 2008 concerned religion. *Expelled: No Intelligence Allowed* was released in April and was fast becoming the top grossing documentary of 2008, only to be pipped to that mantle by *Religulous*, despite the latter's only coming out in October. *Expelled* is fronted by actor-writer-columnist-chat show host Ben Stein, and purports to be a serious attempt to explore systematic discrimination against 'the intelligent design movement', not just by the scientific community but also by government, business and the education system. Stein disposes of Darwinian evolutionists as 'some very smart people [who] believe that we are nothing more than mud animated by lightning'. He goes on to suggest that his freedom to believe in God is being throttled by a quasi-fascistic orthodoxy – he even deploys shots of Hitler and marching storm troopers.[51] In a portentous opener for the film, Stein advises:

It is my duty to get the word out, before it is too late . . . Watching this film will get you in a heap of trouble. You will lose your friends, you may lose your job. You better leave right now. But, if you do leave, will there be anyone left to fight this battle?[52]

This is a knowing invocation of Pastor Martin Niemöller's famous verse about German intellectuals' craven inertia at successive Nazi pogroms, *First They Came . . .*[53] On a Christian chat show promoting the film, Stein invoked the Holocaust before concluding: 'Science leads you to killing people.' There is more, much more, in this vein, as the entertainment paper *Variety* noted:

Even more offensive is the film's attempt to link Darwin's 'survival of the fittest' ideas and Hitler's master-race ambitions (when in doubt, invoke the Holocaust), complete with solemnly scored footage of the experimentation labs at Dachau. Evocations of the Berlin Wall, treated as a symbol of a bullheaded scientific establishment on the verge of collapse, are equally fatuous.[54]

Amid many savage critiques, that of the movie website Rotten Tomatoes was typical: 'Full of patronizing, poorly structured arguments, *Expelled* is a cynical political stunt in the guise of a documentary.'[55] But the equal virulence of supportive blog comments goes some way to explaining the $7.7 million taken at the box office for what is, without doubt, a badly made film. As one large, scary American says in Bill Maher's *Religulous*, 'You start to dispute my God, you gotta problem!'[56]

Religulous, directed by *Borat* director Larry Charles, comes at the subject of belief from the other end of the spectrum. Fronted by well-established comic, satirist and current affairs chat show host Bill Maher, this takes a humorous, but no less serious, pop at the stranglehold Christians have on so much of American public life. Releasing the film a month before the presidential election, Maher is not unaware of the political moment. On a chat show promotional appearance he says:

I preach the gospel of 'I don't know'. And people have had so many religious movies – they've had *The Passion of the Christ*, they've had *The Robe*, they've had *The Ten Commandments* – isn't there time for one, for the tens of millions of rationalists who think like I do, who are afraid that the Sarah Palins of the world are taking over? We've had eight years of George Bush and a faith-based administration. We can't afford another.[57]

In the same interview, Maher observes that 'Religion is a giant elephant in the room of comic gold'.[58] Even at previews, he found that there was an audience craving the release that such humour brings, even as it clearly disappoints Bush supporters. Alongside more serious interviews, Bush archive makes a predictable appearance: 'I believe God wants everybody to be free, that's what I believe. That's part of my foreign policy.' As director Larry Charles says:

This is a provocative subject that is also very, very funny. We're taking a subject that's not usually used for comedy and making it a big laugh-out-loud comedy. Most movies poke gentle fun [at religion]. We stab it to death.[59]

But elsewhere, Maher speaks of a more serious motivation, claiming that:

> Religion makes people not respect other people's lives. We are a nation that is unenlightened because of religion. I do believe that. I think that religion stops people from thinking. I think it justifies crazies. I think flying planes into a building was a faith-based initiative. I think religion is a neurological disorder. If you look at it logically, it's something that was drilled into your head when you were a small child.[60]

The box office takings of over $13 million suggest there is a substantial and receptive audience for this kind of fare, presumably similar to the healthy audience for the relatively unfettered cable chat shows like *Real Time with Bill Maher* on HBO and *The Daily Show with Jon Stewart* on Comedy Central. Despite that, both these religious documentaries would probably have been turned down by Angus Macqueen. Certainly *Expelled* falls well below UK television standards, and *Religulous*'s territory had already been covered more rigorously by Channel 4 with Richard Dawkins's *The Root of All Evil?*.[61]

Surviving

However, Angus Macqueen has left Channel 4 and most of the established documentary filmmakers have left the BBC. Many see their future following in the footsteps of previous generations, moving into drama like Nick Broomfield, Paul Greengrass and Kevin Macdonald. Macdonald's Documentary Oscar for *One Day in September* (1999) and his Best British Film BAFTA for *Touching the Void* (2003) made his transition to mainstream features inevitable, not least because both those successes had substantial dramatic elements in them. *Touching the Void* is the dramatised reconstruction of mountaineer Joe Simpson's extraordinary true story of surviving broken legs and a presumed fatal fall in the Andes. The dramatised scenes are wonderfully done, beautifully shot and lit, and full of real tension, but the real drama is in the documentary footage. It is narrated to camera by Simpson and Simon Yates, the climbing partner who had to cut Simpson's rope, anticipating it would kill him. As an extraordinary documentary series in the first year of Channel 4 demonstrated – *Surviving* (1982) – there is nothing more dramatic and revealing than looking into the eyes of people as they recall extraordinary, life-threatening events that they have survived. This was the approach that producers Darlow Smithson anticipated when originally intending a modest television documentary, but the television rights came expensively bundled with the cinema rights, making it uneconomic unless the bigger film was envisaged. From such serendipity great results can flow, as the enhanced finance allowed the film's awe-inspiring reconstruction of the mountain adventure.

A similar formula was employed by James Marsh's *Man on Wire* (2008), an equally successful documentary about Frenchman Philippe Petit's epic high wire walk between the twin towers of the World Trade Centre in New York in 1974. Petit and his accomplices tell the story, intercut with contemporary footage and black-and-white reconstruction of every aspect save the walk itself. Attracted by the challenge of defying death, just like mountaineers, Petit had conceived this dream as a youth, before the towers had even been built. The film shows previous illegal wire-walks between the towers of Notre-Dame cathedral in Paris and the pylons of the Sydney Harbour Bridge, but the film is really about the pursuit of an obsession, and the meticulous years of preparation and planning that preceded its 45-minute realisation. In that, it is not unlike filmmaking, with the inordinate investment of creative thought, time and resource in an event which passes all too quickly. Neither Petit nor the film can answer directly the question everyone asked: Why did he do it?, but his friend and accomplice Jean-Louis Blondeau and his girlfriend at the time, Annie Alix, come closest, becoming overcome with emotion as they recall the events of 34 years before. Annie says there was always a 'naughty boy' side to Petit, rebelling against his strict upbringing:

> He's excessive, creative – every day is like a work of art for him . . . What excited him most about this, aside from it being a beautiful show, was that it was like a bank robbery. And that excited him enormously.[62]

Petit was arrested after his performance, but charges of trespass and endangerment were dropped in return for doing a bit of juggling for the cameras. Petit became an instant folk hero, changing his life, not necessarily for the better. A groupie took him to bed immediately following his release, and later he split up with his girlfriend. We see little of his life now, other than him practising alone on a wire in a field, as he had done with his friends around him before New York. Facing the wire 400 feet over Manhattan, he had said: 'If I die, what a beautiful death: to die in the exercise of your passion'. The tragedy seems to be that in achieving his dream, his life did end, everything since being anti-climatic, down to earth, looking back as the film does. His closing words suggest he still lives in the bubble of that youth:

> Life should be lived on the edge of life. You have to exercise rebellion, to refuse to taper yourself to rules, to refuse your own success, to refuse to repeat yourself, to see every day, every year, every idea as a challenge. And then you're going to live your life on the tightrope.[63]

Conclusion

Documentary producers live their life on a financial tightrope. Both these films had UK Film Council backing and the investment of broadcasters: *Touching the Void* had Film4 and *Man on Wire* the BBC *Storyville* strand and Discovery Films. *Void* also had a UK distributor on board, Pathé Films. By the time of writing, *Touching the Void* has taken nearly $14 million at the box office worldwide, *Man on Wire* $4.5 million in its first year.[64] These film's success, albeit rare for UK documentary, is instructive in a number of ways. They conflate two of the key elements we have seen prove popular on the big screen: the epic drama of man's conflict with nature in extreme conditions, and deeply personal reflections on the human condition, both in the service of a great narrative. It fulfils that all-genre requirement, 'a good story', and contemporary audiences do not seem to be disaffected by knowing the outcome at the start. Just as Treadwell's death is foretold early in *Grizzly Man*, Simpson's and Petit's survival is apparent from their appearance on film, but these features only serve to reinforce the human interest in their stories. Both address the camera and are compelling characters, engaging not least for their human imperfections.

With the honourable exception of Al Gore, the professorial know-all – familiar as documentary presenters of the past – has largely been replaced by the affable, amusing character you might imagine yourself drinking with in the pub. Michael Moore and Bill Maher bring more of themselves to the screen – Maher interviews his 88-year-old mother in *Religulous* – and make difficult material more digestible. Although these are exalted individuals, much better paid than their more authoritative forebears, their informality relates to the self-referential culture of the time. Just as Morgan Spurlock mainlines hamburgers as a supersize 'me', audiences want larger than life figures who are still 'one of us'. By comparison, it is not just his Neanderthal views that make Ben Stein a throwback to a former age. However, the economic recession has undermined the funding on which the US cinema documentary has tended to rely, much of it from trusts and foundations that wisely did not anticipate profits, the above successes being the exceptions rather than the rule. As Carla Mertes warned, at the January 2009 Sundance festival, for which she programmes the documentary section:

> Foundations and endowments are shrinking, and they're going to be granting less. Documentary filmmakers have traditionally been a very DIY, proud breed, and so I think we'll still see plenty of content being produced, but I think we'll see fewer big-budget, highly produced docs – the *Touching the Voids* and *Man on Wire*.[65]

Increasingly high-quality and affordably available digital technology offers the main avenue of hope in straitened times, and it remains to be seen whether one innovative documentary much discussed at 2009 Sundance stimulates other low-budget originality. Anders Østergaard's *Burma VJ* (2008) combines the work of 30 undercover video-journalists, sponsored by the Oslo-based broadcaster the Democratic Voice of Burma, who bravely used small cameras and mobile phones to record the 2007 uprising led by monks in Burma, and its brutal suppression by the military junta.[66] This was the footage smuggled to Western news media via the internet, but here edited with great skill and augmented by a strong music score and some controversially reconstructed scenes. These left the otherwise sympathetic *Time* reporter Andrew Marshall feeling 'manipulated'. He comments:

> No scene is labelled as a reconstruction. Some are convincingly real, yet others are so simply betrayed as re-enactments by their wooden dialogue that soon I began to anxiously question the authenticity of *every* scene.[67]

It is ironic to end on the old saw: what is documentary 'truth', and how much invention is permissible before it discredits the message. There clearly is much more public support for the partial and personal documentary today, but whether that taste will continue to support the polemical will only be discovered by the box office.

Expert briefing – getting your film seen

While many filmmakers regret the progressive passing of the traditional process of documentaries being commissioned and 100 per cent funded by broadcasters, many others feel liberated by the opportunities afforded by new media and new platforms. Campaigning documentary-maker Jeremy Gilbey says:

> The great news is, we are becoming the commissioning editors now and we have the power to show our own work and we don't need to rely on anyone else . . . the opportunity to tell our stories in the way that we want, with nobody stopping that happening.[68]

That does not just mean uploading to YouTube – although that route has proved so effective for some that the big corporations are muscling in to claw back some of the action. There are plenty of similar sites sharing video material, from myspace.com and revver.com to www.metacafe.com. Many other sites offer different propositions, but are liable to come and go rather faster than book publications, so any of the following information will need to be independently verified:

1   **Quality and control**: www.vimeo.com is an online community of video makers committed to 'respectful, ethical, non-commercial' high-quality video sharing, supporting HD in 1280 x 720 resolution. A free account allows limited upload and storage, while the 'vimeo plus' option offers ten times the storage, unlimited HD upload and domain privacy control of where your videos are embedded on the web. This is exhibition level video sharing, but steadfastly opposed to mercenary motive and unlicensed sampling.

2   **Programming approach**: http://blip.tv has evolved the concept of the online 'show' – a continuing series of video outputs in any style or any subject that parallels the rolling brand of a TV show, but leaves you the content creator in the driving seat. The site offers the choice between a free account and a pro account, and a host of easy to follow tips, from production to distribution and advertising revenue prospects. Advertising, calculated by micro payments on page hits, remains currently the only established form of revenue stream for such web-share sites, but business models are still developing.

3   **Paid TV transfer**: http://current.com introduced the notion of an online site that is an open audition to provide content for the associated cable/satellite channel Current TV.[69] People are invited to make and post video 'pods' of between 3 and 7 minutes – under the rubric VC^2, viewer created content – which, if selected for broadcast, will be paid a small fee (c. $300) in return for the signing over of all rights. The bigger attraction is that some video creators then develop an ongoing and more lucrative supplier relationship with the channel. Another addition – 'make TV in less than 10 mins' – is the invitation to upload viewer comment on the latest film and music releases, which are aggregated on a weekly review show. They also show how to make money from making video ads.

4   **UK TV web access**: While the BBC was the first UK broadcaster to run a comprehensive website – and BBC News continues to invite newsworthy user-generated content – it is Channel 4 that has targeted the aspirant documentary-maker with their 4docs site. This invites 3-minute films of both traditional and experimental kinds, as well as running occasional themed competitions. Its most successful

products have been transmitted on the main channel, in the 3-Minute Wonder slot. At the time of writing, the upload feature is disabled pending a revision of terms of engagement, but the site is a useful source of advice and information and is still visitable at: www.channel4.com/culture/microsites/F/fourdocs/how_to/index.html. ITV Local, which invited videos about community affairs and interests, is currently in abeyance, but promises to relaunch eventually at itv.com/local.

5 **Listings and festivals**: For those more concerned to get on to the film circuit, there are open access sites such as www.archive.org and filmmaker sites such as www.withoutabox.com. The latter lists 3,000 festivals on 5 continents and helps filmmakers manage submissions to them. Withoutabox can arrange listings for films that qualify on www.imdb.com (the movie database), with clips, trailers and stills, and the prospect of adstream revenue. It can also connect filmmakers to www.create space.com, an on-demand distribution platform, which prints, rent and sells DVD copies of films via Amazon. The advantage of this proposition is that it replicates the whole marketing, copying and distribution process, that is often more costly and time-consuming than production, and for which few filmmakers are well-prepared.

6 **Virtual festivals and new vision**: With growing bandwidth, the possibility of the internet not just being the communications interface, but the sole platform, comes closer, with the prospect of changing values. Second Life has yet to host a film festival, but the thought is not inconceivable. http://diydays.com is the website of the Californian 'open source' filmmaking community, which gave birth to the online 'discovery and distribution' film festival in July 2008: http://showcase.fromhereto awesome.com. This is one expression of a form of film distribution/sharing that sees itself as post-capitalist, and certainly post-copyright. They are closely connected to the organisation The League of Noble Peers, who made the *Steal this Film* documentaries, which chart the movement against intellectual property rights and for peer-to-peer file-sharing protocols. One site that aims to aggregate the thinking and practical advice to filmmakers wishing to operate in the open source environment is http://workbook project.com. They are not ignoring financial issues and are building a database on funding and distribution, as well as clearance and delivery issues. The workbook project tag-line neatly encapsulates the more holistic approach today's filmmakers must adopt: 'fund::create::distribute::sustain'.

18 Biopics

....

biopic n. a film based on the life of a famous person

The biographical picture has been a staple of cinema and television since their respective beginnings. In the early days of cinema, it was the most obvious way to approach history entertainingly, offering the leading stars of the day the opportunity to shine as great names, with the most commonly revisited subjects being Napoleon Bonaparte and Abraham Lincoln. John Ford's *Young Mr. Lincoln* (1939), with Henry Fonda in the title role, is still rated one of the greatest biopics of all time, and Abel Gance's silent epic *Napoléon* (1927) has been recently revived, not least due to its then revolutionary use of hand-held cameras and novel three-screen projection, a system called Polyvision, which pre-dated Cinerama by a quarter of a century.[1] As with the whole field of docu-drama (Chapter 15), many directors' approach to real life subjects is to convey authenticity by the use of documentary techniques. Others have used television's once liberal documentary franchise to re-imagine lives in dramatic fashion. Coming at the biopic from either side of the notional drama-doc divide, this popular form further demolishes simplistic distinctions between fact and fiction. It is a porous divide, which the revival of cinema documentary and the growth of celebrity culture have done much to further breach. While biopics may have been popular from the 1920s, only a handful were made each year. Between 2000 and 2009, some 1,000 were made according to one listing,[2] but it is an inexact term and one chapter cannot attempt a comprehensive review. I shall concentrate here on specific territories that have found in the biopic a fruitful genre, such as music – which has evolved from the lives of the great composers to a current obsession with hip-hop artists – and politics – which has developed from heroic hagiographies of Lincoln to the embrace of less sympathetic subjects, from Hitler and the Baader-Meinhoff gang to Presidents Idi Amin and George W. Bush.

A creative force
....

The filmmaker who did more than any other to develop the biopic initiated his film career in the BBC's Music and Arts Department. Ken Russell had worked in dance and photography before his first amateur short, *Amelia and the Angel* (1958), secured him a job working on the arts magazine *Monitor* for Huw Weldon. He found the job making short documentary inserts for this studio show stifling, and the insistence on using stills and archive in preference to dramatisation too limiting. With flamboyant persistence, he managed to persuade his producers to let him make a dramatised documentary about the English composer Edward

Elgar, who had been out of fashion for 30 years. Russell's *Elgar* (1962)[3] had five actors playing him at different stages of his life, but without them talking. The film was credited with helping stimulate a revival of interest in the composer[4] and led to more Russell commissions. Among the most notable are *The Debussy Film* (1965)[5] and *Isadora Duncan: the Biggest Dancer in the World* (1967).[6] The latter prompted Karel Reisz's feature biopic *Isadora* (1968), starring Vanessa Redgrave and winning her Best Actress at the 1969 Cannes Film Festival, which boosted the biopic as a cinema genre and Russell's prospects of making features. He had already made the unsuccessful *French Dressing* (1963) and the Michael Caine spy caper *Billion Dollar Brain* (1967), but his main income was still made at the BBC, where his best work was yet to come.

Song of Summer (1968) sees the full flowering of Russell's genius as a creative interpreter of others' lives, the first such documentary driven by dramatic dialogue.[7] The film is about the last six years of the life of the then nearly blind composer Frederick Delius and his young amanuensis Eric Fenby. Shot on a shoestring, with the Lake District standing in for Norway, this is an emotionally intense study with outstanding performances from Max Aitken as the cantankerous composer and Christopher Gable as the musical hand hired to translate his thoughts. The film was based on Fenby's autobiography *Delius, as I Knew Him*, and Fenby happened to be on set when their original meeting was filmed.[8] Russell turned around to find him wet with tears. 'It took me right back to 1927', he said. 'It was exactly how it happened!'[9] What Fenby was referring to was the emotional truth Russell had intuited, through his total immersion in the music and sources, not that the art director had got the furniture right. Bad biopic is routinely meticulous about design details and has a hole where the heart should be, the empathy for the central characters and what moves them. This was what Russell brought to BBC Music and Arts: he got inside his subjects, whereas the traditional podium arts tended to observe them from outside. Not that Russell was impervious to design features. His first wife, Shirley, was the award-winning costume designer for all of his films up to their divorce in 1978. Re-released on DVD in 2002, Russell says of *Song of Summer*, in the director's commentary, 'This is the best film I ever made. I don't think I would have done a single shot differently'.[10]

'If *Song of Summer* aims for the sublime, *Dance of the Seven Veils*[11] aims for the ridiculous', according to the BFI's Michael Brooke.[12] It is a biopic of the German composer Richard Strauss, but Russell did not like him or his music, calling him 'bombastic, sham and hollow'. Worse, Strauss was seen as a Nazi fellow-traveller, so one of many grotesque sequences in the film has SS thugs carving a Star of David on an old Jewish man's chest, while Strauss encourages his orchestra to play louder to drown out the screams. Once again, Russell emerges as an innovator, because it had not occurred to many people that a biopic could also be a hatchet job, an act of iconoclasm bound to attract fury among the subject's supporters. But it was a time, as Russell remembers, where the BBC had the confidence to stand by such extreme creativity. *Dance of the Seven Veils* was, he says:

> A good example of the sort of film that could never be made outside the BBC, because the lawyers would be on to it in two seconds. I would have had to submit a script to the Strauss family and his publishers Boosey and Hawkes would have come into it, and it would never have happened. The great thing about the BBC is that the quickness of the hand deceives the eye. Before anyone can complain, the film is out. But the price you pay with a really controversial film is that it's usually only shown once.[13]

The Strauss family and publishers were predictably outraged and the film has been banned ever since. Russell continued to court controversy throughout his long feature filmmaking career, with the healthy taste for bawdy that characterises British drama from the Middle Ages to the English Revolution, but which had largely disappeared beneath the crinolines of nineteenth-century prudery. In his autobiography,[14] Russell recalls one of the defining moments of his film-going childhood as being interfered with by a stranger while watching Walt Disney's *Pinocchio* (1940), when he would have been 13. He ran from the cinema, not to return for a long while, but it may well have contributed to his obsession with transgression, his constant desire to shock and disturb through excess, his commitment to interfering with his audience's minds and responses. Joseph Lanza writes that Russell's creative life is 'the product of what Freud calls a "disfigured reminiscence", rife with conflicts between the horrific and the erotic, the neurotic and the visionary, the puerile and the profound'.[15] Russell's stylised feature on the seventeenth-century French church and its infection by witchcraft, *The Devils* (1971), with its orgiastic nuns blasphemously abusing Christ and the Cross, is the film most frequently cited as evidence of a perverted and diseased mind, attracting widespread censorship and condemnatory criticism on release, but overdue for positive reappraisal.[16]

Much of Russell's work is closer to the writer whose work he has three times dramatised, D.H. Lawrence, who died dismissed as a pornographer, but who has since been rehabilitated as one of the greatest English writers, not least since the landmark trial in which *Lady Chatterley's Lover* was judged not to be obscene.[17] *Women in Love* (1969) won an Oscar for Glenda Jackson and a nomination for Russell as Best Director, cementing his position as a leading director, who turned out eight major features over the next seven years, five of them biopics. *The Music Lovers* (1970) was an inventive biopic of the Russian composer Piotr Tchaikovsky, quite distinct from the Russian Igor Talankin's lusher and more reverential biopic, *Tchaikovsky* (1969), which had also been nominated for the previous year's Oscars, for Best Foreign Film. *Savage Messiah* (1972) was a biopic of the French sculptor Henri Gaudier-Brzeska; *Mahler* was a biopic of the Austrian composer and conductor; *Lisztomania* (1975) presented the life of the Polish composer Franz Liszt as a pop star, played by the Who singer Roger Daltrey; and *Valentino* (1977) also deals with celebrity through the loves and losses of the greatest film star of his day, Rudolf Valentino, played by the equally fêted dancer Rudolph Nureyev. Subsequently, Russell made occasional returns to television to make documentaries about composers whose music inspired him: Ralph Vaughan Williams (1984),[18] Anton Bruckner (1990),[19] Arnold Bax (1992)[20] and Bohuslav Martinu (1992).[21]

It is an extraordinary body of work, and one still needing critical re-evaluation, since Russell's commercial star waned and, following several low-budget flops in the 1990s, he has been reduced to making videos in his own back garden. In Italy he would have received the lifetime lionisation of a Fellini or Pasolini; in Britain he has accepted the fleeting nature of fame and fortune with good grace. In his 80s, he remains passionate about film, willingly engages with students as a visiting professor of film studies, and writes copiously for *The Times*. Reticent about over-intellectualising his *oeuvre*, he occasionally lets slip a shard of light that illuminates what he was aiming for in all these musical biopics. One such bonbon is a very prescient recognisation of the sensory orchestration that contemporary students of multimedia identify. 'Design-conscious directors elevate films to art, conjure poetry and deliver emotional impact through synaesthesia, an evocation of other senses and of meaning through stimulating the visual.'[22] Another is that 'When it comes to TV, fiction is truer than fact', as Russell lambasts the takeover of reality television and the disappearance of imaginative drama. He also has little time for the rash of biopics and docu-dramas:

> The number of feature films that boast 'based on true events' is becoming legion, threatening to topple the lost art of storytelling. I am guilty of making some of these 'true stories' myself, having been brought up as a documentary filmmaker.[23]

He invokes the religious power of parable and the narrative skills of Dickens, and is clear that the fact-fiction divide was never significant for him; it was always the story and what it had to tell us:

> Stories are our soul containers, our initiations into a higher perspective. In them we carry our values, our lessons for living, our hopes and dreams, our felt remembrance of humanity as a noble experiment. Stories give us a glimpse of why and who we are. Without them, we feel separate, unrooted, restless, isolated, mistrustful. Through stories, we remember history, communicate feelings, honour the individual and better understand the world which nurtures and redeems us while it also tries and tests us.[24]

Music of other spheres

Bob Dylan, some of whose performances are mentioned in Chapter 14, bestrides the American music landscape like a colossus and has had his fair share of biographical cover. *No Direction Home* (2005) was Martin Scorcese's magisterial two-part documentary just covering the early period of Dylan's career, from his arrival in New York in January 1961 to his first 'retirement' from touring, following his motorbike accident in 1966. The project had originated with producer Jeff Rosen, who had shot ten hours of revealing interview with Dylan in 2000. Scorcese came on board the following year to shape the film, select from the mass of archive and edit a compelling weave of music and comment, from Dylan and his associates. The Alaskan film academic Daniel Griffin is typical of the many critics who find this a fine documentary, with much original detail, but one that does little to unpick the mystique that is Dylan:

> At about the mid-way mark of Martin Scorsese's astounding documentary *No Direction Home*, about the rise and coming-of-age of the American songwriter Bob Dylan, an interviewee articulates the central mystique of Dylan in the simplest way possible, but with the most accurate words I have ever heard concerning the songwriter: 'As he stands on the stage, he somehow conveys to us with his songs that he knows something that we do not' . . . In a way, *No Direction Home* is a continuation of what Scorsese attempted to do in *The Last Temptation of Christ* (the controversial reinterpretation of Jesus' life), *Kundun* (concerning the early years of the Dalai Lama), and *The Aviator* (the Howard Hughes biopic), which was to rip prominent historical characters out of their own clichés and stereotypes and provide them with human faces that only enhance the myths that surround them.[25]

Earlier in Dylan's career, D.A. Pennebaker, who made the documentary of Dylan's 1965 tour, *Don't Look Back*, went on to shoot a documentary about the man himself for ABC's

Stage 67.[26] *Eat the Document* was later edited by Bob Dylan with Howard Alk, the cinematographer who had shot both films, as an extraordinary stream of consciousness that ranged through the artist's psyche. You get flashes of the different Dylans behind the shades: the exhausted legend on tour, the musician jamming with Robbie Robertson and Johnny Cash, the star riding around with John Lennon, and the gnomic figure blanking the press and the audiences who disliked his going electric. But it was all too weird for ABC, who canned it, and the film did not see the light of day until a New York museum showing in 1972.[27] Its shaky camerawork and non-sequential editing would be seen as virtually obligatory today, and is clearly no impediment to enthusiastic viewers, as the impressions on the YouTube site indicate.[28]

A clip of Dylan playing his harmonica taken from *Eat the Document* ends the much more recent cinema biopic, *I'm Not There* (2007). Todd Haynes has clearly drawn on the fragmented self of Dylan that emerges from documentaries such as *Don't Look Back* and *Eat the Document*. His novel approach has six leading actors all playing different aspects of Dylan, reflecting both the influences that made him and the contrasting characteristics within his persona. First a young African-American boy is travelling as 'Woody Guthrie' to meet the aging folksinger, the real Woody Guthrie, on his deathbed. Ben Whishaw plays Arthur Rimbaud, the romantic French poet whom Dylan idolises. Christian Bale plays Jack, the Greenwich Village folk singer who hung out with Joan Baez (Julianne Moore) and is seen later as Pastor John, a born-again Christian. Heath Ledger plays Robbie, the star who gets in deep with other women and loses his wife. Most surprisingly and compellingly of all, Cate Blanchett plays Jude, the electric troubadour of 1965, whom folk audiences called 'Judas'. And Richard Gere plays the ruminative older man, Billy. Some scenes draw directly on extant documentary material, including one in a bootleg out-take of *Eat the Document*, where John Lennon counsels a stoned Dylan in a limousine, saying: 'Do you suffer from sore eyes, groovy forehead, or curly hair? Take Zimdon! . . . Come come, boy, it's only a film. Pull yourself together'.[29] Later, the hell-raising Jude is seen passed out on the floor, with poet Alan Ginsburg standing over him, saying 'He's been in so many psyches', by which time the audience has pretty well grasped the multiple personality idea. At the end, the older Billy is on a train, where he finds the guitar that the young Woody had played, and delivers the final words of the film:

> People are always talking about freedom, and how to live a certain way. 'Course, the more you live a certain way, the less it feels like freedom. Me? I can change during the course of a day. When I wake, I'm one person; when I go to sleep I know for certain I'm somebody else. I don't know who I am most of the time. It's like you got yesterday, today and tomorrow all in the same room. There's no telling what's going to happen.[30]

Generally it is safer to dramatise the lives of subjects who are dead, and cannot sue for libel. But by no means all dead musical legends have been immortalised in biopic form – no Jimi Hendrix, no Janis Joplin, no Frank Zappa, no Bob Marley, no Miles Davis – while plenty have been poorly served by the genre. John Lennon has had more than his fare share of dire drama: *Birth of the Beatles* (1979), *John & Yoko: A Love Story* (1985), *In His Life: The John Lennon Story* (2000) and *The Killing of John Lennon* (2007). Even *Backbeat* (1994), Ian Softley's revisitation of the Beatles' first tour to Hamburg and the loss of original bassist Stuart Sutcliffe, is overrated. Val Kilmer's Jim Morrison in *The Doors* (1991),

Flex Alexander's Michael Jackson in *The Man In The Mirror: The Michael Jackson Story* (2004), Kevin Spacey's Bobby Darin in *Beyond the Sea* (2004), Leo Gregory's Brian Jones in *Stoned* (2005) and Jonathan Rhys Myers's *Elvis* (2005) are among those to which the music publishing companies probably wish they had not licensed the rights.

But there have been two hit music biopics in recent years that have reignited the studios' belief in the form. Jamie Foxx's portrayal of Ray Charles in *Ray* (2004) won him a best Oscar, and the following year Reece Witherspoon won Best Actress for her June Carter in *Walk the Line* (2005), while her co-star as Johnny Cash, Joaquin Phoenix, was pipped to Best Actor by another biopic performance. Philip Seymour Hoffman impersonating the writer Truman Capote in *Capote* (2005) won. A third nominee for that award was David Straithairn for his Ed Murrow in *Good Night and Good Luck* (2005), making it a biopic year at the Oscars. The following year, *Dreamgirls* (2006) – a thinly disguised music biopic about the Diana Ross and the Supremes story – kept up the tradition with a clutch of Oscar nominations and a win for Jennifer Hudson as Best Supporting Actress. And also in 2006, another biopic of Truman Capote, Douglas McGrath's *Infamous*, with Toby Young as Capote, was released, compounding a period of Hollywood's manic mining of twentieth-century creative lives. Where once the cinema might have had one big biopic in a year – like Alan Parker's *Evita* (1976) – they now come out in clutches, imitation being the sincerest form of flatulence.

Pop goes the biopic

In Britain, the form remains more low key and closer to its documentary roots. Alex Cox's *Sid and Nancy* (1986), about the fatal relationship between the Sex Pistols' Sid Vicious and his girlfriend Nancy Spudgeon, clearly owes more to the social realism of earlier English 'kitchen sink dramas' shot by former documentarists such as Lindsay Anderson and Karel Reisz. Anton Corbijn's *Control* (2007) conjures that milieu even more by being shot in Macclesfield in black-and-white. It is a bleak, but beautifully observed, biopic of the troubled Joy Division singer Ian Curtis and his suicide at the age of 23, with a knockout debut performance from Sam Riley as the epileptic, bipolar civil servant, who had difficulty adjusting to his newfound stardom. It also has a powerful script by Matt Greenhalgh, based on Curtis's widow Deborah's memoir, *Touching from a Distance*.[31] Matt Greenhalgh since wrote the script for the latest Lennon biopic, *Nowhere Boy*, being shot in Liverpool at the time of writing under the feature debut direction of Sam Taylor-Wood, the artist responsible for the *David* video installation described in Chapter 16. This is a more localised version of the circularity noted in Hollywood, less imitative, more reflexive, as Britain's relatively small creative community finds common cause and pursues connections, not least those set rolling by Michael Winterbottom's *24 Hour Party People* (2002), his loving tribute to Manchester's Factory Records and late progenitor, Tony Wilson, who was also central to the Joy Division story.

Joy Division were arguably the most important post-punk band, so it is fitting that they are also the subject of one of the best rock documentaries, Grant Gee's *Joy Division: Their Own Story in Their Own Words* (2008). A stylised, formal, cerebral film, it beautifully captures the roots, flavour and impact of their music, the ultimate expression of Factory Records that, in Paul Morley's words, 'made Manchester international, made Manchester cosmic'. It recaptures with photographers the concrete landscapes that the music sprang from, finds extraordinary archive shot throughout the band's brief career, and memorialises the creative genius and tortured soul who was Ian Curtis. It is driven by interviews with the other members of the band and many of the people that were around them, from Curtis's mistress Annik Honoré to their albums' gifted graphic designer, Peter Saville. Above all, the music is given the space to breathe and demonstrate how refreshingly contemporary it sounds 30 years on. As Morley says, 'it's one of the last true stories in pop . . . in a business-dominated culture'.[32]

In the United States, the success of biopics such as *Ray* is compounded by an unusually high secondary income from DVDs, bought by both film fans and music lovers. *Ray* surpassed its US box office takings of $74 million with a combined tally of $80m from DVD, video sales and rental, earning more than $40m (£22m) on the first day of the DVD's release alone.[33] Other music films rushed into production, many of which were instantly forgettable, lucky to make it to DVD. One of the few successes was Darnell Martin's *Cadillac Records* (2008), the story of Chess Records, the crucible of rock and roll, with an outstanding performance as Muddy Waters by Jeffrey Wright, with Mos Def playing Chuck Berry and Beyoncé Knowles as Etta James. The trailer promised the commercial buzz of 'Sex', 'Danger' and 'Freedom', but what this collective biopic delivered was stories as emblematic escapes from the rough south side of Chicago to the fame and fortune that would buy a Cadillac. The nerve that the film hit, even more than *Ray*, was that aspirational quality of such stories which, like reality television, enable an audience to vicariously fantasise about personal transformation, seeing people like themselves making it. None of us will be Napoléon, or Mahler, but many young people still nurture the dream of achieving riches through music or sport.

The most obvious musical arena to profit from this promise is hip-hop. Ironically, it was a white Englishman who made the first notable feature documentary in this area. Nick Broomfield's *Biggie & Tupac* investigated the deaths in 1997 of these two hip-hop artists, implicating Suge Knight, head of Death Row Records, but also suggesting an FBI conspiracy to undermine the growing power of such black icons, by stoking conflict between the East and West coast stars. It deploys Broomfield's trademark doggedness, featuring a lot of himself on camera and soundtrack, but sticking his gun mic. into some dangerous places, asking some awkward questions and getting some intriguing answers. Although generally well received, there is an obvious undertone to reviews at the time, which wonders why it takes this 'whiny' Englishman to bumble into African-American community affairs, imparting a very outside view of a musical milieu he has clearly come to lately.[34] It helped kick start a home-grown hip-hop movie industry.

Notorious (2009) is the dramatised retelling of the story, produced by Biggie Smalls Wallace's manager, Wayne Barrow. Inevitably it takes Biggie's side, bigging up his claim to be 'the greatest rapper in the world', and seeing the story very much from an East coast perspective. But while the tribal conflict produces the necessary drama, the real message is in the lines that everyone wants to hear: 'I'll make you a millionaire by the time you're 21' and 'Can't change the world unless we change ourselves'.[35] The rush release of the DVD, just three months after the film's opening, underlines the demand for a biopic which charts the stratospheric rise from small-time drug dealer to big-time superstar, prompting a rash of hip-hop films to go into production. *Notorious* screenwriter Cheo Hodari Coker has now written a screenplay *Tougher than Leather*, the biopic of another slain hip-hop star, Jason 'Jam-Master Jay' Mizell of the influential hip-hop trio Run-DMC, who was shot dead in his recording studio in Queens, New York, on 30 October 2002. New Line is developing

Figure 18.1
The posthumous biopic of
Biggie Smalls, *Notorious*
(2009), gives the East side
view

Straight Outta Compton, an urban drama about N.W.A. (Niggaz With Attitude), the hip-hop group that helped pioneer the gangsta rap movement in the 1980s and early 1990s. But negotiations apparently broke down between Morgan Creek, producers of a planned biopic on Tupac Shaker, and his family's firm, who hold the rights to his estate, despite a documentary, *Tupac: Resurrection*, making $8 million for Paramount back in 2003.[36] It is ironic that the battles of the streets are now being re-fought in the boardrooms and mansions the music has bought.

Sporting heroics

The African-American command of the sports field has ensured a longer and richer tradition of inspirational biopics. Rafer Johnson was the first black to captain the American Olympic team, carrying the flag into the Olympic stadium in Rome in 1960. Mel Stuart's documentary *The Rafer Johnson Story* (1961), chronicles the struggles and injuries the great decathlon champion endured on his way to this crowning moment of his career. Photo-journalist William Klein's documentary *Muhammed Ali: The Greatest* (1974) celebrates the most famous African-American of all as he regained his world title from George Foreman in the epic 'Rumble in the Jumble', the improbable title fight in Zaire for a $10 million purse put up by the dictatorial President Mobutu. American history director Ken Burns (mentioned in Chapter 3) has contributed to the restitution of the African-American's pre-eminent contribution to sport, with his boxing documentary *Unforgivable Blackness: The Rise and Fall of Jack Johnson* (2004) and his nine-part documentary series *Baseball* (1994). Baseball has produced more biopics than any other sport, from *The Jackie Robinson Story* (1950) – a film starring the African-American in his own life story as the first black in major league baseball, whose arrival at the Brooklyn Dodgers prompted racial abuse, including from his own team members, and even death threats – to the documentary about the Cuban Red Sox legend Luis Triant, *Lost Son Of Havana* (2009). As Howard Good writes:

No other film genre so represents the traditional American belief that any person can achieve success through dint of his own efforts. The belief seems especially pronounced in baseball biopics, whose heroes play what is, after all, 'the national game'.[37]

Robert Redford is reportedly remaking as a big budget feature *The Jackie Robinson Story*, while the original remains one of the most highly rated baseball biopics for its inspirational tale. Redford's film follows on the equally inspirational feature *The Express* (2008), about the tragically short-lived African-American football back Ernie Davis, who was the first black to win the Heisman Trophy,[38] and who became an icon for the developing civil rights movement. However, for sporting heroics, it is hard to beat the heavyweight world champion Muhammed Ali, whose renunciation of his 'slave name' Cassius Clay, joining the Nation of Islam and his refusal of the draft for the Vietnam War, earned him widespread respect, as did his unparalleled deftness in the ring and his ready wit. In 1999, he was named 'Sportsman of the Century' by *Sports Illustrated* and 'Sports Personality of the Century' by the BBC. The big screen biopic followed. Michael Mann's *Ali* (2001), for which Will Smith won the Best Actor Oscar, surfed a popular millennial need for such paeans to the human spirit:

> From the virtuoso opening to the climactic re-creation of Ali's 1974 Zaire bout with George Foreman, Mann achieves a thrilling mix of action and analysis, exploiting and transcending both boxing movie and biopic conventions with a master's ease. Crucially, the film is less a psychological study than a case history of America, from the passing of the Civil Rights Act to the end of the Vietnam War. While Smith's Ali is wholly credible as an individual determined to define and remain true to himself, despite a widespread expectation that African-Americans and sportsmen should quietly accept their lot, the character also becomes an index of racial, religious, political and social changes.[39]

Nothing could be further from this than the documentary made about a later world heavyweight champion, Mike Tyson, which premiered at the Cannes Film Festival. Edited from 30 hours of interviews by director James Toback, *Tyson* (2008) is a brutally frank, uncommented portrait of a former champion with no claim to heroic standing, having been ignominiously banned for biting off part of the ear of the man who finally stole his crown, Evander Holyfield. Before that, Tyson had served three years for the rape of an 18-year-old beauty queen, which crime he denies in the film. But throughout the film Tyson is refreshingly honest about his misogyny, the rough upbringing that fuelled his aggression, and the profligacy that frittered away an estimated $400 million before he filed for bankruptcy:

> I try to live my life the way I possibly can – be who I am. If they [people] really accept me, they are going to have to accept me as I am – my highs and my lows, my vulnerabilities and who I am as a human being. It's just who I am. It is hard for me to put on a front. This is my acting front, this is my outside front, this is my private front – I am just an all-out type of individual and that is what you get.[40]

Such dystopian narratives in the field of dreams have taken longer to achieve popularity.

The movie biopic now most frequently cited as the best of all time is Martin Scorsese's film about the white boxer Jake La Motta, *Raging Bull* (1980), for which Robert de Niro put on 50 pounds and which won him his Best Actor Oscar. The ultimate anti-hero, the foul-mouthed La Motta is consumed by self-hatred, sibling rivalry, insane jealousy-provoking abuse of his wife, all leading to his inevitable decline and failure. As mentioned in Chapter 13, the American audience prefers its heroic characters to be loveable, not crippled by demons, so this film at first met a very mixed reception. But its brave central performance, brilliant editing and cinematography have since seen its acceptance as one of the best films of all time.[41] Shot in a stark, crisply contrasted black-and-white, the film feels like a stylised documentary; the visceral screenplay, by Mardik Martin, was based on Jake La Motta's autobiography of the same name,[42] and the film is rooted in the Italian-American community that Scorcese knows and films so well.

Writing at the time of its re-release in 2007, David Thomson defies the popular reading of *Raging Bull* as being an all too violent and realistic portrait of boxing, and sees in it something much darker: Scorcese's obsession with the conflicted sexuality of American machismo.

> The raging bull here is a figure of remorseless and overwhelming sexual insecurity . . . the Scorsese film is unmatched, in his own work and in American film in general, as a portrait of sexual dread in that vaunted American male, the gangster.[43]

La Motta, at 86, was still alive in 2007 and content with the unheroic portrait that had given him a new lease of life. Too often, the heroic subject retains too much control over the rights in their image to allow a 'warts-and-all' picture, be it drama or documentary. It remains to be seen how independent Spike Lee's long-awaited feature documentary biopic of the richest sportsman of all time, the basketball legend Michael Jordan, who made a second fortune from advertising Nike, can afford to be.

Political impostures

Spike Lee previously shot a major feature biopic in *Malcolm X* (1992), the story of the radical African-American leader that took 25 years to make. Producer Martin Worth had bought the rights to Malcolm X's autobiography in 1967, two years after he was assassinated, and then went through countless writers, stars and would-be financiers before the film was eventually green-lit by Warner Brothers, with Denzel Washington as Malcolm X.[44] Worth had managed to make an Oscar-nominated documentary with material in 1971, also called *Malcolm X*,[45] but remained committed to the possibilities of the feature:

> It's such a great story, a great American story, and it reflects our society in so many ways. Here's a guy who essentially led so many lives. He pulled himself out of the gutter. He went from country boy to hipster and semi-hoodlum. From there he went to prison, where he became a Muslim. Then he was a spiritual leader who evolved into a humanitarian.[46]

Although the movie had become one of the 'great unmade' for so many years – not least because of studio nervousness about the inflammatory subject matter – when its production was eventually announced it attracted a storm of complaint from the African-American community, who feared that its hero's legend would be tarnished by sensational concentration on his earlier life of crime. Criticism was levied at Spike Lee for being a 'Buppie' – 'a young Black city or suburban resident with a well-paid professional job and an affluent lifestyle'[47]

– with protestors taking to the streets and African-American writers saying things like 'We will not let Malcolm X's life be trashed to make middle-class Negroes sleep easier'.[48] When the film overran its budget during post-production, the bond company closed the production down. So important was this project to the evolving sense of African-American identity that the film was finally rescued when Spike Lee not only donated $2 million of his $3 million fee, but persuaded other leading African-Americans to contribute to the costs, with money gifted by the likes of Prince, Michael Jordan, Oprah Winfrey and Bill Cosby. In this important sense, the film carries greater emblematic value than commercial value; the most valuable biopics are ones that are freighted with such historical significance.

Perhaps consumed by this mission, or merely keen to prove himself to his earlier detractors, Spike Lee announced before the film finally opened that he would prefer to be interviewed by black journalists:

I'm doing what every other person in Hollywood does: they dictate who they want to do interviews with. Tom Cruise, Robert Redford, whoever. People throw their weight around. Well, I get many requests now for interviews, and I would like African-Americans to interview me. Spike Lee has never said he only wants black journalists to interview him. What I'm doing is using whatever clout I have to get qualified African-Americans assignments. The real crime is white publications don't have black writers, that's the crime.[49]

While some editors were outraged, others capitulated, including *Rolling Stone, Vogue, Interview* and *Premiere* magazine, whose editor admitted that Lee had made him think about his staffing policy:

Had we had a history of putting a lot of black writers on stories about the movie industry we'd be in a stronger position. But we didn't. It was an interesting challenge he laid down. It caused some personnel changes. We've hired a black writer and a black editor.[50]

Such is the power of emblematic movies that capture the Zeitgeist and gift their makers a whip hand.

The best of American biopics seem to have that knack of defining a key concern of the age. Mike Nichols's *Silkwood* (1983) tells the story of Karen Silkwood, the plutonium plant worker and trade union activist who, having testified to the Atomic Energy Commission about systematic plutonium contamination, was killed on her way to talk to a *New York Times* reporter. Michael Mann's *The Insider* (1999) is about the tobacco company employee who agreed to go on CBS News' *60 Minutes* and reveal that his employers covered up and exploited their knowledge of tobacco's harms and addiction, only for the show to be cravenly spiked by CBS' commercial considerations. Steven Soderbergh's *Erin Brokovich* (2000) is the tale of the eponymous legal assistant whose relentless investigations revealed the long-term poisoning with chromium of the Hinkley town water supply by the Pacific Gas and Electric Company of California, which cost them $333 million, the largest ever corporate payout in a direct action suit in US legal history. Gus van Sant's *Milk* (2008) follows the fortunes of the gay activist Harvey Milk who, when elected to the San Franciso Board of Supervisors in 1977, was the first out gay to be elected to public office, but who was eventually assassinated by his arch-conservative political rival.

All these firms were about important issues and were both commercial and critical successes, earning Oscars for Sean Penn in *Milk* and Julia Roberts in *Erin Brokovich*. Indeed, it is a truth widely held that the surest route to a winning performance is to take the lead in a biopic. From 2000 to 2008, six of the Best Actress Oscars and five of the Best Actor Oscars went to portrayals of real people. Both the identification with real life people and issues, and the age old narrative of the underdog taking on almighty power, owe much to the documentary tradition, and most of these stories had originally been told in documentary form. The BBC first did the *Silkwood* story in 1978; CBS eventually showed the 1996 Jeffrey Wigand *60 Minutes* in February 1999, when the feature was already being made; and *The Times of Harvey Milk* (1984) had already won a Best Documentary Oscar. The reality that these films reflect is less susceptible to the conventional Hollywood cop-out where, however bleak the scenario from which the story unfolds and however corrupt the powerful agencies involved, good and the plucky individual always triumph in the end. In two out of four of these true stories, the plucky individuals died.

One of the better twenty-first century British biopics also trades in that tradition. Joel Schumaker's *Veronica Guerin* (2003) starts with the brutal slaying of the Irish reporter, shot dead for daring to investigate Dublin's drug trade. The film concludes with an epilogue, which captures the seriousness and significance most films cannot aspire to:

> Veronica Guerin's writing turned the tide in the drug war. Her murder galvanised Ireland into action. Thousands of people took to the streets in weekly anti-drug marches, which drove the dealers out of Dublin, and forced the drug barons underground. Within a week of her death, in an emergency session of Parliament, the Government altered the Constitution of the Republic of Ireland to allow the High Court to freeze the assets of suspected drug barons. Everyone in the Republic of Ireland remembers where they were when they heard that Veronica Guerin had been murdered on the Naas Road.[51]

British biopics are normally much less concerned with heroics, but are also enjoying a boom at the current time. One writer alone has been responsible for a clutch of award-garlanded box office successes that have given the genre renewed momentum. Peter Morgan started as a television writer and his first in this genre was for Channel 4.[52] Stephen Frears's *The Deal* (2003) told the story of the pact struck by Tony Blair and Gordon Brown in 1994, which would give Blair an unopposed run at the Labour party leadership in return for standing down in Brown's favour later. Blair's alleged reneging on this deal, and the ensuing inter-necine war between the two, has been credited with incubating the historical failure of the New Labour government. Morgan returned to similar territory for his first feature film, again directed by Stephen Frears, *The Queen* (2006), which concentrated on events surrounding the death of Princess Diana and Blair's attempts to persuade the Queen to recognise popular sentiment. The screenplay won Morgan an Oscar nomination and Helen Mirren Best Actress for her performance as the Queen. That same year Morgan also co-wrote the screenplay for Kevin Macdonald's *The Last King of Scotland* (2006), originally a semi-fictionalised novel by Giles Foden about Uganda's President Idi Amin, which won Forrest Whitaker an Oscar as the tyrant.

Also in 2006, the prolific Morgan's first play opened at the Donmar Warehouse in London. Ron Howard's *Frost/Nixon* dramatised the revealing 1977 television interviews the disgraced President Richard Nixon gave the world's then leading television political interviewer, David

Frost, in which he tacitly admitted his culpability in the Watergate scandal that had lost him the presidency.[53] Michael Sheen took the role of David Frost and Frank Langella played Nixon, parts they would repeat for the film version directed by Ron Howard. *Frost/Nixon* (2008) carries the subtitle in the French version 'l'heure de vérité' (the hour of truth), and it is a tribute to Morgan's skill that he manages to craft drama out of this 30-year-old moment of truth. Next came *The Damned United* (2009), based on David Peace's book on the late, loud-mouthed football manager Brian Clough's disastrously short 44-day tenure as manager of Leeds United, again with Michael Sheen in the lead.[54] At the time of writing, Morgan is directing his debut feature with his own screenplay *The Special Relationship*, concentrating on the accord between Tony Blair (Sheen again) and US President Bill Clinton. Morgan sees this as the final part of the Blair triptych, with *The Deal* and *The Queen*, and also his swansong in the reality field. 'I'm not done with reality, I'm done with it for the time being', he says, relishing escape from the constant criticism that he gets from pedants about the licence the screenwriter inevitably invokes turning facts into a fictional form:

> People are right to question that. They watch a film that is made with real characters. The message is 'We're hoping you believe us'. You may feel betrayed that stuff has been made up, but that's what makes it exciting. People should question what history is and in whose hands it has been written. Researching *Frost/Nixon*, all the players could agree on the simplest details but they had wildly different interpretations of what happened. Those nuances shape our understanding. One person's history is another person's fiction.[55]

Terror revisited

As Morgan the master knows, it is all about storytelling, fact and fiction being interchangeable for the most part. While I have attempted throughout this book to suggest that this signal point is as true of documentary as it is of drama, it is nowhere more apparent than in subject matter bound to divide its audience. The artist Steve McQueen's first feature film, *Hunger* (2009) is the viscerally observed biopic of the first IRA hunger striker to die in the Maze prison in 1981, Bobby Sands, a heroic martyr to the republican community and a terrorist in the government and security forces' eyes. It has split critics between those who call it 'magnificent' and those who see in it an artist's amoral aestheticisation of violence and misery. None deny that it is beautifully shot and powerfully performed, but the conservative Manhattan freesheet *The New York Press* is typical of the detractors:

> You could use art-major terms like 'transgressive' and 'body-conscious' to justify McQueen's aesthetic (close-ups of cell walls decorated with faeces patterned into a spiral like 1980s serialism; studies of Sands' emaciated torso that suggest anorexic Lucien Freuds). But the fact remains: *Hunger* is tough to watch. It merely rewards one's art snobbery and can only be excused as a series of art postures. And eventually, those postures insult the fact of Sands' death-choice and political sacrifice.[56]

McQueen denies that *Hunger* is either an 'art film' or a 'political film', but an idea that he had been obsessed with since a child. It was 'one of the biggest political events in Britain in recent history' but one that had been 'swept under the carpet'.[57] As an artist working in several different media, it was an idea that for McQueen was most suited to the cinematic form:

It's where the idea leads me. If an idea wants to be manifested in paintings or photographs, then that's where it goes. It dictates its shape to me. It has to be like that. The medium can't dictate to me, it's the idea that has to dictate to me. You are the orchestrator but at the same time you are the facilitator. The idea dictates its shape to me, rather than the other way round. I'm not in love with the 35 mm camera any more than I'm in love with the paintbrush. It's the idea I'm in love with.[58]

It's just a case of being particular with detail. It's all about the essence of situations that can translate to audiences, using the camera in a way that's almost like being blind. What I mean by that is using the camera like fingertips, feeling your way through a situation in order to make language as such. [With] a camera, you can address information that usually doesn't get looked at. It's about how you want to illustrate rather than investigate.[59]

This is an artist who once pushed an oil barrel mounted with three video cameras through Manhattan shouting 'Excuse me!', and who won the Turner Prize for his experimental films in 1999. *Hunger* is distinguished by the artist's vision, with exquisitely framed shots, such as a snowflake falling on bloody knuckles, or a prison officer brushing crumbs from his lap. McQueen had considered shooting the whole of *Hunger* without dialogue, and the first hour of it has little, but then comes The Scene – as it has become known – an extraordinary *tour de force* in which Sands, played by Michael Fassbender, and a Catholic Priest, played by Liam Cunningham, discuss the hunger strike for 23 minutes, including an unbroken 17½ minute single shot, reputedly the longest single take in film (as opposed to video) history. It is a bravura performance and while McQueen is no simple apologist for the IRA – he was a war artist in Iraq – this is a deeply political film, as well as a profoundly artistic one.

Terrorism's intentional ability to divide society seems to make mature reflection on film difficult until a generation later. *Hunger* looks back to the events of 27 years ago; Kevin Macdonald's *One Day in September* (1999) appeared 27 years after the events it portrays, the Palestinian kidnapping and killing of Israeli athletes at the 1972 Munich Olympic Games; and *Der Baader Meinhof Komplex/The Baader Meinhof Complex* (2009) covers the history of Germany's notorious terrorist movement over 30 years before, from 1967 to 1977. Germany's troubled post-War history is only now becoming clear for objective reconsideration. Perhaps unsurprisingly, previous films about the leaders of the Red Army Faction (RAF) – Ulrike Meinhof, Andreas Baader and Gudrin Ensslin – have tended to take sides, often portraying them as folk heroes. Even Christopher Roph's *Baader* (2002) essays a largely unsuccessful, uncritical biopic of Baader on the run.

The most outstanding film from the time, *Deutschland im Herbst/Germany in Autumn* (1978) is a portmanteau project made by some of the leading German directors of the day – including Rainer Werner Fassbinder, Heinrich Böll and Volker Schlöndorff – each meditating in different documentary modes on the existential angst that the Red Army Faction had revealed in German society. The film commences with the funeral of the recently slain Daimler-Benz corporation president Hans-Martin Schleyer, shot with nods to the Leni Riefenstahl style to remind us of his Nazi past, and ends with that of the RAF leaders Andreas Baader, Gudrin Ensslin and Jan Carl Raspe, who had reportedly committed suicide but whom the left believe had been assassinated in prison, thus describing the nihilistic arc within which Germany was caught at that time. The most remarked upon sequence is the Fassbinder directed segment, where he talks revealingly and melancholically of his inability to escape the stranglehold of Germany's history. (Fassbinder died of heart failure just five years later, at the age of 37.)

The Baader Meinhof Complex has generally been received well both in Germany and abroad because it achieves a perspective which suggest the culture has finally escaped that stranglehold, even though the last vestiges of the Red Army Faction remained operative until 1999. Written and produced by Bernd Eichinger, who had previously recreated the last days of Hitler in the award-winning *Der Untergang/Downfall* (2004), the film is based on Stefan Aust's definitive biography and a heap of documentary archive and evidence.[60] Shot in documentary style, *The Baader Meinhof Complex* manages vividly to capture the bullet-ridden violence of the terrorist group without portraying them as anti-heroes of the Bonnie and Clyde kind. As Schleyer's son, also Hans-Martin, said to the German newspapers, it was a portrait of '*ein gnadenlose, mileidslose, Mörderbande* – a merciless, ruthless, killer gang':

> Aber nur so kann ein Film auch jungen Leuten vermitteln, wie brutal und blutrünstig die RAF in jener Zeit vorging.

> But [it's] the only way a movie can also teach young people how brutal and bloodthirsty the RAF was being at that time.[61]

Italy has also revisited the demons of its recent past in biopic form. Paolo Sorrentino's *Il Divo* (2009) is subtitled *The Spectacular Life of Giulio Andreotti*. It chronicles the corruption and downfall during his seventh premiership of Italy's longest serving politician, and essays a noirish examination of Italy's bankrupt soul. As one critic remarked, American political biopics are either there 'to humanise an otherwise historically reviled figure' or to burnish an existing halo. The American audience is not accustomed to the cinematic pulverising of the loathsome:

> With its scenes of bodyguarded prowls down Rome's empty streets en route to late-night church confessions, its fetishistic straight-razor shaves, its super close-up reflections in cat's eyes, it's clear that 'Il Divo' aims more for baroque horror than straight political bio. Andreotti is even haunted by a ghost of sorts: that of Aldo Moro – the left-wing former prime minister kidnapped and assassinated by the Red Brigades in 1978, and for whom Andreotti refused to negotiate – an apparition and manifestation of his guilt. And for a while the film's evil elegance works: the swoony steadicam shots through his labyrinthine quarters and classical, centered, almost fascistic framing emphasizing grand moral dissolution.[62]

The New York Times saw *Il Divo* as more of 'a blood-soaked comic opera', in the tradition of Scorcese and Coppola.[63] Ending with Andreotti admitting 'direct and indirect responsibility' for 236 deaths between 1968 and 1984, *Il Divo* gives the megalomaniac these paranoid words in justification:

> We cannot allow the end of the world in the name of what is right. We have a task, a divine task. We must love God greatly to understand how necessary evil is for good. God knows it, and I know it too.

This medieval divine dualism received a religious revival thanks to twenty-first-century terrorism, and duly surfaces in Oliver Stone's George Bush biopic, *W* (2008), with his 2003 State of the Union line, 'You're either with us or you're with the terrorists'. This was Stone's third presidential biopic, following *JFK* (1991) and *Nixon* (1995). He told *Variety* he did not want to make a straightforward anti-Bush polemic:

> Here, I'm the referee, and I want a fair, true portrait of the man. How did Bush go from an alcoholic bum to the most powerful figure in the world? It's like Frank Capra territory on one hand, but I'll also cover the demons in his private life, his bouts with his dad and his conversion to Christianity, which explains a lot of where he is coming from. It includes his belief that God personally chose him to be president of the United States, and his coming into his own with the stunning, pre-emptive attack on Iraq. It will contain surprises for Bush supporters and his detractors.[64]

Journalist detractors, keen to find Stone over-egging the pudding, were astonished to find that all the most improbable scenes in *W* were verifiable, and that Stone had left out some of the more extreme stories for fear that incredulity would undermine the audience response. Truth, as the current bittersweet taste for biopics attest, is not just stranger than fiction, but sometimes unbareable.

Television times

While the screen world continues to blur the boundaries between documented fact and indubitable fiction, television has walked a different path. Despite the occasional serious journalistic documentary series, for instance memorialising the premiership of Tony Blair as he departed office – *The Blair Years* on BBC, a three-part series with David Aaronovich interviewing Blair,[65] and the single documentary *The Rise and Fall of Tony Blair* on Channel 4 written and presented by Andrew Rawnsley[66] – television has fallen into more of a paint-by-numbers approach. Initially, the A&E Channel in the United States started a long-running series called *Biography* in 1987 (following a brief forerunner CBS made in 1962), which did straightforward historical biopic documentaries on the likes of George Washington. Discovering the huge taste for American history that Ken Burns has also served (Chapter 3), the series prospered and was eventually spun into a whole Biography Channel in 1999.

By this time, the agenda had expanded from history to include figures from popular culture and even run lighter lives of the likes of Santa Claus. Writing on behalf of the Parents Television Council in 2006, Christopher Gildemeister regretted the programme's 'mind-numbing focus on current celebrities like Britney Spears'.[67] Worse, it was no longer suitable for children, he commented, as the channel's schedules were tricked out with reruns of series such as the crime drama *Cold Case Files*, biographies of serial killers, and *Notorious*, about mothers who kill their children. He also noted that other, formerly 'improving' channels had followed the same gory path, with Discovery Channel running a series of biopics of the most heinous serial killers, *Most Evil*.

The Biography Channel rebranded in 2007 as *bio*, with the new tagline 'True Story', and is also available in the UK courtesy of Sky. While *Biography* was in its original heyday, Channel 4 launched a long-running strand called *Secret History* in 1991, which took a (for Channel 4 traditional) revisionist approach to history documentary, often controversial biopics of leading political figures of the recent past, from *Harold Wilson – The Final Days* (1996) and Lyndon B. Johnson in *Hello, Mr. President* (1997) to less savoury stories with grabby titles like *The Porn King, the Stripper and the Bent Coppers* (1998) and *The Nazi Officer's Wife* (2003).[68]

In 1994, the BBC launched *Reputations* in response, a series more clearly defined as an historical biopic strand, and one intended to either rehabilitate or undo established historical reputations. The series first aired on BBC2, then moved with much of the serious factual output to BBC4, where *Reputations* still runs as an occasional title, often profiling recently dead entertainers with interesting sex lives that were off limits when still alive, such as Liberace, Frankie Howerd and Kenneth Williams. These featured in a season of programmes, including dramas and arts documentaries, BBC4 ran in 2007 under the umbrella title *Hidden Lives*. This season also included the dramatised Kenneth Williams biopic *Fantabulosa!* (2007), again starring the ubiquitous Michael Sheen, and an *Arena* documentary on the playwright *Joe Orton: Genius Like Us*, originally made in 1982. One advantage of the multi-channel environment is that programmes like these, previously only shown once, now have a much longer shelf-life; but some producers protest that commissioners increasingly favour name recognition as the only guarantee of attracting audiences in the fragmented market, meaning that the same old names keep coming around. For a while no season went by without another programme being made about, but normally not with, David Beckham.

Conclusion

The reductive routine of much such television is merely a video equivalent of what journalists used to call 'a cuttings job', a tired rehash of readily available material. It is a happy accident that 'biopic' rhymes with 'myopic', so short-sighted is much of this work. But the more creative end of the biopic business reflected a simultaneous revival of biography as a creative literary endeavour, becoming one of the most profitable publishing genres. As William Roscoe Thayer's seminal work *The Art of Biography* notes, biography pre-dates the novel by nearly 1,500 years. He goes back to the start of time and notes Man's evolution as a self-conscious being, journeying from 'the outward to the inward'.[69] He reminds us of the great Greek biographer Plutarch, and the lesser Romans Tacitus and Suetonius, whom he denigrates as pandering 'rather too much to scandal and gossip', much like the *bio* channel today. He then drops, like a fragrant grenade, the name of President Theodore T. Roosevelt, whom he happened to be chatting with, and who said:

> How strange motives are! When you did a certain thing, you thought that a single, clear reason determined you, but on looking back you see instead half a dozen mixed motives, which you did not expect at the time.[70]

Thayer says that it may be 100 years or 200 years before the biographer gains sufficient perspective to do an objective job, and even film seems to require a generation to achieve that remove. That distance is what allows Roosevelt's other motives to emerge, that insight which the ambitious filmmaker wants to distinguish their effort, whether it is an imaginative screenwriter like Peter Morgan or a film artist like Steve McQueen. Biopic tells us what it is to be a man, or a woman, in a particular time, what drives and influences them, what a life that merits that interest is truly worth. As Ken Russell established, it is not just a few facts confirming celebrity; it is, or should be, a work of art.

Expert briefing – the art of distillation

Reading a thick, 600 page biography of someone, it is a daunting challenge to see how that may be distilled into one film of any length. In many cases, you will not even have the luxury of someone else having at least prepared the ground in this way. Yet it is possible to extract the life-work of a much-published academic in one short film and have them both content and yet worried that 'nothing is left out'. So how do you go about approaching a documentary biopic?

1   **Get to know your subject**: If they are alive, there is no substitute to time spent talking with them, not just about their work and primary concerns, but also about their private lives, family, distractions and enthusiasms, getting to know how they live, the people, places and things they value. These are what will let you inside the character, giving the human context and telling detail that will enliven your film. If the subject is dead, or unwilling to participate, you can still access that material through friends, business associates, writings about them and other extant material.

2   **Read around your subject**: It is not enough to know the bare bones of their personal story. You need to know what else has been written and made about them, what other people think and say about them, where they fit in their particular firmament. Conflict with another leading light in their field – be they athlete, artist, politician or scientist – may give you the dramatic dynamic you need. Do not rely on the subject alone to give you the story and insight. You will be making the film to frame their picture within the gallery of public value, so make sure you have triangulated the landscape from all the relevant perspectives. As with interviewing generally, it helps to have done this preparation before meeting the subject, so they know you know and they can trust you.

3   **Interrogate your research**: It is easy to get swamped in intensive research, so you need to do more than merely annotate notes, record and log interviews, quotes and references. You need to have people with whom you can discuss that research, preferably not just production team equally immersed in the material, but fresh minds such as your partner or friends, whose interested response, or lack of it, will be a better indicator of what features and facts can grab attention and should make the cut. Were you making a documentary about the innovative Australian composer and pianist Percy Grainger, his sado-masochism and the fact that he had his bedroom set up with mirrors and cameras to record his brutal flagellation by his wife in obsessive detail, meticulously logged including lens settings, would likely get anyone's interest, whether or not they were interested in the music.[71]

4   **Know your archive**: There is a vast amount of film resource available, but often at high cost. You need to know what you can access and afford, and plan that use from the start. So vital is this knowledge that top-end broadcast biopics routinely employ specialist film researchers, whose knowledge and expertise in negotiating copyright contracts is invaluable to the production.

5   **Think in pictures and sound**: All your research from the start should be not least a search for landscapes, locations and key shots that will encapsulate the essence of your subject and storyline. Like McQueen, use the camera as a sensory apparatus to explore the texture of the scene and listen to its rhythm. Sound should equally inform your thinking, from diegetic sound to whatever abstract sound may convey interior

thoughts and emotions. Composers and musicians obviously supply their own score, but music can unlock the story of any subject. The moment you find the right music for your character, or for a key scene in your story, you may well have identified the tenor of your film. At other times, it may be a single shot, a particular line of dialogue or a mood, but it is the 'light bulb moment' you need to illuminate the pathway through the mass of matter in your mind. Only then are you ready to write your script, and it does not arrive until you are ready.

6 **Know your mind**: One reason for unreadiness is that the director/writer has yet to arrive at a clear perspective on their character, they are still confused by the material, they may veer between loving and hating him or her. You need to make up your mind and decide what you think, define your angle and refine your approach accordingly. You may have been driven by an agenda which requires a controversial, iconoclastic or revisionist position to be adopted, but that still necessitates a personal relationship with the subject. A simplistic hatchet job will be no more insightful than an uncritical hagiography. Sir Francis Drake may have been no hero and no better than a ruthless pirate, but why? And would you have acted any better in his position?

7 **Find a frame**: Few biopics successfully cover a whole life, better a contained time frame that encapsulates the life through its most testing time. This need not be a narrative straitjacket; flashbacks and other reflexive devices can be used to open up the frame, but the opportunity to study key moments in detail, rather than a whole life viewed like a drive-by shooting, is clearly preferable. Decide what the single most vital moment in the life story is, and thus your key scene, and work the arc out from there. This may be the start, the apex or the resolution of your film, but the story should roughly equate to that classic three-act structure, with a beginning, middle and end (though not necessarily in that order, as Godard says).

8 **Drop the togas**: If your subject is historical, there should be a clear decision as to whether this is a dramatic or a documentary biopic. Although there remains a current tendency to lace every history documentary with actors in costume, these frequently fail to communicate much beyond the programme's budgetary limitations. Although he has been forced to submit to this imperative, Dr. David Starkey's programmes on Henry VIII demonstrate what history is really about, reinterpreting documentary evidence in such a way as to communicate his passion and its importance without dullness. A passionate advocate, good contributors, and access to the relevant documentary evidence and other archives can make more lasting impact than extras in doublet and hose, or re-enactment armies failing to draw blood.

9 **The minimum need to know**: Successful office politicians use this maxim to define how much information they impart to colleagues and bosses, but it is equally valuable in scripting biopics. Knowing everything, you then need to divest yourself of all but the most salient facts. The script should follow a narrative line, drip-feeding the least information necessary to understand the evolving story. Aim to communicate as much as possible by visual clues, but leave the audience to intuit as much as possible rather than bludgeoning them with commentary. Design interviews to convey as much information as context requires within answers, obviating the need for contextual information.

10 **Script and storyboard**: All the above work should be distilled into a lean working script and, especially if working with creative collaborators, some form of pictorial storyboard, to ensure that everyone is working to the same end. Of all documentary

forms, the biopic clearly needs that level of rigour in planning, if the project is not to disappear beneath a mound of unfocused material and designer facts.

11 **Expect to disappoint**: People's fame, particularly in contemporary celebrity culture, is in large part a projection of their public's aspiration and anxiety, so a filmmaker messing with this is bound to upset the fans. Stars, just like politicians, have their spin doctors who try to control their image and challenge any media that is off-message. Navigating the sea of misinformation is difficult, but it is the journalist-historian-biographer's obligation to get as close to the truth as possible, even if that disappoints the subject or their public. That truth – at 30, even 90 minutes – will necessarily be partial, but should be a reasonable portrait that will stand the test of time, and factually supportable, lest it has to stand the test of an action for defamation – though this is not possible from beyond the grave: you cannot libel the dead.

19 Wildlife

wildlife n. wild animals and plants collectively: a term used esp. of fauna

f you're going out to film an elephant, you have to understand what elephants do.[1] Those for whom the natural world is their domain have always seemed a species set apart and – not least because of the special nature of their knowledge and techniques – they have always tended to work in their own particular environment, with little two-way traffic in personnel and approach with other documentary specialisms. In a culture castigated half a century ago by C.P. Snow as divided into 'two cultures' – where a dominant arts establishment ignored science at its increasing peril – scientists were always in short number at the BBC.[2] Yet, in the city of Bristol, the BBC has quietly grown the world's leading team of natural history programme-makers. The Natural History Unit was founded in 1957 and is now the largest wildlife documentary production house in the world, making about 100 hours of television and 50 hours of radio a year. It also has a commercial arm, Wildvision, supplying programming to commercial outlets such as Discovery's *Animal Planet*.

In the grab-bag commonly called 'Specialist Factual' – Arts, History, Religion and Science – the first two have traditionally grabbed the plaudits, with the BBC's Music and Arts Department regularly winning BAFTA's specialist factual Huw Weldon award. In recent years, it is the NHU that has appeared most frequently in the shortlist of nominees and, in April 2009, it was *Life in Cold Blood* that won it.[3] Despite being presented by the doyen of wildlife presenters, Sir David Attenborough, a series about amphibians and reptiles is an improbable crowd-pleaser. But the art of this area of science film has found a new popularity, mirroring the commercial attraction of the IMAX spectaculars covered in Chapter 17. This chapter concentrates on this form, through the eyes of NHU filmmakers, and reveals how their success is due not just to the freedom to nurture their talent, but also to their observant skills being as keenly trained on other aspects of television production as they are on the wildlife itself. It is a tale that encapsulates the evolutionary inter-breeding of form and function that is the underlying theme of this book. The successors of Charles Darwin turn out to be themselves among the most fit survivors in the struggle for life that is television documentary ecology today.

Life on Earth

As other eternal verities have diminished – from political trust to religious belief – documentaries addressing 'who we are' have been embraced to help fill the vacuum.

Figure 19.1
Sir David Attenborough bows
out with an undiminished
sense of wonder in *Life in
Cold Blood* (2008)

The taste for genealogy reflected in the success of *Who Do You Think You Are?* is one example; history series addressing issues of nationhood, from Simon Schama to Andrew Marr, are another beneficiary; the genre addressing the history of our surrounding flora and fauna, how everything comes to be, is perhaps the most holistic response. *Life in Cold Blood* was the last chapter of Attenborough's life's work presenting documentary series on that theme, from the original *Life on Earth* (1979) to *The Private Life Of Plants* (1995), *The Life of Birds* (1998), *The Life of Mammals* (2002) and *Life in the Undergrowth* (2005):

> The evolutionary history is finished. The endeavour is complete. If you'd asked me 20 years ago whether we'd be attempting such a mammoth task, I'd have said 'Don't be ridiculous'. These programmes tell a particular story and I'm sure others will come along and tell it much better than I did, but I do hope that if people watch it in 50 years' time, it will still have something to say about the world we live in.[4]

As environmental issues have leapt up the public agenda, quite what that 'particular story' is has become more contested. Environmentalists accuse the BBC of underplaying the threats of global warming in programmes that are primarily intended to divert and reassure.[5] Attenborough has been in wildlife filmmaking for 50 years and, as he says, '50 years ago there were no such thing as environmental policies'.[6] Programme-makers were supposed to keep their opinions to themselves, and not do politics, with which terms he was content. So he remained sceptical about climate change and what he called 'crying wolf' until 2006. Then he committed to what had become a widely held orthodoxy. 'The thing that really convinced me was the graphs connecting the increase of carbon dioxide in the environment and the rise in temperature, with the growth of human population and industrialisation.'[7] Voted later that year 'Britain's Greatest Living Icon' by viewers of BBC2's *Culture Show*,[8] Attenborough went on to front documentaries on *Climate Change: Britain Under Threat*[9] and *The Truth About Climate Change*.[10]

Producers at NHU had wrestled with for some years how to integrate environmental science into natural history without frightening away the audience. Alastair Fothergill, executive producer of landmark series *The Blue Planet* and *Planet Earth*, was particularly aware of the changing mood when the latter series aired in 2006:

> I was very concerned when *Planet Earth* was going to be broadcast that the BBC didn't broadcast it on its own, because undoubtedly you could look at it and say 'This is a rose-tinted view of our planet'. But, in the year that *Planet Earth* was broadcast – between the first run and the second run[11] – we did those two big climate change specials and there was a parallel series on BBC4 called *Planet Earth: the Future*. There's also going to be big fund-raising event this summer [2007] called 'Saving Planet Earth', which is like a natural history Red Nose Day.[12]

'Saving Planet Earth' was the name of a new charity, which would have benefited from a live broadcast event day similar to the Comic Relief Red Nose Day, to be called *Planet Relief*, in summer 2008, but nervous BBC executives stepped in to speak out against this and effectively had it banned. Peter Barron, then editor of BBC2's *Newsnight*, announced at the Edinburgh International Television Festival in 2007, that it was: 'not the corporation's job to save the planet. If the BBC is thinking about campaigning on climate change, then that is wrong and not our job.'[13] His then boss, Head of News Peter Horrocks supported him, telling me that it was better for the BBC to seem insipid than lose its reputation for impartiality:

> My view is that *Planet Relief* would have been a strong intervention on one side of an argument, which is contentious in both scientific and political terms, which could not have been balanced by an equivalent response.[14]

Balance is a reductive, two-dimensional concept dependent upon where you insert your virtual fulcrum; it could hypothetically be used to justify giving equal air time to good and evil. Climate change science is not seriously contended, except by fossil-fuel burning corporate interests, which should not have undue sway in non-commercial broadcast media. But, as environmentalist George Monbiot says, 'We have to give them powerful reason why they should see the world from our point of view, as it is against their interests so to do, even if they are a public service broadcaster'.[15] Monbiot also explains that his environmentalist message is 'counter-aspirational' and that, in a competitive, multichannel world, broadcasters are 'desperate' to make people feel good about themselves, not remind them that their time on the planet is limited. Fothergill agrees that they cannot expect audiences to cosy up on the sofa at 9 o'clock on a Sunday evening to be talked to about the negative side of the state of the planet. 'I think you have to inspire people and, I hope . . . motivate them to behave more environmentally sensibly, at least partly motivated by seeing what they might lose.'[16]

Many of the NHU programmes are co-productions, relying for up to 75 per cent of their inevitably high production costs on revenue stream from other broadcasters elsewhere in the world. Their tastes and prejudices are a further constraint on productions. Miles Barton was a producer on *The Life of Birds* and series producer of the award-winning *Life in Cold Blood*. He introduced some environmental subtext into the latter series, but admits that there is a limit to how far the big international co-production series can go with philosophical issues:

With the big, blue chip type of programmes that are going to be sold all the way around the world, the more political, the more complex you make it, the more difficult that is to be assimilated by other broadcasters, other nations and so on. So with those big ones you have to simplify it somewhat and say 'this is what's out there and there are reasons for caring about it'. And then you use other documentaries that are much more targeted and specific and based on that: 'this is what you could do about it, or this is what needs to be done about it'.[17]

That said, Barton points out that NHU programmes have a much richer environmental and human mix than they did a few years ago, reflecting popular concern and a world in which global interconnections are better understood. Nigel Pope, whose series include *Big Cat Diary* and *Orangutan Diary*, goes further, saying that 'the natural history mainstream of ten years ago is pretty darn different to the natural history mainstream of today'.[18] *Orangutan Diary* tracked the orangutans' struggle for survival in the face of rapacious logging that threatened their habitat.[19] Pope says it was hardly a natural history programme at all. Audience comments concentrated on its role as a morality play, showing: 'the best and worst of people. You've got people who are caring for these little things and then you've got these slightly sinister, veiled figures destroying the forest.'[20]

The Zeitgeist has changed. We saw that with the orang-utan series. People were applauding the fact that the BBC was showing the environmental catastrophe. It was seen as a really good thing for the BBC to be doing and, rather than it being a switch-off and alienating people, it drew people in.[21]

Child's eyes, hands-on skills

Today's NHU executives grew up inspired by an earlier generation of wildlife filmmakers, from the German marine explorers Hans and Lottie Hess and their French counterpart Jacques Cousteau to the Belgian Armand and Michaela Denis's series *On Safari* in East Africa and Asia (1955–61), and David Attenborough's own *Zoo Quest* (1954–63). Attenborough was asked to head the new NFU in 1957, but chose to stay in London running his own Travel and Exploration Unit, while the NHU nurtured ornithologist Peter Scott's *Look* and *Faraway Look* (1955–67), animal collector/writer Gerald Durrell's various expeditions (1957–67) and Johnny Morris, whose *Animal Magic* ran from 1962 to 1983. As Alastair Fothergill says, 'The starting point is a passion for the subject, and a lot of the people who work here were little boys like me, who had snakes under my bed'. Unlike other areas of documentary, where a degree of detachment is often an advantage, wildlife does demand that you are steeped in the subject. The Unit needs what he calls 'muddy boot biologists', practical field people, many of whom have degrees in biology or zoology. When he was Head of Department (1992–8), Fothergill resisted the pressure to diversify production to the independent sector, arguing the need to hold on to this in-house expertise, 'a certain body of skills that are unique'.[22]

Miles Barton enthusiastically endorses the value of that collegiality, largely lost elsewhere in a BBC of short-term contracts.

If I want to have a chat with somebody about filming bluebottles, or something, there's someone here that's done that, or possibly an entomologist that's done their PhD on bluebottles . . . We don't have to reinvent the wheel. If somebody's just been filming in Borneo, you have a chat about filming in Borneo – did you use this fixer and so on.[23]

So, what makes the ideal NHU wildlife filmmaker? Fothergill says:

> I want:
> - Passion for the subject
> - Practical knowledge of the subject
> - All the traditional values that the good documentary filmmaker needs, especially story-telling skills
> - Fantastic logistical ability
> - Leadership and creative spark
>
> Of the 250 people who work in Bristol, a handful have all those things.[24]

To that list might be added: a knowledge of contemporary television genres and how they attract their audience. Responsible for some of the most popular series in recent years, Nigel Pope bucks the trend of the home-grown 'muddy boot biologist'. He came to NHU having been executive producer of the Saturday morning children's shows *Live and Kicking* and *The Saturday Show*.[25] He credits that experience with underpinning the success of *Springwatch* and *Autumnwatch*,[26] using the same structure and techniques as for the children's live shows;

> The challenge was to create three weeks of live telly with British wildlife, which was a bit of a tall order quite frankly . . . The thing that really helped was my previous experience in kids' TV . . . we took those conventions and fed them into a natural history context. Instead of the cartoons, you got five- to six-minute films featuring Bill Oddie, Kate Humble or an enthusiastic member of the public and you're intercutting these with the live – or seemingly live – segments, where you're going into the inside of a nesting box, or a family of foxes, or sea eagles, or so forth.[27]

There had been a string of forerunners to the show, from *Badgerwatch* (1977) and *Bird-watch* (1979) to *A Bird in the Nest* (1994/5) and *Britain Goes Wild with Bill Oddie* (2001–3), but not on this scale. With a crew of around a 100 and over 50 cameras, *Springwatch* is the biggest wildlife outside broadcast ever, but what seems to commend it to its audience most is the opportunity to interact with the familiar, with invitations to spot the first cuckoo of spring, etc. creating a flood of postings on the web notice board saying things like 'Dear Bill, come and see my blue-tits; they're the same as yours!'. That opportunity to involve the audience in active exchange is one of the most sought after goals in television, in the belief that it will regenerate audiences and re-engage the young. But Pope remains sceptical about that:

> That's often spoken of as the really big deal but – you know what? – the core audience of shows like *Springwatch* and *Autumnwatch* is pretty old actually, so their interactivity pretty well stops at watching the show on TV. The heart of the success is that sense of ownership and the storytelling. The great advantage of stripping something over three weeks – whether it is blue tits or small furry animals – is that you can really see them grow in front of your eyes, so you don't have to work that hard at making these stories work. You really have that parade of life and death and growth.[28]

What Pope is much clearer about is the need for what he unrepentantly calls 'brand penetration', the need for series that have a proposition that stands out among competing programmes. This he sees as a more important reason for maintaining a multi-platform presence than the false promise of putting the audience in the driving seat. In practice, programme-makers need increasingly to 'box clever', coming up with more sophisticated storytelling approaches and storylines that address audience concerns. He feels that there is also an overemphasis on trying to attract the 16–34 demographic, because natural history is not a genre relevant to that age group, nor do these programmes fit their lifestyles. They tried running a parallel series to the BBC1 *Big Cat Diary*, a behind-the-scenes *Big Cat Uncut*, with gory uncensored kills, on the youth channel BBC3 in 2006 and it got the channel's highest factual programme audience of the year, with an excellent AI (Audience appreciation Index) of 89 per cent, but it was not composed of the 16–34 demographic the channel was aimed at, so the experiment was not repeated.

We have looked elsewhere at the slightly desperate overemphasis on this market, driven by the commercial channels' advertiser priority, but it is also a naive reading of audience behaviour that reduces it to the uni-dimensional profile of its dominant constituent. Just as people's fashion sense and music choice are less dominated by a single prevailing mode these days, viewing options in the multi-platform world are driven more by individual taste than peer pressure; and that taste is fuelled by comfort factors such as familiarity of form and the faces on camera. Children's TV is dependent upon the familiar, friendly faces that front it, and wildlife films too have tended to be presented by characters that convey the first-hand experience of exploration and encounter, from Cousteau's early, literal essays in what Klein calls 'immersive' documentary to the iconic Attenborough. As Attenborough at 82 has withdrawn from his famous role of sitting with the gorillas, or whatever species he was filming, there is a hole in the high ground, but even his eminence does not necessarily cut it abroad. Alastair Fothergill was distressed that Attenborough's beautifully modulated, sparse commentary was cut from *Planet Earth* by co-production partner Discovery for the US transmission, to be replaced by a much more wordy narration by Sigourney Weaver:

> They seem to assume that Americans don't know anything, so they put too many words in . . . and broke the mood of it. I am quite pleased that the DVD, which is the best-selling DVD in America [at the moment], one that has sold over half a million copies, is the BBC version. The Discovery version has sold 27,000.[29]

At a production cost of £16 million, *Planet Earth* was reputedly the most expensive documentary series ever made. It was also the first to be shot in HD (High Definition), a decision made and funded by the co-producers: Discovery and the Japanese broadcaster, NHK. As we have seen, at a time of declining audiences, revenues and budgets, the only way for such high cost work to be made is through co-production, with several end-users sharing the costs. This frequently leads to fearsome, if not fatal, differences between the parties, who invariably have conflicting needs. Each country has different transmission patterns, sometimes different slot lengths, different cultural imperatives and comprehension standards. For instance, as Fothergill says and as we covered in Chapter 12, American producers presume a lower standard of knowledge and attention span in their audience, and require a star name to attract them. Many co-productions have foundered over such irreconcilable differences, but the solution is what is called 'versioning', allowing the partners to re-cut and re-dub to suit their own audiences. This is immensely difficult for a producer who may have sweated blood over some years to produce a work as near to perfection as they possibly can, only to have it mangled by philistines. Fothergill considers himself lucky to largely be above this fray:

> I do hear horrific stories of some of the experiences independents have. Undoubtedly the BBC's basic relationship with Discovery means that in all the co-productions we've made we have editorial control. I am lucky to have done these big landmarks and people want them as they are. It is well over 100 countries that they have sold to and they broadcast them as they are. They just put a local language narration on and it seems to work.[30]

Whatever works

This should not be taken as a reassertion of auteurism in the documentary canon. What Fothergill and his colleagues at the NHU have evolved is a technical mastery of their medium and an equally extensive understanding of what their audiences like.

There remains a Luddite view among some documentary filmmakers that the style their art dictates should be what a grateful television industry should accept, but the boot has been for some time – some would say always – on the other foot. The avid scrutiny of viewing figures and patterns rewards television executives for playing cautious in their commissions. As in so many industries, executive pay has rocketed to reflect that increased power, with commensurate stagnation or reduction in production pay and liberty. Returning series are offered 75 per cent of their first series budget, even if successful. Despite buoyant viewing figures and record sales earnings, NHU suffered a savage one-third cut in its staffing and budgets in 2008, considerably more than the cross-BBC 10 per cent cut. Despite that, the unit's future seems assured, with the expertise still in place, if depleted, and commissions continuing to roll, with the advantage of the extraordinary long lead times many of them have, four or five years in blockbuster cases. These are, however, no grounds for complacency, and threats to programme futures are a constant.

The *Wildlife on One* series, narrated by David Attenborough, ran from 1977 to its decommissioning in 2005. That meant the effective loss of a regular slot on the BBC's premier channel for the NHU, occasional 'blue chip' leviathans such as *Planet Earth* notwithstanding. Nigel Pope thinks that, had they not made some concessions to popular needs, the genre would not have survived:

> Where we struck lucky – or engineered to strike lucky – was in taking on the *Diary* series, the first of which, *Big Cat Diary*, had been successful on BBC2, but not launched into the mainstream consciousness . . . It aired on BBC1 at 7 o'clock and it was a huge success, and that opened the floodgates.
>
> Since then we have done *Elephant Diaries, Chimp Diaries, Bear Diaries* and *Orangutans* . . . it has sort of reinvented a popular natural history genre.[31]

Pope agrees that they have gone out of their way to enhance the familial metaphor in these shows – enabling families at home to view these families in the wild with real empathy – but denies the charge of anthropomorphism, because the experience and emotion is channelled through the presenters. By having each animal group followed by a different presenter, each of them becomes personally identified with their animal families and communicates the elemental emotions of pleasure and pain, gladness and grief:

It's not so much a show about animals as a show about the way that people feel about animals. All the behaviour that you see – lions, leopards and cheetahs – it's conveyed to you by the presenters: Simon King, Jonathan Scott, Saba Douglas-Hamilton. On that level, it's probably one of the most *bona fide* blue-chip behavioural shows that we do.[32]

Presenters interpreting for dumb animals has always been an essential part of the wildlife film, from Johnny Morris onward. What distinguished *Big Cat Diary* and its siblings was its careful appropriation of the mechanics of soap opera. Following the pathway trod by social documentary soaps a decade before – like *Driving Test*, made just across the car park at Bristol – Pope sought advice from the producers of long-running audience favourites such as *Eastenders*:

We deliberately cut it along the lines of a wildlife soap . . . We were fortunate because we have three principal strands, which you can play with and weave around. That's the same as soaps – all use an 'A', 'B' and a 'C' storyline. We apply that to the lions, the leopards and the cheetahs . . . Then we add the cliff-hanger endings, the drama-style pre-titles and the present tense story-lining, which we always use. Even the voiceovers are now recorded in what drama would call ADR – additional dialogue recordings. We don't treat it as a voiceover, we treat it as continuous sync.[33]

The other tradition that *The Big Cat Diary* pioneered on BBC1 was the series being stripped nightly across the week, rather than going out weekly as it had on BBC2. This drew on the success of reality television shows such as *Big Brother* and *I'm a Celebrity* . . . , which were stripped nightly live and followed up on the digital channels. This helped focus the need to construct the narrative as if it was happening in real time, day-to-day across the week. Along with present tense dialogue, each show is engineered to start with the rising sun and end at night. A shoot lasting 29 days is shoe-horned into 5 soap episodes. Pope does not consider this to be deceptive of the audience, or unethical. He says reality TV has created a demand for more structured storytelling. 'I think the audience almost expects a degree of artful manipulation'. No scene selected for the edit is untrue or manufactured in itself. 'We're just watching a jolly good story, very well told'. But he is not uncritical of fellow producers who do misrepresent, like the scene of a polar bear cub being born in David Attenborough's documentary *Polar Bear: Arctic Warrior* (1997), which viewers were not told had actually taken place in Frankfurt Zoo, leaving them to believe it had happened in the wild. 'I think that was unethical,' Pope says. 'That's not even a wild animal; that's an animal in a zoo.'[34] Attenborough has supported his team, saying that it was the only way that they could get the scene, and recently reiterated that: 'I still think it's justified, but that's the closest I have been worried about.'[35] Speaking ten years before, at a Huw Weldon lecture on the subject of misrepresentation in natural history films, entitled 'Unnatural History', Attenborough had said:

As programme-makers, as documentary-makers, we actually invoke fiction much more frequently than we perhaps imagine. As I have said, whoever it was who first said that the camera cannot lie of course was not telling a truth at all. There has never been a less truthful saying than that. The camera is the most convincing of all liars. But in the end it is the motive of the filmmaker that is crucial.[36]

Motives, and the moral values they reflect, change with society. As Pope says, his most interesting storytelling innovations were 'in response to budget cuts. As budgets squeeze, you've got to find ways of using your material in a more interesting way'.[37] He would not justify misrepresentation, nor even the anthropomorphisation that characterises *March of the Penguins* (2005) or *Meerkat Manor*,[38] but recognises the pressure his colleagues are under to find whatever works. Much to Pope's surprise, his successful *Big Cat Diary* was one of the casualties of the 2008 cull.

Wild techniques

Before these innovations in editorial synthesis, technical advances had driven most of the developments in wildlife filming – first with lightweight film gear in the 1960s, then faster film stock and infra-red optics allowing night filming in the 1970s, through digital non-linear editing in the 1990s to this century's developments in HD. As Alastair Fothergill admits, it is the spectacular wildlife photography that brings the audience in and tends to win all the awards. The NHU have consistently upped their own ante; he remembers when *Life on Earth* was pleased to film one lion hunt and kill, whereas 28 years on *Big Cat Diary* showed 4 in a week. But, above all, it is the quality of the images that impresses:

> Often it is technical breakthroughs that have been very important. *The Life of Plants* was a wonderful breakthrough series that showed the audience plants aren't boring. They just happen in a different timescale than you do and, via amazingly elaborate time-lapse photography, suddenly plants became as interesting as cheetahs. And David's recent series, *Life in the Undergrowth*, looked at tiny little invertebrates. Without technical developments in photography, that would have been impossible . . .
>
> Special techniques in photography [that have helped up the ante] include: crittercams, flying cameras, bouldercams, trick photography, CGI . . . creating more excitement, you could argue artificially.[39]

Editorial innovations have also made additional demands on wildlife cinematographers (they actually still call them cameramen, because very few are women). Their default position is holed up alone in a hide for days or weeks on end, to capture a particular wildlife scene on film. With the growth of presenters on location, there is an obvious demand for more sync sound. A lot of this would have been shot on tape, or by a spare crew helicoptered in along with the presenter for the piece to camera after the painstaking work was done, but changing demand and tightened budgets require more flexibility from crews. Even at the high end, with the landmark series shot without presenters, adaptation has been demanded. The introduction of HD on *Planet Earth* made Fothergill and his crew 'very nervous', because they knew how the Super-16 mm Arriflexes they used to use in extreme conditions performed, and they had heard tales of tape cameras freezing up:

> The cameras proved rugged enough, the picture quality is amazing and, for guys used to being in the field for months and months, and never seeing their rushes, it was amazing to be able to analyse their rushes in the field. Most of the cameramen who had sworn on pain of death they didn't want to touch a video camera, would now never go back [to film].[40]

But, as Fothergill notes, even at this cutting edge of modern technology, there are features the back room boys have yet to master:

The one remaining Achilles heel for us is that an enormous amount of wildlife photography is done at variable frame rates – not just the obvious slowing down of a cheetah, but our cameramen know that if you film an elephant at 45 frames per second, they are much more beautiful, and I would say that only about 30 per cent of *Planet Earth* rushes were shot at normal speed. The audience wouldn't realise 90 per cent of the time because it isn't obvious slow motion, but it is creating beauty in the images through varying the frame rate. At the moment there is only one HD camera that offers that, the Panasonic VariCam, and it only offers rates up to 60 frames per second. As soon as somebody brings out a really effective variable speed HD camera, I think film will be dead.[41]

Another innovation digital media have made possible is editing in the field, enabling an essentially tapeless operation after capture. *Big Cat Diary* was all digitised at full resolution on location in the Masai Mara, onto a central digital server called a landshare. At 3 TB, this can hold all 400–500 hours they shot in four weeks, enabling the various production teams to access and edit their own material for the six interwoven storylines: the three wildlife families, and the three presenter lines. Others shot and edited the supplementary materials: the scenics, the travelling material, the sunsets and sunrises. The rough strands were then polished by craft editors, leaving 80–100 scenes with which the production team flew out of Kenya. Then it was down to Nigel Pope, working with just one editor, to craft the final dramatic structure, the three woven storylines with their complementary human followers, played out in a classic five-act structure in each day's episode. 'You always go through the same five acts,' he says. 'Character background; phase of going well; increase of conflict; final showdown; and some form of catharsis.' Although his references and production approach is essentially drawn from drama, Pope also likes the analogy someone drew of himself as a kind of newspaper editor:

That's a really good description. You've got people writing the stories. You've got producers like sub-editors. And you've got a programme editor, or series producer. The number of people involved in the collection of the material is gigantic. The number of people involved in the final, polished edit of the programme is really small – two people, me and an editor – when we get down to the sharp end of the pyramid. One would like to think that this kind of artful storytelling is the kind of thing that will survive.[42]

In the same way that camera crews have had to become more adaptable, the editors also need a broad range of skills. Miles Barton feels that the sheer ratio of raw footage to cut programmes – often more than 100:1 – is difficult for an editor unused to working with such choice, but Bristol has the best of both worlds: a pool of editors familiar with the NHU's needs and methods, but also working in the general features department cutting other sorts of documentary and drama. 'The editors we are working with at the moment [on *Life in Cold Blood*] have just switched from *Casualty*,' he said.

That not only helps import the dramatic pace and storytelling expertise that Pope speaks of, but also challenges any tendency of the wildlife specialist to develop a subject-specific myopia:

You want somebody who will stand back. I like editors who will argue with me and debate it . . . Because this is the danger: You remember half the night you climbed the mountain to get that particular shot, and then the editor says no, 'Its twenty-five seconds that is just boring', it's good that they do that because we're all human. It's impossible not to think of the emotional investment in that particular shot. So that's very healthy in the cutting room. Very few of them are total specialists in these days.[43]

It is a matter of deploying every craft skill and technique to achieve increasingly constructed ends. As Alastair Fothergill says, 'There was a tradition in the past to let the cameraman out in the field, tell him what you want, but you don't know what's going to happen really, get the rushes back and tell your story in the cutting room'. That approximates to the convention of observational documentary that eschews forward planning. There was a parallel tradition of directors who shot miles of film and left them to the editor to make sense of, and craft a film from. Today's financial circumstances demand little is left to chance, and these top producers have to be able to guarantee their commissioners an ever more perfect product, even though wildlife does not respond to direction. Fothergill's solution is to storyboard everything and plan his filming logistics with military precision:

> For *Planet Earth*, *Blue Planet* and *Life in the Freezer*, my team had a storyline that we were constantly evolving. Admittedly it is far less controllable than other areas of documentary. We wanted to film the snow leopard; we had no idea that we were going to get it and our storyline was constantly reacting to the chances Nature threw at us; but at that level we were constantly storyboarding, structurising, actually going out to fit in the sequence. I am very keen to emotionally engage people in the natural world, and its dilemmas, stories and challenges the animals face – and that's about storyboarding . . . Lots of people don't think you should do that. 'How can you possibly storyboard a wildlife film?' The answer is you can, but you have to change it all the time.[44]

Fothergill instances one sequence planned for the Mountains film in *Planet Earth*, where Demoiselle cranes migrate across the Himalayas, through the Kali Gandaki valley, the deepest in the world. Their storyboard required two cameramen sited on opposing mountain tops, who camped there with their respective directors as long as it took to get the shots. Each night they would confer by satellite phone to check off the shots they had got to complete their storyboard. It is a story of the rigour, precision and determination with which this work is approached.

Some techniques do not last, sometimes because overused and quickly tiresome to the audience. Computer generated graphics (CGI) may have become the most important tool in the epic movie world, but its contribution to television has been more patchy. It can suggest the impossible, but is an expensive resource that – like dramatised inserts – can look really naff when spread too thin. It also raises all the issues of credibility and authenticity, with its visualisation restricted by the imaginative limits of its designers. *Walking with Dinosaurs* (1999), combined 'fact and informed speculation with cutting-edge computer graphics and animatronics effects . . . to create the most accurate portrayal of prehistoric animals ever seen on the screen'.[45] Celebrated at the time for its lifelike portrayal and pseudo-scientific authority, it gave birth to a sequel, *Walking with Beasts* (2001) and a prequel, *Walking with Monsters* (2006), neither of which gained the same critical and audience success domestically or internationally, and the genre seems to have ground to a halt. Miles Barton agrees:

Four or five years ago there was CGI in everything and it was a complete craze. I think that has steadied down and it's now more CGI where you need it. So we have one sequence in *Life in Cold Blood*, where David wants to discuss whether dinosaurs were warm or cold blooded. It's still an ongoing issue. So he takes a great big jaw-bone on a cherry-picker [crane] and holds it out and T. Rex comes to life in front of him and runs around and then we look at a young T. Rex and then all the bones dissolve and we find the bones of the young T. Rex imply that they might have been warm blooded, the bone structure. So we have a bit of fun with it, but it's definitely part of the story, and David's in there for scale plus a bit of fun. But that's the only time we use that scale of CGI in the series. We don't sell a series quite so easily just on CGI itself.

Revelation

As mentioned, co-production partners have different requirements, including programme length and, for a long time, the BBC made programmes at 50 minutes, happily fitting hour slots on commercial networks that often take 8–10 minutes' advertising, particularly with prestige products like this. Alastair Fothergill's *The Blue Planet* had been commissioned in 1996 for eight 50-minute episodes, and took nearly five years to make.[46] Four months before transmission, the then Controller BBC1, Lorraine Heggessy, rang Fothergill and said she needed these programmes to run a full hour. 'Well, I am sorry,' he said, 'I can't suddenly conjure up 80 minutes of natural history.' 'You've got to,' she said. Fortunately for Fothergill, the DVD market had already taken off and the extras – particularly the 'Making of' segments – were proving popular, so they had shot quite a lot for this end use. They cut it into ten-minute bolt-ons to the end of each show and 'we got really positive feedback, so with *Planet Earth*, I proposed it from the very beginning':

> They don't give you very much money for it, so what I did was, identify certain shoots where I thought sending a sync. crew was really important. Things like the hunting dogs which we did in Programme 1, which I knew was a 2-week shoot, so I could put a crew in for two weeks. With the snow leopard, which was 24 weeks over 3 years, there's no way a crew could be there, so what we did is put together a Z-1 [camera] with some radio mics. and did it *Video Diary* style, with the director shooting. Actually, I think the rougher they are, the better they are, 'cos then you get the emotional moments that add poignancy. Some of them work really well.[47]

This is where production becomes a triumph for the lucky pragmatist, where serendipity chimes with the Zeitgeist. Had the impossible demand not been made, the brilliant solution would not have had to be found. Had that not happened, the NHU may not have been servicing a new-found thirst for how it works, the sneaky peek behind the scenes. There is something profoundly counter-intuitive about lovingly crafted programmes – undoubtedly some of the most beautiful and sumptuous on television – calmly offering up their technical secrets, with camera crews cowering in an Arctic hut as polar bears bash on the window. But this works for a post-modern, visually literate culture, for whom mystique is very passé. The method does not detract from the magic, and this stuff is widely available elsewhere, on other platforms from digital channels to websites, to the DVD of the series. By embracing that awareness, the NHU have forged yet another weld between the past and the future, between aspirational filmmaking and honest engagement with their public. As Nigel Pope says, it is not about interactivity, but making a sufficient impact to punch through in the public consciousness. 'Soon all this scheduling stuff will disappear in the digital soup,' he prophesies. 'It's about lodging the brand in the public psyche.'[48]

Conclusion

Coincidentally, Psyche was the ancient Greek deification of 'the breath of life', the consort of Eros, the primordial god of lust, love and procreation. These gods' gender characteristics were reassigned in the Judaeo-Christian variants, Adam and Eve; but those ancient myths addressing timeless inquiry about where we come from, and why, are precisely what sustains the natural history genre. It focuses on issues that aspire to the eternal, without claim to theology or mythology. It offers a cogent, scientific worldview that is not immune to change and catastrophe, but manages to maintain a sense of wonder. It invites a materialistic, individualist culture to step outside itself and consider the multiplicity of other life forms with which we share this planet. It may have been slow to embrace the apocalyptic vision of the environmentalist, who cares equally passionately, but who offers little palatable with his diet of greens. Natural history is the rationalist answer to creationism, or so-called 'intelligent design', which threatens to undermine the already patchy teaching of science in schools. It does not presume to an ethno-centric hierarchy of values, nor deny people their right to the comforts of religion. David Attenborough, a lifelong questor for truth, is careful to define himself as an agnostic, not an atheist. What his colleagues bring to our attention is what indubitably is, one reason why they have been loathe to speculate what only might be.

In surviving and evolving, like one of the species they film, the BBC Natural History Unit has shown an unusual flair for riding the 'slings and arrows of outrageous fortune'. They have adapted to change, including contraction, because they believe their collective survival to be important. They know no one else can do the work they do as well and, if their body of expertise were to be disbanded, as it has been in other BBC departments, it would not naturally coalesce anywhere else. When BBC Director-General Mark Thompson announced his plans for the BBC's 'Creative Future', he announced fewer programmes, but bigger and better ones, specifically mentioning more like *Planet Earth*.[49] As *Planet Earth*'s producer, Alastair Fothergill, said, he would not have wanted that series shown without surrounding contextual content. That is what is conspicuously lacking when such product airs on US cable channels, albeit that the show is often over-narrated for the slow of uptake. The problem facing the NHU is to keep up the plurality of their output with reduced means, not falling back on the blue-chip crowd-pleasers that rake in the money and don't rock the boat.

All of which endorses the NHU producer as a fitting microcosm for the documentary filmmaker at large. To survive s/he needs to be expert and adaptable, knowledgeable and fly, creative and commanding. It is not enough to know your subject and the production technology; you have to find ways of redeploying techniques to tell intriguing stories about it, and refresh audiences and their interest. That means being aware of what other programme-makers are doing, why they succeed with audiences, and being open to ways of cannibalising their work to create new hybrids. Documentary is not a finite form, but a set of techniques and sensibilities that is constantly reinventing the form and the purposes it is put to. Perhaps the most dangerous and difficult task is to remain clear-sighted as to the real value and impact of what our films achieve, and still resist pressures to prostitute talent for gain.

Expert briefing – financing the film

As the market and opportunities change, so do the ways of financing film. Although the traditional one-stop shop of 100 per cent front-end financing by BBC Documentaries or Channel 4 is a diminishing prospect, there are other options before you get to the self-financing freedom favoured by the open source aficionados of the net. This is a necessarily incomplete survey of different routes from conception to completion:

1 **Traditional TV**: All the major broadcasters have websites detailing their documentary wish lists and terms of trade. ITV has largely moved out of documentary, and one-offs are rare on the BBC, save *Storyville* (BBC4), which is for established filmmakers. Most broadcasters – terrestrial such as Five and digital such as Sky and Virgin – are more interested in series and formats, which only leaves Channel 4 actively chasing one-offs, for its *Cutting Edge* series and its 25' first-time director slot, *First Cut*. The latter's Commissioning Editor, Aysha Rafaele, writes on the Channel 4 producers' website:

> Whether you are an AP or a film school graduate I am most excited by people who have a keen understanding of television grammar – who watch documentaries with passion and a critical eye – and who can talk to me with authority about films they have loved and how they would want to make theirs. I want to give films to directors who love and understand the medium of telly, who 'get' the rigours and demands it places on directors and understand the possibilities inherent in the medium and who want to push at those possibilities – but never with a contempt for their audience.[50]

2 **Umbrella deals**: Even if your approach and pitch are successful – in the face of the competition of thousands – ingénues will be 'warehoused' with companies that have an established track in producing films on time and budget, and to the commissioner's demands. That will, in effect, mean you signing over control of, and most of the financial interest in, your show. Just as with inventors on *Dragon's Den*, this will be worth it. You should get the director role, credit and pay – though you could be supplanted by established talent – but are less likely to get a share of the profit (the production fee, calculated as a percentage of the net production budget). You may be offered a small percentage of the 'back-end' – secondary sales and rights which, after creative accountancy has deducted overheads, is rarely worth very much. First-timers are better advised to try and strike a deal at the development stage with an appropriate independent producer, ideally insisting on at least 5 per cent of the production fee, or a commensurate flat fee of at least £5,000 on commission. If the company believes in you and your project, they should invest in and help shape the project, and will certainly have better access to, and success with, targeting and pitching.

3 **Ideas and access**: Most commissioners repeat the mantra that it is 'the idea' that counts, but there is no copyright in ideas and the only tradable commodity, other than established talent, is access. If your idea involves a particular person or place, you should have secured exclusive access to that feature, and approached the producer or commissioner whose output suggests they may be interested in it, with proof of your ownership. Whereas once there was a general caution about subject matter that might glean a promotional benefit from the film, now this is more widely accepted as a feature of trade. Product placement is only banned where obvious and/or paid for and this proscription is about to be relaxed.

4 **Taster tapes**: The other mantra is 'What's the story?' i.e. what is compelling about this subject? Your passionate advocacy and well-focused expertise is a given; but few will trust you, or their own imagination, to be sure that what they will get on screen is golden. If your human subject is a charismatic performer, or your institutional access a hitherto unseen secret place, then video footage can confirm that and your access to it. It is usually unwise to attempt to demonstrate the style of the film and its post-production polish, unless you have the actual craftsmen and resources that could achieve that, which then becomes a pilot and may undermine your appeal for funding. Acquisitions and completion funding pay significantly less than an original commission.

5 **Development funding**: Somewhat harder to get in times of recession, but an established half-way house for prospective commissioners is to put up a few thousand pounds to finance an exploratory shoot, whose specific delivery requirements will enable them then to decide whether to commit the necessary full funding. Even some independents will do this. For a first-time filmmaker, it is important to not undertake this without: a) understanding and agreeing the contractual terms that this will tie you to; and b) understanding and complying with the delivery requirements the development deal sets.

6 **Co-production**: Not for the faint-hearted or inexperienced, this is developing as the only way to finance big budget documentaries. It is considered vital to first land a domestic broadcaster, i.e. one in your own country, before approaching overseas broadcasters. People are much more confident of buying in behind the BBC or Channel 4, and they reason: if you cannot sell it to your own market, why should they buy? Just as with the absolute prerequisite of understanding your home market needs, you need to acquaint yourself with the very different cultural requirements of prospective partner nations. Few achieve the nirvana that every nation will buy the same product, such as *Planet Earth*; more realistic to agree viable versioning to serve the different needs, and ensure the production budget, particularly in post, will cover it.

7 **Commercial interests**: Despite the mid-twentieth-century BBC piety – where cornflake packets and car logos were covered up and no brand name mentioned – corporate richesse has been behind many fine documentaries, long before the current vogue for corporate sponsored television entertainment. Grierson worked for the Empire Marketing Board, which begat the GPO Film Unit, home of the great English documentary filmmakers in the 1930s. The National Coal Board sponsored 1,173 films between 1946 and 1984. Eurostar fully financed Shane Meadows's low-budget feature *Somers Town* (2008). Today's sophisticated marketeers are well aware of the power of film among the young and its viral impact through internet sharing. Imaginative pitching of lateral brand association in films of documentary value is well within the compass of corporate PR.

8 **Agencies and networks**: Channel 4 funds Britdoc, a central clearing house for helping British documentaries with theatre and world potential find funding. Their Goodpitch@Hotdocs initiative 'brings together inspiring social-purpose film projects and a group of expert participants from charities, foundations, brands and media to form powerful alliances around groundbreaking films'.[51] It is run in conjunction with the Sundance Documentary Institute, which also has an active programme encouraging documentary development, with workshops (i.e. the Film Music workshop the Francis brothers attended in developing Black Gold), screenings and networking for often

isolated filmmakers.[52] Britdoc also runs an annual documentary festival in July, with a Pitching Forum and other networking events to help you to find partners and finance. The UK Film Council is only interested in documentaries destined to be cinema features.[53] But the European Documentary Network does offer the kind of support documentary filmmakers need on a pan-European basis.[54]

9 **Foundations**: There are many rich endowments that sponsor work in particular fields. The UK-based Wellcome Trust finances a wide range of activities in the area of health, including films.[55] The USA is considerably better furnished with such sources. The Hartley Film Foundation sponsors films about religion;[56] the US The National Educational Association is a source for educational initiatives;[57] the National Assembly of State Art Agencies is worth approaching for art films;[58] The National Endowment for the Humanities[59] covers all forms of cultural endeavour. The San Francisco Film Arts Foundation offers a full prospectus of training and gear sourcing to help with funding and distribution.[60] Even the federal government is a potential source for funding: FederalFundingPrograms.org (FFP) offers up to half a million dollars to start a business,[61] which apparently can include film.

10 **Self-financing**: Not necessarily as daunting a prospect as it may seem, this has the inestimable advantage of making you your own master, accountable to no one, save perhaps your bank manager. Even s/he may be approached for a business loan secured against future earnings. The relative cheapness of cameras, stock and editing software makes DIY a more realistic option than ever before. The internet is evolving exponentially as the most important distribution platform, to which entry is free. Ways of doing this are still evolving, but are mentioned in Chapter 17's expert briefing. Even releasing your material for free distribution and use, under the Creative Commons[62] agreement, may prove a long-term benefit in terms of getting your work and talent noticed. What is clear is that the worlds of production and distribution are undergoing a seismic change, and the conventional filters of distribution are rapidly becoming obsolete. The filmmakers of tomorrow need to seize control of the means of production and distribution.

Notes

....

Introduction

1   D. Blunkett, *The Blunkett Tapes: My Life in the Bear Pit*, 2006.
2   J. Grierson, 'First principles of documentary', in Forsyth Hardy (ed.) *Grierson on Documentary*, 1979.

Part I Talk to the camera

1   Bill Nichols, *Introduction to Documentary*, 2001, pp. 105–7.
2   Source: Center for Media and Public Affairs at George Mason University & Media Tenor, 19 October 2004.

1 Reportage

1   All dictionary definitions taken from *Collins English Dictionary*, 4th edn, 2006.
2   Ed Braman (ed.) *Unreported World*, Channel 4, in interview with author.
3   John Pilger, *Tell Me No Lies*, 2005.
4   John Pilger, *Guardian*, 14 September 2006.
5   Richard Lindley, *Panorama: Fifty Years of Pride and Paranoia*, 2003, p. ix.
6   *Harvest of Shame* was voted by a 1999 New York University poll the 11th most influential work of journalism in any media in the twentieth century; Murrow's investigation of McCarthy was 10th, and his wartime radio broadcasts 4th, *The New York Times*, 1 March 1999.
7   Mary Ann Watson interview on Museum of Broadcast Communications web documentary *The Great Debates & Beyond: The History of Televised Presidential Debates*, 2000.
8   Institute of Commonwealth Studies library catalogue.
9   *World in Action: The Quiet Mutiny*, Granada TV, 28 September 1970.
10   Ibid.
11   BBC Written Archives Centre, T32/266/2, 22 June 1953, quoted in Richard Lindley, *Panorama: Fifty Years of Pride and Paranoia*, 2003, p. 3.
12   Brand and Ross: BBC statement, 29 October 2008, http://news.bbc.co.uk/1/hi/entertainment/7697354.stm.
13   James Robinson, 'Insiders fear cut-down *Panorama* will lead to narrower horizons', *The Observer*, 17 December 2006.
14   *Provos*, 1997, *Loyalists*, 1999, and *Brits*, 2000, BBC TV.
15   Peter Taylor, *Provos: The IRA and Sinn Fein*, 1998; *Loyalists*, 2000; and *Brits: The War Against the IRA*, 2002.
16   From October 1988 to 1994, broadcasters were banned from broadcasting the voices of terrorists, a ban that was effectively circumnavigated by having their words being voiced by actors.

17   BBC obituary for Sir Charles Wheeler, 4 July 2008, http://news.bbc.co.uk/1/hi/entertainment/7402172.stm.
18   BBC Current Affairs meeting, Lime Grove, July 1988, http://news.bbc.co.uk/1/hi/programmes/newsnight/7499768.stm.
19   BBC Written Archives Centre.
20   Nicholas Wright, *The Reporter*, London: Nick Hern Books, 2007.
21   *This Week: Death on the Rock*, Thames for ITV, 28 April 1988.
22   See Roger Bolton, *Death on the Rock and Other Stories*, 1990.
23   Patricia Holland, *The Angry Buzz: This Week and Current Affairs Television*, 2006, p. 205.
24   Charles Lewis speaking at the Frontline Club, London, 20 July 2006.
25   *Panorama – Cocaine: Alex James in Colombia* was first broadcast on BBC1, 28 January 2008.
26   Ben Rich, BBC website, Friday, 16 May 2003.
27   Stephen Pile, *The Daily Telegraph*, 7 June 2003.
28   Ibid.
29   www.samirhussein.com/gallery_30800.html.
30   Kevin Sutcliffe talking to the author, 27 March 2007.
31   James Curran and Jean Seaton, *Power without Responsibility*, 2003, p. 375.
32   Jon Snow, *Shooting History*, London: Harper Perennial, 2005, p. 18.
33   *Dispatches: Fighting the Taliban* and *Meeting the Taliban*, October Films for Channel 4, 8 and 11 January 2007.
34   *Video Diaries: Nightmare in Paradise*, BBC2, 1993.
35   Ed Braman, interviewed by the author, 10 April 2007.
36   *Dossier: The Media In Times of War*, European Broadcasting Union website report 2004, www.ebu.ch/CMSimages/en/online_16_e_trauma-journalistes_tcm6-12041.pdf.
37   National Union of Journalists statement, 13 October 2006, http://news.bbc.co.uk/1/hi/uk/6046950.stm.
38   *Journalists Killed in 2007*, Committee for the Protection of Journalists website, http://cpj.org/deadly/2007.php.
39   Stewart Purvis, former ITN Chief Executive, Professor of Television Journalism at City University, quoted in Vin Ray, *The Television News Handbook*, London: Macmillan, 2003.
40   Mischa Glenny in interview with the author, Beograd, February 1993.
41   John Simpson, *News from No Man's Land: Reporting the World*, 2002.
42   James Curran and Jean Seaton, *Power without Responsibility*, 2003, p. 336.
43   Andrew Marr, *My Trade: A Short History of British Journalism*, 2004.
44   http://pewresearch.org/pubs/1133/decline-print-newspapers-increased-online-news.
45   Ben Hammersley talking to Kevin Marsh at the Frontline Club, London, 26 September 2006.
46   Chris Shaw, Senior Programme Controller, News and Current Affairs, Channel 5, talking at Edinburgh International Television Festival, 24 August 2008.
47   Andrew Keen, talking at the BBC Media Futures Conference, Alexandra Palace, London, 20 June 2008.

2   Exposé: investigations, undercover and the so-jo

1   Roger Cook started on BBC Radio 4 in 1971, with *Checkpoint*, before moving to ITV with *The Cook Report*, 1985–98.
2   NBC website, January 2007, www.nbclosangeles.com/news/local/InvestigativeTeam.html.
3   CNN website, January 2007, www.cnn.com/CNN/Programs/siu/.
4   Channel 4 website, January 2007, www.channel4.com/news/dispatches/dispatches_home.html.
5   news.bbc.co.uk/1/hi/entertainment/986437.stm.
6   *MacIntyre Undercover: Fashion Victims*, BBC1, 29 November 1999.
7   Donald MacIntyre quoted in Michael Bromley, 'Subterfuge as public service: investigative journalism as idealized journalism', in Stuart Allan (ed.), *Journalism: Critical Issues*, 2005.

8 *MacIntyre's Big Sting*, 3 series, True North Productions for Five TV, 2004–6.
9 Gavin MacFadyen talking to the author, 5 February 2009.
10 *The Secret Policeman*, produced by Simon Ford, first broadcast on BBC1, 21 October 2003.
11 The inquiry was ordered by Labour Home Secretary Jack Straw after a long battle fought by the parents for justice, following police failure to convict the perpetrators of the murder of their son in 1993. For the report, see www.archive.official-documents.co.uk/document/cm42/4262/4262.htm.
12 'Anger after police racism film', BBC website, 22 October 2003, http://news.bbc.co.uk/1/hi/uk/3212442.stm.
13 Glen del Medico being interviewed by Michael Cockerell on the occasion of his retirement, 6 July 2004, www.guardian.co.uk/media/2004/jul/07/bbc.
14 Ian Burrell, 'Blunkett attacks BBC secret film of racist police trainee', *The Independent*, 20 October 2003.
15 *The Secret Agent*, produced by Simon Ford, first transmitted on BBC1, 15 July 2004.
16 Tom Uttley, 'The BNP is thoroughly nasty, so why did 750,000 people vote for it?', *The Daily Telegraph*, 16 July 2004.
17 www.tcij.org/.
18 Hugo de Burgh, *Investigative Journalism: Context and Practice*, 2000.
19 www.publicintegrity.org/.
20 http://centerforinvestigativereporting.org/about.
21 Ibid.
22 Upton Sinclair, *The Jungle*, New York: Prentice Hall, 1906, available in Penguin Classics, 2005.
23 Miller Center on Public Affairs, American President Online Reference Resource, http://millercenter.org/academic/americanpresident/roosevelt/essays/biography/4.
24 John Bunyan, *Pilgrim's Progress*, first published London 1678, available in Penguin Classics, 2008.
25 Bob Woodward and Carl Bernstein, *All the President's Men*, 1974.
26 *All the President's Men*, directed by Alan J. Pakula, USA, 1976.
27 Douglass K. Daniel, 'Best of times and worst of times: investigative reporting in post-Watergate America', in Marilyn Greenwald and Josph Bernt (eds), *The Big Chill: Investigative Reporting in the Current Media Environment*, 2000, p. 12.
28 Ibid.
29 *The Sunday Times* Insight Team, *Ulster*, London: Penguin Books, 1972.
30 Steven Barnett, 'Opportunity or threat: the BBC, investigative journalism and the Hutton report', in Stuart Allan (ed.), *Journalism: Critical Issues*, 2005, p. 329.
31 Ian Hargreaves, *Journalism: Truth or Dare?*, 2003, p. 180.
32 Charles Lewis talking to Bob Garfield on National Public Radio, 4 March 2005. *On the Media: The Digging Life*, copyright WNYC Radio.
33 www.centerforinvestigativereporting.org/.
34 www.propublica.org/.
35 David Swensen and Michael Schmidt, 'News you can endow', *The New York Times*, 2 January 2009, www.nytimes.com/2009/01/28/opinion/28swensen.html?pagewanted=1&_r=2.
36 Gavin MacFadyen talking to the author, 5 February 2009.
37 Nick Davies, *Flat Earth News*, 2008.
38 Nick Davies, 'Trust me, dear reader', *Guardian*, 26 May 2008.
39 Philip Webster, '"Peers-for-sale" claim brings call for police investigation', *The Sunday Times*, 26 January 2009; video release, *Times* online, 30 January 2009.
40 Sharon Tiller, speaking at the Berkeley Graduate School of Journalism 'Crisis in news: investigative reporting on the web' conference, 26 April 2008.
41 Steven Talbot, speaking at the same conference.
42 Charles Lewis interviewed by John McQuaid, posted 20 November 2006, www.newassignment.net.
43 Sharon Tiller, speaking at the Berkeley Graduate School of Journalism 'Crisis in news: investigative reporting on the web' conference, 26 April 2008.

44   Kevin Sites, quoted in Annaliza Savage, 'Video blogger Kevin Sites keeps one foot in the war zone', *Wired*, 18 April 2008, www.wired.com/politics/security/news/2008/04/sites_interview.

45   Kevin Sites in video interview with *Wired*, posted 18 April 2008, www.wired.com/politics/security/news/2008/04/sites_interview.

46   Hot Zone docs. First posted weekly from 2 October 2007, http://hotzone.yahoo.com/.

47   http://viewmagazine.tv.

48   Ibid.

49   David Dunkley Gyimah, talking at the Apple Store, London, 27 March 2008.

50   Ibid.

51   Charles Lewis interviewed by John McQuaid, posted 20 November 2006, www.newassignment.net.

52   Steve Outing, 'Investigative journalism: will it survive?', *Editor & Publisher*, 16 November 2005.

53   Ibid.

54   Sharon Tiller, speaking at the Berkeley Graduate School of Journalism 'Crisis in news: investigative reporting on the web' conference, 26 April 2008.

55   Rob Spence, *Eyeborg blog*, www.eyeborgblog.com/.

56   D.G. Compton, *The Continuous Katherine Mortenhoe, or The Unsleeping Eye*, New York: DAW Books, 1974.

57   *Titicut Follies*, directed by Fred Wiseman, USA, 1967.

58   Robert Coles, 'Stripped bare at the follies', *The New Republic*, 20 January 1986, 18: 28–30.

59   Nursing & Midwifery Council press release, 17 April 2009, www.nmc-uk.org/aArticle.aspx?ArticleID=3668.

60   Ibid.

61   *Dispatches: Undercover Teacher*, first transmitted by Channel 4, July 2005.

62   Disciplinary order made by the GTC, 25 March 2009, www.gtce.org.uk/regulation/disciplinary_orders/250309/.

63   Kevin Sutcliffe, speaking to Channel 4 website, 26 March 2009, www.channel4sales.com/news/26/03/2009/undercover+teacher+stands+by+channel+4+documentary+exposing+ofsted+deception.

64   Office of Public Sector Information, *Public Interest Disclosure Act* 1998, Section 1: 43B, www.opsi.gov.uk/acts/acts1998/ukpga_19980023_en_1#l1g1.

65   Clay Shirky, *Here Comes Everybody*, 2008, pp. 66 ff.

66   Gavin MacFadyen, talking to the author, 5 February 2009.

67   http://slewfootsnoop.wordpress.com.

68   http://pipl.com.

69   *The Times* online 5 March 2007, www.timesonline.co.uk/tol/global/article1471409.ece?token=null&offset=0&page=1.

70   Heather Brooke, *Your Right to Know – New Edition: A Citizen's Guide to the Freedom of Information Act*, 2006.

3   From lectures to landmarks: history and ideas

1   A.J.P. Taylor, *The Origins of the Second World War*, 1961, 1996.

2   'MAD is an evolutionary defense strategy based on the concept that neither the United States nor its enemies will ever start a nuclear war because the other side will retaliate massively and unacceptably. MAD is a product of the 1950s' US doctrine of massive retaliation, and despite attempts to redefine it in contemporary terms like *flexible response* and *nuclear deterrence*, it has remained the central theme of American defense planning for well over three decades', wrote USAF Colonel Alan J. Parrington in 'Mutually Assured Destruction Revisited' in the winter 1997 edition of *Airpower Journal*, www.airpower.maxwell.af.mil/airchronicles/apj/apj97/win97/parrin.html.

3   Edward Gibbon, *The History of the Decline and Fall of the Roman Empire*, London: Strahan & Cadell, 1766–88, pp. 1776–89.
4   A.J.P. Taylor, *A Personal History*, New York: Atheneum, 1983, p. 229.
5   A.J.P. Taylor, 'Accident prone, or what happened next', in A.J.P. Taylor, *From Napoleon to the Second International: Essays on Nineteenth Century Europe*, edited with an introduction by Chris Wrigley, Harmondsworth: H. Hamilton, 1993, p. 21.
6   Benjamin Carter Hett, ' "Goak here": A.J.P. Taylor and *The Origins of the Second World War*', *Canadian Journal of History*, August 1996.
7   *The Independent*, London, 15 February 2002.
8   *The Northern Echo*, Saturday, 16 March 2002.
9   *The Daily Telegraph*, 14 February, 2002.
10 Caroline Frost, *David Starkey: Laughing All the Way to the Library*, BBC News profile, Friday, 8 March 2002, www.dugbert.com/caroline/1860744.html.
11 *Civilisation: A Personal View by Kenneth Clark*, first transmitted on BBC2, 23 February–18 May 1969.
12 Kenneth Clark, *The Fallacies of Hope*, episode 12 of *Civilisation*, BBC2, 1969, BBC DVD 2005.
13 *Ways of Seeing*, produced by Mike Dibb, first episode (of four) broadcast BBC2, 8 January 1972.
14 Kenneth Clark, *The Nude*, 1956.
15 John Berger, *Ways of Seeing*, 1972, p. 64.
16 Berger, ibid., p. 47.
17 *The Shock of the New: Art and the Century of Change*, produced by Lorna Pegram, BBC2, 1980.
18 Robert Hughes, *The Shock of the New: Art and the Century of Change*, 1980, p. 7
19 Hughes, ibid., p. 111.
20 Robert Hughes, 'That's showbusiness', *Guardian*, 30 June 2004.
21 *The Ascent of Man*, produced by Adrian Malone, BBC1 1973.
22 Sean Cubbitt, 'The museum of broadcast communications', www.museum.tv/archives/etv/A/htmlA/ascentofman/ascentofman.htm.
23 *Men of Ideas*, presented by Bryan Magee, first part (of 15) broadcast BBC2, 19 January 1978.
24 Bryan Magee, *Men of Ideas: Some Creators of Contemporary Philosophy*, 1978.
25 *The Great Philosophers*, presented by Bryan Magee, first part (of 15) transmitted BBC2, 6 September 1987.
26 Robert Kee, *Ireland: A History*, 1980, p. 15.
27 Michael Wood, paper to Institute of Historical Research conference on History in British Education, 15 February 2005, www.history.ac.uk/education/conference/wood.html.
28 David Herman, *Guardian*, Saturday, 1 November 2003.
29 *Shoah*, directed by Claude Lanzmann, 1985, runs 9½ hours and was shown in 9 parts on Channel 4. It features testimony of witnesses to the Holocaust and Lanzmann has said: 'It is not a documentary'. See: 'Seminar with Claude Lanzmann', *Yale French Studies*, 1991, 79 (96). 'Wank week' was announced in autumn 2006 for spring 2007, but 'put on hold' following adverse press comment over *Celebrity Big Brother* in January 2007.
30 Jeremy Isaacs, 'Too much reality', *Prospect Magazine*, 29 December 2006.
31 *Mail on Sunday*, 1 December 2002.
32 *Vogue*, Photo-feature, October 2003.
33 *Time Out*, 2 November 2005.
34 Angela Piccini, 'TV in BA', *British Archaeology*, March 2004, 75.
35 *Henry VIII: Mind of a Tyrant*, presented by David Starkey, first episode (of 4), Channel 4, 3 April 2009.
36 *Radio Times*, 1 April 2009.
37 Bettany Hughes, *Helen of Troy: Goddess, Princess, Whore*, 2005.
38 Paul Cartledge, puff found on Bettany Hughes website, www.bettanyhughes.co.uk/books.htm.

39   Francis Fukiyama, *The End of History and the Last Man*, 1993.
40   *The English Civil War*, presented by Tristram Hunt, first episode (of four), BBC2, 7 January 2002.
41   *Castles*, presented by Marc Morris, 6 episodes, Channel 4, May–June 2003.
42   *Simon Schama's A History of Britain*, BBC TV and BBC Books, 2000–2.
43   Simon Schama, *Citizens: A Chronicle of the French Revolution*, New York: Alfred A Knopf; and London: Penguin Books, 1989.
44   Simon Schama, *Dead Certainties: Unwarranted Speculations*, 1991, 1998.
45   To Jeremy Isaac's distaste, Peaches Geldof, teen presenter and socialite, presented *The Beginner's Guide to Islam* on Channel 4 in September 2006.
46   *Rough Crossings*, directed by Stephen Condie, BBC2, 23 March 2007.
47   *Wikipedia*, http://en.wikipedia.org/wiki/Superdon.
48   Andrew Wilson, *Broadcast Now* website, 8 February 2007, www.broadcastnow.co.uk/broadcastnowBlogEntry.aspx?BlogEntryID=76.
49   Simon Schama, *Simon Schama's Power of Art*, 2006, p. 7.
50   Ibid.
51   BBC Worldwide annual review, 2007/8, www.bbcworldwide.com/annualreviews/review2008/Sales_Distribution.aspx.
52   Lewis and Clark, *The Journey of the Corps of Discovery*, first transmitted on PBS, 11 February 2009.
53   Virginia Heffernan, 'America's arty history teacher', *The New York Times*, 11 September 2004.
54   *Ken Burns' America*, DVD, 2004.
55   Curtis White, *The Middle Mind: Why Consumer Culture is Turning Us into the Living Dead*, 2005.
56   Ibid.
57   *The World at War*, produced by Jeremy Isaacs, first part (of 26) transmitted on ITV, September 1973.
58   Richard Holmes, *The World at War: The Landmark Oral History from the Previously Unpublished Archives*, 2007.
59   Robert J. McNamara, quoted on www.imdb.com.
60   *Death of Apartheid*, produced by Brian Lapping Associates, first part (of six) transmitted Discovery, 3 July 1995.
61   *Death of Yugoslavia*, produced by Brian Lapping Associates, first part (of six) transmitted BBC2, 3 September 1995.
62   Herbert Marcuse (1898–1979) was the German philosopher and political theorist whose critique of popular culture was enormously influential in post-War America.
63   *Century of the Self*, written and directed by Adam Curtis, first part (of four) transmitted BBC2, 17 March 2002.
64   *The Power of Nightmares*, written and directed by Adam Curtis, first part (of three) transmitted BBC2, 20 October 2004.
65   *The Trap: What Happened to Our Dream of Freedom*, written and directed by Adam Curtis, first part (of three) transmitted BBC2, 11 March 2007.
66   Andrew Orlowski, 'Adam Curtis: the TV elite has lost the plot', *The Register*, 20 November 2007, www.theregister.co.uk/2007/11/20/adam_curtis_interview.
67   *Monty Python's Flying Circus* was a legendary comedy sketch show broadcast by the BBC from 1969 to 1974. The team went on to make five films and international careers.
68   *Great Railway Journeys of the World: Confessions of a Train Spotter*, presented by Michael Palin, BBC1, 27 November 1980.
69   *Michael Palin: Round the World in Eighty Days*, directed by Roger Mills, first part (of seven) broadcast BBC1, 11 October 1989.
70   *Paul Merton in China*, first broadcast on Five, 21 May 2007, *Paul Merton in India*, Five, 8 October 2008.
71   *Stephen Fry in America*, first broadcast on BBC1, 12 October–16 November 2008.

72   Richard Klein, now Controller BBC4, interviewed by the author, 29 June 2007.
73   www.barb.co.uk/.
74   Commissioner conversation with the author.
75   www.channel4.com/corporate/4producers/commissioning/documentaries.html.
76   www.bbc.co.uk/commissioning/tv/network/channels/.
77   Adam Curtis talking to Tim Adams, 'The exorcist', *The Observer*, 24 October 2004.
78   Adam Curtis talking to Errol Morris, 31 October 2005, www.errolmorris.com/content/interview/believer0406.html.
79   *The Government Inspector*, written and directed by Peter Kosminsky, first broadcast, Channel 4, 17 March 2005.
80   Peter Kosminsky talking to Michael Berkeley *Private Passions*, BBC Radio 3, 15 February 2009.

4   *Vox populi*: the voice of the people

1   Andy Warhol, *Warhol*, catalogue for retrospective at Moderna Museet, Stockholm: Harper Books, 1968.
2   *You've Been Framed*, produced by Granada for ITV, 1990–present.
3   *America's Funniest Home Videos*, produced by Vin di Bona for ABC, 1989–present.
4   The newsreel footage of Mexican military campaigns 'flooded the theaters' in the 1910s and formed the basis of Carmen Toscano's *Memorias de un mexicano / Memories of a Mexican* (1950) and Gustavo Carrero's *Epopeyas de la Revolución/Epics from the Revolution* (1960). See Isabel Arredondo, 'Mexico', in I Aitken (ed.), *Encyclopedia of the Documentary Film*, 2005.
5   Graham Roberts, *Forward Soviet! History and Non-fiction Film in the USSR*, New York: I.B.Tauris, 1999.
6   Martin Skoll, *Hundred Years of Czech Documentary Film, 1898–1998: A Brief History of Czech Non-fiction Film / Cesky dokumentarni film*, Prague: Mala Skala, 2000.
7   Jack C. Ellis, *John Grierson: Life, Contributions, Influence*, Carbondale, IL: Southern Illinois University Press, 2000.
8   Quoted in Elizabeth Sussex, *The Rise and Fall of British Documentary: The Story of the Film Movement Founded by John Grierson*, Berkeley, CA: University of California Press, 1975.
9   Peter Lee-Wright, *Child Slaves*, London: Earthscan Publications 1990.
10 Paul Rotha, *Documentary Film: The Use of the Film Medium to Interpret Creatively and in Social Terms the Life of the People as it Exists in Reality*, London: Faber, 1952.
11 John Grierson in Forsyth Hardy (ed.) *Grierson on Documentary*, 1946 and 1979.
12 A. William Bluem, *Documentary in American Television*, New York: Hastings House 1965.
13 Prime Minister Margaret Thatcher speaking to the 1922 Committee during the miners' strike, 8 July 1984 – archived notes p.8, www.margaretthatcher.org/speeches/displaydocument.asp?docid=105563.
14 Bill Nichols, *Introduction to Documentary*, 2001.
15 Mike Grigsby, *Working the Land*, ITV, 10 January 1972.
16 www.amber-online.com/sections/about-us.
17 *Maybe*, Amber Films Collective, 1969.
18 *Byker*, Amber Films Collective, Channel 4 1983.
19 www.amber-online.com/history_chapters/1979–1990.
20 Bill Nichols, *Introduction to Documentary*, 2001.
21 Mike Fentiman, interview with author, 14 September 2007.
22 In April 2007, Geordie duo Anthony McPartlin and Declan Donnelly reportedly signed a 2½-year £40 million contract to present shows on ITV, including *I'm A Celebrity . . . Get Me Out Of Here!*, *Ant & Dec's Saturday Night Takeaway* and *Britain's Got Talent*. Darren Davidson, 'ITV extends Ant and Dec contract to 2009', *Brand Republic*, www.brandrepublic.com/news/650825/itv-extends-ant-dec-contract-2009/.

23 In 2007, Jonathan Ross reportedly signed a three-year, £16 million contract to present *The Jonathan Ross Show*, 2001–present, the *Film* . . . review programme on BBC1, and his Saturday morning show on Radio 2.
24 Sean Langan, interview with author, 12 July 2007.
25 Roly Keating, speaking at Televisual Intelligent Factual Festival, BAFTA, London May 2007.
26 Anthony Lilley, Huw Weldon Memorial Lecture, Royal Television Society, 13 September 2007.
27 Ibid.
28 Interview conducted by the author at BBC Television Centre, April 2007.
29 Raymond Snoddy, 'Chris Cramer: meet the future of TV news', *The Independent*, 19 February 2007.
30 Buncefield oil depot suffered a major explosion on 11 December 2005 and fire that raged for some days.
31 Ben Brown, interviewed at BBC Television Centre by the author, 19 April 2007.
32 http://slashdot.org/ 'News for nerds, stuff that matters'.
33 http://digg.com/ 'If your submission rocks and receives enough Diggs, it is promoted to the front page'.
34 http://twitter.com/ 'What are you doing?' in 140 characters.
35 Peter Horrocks, St Anne's College/Reuters Institute lecture, 28 November 2006.
36 BBC News website 'Your news, your pictures', http://news.bbc.co.uk/1/hi/talking_point/2780295.stm.
37 *Down Your Way*, 1946–92, was a venerable BBC programme (Home Service/Radio 4) that visited towns, talked to people and played their choice of music.
38 Interview conducted by the author at BBC Television Centre, April 2007.
39 http://uk.current.tv/uploads.htm 'Viewer-created content. Make a pod. Get on tv. Get paid'.
40 Some web broadcasters, such as 4docs, settle for a verbal agreement recorded on camera.

Part II Observe the people

1 John Berger, *Ways of Seeing*, 1972, p. 18.
2 Ibid., p. 17. Also see Dziga Vertov, *Kino-Eye: The Writings of Dziga Vertov*, edited by A. Michelson, trans. Kevin O'Brien, 1984, 1992.
3 David Stuckler, Lawrence King and Martin McKee, 'Mass privatisation and the post-communist mortality crisis: a cross-national analysis', *The Lancet*, 31 January 2009–6 February 2009, 373 (9661): 399–407.
4 *The Russian Godfathers*, directed by Patrick Forbes, first transmitted on BBC2, 8 December 2005.
5 Vladimir Putin was elected President of Russia on 26 March 2000, re-elected in 2004 and, constitutionally denied a third term, became Prime Minister on 8 May 2008.
6 Roman Abramovich bought Chelsea Football Club in a deal worth £140 million on 1 July 2003.

5 Real life

1 *Encarta World Dictionary*.
2 *The Royal Family* was jointly produced by the BBC and ITV and first shown on 21 February 1969.
3 *Sun* newspaper, 12 July 2007.
4 *Monarchy: The Royal Family at Work*, first transmitted on BBC1, 26 November 2007.
5 Stella Bruzzi, *New Documentary: A Critical Introduction*, 2000, p. 69.
6 Stephen Mamber, 'Cinéma vérité in America', *Screen*, summer 1972, 13 (2).
7 Jean Rouch, in G. Roy Levin, *Documentary Explorations: 15 Interviews with Film-Makers* (1st edn), 1971, p. 136.
8 Robert Drew, 'Narration can be a killer', reprinted in Kevin Macdonald and Mark Cousins (eds), *Imagining Reality: The Faber Book of Documentary*, 1996, pp. 271–3.

9   Quoted by Brian Winston, 'The documentary film as scientific inscription', in Michael Renov (ed.), *Theorising Documentary*, 1993, p. 43.
10   Stella Bruzzi, *New Documentary: A Critical Introduction*, 2000, p. 70.
11   Alan Rosenthal, 'Emile de Antonio: an interview', *Film Quarterly*, Fall 1978, 31 (1), quoted in Stella Bruzzi, *New Documentary: A Critical Introduction*, 2000, p. 70.
12   Kaleem Aftab and Alexandra Weltz, 'Fred Wiseman', www.iol.ie/galfim/filmwest.
13   London *Evening News*, 10 February 1956.
14   www.bfi.org.uk/booksvideo/video/details/freecinema/.
15   Lindsay Anderson, 'Only connect: some aspects of the work of Humphrey Jennings', *Sight and Sound*, April–June 1954.
16   Ibid.
17   *Free Cinema* programme leaflet, quoted in Richard Armstrong, 'Free Cinema', review of *Free Cinema* DVD, BFI *Sense of Cinema* web magazine, 2006, http://archive.sensesofcinema. com/contents/dvd/06/39/free_cinema.html.
18   Four US number one hits in 1956, commencing with *Heartbreak Hotel* in March.
19   *And God Created Woman* (1956), directed by Bardot's husband Roger Vadim, was a hit in London and then the most successful European film ever in the USA.
20   *Free Cinema* programme leaflet, quoted in Richard Armstrong, 'Free Cinema', review of *Free Cinema* DVD, BFI *Sense of Cinema* web magazine, 2006, http://archive.sensesofcinema. com/contents/dvd/06/39/free_cinema.html.
21   Bill Nichols, *Introduction to Documentary*, 2001.
22   Margaret Mead, *TV Guide*, 6 January 1973.
23   *The New York Times*, 8 February 1973.
24   Jeffrey Ruoff, *An American Family: A Televised Life*, 2001.
25   Jeffrey Ruoff, 'Can a documentary be made of real life? The reception of "An American Family"', in Peter Ian Crawford and Sigurjón Baldur Hafsteinsson (eds), *The Construction of the Viewer: Media Ethnography and the Anthropology of Audiences*, Denmark: Intervention Press, 1996, pp. 70–296.
26   Ibid.
27   Angela Mason aka Sylvia Thomas, *The Daily Mail*, 7 July 2007.
28   Roger Graef, *Police: An Allegation of Rape*, BBC1, 1982.
29   Of the 11,766 allegations of rape made in 2002 there were just 655 convictions (5.6 per cent), 258 of which had come from a guilty plea. Only 14 per cent of cases pursued made it to trial. Source: Home Office, 2005.
30   Nina Hobson, *Dispatches: Undercover Copper*, 27 April 2006.
31   John Corner, *The Art of Record: A Critical Introduction to Documentary*, 1996.
32   Michael Waldman, *Queens: A Cambridge College*, BBC1, 1984.
33   www.channel4.com/culture/microsites/C/cutting_edge/index.html.
34   ITC annual report 1998, www.ofcom.org.uk/static/archive/itc/itc_publications/annual_ report/1998/programme_regulation.asp.html.
35   *Guardian* newspaper, 5 May 1998.
36   Brian Winston, *The Primrose Path: Faking UK Television Documentary, 'Docuglitz' and Docusoap*, La Trobe University, Australia, website, www.latrobe.edu.au/screeningthepast/ firstrelease/fr1199/bwfr8b.htm.
37   Brian Winston, 'Ethics', in Alan Rosenthal and John Corner (eds), *New Challenges for Documentary*, 2nd edn, 2005, p. 180.
38   Stella Bruzzi, *New Documentary: A Critical Introduction*, 2000, pp. 121ff.
39   Chris Terrill, quoted in ibid., p. 90.
40   Marks & Spencer Plc v. Granada Television Ltd, 23 February 1998.
41   Mark Thompson, *Guardian*, 24 August 2007.
42   Brian Woods, *Evicted*, BBC1, 29 November 2006.
43   Paul Watson, *Rain In My Heart*, BBC2.
44   Christaan Harden on dfg docs website, www.dfgdocs.com/resources/Doc_Reviews/75.aspx.

45 BBC Radio 4 *Today* programme, 31 July 2007.
46 *Sylvania Waters*, produced by Paul Watson, ABC & BB.
47 *Keeping Up Appearances*, written by Roy Clarke, BBC1, 1990–5.
48 *Video Nation*, produced by Chris Mohr and Mary Rose, BBC2, 1993–2001, available online at www.bbc.co.uk/videonation/.

6   Docu-soap and mocu-soap

1 *Collins English Dictionary*, 4th edn, 2006, which adds: 'so called because manufacturers of soap were typical sponsors'.
2 Stella Bruzzi, *New Documentary: A Critical Introduction*, 2000.
3 *Children's Hospital* ran on BBC1 from 1993 to 2001; its original producer, Richard Bradley, is MD of Lion TV.
4 Annette Hill, 'Fearful and safe: audience response to British reality programming', *Television and New Media*, 2 May 2000.
5 The watershed is an agreement in British television broadcasting that sex, violence and bad language should not be shown before 9.00 pm. 'Material unsuitable for children should not, in general, be shown before 2100 or after 0530', www.ofcom.org.uk/tv/ifi/codes/bcode/protectingu18/.
6 Rupert Smith, *Guardian*, 19 January 2000.
7 *Vet School* ran for one series on BBC1 in 1996 and *Vets in Practice* ran for eight series from 26 July 1997 to 31 December 2002.
8 *Driving School* ran in 6 x 30 minute episodes on BBC1 from 10 June to 15 July 1997.
9 *Clampers* ran for six weeks on BBC1 from 11 May 1998.
10 *Airport* ran for ten series from 1996 to 2005, the first year on BBC2, thereafter on BBC1.
11 *Airline* debuted on ITV on 6 March 1998 and ran for 10 series of varying lengths until 2007.
12 Ray Webster, 'Highs and lows of letting ITV's cameras loose at 30,000 feet', *The Observer*, 27 August 2000.
13 *Luton Airport*, Screenchannel Productions for ITV1, May 2005.
14 Joe Houlihan, *The Independent*, 22 February 2000.
15 www.bbc.co.uk/pressoffice/pressreleases/stories/2002/07_july/17/annual_report.shtml.
16 Joe Houlihan, *The Independent*, 22 February 2000.
17 *Hotel*, BBC TV, 1997, 8-part series peaked with an audience of 11 million viewers.
18 *Fawlty Towers*, BBC TV, 1975 and 1979, 2 x 6-part comedy series written by and starring John Cleese and Connie Booth, voted by the British Film Institute (BFI TV 100) as the best British TV show of all time.
19 Stella Bruzzi, *New Documentary: A Critical Introduction*, 2000, p. 85.
20 *Trouble at the Top*, BBC TV, 1997–2005 (9 series).
21 *Blood on the Carpet*, BBC TV, 1999 and 2001 (2 series).
22 *Crisis at the Castle*, BBC TV, 2007 (3-part series).
23 Richard Klein, interview with the author, 29 June 2007.
24 *NYPD Blue*, written and produced by Steve Bochco and David Milch for ABC TV, 1993–2005.
25 *The Comic Strip Presents . . .* debuted on the first night of Channel 4, 2 November 1982, with *Five Go Mad in Dorset* and continued with five series and nine specials until *Sex Actually*, 28 December 2005.
26 The band's 17th album, released on 17 March 1992. It eventually reached the 61st spot on the Billboard charts. The 21-city tour of the United States and England that began on 17 May 1992, at an Air Force base in Colorado Springs, Colorado, and culminated in a sell-out on 7 July at London's famed Royal Albert Hall, www.spinaltapfan.com/atozed/TAP00069.htm.
27 A further Spinal Tap 30-city 'Unwigged and Unplugged' tour began in Vancouver on 17 April 2009.
28 *All You Need is Cash* debuted on NBC on 22 March 1978 and was shown on BBC2 on 27 March 1978.
29 *New York Time Movie Guide*, 8 December 2006, www.nytimes.com/2006/12/08/movies.

30   *The Thick of It*, first transmitted on BBC4, 19 May 2005.
31   *In the Loop*, directed by Armando Ianucci, released in the UK, 17 April 2009.
32   David D'Arcy, 'In the loop', *Screen International's ScreenDaily.com*, 20 January 2009, www.screendaily.com/ScreenDailyArticle.aspx?intStoryID=42617&strSearch=in%20the%20loop&strCallingPage=ScreenDailySearchSite.aspx.
33   *Anyone For Pennis*, 1995; *VIP – Very Important Pennis*, 1996; *Dennis Pennis RIP: Too Rude to Live*, 1997.
34   *Da Ali G Show*, Channel 4, March–May 2000.
35   *Ali G in da USA*, Channel 4/HBO.
36   *Ali G Indahouse: The Movie*, directed by Mark Mylod, 2002.
37   *Borat: Cultural Learnings of America for Make Benefit Glorious Nation of Kazakhstan*, directed by Larry Charles, 2006.
38   *Brüno*, directed by Larry Charles with the mischievous working title: *Bruno: Delicious Journeys Through America for the Purpose of Making Heterosexual Males Visibly Uncomfortable in the Presence of a Gay Foreigner in a Mesh T-Shirt*, 2009.
39   Craig Hight and Jane Roscoe, *Faking It: Mock Documentary and the Subversion of Factuality*, 2001, pp. 117–18.
40   Peter Jackson, interviewed in *Midwest Art Magazine*, 1996, 10 (23).
41   *Alien Autopsy: Fact or Fiction?*, director Ray Santilli, first aired Fox TV, 28 August 1995.
42   Marc Horne, *The Sunday Times*, 16 April 2006.
43   *Alien Abduction: Incident in Lake County*, director Dean Alioto, first aired UPN, 20 January 1998.
44   Craig Hight and Jane Roscoe, *Faking It: Mock Documentary and the Subversion of Factuality* 2001, p. 155.
45   *De Grote Donor Show/The Big Donor Show*, produced by BNN, Netherlands, transmitted on 1 June 2007.
46   Anne-Marie Walsh, 'Kidney donor reality TV show sparks fury', *The Independent*, 30 May 2007.
47   'TV kidney competition was a hoax', BBC News website, 2 June 2007, http://news.bbc.co.uk/1/hi/entertainment/6714063.stm.
48   Larry David, *Curb Your Enthusiasm*, HBO, 15 October 2000.
49   John Betjeman, 'Slough' in *Continual Dew*, London: John Murray 1937: 'Come friendly bombs and fall on Slough! It isn't fit for humans now.'
50   Tad Friend, *The New Yorker*, 11 December 2006.
51   Ibid.
52   *The Armstrongs*, BBC2, February–May 2006.

7   Extreme television: flashing lights and freak shows

1   Sky customer website, accessed Sunday, 23 September 2007, http://mysky.sky.com/portal/site/skycom/.
2   Eric Hobsbawm, *Age of Extremes*, 1994.
3   www.realitytv.co.uk/show, accessed on 24 September 2007.
4   'Approximately 40 people die each year in RTIs involving the police, with the majority of deaths being the result of a police pursuit. No official figures exist, but we estimate that there were between 11,000 and 19,000 police pursuits in England and Wales during 2005/6 and that between 1 and 11 pursuits out of every 1,000 lead to a death.' *Police Road Traffic Incidents: A Study of Cases Involving Serious and Fatal Injuries,* London: Independent Police Complaints Commission, September 2007, p. vi.
5   *Rail Cops*, BBC1, January–March 2003.
6   *Sky Cops*, BBC1, September 2006.
7   *Girl Cops*, BBC1, February–April 2006.
8   *Shaping A Fairer Future*, Women & Work Commission, 2006.
9   *Police Camera Action!* Optomen Productions for Carlton TV, 1994–2002.
10   *World's Wildest Police Videos*, Fox TV, 1998–2002.

11   Ann Johnson and Ted Prosise, *Narrating Encounters With the Police: World's Wildest Police Videos*, 4 May 2001, http://reviews.media-culture.org.au/features/realitytv/wwpv-c.html.
12   Ibid.
13   www.realitytv.co.uk/show, accessed on 24 September 2007.
14   *Cops With Cameras*, ITV1, February 2007.
15   Sam Wollaston, *Guardian*, 28 February 2007.
16   http://policelockerroom.blogspot.com/2007/03/cops-with-cameras.html.
17   Ibid.
18   David L. Altheide, 'The news media, the problem frame, and the production of fear', *The Sociological Quarterly*, 1997, 38 (4): 647–68.
19   *Crimewatch UK*, BBC1, 1984.
20   *Aktenzeichen XY . . . ungelöst*, ZDF, 1967.
21   *Crimewatch UK*, BBC1, 8 July 1997.
22   Katie Thompson, quoted in Deborah Jermyn, *Crime Watching: Investigating Real Crime TV*, London: I.B. Tauris, 2006.
23   Deborah Jermyn, ibid.
24   www.amw.com/line-of-duty, accessed 28 September 2007.
25   www.amw.com/fugitives/amw_dirty_dozen.cfm, accessed 28 September 2007.
26   'On 30 June 2006, 2,245,189 prisoners were held in Federal or State prisons or in local jails – an increase of 2.8 per cent from mid-year 2005, less than the average annual growth of 3.4 per cent since year end 1995. At year end 2005 there were 3,145 black male sentenced prison inmates per 100,000 black males in the United States, compared to 1,244 Hispanic male inmates per 100,000 Hispanic males and 471 white male inmates per 100,000 white males.' US Department of Justice Bureau of Justice Statistics, www.ojp.usdoj.gov/bjs/prisons.htm, accessed 28 September 2007.
27   *Human Rights Watch*, 2 (12) (G); *Punishment and Prejudice: Racial Disparities in the War on Drugs*, May 2000, www.hrw.org/reports/2000/usa/Rcedrg00-01.htm.
28   www.hybridfilms.tv/productions.html.
29   www.artaid.org/artaidESU.html.
30   *Brotherhood – Life in the FDNY*, directed by Lilibet Foster, USA, 2004.
31   BBC News online, 30 May 2000, http://news.bbc.co.uk/1/low/entertainment/769741.stm.
32   Caryn James, *The New York Times*, 5 December 2000, http://query.nytimes.com/gst/fullpage.html?res=9403E5DF143CF936A35751C1A9669C8B63.
33   See Chapter 5.
34   *The Human Body*, BBC1, July–September 1998.
35   *Anatomy for Beginners*, Channel 4, November 2002. See www.channel4.com/science/microsites/A/anatomy/index.html.
36   Reported by BBC News online, 27 January 2003. See http://news.bbc.co.uk/1/hi/entertainment/tv_and_radio/2696517.stm.
37   *Extraordinary People*, Five. See www.five.tv/programmes/extraordinarypeople/.
38   *BodyShock*, Channel 4. See www.channel4.com/more4/documentaries/doc-feature.jsp?id=29&pageParam=2&letter=.
39   *Half Ton Hospital*, *Tonight* special for ITV1, March 2007.
40   *The Boy Whose Skin Fell Off*, Channel 4, March 2004.
41   Mark Lawson, *Guardian*, 8 March 2004.
42   *The Boy Whose Skin Fell Off*, Channel 4, update shown September 2004.
43   www.bbc.co.uk/ouch/columnists/laurence/260207_index.shtml.
44   *Executions*, EduVision Films Ltd, 1995.
45   *The Bridge*, directed by Eric Steel, USA, 2007.
46   *The Bridge of Death*, ABC News online, 20 October 2006.
47   Howard Feinstein, 'Get your suicides here, folks', *Guardian*, 23 June 2006.
48   Ibid.
49   Ibid.

50   Stephen Holden, *The New York Times*, 27 October 2006.
51   Benjamin Sacher, *The Daily Telegraph*, 21 July 2007.
52   Paul Watson, Goldsmiths College, 17 October 2007.
53   *The World's Biggest Boy*, the Russian Dzhambulat Khotokhov was 16 stone at the age of 7, and the subject of a Channel 4 *BodyShock* film in March 2007.
54   *The Woman With Half A Body*. Coloradan Rosemarie Siggins had her legs amputated as a child due to a genetic condition, but remains fiercely independent and mobile on her arms and a skateboard, as an *Extraordinary Lives* film revealed in February 2007.
55   Joseph Carey Merrick (1862–90) was known as 'The Elephant Man' because of his colossal cranial deformities, which caused him to be exhibited as a sideshow freak, until such sideshows were banned in the UK in 1886. His case was taken up by the leading physician Sir Frederick Treves, who arranged accommodation and care for him at the London Hospital, until he died from his condition at the age of 27. Thanks to this acceptance, he became a popular figure and a favourite of Queen Victoria.
56   *The Elephant Man*, director David Lynch, 1980, starring John Hurt.

Part III Change the mind

8   Education

1   *Look Around You*, written by and starring Robert Popper and Peter Serafinowicz, Talkback Thames for BBC2, 2002 and 2005.
2   http://tv.cream.org/lookin/schools/index.htm.
3   *Maths-in-a-Box*, *Maths File*, *Wondermaths*, all BBC Schools.
4   Kevin Lygo, Channel 4 Statement of Policy for 2007.
5   Sean Dodson, *Guardian*, 7 March 2006.
6   Mike Flood Page, interview with the author, 10 March 2008.
7   BBC Trust Press Release, 17 March 2007.
8   Quoted in A.E. Musson, *Trade Union and Social History*, London: Routledge, 2006, p. 186.
9   Quoted in Asa Briggs, *History of Broadcasting in the United Kingdom*, 1995, p. 484.
10   *Milestones in Working Class History*, BBC1, November–December 1975.
11   *The Past at Work*, BBC2, March–April 1980.
12   *On The Move*, BBC1, October–December 1975. By the end of the first series, 10,000 people had contacted the national helpline.
13   *Parosi*, BBC1, October 1977–April 1978. *Parosi* (literally *Neighbours*) pre-dated the eponymous Australian soap by eight years and featured an Indian and a Pakistani family living next door to each other in a multicultural West London suburb. The series was written by Dilip Hiro and Naseem Khan.
14   *Delia Smith's Cookery Course*, BBC2, 1978–80.
15   *Bellamy on Botany*, BBC1, 1973.
16   John Berger, *Ways of Seeing*, 1972, p. 153.
17   *Ways of Seeing*, BBC2, 1972.
18   *Rough Science*, BBC2, 30 episodes from 26 May 2000 to 7 December 2005.
19   *Renaissance Secrets*, BBC2, November–December 1999.
20   *Coast*, BBC2, 2005–9.
21   Thirteen/WNET *NTTI Evaluation Results: National Teacher Training Institute, 2001–2 final report*, New York: Thirteen/WNET, 2002, www.thirteen.org/edonline/ntti/index.html.
22   K. Shephard, 'Questioning, promoting, and evaluating the use of streaming video to support student learning', *British Journal of Educational Technology*, 2003, 34 (3): 295–308.
23   R. Reed, 'Streaming technology improves student achievement', *T.H.E. Journal*, February 2003.
24   F.J. Boser, G.S. Meyer, A.J. Roberto and C.G. Inge, 'A report on the effect of the Unitedstreaming™ application on educational performance', *United Learning*, August 2003.

25   *Television Goes to School. The Impact of Video on Student Learning in Formal Education*, Centre for Public Broadcasting, 2004.
26   *Ingenious Africa*, Episode 1, Thought Films, 2006.
27   Sophie Chauchard-Stuart, 'Mirror to reality', *The Independent*, 8 April 1997.
28   DigitalArts online, 20 November 2006, www.digitalartsonline.co.uk/features/index.cfm?feature id=1533.
29   Royal Television Society Educational television Awards 2006, www.rts.org.uk/Information_ page_+_3_pic_det.asp?id=16779.
30   Mike Flood Page, interview with the author, 10 March 2008.
31   www.channel4.com/learning/breakingthenews/index.html.
32   Mike Flood Page, interview with the author, 10 March 2008.
33   *Breaking the News*, Channel 4, 29 November 2005.
34   www.teachers.tv/video.
35   R. Canale and S. Wills, 'Producing professional interactive multimedia: project management issues', *British Journal of Educational Technology*, 1995, 26 (2): 84–93.

9   Propaganda

1   *Internet Filtering in China in 2004–2005: A Country Study*, 2005, Harvard. For a more up-to-date review, see http://opennet.net/sites/opennet.net/files/ONI_China_2009.pdf.
2   Ewen MacAskill, 'Yahoo! forced to apologise to Chinese dissidents over crackdown on journalists', *Guardian*, 14 November 2007.
3   Bruce Einhorn, 'How China controls the Internet', *Business Week*, 13 January 2006.
4   www.opennetinitiative.net/research/profiles/uae.
5   Niccolò Machiavelli, *Il Principe*, trans. W.K. Marriott, www.digilander.libero.it/il_machiavelli/ translate_english/machiavelli_the_prince.html.
6   Dziga Vertov, *Kino-Eye: The Writings of Dziga Vertov*, edited by Annette Michelson, trans. Kevin O'Brien, 1984, 1992.
7   Esfir Shub, *Zhizn moya-kinematograf / Cinema is my Life*, 1972, p. 18.
8   Marina Burke, 'Esther Shub', in Ian Aitken (ed.), *Encyclopedia of the Documentary Film*, 2006, p. 1221.
9   Footage discovered in a museum in Bratsk by the author.
10   Philip Woods, 'Film propaganda in India 1914–1923', *Historical Journal of Film, Radio and Television*, October 1995.
11   *The Real Glory*, directed by Henry Hathaway, 1939.
12   Prem Chowdhry, *Colonial India and the Making of Empire Cinema: Image, Ideology and Identity*, 2000.
13   *Submission*, directed by Theo van Gogh, first broadcast on VPRO, 29 August 2004.
14   *Dispatches: Undercover Mosque*, first broadcast on Channel 4, 15 January 2007.
15   Richard M. Barsam, *Film Guide to Triumph of the Will*, 1975.
16   Keith Williams, 'Humphrey Jennings' in Ian Aitken (ed.), *Encyclopedia of the Documentary Film*, 2006, p. 680.
17   Humphrey Jennings's letter to his wife, 29 January 1943, in Kevin Jackson (ed.), *The Humphrey Jennings Film Reader*, 1993, p. 76 ('the Fire one' = *Fires Were Started*).
18   Ibid.
19   Richard M. Barsam, *Non-fiction Film: A Critical History*, 1992.
20   *The Battle of Midway*, directed by John Ford, released on 14 September 1942.
21   *The Battle of Britain*, directed by Frank Capra, 1943. See Internet Archive at www.archive.org.
22   *The Battle of China*, directed by Frank Capra, 1944. See Internet Archive at www.archive.org.
23   *The Battle of Russia*, directed by Anatole Litvak, 1944. See Internet Archive at www.archive.org.
24   George Orwell, *1984*, London: Secker & Warburg, 1949, p. 156.
25   'UK: human rights: a broken promise', Amnesty International, published 23 February 2006, www.amnesty.org/en/library/asset/EUR45/004/2006/en/ce28dddd-d45b-11dd-8743-d305 bea2b2c7/eur450042006en.html.

26 Clement Atlee quoted on COI site at the National Archives, www.nationalarchives.gov.uk/films/aboutfilms.htm.

27 *The Berlin Airlift*, 1949, www.nationalarchives.gov.uk/films/1945to1951/filmpage_ba.htm.

28 *Operation Hurricane*, directed by Ronald Stark, 1953, www.nationalarchives.gov.uk/films/1951to1964/popup/transcript/trans_oper_hurr.htm.

29 *Communism*, Coronet Instructional Films, 1952, see www.archive.org/details/Communis1952.

30 *A New Look at the H-Bomb*, available on the DVD collection *Atomic Testing: Declassified*, 2007, and at http://video.google.com/videoplay?docid=-2967874724943351515.

31 *Duck and Cover*, directed by Anthony Rizzo for US Federal Civil Defense Administration, 1951.

32 'Pre-emptive nuclear strike a key option NATO told', *Guardian*, 22 January 2008, p. 1.

33 Stella Bruzzi, *New Documentary: A Critical Introduction*, 2000, p. 35.

34 Erik Barnouw, *Documentary: A History of the Non-fiction Film*, 2nd edn, 1993, p. 345.

35 Ibid.

36 BBC Arabic TV started 12 hours a day on 11 March 2008; 24-hour programmes began 19 January 2009.

37 BBC Persian TV was launched on 14 January 2009 to broadcast 8 hours a day to Iran and Afghanistan.

38 George W. Bush, in his 'war whoop' speech to the US Congress, 20 September 2001.

39 Norman Solomon, *War Made Easy: How Presidents and Pundits Keep Spinning Us to Death*, 2005.

40 Iraq reporter unlawfully killed, BBC News website, 13 October 2006, http://news.bbc.co.uk/1/hi/uk/6046950.stm.

41 Quoted in Stephen Grey, 'A lack of cover', *Guardian*, 5 June 2009.

42 Ibid.

43 Ibid.

44 *The New York Times* masthead slogan since 1896.

45 *Propaganda™* website, www.propaganda.co.uk/index.php/how.

46 Ofcom revised ruling, 13 December 2006, www.ofcom.org.uk/consult/condocs/tvappeals/broadcast_appeals/.

47 George Orwell, 'Politics and the English Language', London, Horizon, 1946, vol. 13, issue 76, pp. 252–65; reprinted in *Shooting an Elephant and Other Essays*, Secker & Warburg, 1950. Available online at www.orwell.ru/library/essays/politics/english/e_polit.

48 George Orwell, *1984*, London: Secker & Warburg, 1949.

49 Martin Luther King's speech, on the steps of the Lincoln Memorial, Washington DC, 28 August 1963.

50 Julian Henriques, speaking at Goldsmiths Screen School seminar on Synaesthesia, 24 March 2009.

51 Elias Canetti, *Crowds & Power*, 1962, p. 15.

52 Richard Eden 'Paediatrician attack: "People don't want no paedophiles here"', *The Daily Telegraph*, 3 September 2000, www.telegraph.co.uk/news/uknews/1353904/Paediatrician-attack-People-dont-want-no-paedophiles-here.html.

10 Polemic
....

1 Channel 4 website, www.channel4.com/culture/microsites/W/wtc4/history/timeline.html.

2 Victor Schonfeld, 'Shock and awe', *Guardian*, 5 July 2007.

3 *Hugh's Chicken Run*, Channel 4, 7–9 January 2008.

4 *Jamie's Kitchen*, Channel 4, November–December 2002.

5 *Jamie's School Dinners*, Channel 4, February–March 2005.

6 Maggie Brown, *A Licence to be Different: The Story of Channel 4*, 2007, p. 278.

7 *The Great Global Warming Swindle*, Wag Productions for Channel 4, first broadcast March 2007.

8 Geoffrey Lean, 'Climate change: an inconvenient truth . . . for C4', *The Independent*, 11 March 2007, http://news.independent.co.uk/environment/climate_change/article2347526.ece.

9   'Heat is on for deniers of global warming', *The Observer*, Sunday, 11 March 2007.

10   Martin Durkin, speaking at Televisual Intelligent Factual Festival, BAFTA, London, 23 May 2007.

11   Alan Hayling, speaking at Televisual Intelligent Factual Festival, BAFTA, London, 23 May 2007.

12   ITC ruling, archived at Ofcom, www.ofcom.org.uk/static/archive/itc/itc_publications/complaints_ reports/programme_complaints/show_complaint.asp-prog_complaint_id=40.html.

13   George Monbiot, 'The revolution has been televised', *Guardian*, 18 December 1997, www. monbiot.com/archives/1997/12/18/the-revolution-has-been-televised/.

14   www.channel4.com/science/microsites/G/great_global_warming_swindle/index.html.

15   *Empire*, Channel 4, first broadcast January 2003.

16   Niall Ferguson speaking on Channel 4 website following transmission of his first programme 9 January 2003, www.channel4.com/community/showcards/E/Empire_-_Niall_Ferguson.html.

17   Andrew Roberts, *The Times*, 8 January 2003.

18   Priyamvada Gopal, 'The story peddled by imperial apologists is a poisonous fairytale', *Guardian*, 28 June 2006.

19   David Smith, 'Niall Ferguson: the empire rebuilder', *The Observer*, Sunday, 18 June 2006.

20   *Colossus*, Channel 4, June 2004.

21   *The War of the World*, Channel 4, June–July 2006.

22   Niall Ferguson, *Colossus: The Rise and Fall of the American Empire*, 2004, p. 301.

23   Niall Ferguson, BBC website, http://news.bbc.co.uk/1/hi/programmes/this_week/5086488. stm.

24   Benjamin Wallace-Wells 'Right man's burden: why empire enthusiast Niall Ferguson won't change his mind', *The Washington Monthly*, June 2006.

25   Ibid.

26   Gary Edgerton, quoted in Leger Grindon, 'Ken Burns', *Encylopedia of the Documentary Film*, 2005, p. 157.

27   Frederick Douglass, quoted in *The American Civil War*, produced by Ken and Ric Burns for PBS, 1990.

28   Nancy Franklin 'In the trenches: Ken Burns on the Second World War', *The New Yorker*, 24 September 2007.

29   Alfred Dreyfus was a Jewish army officer falsely imprisoned for treason. The prominent novelist Emile Zola addressed an open letter to the President of the Republic, published in *L'Aurore* on 13 January 1898, accusing the generals whose conspiracy and cover-up had gerrymandered the court-martial and led to the truly guilty man being found innocent. Zola was subsequently found guilty of criminal libel and had to flee to England to escape jail, but his incendiary polemic eventually led to Dreyfus's release and rehabilitation.

30   Janet Street-Porter, 'Talent versus television', 20th James MacTaggart Lecture, Edinburgh, August 1995.

31   Janet Street-Porter, *J'Accuse: Technonerds*, Channel 4, 19 March 1996.

32   Tom Paulin, *J'Accuse: Virginia Woolf*, Channel 4, March 1991.

33   Hunter Davis, *J'Accuse: Manchester United*, Channel 4, 4 April 1995.

34   Alison Pearson, *J'Accuse: The News*, Channel 4, 1 November 1994.

35   Ibid.

36   William Shawcross, *J'Accuse Jacques*, Channel 4, 21 March 2003.

37   Gary Younge, *J'Accuse: Uncle Sam*, Channel 4, 28 March 2003.

38   Chris Hitchens, *Hell's Angel: Mother Teresa of Calcutta*, Channel 4, 1994.

39   Ibid.

40   Ibid.

41   Chris Hitchens, *God Is Not Great*, 2007.

42   Richard Dawkins, *The Root of All Evil?*, Channel 4, January 2006.

43   Ibid.

44   Richard Dawkins, *The God Delusion*, 2006.

45   *The Jeremy Vine Show*, BBC Radio 2, 5 January 2006.

46 Richard Dawkins, 'Diary', *New Statesman*, 30 January 2006.
47 Alister McGrath, *Dawkins' God: Genes, Memes and the Meaning of Life*, Oxford: Blackwell, 2005.
48 www.citychurchsf.org/openforum.htm.
49 www.alternet.org/story/47052/.
50 Richard Dawkins presents *Root of All Evil? The Uncut Interviews*, www.RichardDawkins.net.
51 Alister McGrath and Joanna Collicut McGrath, *The Dawkins Delusion? Atheist Fundamentalism and the Denial of the Divine*, 2007.
52 *TV Nation* Pilot (Show 1) segment summaries, NBC, 19 July 1994, www.dogeatdogfilms.com/tv/tvarchive.html.
53 *The Awful Truth*, Channel 4, 11 April–27 June 1999; and 17 May–5 July 2000.
54 Michael Moore, *Stupid White Men . . . and Other Sorry Excuses for the State of the Nation!*, 2001.
55 *Fahrenheit 9/11*, 2004.
56 www.mooreexposed.com; www.moorelies.com.
57 David T. Hardy and Jason Clarke, *Michael Moore is a Big Fat Stupid White Man*, 2004.
58 *Fahrenhype 9/11*, directed by Alan Peterson, 2004.
59 *Michael Moore Hates America*, directed by Michael Wilson, 2004.
60 *Manufacturing Dissent*, directed by Rick Caine and Debbie Melnyk, 2007.
61 *The Mark Thomas Comedy Product*, Channel 4, 1996–2002.
62 *Dispatches: Mark Thomas – Weapons Inspector*, Channel 4, 2003; *Dispatches: Mark Thomas – Debt Collector*, Channel 4, 2003; *Dispatches: After School Arms Club*, Channel 4, 2006; *Dispatches: Mark Thomas on Coca-Cola*, Channel 4, 2007.
63 Mark Thomas, *As Used on the Famous Nelson Mandela: Underground Adventures in the Arms and Torture Trade*, 2006.
64 James Hawes, 'War on shifty arms dealers', *The Daily Telegraph*, 13 August 2006, www.telegraph.co.uk/arts/main.jhtml?xml=/arts/2006/08/13/botho29.xml.
65 *Brass Eye*, Channel 4, February 1997.
66 Hansard, 23 July 1996: Column 169.
67 Chris Morris, press release for *Brass Eye*, January 1997.
68 See Guy-Ernest Debord, *La Société du Spectacle / The Society of the Spectacle*, 1967.
69 *Brass Eye Special: Paedogeddon*, 26 July 2001.
70 Euan Ferguson, *The Observer*, 5 August 2001.
71 Jonathan Swift, *A Modest Proposal*, pamphlet, 1729, downloadable at: www.gutenberg.org/etext/1080.
72 *Nathan Barley*, Channel 4, 11 February–18 March 2005.
73 *The IT Crowd*, Series I, Channel 4, February–March 2006.
74 Richard Brooks 'Satirist turns terrorists into Dad's Army', *The Sunday Times*, 13 January 2008.
75 Michel Foucault, 'Ethics', interviewed by Paul Rabinow in May 1984, just before Foucault's death. Paul Rabinow and Michel Rose, *Essential Works of Foucault*, Vol. 1, trans. Lydia Davis, 1997.
76 Michael Warner, 'Uncritical Reading', in Jane Gallop (ed.), *Polemic: Critical or Uncritical*, 2004.
77 George Orwell, *Notes on Nationalism*, essay first published in *Polemic*, 1, October 1945. Available online at http://orwell.ru/library/essays/nationalism/english/e_nat.
78 Ibid.

11 Liberation

1 Lee Gomes, 'Will all of us get our 15 minutes on a YouTube video?' *Wall Street Journal*, 30 August 2006.
2 'Google closes YouTube deal', Reuters, 14 November 2006.
3 www.youtube.com.
4 See www.unreportedworld.blogspot.com/.

5   *Visit Palestine*, directed by Katie Barlow, 2006.

6   Peter Bradshaw, 'Visit Palestine', *Guardian*, 31 March 2006.

7   Ken Loach, quoted on the *Visit Palestine* website, www.visit-palestine.com.

8   Naomi Klein, *No Logo: Taking Aim at the Brand Bullies*, 2000.

9   *The Take*, directed by Avi Lewis, 2004, see http://thetake.org/index.cfm?page_name= synopsis.

10   *Not A Love Story*, directed by Bonnie Sherr Klein, 1981.

11   Jill McGreal, '*Not a Love Story*: feminism and pornography', *Undercut*, 6, 1985.

12   See T. Grimes, J. Anderson and L. Bergen, *Media Violence and Aggression*, 2008.

13   Quoted by John Turnbull, 'Souls on the line: Guatemala City sex workers turn to football for a sense of who they are', 30 June 2007, www.theglobalgame.com.

14   Quoted by Catherine Elton, 'Prostitutes win respect with soccer', *Miami Herald*, 31 October 2004.

15   www.wmm.com/filmcatalog/titleindex/browse_titles.shtml.

16   *Sentenced to Marriage*, directed by Anat Zuria, Israel, 2004.

17   Donato Totaro, 'Women united: sentenced to marriage and highway courtesans', 31 July 2006, 10 (7), www.Offscreen.com.

18   *The Greatest Silence: Rape in the Congo*, directed by Liz Jackson, 2006.

19   Ibid.

20   *The Heart of Kampala*, directed by Winnie Gamisha and Andreas Frowein, 2005.

21   Winnie Gamisha, interviewed by Ogovo Ondego, 'Living for film, family, women's liberation and Africa', www.artmatters.info/film/articles/tezran.php.

22   Quoted on *About Documentaries* website, http://documentaries.about.com/od/popular docsubjects/a/iraqwar.htm.

23   *The Dreams of Sparrows*, Harbinger Films, directed by Hayder Mousa Daffar, 2005.

24   Iraq Eye press release, New York, 26 September 2006, www.iraqeye.org/sorospr.pdf.

25   www.youtube.com/iraqeyetv.

26   Jonathan Rosenbaum, *Chicago Reader*, 3 August 2007, www.chicagoreader.com/features/ stories/moviereviews/2007/070803/.

27   Ibid.

28   Charles Burnett, quoted in *Lumière Reader*, www.lumiere.net.nz/reader/item/1186.

29   Miles and Rosenblum, quoted by Karen Everhart Bedford in *Current*, 20 September 1993.

30   Fernando Solanas and Octavio Getino, *Towards a Third Cinema: Notes and Experiences for the Development of a Cinema of Liberation in the Third World*, 1969, p. 23.

31   Richard Meran Barsam, *Non-fiction Film: A Critical History*, 1992, p. 373.

32   Alberto Elena and Marina Diaz Lopez, *The Cinema of Latin America*, 2003, p. 119.

33   Peter Matthews, '*The Battle of Algiers*: bombs and boomerangs', www.criterion.com/current/ posts/342.

34   'National liberation, national renaissance, the restoration of nationhood to the people, common-wealth: whatever may be the headings used or the new formulas introduced, decolonization is always a violent phenomenon'. Quoted in Frantz Fanon, *Les Damnés de la Terre / The Wretched of the Earth*, 1963.

35   Ibid.

36   Teshome Gabriel, 'The Third Cinema question: notes and reflections', in Jim Pines and Paul Willemen, *Questions of Third Cinema*, 1990, p. 14.

37   Chris Berry, 'Poisonous weeds or national treasures: Chinese left cinema in the 1930s', *Jump Cut*, March 1989, 34: 87–94.

38   Wu Wengiuang, quoted in Weimin Zhang, 'Bumming in Beijng', in Ian Aitken (ed.), *Encyclo-pedia of the Documentary Film*, 2006.

39   Ernest Larsen, 'Video Vérité from Beijing', *Art in America*, September 1998: 53 and 55.

40   Bérénice Reynaud, 'Dancing with pyself, drifting with my camera: the emotional vagabonds of China's new documentary', *Senses of Cinema*, September 2003, www.sensesofcinema. com/contents/03/28/chinas_new_documentary.html.

41   Paola Voci, 'Quasi-documentary, cellflix and spoofs: Chinese movies' other visual pleasures', *Senses of Cinema*, 2006, www.sensesofcinema.com/contents/06/41/other-chinese-movies-pleasures.html.
42   David Dunkley Gyimah in conversation with the author, 25 March 2008.
43   http://oneworldmedia.org.uk/awards.
44   www.btselem.org/.
45   Rory McCarthy, 'Cameras for action', *Guardian*, 22 June 2009.
46   Ibid.

Part IV Entertainment for all

1   Peter Fincham, McTaggart lecture, Edinburgh International Television Festival, 23 August 2008.
2   Melvyn Bragg, speaking on a panel discussion at Edinburgh International Television Festival, 22 August 2008.

12 Formats and reality TV

1   www.bfi.org.uk/archive.
2   *7 Up*, ITV, 5 May 1964.
3   *7 plus Seven*, ITV, 15 December 1970.
4   Roger Ebert, *Fifty Greatest Documentaries*, Channel 4, 9 October 2005.
5   *7 Up 2000*, BBC1, 13 April 2000; and *14 Up 2000*, BBC1, 16 and 23 September 2007.
6   Stella Bruzzi, *New Documentary: A Critical Introduction*, 2000, p. 103.
7   Annette Hill, *Reality TV: Audiences and Popular Factual Television*, 2005, p. 177.
8   Natasha Forrest, *Wife Swap*, The F-Word, 16 February 2003, www.thefword.org.uk/reviews/2003/02/wife_swap.
9   Annette Hill, *Reality TV: Audiences and Popular Factual Television*, 2005, p. 117.
10 'Sadistic *Wife Swap* nearly cost me my sanity, says TV presenter Anna Courtenay', *The Daily Mail*, 10 February 2008.
11 'TV producers sued by "gay" wife swap man', *Metro*, 9 December 2005.
12 Richard Klein, interviewed by the author, 29 June 2007.
13 Stuart Jeffries, 'Where did it all go wrong?', *Guardian*, 22 March 2007.
14 Stephen Lambert, 'Innovate and experiment', *Guardian: Comment is Free*, 24 March 2007.
15 *The Secret Millionaire*, RDF Media for Channel 4, 2006–8.
16 *Saturday Night*, produced and directed by Brian Hill, Century Films for BBC2, 3 April 1996.
17 Simon Armitage, quoted in Maxine Baker, *Documentary in the Digital Age*, 2006, p. 164.
18 *Drinking for England*, produced and directed by Brian Hill, Century Films for BBC2, 28 October 1998.
19 Maxine Baker, *Documentary in the Digital Age*, 2006, p. 161.
20 Jane Roscoe, Opening address to the symposium, *Documentary – The Non-conformists*, Sydney, Australia, 10–12 September 2004.
21 Derek Paget and Jane Roscoe, 'Giving voice: performance and authenticity in the documentary musical'. Also available online at www.ejumpcut.org/archive/jc48.2006/Musical Docy/index.html.
22 *Feltham Sings*, produced by Roger Graef and directed by Brian Hill, Century Films & Films of Record for Channel 4, 17 December 2002.
23 Maxine Baker, *Documentary in the Digital Age*, 2006, p. 168.
24 Paget and Roscoe, 'Giving voice'.
25 *Songbirds*, produced and directed by Brian Hill, Century Films for Channel 4, December 2005.
26 *Pornography: The Musical*, produced and directed by Brian Hill, Century Films for Channel 4, 21 October 2003.

27   Simon Boswell, quoted in Paget and Roscoe, 'Giving voice'.

28   *The Seven Sins of England*, directed by Joe Bullman, Channel 4, 8 May 2007.

29   www.channel4.com/culture/microsites/S/seven_sins/index.html.

30   Gerard Gilbert, 'The Seven Sins of England', *The Independent*, 5 May 2007.

31   *Kilroy*, BBC1, 1987–2004, suspended after presenter Robert Kilroy-Silk's *Sunday Express*, 4 January 2004, column described Arabs as 'suicide bombers' and 'limb amputators'.

32   *The Jeremy Kyle Show*, ITV 2005–present, described by Judge Alan Berg as 'human bear-baiting which goes under the guise of entertainment'.

33   *The Jerry Springer Show*, WMAQ-TV/NBC, 1991–present, progenitor of so-called 'trash TV' and unrepentantly called 'a freak show' by its multimillionaire host.

34   *Ricki Lake*, Garth Ancier/CBS, 1994–2004.

35   Annette Hill, *Reality TV: Audiences and Popular Factual Television*, 2005, p. 23.

36   Sjaak Nouwt, Berend R. de Vries and Dorus van der Burgt, 'Camera surveillance and privacy in the Netherlands', in S. Nouwt, B.R. de Vries, J. Prins and C. Prins, *Reasonable Expectations of Privacy? Eleven Country Reports on Camera Surveillance and Workplace Privacy*, 2005.

37   *Broadcast*, 1 August 2003.

38   Andy Warhol, quoted in catalogue for his first European retrospective at the Moderna Museet, Amsterdam, 1968.

39   Evan Marriott, John Saade, Joe Borgenicht and Daniel Chen, *The Reality TV Handbook: An Insider's Guide: How To: Ace a Casting Interview, Form an Alliance, Swallow a Live Bug, and Capitalize on Your 15 Minutes of Fame*, 2004, p. 40.

40   Rick Kissell 'Survivor finale racks up phenomenal ratings', *Variety*, 25 August 2000.

41   BBC News website, 24 August 2000, http://news.bbc.co.uk/1/hi/entertainment/894244.stm.

42   Caryn James, 'Critic's notebook: Machiavelli, on a desert isle, meets TV's reality. Unreal', *The New York Times*, 20 August 2000.

43   Joseph Campbell was a revered American professor of comparative mythology, whose work became widely known through the PBS series *The Power of Myth*, 1988, and who was recognised by filmmaker George Lucas as a key influence on his *Star Wars* films. Probst is referencing his best-known saying: 'Follow your bliss.'

44   '*Survivor* host Jeff Probst media teleconference', *SurvivorFever.net*, 29 January 2008, www.survivorfever.net/s16_jp_teleconference.html.

45   Since writing, Jade Goody died of cervical cancer, aged 27, on 22 March 2009. She had been told of her terminal condition while appearing on the Indian version of *Big Brother*, and chose to live out the last weeks of her life with documentary television cameras, securing significant earnings to bequeath to her children.

46   *Celebrity Big Brother*, 19 January 2007, was Channel 4's top rated show of 2007, with 8.7 million viewers, a 41.9 per cent share.

47   Roly Keating quoted in BBC press release, 7 February 2006, www.bbc.co.uk/pressoffice/pressreleases/stories/2006/02_february/07/apprentice.shtml.

48   Jonathan Freedland, 'What *The Apprentice* says about Blair's Britain: only profit matters', *Guardian*, 3 May 2006.

49   Dan Adamson, interviewed by the author at Goldsmiths, 9 June 2006.

50   Helen Veale, interviewed by the author, 21 November 2007.

51   *Dumped*, outline for Channel 4, 2–5 September 2007.

52   *Jamie's School Dinners*, Channel 4, 23 February–16 March 2005.

53   *Hugh's Chicken Run*, Channel 4, 7–9 January 2008.

54   *The Woman Who Stops Traffic*, Channel 4, 26 February–11 March 2008.

55   Daisy Goodwin, speaking at the Televisual Intelligent Factual Festival, 23 May 2007.

56   Ibid.

57   Deployed as metaphor. There is no incontrovertible evidence for the veracity of this image, probably invented for propagandistic purposes in the sixteenth century and enthusiastically promoted by Hollywood.

68   'The 100 best TV shows of all time', as chosen by *The Times* TV critic James Poniewozik, www.time.com/time/specials/2007/article/0,28804,1651341_1659196_1652735,00.html.

59   Vicki Barrass, interviewed by the author, 29 May 2007.
60   Angus Macqueen, interviewed by the author, 10 October 2007.
61   Ibid.
62   Michael Schneider, 'Layoffs get the reality TV treatment', *Variety*, 7 April 2009, www.variety.
     com/article/VR1118002236.html?categoryid=14&cs=1&query=Someone%27s+Gotta+Go.
63   Ibid.
64   James Robinson, 'Moment of truth as lie detector quiz show is banned', *Guardian*, 25 June
     2009.
65   *The Phantom of the Paradise*, directed by Brian de Palma, 1974.

13   Lifestyle: house and garden, makeover and motors, food and travel

1   *Top Gear*, BBC2, 2 December 2007, 8.4 million = 28.1 per cent share; *Celebrity Big Brother*,
     Channel 4, 17 January 2007, 8.7 million = 41.9 per cent share. Source: *Guardian*, www.
     guardian.co.uk/media/2007/dec/13/television.
2   Royal Television Society, www.rts.org.uk/Information_page_+_3_pic_det.asp?sec_id=503&id
     =34996.
3   *Fifth Gear*, Five, 2002–present.
4   Michel Foucault, *Histoire de la sexualité, III: le souci de soi / The History of Sexuality*, Vol. III:
     The Care of the Self, 1984, 1986.
5   Ulrich Beck in Beck and Beck-Gernsheim, *Individualization: Institutionalized Individualism and
     Its Social and Political Consequences*, 2002, p. 22.
6   Ibid., p. 26.
7   Barry Bucknell (1912–2003) appeared in *About the Home*, 1956/7, *Do It Yourself with Barry
     Bucknell*, 1958–60, and *Bucknell's House*, 1962–3 (all BBC).
8   *Changing Rooms*, BBC2, 1996, BBC1, 1997–2004.
9   *Home Front*, BBC2, 1999–2002.
10   Anthony Giddens, *Modernity and Self-identity*, 1991, p. 54.
11   www.bbc.co.uk/lifestyle/tv_and_radio/index_by_category.shtml.
12   *BBC Gardeners' World* magazine, monthly.
13   www.gardenersworld.com.
14   *BBC Gardeners' World Live*, 1992–present.
15   *Growing Out of Trouble*, BBC2, December 2006; and Monty Don, *Growing Out of Trouble*,
     2006.
16   *Grand Designs*, Talkback Thames for Channel 4, 1999–present.
17   *Grand Designs Live*, Talkback Thames for Channel 4, 4–9 May 2008.
18   www.granddesignsawards.com/.
19   Kevin McCloud, quoted by Tamsin Blanchard, 'Building sight', *The Observer*, 2 November
     2003.
20   *Grand Designs* was Channel 4's third most watched programme in 2007, with 5.8 million on
     28 February, an audience share of 25.3 per cent. Source: www.guardian.co.uk/media/2007/
     dec/13/television.
21   www.channel4.com/4homes/on-tv/kevin-s-big-town-plan/kevin-mccloud-and-the-big-town-
     plan-regenerate-your-town-08-08-11_p_1.html.
22   *Property Ladder*, Talkback Thames for Channel 4, 2000–present.
23   *Location, Location, Location*, IWC Media for Channel 4, 2001–present. Programmes
     increased to 60 minutes long, and featuring 2 couples, from the 2007 series.
24   Kirstie Allsop quoted in 'Tories hire queen of property TV Kirstie Allsopp to liven up policy',
     The Daily Mail, 21 October 2007.
25   RICS housing market survey December 2007, www.rics.org/NR/rdonlyres/65944DC4-61D8-
     429D-8FA5-D31693B7D3AE/0/RICSHousingMarketSurveyDecember2007WEB.pdf.
26   Sarah Beeny and Kirstie Allsopp, quoted by Jon Henley, 'Repossession, repossession',
     Guardian, 10 April 2008.

27   Land Registry House Price Index, figures released 27 March 2009, www1.landregistry.gov.uk/assets/library/documents/hpireport2732009e.pdf.
28   www.channel4.com/4homes/on-tv/location-location-location/about-phil-spener/about-phil-spencer-08-06-24_p_1.html (accessed 12 April 2009).
29   *A Place in the Sun*, FreeForm for Channel 4, 2000–present.
30   www.channel4sales.com/news/home?year=&month=&id=549.
31   www.statistics.gov.uk/.
32   Peter Allen, 'British retirees in France lose free health care', *The Daily Telegraph*, 3 September 2007.
33   *How to Cheat at Cooking*, BBC2, 10 March to 14 April 2008.
34   Alun Palmer, 'Jamie Oliver's chicken crusade', *The Daily Mirror*, 7 January 2007, www.mirror.co.uk/news/topstories/2008/01/07/jamie-oliver-s-chicken-crusade-89520-20277197/.
35   James Hall, 'Jamie writes off Sainsbury's chicken comments', *The Daily Telegraph*, 12 January 2008.
36   Jamie Oliver letter published on blogsite.
37   *The Naked Chef*, BBC2, 1999.
38   *Jamie's Kitchen*, TalkbackThames for Channel 4, 2002.
39   *Jamie's School Dinners*, TalkbackThames for Channel 4, 2005.
40   BBC Editorial Guidelines, 'Conflicts of interest: on-air talent and commercial advertising', www.bbc.co.uk/guidelines/editorialguidelines/advice/conflicts/7onairtalentand.shtml.
41   'I want to change our approach on product placement. We'll consult on this and would hope to have any change in place in the New Year', Ben Bradshaw, DCMS Secretary, addressing RTS Conference, Cambridge, 16 September 2009.
42   Kirsty Fairclough, *First International Conference of Lifestyle Television*, University of Salford, 25–7 April 2007.
43   *In Search of Perfection*, BBC2, 16 October–19 December 2007.
44   Heston Blumenthal, quoted by Jay Rayner, 'Molecular gastronomy is dead', *The Observer*, 14 October 2007.
45   *Come Dine With Me*, Channel 4, 10 January 2005–present.
46   *What Not to Wear*, BBC2, 2001–3, BBC1, 2004–8.
47   Vicki Barrass, interviewed by the author, 29 May 2007.
48   Ibid.
49   *Trinny and Susannah Undress . . .*, ITV.
50   *How to Look Good Naked*, Maverick for Channel 4, 27 June 2006–present.
51   *How to Look Good Naked*, Maverick and RDF USA for Lifetime TV, January–March 2008.
52   *Queer Eye for the Straight Guy*, Scout Productions for Bravo, July 2003–October 2007.
53   Abigail Harvey, interviewed by the author in New York, 18 June 2007.
54   Ibid.
55   Vicki Barrass, interviewed by the author, 29 May 2007.
56   Abigail Harvey, interviewed by the author in New York, 18 June 2007.
57   *Extreme Makeover*, Lighthearted Entertainment for ABC, 2002–7.
58   Deleese Williams on Court TV, www.courttv.com/news/2006/1006/extreme_makeover_ctv.html?page=1.
59   Annette Hill, *Reality TV: Audiences and Popular Factual Television*, 2005, p. 133.
60   *Dr 90210*, E! Entertainment, 2004–present.
61   *I Want a Famous Face*, MTV, 2004–present.
62   *The Swan*, Fremantle for Fox TV, 7 April–20 December 2004.
63   Robert Bianco, 'There's nothing beautiful about The Swan', *USA Today*, 11 April 2004.
64   http://ww3.komotv.com/Global/story.asp?S=1880407.
65   Richard D'Amico, 'Plastic surgery is real, not reality TV', *Virtual Mentor – The American Medical Association Journal of Ethics*, March 2007, 9 (3): 215–18.
66   Ibid.
67   Brian Lowry, 'The Swan', *Variety*, 8 April 2004.

68 Matthew Gilbert, 'Famous face is not a pretty sight', *Boston Globe*, 29 March 2004.
69 *All New Cosmetic Surgery Live*, Five, 2004–5, www.five.tv/home/frameset/?content=1171 2466&.
70 Adam Searle, President of the BAAPS, 25 April 2005, www.baaps.org.uk/content/view/ 130/62/.
71 Richard Jinman, 'Time to renew lifestyle TV', *Sydney Morning Herald*, 3 November 2004, www.smh.com.au/articles/2004/11/02/1099362142968.html?from=storyrhs.
72 Alicia Androich, 'The facts of lifestyle', *Real Screen*, 1 January 2008, www.realscreen.com/ articles/magazine/20080101/page45.html.
73 Tania Lewis, ' "He needs to face his fears with these five queers!": Queer eye for the straight guy, makeover TV, and the lifestyle expert', *Television & New Media*, 2007, 8: 292, http:// tvn.sagepub.com/cgi/reprint/8/4/285. Also see: Tania Lewis, *Smart Living: Lifestyle Media and Popular Expertise*, 2008.
74 Ibid., p. 306.

14 Performance and performers

1 *The Ed Sullivan Show*, CBS, 20 June 1948–6 July 1971, featured the Beatles three times in February 1964.
2 *Sunday Night at the London Palladium*, ATV for ITV, 25 September 1955–1 July 1967.
3 *Don't Look Back*, directed by D.A. Pennebaker, USA, 1967
4 David Baker, ' "I'm glad I'm not me!" Marking transitivity', in *'Don't Look Back'*, *Screening the Past*, website, www.latrobe.edu.au/screeningthepast/firstrelease/fr_18/DBfr18b.html#fn23.
5 *A Hard Day's Night*, directed by Richard Lester, 1964.
6 Allan Kozinn, 'They came, they sang, they conquered', *The New York Times*, 6 February 2004.
7 Albert and David Maysles, *'What's Happening! The Beatles in the USA*, Granada/CBS, 1964, re-released as *The Beatles: The First US Visit*, Apple Corps, 2004.
8 David Maysles, interviewed by James Blue, *Film Comment*, autumn 1964, 2 (4), reprinted in Kevin Macdonald and Mark Cousins, *Imagining Reality: The Faber Book of Documentary*, 1996.
9 *Stones in the Park*, Granada TV for ITV, 1969.
10 *Sympathy for the Devil*, directed by Jean-Luc Godard, 1968; both versions on Fabulous Pictures DVD, 2006.
11 *World in Action: Mick Jagger*, Granada for ITV, 31 July 1967; *World in Action* DVD compilation, 2005.
12 *Stones in the Park*, Granada TV for ITV, 1969.
13 Bill Nichols, *Introduction to Documentary*, 2001, pp. 131 and 137.
14 *Monterey Pop*, directed by D.A. Pennebaker, USA, 1967.
15 Rod Phillips, 'Monterey pop', in Ian Aitken (ed.), in *Encyclopedia of the Documentary Film*, 2006.
16 'How Woodstock happened', *The Times Herald-Record*, Woodstock commemorative edn, 1994.
17 'The Message of History's Biggest Happening' *Time* magazine, 29 August 1969, pp. 32–3.
18 *Woodstock*, directed by Michael Wadleigh, Warner Brothers, 1970; re-released, 225 minutes director's cut, 1994.
19 *Gimme Shelter*, directed by Albert and David Maysles, USA, 1970.
20 *Shine a Light*, directed by Martin Scorsese, USA, 2008.
21 www.salon.com/ent/review/2008/04/04/shine_a_light/.
22 *Don't Look Back*, directed by D.A. Pennebaker, USA, 1967.
23 *Easy Rider*, directed by Dennis Hopper, USA, 1969.
24 *The Last Waltz*, directed by Martin Scorsese, USA, 1978.
25 Michael Wilmington, 'Movie release: *The Last Waltz*', *The Chicago Tribune*, 18 April 2002.

26   Magazine sizes vary, but a standard 1,000 feet (300 m) runs about 11 minutes at 24 frames per second.

27   Having failed to build up an adequate subscriber base to pay the exorbitant fees it bid for the premiership, Setanta defaulted on payments in June 2009, was stripped of its Premiership rights and collapsed as a UK pay-channel on 26 June 2009.

28   *Football as Never Before*, directed by Hellmuth Costard, Germany, 1970.

29   *Zidane: un portrait du 21e siècle*, directed by Douglas Gordon and Philippe Parreno, France, 2006.

30   Johnny Ray Huston 'The mark of Zidane', *San Francisco Bay Guardian*, 16 May 2007.

31   *Kobe Doin' Work*, directed by Spike Lee, premiered at the Tribeca Film Festival, 25 April 2009 and transmitted 16 May 2009 on the ESPN channel. Not one of Lee's better works, this is widely ascribed to Bryant insisting on creative control, though Lee denies this.

32   Spike Lee talking to Jason Solomons, 'Trash Cannes', *The Observer*, 25 May 2008.

33   *Olympia*, directed by Leni Riefensthal, Germany, 1936.

34   *The Triumph of the Will*, directed by Leni Riefensthal, Germany, 1934.

35   *Joe Louis: America's Hero . . . Betrayed*, HBO, 23 February 2008.

36   *When We Were Kings*, directed by Leon Gast, USA, 1996.

37   Leger Grindon, '*When We Were Kings*', in Ian Aitken (ed.), *Encyclopedia of the Documentary Film*, 2006.

38   *Hoop Dreams*, directed by Steve James, USA, 1994.

39   Still unresolved at time of going to press.

40   Google search 26 May 2008 revealed: 7,940,000 results for 'skateboard videos'; 10,700,00 for 'running videos'; 11,700,000 for 'football videos'. On 26 June 2009, the same Google search terms yielded: 8,630,000 for skateboard, 85,900,000 for running and 86,800,000 for football.

41   Defendants' Answer to Amended Complaint and Demand for Jury Trial, www.youtubeclass action.com/courtdox/DefAnswertoAmdCplt.pdf.

42   Andrew Keen, speaking at Media Futures Conference, London, 20 June 2008.

43   Ibid.

44   www.amazon.co.uk (accessed 16 July 2008).

45   Ibid.

46   *The Daily Mirror*, 2 December 1976.

47   Stephen Dalton, 'Joe Strummer: the film', *The Times*, 12 May 2007.

48   Simon Garfield, 'This blissful film lasts for 35 years', *The Observer*, 26 March 2006.

49   Ibid.

50   Glastonbury 2009 prices.

51   Glastonbury 2008 was notable for not selling out, blamed by some (notably Oasis's Noel Gallagher) on choosing top hip-hop artist Jay-Z to headline.

52   Source: www.telegraph.com, 25 May 2008.

53   *Hitwise*, 25 June 2008, www.hitwise.com/press-center/hitwiseHS2004/google-increase-twentysix.php.

54   *Hitwise*, 26 March 2008, www.hitwise.co.uk/press-center/hitwiseHS2004/video.php.

55   Harry Wallop, 'BT calls for BBC to fund the costs of iPlayer', *The Daily Telegraph*, 10 June 2009.

56   John Roese, 'Personal view: Satisfying the bandwidth monster in all of us', *Financial Times*, 23 June 2008.

57   Jürgen Habermas, *The Structural Transformation of the Public Sphere*, 1989.

58   Andrew Keen, speaking at Media Futures Conference, London, 20 June 2008.

59   *Katie & Peter: The Next Chapter*, ITV2, 27 March–3 July 2008.

60   Unreality TV blog, www.unrealitytv.co.uk/reality-tv/katie-price-and-peter-andre-return-in-the-next-chapter/.

61   'Celebrity couple make paper pay', 2 July 2008, http://news.sky.com/skynews/Home/Showbiz-News/Model-Katie-Price-In-High-Court-Over-News-Of-World-Nanny-Story/Article/200807 115021026?f=rss.

62   Natalie Trombetta, 'Katie Price and Peter Andre split after four years of marriage', *The Daily Mail*, 13 May 2009, www.dailymail.co.uk/tvshowbiz/article-1180575/Its-Katie-Price-Peter-Andre-split-years-marriage.html.
63   *Geri*, directed by Molly Dineen, Channel 4, 5 May 1999.
64   'Molly Dineen', in David Goldsmith, *The Documentary Makers: Interviews with 15 of the Best in the Business*, London: RotoVision, 2003.
65   See Ian Goode, 'Living with fame: *Geri* and *Living with Michael Jackson*', *Social Semiotics*, June 2008, 18 (2).
66   Sean Redmond, 'I confess', *Social Semiotics*, June 2008, 18 (2).
67   *Madonna: Truth or Dare*, directed by Alek Kashishian, 1991.
68   Ibid.
69   Marcus Aurelius, *The Thoughts of Marcus Aurelius Antoninus*, Charleston: BiblioBazaar, 2008.
70   William Shakespeare, *As You Like It*, Act 2, Scene 7.
71   Sean O'Casey, *Sunset and Evening Star*, 1954, reprinted in *Autobiographies II*, New York: Carroll & Graf, 1984.

15 Drama-doc and docu-drama

1   Jimmy McGovern, 'The power of truth', *Guardian*, 10 June 2004.
2   José Padilha, quoted in Sheila Johnston, '*Elite Squad*: the movie that shook Brazil', *The Daily Telegraph*, 18 July 2008.
3   Ibid.
4   *Culloden*, directed by Peter Watkins, first broadcast on BBC TV, 5 December 1964.
5   *The War Game*, directed by Peter Watkins, first transmitted on BBC1, 31 July 1985.
6   Phillip Drummond, '*The War Game*', online Museum of Broadcast Communications, www.museum.tv/archlves/etv/W/htmlW/wargamethe/wargamethe.htm.
7   Patrick Murphy and John Cook, in Ian Aitken (ed.), *Encyclopedia of the Documentary Film*, 2006, pp. 14–16.
8   Kenneth Tynan, 'A warning masterpiece', *The Observer*, 13 February 1966.
9   Phillip Drummond, '*The War Game*', online Museum of Broadcast Communications, www.museum.tv/archives/etv/W/html/wargamethe/wargamethe.htm.
10   Dave Rolinson, 'Drama documentary'; BFI, www.screenonline.org.uk/tv/id/1103146/index.html.
11   *Z Cars* was a police drama series, created by Troy Kennedy Martin and Allan Prior, which ran on BBC1 from 1962 to 1978.
12   *Up the Junction*, directed by Ken Loach, BBC, first broadcast 3 November 1965.
13   *Cathy Come Home*, directed by Ken Loach, BBC, first broadcast 16 November 1966.
14   *In Two Minds*, directed by Ken Loach, BBC, first broadcast 1 March 1967.
15   R.D. Laing, *Sanity, Madness and the Family*, Vol. 1: *Families of Schizophrenics*, 1964.
16   Ken Loach quoted by Kevin Sherman, 'United Kingdom', in Ian Aitken (ed.), *Encyclopedia of the Documentary Film*, 2006, p. 1375.
17   *Days of Hope*, directed by Ken Loach, first broadcast 11 September 1975.
18   Tony Garnett, quoted in Ros Cranston, '*Days of Hope*', BFI, www.screenonline.org.uk/tv/id/467647/index.html.
19   *Death of a Princess*, directed by Anthony Thomas for ATV/WGBH, first transmitted on ITV 9 April 1980.
20   Saudi Embassy, London, press release, 11 April 1980.
21   Quoted in David Brockman, '*Death of a Princess*', *Transdiffusion*, 2 July 2005, www.transdiffusion.org/emc/behindthescreens/princess.php.
22   Bill Nichols, *Introduction to Documentary*, 2001, p. 20.
23   Paul Swann, *The British Documentary Film Movement 1926–1946*, 1989.
24   Lindsay Anderson, 'Only connect: some aspects of the work of Humphrey Jennings', *Sight and Sound*, April–June 1954.

25   Kevin Macdonald, quoted in Maxine Baker, *Documentary in the Digital Age*, 2006, p. 109.
26   Ibid., p. 110.
27   *The Life and Times of Rosie the Riveter*, directed by Connie Field, 1981.
28   Quoted in Judith Williamson, 'When the boys came home', *City Limits*, November 1981, p. 45.
29   Erik Barnouw, *Documentary: A History of the Non-fiction Film*, 1974, p. 185.
30   *The Thin Blue Line*, directed by Errol Morris, 1988.
31   Terrence Rafferty, 'The Thin Blue Line', *The New Yorker*, 5 September 1988.
32   Leslie Woodhead, talking to Prague Radio, 12 March 2007, www.radio.cz/en/article/89252.
33   *The Man Who Wouldn't Keep Quiet*, directed by Leslie Woodhead, first transmitted on ITV, 4 November 1970.
34   *Strike*, directed by Leslie Woodhead, 1981.
35   *Invasion*, directed by Leslie Woodhead, 1980.
36   Leslie Woodhead, talking to Prague Radio, 12 March 2007.
37   *Why Lockerbie?* directed by Leslie Woodhead, 1991.
38   *A Cry from the Grave*, directed by Leslie Woodhead, first transmitted on BBC2, 27 November 1999.
39   *Children of Beslan*, directed by Leslie Woodhead and Ewa Ewart, first transmitted on BBC2, 30 August 2005.
40   *The Fix*, directed by Paul Greengrass, first transmitted on ITV, 4 October 1997.
41   *The Murder of Stephen Lawrence*, directed by Paul Greengrass, first transmitted on ITV, 18 February 1999.
42   *The Stephen Lawrence Story*, directed by Kelvin Richard, first transmitted on Channel 4, 15 February 1997.
43   *Bloody Sunday*, directed by Paul Greengrass, first transmitted on ITV, 25 January 2002.
44   Desson Thomas, 'For Paul Greengrass, a connecting flight', *Washington Post*, 1 May 2006.
45   Ibid.
46   *Sunday*, directed by Jimmy McGovern, first transmitted on Channel 4, 28 January 2002.
47   *Hillsborough*, directed by Charles McDougall, first transmitted on ITV, 5 December 1996.
48   Dave Rolinson, 'Hillsborough', *BFI Screen Online*, www.screenonline.org.uk/tv/id/1052988/index.html.
49   *Dockers*, directed by Bill Anderson, first transmitted on Channel 4, 11 June 1999.
50   *Writing the Wrongs*, produced by Planet Wild, first transmitted on Channel 4, 11 June 1999.
51   Jimmy McGovern in *Writing the Wrongs*.
52   Jimmy McGovern, 'The power of truth', *Guardian*, 10 June 2004.
53   Jimmy McGovern, *Edgeways*, 1 April 2005, 13, www.edgehill.ac.uk/edgeways/issue13/inconversation.htm.
54   *Little Angels*, directed by Paul McGuigan, first transmitted BBC2, 13 August 2002.
55   Paul McGuigan, 'Director defends drug-taking scenes', BBC News website, 12 August 2002, http://news.bbc.co.uk/1/hi/uk/2179062.stm.
56   Jimmy McGovern, 'The power of truth', *Guardian*, 10 June 2004.
57   Margaret Lockwood Smith, quoted in Nicole Martin, 'Marchioness families ask ITV to drop drama', *The Daily Telegraph*, 24 August 2007.
58   Nick Elliott: 'Marchioness docu-drama will not be shown in its current form', *Guardian Organgrinder*, 25 August 2007.
59   *Ghosts*, directed by Nick Broomfield was first released in cinemas, 12 January 2007, then broadcast on More 4, April 2007.
60   Nick Broomfield, Televisual Intelligent Factual Festival, BAFTA, London, 22 May 2007.
61   Ibid.
62   J.C. Wilsher and Isabelle Grey, 'Drama documentary', *UK Writer*, New Year 2007.
63   Mark Lawson, 'TV Matters', *Guardian*, 16 November 2006.
64   *Murder at Harvard*, directed by Erik Stange, for *American Experience*, WGBH Boston, first transmitted on BBC2, *Timewatch*, 14 December 2002.
65   Simon Schama, *Dead Certainties (Unwarranted Speculations)*, 1991.

66   William Boyd, 'Dead uncertainties', *The Sunday Times*, 9 June 1991.

67   Linda Colley, 'Fabricating the past', *The Times Literary Supplement*, 14 June 1991, p. 5.

68   Martin Smith, 'History and the media: are you being hoodwinked?, *History Today*, March 2003, 53 (3): 28.

69   *The BBC's Editorial Values for News and Factual Programme Makers*, p. 8, www.bbc.co.uk/guidelines/editorialguidelines/edguide/.

70   Martin Smith, 'History and the media: are you being hoodwinked?, *History Today*, March 2003, 53 (3): 28.

71   *The Verdict*, made by RDF Media, first transmitted on BBC2, 11–15 February 2007.

72   Richard Klein, interviewed by the author, 29 June 2007.

73   *Consent*, directed by Brian Hill, first transmitted on Channel 4, 21 January 2007.

74   Stuart Jefferies, 'Twelve angry celebs', *Guardian*, 13 January 2007.

75   'Verdict show is trivialising rape', *Yahoo! News*, 12 February 2007.

76   Conviction rates of rape reported had fallen to 5.6 per cent in 2002. Source: Liz Kelly, Jo Lovett and Linda Regan, *A Gap or a Chasm? Attrition in Reported Rape Cases*, Home Office Research Study 293. Improved CPS procedures have led to a reported rise of 6.5 per cent at the time of writing, April 2009.

77   Richard Klein, interviewed by the author, 29 June 2007.

16 Art and anarchy

1   Guy-Ernest Debord, *La Société du Spectacle / The Society of the Spectacle*, 1967.

2   Guy-Ernest Debord, *Report on the Construction of Situations and on the International Situationist Tendency's Conditions of Organization and Action*, June 1957, www.bopsecrets.org/SI/report.htm.

3   Stuart Elliott 'Advertising: a new ranking of the "50 best" television commercials ever made', *The New York Times*, 14 March 1995, www.nytimes.com/1995/03/14/business/media-business-advertising-new-ranking-50-best-television-commercials-ever-made.html.

4   Steve Jobs, speaking at Apple Event, Fall 1983, www.youtube.com/watch?v=ISiQA6KKyJo.

5   Adelia Cellini, 'The story behind Apple's "1984" TV commercial: *Big Brother* at 20', *MacWorld*, January 2004.

6   *L'Arrivée d'un Train en Gare de la Ciotat / Arrival of a Train at a Station*, directed by Auguste and Louis Lumière, 1895, one of the first documentaries, shot in one shot on a single 50 second film roll.

7   *Un Chien Andalou*, directed by Luis Buñuel and Salvador Dali, 1924.

8   For example, *Ballet Mécanique*, directed by Fernad Léger, 1924; *Film is Rhythm*, directed by Hans Richter, incorporating *Rhythmus 21*, 1921, *Rhythmus 23*, 1923 and *Rhythmus 25*, 1925. See also Thomas Elsaesser, 'Dada/cinema?', in Rudolf E. Kuenzli (ed.), *Dada and Surrealist Films*, 1987.

9   Amos Vogel, *Film as a Subversive Art*, 1974, p. 19, quoting Erich Neuman, *Art and the Creative Unconscious*, 1959, p. 112.

10   Don McLaughlin, quoted in Amos Vogel, *Film as a Subversive Art*, 1974, p. 78.

11   Stan Brakhage, *Metaphors on Vision*, 1960, republished in Bruce McPherson (ed.), *Essential Brakhage: Selected Writings on Filmmaking*, 2001.

12   Brian Frye, 'Stan Brakhage', *Senses of Cinema*, September 2002, http://archive.sensesofcinema.com/contents/directors/02/brakhage.html.

13   Bill Nichols, *Representing Reality: Issues and Concepts in Documentary Cinema*, 1991, p. 81.

14   Bart Testa, 'Seeing with experimental eyes: Stan Brakhage's *The Act of Seeing with One's Own Eyes*', in Barry Keith Grant and Jeanette Sloniowski (eds), *Documenting the Documentary*, Detroit: Wayne State University Press, 1998, p. 284.

15   Quoted in Amos Vogel, *Film as a Subversive Art*, 1974, p. 104.

16   Stephen Dwoskin, 'Reflections: the self, the world and others, and how all these things melt together in film', *Trafic*, summer 2004, 50.

17   Ibid.
18   Stephen Dwoskin, *Film Is . . . the International Free Cinema*, 1975.
19   Gary Morris, 'Sorry, it had to be done! Radical actioner Kurt Kren', *Bright Lights Film Journal*, 24 April 1994, online, www.brightlightsfilm.com/24/kren.html.
20   Ibid.
21   Amos Vogel, *Film as a Subversive Art*, 1974, p. 199.
22   Kurt Kren, quoted by Morris, 'Sorry, it had to be done! Radical actioner Kurt Kren', *Bright Lights Film Journal*, 24 April 1994, online, www.brightlightsfilm.com/24/kren.html.
23   Amos Vogel, *Film as a Subversive Art*, 1974, p. 234.
24   Stan Brakhage, quoted in Laura Gildersleeve, 'Good for him! Four films by Stan Brakhage', *American Chronicle*, online, 19 March 2008, www.americanchronicle.com/articles/view/55815.
25   Stan Brakhage, quoted in Donovan Juan, 'Stan Brakhage and the newer laocoon of film', *The Minute Hands*, Juan's arts blogspot, posted 2 January 2008, http://theminutehands.blogspot.com/2008/01/stan-brakhage-and-newer-laocoon-of-film.html.
26   Jonas Mekas, *Movie Journal: The Rise of a New American Cinema 1959–71*, 1972, p. 236.
27   Jonas Mekas, *Just Like A Shadow*, 2000.
28   *As I Was Moving Ahead I Saw Brief Glimpses of Beauty*, directed by Jonas Mekas, 2000.
29   Genevieve Yue, 'Jonas Mekas', *Senses of Cinema*, January 2005, http://archive.sensesofcinema.com/contents/directors/05/mekas.html#6.
30   *Trying to Kiss the Moon*, directed by Stephen Dwoskin, 1994.
31   *Intoxicated by my Illness*, directed by Stephen Dwoskin, 2001.
32   Stephen Dwoskin, 'Fragments of a filmmaker's work', *Lussas: Le Village Documentaire*, words recorded by Maureen Loiret in Brixton, 21 August 2008, www.lussasdoc.com/etatsgeneraux/2008/programmation.php?id=117&loc=en.
33   Rachel Spence, 'Quattrocento art and Bill Viola's videos', *Financial Times*, 1 November 2008.
34   *San Francisco Museum of Modern Art* online catalogue for Bill Viola, www.sfmoma.org/media/features/viola/fr_videotapes1.html.
35   John Haber, 'Bill Viola at the Whitney', May 1998, www.haberarts.com/viola2.htm.
36   Rachel Spence, 'Quattrocento art and Bill Viola's videos', *Financial Times*, 1 November 2008
37   Bill Viola talking about his video installation, *The Messenger* (1996), to Martin Gayford, 'Viola's video altarpieces to grace St Paul's', bloomberg.com, 18 January 2009.
38   See N. Salomon, L. Tickner, M. Kelly, P. Smith and A. Jones, 'The gendered subject', in Donald Preziosi (ed.), *The Art of Art History*, 1998, pp. 344ff.
39   Richard Dorment, 'Beckham, the sleeping beauty', *The Daily Telegraph*, 28 April 2004, www.telegraph.co.uk/culture/art/3616013/Beckham-the-sleeping-beauty.html.
40   Dominique Païni, *Chantal Ackerman*, published to accompany the exhibition *Chantal Ackerman* at Camden Arts Centre, London, 11 July–14 September 2008.
41   Chantal Ackerman, speaking to Miriam Rosen, 'In her own time', trans. Jeanine Herman, *ArtForum*, 20 April 2004.
42   Alice Correia, 'Interpreting Jeremy Deller's *The Battle of Orgreave*', *Visual Culture in Britain*, 7 (2), winter 2006: 93–112.
43   Emma Brockes 'It's art, but is it porn?', *Guardian*, 5 November 2002, www.guardian.co.uk/artanddesign/2002/nov/05/turnerprize2002.turnerprize.
44   The title is a knowing appropriation of that of a leading work on the history of avante-garde art: Hal Foster, *The Return of the Real: Avant-garde at the End of the Century*, 1996.
45   Phil Collins, talking on the Tate website, www.tate.org.uk/britain/turnerprize/2006/philcollins.htm.
46   Victoria Miro gallery press release for *The Return of the Real*, 6 October–10 November 2007 show, www.victoria-miro.com/exhibitions/_381/?a=8.
47   Ibid.
48   T.J. Demos on the Otolith Group, *ArtForum*, September 2006.
49   Renzo Martens, speaking at the London School of Economics, 4 June 2009.

50   Ibid.
51   Jean Rouch, quoted in André Bazin, *What is Cinema?*, trans. Hugh Gray, 1967, p. 16.
52   Charlotte Higgins, 'The art of seduction: sex through the ages, from every possible angle',
     Guardian, 10 October 2007, www.guardian.co.uk/uk/2007/oct/10/art.artnews.
53   Kenneth Clark, *The Nude*, 1956.
54   Kenneth Clark, quoted in Tom Lubbock, 'The art of seduction', *The Independent*, 27 October
     2007, www.independent.co.uk/arts-entertainment/art/features/the-art-of-seduction-759174.
     html.
55   Ross McElwee, quoted in Scott Macdonald, *A Critical Cinema: Interviews with Independent
     Filmmakers*, 1992.
56   See Charles W. Morris, *Writings on the General Theory of Signs*, 1971; and Umberto Eco,
     A Theory of Semiotics (Advances in Semiotics), 1978.
57   *The Shining*, directed by Stanley Kubrick, 1980.
58   *The Blair Witch Project*, directed by Daniel Myrick and Eduardo Sánchez, 1999, cost $22,000
     to make and grossed over $248 million worldwide, making it the highest ratio return on any
     film investment.
59   Nixon campaign scripts reproduced in Joe McGinniss, *The Selling of the President*, 1970.

Part V Watch the figures

1   *40 Minutes* ran 324 editions on BBC2 between 1 October 1981 and 9 April 1994.
2   Roger Graef, talking at televisual conference, July 2007.
3   Nick Fraser, talking to BBC4 website, October 2004, www.bbc.co.uk/bbcfour/documentaries/
    storyvllle/nick-fraser-interview.shtml.
4   Clay Shirky, *Here Comes Everybody*, 2008.
5   Ibid.
6   Marc Francis, speaking to the author at Goldsmiths, 24 October 2007.
7   *Black Gold*, produced and directed by Marc and Nick Francis, was shown on More 4,
    3 February 2009 and under the *Independent Lens* banner on PBS.

17 Box office

1   Marilyn Gaunt, 'From eight-man crew to one-woman band: my life in television documentary',
    in Thomas Austin and Wilma de Jong (eds), *Rethinking Documentary: New Perspectives, New
    Practices*, 2009, p. 156.
2   Angus Macqueen, talking to the author, July 2007.
3   Jess Search, 'Picture perfect partners, cool brands promotional feature', http://britdoc.org/
    assets/media/docs/foundation_observer.pdf. Accessed 19 January 2009; website now
    redesigned.
4   *The Day after Peace* (2009) charts Jeremy Gilley's involvement of world leaders and film stars
    in his one-man campaign to get the world to adopt an annual Peace Day.
5   Mojo Box Office website, www.boxofficemojo.com/genres/chart/?id=documentary.htm.
6   Michael Moore at Academy Awards ceremony, Hollywood, 24 March 2003.
7   Christopher Hitchens, in 'Unfairenheit 9/11', *Slate*, 21 June 2004, attacks Moore at length
    for being 'inconsistent', 'hypocritical', 'opportunistic' and 'morally frivolous', www.slate.com/
    id/2102723/.
8   *The Corporation*, directed by Mark Achbar and Jennifer Abbott, 2003.
9   'The lunatic you work for', *The Economist*, 6 May 2004.
10 Roger Ebert, 'The corporation', *Chicago Sunday Times*, 16 July 2004.
11 Thomas Austin and Wilma de Jong (eds), *Rethinking Documentary: New Perspectives, New
    Practices*, 2009, p. 24
12 Bethany McLean, question 'Is Enron over-priced?', *Fortune*, 5 March 2001.

13   In 1720, a debt-ridden UK government granted the South Sea Company a monopoly on trade with Spain's thirteen South American colonies and shares quickly escalated as the country, led by politicians and the Royal Family, speculated wildly on promised profits. The South Sea Bubble then burst, bankrupting thousands.

14   Gore, *An Inconvenient Truth*, directed by Davis Guggenheim, 2006.

15   McClure, 'Travel adventuring: Greg MacGillivray', in *Travel Adventure Cinema*, 9 November 2008, www.traveladventurecinema.com/story.php?content=1226279615.

16   Jill Hecht Maxwell, 'In a former life: Greg MacGillivray', *Inc. magazine*, August 2001, www.inc.com/magazine/20010801/23231.html.

17   *Grand Canyon Adventure*, Interview with director/producer Greg MacGillivray. *Big Movie Zone*, 7 April 2008, www.bigmoviezone.com/articles/index.html?uniq=314.

18   MacGillivray Freeman Films company profile, www.macfreefilms.com/company.htm.

19   Wade Holden, quoted in Desson Thompson 'March of the cuddly-wuddly documentaries', *Washington Post*, 29 July 2007.

20   'The numbers', 29 January 2009, www.the-numbers.com/market/Genres/Documentary.php.

21   Anthony Breznican, 'Penguins' progress', *USA Today*, 28 November 2006.

22   Desson Thompson, 'March of the cuddly-wuddly documentaries', *Washington Post*, 29 July 2007.

23   Ibid.

24   Todd Gilchrist, 'Arctic tale review', ign movies.com, 27 July 2007, http://uk.movies.ign.com/articles/807/807434p1.html.

25   *Grizzly Man*, directed by Werner Herzog, 2005.

26   Ibid.

27   Peter Bradshaw, '*Grizzly Man*', *Guardian*, 3 February 2006.

28   Robert Ebert, '*Grizzly Man*', *Chicago Sunday Times*, 12 August 2005.

29   Thomas Austin, ' ". . .to leave the confinements of his humanness": authorial voice, death and constructions of nature in Werner Herzog's *Grizzly Man*', in Thomas Austin and Wilma de Jong (eds), *Rethinking Documentary: New Perspectives, New Practices*, 2009, p. 55.

30   Paul Cronin (ed.), *Herzog on Herzog*, 2002, p. 301.

31   Michael Renov, 'First-person films', in Thomas Austin and Wilma de Jong (eds), *Rethinking Documentary: New Perspectives, New Practices*, 2009, p. 41.

32   Ibid., p. 42.

33   Ibid., p. 45.

34   Megan Ratner, 'A memoir of circumstance and substance', *Bright Lights Film Journal*, February 2004, 43, www.brightlightsfilm.com/43/myarch.htm.

35   *The Fog of War*, directed by Errol Morris, 2003.

36   'Video shows Bush Katrina warning', BBC News website, 2 March 2006, http://news.bbc.co.uk/1/hi/world/americas/4765058.stm.

37   Barack Obama, Inauguration speech, Washington, 20 January 2009.

38   George W. Bush, White House press conference, 6 November 2001.

39   *Taxi to the Dark Side*, directed by Alex Gibney, 2007.

40   Ibid.

41   Missy Schwartz, 'Errol Morris: his new Iraq documentary', ew.com, www.ew.com/ew/article/0,,20195530,00.html.

42   Philip Gourevich and Errol Morris, 'Exposure: the woman behind the camera at Abu Ghraib', *The New Yorker*, 24 March 2008, www.newyorker.com/reporting/2008/03/24/080324fa_fact_gourevitch?

43   Ibid.

44   Ibid.

45   *Standard Operating Procedure*, directed by Errol Morris, 2008.

46   Maxine Baker, *Documentary in the Digital Age*, London: Focal Press, 2006, p. 8.

47   Missy Schwartz, 'Errol Morris: his new Iraq documentary', ew.com, www.ew.com/ew/article/0,,20195530,00.html.

48 *Taxi to the Dark Side*, directed by Alex Gibney, 2007.
49 Tony Blair, talking to David Aaronovich on *The Blair Years*, BBC1, 17 November 2007.
50 President George W. Bush, National Cathedral, Washington DC, 2 October 2001.
51 *Expelled: No Intelligence Allowed*, directed by Nathan Frankowski, 2008.
52 Ibid.
53 See Holocaust survivor's website, http://isurvived.org/home.html#prologue.
54 Justin Chang '*Expelled: No Intelligence Allowed*', *Variety*, 11 April 2008.
55 http://uk.rottentomatoes.com/m/expelled_no_intelligence_allowed/.
56 *Religulous*, directed by Larry Charles, 2008.
57 Bill Maher on *The Early Show with Harry Smith*, CBS News, 29 September 2008.
58 Ibid.
59 Larry Charles, quoted in Bruce Demara, 'Maher preaches to the TIFF choir', *Toronto Star*, 10 September 2007, www.thestar.com/entertainment/article/254761.
60 Bill Maher on Scarborough Country, MSNBC TV, 15 February 2005, www.msnbc.msn.com/id/6980984.
61 Richard Dawkins's 2-part *The Root of All Evil?*, Channel 4, first broadcast 4 and 11 January 2006.
62 *Man on Wire*, directed by James Marsh, 2008.
63 Ibid.
64 www.the-numbers.com/movies/series/Documentary.php.
65 Carla Mertes, quoted by Andrew Smith, 'Touching the void', *Guardian*, 30 January 2009.
66 *Burma VJ*, directed by Anders Østergaard, Denmark, 2008.
67 Andrew Marshall, '*Burma VJ*, truth as casualty', *Time Magazine*, 29 January 2009
68 Britdoc conference with NGOs (The Third Sector), 2008, http://britdoc.org/britdoc/third_sector/.
69 In the UK, Current TV is found on Sky channel 183 and Virgin Media 155; for US channels carrying Current TV see http://current.com/tv_shows.htm.

18 Biopics

1 Cinéaste Kevin Brownlow collected material for *Napoléon*'s revival, the most recent showing of which on three screens ran 5½ hours at the Royal Festival Hall in December 2004, with a live orchestra.
2 http://en.wikipedia.org/wiki/List_of_biographical_films.
3 *Elgar*, directed by Ken Russell, first transmitted BBC1, 11 November 1962.
4 Michael Kennedy, *Portrait of Elgar*, 1968.
5 *The Debussy Film*, directed by Ken Russell, first transmitted BBC1, 18 May 1965.
6 *Isadora Duncan: The Biggest Dancer in the World*, directed by Ken Russell, first transmitted BBC1, 22 September 1966.
7 *Song of Summer*, directed by Ken Russell, first transmitted BBC1, 15 September 1968.
8 Eric Fenby, *Delius, As I Knew Him*, 1936.
9 Ian Lace, *Film Music on the Web*, www.musicweb-international.com/film/2002/Jan02/DVD_delius.html.
10 Ken Russell, *Song of Summer*, BBC 1968, British Film Institute, DVD BFIVD518.
11 *Dance of the Seven Veils*, directed by Ken Russell, first transmitted BBC1, 15 February 1970.
12 Michael Brooke, '*Dance of the Seven Veils* (1970)', BFI online, www.screenonline.org.uk/tv/id/482892/.
13 John Baxter, *An Appalling Talent: Ken Russell*, 1973.
14 Ken Russell, *A British Picture: An Autobiography*, 1989, 2008.
15 Joseph Lanza, *Phallic Frenzy: Ken Russell and His Films*, 2007, p. 2.
16 A forthcoming biography of Ken Russell by Linda Ruth Williams promises to put the record straight.

17   The trial of Penguin Books under the Obscene Publications Act lasted from 20 October to 2 November 1960.

18   *Ralph Vaughan Williams*, directed by Ken Russell, *South Bank Show*, ITV, 8 April 1984.

19   *The Strange Affliction of Anton Bruckner*, directed by Ken Russell, *South Bank Show*, ITV, 14 October 1990.

20   *The Secret Life of Arnold Bax*, directed by Ken Russell, *South Bank Show*, 22 November 1992.

21   *The Mystery of Dr Martinu*, directed by Ken Russell, BBC2, 16 May 1992.

22   Ken Russell, 'The films designed to delight', *The Times*, 31 January 2008, http://entertainment. timesonline.co.uk/tol/arts_and_entertainment/film/article3278581.ece.

23   Ken Russell, 'When it comes to TV, fiction is truer than fact', *The Times*, 20 January 2009, http://entertainment.timesonline.co.uk/tol/arts_and_entertainment/tv_and_radio/article5547505.ece.

24   Ibid.

25   'No Direction Home', *Film as Art: Daniel Griffin's Guide to Cinema*, http://uashome.alaska. edu/~dfgriffin/website/nodirectionhome.htm.

26   *ABC Stage 67* was an innovative but unsuccessful attempt to run a weekly strand including dramas, documentaries, variety and musicals. It ran for one season, from 14 September 1967 to 4 May 1968.

27   *Eat the Document*, directed by Bob Dylan with Howard Alk, 1972, first screened at New York's Academy of Music and the Whitney Museum of American Art.

28   *Eat the Document*, clips available on www.youtube.com/watch?v=GhKhTtQpe6o&feature=related.

29   *I'm Not There*, directed by Todd Haynes, 2007.

30   Ibid.

31   Deborah Curtis, *Touching the Distance*, 1995.

32   *Joy Division: Their Own Story in Their Own Words*, directed by Grant Gee, 2008.

33   'Ray DVD beats box office takings', BBC News online, 10 February 2005, http://news.bbc.co. uk/1/hi/4252929.stm.

34   For example, www.haro-online.com/movies/biggie_and_tupac.html.

35   *Notorious*, directed by George Tillman, Jnr, 2009.

36   Steven Zeitchik and Matthew Belloni, 'Tupac biopic at center of legal battle', *Billboard*, 19 February 2009, www.billboard.com/bbcom/news/shakur-biopic-at-center-of-legal-battle-1003942843.story.

37   Howard Good, *Diamond in the Dark: America, Baseball and the Movies*, 1995, p. 55.

38   The Heisman Memorial Trophy Award is the most prestigious annual award for the most outstanding player in American college football.

39   *Ali*, directed by Michael Mann, 2001, listing in *Time Out Film Guide 2009*, London: Time Out, 2008.

40   *Tyson*, directed by James Toback, 2008.

41   The American Film Institute has *Raging Bull* as the best sports film of all time and 4th in all-time best 100, http://connect.afi.com/site/DocServer/TOP10.pdf?docID=441.

42   Jake La Motta, *Raging Bull*, 1970.

43   David Thomson, 'Animal Instinct', *Guardian*, 10 August 2007, www.guardian.co.uk/film/2007/ aug/10/martinscorsese.robertdeniro.

44   Malcolm X with Alex Haley, *The Autobiography of Malcolm X*, 1965.

45   *Malcolm X*, directed by Arnold Perl, 1971.

46   Bernard Weinraub, 'A movie producer remembers the human side of Malcolm X', *The New York Times*, 23 November 1992, www.nytimes.com/1992/11/23/movies/a-movie-producer-remembers-the-human-side-of-malcolm-x.html.

47   *The American Heritage® Dictionary of the English Language*, 4th edn, Boston, MA: Houghton Mifflin, 2000.

48   Amira Bakara, spokesman for the United Front to Preserve the Legacy of Malcolm X, quoted in David Ansen and Spike Lee, 'The battle for Malcolm X', *Newsweek*, 26 August 1996, www. newsweek.com/id/122433/output/.

49 Spike Lee in Bernard Weinraub, 'Spike Lee's request: black interviewers only', *The New York Times*, 29 October 1992, www.nytimes.com/1992/10/29/movies/spike-lee-s-request-black-interviewers-only.html.
50 Ibid.
51 *Veronica Guerin*, directed by Joel Schumacher, UK-Eire, 2003.
52 *The Deal*, directed by Stephen Frears, first transmitted on Channel 4, 28 September 2003.
53 *David Frost Interviews Richard Nixon*, produced by Paradine Productions, first transmitted 19 May 1977.
54 David Peace, *The Damned United*, 2006.
55 Tim Teeman, '*The Damned United*'s Peter Morgan say it's time to leave reality behind', *The Times*, 21 March 2009, http://entertainment.timesonline.co.uk/tol/arts_and_entertainment/film/article5944527.ece.
56 Armand White, 'Steve McQueen's *Hunger*', *New York Press*, 18 March 2009, www.nypress.com/article-19539-steve-mcqueens-hunger.html.
57 Sean O'Hagan, 'McQueen and country', *The Observer*, 12 October 2008, www.guardian.co.uk/film/2008/oct/12/2.
58 Rob Carnevale, '*Hunger* – Steve McQueen Interview, *indielondon*, www.indielondon.co.uk/Film-Review/hunger-steve-mcqueen-interview.
59 Aaron Hills, 'Steve McQueen touches history in *Hunger*', ifc.com, www.ifc.com/news/2009/03/steve-mcqueen-on-hunger.php?page=1.
60 Stefan Aust, *The Baader-Meinhof Complex*, 2008.
61 'Schnelle von Buback, Lob von Schleyer' / 'Censure from Buback, Praise from Schleyer', *Der Spiegel* online (trans. by author), www.spiegel.de/kultur/kino/0,1518,578833,00.html.
62 Michael Koresky, 'Out for blood: Paolo Sorrentino's *Il Divo*', *indieWire*, www.indiewire.com/article/out_for_blood_paolo_sorrentinos_il_divo/.
63 Stephen Holden, 'Out of Fellini and into *The Godfather*: a politician's life', *The New York Times*, 24 April 2009, http://movies.nytimes.com/2009/04/24/movies/24divo.html.
64 Michael Fleming, 'Oliver Stone votes for Bush project', *Variety*, 20 January 2008, www.variety.com/index.asp?layout=awardcentral&jump=contenders&id=director&articleid=VR1117979349&cs=1.
65 *The Blair Years*, first part (of 3) transmitted BBC1, 18 November 2007, based on Alastair Campbell, *The Blair Years*, London: Arrow Books, 2007.
66 *The Rise and Fall of Tony Blair*, written and presented by Andrew Rawnsley, Channel 4, 23 June 2007.
67 Christopher Gildemeister, 'Entertainment industry news for the week of 16 October 2006', Parents Television Council, www.parentstv.org/PTC/publications/culturewatch/2006/1016.asp.
68 Between 19 November 2003 and 12 June 2004, 95 original documentaries were transmitted under Channel 4's *Secret History* title.
69 William Roscoe Thayer, *The Art of Biography*, 1920, p. 34.
70 Ibid., p. 24.
71 John Bird, *Percy Grainger*, 1999.

19 Wildlife

....

1 Alastair Fothergill, interviewed by the author, 17 July 2008.
2 C.P. Snow's Rede lecture, *The Two Cultures and the Scientific Revolution* was delivered in the Senate House, Cambridge on 7 May 1959. C.P. Snow, *The Two Cultures*, 1993.
3 *Life in Cold Blood*, produced by BBC Natural History Unit, first transmitted on BBC1, 4 February 2008.
4 David Attenborough interviewed by Jeremy Paxman, 'The last word', *Radio Times*, 26 January 2008.
5 For example, George Monbiot, see http://video.google.com/videoplay?docid=-7446813467523135314.

6   David Attenborough: 'Climate change is the major challenge facing the world', *The Independent*, 26 May 2006.

7   Ibid.

8   www.bbc.co.uk/pressoffice/pressreleases/stories/2006/12_december/16/icon.shtml.

9   *Climate Change: Britain Under Threat*, a BBC Open University co-production, BBC1, 21 January 2007.

10   *The Truth about Climate Change*, first broadcast BBC2, 22 October 2006.

11   *Planet Earth*, produced by Alastair Fothergill, was transmitted in two runs on BBC1, from 5 March to 2 April 2006, and from 5 November to December 2006.

12   Alastair Fothergill, interviewed by the author, 17 July 2008.

13   Peter Barron, quoted in Adam Sherwin, 'BBC scraps plans for day-long special on climate change', *The Times*, 6 September 2007, http://entertainment.timesonline.co.uk/tol/arts_and_entertainment/ tv_and_radio/article2393266.ece. In July 2008, Barron announced he was leaving the BBC to become Google UK's Head of Communications and Public Affairs.

14   Peter Horrocks, interviewed by the author, 4 April 2008.

15   George Monbiot, http://video.google.com/videoplay?docid=-7446813467523135314.

16   Alastair Fothergill, interviewed by the author, 17 July 2008.

17   Miles Barton, interviewed by the author, 10 July 2007.

18   Nigel Pope, interviewed by the author, 10 May 2007.

19   *Orangutan Diary*, first aired on BBC1, 2–6 April 2007.

20   Ibid.

21   Ibid.

22   Alastair Fothergill, interviewed by the author, 17 July 2008.

23   Miles Barton, interviewed by the author, 10 July 2007.

24   Alastair Fothergill, interviewed by the author, 17 July 2008. In October 2007, the BBC announced cuts in staff and budget for the NHU of one-third, significantly more than the 105 cuts being made across BBC production.

25   *Live and Kicking* ran on BBC1 Saturday mornings from 2 October 1993 to 15 September 2001; *The Saturday Show* followed, from 22 September 2001 to 3 September 2005.

26   *Springwatch* ran on BBC2 from 22 September 2001 to 3 September 2005, and annually since; *Autumnwatch* ran first as a two-week series on BBC2 from 2 to 12 October 2006.

27   Nigel Pope, interviewed by the author, 10 May 2007.

28   Ibid.

29   Alastair Fothergill, interviewed by the author, 17 July 2008. The DVD of the BBC series *Planet Earth* had sold over 2.65 million by May 2009, making $147 million. Source: www.the-numbers.com/dvd/charts/annual/2007.php.

30   Alastair Fothergill, interviewed by the author, 17 July 2008.

31   Nigel Pope, interviewed by the author, 10 May 2007.

32   Ibid.

33   Ibid.

34   Ibid.

35   Sir David Attenborough talking to Bob McKeown, on the release of *Cruel Camera*, produced by CBC and first shown 16 January 2008, www.cbc.ca/fifth/cruelcamera/attenborough.html.

36   Ibid.

37   Nigel Pope, interviewed by the author, 10 May 2007.

38   *Meerkat Manor*, produced by Oxford Scientific Films for Animal Planet International, 2005–9.

39   Alastair Fothergill, interviewed by the author, 17 July 2008.

40   Ibid.

41   Ibid.

42   Nigel Pope, interviewed by the author, 10 May 2007.

43   Miles Barton, interviewed by the author, 10 July 2007.

44   Alastair Fothergill, interviewed by the author, 17 July 2008.

45   *Walking with Dinosaurs*, first episode (of six) broadcast BBC1, 16 April 1999.

46 *The Blue Planet*, produced by Alastair Fothergill for BBC NHU, first transmitted BBC1, 12 September–31 October 2001.
47 Alastair Fothergill, interviewed by the author, 17 July 2008.
48 Nigel Pope, interviewed by the author, 10 May 2007.
49 Mark Thompson, Speech to BBC staff on delivering Creative Future, 18 October 2007, www.bbc.co.uk/pressoffice/speeches/stories/thompson_staff_181007.shtml.
50 www.channel4.com/corporate/4producers/commissioning/documentaries.html.
51 http://britdoc.org/real_good/hotdocs/.
52 http://docsource.sundance.org/.
53 www.ukfilmcouncil.org.uk/featuredocs.
54 www.edn.dk/art.lasso?nn=1.
55 www.wellcome.ac.uk/Funding/index.htm.
56 http://hartleyfoundation.org/grants.
57 www.nea.org/index.html.
58 www.nasaa-arts.org/aoa/grant_makers.shtml.
59 www.neh.gov/.
60 www.filmarts.org/.
61 www.federalfundingprograms.org/.
62 http://creativecommons.org/.

Bibliography

Aaron, M. (ed.) (2004) *New Queer Cinema*, Brunswick, NJ: Rutgers University Press.

Aitken, I. (ed.) (2005) *Encyclopedia of the Documentary Film*, London: Routledge.

Allan, S. (ed.) (2005) *Journalism: Critical Issues*, Maidenhead: Open University Press.

Altheide, D.L. (1997) 'The news media, the problem frame, and the production of fear', *The Sociological Quarterly*, 38 (4): 647–68.

Anderson, L. (1954) 'Only connect: some aspects of the work of Humphrey Jennings', *Sight and Sound*, April–June.

Andrejevic, M. (2004) *Reality TV: The Work of Being Watched*, Lanham, MD: Rowman & Littlefield.

Armstrong, R. (2005) *Understanding Realism (Understanding the Moving Image)*, London: BFI.

Aust, S. (2008) *The Baader-Meinhof Complex*, London: Bodley Head.

Austin, T. and de Jong, W. (eds) (2009) *Rethinking Documentary: New Perspectives, New Practices*, Maidenhead: Open University Press/McGraw-Hill.

Baker, M. (2006) *Documentary in the Digital Age*, London: Focal Press.

Barnett, S. (2005) 'Opportunity or threat: the BBC, investigative journalism and the Hutton report', in S. Allen (ed.), *Journalism: Critical Issues*, Maidenhead: Open University Press.

Barnouw, E. (1974, 1983, 1993) *Documentary: A History of the Non-fiction Film*, Oxford: Oxford University Press.

Barsam, R.M. (1975) *Film Guide to Triumph of the Will*, Bloomington, IN: Indiana University Press.

—— (1992) *Non-fiction Film: A Critical History*, Bloomington, IN: Indiana University Press.

Barthes, R. (1957, 1972, 2000) *Mythologies*, Paris: Editions du Seuil; London: Jonathan Cape; London: Vintage, new edn.

—— (1978, 1993) *Image – Music – Text*, New York: Hill & Wang.

Baxter, J. (1973) *An Appalling Talent: Ken Russell*, London: Michael Joseph.

Bazin, A. (1967, 1971) *What Is Cinema?*, Vols I and II, trans. Hugh Gray. Berkeley, CA: University of California Press.

Beck, U. and Bech-Gernsheim, E. (2002) *Individualizatio: Institutionalized Individualism and its Social and Political Consequences*, London: Sage.

Berger, J. (1972) *Ways of Seeing*, London: BBC/Penguin Books.

—— (1980, 1991) *About Looking*, New York: Vintage International.

Bernard, Sheila Curran (2004) *Documentary Storytelling for Film and Videomakers*, Oxford: Focal Press.

Berry, C. (2003, 2008) *Chinese Films in Focus II*, London: BFI.

—— (2008) *Postsocialist Cinema in Post-Mao China: The Cultural Revolution after the Cultural Revolution*, London: Routledge.

Bignell, J. and Orlebar, J. (2005) *The Television Handbook*, London: Routledge.

Bird, J. (1999) *Percy Grainger*, Oxford: Oxford University Press.

Blunkett, D. (2006) *The Blunkett Tapes: My Life in the Bear Pit*, London: Bloomsbury.

Bolton, R. (1990) *Death on the Rock and Other Stories*, London: W.H. Allen and Virgin Books.

Bordwell, D. (1985) *Narration in the Fiction Film*, Madison, WI: University of Wisconsin Press.

Boser, F.J., Meyer, G.S., Roberto, A.J. and Inge, C.G. (2003) A report on the effect of the Unitedstreaming™ application on educational performance, *United Learning*, August.

Bourdieu, P. (1993) *The Field of Cultural Production*, Cambridge: Polity Press.
—— (1998) *On Television*, New York: New Press.
Bourriaud, N. (2000) *Postproduction. Culture as Screenplay: How Art Reprograms the World*, New York: Lucas & Sternberg.
Bousé, D. (2000) *Wildlife Films*, Philadelphia, PA: Philadelphia University Press.
Boyle, R. (2006) *Sports Journalism: Context and Issues*, London: Sage.
Bradley, R. *et al*. (1994) *Children's Hospital*, London: Penguin Character Books.
Briggs, A. (1995) *History of Broadcasting in the United Kingdom*, Oxford: Oxford University Press.
Bronowski, J. (1973) *The Ascent of Man*, London: Little Brown & Co.
Brooke, H. (2006) *Your Right to Know – New Edition: A Citizen's Guide to the Freedom of Information Act*, London: Pluto Press.
Brooker, W. and Jermyn, D. (eds) (2003) *The Audience Studies Reader*, London: Routledge.
Brown, M. (2007) *A Licence to be Different: The Story of Channel 4*, London: BFI.
Bruzzi, S. (2000, 2006) *New Documentary: A Critical Introduction*, London: Routledge.
—— (2007) *Seven Up*, London: BFI.
Burt, J. (2002) *Animals in Film*, London: Reaktion Books.
Burton, J. (1986) *Cinema and Social Change in Latin America: Conversations with Filmmakers*, Austin, TX: University of Texas Press.
Canetti, E. (1962, 1973, 1984) *Crowds and Power*, London: Victor Gollancz.
Cashmore, C. (2005) *Making Sense of Sports*, 4th edn, Abingdon: Routledge.
—— (2006) *Celebrity Culture: Key Ideas*, Abingdon: Routledge.
Center for Public Integrity (2000) *Citizen Muckraking: Stories and Tools for Defeating the Goliaths of Our Day*, Monroe, ME: Common Courage Press.
Centre for Public Broadcasting (2004) *Television Goes to School. The Impact of Video on Student Learning in Formal Education*, New York: Education Development Center.
Chanan, M. (2007) *The Politics of Documentary*, London: BFI.
Chapman, J. (2007) *Documentary in Practice*, Cambridge: Polity Press.
Chowdhry, P. (2000) *Colonial India and the Making of Empire Cinema: Image, Ideology and Identity*, Manchester: Manchester University Press.
Clark, K. (1956) *The Nude*, London: John Murray.
—— (1969) *Civilisation: A Personal View*, New York: Harper & Row.
Corner, J. (1996) *The Art of Record: A Critical Introduction to Documentary*, Manchester: Manchester University Press.
Correia, A. (2006) 'Interpreting Jeremy Deller's *The Battle of Orgreave*', *Visual Culture in Britain*, 7 (2), winter.
Couldry, N. (2003) *Media Rituals: A Critical Approach*, London: Routledge.
Coyer, K., Dowmunt, T. and Fountain, A. (2007) *The Alternative Media Handbook*, London: Routledge.
Cronin, P. (ed.) (2002) *Herzog on Herzog*, London: Faber & Faber.
Curran, J. (2002) *Media and Power: Communication and Society*, London: Routledge.
—— and Seaton, J. (2003) *Power without Responsibility: The Press and Broadcasting in Britain*, London: Routledge.
Curtis, D. (1995) *Touching the Distance*, London: Faber & Faber.
Daniel, D.K. (2000) 'Best of times and worst of times: investigative reporting in post-Watergate America', in M. Greenwald and J. Bernt (eds), *The Big Chill: Investigative Reporting in the Current Media Environment*, Ames, IA: Iowa State University Press.
Davies, N. (2008) *Flat Earth News: An Award-winning Reporter Exposes Falsehood, Distortion and Propaganda in the Global Media*, London: Chatto & Windus.
Dawkins, R. (2006) *The God Delusion*, London: Bantam Press.
Debord, G.-E. (1967, 1977) *La Société du Spectacle / The Society of the Spectacle*, Paris: Editions Buchet-Chastel; Detroit: Black & Red.
de Burgh, H. (2000) *Investigative Journalism: Context and Practice*, London: Routledge.
Don, M. (2006) *Growing Out of Trouble*, London: Hodder & Stoughton.
Dornfield, B. (1998) *Producing Public Television, Producing Public Culture*, Princeton, NJ: Princeton University Press.

Dovey, J. (2000) *Freakshow: First Person Media and Factual TV*, London: Pluto Press.

Dowmunt, T., Dunford, M. and van Hemert, N. (eds) (2007) *Inclusion Through Media*, London: Goldsmiths.

Dwoskin, S. (1975) *Film Is . . . The International Free Cinema*, London: Peter Owen.

—— (2004) 'Reflections: the self, the world and others, and how all these things melt together in film', *Trafic*, 50, summer.

Eco, U. (1978) *A Theory of Semiotics (Advances in Semiotics)*, Bloomington, IN: Indiana University Press.

Edwards, D. and Cromwell, D. (2006) *Guardians of Power: The Myth of the Liberal Media*, London: Pluto Press.

Elena, A. and Lopez, M.D. (2003) *The Cinema of Latin America*, London: Wallflower Press.

Ellis, J. (2000) *Seeing Things: Television in the Age of Uncertainty*, London: I.B. Tauris.

—— and McLane, B.A. (2005) *A New History of Documentary Film*, London: Continuum.

Fanon, F. (1961, 1963, 2001) *Les Damnés de la Terre / The Wretched of the Earth*, trans. C. Farrington, London: Penguin Books.

Fenby, E. (1936) *Delius, As I Knew Him*, London: Fenby Press.

Fenton, N. (ed.) (2009) *New Media, Old News: Journalism and Democracy in the Digital Age*, London: Sage.

Ferguson, N. (2002) *Empire: How Britain Made the Modern World*, London: Allen Lane.

—— (2004) *Colossus: The Rise and Fall of the American Empire*, New York: Penguin Press.

Foster, G.A. (1997) *Women Filmmakers of the African and Asian Diaspora: Decolonizing the Gaze, Locating Subjectivity*, Carbondale, IL: University of Southern Illinois Press.

Foster, H. (1996) *The Return of the Real: Avant-garde at the End of the Century*, Cambridge, MA: MIT Press.

Foucault, M. (1984,1986) *Histoire de la sexuality, III: le souci de soi / The History of Sexuality, Vol. III, The Care of the Self*, Paris: Pantheon; New York: Allen Lane.

Fukiyama, F. (1993) *The End of History and the Last Man*, New York: Penguin Books.

Gallop, J. (ed.) (2004) *Polemic: Critical or Uncritical*, London: Routledge.

Gever, M., Greyson, J. and Parmar, P. (eds) (1993) *Queer Looks: Perspectives on Lesbian and Gay Film and Video*, New York: Routledge

Giddens, A. (1991) *Modernity and Self-Identity*, London: Polity Press.

Good, H. (1995) *Diamond in the Dark: America, Baseball and the Movies*, Lanham, MD: Scarecrow Press.

Gore, A. (1992) *Earth in the Balance: Foraging a New Common Purpose*, London: Earthscan.

—— (2006) *An Inconvenient Truth*, London: Bloomsbury.

Grant, B. and Sloniowski, J. (eds) (1998) *Documenting the Documentary: Close Readings of Documentary Film and Video*, Detroit, MI: Wayne State University Press.

Grey, S. (2007) *Ghost Plane: The True Story of the CIA Rendition and Torture Programme*, London: St Martin's Griffin.

—— (2009) *Operation Snakebite: The Explosive True Story of an Afghan Desert Siege*, New York: Viking.

Grierson, J. and Hardy, F. (eds) (1979) *Grierson on Documentary*, London: Faber & Faber.

Grimes, T., Anderson, J. and Bergen, L. (2008) *Media Violence and Aggression: Science and Ideology*, London: Sage.

Habermas, J. (1962, 1989) *Strukturwandel der Öffentlichkeit. Untersuchungen zu einer Kategorie der bürgerlichen Gesellschaft / The Structural Transformation of the Public Sphere: An Inquiry into a Category of Bourgeois Society*, trans. Burger and Lawrence, Cambridge: Polity Press.

Harcup, T. (2003, 2009) *Journalism: Principles and Practice*, London: Sage.

—— (2007) *The Ethical Journalist*, London: Sage.

Hardy, D.T. and Clarke, J. (2004) *Michael Moore is a Big Fat Stupid White Man*, New York: HarperCollins.

Hardy, F. (ed.) (1979) *Grierson on Documentary*, London: Faber.

Hargreaves, I. (2003) *Journalism: Truth or Dare?* Oxford: Oxford University Press.

Hart, S.M. (2004) *A Companion to Latin American Film*, Woodbridge: Tamesis.

Hartley, J. (1999) *Uses of Television*, London: Routledge.

Heider, K.G. (1976) *Ethnographic Film*, Austin, TX: University of Texas Press.

Hesmondalgh, D. (2006) *Media Production*, Maidenhead: Open University Press.

Hight, C. (2010) *Television Mockumentary: Reflexivity, Satire and Play in Televisual Space*, Manchester: Manchester University Press.

—— and Roscoe, J. (2001) *Faking It: Mock Documentary and the Subversion of Factuality*, Manchester: Manchester University Press.

Hill, A. (2005) *Reality TV: Audiences and Popular Factual Television*, London: Routledge.

—— (2007) *Restyling Factual Television*, London: Routledge.

Hitchens, C. (2007) *God Is Not Great*, New York: Atlantic Books.

Hobsbawm, E. (1994) *Age of Extremes: The Short Twentieth Century 1914–1991*, London: Michael Joseph.

Holland, P. (2006) *The Angry Buzz: This Week and Current Affairs Television*, London: I.B. Tauris.

Holmes, R. (2007) *The World at War: The Landmark Oral History from the Previously Unpublished Archives*, London: Ebury Press.

Holmes, S. and Jermyn, D. (eds) (2004) *Understanding Reality TV*, London: Routledge.

—— and Redmond, S. (eds) (2007) *A Reader in Stardom and Celebrity*, London: Sage.

Hughes, B. (2005) *Helen of Troy: Goddess, Princess, Whore*, London: Jonathan Cape.

Hughes, R. (1980) *The Shock of the New: Art and the Century of Change*, London: BBC Books.

Ivens, J. (1969) *The Camera and I*, New York: International Publishers.

Jackson, K. (ed.) (1993) *The Humphrey Jennings Reader*, Manchester: Carcanet.

Jacobs, L. (ed.) (1971) *The Documentary Tradition: From Nanook to Woodstock*, New York: Hopkinson & Blake.

Jenkins, H. and Thorburn, D. (eds) (2004) *Democracy and New Media*, Cambridge, MA: MIT Press.

Jenkins, R. (2002) *Pierre Bourdieu*, London: Routledge.

Jermyn, D. (2006) *Crime Watching: Investigating Real Crime TV*, London: IB Tauris.

Johnson, S. (2005) *Everything Bad is Good for You: How Today's Popular Culture is Actually Making Us Smarter*, New York: Riverhead Books.

Juhasz, A. and Lerner, J. (eds) (2006) *F is for Phony: Fake Documentary and Truth's Undoing*, Minneapolis, MN: Minnesota University Press.

Kee, R. (1980) *Ireland: A History*, London: Weidenfeld & Nicolson.

Kennedy, M. (1968) *Portrait of Elgar*, Oxford: Oxford University Press.

Kilborn, R. (2003) *Staging the Real: Factual TV programming in the Age of Big Brother*, Manchester: Manchester University Press.

—— and Izod, J. (1997) *An Introduction to Television Documentary: Confronting Reality*, Manchester: Manchester University Press.

Klein, N. (2000) *No Logo: Taking Aim at the Brand Bullies*, Toronto: Knopf Canada.

Kochberg, S. (ed.) (2002) *Introduction to Documentary Production: A Guide for Media Students*, London: Wallflower Press.

Kuenzli, R.E. (ed.) (1987) *Dada and Surrealist Films*, New York: Rudolf & Owens.

Laing, R.D. (1964) *Sanity, Madness and the Family*, Vol. 1: *Families of Schizophrenics*, London: Tavistock Publications.

La Motta, J. (1970) *Raging Bull*, Upper Saddle River, NJ: Prentice-Hall.

Lanza, J. (2007) *Phallic Frenzy: Ken Russell and His Films*, Chicago, IL: Chicago Review Press.

Lee-Wright, P. (1990) *Child Slaves*, London: Earthscan Publications.

—— (2008) 'Virtual news: BBC news at a "future media and technology" crossroads', *Convergence: The International Journal of Research into New Media Technologies*, 14 (3).

—— (2009) 'Culture shock: new media and prganisational change in the BBC', in N. Fenton (ed.), *New Media, Old News: Journalism and Democracy in the Digital Age*, London: Sage.

Levin, G.R. (1971) *Documentary Explorations: 15 Interviews with Film-Makers*, New York: Anchor Doubleday.

Lewis, C. (ed.) (2004) *The Corruption Notebooks*, Washington, DC: Public Integrity Books.

—— (2004) *The Buying of the President*, New York: Harper Collins/Perennial.

Lewis, T. (2008) *Smart Living: Lifestyle Media and Popular Expertise*, New York: Peter Lang.

Lindley, R. (2003) *Panorama: Fifty Years of Pride and Paranoia*, Petersfield: Politicos.

Lipkin, S.N. (2002) *Real Emotional Logic: Film and Television Docudrama as Persuasive Practice*, Carbondale, IL: Southern Illinois University Press.

Lippit, A. (2000) *Electric Animal: Towards a Rhetoric of Wildlife*, Minneapolis, MN: University of Minnesota Press.

Lister, M., Dovey, J., Giddings, S., Grant, I. and Kelly, K. (2003) *New Media: A Critical Introduction*, London: Routledge.

Loizos, P. (1993) *Innovation in Ethnographic Film: From Innocence to Self-Consciousness, 1955–1985*, Manchester: Manchester University Press.

Lovell, T. (1980) *Pictures of Reality: Aesthetics, Politics and Pleasure*, London: British Film Institute.

Macdonald, K. and Cousins, M. (1996) *Imagining Reality: The Faber Book of Documentary*, London: Faber.

Macdonald, M. (1998) 'Publicizing the personal: women's voices in British television documentaries', in C. Carter, G. Branston and S. Allan (eds), *News, Gender and Power*, London: Routledge.

Macdonald, S. (1992) *A Critical Cinema: Interviews with Independent Filmmakers*, Berkeley, CA: University of California Press.

MacDougall, D. (1998) *Transcultural Cinema*, Princeton, NJ: Princeton University Press.

—— (2006) *The Corporeal Image: Film, Ethnography and the Senses*, Princeton, NJ: Princeton University Press.

McGinniss, J. (1970) *The Selling of the President*, London: André Deutsch.

McGrath, A. and McGrath, J.C. (2007) *The Dawkins Delusion? Atheist Fundamentalism and the Denial of the Divine*, London: SPCK.

McKee, R. (1999) *Story: Substance, Structure, Style and the Principles of Screen Writing*, London: Methuen.

McLean, B. and Elkind, P. (2003) *The Smartest Guys in the Room: The Amazing Rise and Scandalous Fall of Enron*, New York: Viking.

McLeod, K. (2005) *Freedom of Expression: Overzealous Copyright Bozos and Other Enemies of Creativity*, New York: Doubleday.

McPherson, B. (ed.) (2001) *Essential Brakhage: Selected Writings on Filmmaking*, New York: McPherson & Co.

Magee, B. (1978) *Men of Ideas: Some Creators of Contemporary Philosophy*, Oxford: Oxford University Press.

Mansfield, G. (1996) *Vets School*, London: BBC Books.

Marr, A. (2004) *My Trade: A Short History of British Journalism*, London: Macmillan.

Marriott, E., Saade, J., Borgenicht, J. and Chen, D. (2004) *The Reality TV Handbook: An Insider's Guide: How To Ace a Casting Interview, Form an Alliance, Swallow a Live Bug, and Capitalize on Your 15 Minutes of Fame*, Philadelphia, PA: Quirk Books.

Martin, M. (ed.) (1997) *New Latin American Cinema*, Detroit, MI: Wayne State University Press.

Meigh-Andrews, C. (2006) *A History of Video Art: The Development of Form and Function*, Oxford: Berg.

Mekas, J. (1972) *Movie Journal: The Rise of a New American Cinema 1959–71*, New York: Macmillan.

—— (2000) *Just Like a Shadow*, New York: Steidl.

Minkel, W. (2003) 'The once and future video', *School Library Journal*, 49 (1): 52.

Mitchell, J. (2004) *Genre and Television: From Cop Shows to Cartoons in American Culture*, London and New York: Routledge.

Moore, M. (2001) *Stupid White Men . . . and Other Sorry Excuses for the State of the Nation!*, New York: HarperCollins.

Morris, C.W. (1971) *Writings on the General Theory of Signs*, The Hague: Mouton.

Murray, S. and Oullette, L. (eds) (2004) *Reality TV: Remaking Television Culture*, New York: New York University Press.

Neuman, E. (1959) *Art and the Creative Unconscious*, Princeton, NJ: Princeton University Press.

Nichols, B. (1991) *Representing Reality: Issues and Concepts in Documentary*, Bloomington, IN: Indiana University Press.

—— (2001) *Introduction to Documentary*, Bloomington, IN: Indiana University Press.

Nouwt, S., de Vries, B.R., Prins, J. and Prins, C. (2005) *Reasonable Expectations of Privacy? Eleven Country Reports on Camera Surveillance and Workplace Privacy*, The Hague: Asser Press.

Oullette, L. (2002) *Viewers Like You? How Public TV Failed the People*, New York: Columbia University Press.

—— and Hay, J. (2008) *Better Living through Reality TV: Television and Post-Welfare Citizenship*, Oxford: Wiley-Blackwell.

Paget, D. (1998) *No Other Way to Tell it: Dramadoc/Docudrama on Television*, Manchester: Manchester University Press.

—— and Roscoe, J. (2006) 'Giving voice: performance and authenticity in the documentary musical', *Jump Cut: A Review of Contemporary Media*, 48, winter.

Peace, D. (2006) *The Damned United*, London: Faber & Faber.

Pilger, J. (2005) *Tell Me No Lies*, London: Vintage.

Pines, J. and Willemen, P. (1990) *Questions of Third Cinema*, London: BFI.

Preziosi, D. (ed.) (1998) *The Art of Art History*, Oxford: Oxford University Press.

Rabiger, M. (2004) *Directing the Documentary*, Amsterdam: Focal Press.

Rabinow, P. and Rose, M. (1997) *Essential Works of Foucault*, Vol. 1, New York: The New Press.

Redmond, S. (2008) 'I confess', *Social Semiotics*, June.

—— and Holmes, S. (eds) (2008) *Stardom and Celebrity: A Reader*, London: Sage.

Renov, M. (ed.) (1993) *Theorising Documentary*, London and New York: Routledge.

—— (2004) *The Subject of Documentary*, Minneapolis, MN: University of Minnesota Press.

Reynaud, B. (2003) 'Dancing with myself, drifting with my camera: the emotional vagabonds of China's new documentary', *Senses of Cinema*, September.

Robin, D. and Jaffe, I. (1999) *Redirecting the Gaze: Gender, Theory and Cinema in the Third World*, Albany, NY: State University of New York Press.

Rony, F.T. (1996) *The Third Eye: Race, Cinema and Ethnographic Spectacle*, Durham, NC: Duke University Press.

Rosenthal, A. and Corner, J. (eds) (2005) *New Challenges for Documentary*, 2nd edn, Manchester: Manchester University Press.

Rotha, P. (1952) *The Documentary Film*, 2nd edn, London: Faber & Faber.

Rouch, J. (2003) *Ciné-Ethnography*, Minneapolis, MN: University of Minnesota Press.

Rubin, H.J. and Rubin, I.S. (1995) *Qualitative Interviewing: The Art of Hearing Data*, London: Sage.

Ruoff, J. (2001) *An American Family: A Televised Life*, Minneapolis, MN: University of Minnesota Press.

Russell, K. (1989, 2008) *A British Picture: An Autobiography*, London: Heinemann; revised edn, London: Southbank Publishing.

Schama, S. (1991, 1998) *Dead Certainties (Unwarranted Speculations)*, London: Granta Books; and London: Penguin.

—— (2000, 2001, 2002) *A History of Britain* (3 vols), London: BBC Books.

—— (2006) *Simon Schama's Power of Art*, London: BBC Books.

Seaton, J. (2005) *Carnage and the Media: The Making and Breaking of News about Violence*, London: Allen Lane.

—— (forthcoming, 2010) *What's the Point of the BBC?*, London: Continuum Books.

Shepherd, K. (2003) 'Questioning, promoting, and evaluating the use of streaming video to support student learning', *British Journal of Educational Technology*, 34 (3): 295–308.

Shirky, C. (2008) *Here Comes Everybody*, New York: Penguin Books.

Shub, Esfir (1972) *Zhizn moya-kinematograf* (*Cinema is my Life*), Moscow: Isskustvo, p. 18.

Silverstone, R. (1985) *Framing Science: The Making of a BBC Documentary*, London: BFI.

—— (1994) *Television and Everyday Life*, London: Routledge.

—— (2007) *Media and Morality: On the Rise of the Mediapolis*, Cambridge: Polity Press.

Simpson, Joe (1988) *Touching the Void*, London: Jonathan Cape.

Simpson, John (2002) *No Man's Land: Reporting the World*, London: Macmillan.

Sites, K. (2007) *In the Hot Zone: One Man, One Year, Twenty Wars*, New York: Harper Perennial.

Sitney, P.A. (ed.) (1978) *The Avant-Garde Film: A Reader of Theory and Criticism*, New York: New York University Press.

Smith, M. (2003) 'History and the media: are you being hoodwinked?', *History Today*, March.

Snow, C.P. (1993) *The Two Cultures*, Cambridge: Cambridge University Press.

Solanas, F. and Getino, O. (1969) 'Towards a Third Cinema: notes and experiences for the development of a cinema of liberation in the Third World', *Tricontinental*, Havana.

Solomon, N. (2005) *War Made Easy: How Presidents and Pundits Keep Spinning Us to Death*, Hoboken, NJ: John Wiley & Sons.

Strossen, N. (1995) *Defending Pornography: Free Speech, Sex and the Fight for Women's Rights*, New York: Simon & Schuster.

Sugar, A. (2005) *The Apprentice: How to Get Hired and Not Fired*, London: BBC Books.

Swann, P. (1989) *The British Documentary Film Movement 1926–1946*, Cambridge: Cambridge University Press.

Tapper, R. (ed.) (2002) *The New Iranian Cinema: Politics, Representation and Identity*, London: I.B. Tauris.

Tate (2006) *Making History: Art and Documentary in Britain from 1929 to Now*, Liverpool: Tate.

Taylor, A.J.P. (1961, 1996) *The Origins of the Second World War*, London: Penguin Books; London: Simon & Schuster.

Taylor, P. (1998) *Provos: The IRA and Sinn Fein*, London: Bloomsbury.

—— (2000) *Loyalists*, London: Bloomsbury.

—— (2002) *Brits: The War against the IRA*, London: Bloomsbury.

Thayer, W.R. (1920) *The Art of Biography*, New York: Charles Scribner's Sons.

Thomas, M. (2006) *As Used on the Famous Nelson Mandela: Underground Adventures in the Arms and Torture Trade*, London: Ebury Press.

Thumin, J. (2002) *Small Screen, Big Ideas: Television in the 1950s*, London: I.B. Tauris.

Tunstall, J. (1994) *The Media are American: Anglo-American Media in the World*, London: Constable.

Vaughan, D. (1999) *For Documentary: Twelve Essays*, Berkeley, CA: University of California Press.

Vertov, D. (1984, 1992) *Kino-Eye: The Writings of Dziga Vertov*, edited by A. Michelson, trans. K. O'Brien, London: Pluto Press; Berkeley, CA: University of California Press.

Vogel, A. (1974) *Film as a Subversive Art*, London: Weidenfeld & Nicholson.

Waldman, D. and Walker, J. (eds) (1999) *Feminism and Documentary*, Minneapolis, MN: University of Minnesota Press.

Ward, P. (2005) *Documentary: The Margins of Reality*, London: Wallflower Press.

Waugh, T. (ed.) (1984) *'Show Us Life': Towards a History and Aesthetics of the Committed Documentary*, Metuchen, NJ: The Scarecrow Press.

White, C. (2005) *The Middle Mind: Why Consumer Culture Is Turning Us into the Living Dead*, London: Penguin Books.

Wilsher, J.C. and Grey, I. (2007) 'Drama documentary', *UK Writer*, Writers' Guild.

Winston, B. (1995) *Claiming the Real: The Documentary Film Revisited*, London: BFI.

—— (2000) *Lies, Damn Lies and Documentaries*, London: BFI.

Woods, P. (1995) 'Film propaganda in India 1914–1923,' *Historical Journal of Film, Radio and Television*, October.

Woodward, B. and Bernstein, C. (1974) *All the President's Men*, New York: Simon & Schuster.

X, Malcolm with Haley, A. (1965) *The Autobiography of Malcolm X*, London: Penguin.

Yingchi, C. (2007) *Chinese Documentaries: From Dogma to Polyphony*, London: Routledge.

Selective webography

This selective webography includes website/organisation definitions *in their own words*. Listing here does not confirm that the sites will always fulfil their declared objectives nor confer any special status. All web sources should routinely be cross-referenced.

www.amnesty.org – 'a worldwide movement of people who campaign for internationally recognized human rights for all'
www.archive.org – 'building a digital library of internet sites and other cultural artefacts in digital form'
www.barb.co.uk – Broadcasters Audience Research Board
www.bbc.co.uk/history – 'The BBC is putting some of the treasures of its archive online'
www.bbc.co.uk/videonation – 'your views and experiences on camera and online'
www.bettanyhughes.co.uk – 'historian, author, broadcaster'
http://billviola.com – 'a pioneer in the medium of video art'
http://blogs.channel4.com/fourdocs – 'an online documentary channel'
www.boxofficemojo.com – reviews and box office
www.btselem.org – 'the Israeli information centre for human rights in the occupied territories'
www.channel4.com/corporate/4producers – 'Channel 4's online commissioning guide. If you want to make a TV programme or a film for us, you'll find everything you need right here'
www.creativecommons.org – 'Share, Remix, Reuse – Legally . . . a nonprofit organization that increases sharing and improves collaboration'
http://current.com – 'get creative, get on TV, get paid'
www.dfgdocs.com – 'a one-stop shop for documentary, created especially for all of you interested in the art and craft of documentary filmmaking'
www.documentary-film.net – 'watch films online, in full and high quality'
www.ejumpcut.org – 'a review of contemporary media'
http://freeonlinedocumentary.com – 'watch the best online documentaries for free'
http://frontlineclub.com – 'championing independent journalism'
http://hotzone.yahoo.com – AP top stories and 'You Witness News'
http://imdb.com – The Internet Movie Database
www.iraqeye.org – 'Iraq from an Iraqi's perspective'
http://jobs.guardian.co.uk/jobs/media – 'Find the latest media jobs including work in TV, entertainment and radio jobs'
http://nomadsland.com – 'a social network devoted to documentaries, local film clubs, community screenings and all visual social issue media'
http://onebigtorrent.org – 'sharing material that deals with or is relevant to issues of social justice, progressive and radical politics, independent media, ecology'
http://oneworldmedia.org.uk – 'a UK-based organisation which aims to increase global understanding through effective use of the media'
http://onlinefilm.org – 'a legal distribution platform for the low-cost distribution and marketing of German and European films via the internet'
http://opennet.net – 'ONI's mission is to identify and document internet filtering and surveillance'

www.pbs.org/wgbh/pages/frontline/view – 'thought-provoking journalism on air and online'

http://popmatters.com – 'feature essays about any aspect of popular culture, current or past'

www.realityblurred.com – 'Babysitting television's bastard child with reality TV news, reviews and analysis'

www.rts.org.uk – 'The Royal Television Society is the leading forum for discussion and debate on all aspects of the television community'

www.searchsystems.net – 'the original, largest, most up-to-date and reliable directory of public records'

http://sensesofcinema.com – 'an online journal devoted to the serious and eclectic discussion of cinema'

http://slewfootsnoop.wordpress.com – 'Tips, tricks and sources for journalists doing online research'

www.teachers.tv – 'Thousands of education programmes on TV and online'

www.the-numbers.com – 'box office data, movie stars, idle speculation'

www.tvcream.co.uk – enthusiast reviews and archive

www.unreportedworld.blogspot.com – 'Screening films produced with conscience and commitment to open and free expression'

http://viewmagazine.tv – 'cine-videojournalism and video new wave storytelling'

www.wired.com – 'unfold the universe of virtualisation'

www.withoutabox.com – 'a worldwide audience for filmmakers, a complete online management system for film festivals'

www.wmm.com – 'Women Make Movies: films by and about women'

www.youtube.com/iraqeyetv – The Iraq Eye Media Group *iraqeyetv*'s channel

Also see Chapters 17 and 19 expert briefings: 'Getting your film seen' (pp. 333–4) and 'Financing the film' (pp. 368–70).

Index